Communications
in Computer and Information Science   208

Qingyuan Zhou (Ed.)

Applied Economics, Business and Development

International Symposium, ISAEBD 2011
Dalian, China, August 6-7, 2011
Proceedings, Part I

 Springer

Volume Editor

Qingyuan Zhou
Jiangsu Teachers University of Technology
Yuying Road No. 2
Changzhou, Jiangsu Province, 213001, China
E-mail: zqyconference@gmail.com

ISSN 1865-0929   e-ISSN 1865-0937
ISBN 978-3-642-23022-6   e-ISBN 978-3-642-23023-3
DOI 10.1007/978-3-642-23023-3
Springer Heidelberg Dordrecht London New York

Library of Congress Control Number: 2011933608

CR Subject Classification (1998): H.4, H.3, C.2, I.2, D.2, J.1

Typesetting: Camera-ready by author, data conversion by Scientific Publishing Services, Chennai, India

Printed on acid-free paper

Springer is part of Springer Science+Business Media (www.springer.com)

Preface

It is our pleasure to welcome you to the proceedings of the 2011 International Symposium on Applied Economics, Business and Development (ISAEBD 2011) which was held in Dalian, China. ISAEBD 2011 was the first conference dedicated to issues related to applied economics, business and development. This conference aims to provide a high-level international forum for researchers to present and discuss the recent advances in related issues, covering various research areas including economics, management, education and its applications.

The conference is sponsored by the Hong Kong Education Society, International Material Science Society and Information Engineering Research Institute. Their support is very important for our conference.

The conference was both stimulating and informative with an interesting array of keynote and invited speakers from all over the world. Delegates had a wide range of sessions to choose from.

The program consisted of invited sessions, technical workshops and discussions with eminent speakers covering a wide range of topics in applied economics, business and development. This rich program provided all attendees with the opportunity to meet and interact with one another.

We would like to thank the organization staff, the members of the Program Committees and the reviewers for their hard work.

We hope the attendees of ISAEBD 2011 had an enjoyable scientific gathering in Dalian, China. We look forward to seeing all of you at the next ISAEBD event.

Qingyuan Zhou

ISAEBD 2011 Organization

Honorary Conference Chairs

Chin-Chen Chang	Feng Chia University, Taiwan
Chris Price	Aberystwyth University, UK

General Chairs

Qinyuan Zhou	Jiangsu Teachers University of Technology, China
Junwu Zhu	Yangzhou University, China

Program Chairs

Honghua Tan	Wuhan Institute of Technology , China
Qihai Zhou	Southwestern University of Finance and Economics, China

Publication Chair

Mark Zhou	Hong Kong Education Society, Hong Kong

Local Chair

He Ping	Liaoning Police Academy, China

International Program Committee

Ming-Jyi Jang	Far-East University, Taiwan
Tzuu-Hseng S. Li	National Cheng Kung University, Taiwan
Yanwen Wu	Huazhong Normal University, China
Teh-Lu Liao	National Cheng Kung University, Taiwan
Yi-Pin Kuo	Far-East University, Taiwan
Qingtang Liu	Huazhong Normal University, China
Wei-Chang Du	I-Shou University, Taiwan
Jiuming Yang	Huazhong Normal University, China
Hui Jiang	Wuhan Golden Bridge-Network Security Technocogy Co. Ltd., China
Zhonghua Wang	Huazhong Normal University, China
Jun-Juh Yan	Shu-Te University, Taiwan
Dong Huang	Huazhong University of Science and Technology, China
JunQi Wu	Huazhong Normal University, China

Table of Contents – Part I

Stability Analysis for Various Business Forms

Ai-nong Zhou

Department of Economic Management, Guangzhou Institute of Railway Technology,
Guangzhou, 510430, P.R. China

Abstract. There exist numerous types of business forms at different periods all over the world. This paper compares the stabilities of three business forms based on the decision-makers: Corporations with individual decisions (CIDs), multi-person decision corporations (MDCs) and stock corporations (SCs). Three business forms are first modeled as evolutionary graphs, respectively. By the existing results in the evolutionary graph theory (EGT), we then find that stock corporations (SCs) are more stable than MDCs while MDCs are more stable than CIDs.

Keywords: Evolutionary graph, business forms, stability, fixation probability.

1 Introduction

The legal business forms have evolved in the past years almost in all countries and there now exists great difference about business forms all over the world[14,2,10,8] and the references mentioned therein. The business forms of European and the United States are discussed and the changes of the business forms are addressed[14]. The firms of Denmark were investigated and analyzed [2].

The forms of the business are determined by multiple factors, such as partnership, stability, culture, law, efficiency and so on. Although the laws of the business forms, were all originated from the Roman *Societas*, there now exists drastic difference in the laws of the business forms. Moreover, there exists a dramatic debate in the law community about the business forms, which motivate us to further investigate them.

In the Middle Ages, trade revived and mediaeval merchants sought a suitable business organization form meshed with contemporary society and economic situations. At that time, the advantageous business forms are small, in general family owned, commercial firms. In many developing countries, private businesses are still very popular now. This paper focuses on the features of the firms to make decisions, which is not the owner of firms. Almost all of these businesses are also fallen into the communities of corporations with individual decisions(CIDs) and multi-person decision corporations (MDCs).

A stock corporation, also referred to as the ``general corporation" or ``open corporation". The Stockholders are the owners of the stock corporation. Typically, holders of common stock have the right to one vote for each share they own to elect the members of the Board of Directors and to vote on certain other matters of major significance to the company. According to the Delaware General Corporation Law, any

Q. Zhou (Ed.): ISAEBD 2011, Part I, CCIS 208, pp. 1–7, 2011.

stockholder who holds a majority of the shares of issued stock can control the company. This is sometimes referred to as a ``majority shareholder''. Majority shareholders take on a heightened responsibility to minority shareholders, see the following web page [15]. There are many further researches on SCs recently[13]. Fiegener [3] investigated that the chief executive officers (CEOs) of small private corporations involve the board of directors in strategic decisions. There also exist some researches on more complex cases about firms[1].

There exist numerous factors to affect the forms to make decisions in the firms. We aim to analyze the stabilities of the business with three types of forms, including CIDs, MDCs and SCs, which also has the crucial effects on the forms of businesses.

To analyze the stability of businesses, we resort to evolutionary graph theory (EGT) in this paper. We now introduce EGT briefly. Evolutionary graphs were initially proposed in[5] and developed by[7,16,9,12]. EGT is another measure to implement evolutionary dynamic where the individuals in a population are all posed on a graph. Evolutionary graphs (EGs) give a rational explanation for the evolutionary dynamic affected by the population structures.

In [5], isothermal structure, K-star structure and directed cycle graphs are introduced and analyzed, respectively. In [7], EGs on two levels are proposed and discussed. Furthermore, an interesting result, EGs on two levels being more stable, is obtained. Directed cycle EGs and regular random graphs were discussed again and a condition that the cooperation will overwhelm over defector is obtained[12].

For EGs, two crucial definitions are fitness and fixation probability, respectively. Fitness reflects the fit degree of the individuals in a group and the invader (or a mutant in biological field). After an invader enters a group or a mutant appears in a population, the invader may leave or may stay in this group. The fixation probability is the probability that an invader (or a mutant in biological field) takes over the group or population. The fixation probability is therefore a highly suitable index rank the stability. When the fixation probability is smaller, this group is more stable. On the contrary, the corresponding group is less stable.

We just consider some special corporations, in which there are identical properties in some specific aspects for all individuals, in this work. Namely, in this paper, all members in the corporations of this paper play the (approximately) identical roles to decide something about firms. For instances, all stocks in a stock corporation have the identical effect on the decision of the corporation because each share has the same role in this type of the corporation. There exist multiple reasons to do in this way. Firstly, for a large corporation, there exist numerous members, which is suitable for EGT. Secondly, we assume that all members, in a firm or in a department of this firm, have the identical roles in some aspects, while we just consider these factors and EGT is appeal. Thirdly, we always assume that there exists fixed number of labors in a firm, which is also convenient to employ EGT. It is rational to employ an index, fixation probability in evolutionary graph theory to label the suitable degree of a corporation.

In biological field, the fitness of an individual is determined by many complicated factors, such as climate, payoff function and so on. Similar to that in the biological field, we further point out that the fitness of a corporation is determined by numerous factors, such as belief, culture, industries, organization structures, benefits, laws and so on. The fitness of a corporation is highly similar to that in biological field, which is also very difficult to determine the exact form of it because a single factor may play decisive roles in reality in many situations.

Actually, we can obtain the fitness of an invading corporation by testing the number of the corporations entering some industry and the number of corporations leaving this industry. Assume that they are n_1, n_2, respectively. We can calculate the fitness by the formulation $r = n_1 / n_2$, which is similar to that in biological field.

There mainly are two contributions in this paper: On one hand, evolutionary graph theory, a very young theory in biological field which is successful to explain evolutionary theory, is now extended to the social fields, especially, in economics, and, many interesting results of EGT are employed to analyze the stabilities of the corporations in this paper. On the other hand, the stabilities of business forms are successfully explained by EGT. We further point that the fitness of other problems can be similarly obtained. It is therefore rational to extend EGT to various social fields because the corresponding fitness can be calculated. Motivated by the excellent papers[4,6,11], we aim to introduce EGT to the economic field.

2 The Models

We now model firms with CIDs, MDCs and SCs by evolutionary graph approaches, respectively. There are all N members in a CID, an MDC and an SC in this section.

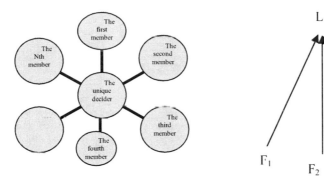

Fig. 1. CID with N members

Fig. 2. 1-star EG based on CID with N vertices

Apparently, CIDs can be modeled as Stackelberg games and MDCs can be modeled as multi-leader-follower games. When we model CIDs as EGs, we regard all staff except the unique decider as the vertices in the lower level, see the vertices $(F_1, F_2, \cdots, F_N)$ in Fig. 2. The vertex L in Fig. 2 stands for the unique decider. In a CID, the positions of the members seem to like a 1-star EG. CIDs, modeled as 1-star EGs, are formally given as follows, see it in detail in Fig. 2 and Fig. 1.

We also model MDCs as EGs in Fig. 3, which is similar to EGs on two levels in [7]. MDCs are modeled as an evolutionary graph on two levels, which is given as follows. The vertexes, $(F_1, F_2, \cdots, F_N)$, in the lower level, stand for all the staffs (to simplify the problem, all the middle and fist line mangers are also regarded as vertices in the lower level.) The deciders are vertices in the upper level of EG in Fig. 3, see the vertices $(L_1, L_2, \cdots, L_M)$ in EG.

SCs are now modeled as another EG with two levels, which is following introduced in detail. In an SC, the CEO (Chief Executive Officer), is regarded as a vertex C, and the members of the Board of Directors (BD), put on EG of Fig. 4 as vertices $(L_1, L_2, \cdots, L_M)$, consist in an evolutionary graph.

Furthermore, the CEO, vertex C in the corresponding EG, and the members in the corporation (including all middle managers, first line managers and the average staffs), put on EG of Fig. 4 as vertices $(F_1, F_2, \cdots, F_N)$ in EG, lie in another EG (see Fig. 4).

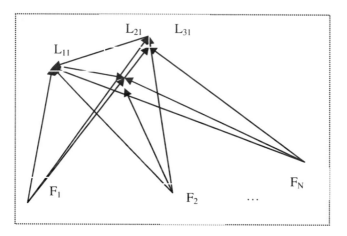

Fig. 3. EG on two levels based on MDCs (m=3) with 3 vertices (L1, L2 and L3) in the upper level and N vertices ($F_1, F_2, \cdots, F_N$) in the Lower level

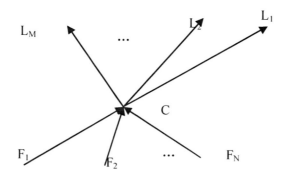

Fig. 4. EG on two levels based on SCs, the first evolutionary sub-graph with M vertices and N vertices in the second evolutionary sub-graph

CIDs are hence modeled as 1-star EGs in Fig. 2. MDCs are modeled as EGs on two levels in Fig. 3 while SCs are modeled as another type of EGs on two levels in Fig. 4. The structure of EGs based on SCs differs greatly from those based on MDCs. We will compare the stabilities of three EGs in the next section.

For all EGs in this paper, we always assume, except specific explanation, that the fitness in this EGs is 1 and r for a mutant or an invader. CIDs are rationally modeled as a 1-star evolutionary graph with N vertices. By the conclusion in Lieberman [5], we can calculate the fixation probability of Fig. 2. The corresponding fixation probability is directly given by the following formulation

$$\rho_1 = (1 - 1/r)/(1 - 1/r^N) \tag{1}$$

MDCs are modeled as an EG on two levels in Fig. 3, which was also introduced in the paper of Nie's (Nie, 2008). If there are m deciders and N followers, the fixation probability is then given as follows, according to the result of Nie[7].

$$\rho_2 = \frac{1 - 1/r}{1 - 1/r^N} \frac{1 - 1/r}{1 - 1/r^m}. \tag{2}$$

By the equations (1) and (2), the following conclusion is immediately obtained

Theorem 1. Under the same conditions, MDCs are more stable than CIDs.

Proof: We first show that $1 \geq \rho_1 \geq 0$ for $N > 1$ and for all $r > 0, r \neq 1$. When $r > 0, r \neq 1$, (1) yields $\rho_1 = \dfrac{1 - 1/r}{1 - 1/r^N} = \dfrac{1}{1 + 1/r + \cdots + 1/r^{N-1}}$. We consequently obtain that $1 \geq \rho_1 \geq 0$ for $N > 1$ and for all $r > 0, r \neq 1$. By the way similar to the above, we also have $0 < (1 - 1/r)/(1 - 1/r^m) < 1$ for all $m > 1$ and for any $r > 0, r \neq 1$. We immediately obtain that $\rho_1 > \rho_2 = (1 - 1/r)^2/[(1 - 1/r^N)(1 - 1/r^m)]$ for all $N > 1, m > 1$ and for any $r > 0, r \neq 1$. We therefore obtain that the fixation probability of the 1-star EG, or that in Figure 2, is larger than that of EG on two levels with the same number of vertexes in the lower level, or the EG in Fig. 3. By the definition of the fixation probability and the relation between the fixation probability and the stability, CIDs are accordingly easier to attack by others and we immediately have that MDCs are more stable than CIDs if there are all N staffs. The result is obtained. ∎

SCs are formally modeled as another EG on two levels. In an SC, the CEO (Chief Executive Officer) and the members of the Board of Directors (BD) consist in an evolutionary sub-graph (for convenience, we call it the first evolutionary sub-graph). On the other hand, the CEO and the members in the corporation lie in another evolutionary sub-graph (see Fig. 4) (We call this the second evolutionary sub-graph).

We assume that the fitness of the members in BD is 1 and $\tilde{r}$ for others. We also assume that the fitness is 1 for all staffs and r for others. In general, $r \neq \tilde{r}$ and $\tilde{r}$ is close to 1 because BD is more open to the society than a corporation. We now consider the fixation probability to Fig. 4, EG based on SC. Similar to the analysis and the results of Nie [7], when an EG of Fig. 4 is invaded, the invader receives the defense from two evolutionary sub-graphs. When an invader enters the first evolutionary sub-graph, according to the result[5], the probability to take over all this sub-graph is $(1-1/r)/(1-1/r^N)$.

When an invader enters the second evolutionary sub-graph, the probability to take over all this sub-graph is $(1-1/\tilde{r})/(1-1/\tilde{r}^M)$. The fixation probability of EG in Fig. 4 is therefore given as follows:

$$\rho_3 = (1-\frac{1}{r})(1-\frac{1}{\tilde{r}})/[(1-\frac{1}{r^N})(1-\frac{1}{\tilde{r}^M})] \qquad (3)$$

We further note that the fixation probability of EG in Fig. 4 is identical no matter the invader enters this EG from the first or from the second sub-graph.

In general, the number of the members in BD for an SC is in general much larger than that of the deciders in an MDC, or $M > m$. Furthermore, $1 > \tilde{r} > r$ because BD is more open than other organizations or the group of the staffs in a corporation. We then have the following conclusion

Theorem 2. If $M > m, 1 > \tilde{r} > r$ and $\tilde{r}^M < r^m$, SC is more stable than MDc.

Proof: According to $M > m$ and $1 > \tilde{r} > r$, by simple calculation we immediately have the following formulation $1/r > 1/\tilde{r} > 1$ or $1/r - 1 > 1/\tilde{r} - 1$. On the other hand, $\tilde{r}^M < r^m$ yilelds $1 < 1/r^m < 1/\tilde{r}^M$, or $1/r^m - 1 < 1/\tilde{r}^M - 1$. Combined the above two inequalities, we immediately obtain

$$\frac{1}{1+\frac{1}{r}+\frac{1}{r^2}+\cdots+\frac{1}{r^{m-1}}} = \frac{1-1/r}{1-\frac{1}{r^m}} > \frac{1-1/\tilde{r}}{1-\frac{1}{\tilde{r}^M}} = \frac{1}{1+\frac{1}{\tilde{r}}+\frac{1}{\tilde{r}^2}+\cdots+\frac{1}{\tilde{r}^{M-1}}} . \qquad (4)$$

We therefore obtain that $\rho_3 < \rho_2$. The fixation probability of the EG in Fig. 4 is less than that of EG, modeled from MDC. By virtue of the definition of the fixation probability and the relation between the fixation probability and the stability, MDCs are easier to attack by others than SCs. Under the same conditions, SC is more stable than MDC. The result is obtained and the proof is complete. ∎

We assume that $\tilde{r}^M < r^m$, $M > m$ and $1 > \tilde{r} > r$ in the above result, which means that the number of members of BD is in general much larger than the number of the deciders in an MDC, and BD is more open to the public than the staffs in an MDC. In general, $m = 2$ or 3, while M is greater than 20 in practice. These assumptions are therefore extremely rational.

In summary, we find that SCs are more stable than MDCs, while MDCs are more stable than CIDs according to Theorem 1 and Theorem 2. This is also a main factor that the forms of SC are very popular all over the world. By the way, the form of SC also has the advantage of the CID because the BD has not direct effect on the staff or the managers of the corporation in an SC.

3 Concluding Remarks

Based on evolutionary graph theory (EGT), three business forms are compared. We find that the form of SCs is more stable than that of MDCs and similar result also holds for MDCs and CIDs. We resort to evolutionary graph theory (EGT) to analyze the social phenomena, and, argue some practical and useful conclusions.EGT, as an infant in both biological field and mathematics, it is very suitable for many social phenomena. It is important to extend EGT to more comprehensive cases in economics. There exists many researching topics on EGT, see in the paper of Lieberman et al.[5].

The stability of different forms of businesses is considered in this paper. It is the crucial factor to determine the forms of business. There exist many other factors, which also play important roles to determine the forms of businesses. It is also the further topics to investigate. About the fitness of a corporation, it is also a further interesting researching topic. Resorting to evolutionary graph theory, we consider the business forms. It is extremely important to extend EGT to more extensive situations.

References

1. Birkinshaw, J., Lingblad, M.: Intrafirm competition and charter evolution in the multibusiness firm. Organization Science 16(6), 674–686 (2005)
2. Eriksson, T., Kuhn, J.M.: Firm spin-offs in Denmark 1981-2000-patterns of entry and exit. Int. J. Industrial Organization 24(5), 1021–1040 (2006)
3. Fiegener, M.K.: Determinants of board participation in the strategic decision of small corporations. Entrepreneurship Theory and Practice 29(5), 627–650 (2005)
4. Friedman, D.: Evolutionary games in economics. Econometrica 59(3), 637–666 (1991)
5. Lieberman, E., Hauert, C., Nowak, M.A.: Evolutionary dynamics on graphs. Nature 433, 312–316 (2005)
6. Netzer, N.: Evolution of time preferences and attitudes toward risk. American Economic Review 99(3), 937–955 (2009)
7. Nie, P.Y.: Evolutionary graphs on two levels. Ars Combinatoria 86, 115–120 (2008)
8. Nie, P.Y.: Spatial technology spillover. Economic Computation and Economic Cybernetics Studies and Research 44(4), 213–223 (2010)
9. Nie, P.Y., Zhang, P.A.: Fixation time for evolutionary graphs. Int. J. Modern Physics B 24(27), 5285–5293 (2010)
10. Nie, P.Y.: Commitment for storable goods under vertical integration. Economic Modelling 26(2), 414–417 (2009)
11. Nie, P.Y.: Selection games in economics. Applied Economics Letters 14, 223–225 (2007)
12. Ohtsuki, H., Hauert, C., Lieberman, E., Nowak, M.A.: A simple rule for the evolution of cooperation on graphs and social networks. Nature 441, 502–505 (2006)
13. Rappaport, A.: 10 ways to create shareholder values. Harv. Bus. Rev. 84(9), 66 (2006)
14. Vermeulen, E.P.M.: The Evolution of Legal Business Forms in Europe and the United States. Kluwer Law International, The Hague (2003)
15. https://www.delawareinc.com/101/11visa.cfm?pageid=10042
16. Zhang, P.A., Nie, P.Y., Hu, D.Q.: Bi-level evolutionary graphs with multi-fitness. IET Systems Biology 4(1), 33–38 (2010)

Layout Model and Its Optimization for Man-to-Part Order Picking System

Shizhen Li[*]

Yangtze University, Jinzhou 434023, China
ShizhenLi2011@126.com

Abstract. It established the general layout model for picking area of man-to-part order picking system, and it has carried on the specific analysis to the average expected walk distance under the various storage strategies and path strategies through using some of the conclusions of previous studies. The layout model has universality, and the different average expected walk distances can generate different layout modules. According to the composition characteristics of the model, it uses a numerical example to show the method of solving for model and obtains the relevant conclusions of the layout of order picking system.

Keywords: Man-to-part order picking system, layout, model, optimization.

1 Introduction

Minimizing the operating time of order picking is the goal of all order picking systems, and this goal can be realized through many kinds of ways. Under the given warehouse layout conditions, it can shorten the order picking time and improve the order picking efficiency through adopting the optimized picking path, the orders' partial picking and appropriate storage strategy. However, whether the layout of the order picking system itself is good or not also is a crucial factor which can affect the order picking efficiency, the difference is that the former belongs to operational level and the latter belongs to the design level. The system layouts which have different qualities may be almost same in construction costs, but their impacts on future operations will be very different. Sometimes the ratio between the actual removal expense and the effective removal expense of the facility's layout which does not meet the design principles of the logistics system even reaches 332% [1]. Therefore, in the stage of initial planning and layout, it should make comprehensive consideration and planning to hope to play the maximum performance of the order picking system.

---

[*] The key project of science and technology of Hubei provincial Department of Education (D20081203).

Q. Zhou (Ed.): ISAEBD 2011, Part I, CCIS 208, pp. 8–14, 2011.
© Springer-Verlag Berlin Heidelberg 2011

2 The Order Picking System and Operational Assumptions

It considers the low level man-to-part level walk picking system. The pickers walk or drive to the picking area and remove the needed products from the storage position. The pickers and the car can walk from the two opposite directions in the laneway; the goods are stored on the shelves on both sides of the laneway. The relevant assumptions are as follows: (1) The picking area is composed of a series of determined rectangular shelves, each shelf stores at least more than one type of products. (2) The maximum cargo space' height is less than 2 meters [2], the pickers can remove the products in any positions without using any tools. (3) Ignore the additional time on the vertical direction which is caused by the shelf's height. (4) The narrow laneway picking system, namely the pickers can remove the items on both two sides of the shelf at the same time, and it do not need the additional time of shifting from one side of the shelf to another. (5) A picking order is equal to an order (the order does not be picked) or a batch of orders (batch picking). (6) There is no demand correlation among the picked products, namely the probability of a product which appears in the order is not affected by the other products in the order.

3 The Layout Model for Picking Area

The working time of picking is composed of the following three parts[2-3]: (1) the walking time from the beginning to the first item to be picked, the shifting time between each item to be picked and the time from the last item to be picked to the end can be regarded as the sum of the walking time in the storage channel and the lateral channel; (2) the processing time in the storage position point: such as the time of finding goods, removing the goods and documents processing; (3) the management time of the path's start and end: the time of managing and starting the task, for example, the time of obtaining and depositing the picking equipments, and the time of obtaining the picking orders. It supposes that the time of management and processing has nothing to do with the storage position strategy and the path strategy, and the walking time is the monotonic increasing function of the walking distance, the goal of minimum picking time is equal to the minimum picking distance[4-7]. Here takes the minimum average walking distance as the goal to establish the layout model.

4 The Analysis of the Average Expected Walking Distance

4.1 The Average Walking Distance under the Random Storage Strategy

The random distribution strategy except to its many advantages, such as the high space utilization and the strong flexibility, usually also is the benchmarking of improving the other storage strategy, besides, the random storage is used more in practice, when the market changes too quick and it can obtain the demand frequency of products statistics, it usually only uses the random storage strategy. Here firstly analyzes the walking distance under the random storage strategy, and then carries on analysis to the walking distance under the other strategies on the basis of this. It supposes Dc to express the distance which walks along x direction in front and rear channels in Figure 1, and Da expresses the distance which walks along y direction of storage shelf, the area of the storage area A=xy, r=y/x is called the warehouse's shape factor. Because the starting and the ending are at the same location, no matter which path strategy is used, the walking distance of the x direction is only related to the number of distribution laneways of the products to be picked, its expression can unified be expressed as[124]:

$$E[D_c] = w_a \left[n - 1 - 2 \sum_{i=1}^{n-1} (\frac{i}{n})^m \right] + w_a \sum_{i=1}^{n} \left\{ (|i - d| + |i - n + d - 1|) \times \left[\left(\frac{i}{n} \right)^m - \left(\frac{i-1}{n} \right)^m \right] \right\}$$

The walking distance in the picking laneway along the y direction has the relationship with the path strategy, and it is expressed by the mark $E[D_a^x]$, here x expresses the appropriate path strategy. Thus the pickers' average expected walking distance in picking area can be expressed by $E[D_a^x]$ which is related to the path strategy and $E[D_c]$ which has no relationship with the path strategy two parts, that is: $D_m^x(n, y, d) = E[D_a^x] + E[D_c]$.

It can respectively determine the expressions of $E[D_a^x]$ according to the different path strategies in bibliography [2-4, 8], such as the traversing strategy, the midpoint strategy and the maximum gap strategy and so on.

4.2   The Average Walking Distance under the Classified Storage Strategy

The bibliography [3] proves that under the random storage strategy d=(n+1)/2, namely, when the entrance is in the middle position of the front channel, the average expected walking distance is shortest. Based on this conclusion, under the classified storage strategy, it supposes that the position of the entrance of the layout model is sure to be located in the middle of the front channel, and in order to be advantageous for the analysis, its channel number is bilateral symmetry as the Figure 1. It respectively adopts different path strategies to calculate the average expected walking distance according to the different classification layout situation.

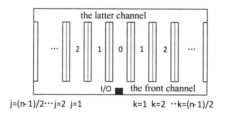

Fig. 1. The laneway's numbering method when the number of laneways is the odd number

It carries on the ordering for the goods according to COI principle; storing the goods which have low COI value near the entrance is the common method of the classified storage strategy. The ABC classified storage curve which is based on the COI principle can be expressed by the function as follows[2, 8]:

$$F(x) = \frac{(1 + s)x}{s + x}, \quad 0 \le x \le 1, \quad F(x) \ge 0, \quad s \ge 0 \text{且} s + x \ne 0$$

In the formula, x expresses the ratio between the needed storage space and the total storage space; s is the shape factor and expresses the deflection extent of the curve. The greater the s value is, the more gently the ABC curve is, for example, the 50/20, 60/20, 70/20, 80/20 ABC curve under the COI storage principle, the values of s are respectively 0.33, 0.20, 0.12 and 0.07.

4.2.1 The Return Strategy of the Cross Laneway Mode

The expected walking total distance of picking process likewise is composed of the walking distance of picking channel and the walking distance of front and rear channel two parts. In the mode of cross laneway storage, each picking laneway has the same access frequency; the ABC curve which is based on COI principle in each laneway is same. Therefore, the number of expected picking laneway is the same as that of the random storage strategy, namely $E[A] = n\left[1 - (\frac{n-1}{n})^m\right]$.

Thus the expected picking number in each laneway is $q = \frac{m}{E[A]}$. The distance of the return part depends on the position of the item which is the farthest from the front channel in the laneway, and these q items can be regarded as the random variable according to F(x) distribution, so the ration R that the expected value of the farthest picking position in a laneway accounts for the length of laneway can be expressed [2]:

$$R(q) = \int_0^1 \frac{dF^q(x)}{dx}.x.dx = \int_0^1 q\left[\frac{(1+s)x}{s+x}\right]^{q-1}.\frac{(1+s)s}{(s+x)^2}.x.dx$$

$$E[D_a^R] = E[A]\left[w_c + 2lR(q)\right] \qquad (2)$$

4.2.2 The Traversing Strategy of the Mode within Laneway [8]

Under the classification storage mode within the laneway, the products' distributions of the storage area in the left and right two sides of I/O are symmetrical, the probability of having a picking position for the two laneways which are in the symmetrical position which is determined by F (x) is same. It should distinguish the odd number and even number of the laneways' number, when n is the odd number, the probability of a laneway k which has a picking product is:

$$P_k = \begin{cases} F(1/n) & k=0 \\ \frac{1}{2}\left[F(\frac{2k+1}{n}) - F(\frac{2k-1}{n})\right] & k=1,\ldots(n-1)/2 \end{cases}$$

The laneway j has the same probability with the laneway which is symmetric with k.

When n is the even number, the expression for the probability of laneway k which has a picking product is:

$$P_k = \frac{1}{2}\left[F(\frac{2k}{n}) - F(\frac{2k-2}{n})\right] \qquad k=1,\ldots n/2$$

Obviously, the probability of no picking goods in the laneway is $(1-P_k)^m$ Therefore, there is at least a picking product in the laneway, the probability for the pickers to traverse these laneways is $1-(1-P_k)^m$. It can calculate the expected walking distance in the picking laneways after knowing the probability of different circumstances.

$$E[D_n^x] = \begin{cases} (y+w_a)\left\{1-\left[1-F\left(\frac{1}{n}\right)\right]^m + 2\sum_{k=1}^{(n-1)/2}\left\{1-\left\{1-\frac{1}{2}\left[F(\frac{2k+1}{n})-F(\frac{2k-1}{n})\right]\right\}^m\right\}\right\} & n \text{ is the odd number} \\ 2(y+w_a)\sum_{k=1}^{n/2}\left\{1-\left\{1-\frac{1}{2}\left[F(\frac{2k}{n})-F(\frac{2k-2}{n})\right]\right\}^m\right\} & n \text{ is the even number} \end{cases} \tag{2-5}$$

5 The Numerical Examples of Layout Optimization for Order Picking Area

According to the total length of different shelves, it uses the layout model to determine the best layout structure of the picking area. In the situation of certain total length of shelf, with the increase in the number of laneways, the length of the laneway will be gradually reduced. Thus the length of shelf y in each laneway is equal to 1/2 of the ratio of the shelf's total length L and the number of the laneways. Because it has been demonstrated that the entrance is in the middle of the front channel to be the best position, therefore the example sets the entrance position in the middle of the front channel. It can get the best layout of picking area which relates to the walking distance through considering the number of laneways under the minimum path length.

Because the minimum path length has the relationship with the storage strategy and the path strategy, here takes the traversing strategy of the random storage strategy as the example to carry on optimizing layout for the picking area that its total length of the shelf surface L is 300 meters and the laneway center distance wa is 4 meters. When the entrance is in the middle position, d= (n+1)/2, for simplicity, the walking distance of the picking laneway uses the formula which is similar to formula (1). According to the above assumption, the picking walking distance can be simplified as:

$$D_w^x(n, y, d) = E[D_a^x] + E[D_c]$$
$$= yn[1-(\frac{n-1}{n})^m] + 0.5y$$
$$+ w_a\left[n-1-2\sum_{i=1}^{i-1}(\frac{i}{n})^m\right] + w_a\sum_{i=1}^{i}\left\{(|2i-n-1|)\times\left[\left(\frac{i}{n}\right)^m - \left(\frac{i-1}{n}\right)^m\right]\right\}$$

Thus the layout optimization model can be written as follows:

$$Z = \min\left\{ \begin{aligned} &yn[1-(\frac{n-1}{n})^m] + 0.5y \\ &+w_a\left[n-1-2\sum_{i=1}^{n-1}(\frac{i}{n})^m\right] + w_a\sum_{i=1}^{n}\left\{(|2i-n-1|)\times\left[\left(\frac{i}{n}\right)^m - \left(\frac{i-1}{n}\right)^m\right]\right\} \end{aligned} \right\}$$

$$2y \times n = L$$
$$1 \leq n \leq L/2, \quad \text{and uses integers}$$
when n is equal to 1 $E[D_c]=0$ \qquad the expression of the objective function is in the second line
$$y \geq 1$$

The layout model is the nonlinear function, in addition to asking the laneway's number to use integers, there also has the absolute value computation which relates to the variables in the objective function, and the variable also is emerged in the upper limit of summation, at present, this model is difficult to be solved through using the authority software of MATALAB and LINGO and so on. But after careful analysis, it is not difficult to find that the first constraint is an integer, the dependent variable y can be directly replaced by the variable n to be substituted into the objective function, at this time the objective function is changed into a function of one variable which only has one variable. It can be seen from the second constraint that when L is equal to 300, the value of n is the integer between 1 and 150, the solution space of the model is very small, and the layout structure only has 150 possibilities (it arranges the shelves symmetrically on both sides of the laneway), namely from 150 meters length of a laneway to 1 meter of 150 long laneways. In the case of a small number of solutions, the exhaustive algorithm is a very competitive algorithm, and it will certainly be able to get the exact optimal solution. In this paper's layout model for order picking area, the number of laneways of shelves' layout is not a great number, and it uses the integers, belongs to the discrete problem and its solution space is very small, the exhaustive algorithm can draw the results on the computer less than a second after inputting the correlative data. In order to ensure the correction and effectiveness of the results, it firstly does not consider the integer requirements for n and carries on the integer processing for the upper limited variable in summation; it firstly regards the model as the real number planning, and transfers the bounded scalar nonlinear minimization procedures of METNABLE to obtain the real solutions, then carries on the integer solutions searching around the real solutions, the obtained results are consistent with that of exhaustive algorithm. The following carries on the specific analysis for the computed results.

When L is equal to 300 meters and wa is equal to 3 meters, the distribution of the optimal laneway number has 6 kinds of situations; it is as the Table 1.

Table 1. The distribution of the laneway number when L is 300 meters and wa is 3 meters

The size of the picking order m	1	2~5	6~11	12~17	18~19	≥20
The optimal laneways number n*	11	10	15	10	5	3

It can draw the conclusion from this that when the total length of the shelf is certain, in the picking system layout of narrow laneway, the smaller the picking order is, the greater the number of optimal laneway is; the greater the picking order is, the small the number of optimal laneway is. In the case of the same number of laneway, the more the number of items to be picked is, the longer the expected walking path is. When the size of the picking order reaches to a certain extent, the optimal number of laneway is no longer to change. But in the layout of the greater picking order system, along with the increase of the items in the picking order, in the range of a small number of laneways, the laneway's number—the expected path length curve can present the jumping or fluctuation phenomena in varying degrees. This phenomenon can be explained that if the number of laneways in picking area is odd number and all the laneways must be visited, thus there is a part of distance which needs to return the entrance and walk repetitively in the last laneway to be visited. If the quantity of the goods to be picked is great, the probability of all the laneways to be visited can be increased, it leads to the increase of the distance which needs to walk repetitively for the last laneway. Along with the increase of the number of laneways, this phenomenon can be reduced. Because when the quantity of the items to be picked is certain, if the quantity of the laneways' number can be increased, so the probability of all the laneways to be visited can be reduced. The numerical calculations also show that when the total length of the shelf is certain, if it hopes to arrange the least number of laneways, it must meet that the items of the picking order reach certain quantity; when the number of picking goods' items exceeds this value, the value of the optimal laneway's number is no longer to change and keeps a fixed value. It can be seen from the situation of the jumping of the smallest number of laneways, the differences between the total lengths of the shelf and the shortest path lengths which are corresponded to the values of two alternate laneways are smaller. Besides, according to these characteristics, when it makes the specific layout decision, it also can be according to the size of the area of the picking area and the actual shape to select a layout of laneway which is the most fitting the actual.

6 Conclusion

It has established the picking area's layout model for man-to-part order picking system, it has carried on the specific analysis to the average expected walk distance under the various storage strategies and path strategies through using some of the conclusions of previous studies, and it uses examples to show the solving method of the model. It is worth noting that the layout model has universality, the different average expected walking distances can generate different layout models, when the distribution centers make layout decisions, they can use different layout model to design and optimize according to their actual situation.

References

1. Jiashan, W.: The Facilities' Planning and Design. Industrial Engineering (1), 11–14 (1998)
2. Caron, F., Marchet, G., Perego, A.: Routing policies and COI-based storage policies in picker-to-part systems. International Journal of Production Research 36(3), 713–732 (1998)
3. Roodbergen, K.J., Vis, I.F.A.: A model for warehouse layout. IIE Transactions 38, 799–811 (2006)
4. Goetschalckx, M., Ratliff, D.H.: Order picking in an aisle. IIE Transactions 20, 531–562 (1988b)
5. Donald Ratliff, H., Rosenthal, A.S.: Order-picking in a rectangular warehouse: a solvable case of the traveling salesman problem. Operation Research 31(3), 507–521 (1983)
6. Jarvis, J.M., McDowell, E.D.: Optimal product layout in an order picking warehouse. IIE Transactions 23(1), 93–102 (1991)
7. Hall, R.W.: Distance approximations for routing manual pickers in a warehouse. IIE Transactions 25(4), 76–87 (1993)
8. Hwang, H., Oh, Y.H., Lee, Y.K.: An evaluation of routing policies for order-picking operations in low-level picker-to-part system. Int. J. Prod. Res. 42(18), 3873–3889 (2004)
9. Guenov, M., Raeside, R.: Zone shape in class based storage and multi-command order picking when storage/retrieval machines are used. European Journal of Operational Research 58(1), 37–47 (1992)

Research on the Construction of Private Enterprise Culture in Zhejiang – A Case Study of Jinhua City

Fanghua Sun

College of Economics and Management, Zhejiang Normal University,
Jinhua, Zhejiang, China
sunfanghua@zjnu.cn

Abstract. In the background where the market economy constantly improves and the social system gradually improves, to explore and research the role of private enterprise culture in sustainable development have important and far-reaching theoretical and practical significances. Based on the empirical analysis of the construction of private enterprise culture in Jinhua, the paper focuses on the status and the existing problems of the construction of private enterprise culture in Jinhua and proposes strategies on the construction of private enterprise culture in Jinhua.

Keywords: Private Enterprise, Enterprise Culture, Learning Organization.

1 Research and Analysis on the Construction of Private Enterprise Culture in Jinhua

Private economy is a major feature and advantage of Jinhua. The city's private economy accounts for more than 90% of the total economy, which dominates in the economic development and brings the emergence of a large number of well-known enterprises. The author deeply learns about the economic development of the private enterprises in Jinhua, concerns the basic status of the construction of private enterprise culture in Jinhua, and conducts a full investigation:

1.1 Survey Description

The respondents of survey are 45 representative private enterprises in Jinhua area, which basically reflect the status of the construction of private enterprise culture in Jinhua. The contents of survey include the cognition and the status quo of enterprise culture, the basic situation and the performance of construction of enterprise culture; the type of survey: enclosed questionnaire; sampling range: private enterprises in Jinhua.

In this survey, 45 companies are surveyed, to which 450 questionnaires are sent. And 340 questionnaires are returned, with the recovery rate reaching 75.56%. There are 300 valid questionnaires, with the efficiency of 88.24%; the survey questionnaires are mainly targeted at the junior and senior management staff in the enterprise, accounting respectively for 36.67% and 53.33%.

Q. Zhou (Ed.): ISAEBD 2011, Part I, CCIS 208, pp. 15–21, 2011.

1.2 Empirical Analysis of Survey Results

1.2.1 Cognition of Private Enterprise Culture

(1) The basic understanding of the concept of enterprise culture.

Enterprise culture is in a certain social context the unique values, beliefs, codes of conduct, business philosophy and business ethics formed in the long process of enterprise operation and development. The survey results show that on average 90% of the respondents agree on the concept above. Enterprise culture is generally considered a kind of management tools and management methods. The respondents especially reach a consensus on "the core content of enterprise culture is the shared values and code of conduct among employees ". 26% of people's understandings of enterprise culture still only stay on the shallow level and the surface, for example, enterprise culture is just the culture of boss, just to enrich the cultural life of the staff, to design and upgrade the enterprise image.

(2) The understanding of relationship between enterprise culture and enterprise development

Many enterprises generally agree that good enterprise culture has a direct or indirect impact on the survival and development of enterprises. Among them, 60% of respondents believe that it has a great impact, which to a certain extent reflects the public already has a certain cognition level about the role of the impact of enterprise culture. At the same time, the competitive advantage of enterprise culture as the core one of enterprise is gradually revealed. As the companies-pursued concept of improving the quality and brand firmly established, the concept of culture is gradually becoming the fashionable "word" entrepreneurs keen to talk of at their leisure.

Table 1. Major competitive advantages of enterprises

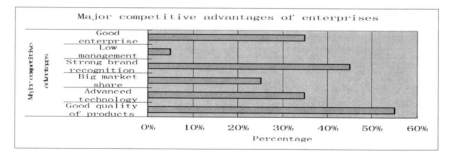

(3) The main factors of enterprise culture

Internal factors: The individual concept of entrepreneurs、 Traditions of entrepreneurs、(Institutional environment、Industry Culture)

External factors: Social culture、Market environment 、Customer factors 、Foreign culture、(Institutional environment、Industry Culture)

Internal factors / external factors = 100/85.8325 = 1.165 ⇒ the influence of internal factors> External factors influence

Table 2. The main factors of enterprise culture

Influencing factors	Great impact	Respectively great impact	General impact	No impact
The individual concept of entrepreneurs	50%	50%		
Traditions of entrepreneurs	23.33%	50%	26.67%	
Institutional environment	33.33%	46.67%	20%	
Social culture	10%	63.33%	20%	6.67%
Industry Culture	10%	66.67%	20%	3.33%
Market environment	10%	50%	30%	10%
Customer factors	20%	45%	15%	20%
Customer factors	3.33%	16.67%	60%	20%

It demonstrates the impacts of the influencing factors weaken from the individual concept of entrepreneurs to the foreign culture in order, showing the characteristics of the influencing factors of enterprise culture drop from the inside to outside. It then decides the construction of enterprise culture must to be an inside-out and top-down process. It is not hard to see that the key influencing factor of private enterprise culture is the entrepreneurs' personal factors.

1.2.2 The Status of Private Enterprise Culture

"Denison organizational culture model" is created by the well-known professor Daniel • Denison of the Swiss International Department of Management (IMD), which is one of the most effective and practical models to measure the organizational culture.

Table 3. Denison Organizational Culture Assessment Method

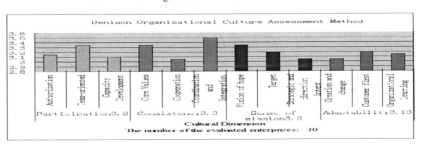

As is shown in Table 3, firstly, the four dimensions comprehensively reflect the overall level of the culture of the city's private enterprises is not high. In the twelve small dimensions, only the four dimensions of team-oriented, core values, coordination and integration and the vision of hope, etc. are higher than the average value of 3.208. Secondly, the adaptability of private enterprise culture in terms of dimension is slightly lacking compared to other dimensions, which shows that private enterprises need to be improved in the company's flexibility and ability to deal with the rival of the external environment. 30% of the respondents believe that "the enterprise culture of their own businesses do not adapt to the realities of business", which confirm the fact inferred above. Moreover, their awareness of innovation and learning is insufficient. If enterprise culture can encourage and support activities of innovation, it will further enhance the opportunity of innovative products or the commercialization of services. Almost eighty percent of the respondents believe that the enterprise culture of their own business needs to be innovated, and almost twenty percent believe it needs badly.

1.3 Basic Status of the Construction of Enterprise Culture

Business operators on the construction of enterprise culture determine the basic status. The survey involves the organizational leadership, achievement form, stage and other issues of enterprise culture construction, and also business operators' familiarity with enterprise culture at all levels and evaluation of the status quo of enterprise culture.

Organizational leadership: The private economic determines that the main responsible people of enterprise culture are general manager and human resources manager, who account respectively for 30% and 33.33%. The economic structure and model of private enterprises determines in the early stage of development, it is not possible to set up special departments to take charge of the construction of enterprise culture, which from one side reflects there is still a gap on the enterprise operators' awareness of the importance of enterprise culture. The good news is there are around seventy percent of enterprises have the relevant departments responsible for enterprise culture.

Expert guidance: It is very important and has a "the crucial point" meaning to get the right guidance of "famous teacher" in the process of the construction of enterprise culture for enterprises. Unfortunately, 60% of the companies do not hire experts to do the guidance.

The stage: When asked about what stage their construction of the enterprise culture is in, the enterprises respond as the results show that there are 0 "not started" , 40% "brewing and exploring stage", 46.67%"basic formed stage", and 13.33% " deepening and improving stage". It is not difficult to find in our city the construction of private enterprise culture is in the stage of "brewing and exploring" and "basic formed", not" evolved "to the stage of self-conscious implementation of their own cultural management.

Major difficulties: The major difficulties encountered in the process of the construction are successively 50% "lack of consensus within", 30% "low qualities of the workers", 26.67% "lack of motivation", 20% "lack of a favorable external environment" 30%" do not know how to do " and 10% " do not know the meaning of enterprise culture".

2 Deep Analysis of the Existing Problems of the Construction of Private Enterprise Culture in Jinhua

2.1 Private Enterprises' Misunderstanding of Enterprise Culture

At present, there are mainly two typical misunderstandings of the construction of enterprise culture for private enterprises in Jinhua: First, they think the enterprise culture construction is equivalent to general arts and sports activities (the enterprises who agreed accounting for 26.67%), and the motive of publicity is more than the actual content of itself, just to make the enterprise culture construction simplistic and superficial; Second, 50% of them think the enterprise culture is equivalent to shaping the corporate image. Such understanding makes the enterprise culture unilateral. The corporate image shaping is an external forms and means to achieve running and development goals of private enterprise, but cannot covers all the enterprise culture.

2.2 The Cultivation of Private Enterprise Culture Is at the Low Level

As is shown in the survey, the majority of private enterprise culture construction is still in the stage of "brewing and exploring" and "basic formed". Apart from a few private enterprises (26.67%) has entered the stage of self-conscious implementation of cultural management, most private enterprises lack a deep understanding of the importance of enterprise culture. They do not care about or beyond their grasp on careful management of the implementation of enterprise culture. The existing value throughout enterprise running, many are formed in the spontaneous and unconscious accumulation of their long-term operation, with a strong color of experience, fragmented and unstable; some enterprises have put forward the business philosophy, mission and values in form of text, but often with a character of general, imitation and lack of vitality, thus making it difficult to have a strong influence on enterprise.

2.3 The Private Enterprise Culture Lack of Innovative Spirit

Some private enterprise thought their old enterprise culture, which has been deeply rooted, had promoted the development of enterprises, and therefore do not want to or could not bear to be innovative. In fact, if the original positive enterprise culture is not updated in time, it will become negative enterprise culture, thus impeding the development of enterprises, making the enterprise culture lack of the adaptability to environment. The real enterprise culture is a dynamic system, which must be progressive and make new ideas, new knowledge, new technologies and new management enrich the enterprises, thus constantly adapting to the needs of the social environment[6]

2.4 Lack of Entrepreneurs with Both Ability and Integrity

Currently, most private enterprise culture is too rigid and lack in flexibility. In the subconscious of Chinese people, the thinking of officialdom standard has been influencing on the growth of the Chinese entrepreneurs. Although the educational level of private entrepreneurs has been generally improved, due to the various constraints of the external environment and internal quality, the entrepreneurs with ability and integrity, excellent management skills and strategic vision are lacked. Most of these entrepreneurs are content with the status quo or enjoy the existing results. Many private entrepreneurs who lack of goals and vision of making enterprise bigger and stronger do not take enterprise as their own career and life, but as a display of the symbol of their status and strength, not to mention to expand the construction of enterprise culture with far-sighted thought.

3 Strategy Analysis of the Construction of Private Enterprise Culture in Jinhua

3.1 Attach Great Importance to the Construction of Enterprise Culture

With the arrival of China's full market economy era, the entrepreneurs in Jinhua must clearly recognize that in the fierce market competition conditions, reforming of enterprise needs culture for support, production and operation need culture for promotion, market strategy needs culture for development, enterprise management needs culture for regulation, enterprise image needs culture for shaping, and enterprise reputation needs culture for transmission. Based on the full recognition of the importance of enterprise culture, it is proposed to deep understand the connotation of enterprise culture, take the deep enterprise culture as the starting point, to find the enterprise actual cultural heritage and values with local characteristics. Besides, it is proposed to overcome a variety of one-sided understanding of enterprise culture, and get rid of the various errors in the construction of enterprise culture.

3.2 To Establish Long-Term Goal and Shape Enterprise Core Values

How the role of enterprise culture to inspire plays to a large extent lies in the success of the exploration of enterprise personality. During the construction of enterprise culture, we must fully analyze internal and external factors, refine the core values. We must first consider the characteristics of the industry and know that the enterprise culture of different sectors has its own characteristics; Secondly, we must consider the component of enterprise culture and its members, and know that the different types of people and their combination will affect the formation of enterprise culture.In addition, it's proposed to establish brand awareness and strengthen enterprise character. Brand is the most important form of enterprise intangible assets, the symbol of credit, also the most important means of operation in enterprise running activities.

3.3 There Must Be Innovative Awareness and "Harmony" Atmosphere

If enterprises want to be competitive, they should capture information from customer, market and other aspects, thus absorbing new ideas and creating favorable environment and atmosphere for innovation. There are such key aspects: First, abandon some parts of traditional spirit of enterprise culture, which are not adapt to market economy and knowledge economy demands, abandoning the obsolete and the old thoughts and ideas with no inspiring function. Second, promote the enterprise culture whose forerunner is the spirit of innovation. Third, based on the re-examination of enterprise spiritual and cultural content, according to the new strategic objectives of enterprises in development stage, establish a new core spirit of enterprise and arouse the enthusiasm of a high degree of innovation of the entire staff, so that all staff together can achieve common goals. Meanwhile, enterprises not only need internal "harmony" so that employees can work in unity and solidarity, thus facing together the enterprises difficulties and crises; but also need external "harmony" with the Government, trying to get extensive support from the Government; besides need "harmony" with other enterprises, develop themselves in competition and joint, and thus being invincible.

3.4 Emphasize on the Entrepreneurial Factors and Bring It into Play

Entrepreneurs are the basic elements of enterprise core competitiveness, also the key to cultivate the unique and positive enterprise culture. Internationally competitive entrepreneurs must have both ability and integrity, with excellent management skills and strategic vision, take enterprise as their own careers and lives; with the "three-Quotient": high IQ, high EQ, high CQ, also have four abilities: innovation ability, adaptability, public relations ability and multicultural coordination ability. Entrepreneurs have to learn use vertical thinking, reverse thinking and lateral thinking to think creatively, especially in strategic thinking, and in accordance with changes in the international market and new enterprise "scene" to fix enterprise strategy and business strategy, to adjust their approach to leadership and management, then to guide and influence employees into "confident and capable" state, thus making them innovate and meet the challenge.

3.5 Enhance Organizational Learning and Create Learning Organizations

Now the competition among enterprises is not only the competition of the capital, existing technology and stock of talent, but competition of enterprise learning capacity, that is the competition of employees' and organizational learning motivation, learning perseverance and ability to learn. Successful companies will be learning organizations. If entrepreneurs want to maintain sustainable competitive advantage, the only way is to learn better and faster than the competitors. Therefore, the shaping of new learning enterprise culture in the enterprise's growth and development is crucial. Enterprises should strengthen organizational learning and create learning organizations. Learning is no longer a matter of individual employees, but the responsibilities and obligations of the organization's all members, is an investment in intellectual capital, and is the process of accumulation of knowledge and value for enterprises. Only in this way, enterprises can gain advantages in the competition, then to obtain long-term development.

References

1. Philip, Harris, R., Moran (eds.): Cross-cultural Management Tutorial, pp. 39–52. Xinhua Publishing Press (2002)
2. Luo, C.: Enterprise Culture, pp. 121–157. China Renmin University Press (1999)
3. De, Z.: Corporate Culture and CI planning, pp. 32–57. Tsinghua University Press (2000)

A Pragmatic Study of Irony in Samuel Beckett's Plays

Lihua Huang

School of Foreign Languages, Nanchang Hangkong University, Nanchang,
Jiangxi, China
LihuaHuang2011@126.com

Abstract. Irony is one of the salient characteristics in Samuel Beckett's plays.
The paper attempts to apply post-Gricean theories of pragmatics to analyze both
"echoic mention" and "allusional pretense" ironies in order to reveal the
different subjects implied in Beckett's plays. Through analysis, the paper finds
that Beckett always used the ironic techniques to build his own unique narrative
mode: making oneself alienate himself/herself from the past memories which
are painful and fragmented.

Keywords: Samuel Beckett, dramatic utterances, irony, echoic mention,
allusional pretense.

1 Introduction

Pragmatic study of irony can be dated back to 1970s'Grice. Grice regards irony as a
violation of "maxim of quality" in the dialogue that it connotates antonymy which the
ironic dialogue expresses. For instance, the addressor invariably depicts an obviously
"bad" thing as a "good" one. But, the addressor not only expresses the reverse
meaning of irony under certain circumstances. Therefore, Grice's method turns to be
insufficient of explaining uncertainty of irony. Developing Grice's theory, Sperber
and Wilson put forward a newly ironic theory "echoic mention". It is said that irony
does not describe what the addressor's thinking but the others'. The addressor makes
use of the dialogue to express an attitude that reflects thinking in the dialogue, or an
attitude aiming at the person who has expressed a dialogue and upholded thinking.
Irony belongs to the second level of interpretation of one's thinking, which is defined
as echoic explanation. During the explanation, the addressor deviates himself from
echoic thinking. The attitude expressed by irony is usually refusal or disagreement.
[1] (Sperber and 1996:238-243)

However, the word "echo" is ambiguous and used to arousing misunderstanding.
That is because "not all the ironic echo can be easily recognized. The echoed thinking
might not be depicted in the dialogue; not a specific person but a certain type of
people or common people might understand the echoed thinking; or it is just a kind of
cultural aspiration or cultural norms."[2] (Wilson and Sperber 1989:60) Then, Sperber
and Wilson(1986) Turned "echoic mention" into "echoic interpretation". Many newly
ironic theory have come into being from then on such as pretense theory by Clark and
Gerrig(1984), echoic reminder by Kreuz and Glucksberg(1989) and allusional
pretense based on the above theories by Kumon-Nakamura(1995) and so on.

Q. Zhou (Ed.): ISAEBD 2011, Part I, CCIS 208, pp. 22–27, 2011.
© Springer-Verlag Berlin Heidelberg 2011

Although the updated theories each time seem to enrich the explaining and describing efforts to the previous, irony in specific context is not likely to be interpreted. For example, there are two people coming to a door at the same time. One of them opened the door and came in after the door swing to close behind him. The other happened to carry a big box, saying to the former one:

1.1 a. Thank You for Your Letting the Door Open

  b. Thank you for Your Closing the Door

There exists an obvious but not easily attentive fact that(1a)and(1b)both can be understood as irony. The addressor of(1a)makes use of echoic reminder in counter-fact context, while(1b)does not. Meanwhile, both(1a)and(1b)possess the nature of "pragmatic dishonesty" and "inappropriate relation". But they cannot explain the dialogues above which seem to be ironic and have contradictory premises. Thus, the "echo theory" and its variants theories cannot be justified. That is not a unique situation. Take another dialogue for example, when a car ahead suddenly turned left without any indicator light, a driver commented:

1.2 a. I like People to Bright the Indicator Light before They Turn around

  b. I like People not to Bright Indicator Light before They Turn around

Just like(1a) and(1b), both (2a) and(2b)have ironic meanings. (1a) and(2a)refer to things not happened, while (1b) and(2b)indicate things have already happened and the effects of irony seem alike. That comes to a question that how a dialogue has the same ironic effect with the other of contradictory premise. In the view of this, Yoshihiko Kihara(2005)proposed an integrated method— mutually manifest expectation space. That is to say, in the absence of any significant context to create a circumstance, one's aspiration is to make the intention of speaker be understood by the listeners. It can help us explain the following questions: how could irony reach its expected effects; how could ironic and possible assertion A and the opposite A express with the same contents; why is irony used to criticize not to praise mostly; and why does the negative irony need no dominant premise while affirmative irony needs.

Samuel Beckett (1906-1989) is one of the most important playwrights in 20th century. His plays are not confined to traditional dramatic forms with variety of writing skills such as humor, irony, parody and metaphor etc. As the comments of Nobel Prize to him in 1969 said, "with a peculiar form of his novels and plays, modern people get inspired from the spirit of weary." After reading his dramas, the author find that irony is the most prominent writing skill and expressed throughout Beckett's plays. Due to the limitation of space the article will use the above post-Gricean pragmatic theories related to analyze "echoic mention" and "allusional pretense" in Beckett's plays, in order to reveal the dramas of different themes and deepen our understanding toward Beckett.

2 "Echoic Mention" of Irony in Backett's Plays

Generally speaking, Backett's plays set an example for modern dramas. "Echoic mention" can be embodied in his varied dizzying theatrical dialogues. According to

Sperber and Wilson, to understand irony requires two steps: firstly, it is necessary to recognize the fact that the view proposed is not on behalf of addressor' thinking but just an echo. Secondly, it is also necessary to believe that the use of irony by the addressor is to make him deviate from the contents and take for fun.[3] (S'hiri 1992:127) Beckett's drama "Happy Days" created in 1960 can best describe that problem. The theme of this play concludes at the significance of "self-understanding", "anisotropic dialectics", "gazes from the third party" and "redemptive power" of language without any body languages. In the act one, in the open arena and under the glare of lights, the heroine Winnie is buried in a mound. The soil has crammed to her waist; then in the act two, soil has buried to her neck. Winnie continuously repeats such hopeful messages to her husband Willie who hides behind her, standing in a hole nearby until the end of the act: "Ah, it will be another happy day!"[4] (Beckett 1961:31) Literally speaking, it seems like Winnie's positive thinking. But actually, it is just an echo which does not belong to her factual idea dramatically. Winnie deeply knows that there is no happiness in the future for her except gradually caught in the mound. After she realizes her predicament, she tries to make use of the redemptive power of language to get rid of the plight and keep a positive and active philosophy of life. At the end of the second act, Winnie singing lyric minor towards Willie is the best witness. "Winnie: ... Please listen, while shaking dance is telling, dear, love me! Every time the fingers touching tell me what I need, To tell you, it's true, it's true, you still love me!"(ibid. :31)Here, Backett uses "echoic mention" repeatedly with the purpose of describing a negative and disagreeable attitude. Meanwhile, addressor can deviate from that it. As for Winnie, her intention is to tell her husband that she lives comfortably now and need not anyone to interrupt her peaceful atmosphere, even if she knows that she is dying. While as for Willie, he does not response to Winnie's words and actions, but quietly stares at her. As far as the author is concerned, two reasons can be concluded from that. One the one hand, Willie might be a passionate person or a ruthless one; on the other hand, according to Yoshihiko Kihara's "mutually manifest expectation space", without any significant context to create a circumstance, an addressor of typical irony expresses his aspiration in the circumstance, which will not come true in the real space.[5] (Kihara 2005:513) That's to say, the echoic mention only refers to the addressor's aspiration. Willie might have understood what his wife thinks and aspires, so he does not need any reaction or help her proactively. Therefore, he keeps silence all the time, which is the real intention of the method of "gazes from the third party".

Another important drama "Karapp's Last Tape" (1957) written in Backett's early period shows a one-act play that the hero Karapp remodels his identity with the help of listening to the recordings of anecdotes. The identity of Karapp is displayed by varied ironic monologues. At the beginning of the drama, 69-year-old Karapp is listening to a recording when he was 39. Karapp recalls: "I sat there in the chilly wind, and I wish my mother died."[6] (Beckett 1991:1276) That is not a pure demonstration, but an "echoic mention" because the monologue is very ambiguous. Karapp does not sure his mother died, and the expression implies a response to others' views and dialogues. It is indicated from Karapp that it's ridiculous, artificial, inappropriate or inadvisable. Therefore, what Karapp says conveys his attention: it is absurd to think his mother will die; it is stupid that his friends let him believe that his mother will die; he views that his friends' assertion is naïve etc. Karapp "echoes" the belief or the dialogue with the same contents in his response in order to express a critical or sneering attitude. In short, based on the difference between the actual method described in the monologue and the real situation of the whole story, the discourse expressed by the addressor's attributable words or ideas possesses a deviation of the attitude. As for this play, Karapp makes use of "echo" language to remodel his sensation when listening to his mother's death. Karapp keeps trying to eliminate the ambiguous relationship between he and his mother. Reviewing the past event after 30 years reveals his effort to get rid of his passion to his mother.

3   "Allusional Pretense " of Irony in Backett's Plays

The theoretical basis of pretense is Grice's (1975, 1978) pragmatic substitute and Fowler's (1965) double-audience postulate. Later, Clark and Greg from Stanford University summarized pretense theory based on the above two. It is said that Addressor pretends to implement a speaking act, looking forward to seeing through the camouflage by his listeners and acknowledging ironic and critical attitude behind it. "allusional pretense" is concluded by Kumon-Nakamura (1995) on the basis of "echoic mention" from Sperber and Wilson and "pretense theory" from Clark and Greg. The theory is that ironic speech must have several essential characteristics. Firstly, it co notates (not echo) former views and acts etc. Secondly, all the intentionally ironic speeches contain "pragmatic insincerity". Words and acts in communication must be appropriate with four conditions: (a)Propositional contents of discourse is suitable and felicitous, (b)status between addressor and listener is equivalent and proper, (c)the state of mind implied in the discourse is right and sincere, (d)Listener sincerely feels and understands the addressor.[7] (Kumon-Nakamura et al 1995) If any one of felicity conditions is violated, it will be regarded as pragmatic insincerity.

There is no doubt that "allusional pretense" is embodied in Backett's play, especially in his famous drama "waiting for Godot" (1954). Two homeless people, Vladimir and Estragon are waiting for Godot, a very important person for them day by day, as Vladimir states: "Thanks to Godot, we are saved! Let's welcome him!"[8] (Beckett 1954:47) These words indicate Chapter 25 in Matthew: "Then the kingdom of heaven will be like ten virgins, who took their lamps, and went out to meet the bridegroom." In the bible, the bridegroom came and brought them to the wedding eventually (the image to redeem and protect). However, in the play, Vladimir is wrong because Godot does not appear in the end; they are not redeemed or protected by God. Also the dramatic scenes allude to many situations in the bible. As a addressor A, Vladimir says unconsciously "we are saved! Let us welcome him!" He pretends to be an outsiders S' (just like the people accompanying bridegroom in Chapter 25 in Matthew) to ask an unwitting listener A' to welcome Godot. The intention is to let listener A'(Estragon) realize the camouflage and make fun of addressor S' , believer A' and the discourse itself in reality. While the actual listeners A (audience) issue the same sigh as Vladimir says "the last hope left is for us to disappear" after recognizing the fact and feeling a little bit relax. Unfortunately, Vladimir and Estragon continue to wait for Godot, hoping for salvation with confusion. Backett takes an ironic mockery of Vladimir and Estragon who has had many impractical wishes through the method of "allusional pretense" in this play.

Then, we continue to analyze another play "Endgame" (1958) written in Backett's early period. In this play, hero Hamm and his servant Clov are talking about the barren state of the world. Clov is angry to his master Hamm of pretended ignorance:

When the old mother Pegg ask you to lend her some lamp oil, you tell her to go to hell. Do you know what happened then? No?

[STOP]

Do you know what the old mother died of? She died of darkness.[9] (Beckett 1958: 75) Here, the accusation towards Hamm from Clov also implies the story in Chapter 25 in Matthew. After the five foolish virgins arose, they suddenly realized they took no oil with. So the foolish said to the wise: "Give us some of your oil, for our lamps are going out." But the wise answered: "What if there isn't enough for us and you? You go rather to those who sell, and buy for yourselves."(Matthew 25:1-13) Clov's accusation discourse echoes "oil", "lamp", "hell" and "darkness" and so on in the story of bible. Those intensified ironic meaning strengthen helplessness in the play. Meanwhile, Hamm is quite like God. He pretends to be ignorant. He cannot provide possible methods to live whether it is a piece of bread in the wild or the oil in darkness. His disguise has a great deceptive effect to his servant Clov and makes him very painful. Clove wants to rebel but has to obey; He wants to kill Hamm but dares not because he cannot live without Hamm. Without Hamm's instruction, Clov does not know how to open the store room. To some extent, the accusation towards Hamm from Clov possesses pragmatic insincerity for it violates one suitable condition in ironic communication. That is,(b)status between addressor and listener is equivalent and proper, or (c)he state of mind implied in the discourse is right and sincere. Even though, the alluding itself does not change or increase pessimistic fact or sense of homelessness, it just enhance the existing images like "oil", "lamp", "hell" and "darkness" etc. These images are so simulated and deceptive that listeners need to recognize them with the help of other memories. Therefore, in addition to sense of helplessness, a huge sense of loss soaks in the play. Such sense of loss is not only suitable for this specific scene, but also for any situation in history. The genius of Backett relies on the use of the ironic pretense —"allusional pretense". He makes use of the bible story people are familiar with to universalize one of the themes that depicts sense of loss.

4 Conclusion

Samuel Backett is the world-renowned master of theatre of absurd in 20th century. He cleverly blends irony into his skillful method of writing during the creation of dramas, highlighting multiple themes like "self-understanding", "helplessness", "loss", "anxiety", "silence", "gazes from the third part" and "salvation" in the dramatic discourse. With the use of ironic discourse, Backett tries to negate "Proustian imagery" narration and create "Backettian narration". It helps us to get rid of miserable memories with absent self-image in the past. The application of ironic discourse can be considered to be a miniature of Backett's toilsome exploration for the new theatrical form all his life. But we have been shaken deep in our hearts by his ironic discourses, as his Nobel Prize comments say: "Because of his newly forms of novels and dramas, our modern people can get excited from poverty."

References

1. Sperber, D., Wilson, D.: Relevance: Communication and Cognition. Basil Backwell (1986)
2. Sperber, D., Wilson, D.: On verbal irony. Lingua 87, 53–76 (1989)
3. S'hiri, S.: A Pragmatics of Verbal Irony in Literary Discourse: An Example from Drama. Edinburgh Working Papers in Linguistics 3, 124–134 (1992)
4. Beckett, S.: Happy Days. Grove, New York (1961)
5. Kihara, Y.: The mental space structure of verbal irony. Cognitive Linguistics 16(3), 513–530 (2005)
6. Beckett, S.: Krapp's Last Tape. In: Comley, N.R., Klaus, C.H., Scholes, R., Silverman, M. (eds.) Elements of Literature, Essay, Fiction, Poetry, Film, pp. 1273–1279. Oxford University Press, New York (1991)
7. Kumon-Nakamura, S., Glucksberg, S., Brown, M.: How about another piece of pie: The allusional pretence theory of discourse irony. Journal of Experimental Psychology: General 124, 3–21 (1995)
8. Beckett, S.: Waiting for Godot. Grove Press, New York (1954)
9. Beckett, S.: Endgame. Grove Press, New York (1958)

Effects of Strategic Consumer Behavior on Radical New Product Capacity Decision

Guojun Ji and Guangyong Yang

School of Management, Xiamen University, Xiamen 361005, China
jiking@xmu.edu.cn, xmdxygy@126.com

Abstract. When radical new product is introduced to market, capacity and demand behave highly mismatch, so capacity decision has been a key issue that innovator need to consider. We consider three types of consumers: myopic consumers, strategic consumers and bargain-hunters, in which strategic consumers choose inter-temporal purchase timing. Firstly, we find that when the fraction of strategic consumers grows to some level, an extra fraction of strategic consumers will not influence the innovator's capacity decision without speculator cases. Secondly, we study speculative behavior case, our results show that if speculator is risk averse, it's no impact on innovator; if speculator behaves risk preference, innovator's optimal capacity and quantity hoarded by speculator's decrease in fraction of strategic customers and capacity cost. Finally, we show that speculator can alleviate mismatch risk between supply and demand, however, only fraction of strategic customers higher than some threshold level, speculator can increase innovator's profits.

Keywords: strategic consumers, speculative behavior, radical new product, rational expectation.

1 Introduction

With shrinkage of product life cycle, increase of technological complexity as well as rationality of customer purchase behavior, product innovation has been a competitive weapon for innovator sustainable development. Generally, Product innovation involved radical innovation and incremental innovation. According to report by PDMA, incremental innovation was negative correlated to innovator's performance, however, radical innovation is closed correlated to innovator's performance (Adams 2004). Radical innovation can be achieved by following two strategies, significant technological innovation as well as redefining product value to customer. Kodak cooperation captures digital video market by investing radical technology (Fobers 2003), whereas success of Apple company iPod is attributed to new function of experience, namely, not only listen music, but rather download music from websites. These two radical new strategies focus on long term benefits, so they play a vital role in constructing company competitive capability.

However, radical new product introduced to market, its intrinsic attributes is not judged, capacity and demand behave highly mismatch, so capacity decision is a key

Q. Zhou (Ed.): ISAEBD 2011, Part I, CCIS 208, pp. 28–34, 2011.

issue that innovator need to consider. On the other hand, with rapid introduction of new product, customers believe that now hot product will be obsolete in tomorrow, their purchase decision characterizes rationally, that is, utilizing strategic waiting to purchase product at lowest price in future. Due to mismatch between capacity and demand, innovator capacity may be stock out, this attract speculator entry market to obtain arbitrage revenue. Take Apple's iPhone as an example, when it was introduced to market, shortage of capacity ever attract speculator. Based on these considerations, this paper study that optimal capacity decision innovator faces in the presence of strategic customers.

This paper has following three conclusions: (a) when the fraction of strategic consumers grows to some level, an extra fraction of strategic consumers will not influence the innovator capacity and profits without speculator cases. (b) If speculator behaves risk preference, innovator's optimal capacity and quantity hoarded by speculator decrease in fraction of strategic customers and capacity cost. (c) Speculator can alleviate mismatch risk between supply and demand.

The papers that study on impact of radical innovation on innovator core competitive ability include, Bhaskaran and Krishnan (2009) show that investment sharing is more attractive for new-to-the-world product projects with significant timing uncertainty. Chao and Kavadias (2008) find that environmental complexity shifts the balance toward radical innovation. Karim (2009) explores radical innovation from dynamic capacity and organization learning ability perspective. These papers mainly study radical new product from technology, environment as well as process perspectives. We study radical new product capacity decision from supply chain perspective in the presence of heterogeneous customers.

Other stream of research involved strategic customer behavior. Lai et al. (2010) examine the impact of a posterior price matching policy on consumers' purchasing behavior. Levin et al. (2009) present a dynamic pricing model for oligopolistic firms selling differentiated perishable goods to multiple finite segments of strategic consumers who may time their purchases. These papers use dynamic pricing model to study strategic customer behavior and dynamic pricing, but based on radical new product. Su and Zhang (2008) show that the seller's profit can be improved by promising either that quantities available will be limited or that prices will be kept high. These papers focus on fixed capacity.

2 Model

We consider an innovator sells radical new product in two periods. Let t_i denotes i-period, $i=1, 2$. Sell price in first period and second period is p_1 and p_2, respectively, $p_1 \geq p_2$. We assume that radical product introduced to market, capacity that can be used to sell is limited. The unit production or purchase cost is c.

Based on product value, we refer to customer that can purchase product in first period as high end customer and customer that only purchase product in second period as low end customer. High end and low end customer's valuation is V_H and V_L, respectively. We assume $V_L < c < p_1 < V_H$. We also assume that amount of high end customers is large so that impact of individual customer on market is negligible. Let X denotes that amount of high end customers is a random variable. We define $F(\cdot)$

and $f(\cdot)$ to be, respectively, the distribution and density functions of X, with $\overline{F}(\cdot) = 1 - F(\cdot)$.

(a) Strategic customer: fraction of strategic customer in high end customer is α. Strategic customer is risk neutral, their valuation is not variable over time, that is, not loss of utility for radical new product. Strategic customers rationally expect product availability in second period and choose inter-temporal purchase timing. Rational expectation hypothesis states that economic outcomes do not differ systematically from what people expect them to be (Muth 1961). (b) Myopic customer: fraction of myopic customer in high end customer is $1-\alpha$. We assume $V_H > p_1$ so that all myopic customers purchase products in first period. (c) Bargain hunter: all low end customers are bargain hunter. We assume that there has been a large number of bargain hunter, hence, the innovator can always sell all leftovers at a sufficiently low price. However, once demand exceeds capacity, we assume efficient rationing, so low end consumers have the lowest priority.

Assumption 1. A random variable X satisfies the monotone scaled likelihood ratio (MSLR) property. That is, for all $0 \leq \varepsilon \leq 1$, $f(\varepsilon X)/f(X)$ is monotonic in X.

3   Capacity Decision without Speculator

This section analyzes a sub-game perfect equilibrium between innovator and strategic customers, and explores impact of strategic customer behavior on optimal capacity decision.

We use $\tilde{\beta}$ denote innovator's belief on fraction of strategic customers who buy in the second period. Innovator infers that fraction of strategic customers who buy in the first period is $\xi = 1 - \alpha\tilde{\beta}$ and demand is ξX. Total amount of strategic customers in second period is $\alpha\tilde{\beta}X$. Leftovers at the end of first period are $L = (q - \xi X)^+$. a) If $\xi X \geq q$, we have $L = 0$ and ignore pricing decision in second period, b) If $\xi X < q$, we have $L > 0$, innovator has two choices in second period, that is, Only selling to strategic customers or cleaning leftovers L at the discount price.

We use R_2 denote innovator's revenue in second period,

$$R_2 = \begin{cases} V_L L & \text{if } p_2 = V_L, \\ p_1 \min(\alpha\tilde{\beta}X, L) & \text{if } p_2 = p_1. \end{cases}$$

Lemma 1. *Let* $\lambda = V_L / [V_L + (p_1 - V_L)\alpha\tilde{\beta}]$, *innovator's optimal price in second period*

is $p_2(X) = \begin{cases} V_L & \text{if } X < \lambda q \\ p_1 & \text{if } \lambda q \leq X < q/\xi. \end{cases}$

Lemma 1 illustrate that if demands are very high, innovator keep price constant, otherwise, clean the leftovers at the price V_L.

Strategic customer tradeoffs expected surplus in first period with second period to select purchase timing. The expected surplus in first period is

$$u_1 = V_H - p_1 \tag{1}$$

The expected surplus in second period is

$$u_2 = F(\lambda q)(V_H - V_L) + [F(q) - F(\lambda q)](V_H - p_1) + \int_{l}^{q/\xi} \frac{q - \xi X}{(1-\xi)X} dF(X)(V_H - p_1) \qquad (2)$$

Thus, strategic customer purchasing product between first period and second period is indifferent if and only if

$$u_1 - u_2 = [\overline{F}(q) - \int_{l}^{q/\xi} \frac{q - \xi X}{(1-\xi)X} dF(X)](V_H - p_1) - F(\lambda q)(p_1 - V_L) = 0 \qquad (3)$$

We use $\tilde{q}$ denote strategic customers' belief on innovator's capacity. Based on equation (2), we have the following lemma 2.

Lemma 2. *Fraction of strategic customers who buy in the second period satisfy* $\lim_{\tilde{q} \to 0} \beta^*(\tilde{q}) = 0$, $\lim_{\tilde{q} \to +\infty} \beta^*(\tilde{q}) = 1$.

We use $\Pi(q, \tilde{\beta})$ denote innovator's expected profits, which depend on belief on Fraction of strategic customers who buy in the second period.

$$\Pi(q, \tilde{\beta}) = p_1 q \overline{F}(\frac{q}{\xi}) + \int_{l}^{\frac{q}{\xi}} [p_1 \xi X + p_1(q - \xi X)] dF(X)$$

$$+ \int_{\lambda q}^{q} [p_1 \xi X + p_1 \tilde{\beta} \alpha X] dF(X) + \int_{}^{\lambda q} [p_1 \xi X + V_L(q - \xi X)] dF(X) - cq \qquad (4)$$

Based on equation (5), we have the following lemma 3.

Lemma 3. *Innovator's expected profits* $\Pi(q, \tilde{\beta})$ *is quasi-concave in* q, *optimal capacity* q^* *is determined by following first-order condition*

$$d\Pi(q, \tilde{\beta})/dq = p_1 \overline{F}(q) + V_L F(\lambda q) - c = 0 \qquad (5)$$

Proposition 1. *There exists a sub-game perfect equilibrium between innovator and strategic customers,* (q^*, β^*).

Corollary 1. *There exists a threshold* $\alpha^\circ \in [0,1]$ *such that for* $\alpha > \alpha^\circ$, *a sub-game perfect equilibrium is* (q_2^*, β_2^*), *in which* $\beta^* < 1$. *For* $\alpha \leq \alpha^\circ$, *a sub-game perfect equilibrium is* $(q_1^*, 1)$, *and* $q_1^* \geq q_2^*$.

Corollary 1 shows that when fraction of strategic customers who buy in the second period, α, is large, the probability of obtaining product in second period decreases so that more strategic customers purchase product early. In contrast, when α is small, the probability of obtaining product in second period increases so that more strategic customers purchase product lately. In other words, when α is small, strategic customer behavior has little impact on innovator, at this time, innovator sells more product to myopic customers, which in turn increase capacity.

4 Capacity Decision with Speculator

We assume a single speculator entry the market and innovator's sell price is fixed over time, that is, $p_2 = p_1$.

Speculator purchases products in first period in order to reselling products at the higher price in second period. But, clearance price in second period is determined by total capacity and demand, so speculator also faces risk that price lower than ever. For exposition, we regard to speculator's market as secondary market, such as website market, innovator's market as primary market. Let A denote quantity hoarded by speculator, symbol "^" denote with speculator case, π denote speculator's expected profits.

Assumption 2. $\pi \geq \underline{\pi}$.

This assumption shows that speculator entry market if and only if his expected profits must exceed his reservation profits.

Total capacity in second period is $L+A$, in which L was leftovers at the end of first period. We still use $\tilde{\beta}$ denote innovator's belief on fraction of strategic customers who buy in the second period. Innovator infers fraction of strategic customers who purchase products in first period is also $\xi = 1 - \alpha\tilde{\beta}$, the demand in first period is ξX +A. Total amount of strategic customers in second period is still $\alpha\tilde{\beta}X$. Because there has been primary market and secondary market in second period simultaneously, clearance price $\hat{p}_2$ is determined by total capacity and demand.

Lemma 4. *Speculator's optimal price in secondary market is*

$$\hat{p}_2(X) = \begin{cases} V_L & if \quad X < A/(\alpha\tilde{\beta}) \\ p_1 & if \quad A/(\alpha\tilde{\beta}) \leq X < q \\ V_H & if \quad X \geq q. \end{cases}$$

Speculator's expected profits is as follows

$$\pi = AV_H \overline{F}(q) + p_1 A[F(q) - F(A/(\alpha\tilde{\beta}))] + V_L AF(A/(\alpha\tilde{\beta})) - p_1 A \qquad (6)$$

According to assumption 2, we have

$$F(A/\alpha\tilde{\beta}) = k_1 \overline{F}(q) - k_2 \qquad (7)$$

where $k_1 = (V_H - p_1)/(p_1 - V_L)$, $k_2 = \underline{\pi}/(p_1 - V_L)$.

Strategic customer's expected surplus in first period is

$$u_1 = V_H - p_1 \qquad (8)$$

We use μ denote expected surplus difference between first period and second period,

$$\mu = u_1 - u_2 = [\overline{F}(q) - \int_l^{\frac{q-A}{\xi}} \frac{q - \xi X - A}{\alpha\tilde{\beta}X} dF(X)](V_H - p_1) - F(A/(\alpha\tilde{\beta}))(p_1 - V_L)$$

Lemma 5. *There exists a reservation profits threshold $\underline{\pi}_\Re$ such that for $\underline{\pi} > \underline{\pi}_\Re$, all strategic customer purchase product early, that is, $\hat{\beta}^* = 0$, for $\underline{\pi} = \underline{\pi}_\Re$, only some part of strategic customer purchase product lately, for $\underline{\pi} < \underline{\pi}_\Re$, all strategic customer purchase product lately, that is, $\hat{\beta}^* = 1$.*

For exposition, we only focus on $\underline{\pi} < \underline{\pi}_\Re$ case. Without loss of generality, we assume $\underline{\pi}_\Re = 0$. Hence, we have $\hat{\beta}^* = 1$, and following expected profits,

$$\hat{\Pi}(q,A) = p_1 q \overline{F}(q) + p_1 A F(A/\alpha) - cq + p_1 \int_0^q X dF(X) - p_1 \alpha \int_0^{A/\alpha} X dF(X) \qquad (9)$$

Proposition 2. a) *All strategic customers purchase products lately.* b) *Suppose that $f(0) = 0$, innovator's optimal capacity $\hat{q}^*$ is characterized by following first-order condition $d\hat{\Pi}(q)/dq = (p_1\overline{F}(q) - c)f[F^{-1}(k_1\overline{F}(q))] - \alpha p_1 k_1^2 \overline{F}(q)f(q) = 0$. Optimal quantity hoarded by speculator is $A^* = \alpha F^{-1}[k_1\overline{F}(\hat{q}^*)]$.*

Proposition 3. a) $\hat{q}^* < q^*$. b) *There exists a fraction of strategic customers threshold $\alpha^* \in [0, \alpha^*]$ such that for $\alpha < \alpha^*$, we have $\Pi^* > \hat{\Pi}^*$, for $\alpha \geq \alpha^*$, we have $\Pi^* \leq \hat{\Pi}^*$.*

Proposition 3 shows that speculator can alleviate mismatch risk between demand and supply. But only when fraction of strategic customer is large, speculator helps to increase innovator's profits.

5 Conclusions

Radical new product is introduced to market under demand uncertainty, mismatch between capacity and capacity is large, so capacity decision has been a core issue that innovator need to cope with. On the other hand, sophisticated customers utilize strategic waiting to obtain much surplus by inter-temporal purchase timing decision. This paper considers three types of customers, myopic customer who behaves blindly purchase, strategic customer who rationally purchase, as well as bargain hunter who behaves a good deal.

This paper has following conclusions: when the fraction of strategic consumers grows to some level, an extra fraction of strategic consumers will not influence the innovator's capacity and profits without speculator cases. Speculator alleviate mismatch risk between capacity and demand, but, only fraction of strategic customers higher than some threshold, speculator can help to increase innovator's profits.

The further research can be extended from following perspective. First, we focus on impact of speculative behavior on innovator's capacity decision. Exploring effects of other ownership, such as imitator and competitor, on innovator's capacity decision can further test robustness of conclusions of this paper. Second, we consider a single innovator case. It can be extended to decentralized supply chain or oligopoly competition cases. Finally, studying revenue management mechanisms of radical new product has more theoretical and practical meanings for supply chain innovation and coordination.

Acknowledgments. This research was sponsored by the National Nature Science Foundation of China (70971111), and the Nature Science Foundation of Fujian, China (2009J01313).

References

1. Adams, M., Boike, D.: The PDMA foundation 2004 comparative performance assessment study. Visions 28(3), 26–29 (2004)
2. Fobers.: Can Kodak make up for lost moments? (October 6, 2003)

3. Bhaskaran, S.R., Krishnan, V.: Effort, revenue, and cost sharing mechanisms for collaborative new product development. Management Sci. 55(7), 1152–1169 (2009)
4. Chao, R.O., Kavadias, S.: A Theoretical framework for managing the new product development portfolio: When and how to use strategic buckets. Management Sci. 54(5), 907–921 (2009)
5. Karim, S.: Business unit reorganization and innovation in new product markets. Management Sci. 55(7), 1237–1254 (2009)
6. Lai, G., Debo, L.G., Sycara, K.: Buy now and match later: The impact of posterior price matching on profit with strategic consumers. Manufacturing and Service Operation Management 12(1), 33–55 (2010)
7. Levin, Y., McGill, J., Nediak, M.: Dynamic pricing in the presence of strategic consumers and oligopolistic competition. Management Science 55(1), 32–46 (2009)
8. Su, X., Zhang, F.: Strategic customer behavior, commitment, and supply chain performance. Management Sci. 54(10), 1759–1773 (2008)
9. Muth, J.F.: Rational expectations and the theory of price movements. Econometrica 29, 315–335 (1961)

Appendix

Proof of lemma 3. According to assumption 1, $f(\lambda q)/f(q)$ is a monotonic function of q, so $d^2\Pi/dq^2 = 0$ has only a solution. Because $\lim_{q\to 0} d\Pi/dq = p_1 - c > 0$, $\lim_{q\to +\infty} d\Pi/dq = V_L - c < 0$, hence, $d\Pi/dq = 0$ has only a solution.

Proof of Proposition 2. We construct Lagrange function as follows

$$\max H(q, A) = \hat{\Pi}(q, A) + \delta\pi,$$

$$\begin{cases} \dfrac{\partial H}{\partial q} = \dfrac{\partial \hat{\Pi}}{\partial q} + \delta\dfrac{\partial \pi}{\partial q} = 0 & \text{(A1)} \\[2mm] \dfrac{\partial H}{\partial A} = \dfrac{\partial \hat{\Pi}}{\partial A} + \delta\dfrac{\partial \pi}{\partial A} = 0 & \text{(A2)} \\[2mm] \dfrac{\partial H}{\partial \delta} = \pi = 0 & \text{(A3)} \end{cases}$$

Solving equation (A2) and (A3) simultaneously, we have

$$[p_1\overline{F}(q) - c]f(\frac{A}{\alpha}) - \alpha p_1 k_1 F(\frac{A}{\alpha})f(q) = 0 \tag{A4}$$

$$\frac{d\hat{\Pi}}{dq} = (p_1\overline{F}(q) - c)f[F^{-1}(k_1\overline{F}(q))] - \alpha p_1 k_1^2 \overline{F}(q)f(q) = 0 \tag{A5}$$

a) If $p_1\overline{F}(q) < c$, namely, $q > F^{-1}[(p_1 - c)/p_1]$, we have $d\hat{\Pi}/dq < 0$, hence, $\lim_{q\to+\infty} d\hat{\Pi}/dq \leq 0$.

b) Because of $\lim_{q\to 0}\dfrac{d\hat{\Pi}}{dq} = (p_1 - c)f[F^{-1}(k_1)] - \alpha p_1 k_1^2 f(0)]$, suppose that $f(0) = 0$, we have $\lim_{q\to 0} d\hat{\Pi}/dq > 0$. Combined a) with b), a solution $\hat{q}^*$ to (A5) must exist. Further, according to equation (11), we have $A^* = \alpha F^{-1}[k_1\overline{F}(\hat{q}^*)]$.

The Effect That Project Management Certification Has on Employability: Agents' Perceptions from Spain

Ignacio de los Ríos-Carmenado[1], José M. Díaz-Puente[1],
and Jesús Martínez-Almela[2]

[1] Agricultural Engineering School, Technical University of Madrid,
Avenida Complutense S/N, 28040 Madrid, Spain
{ignacio.delosrios,jm.diazpuente}@upm.es
[2] Industrial Engineering School, Technical University of Valencia,
Camino de la Vera S/N, 46022 Valencia, Spain
jma@bioagroprojects.com

Abstract. This study analyses the effects that the project management certification has on employability. This analysis started with a participative process in which various groups of experts who are involved in the certification of people were consulted. A personal interview was carried out amongst 106 professionals —certifying bodies, training institutions, the civil service, and international organisations— and amongst professional who are certified in project management by the International Project Management Association in Spain. The results show that the certification emerges as a powerful tool for improving employability. The effects are demonstrated across two complementary aspects: internal company aspects and external aspects relating to the labour market. Finally, by compiling the different agents' opinions, a series of measures emerge for improving the accreditation processes as an employability tool and increasing the mutual learning between public and private actors.

Keywords: employability, project management, professional skills, certification systems.

1 Introduction

The link between training [45] accreditation of professional skills [25] and employment is a subject which has been discussed for some time; however, it is especially pertinent during times of crisis. In an economic environment with such a competitive labour market, staying in a job or finding a new job becomes of paramount importance for many people. In this context, skill-based training has emanated as a key factor for employability at an international level.

On the other hand, since the 1970s, the evolution of integrated economies and societies in the OECD has transformed life-long learning as a key objective for training and education policies. The concept of employability is often raised in international debates [41], [27] and is understood as the aptitude for working competently within a labour market [34]. Several studies have concluded that the skill

Q. Zhou (Ed.): ISAEBD 2011, Part I, CCIS 208, pp. 35–47, 2011.
© Springer-Verlag Berlin Heidelberg 2011

level within the population is linked to employability and that these skills should be adapted quickly in order to respond innovatively to the structural changes that are currently being experienced. This so-called life-long learning [36] is in response to said challenge and was adopted as a political objective for the member states of the OECD in 1996 [34]. Certification systems for professional skills are seen as tools that aim to improve people's employability and learning [20]. Therefore, the concepts of life-long learning and employability are strongly linked to these systems which are focused on skills and learning from a particular job [33], [34].

Currently, there are several active certification models for personal skills —both professional and industrial— most of which are recognised internationally. In Spain there are currently five certified organisations for professional skills which are better known and more credible for the following reasons: a) their certifying bodies are internationally recognised and they apply rules at an international level; b) they are accredited by the National Accreditation Body (ENAC), according to the applicable international standard ISO/IEC 17024: 2003 and other stipulated accreditation requirements for organisations that certify people; c) they are based on models which have a voluntary element by which certain professionals improve public recognition of their skills and abilities.

In Spain there are five such certification models for professional skills which meet these three requirements. They are associated with different areas; The European Organization for Quality (EOQ), The International Project Management Association (IPMA), The Project Management Institute (PMI), People Capability Maturity Model (P–CMM), and Coaching.

This study investigates in Spain the effect that the project management certification —IPMA's universal *four level certification system*— has on employability. This universal system has been present in Spain since the year 2000 through AEIPRO (Asociación Española de Ingeniería de Proyectos, Spanish Association of Project Engineering) and it's Project Management Certification Body (OCDP). This study will analyse the work already carried out, as well as the results of a participative process — including interviews and surveys— carried out with all the agents who are involved in certification processes. An estimate of the effects of the project management certification (4-L-C system) is made within the professional context of Spain and partly from the point of view of the various agents involved: companies, people certification organisations, people who are certified, the civil service, international organisations and agents responsible for training. The basic terms for project management certification are derived from the ISO/IEC 17024 standard 'General requirements for bodies operating certification of persons'.

The result of the study brings together the lessons learnt regarding the project management certification and its positive results as an employability tool. The study has also been used to collate suggestions and proposals —suitable for the Spanish and international context— which help to improve the professional certification systems. These measures are primarily focused on mitigating the lack of information regarding professional certification processes, as well as the lack of integration and coordination between the different actors involved in these processes.

2   Method

At a global level, the regulations for organisations that certify people emanate from the international standard for conformity assessment and general requirements [29]. This rule sets out the criteria which these certification bodies must comply with for their accreditation. One of these criteria requires the certification body to define a process for pro-actively ensuring that certified people comply with the relevant regulations for that particular certification scheme. In accordance with the international regulation, the control process can include an evaluation process, information from the relevant authorities, structured interviews, and other regular analysis mechanisms, in order to validate the results of the certification scheme [13].

This study focuses on the regulation and quality control system used by AEIPRO's Project Management Certification Body (OCDP), as a body linked to the IPMA in Spain [1]. Similarly, the research focuses on the studies carried out by the Office for Economics and Employment of the Regional Government of Madrid which it uses to improve its employment policies [44].

In this context, the methodological focus was based on the creation of a series of key questions which were answered using participative methods; direct interviews and questionnaires sent to relevant agents [37], [46]. The study relied on cooperation with Madrid's regional government and external agents belonging to various certification bodies and international organisations, the private sector, the civil service and universities. For the first time, this participative method enabled the study to be supported by all the leading figures involved in the project management skills certification system. All their knowledge, perceptions and experience was analysed and compared in the study. With this participative and pluralist approach [30], [24] it was expected that all the agents involved would benefit greatly from their participation in the evaluation work [22]. This approach also enabled the following objectives: a) take advantage of everyone's contributions and ensure that the main source of information is the knowledge and experience of the agents involved [2], [13], [39] with skill certification systems; b) facilitate the agents' learning [38] by identifying best practice and providing guidance on possible measures for perfecting these actions; c) achieve greater involvement from people [23] and improve links between agents, given that participation is such an important source of dynamics and cooperation; and d) position the analysis of the problems and the effects from the point of view of the beneficiaries of the actions.

2.1   Sources of Information

The investigation's methodology combined two complementary information sources. On one hand, a secondary source, consisting of information already generated by other studies, official publications, statistics from the personal [28], scientific documentation and international experiences with regards to professional skills, certification models and project management discipline [43], [47], [26], [16], [35]. On the other hand, a primary source of information, consisting of empirical knowledge based on the leading figures' experiences and perceptions. The participative methodology was supported by the five types of agent involved in the process of certifying people: a) professionals who work in companies' human resources departments; b) professionals who work in bodies that certify people; c) training agents; d) public sector agents and those from international organisations; and e) people certified by the project management certification system in Spain. Two participatory methods were designed —a personal interview and one questionnaire— which were sent to 106 experts and professionals. Whilst the questionnaires were completed during March and April 2009, the interviews lasted until June 2009.

Table 1. Sources of information

Method	Sources	Population	Sample
Interview with experts	ENAC, certification & training bodies	65 experts	46 experts (from businesses, certification bodies, training bodies, civil service and international experts
Questionnaire	IPMA Certification Yearbook. ODCP	245 professionals certified in Spain	60 certified professionals

The first method involved personally *interviewing experts*. The interview script was structured in three blocks of questions which aimed to obtain opinions from three different focus points: a) skills in the labour market; b) the effects that certification has on employability; and c) the link between training-certification-employability.

The second participative method was the *questionnaire for certified people*, which were carried out by the Spanish Certification Body. The questionnaires sample was extracted from the professionals who have been certified by the project management 4-L-C system in Spain and appear in AEIPRO's Certification Body directory and the IPMA Certification Yearbook (IPMA, 2009). The questionnaire was designed with the cooperation of AEIPRO's Project Management Certification Body and was completed by individuals certified in Spain. People's contributions were voluntary and anonymous. The questionnaire was structured in four parts: a) the certified person's personal information; b) assessment of the general effects of certifying people; c) assessment of skills with regards to employability; d) assessment of the effects of certification at company level; and e) assessment of the effects of certification on an individual and global level.

2.2 Verification of the Representation

Personal Interviews with the Experts: The participative process covered all aspects of the certification process: business environment, certification bodies, training bodies, public organisations and international experts, as well as certified individuals. Face-to-face interviews were carried out with all the directors of the certification bodies of institutions that are currently accredited in Spain by the ENAC for meeting the criteria required for certifying people.

Questionnaire for certified people: A specific group of people were interviewed, all of whom are certified by AEIPRO's Project Management Certification Body. These certified professionals are people who have demonstrated their competency in project management, through an external evaluation. The distribution of the interviews by levels of certification is in Table 2.

Table 2. Participative methods used

Levels of certification[1]	% of population certified	% of the interviews
Certified Projects Director (Level A)	0.5%	2%
Certified Senior Project Manager (Level B)	5%	8%
Certified Project Manager (Level C)	22%	21%
Certified Project Management Associate (Level D)	73%	69%

The Project Management Certification Body (OCDP) sent this survey to 245 people, with a response rate of 24%. The representativeness of the sample and the errors are acceptable from the statistical point of view, and therefore the size of the sample was not increased [12]. The professionals interviewed are all at different stages of the Project Management Certification system. The representation of the sample was analysed and compared with the percentage of certified people according to the different levels, as per IPMA's directories [28]. All the people surveyed are currently working, which demonstrates that this professional certification can guarantee ongoing employment. With regards to professional experience, 69% have over 10 years of experience, whilst 12% have less than five years of experience. This group has a mainly technical background (71% are engineers), although it also includes professionals with a non-technical background (29% are graduates).

3 Results

3.1 The Effects That the Project Management Certification Has on Employability

All the experts that were interviewed across the various areas involved agree that the certification of skills is a good tool in terms of employability. 50% of the experts that were interviewed valued the way in which the certification helps when it comes to making up for any shortfalls in employees' behavioural and contextual skills. Behavioural competences are the most highly rated by all the experts and they highlight ethics and appreciation of values as areas for improvement; these behavioural competences cover the project manager's attitudes and skills. 45% of the experts consider that the certification processes have effects on continuous development and improving employees' competitive advantage; something that is considered necessary for maintaining employability. Table 3 shows the ratings of the effects that the project management certification has on employability, according to the opinions of the certified people that were surveyed.

---

[1] *Certified Projects Director (Level A):* is able to direct an important portfolio or programme, an advanced level of knowledge and experience would be required; *Certified Senior Project Manager (Level B)*: is able to manage a complex project; *Certified Project Manager (Level C)*: is able to lead a project with limited complexity; *Certified Project Management Associate (Level D)*: is able to apply project management knowledge when he participates in a project.

Table 3. The effects that certification has on employability

The effects of certification	Low	Medium	High
Improved employee performance	8%	28%	59%
Improved skill-based training	8%	36%	51%
Improvements in companies' competitiveness	10%	33%	51%
Improved career progression	5%	44%	46%
Increase the company's credibility	5%	46%	44%
Improved efficiency of team working	5%	49%	41%
Improved communication	3%	51%	38%
Improve the company's productivity	8%	54%	33%
Improved conflict management	5%	59%	31%
Improved employment policies	15%	51%	23%

Note: Low (1-2), Medium (3-4) and High (5-6). Source: Survey of certified people, 2009

It is evident that as the level of responsibility increases (i.e. at higher certification levels), organisational-wide effects become most relevant, followed by the level of team working; whilst effects at an individual level become less valued. This confirms the idea that the certification culture has effects that go further than employees' personal benefits, and indeed affects the institution or company as a whole, starting with the improvements in human resources [32], [9]. Furthermore, the average global rating of the effects increases gradually as we move from the levels with least responsibility (Certified Project Management Associate) to the highest certification levels (Projects Director).

Approximately 85% of those surveyed consider – with a medium (33%) or high (51%) rating – that certification enables organisations to improve competitiveness (both companies and institutions). The rating for this effect increases as we move from the levels with least responsibility to the highest certification levels.

The effect that certification has in terms of an organisation's productivity is another of the most valued factors —with a medium-high rating amongst 87% of those surveyed— which indicates that professionals consider that certification represents a contribution to an organisation's performance, from the point of view of improving the efficiency and effectiveness of their workforce. Approximately 90% of those surveyed consider that certification has an important effect on the reliability of an organisation (company or institution).

In terms of personal factors, approximately 90% consider that certification plays an important part in improving personal performance within an organisation. Similarly, 90 % of certified people highly rate certification in order to advance or achieve promotion, as well as for developing skills. Other positive effects of certifying people that those surveyed give a high rating to (approximately 90%) include: effective team working, followed by improvements in communication and conflict & crisis management.

3.2   The Effects That a 'Certification Culture' Has on Employability

The general results of the participative processes demonstrate that the incorporation of an project management certification culture within companies has effects on two complementary factors with regards to employability. Firstly, there are effects that influence internal factors in terms of the employees' professional profile, which will be referred to as the effects on internal employability. Secondly, there are effects that are linked to the level of employees' competitiveness in the context of the labour market, which will be referred to as effects on external employability. Table 4 shows the global results of the ratings made by the certified professionals who were surveyed on the different effects which were considered.

Table 4. The effects that 'project management certification culture'

The effects of a 'certification culture'	Low	Average	High
Improve training and learning processes	5%	49%	41%
Improve public recognition for professionals	5%	33%	56%
Progress towards an understanding of total quality	5%	54%	33%
Improve efficiency in the civil service	8%	62%	23%
Improve the quality of the civil service	8%	59%	26%
Improve the management of human resources in companies	10%	49%	36%
Enhance recruitment and selection processes	8%	44%	41%
Improve companies' productivity	15%	72%	10%
Improve employment policies	10%	56%	23%
Higher expectation of employees' performance	13%	41%	38%
Enhance international business, and relationships	5%	41%	36%
Increase focus on consumers' rights	15%	46%	18%

Note: Low (1-2), Medium (3-4) and High (5-6). Source: Survey of certified people, 2009

The effects that are most highly rated by certified professionals are the improvements in the recognition of professionals (56%), followed by the improvements in training and employees' learning processes and the improvements in recruitment and selection processes. In terms of the effects that are most linked to the company or organisation, those with the highest rating (high or very high) are the improvements in recruitment and selection processes (85% of those interviewed), and the public recognition of professionals (90% of those surveyed). This can be turned into a competitive advantage for certification, given that it reduces companies' costs when recruiting and training professionals for a particular position. The certified professionals who were interviewed award a high score to the effects on improved international relationships and they link the certification with the concept of quality. This can be explained because the project management certification is endorsed by an internationally recognised model. A high percentage of the certified professionals who were interviewed (90%) consider that certification could be an improvement mechanism for educational quality and training programmes; whilst 80% consider that it could be a tool for improving employment policies.

We can conclude that the certification of professional skills —project management— is seen as a strategic element for improving employability, and complements professional development for individuals and organisations. Furthermore, it establishes a link between training processes and the demands of the labour market, building a bridge between training and employment, in line with the trends of the European Higher Education Area.

3.3 Improvements in Employability amongst Certified People

75% of the experts who were interviewed consider that the project management certification can improve employability for graduates; that is, their suitability with regards to meeting companies' requirements for a particular job role. These experts consider that certification can act as a mechanism for improving employability, establishing a link between training and the demands of the labour market. Nearly 85% of the people who were surveyed consider that the project management certification is a professional tool that has positive effects on their own professional career. As can be seen in Table 5, the most valued effects amongst those surveyed are the improvements in experience and knowledge, improvements to contextual skills for developing their professional activity.

Table 5. Evaluation of the effects that certification has on improving employability

The effects evaluated by different professionals	Level	Average
Improve my knowledge and new experiences	Very High	4.8
It has allowed me to improve my behavioural skills	Very High	4.8
It has allowed me to improve my contextual skills	Very High	4.7
It has allowed me to establish new professional contacts	Very High	4.5
It is a professional development tool	Very High	4.5
It has allowed me to improve my technical skills	High	4.3
Improve the quality of project management	High	4.2
It has allowed me to increase the international work	Medium	3.8
It has helped my career progression	Medium	3.4

Note: Low (1-2), Medium (3-4) and High (5-6). Source: Survey of certified people, 2009

All of the professionals who were interviewed were already working when they became certified. As a result, the effects that the project management certification has on finding a job cannot be quantified. The effects of certification are aimed at improving both external and internal employability. Approximately 45% of those interviewed highly rate certification, as a professional development tool.

In order to evaluate the effects that certification has on employability and one's professional career, a further four criteria were considered in terms of following the certified professionals: a) new projects carried out after certification, b) new functions and responsibilities developed after certification, c) extra training carried out and, d) new experiences obtained after certification. In terms of these four criteria, a range of results was obtained. The majority of certified professionals (87%) have taken on new responsibilities in new projects following on from their certification. 72% have taken on new roles and responsibilities in the project/programme/portfolio management field. 80% have improved their training since becoming certified, going on to receive further training. 21% have been involved in higher education through postgraduate study, and 36% through professional specialisation courses. Finally, 70% have increased their area of professional activity with a large range of new experiences, in particular consultancy and advisory roles, project management, teaching and research.

Participants were also asked to rate the skills they value most in terms of employability. The certified professionals who were surveyed consider that the skills that have the most influence on employability are behavioural (4.5), followed by technical (4.3), and contextual (4.1). They highlight 6 behavioural skills: ethics, compromise and motivation, leadership, conflict & crisis management, creativity, and efficiency; and 5 "technical" skills that are strongly linked to the professional capacity for integrating social aspects in the professional arena: team working, problem resolution, relationships with interested parties, project organisation, and communication.

4 Conclusion

The global results and opinions of the various agents demonstrate that the project management certification is an employability tool that has an effect on two complementary factors: on internal aspects of companies and organisations (internal employability) and on external factors in relation to the labour market (external employability).

From the professional and business world, 93% of the experts stated that the project management certification has a high usage potential as an employability tool. It is considered as an added-value tool offered to employees and companies, but at a secondary level when it comes to hiring somebody. There is still a great lack of knowledge about certification systems in the business world. The results of this study support Baker's [4] findings which state that when candidates are recruited they are evaluated through other mechanisms such as references from previous employers, psychological tests or other internal tools within the company. However, it can be seen that, in accordance with other studies [7], [14], [6] skill-based factors are considers to be important for professional performance within companies and they are considered when it comes to evaluating candidates' employability.

From within this business environment the benefits of certification which stand out the most are that it improves the company/organisations' competitiveness and it provides the employee and company with the confidence to perform well. From within this business environment it is evident that there is not a sufficient connection between training and the demands of the labour market (in accordance with the results of [6], [21]). Similarly, 75% of the experts who were interviewed consider that professionals do not meet the companies' requirements when applying for a job, whilst 50% consider that there is a shortfall in behavioural skills; as explained in a study by Cannon [10] or the Tunning Project [42].

Training experts agree that skills certification models such as the universal four-level-certification system represent a clear path between skill-based training and employability. The new context of The European Higher Education Area offers opportunities for professional skills to be included in training processes, strives to adapt to the need for comprehensive training (with values) and is orientated towards improving the employability of graduates. Certification is considered as a tool for connecting external agents (across different professional sectors) to training processes. However, for this connection to be efficient it must be accompanied by changes in learning processes (see [8]).

Experts from project management bodies in Spain, Germany, France, UK, Portugal and Switzerland consider that the model is clearly expanding and has direct, obvious effects on individuals' employability and on the companies in which the employees are based. The official figures according to the IPMA Certification Yearbook [28] show the increasing number of professionals and organizations that have become involved in these processes as a strategy for improving performance. The tracking/monitoring of certified professionals by these bodies guarantees the benefits for individuals.

International debates raise the concept of "employability", which is understood as "the aptitude for working competently within the labour market" [33]. The opinions of experts from international bodies reflect the global tendencies for promoting the integration of skills in areas such as education and work [34]. A great deal of emphasis is placed on countries designing and implementing specific strategies that allow improvements in the quality of human capital [14] and the equilibrium of ever-changing labour markets.

Experts from different countries have been interviewed as well as Quality Agencies, Accreditation, Certification and Testing bodies. Generally, the responses stress the need for linking certification systems with life-long learning and redefining current policies. Amongst these replies, ideas stand out such as the need for motivating employees to gain certification, linking education, certification and employment, embedding measures for increasing the level of voluntary certification, expanding the number of certification systems and making certification systems more transparent, in accordance with international requirements.

Amongst those individuals who are certified, the most valued effect of the project management certification (in terms of employability) is the improvement in their own professional development. Approximately 85% of the professionals who were interviewed consider that the project management certification tool has an influence on improving their professional career. Furthermore, all the professionals state that the effects of certification go beyond personal benefits and impact other aspects of team working and the company/institution as a whole.

Finally, in addition to collating the opinions of the different agents, a number of proposals are also made for improving certification as an employability tool and for promoting mutual learning between public and private actors. These proposals respond to the main arguments highlighted by all the agents involved; the lack of information regarding professional certification processes (i.e. systems, benefits etc.); and the need for better integration/coordination between the different actors involved and qualification systems/certification processes.

With regards to the lack of information available, it was stressed that there is a need for encouraging employees to become professionally certified. Some ideas are suggested, such as: promoting professional certification with assistance for unemployed professionals, help for companies to reduce the cost of certifying their professionals, or help for companies to increase training programmes which could lead to professional certification. In this respect, there was also talk of investing more resources into educational innovation targeted at gaining professional skills. It is about communicating the benefits of certification in terms of employability and creating a culture that promotes certifications with a voluntary characteristic.

As for the lack of coordination between the different actors involved, they were encouraged to create new mechanisms for linking education, certification and employment; creating strategic alliances between these actors with the purpose of improving employability; unifying evaluation processes for professional skills; diversifying systems for certifying people, increasing options, making them more transparent, in accordance with the international requirements (ISO 17024) and giving them a more progressive characteristic. There was also an emphasis on the need to improve the management of qualification systems and the link to certification systems, in order to improve the relationship between the two. There was a discussion around helping certifying bodies to supervise and monitor their certified professionals, with a view to improving their quality control systems and the way in which the certifications are used.

Until now promotion and dissemination efforts have been focused on each agent's individual initiatives, with the exception of the civil service, whose initiatives have been primarily focused on qualification systems (work skills). The previous proposals are raised in view of the need to incorporate the different agents involved in the certification process (private and public) who have participated in this study.

References

1. AEIPRO, NCB3.1: Bases para la competencia en Dirección de Proyectos. UPV-AEIPRO Traducción y Adaptación: J. Martínez-Almela (2010)
2. Argyris, C., Schön, D.: Organisational Learning: A Theory of Action Perspective. Addison Wesley, Bostan (1978)
3. Arnnold, J., Mackenzie, K.: Self-ratings and supervisor ratings of graduate employees competences during early career. Journal of Occupation and Organizational Psychology 65, 235–250 (1992)
4. Baker, B.: MCI Management Competences and APL: The way forward for Management Education, Training and Development? J. of Industrial Training 15(9), 17–26 (1991)
5. Barnard, C.: The functions of the executive. Harvard University Press, Cambridge (1968)
6. Bergenhenegouwen, G., Horn, H., Mooijman, E.: Competence development - a challenge for HUM professionals: core competences of organizations as guidelines for the development of employees. J. of European Industrial Training 29(2), 55–92 (1996)
7. Birchall, D., Hee, T., Gay, K.: Competences for international managers. Singapore Institute of Management (1982)
8. Boyatzis, R., Stubbs, E., Taylor, N.: Learning Cognitive and Emotional Intelligence Competencies Through Graduate Managemente Education. Academy of Management Learning and Education 1(2), 150–162 (2002)

9. Brisgstock, K.: The Graduate attributes we've overlooked: enhancing graduate employability through career management skills. Higher Education Research & Development 28(1), 31–44 (2009)
10. Cannon, F.: Business-driven management development: developing competences which drive business performance. Journal of European Industrial Training 19(2), 26–31 (1995)
11. Caupin, G., Carvalho, N.P., Alba, J.: Revalidation AEIPRO Certification. Certification Validation Management Board. In: IPMA (2009)
12. Cea, M.: Metodología cuantitativa. Estrategias y técnicas de investigación social. Madrid: Síntesis (2001)
13. Chambers, R.: Participatory rural appraisal (PRA): Analysis of experience. World Development 22(9), 1253–1268 (1994)
14. Cheetham, G., Chivers, G.: Towards a holistic model of professional competence. Journal of European Industrial Training 20(5), 20–30 (1996)
15. Cheetham, G., Chivers, G.: The reflective (and competent) practitiones: a model of professional competence which seeks to harmonise the reflective practitioner and compentence-based approaches. J. European Industrial Training 22(7), 267–276 (1998)
16. Crawford, L.H., Hobbs, J.B., Turner, J.R: Project categorization systems: aligning capability with strategy for better results. In: PMI, Upper Darby, PA (2005)
17. Day, G.: Working with the grain? Towards sustainable rural and community development. Journal of Rural Studies 14(1), 89–105 (1998)
18. Delemare, F., Winterton, J.: What is Competence? Human Resource Development International 8(1), 27–46 (2001)
19. De los Ríos, I., Cazorla, A., Díaz, J.M., Yagüe, J.L.: Project–based learning in engineering higher education: two decades of teaching competences in real environments. Procedia – Social and Behavioral Sciences 2(2), 1368–1378 (2010)
20. De los Ríos-Carmenado, I., Ros, A., Ortiz, I., Fernández, A., Del Río, M., Romera, A.: Cooperative model for learning and assessment of behavioural competences in project management according to IPMA-NCB model. Selected Proceedings 13th International Congress on Project Engineering. AEIPRO. IPMA, pp. 499–512 (2010)
21. De los Ríos-Carmenado, I., Díaz-Puente, J.M., Yagüe, J.L., Romera, A., Rodriguez, F.: The integration of project management skills in postgraduate programmes. In: Selected Proceedings 14th International Congress Project Engineering. International Project Management Association, pp. 295–310 (2011)
22. Díaz-Puente, J.M., Yagüe, J.L., Afonso, A.: Building Evaluation Capacity in Spain: A Case Study of Rural Development and Empowerment in the European Union. Evaluation Review 32(5), 478–506 (2008)
23. Díaz-Puente, J.M., Cazorla, A., De los Ríos, I.: Empowering Communities through Evaluation: Some Lessons from Rural Spain. Community Development Journal 44(1), 53–67 (2009)
24. Díaz-Puente, J., Cazorla, A., De los Ríos, I.: Policy Support for the Diffusion of Innovation among SMEs: An Evaluation Study in the Spanish Region of Madrid. European Planning Studies 17(3), 365–389 (2009)
25. Fitzenberger, B., Speckesser, S.: Employment effects of the provision of specific professional skills and techniques in Germany. Empirical Economics 32, 529–573 (2007)
26. Geraldi, J., Turner, J.R., Maylor, H., Söderholm, A., Hobday, M., Brady, T.: Innovation in project management: Voices of researchers. International Journal of Project Management 26(5), 586–589 (2008)

27. Hallier, J.: Rhetoric but whose reality? The influence of employability messages on employee mobility tactics and work group identification. International Journal of Human Resource Management 20(4), 846–868 (2009)
28. IPMA, I. P.: IPMA Certification Yearbook 2009. Editors: Werner Schmehr, Hans Knoepfel (2009)
29. ISO/IEC:17024: Conformity assessment. General requirements for bodies operating certification of persons. Switzerland International Organization for Standardization (2003)
30. Leviton, L.: Building evaluation's collective capacity. American Journal of Evaluation 22(1), 1–12 (2001)
31. Martín-Fernández, S., De los Ríos-Carmenado, I., Cazorla, A., Martinez-Falero, E.: Pilot study on the influence of stress caused by the need to combine work and family on occupational accidents in working women. Safety Science 47(2), 192–198 (2008)
32. Moreau, M., Leathwood, L.: Graduates, employment and the discourse of employability: a critical analysis. Journal of Education and Work 16(4), 305–324 (2006)
33. OECD: What Competences de we need for a successful life and a well-functioning society. OECD, Paris (2005)
34. OCDE: Sistemas de cualificaciones. Puentes para el aprendizaje a lo largo de la vida. Madrid: INCUA. OCDE (2008).
35. Ono, D.: Upgrading skills using the US Project Management Institute body of knowledge. International Journal of Project Management 13(2), 137–140 (1995)
36. Pang, M., Chua, B.-L., Chu, C.W.L.: Learning to stay ahead in an uncertain environment. International Journal of Human Resource Management 19(7), 1383–1394 (2008)
37. Patton, M.Q.: Utilization-Focused Evaluation: The New Century Text, 3rd edn. Sage, Thousand Oaks (1997)
38. Preskill, H., Torres, R.: Evaluative Inquiry for Learning in Organization. Sage Publications, Thousand Oaks (1999)
39. Rondinelli, D.A.: Development Projects as Policy Experiments: An Adaptive Approach to Development Administration. Routledge, London (1993)
40. Schkolnick, M.: Certificación por competencias como parte del sistema de protección social: la experiencia de países desarrollados y lineamientos para América Latina CEPAL. Santiago de Chile: Serie Políticas Sociales No 113, División de Desarrollo Social (2005)
41. Scholarios, D., Van der Heijden, B., Van der Schoot, E., Bozionelos, N.: Employability and the psychological contract in European ICT sector SMEs. International Journal of Human Resource Management 19(6), 1035–1055 (2008)
42. Tunning Project: Tunning Educational Structures in Europe. Bilbao: Publicaciones de la Universidad de Deusto (2006)
43. Turner, J.R.: International Project Management Association global qualification, certification and accreditation. International Journal of Project Management 14(1), 1–6 (1996)
44. UPM–Comunidad de Madrid: Modelos internacionales de certificación de competencias profesionales como herramienta de empleabilidad: aplicación a la Comunidad de Madrid. Madrid: "Panorama Laboral". Comunidad de Madrid (2009)
45. Van de Wiele, P.: The impact of training participation and training costs on firm productivity in Belgium. International Journal of Human Resource Management 21(4), 582–599 (2010)
46. Whyte, W.F.: Participatory Action Research. Sage, Newbury Park (1991)
47. Winter, M., Smith, C., Morris, P., Cicmil, S.: Directions for future research in project management: the main findings of a UK government–funded research network. International Journal of Project Management 24(8), 638–649 (2006)

Social Involvement in Rural Areas. A Methodological Approach

José M. Díaz-Puente[1], Francisco J. Gallego[2], and Pablo Vidueira[1]

[1] Agricultural Engineering School, Technical University of Madrid,
Avenida Complutense S/N, 28040 Madrid, Spain
{jm.diazpuente@,pvm@alumnos.}upm.es
[2] Institute of Community Development of Cuenca.
Calle Segóbriga, 7, 16001, Cuenca, Spain
fgallego@idccuenca.org

Abstract. Community development must be accompanied by a social involvement process which creates functional groups of citizens capable of taking responsibility for their own development. It is important that this process promotes a structure for all population groups and provides the appropriate institutional and technical support. The present paper addresses these issues from a methodological approach based on over 25 years of experience by the Institute of Community Development of Cuenca in revitalizing rural areas of the Spanish province of Cuenca. The long-term perspective of this experience provides some keys which can be used to successfully support the process of social involvement in rural areas.

Keywords: Community development, Social Involvement, Social Structure, Partnership.

1 Introduction

Efforts to streamline the network of associations began with community organization. This concept is understood as a process where the community strives to control its problems and reach solutions through its organizations and institutions [23]. Therefore, the existence of organized groups of individuals acting together is essential [37], as well as the role of external actors in collaborating with the community throughout this process [30].

This role for the community depends on the existence of functional citizens' groups that promote individual participation, as well as the community's ability to be an active and responsible agent in the development process [43]. That is why the social involvement process is so essential and must always play a key role in the process of community development. The goal is to open channels for participation through which individuals can identify and prioritize their needs, and to encourage the work for supporting the development of the community [32], [20].

However, the presence of this boost to encourage participation does not guarantee that a genuine process of community development will take place [18]. The process of

Q. Zhou (Ed.): ISAEBD 2011, Part I, CCIS 208, pp. 48–55, 2011.

revitalization should be inclusive with all population groups. Numerous studies show the failure of development processes that only include certain groups of people [18], [35], [39], [6], [38], [22].

Similarly, it is crucial to the success of this process that the community is provided with the appropriate technical support [2] and with the support of public institutions [43], [2], [9], throughout the process of identification and prioritization of needs, as well as in creating development measures and in the analysis of resource availability.

Since the late nineties, within the framework of the LEADER Initiative, there has been a lot of research carried out regarding the changing role of public institutions and the processes targeting rural development [11], [29], [42], [46], [40], [19], [8]. The gradual democratization of developed countries has led to a change in the perception of development from traditional top-down approaches (welfare) to bottom-up approaches, based on the direct use of national resources [44], [33], [10]. This change is essential for the viability of social structuring process [26], [7], and also has allowed to non-state organizations —which have the ability to mobilize local potential [10]— to take on a very important role as community partners in the development process. This role is especially important in terms of the organization within society [35], [25], [12] and even more so in areas with low population density, which can be characterized by intense isolation and rural exodus [38]. The contribution made by these associations is needed in order to achieve a more inclusive and participatory form of development [39], [22]. Public institutions need to trust that these associations and local actors are able to carry out proper management of the development process [26].

This article focuses on the social involvement model implemented by the Institute of Community Development of Cuenca (hereafter IDC Cuenca) during over 25 years in underpopulated rural areas. Based on this long term perspective, the article discusses a model founded on social inclusion and the promotion of participation by all sectors of the population by providing encouragement and support, prioritizing its most pressing needs, and seeking innovative responses to these needs. It will also seek to provide solutions with regard to the relationship between public institutions and local associations and the role played by these associations in the development process. This issue is crucial in determining the effectiveness of development programmes. It concerns individuals, partnerships and policy makers alike [2], [3].

2 Context

2.1 Institutional Context: The IDC of Cuenca

The IDC of Cuenca is a non-profit association founded in 1984 with the intention of promoting community development in depressed rural areas within the province of Cuenca, Spain. For over 25 years, it has been working to achieve three main objectives. Its first objective is to upgrade human resources and the structure of society in order to encourage a process of development within a framework of equality that improves quality of life and avoids further depopulation of rural communities. Its second objective is to preserve and enhance the regional identity, rural culture and natural resources. Finally, the association attempts to build on current innovation and quality practices in agriculture and promote entrepreneurship through the incorporation of new techniques and technologies.

These objectives are achieved through a methodology founded on ensuring access to information, improving training opportunities and encouraging the creation of a dynamic body of actors. The IDC seeks to encourage the development of these processes through promotional strategies, a thorough knowledge of the reality of the situation within the region and the formation of links within the population. After 25 years, this methodology has been shown to be capable of responding both to the needs as perceived by the local population and the more specific and urgent needs of the development process, reconciling the two with the initial context of each individual community. Thus, the IDC has established itself as an association for the development of far-reaching growth within the territory and, as discussed below, has spearheaded numerous development processes within the Cuenca province.

2.2 Regional Background: The Province of Cuenca

The province of Cuenca is located in Spain, in the the central-eastern area of the country. The province covers 17,141 km^2 [14] and has 217,363 inhabitants [16]. The population density of the province is 12.68 inhabitants per km^2 [16], well below the national average of 90.6 inhabitants per km^2 [17] and the European Union average of 113.5 inhabitants per km^2 [17]. Of the 238 municipalities within the province, almost 80% (186 municipalities) have a population density of less than 10 inhabitants per km^2, and 111 municipalities have less than 4 persons per km^2 [15]. Currently, the majority of the province is suffering the effects of depopulation, as demonstrated by the loss of 34,208 inhabitants (13%) since 1970 [13], and it is classified as a disadvantaged area at risk of depopulation by the Spanish Agricultural White Paper [27].

The area is characterized by a marked trend towards the predominance of agriculture, lack of training and service offerings, communication deficiencies —initially relating to poor road infrastructure and currently linked to deficits in information technology and communications— and social dislocation. IDC Cuenca is working to reverse these trends. In some cases, however, they continue to drive individuals away from the area.

These trends were reflected in Spain's Sustainable Rural Development Program for 2010-2014 (regulated by Law 45/2007), in which three of the five regions of Cuenca are among the rural areas identified as development targets due to low population density, the predominance of agricultural activity, low income levels, the significant extent of its geographic isolation and the difficulties of regional restructuring. The two remaining regions are classified as intermediate rural areas, which are areas that have low to medium population density, diversified employment, low to medium income levels and are geographically remote from major urban centers [28].

3 Methodology of the Social Development Process

The IDC has promoted Cuenca over the course of the past 25 years, implementing a process of community development in its less populated rural areas and expending much of its effort in revitalizing the network of local associations and creating partnerships. This has primarily occurred in the form of locating and securing the cooperation of agencies and public and private entities in promoting the idea of development through potential synergies between endogenous and exogenous growth in the area [7]. This dynamic process, spearheaded by the IDC, has a number of distinctive features and methods. It is precisely these methods that have allowed this process to be ongoing today after 25 years.

Among these methods is the concept of social involvement as a process [36], [5] which begins as a set of successive and coherent phases. Another significant feature is the initiation of an established self-identity [31], [1] which seeks to unite the local population through an appreciation of its region, reinforcing their involvement in the development process once it begins. The third methodological feature of this process is the establishment of links between the association and the local population. Finally, this process places a strong emphasis on the analysis of social involvement and community development experiences in other areas. These can serve as the basis for the design of operational partnership models.

In addition to these methods, the IDC's work in the field of social involvement employs two main tools. The first is promotion, encouraging people to get involved in the process and, consequently, in their transformation into agents of change and growth within their own region [4]. The second is the accompaniment of this process with technical assistance in resolving all of the existing needs in the region through training, planning methodologies and tools, and providing an accountability framework for the implementation, monitoring and evaluation of initiatives [8].

Driven by promotional activities, a series of operational models to guide the structure and functioning of these associations have been designed. These models should be flexible in order to respond to the situation and the needs identified by the local population.

The social development process begins by channeling the established needs of the population through tailored operative models. These early experiences will be deemed successful if they manage to address the needs expressed by the population. To this end, the IDC provides support in the form of technical assistance and collaboration with its local associations. Positive results are used as a source of inspiration and motivation for groups not yet firmly rooted in the social structuring process. This encourages the population to continue its development process. Responding to their needs through partnership projects leads to an improvement in social structure and provides increased stimulation for other groups. Figure 1 outlines the methodology of the social involvement process implemented by the IDC over the course of the past 25 years.

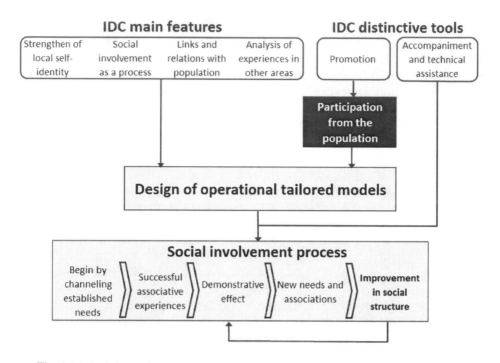

Fig. 1. Methodology of social involvement process implemented by the IDC of Cuenca

4   Conclusions

Social development is one of the strongest guarantees for the progression of any development program [41] and is particularly important in areas with low population density. The model analyzed in this paper begins by encouraging people, in this case through the endogenous culture, and prompting them to unite because of their appreciation of the region and their interest in improving their living conditions. This methodological factor has also facilitated the entry of the IDC into the region in a way which is close to the population. The cooperative work created ties and mutual understanding between the IDC and local population.

The elements that act as stimuli are usually outside the community. In addition to culture, there are other factors such as perceived threats to their interests [2], the positive stimulus of an external agent [30] or the demonstration effect.   The demonstration effect —when a group is organized and plunged into the development process and becomes a stimulus for other groups in the territory— is deeply rooted in rural areas and is essential in the social involvement process.

Another important methodological aspect is to have a defined working philosophy and the ability to adapt to the various initiatives that will be carried out. This can be seen throughout the work of the IDC although the cultural caravan is a prime example of something that was not proposed directly by the IDC Cuenca, but rather the provincial council under agreement with the IDC. However, the IDC learned to apply their principles to the activities in order to achieve the results shown above.

However, the community must have a full sense of ownership over the development process [2]. Therefore, it is necessary that the community is involved in determining those who actually require immediate help, rather than relying on the perspective of an external agent that will identify those who appear most urgent. Addressing the needs felt by the population unites individuals in achieving these goals. Actions to address needs not generating consensus results in division between those who agree and those who do not. Shared experiences adapted to the prioritised needs of the population should be based on flexible models which can provide innovative responses to those needs within their own specific context. In addition to the experience of the IDC Cuenca, it is clear that the response to these perceived needs will reveal new ones which encourage the continuation of the community development process [34].

Finally, the IDC's technical assistance and aid for associations emerging in the territory is of crucial importance. One aspect of this assistance targets the achievement, through partnerships, of plans that will provide content for the process and act as a force for greater cohesion among its members. Ongoing educational programmes, designed to strengthen awareness of the local situation and provide the population with new skills that promote social participation and develop leaders for the new development processes, are also crucial in this regard.

The process of social structuring encouraged by the Cuenca IDC has followed a specific guideline: associations arise as a consequence of the desire and will of their members to contribute to the achievement of certain objectives within their community. In this context, the role of the IDC is to encourage and facilitate this process through its tools and methodological characteristics. The role of this process of social activism is to promote social structure and enable people to address various aspects of their development according to their own needs [2]. This development becomes sustainable when the associations generate it themselves by forming new partnerships that continue to deepen through increased structuring of their society and additional improvements in the quality of life of their region's population.

References

1. Andolina, R., Radcliffe, S., Laurie, N.: Development and culture. Transnational identity making in Bolivia. Polit. Geogr. 24, 678–702 (2005)
2. Armstrong, J.: Making Community Involvement in Urban Regeneration Happen - Lessons from the United Kingdom. Community Dev. J. 28, 355–361 (1993)
3. Borek, T., Falkowski, J., Giejbowicz, E., Janiak, K., Poslednik, A., Zielin, Ska, M.: Inicjatywa doswiadczenia LEADER +-i pierwsze Rozwoju Szansa. Fundacja dla pomocy Programow Rolnictwa, Warszawa (2006)
4. Caride, J.A.: La animación sociocultural y el desarrollo comunitario como educación social. Revista de Educación 336, 73–88 (2005)
5. Clark, D., Southern, R., Beer, J.: Rural governance, community empowerment and the new institutionalism: a Case Study of the Isle of Wight. J. Rural Stud. 23, 254–266 (2007)
6. Considine, M.: Local Partnerships: Different Histories, Common Challenges - a synthesis. In OECD (ed.) Managing Decentralisation: a New Role for Labour Market Policy, Organisation for Economic Co-operation and Development, Paris (2003)

7. Díaz-Puente, J.M., Yagüe, J.L., Afonso, A.: Building Evaluation Capacity in Spain: a case study of Rural Development and empowerment in the European Union. Evaluation Rew. 32, 478–506 (2008)
8. Díaz-Puente, J.M., Cazorla, A., de los Rios, I.: Empowering Communities Through Evaluation: some lessons from rural Spain. Community Dev. J. 44, 53–67 (2009)
9. Edwards, B., Goodwin, M., Pemberton, S., Woods, M.: Partnerships, power, and scale in rural governance. Environ. Plann. C. 19, 289–310 (2001)
10. Furmankiewicz, M., Thomson, N., Zielinska, M.: Area-based partnerships in rural Poland: the post-accession experience. J. Rural Stud. 26, 52–62 (2010)
11. Goodwin, M.: The Governance of Rural Areas: Some Emerging Research Issues and Agendas. J. Rural Stud. 14, 5–12 (1998)
12. Grochowski, M., Regulska, J.: New partnership and Collaboration: Local Government and Its Supporting Institutions - The case of Poland. In: Amna, E. and Montin, S., (Eds.) Towards a New Concept of Local Self-government? Recent Local Government Legislation in Comparative Perspective, Fagbokforlaget, Bergen (2000)
13. Instituto Nacional de Estadística,
    http://www.ine.es/inebaseweb/
    treeNavigation.do?tn=92693&tns=141136#141136
14. Instituto Nacional de Estadística,
    http://www.ine.es/jaxi/tabla.do?path=/t43/a011/a1998/10/
    &file=t10031.px&type=pcaxis
15. Instituto Nacional de Estadística,
    http://www.ine.es/jaxi/tabla.do?path=/t43/a011/a1998/
    densidad/10/&file=t10051.px&type=pcaxis&L=0
16. Instituto Nacional de Estadística,
    http://www.ine.es/jaxi/tabla.do?path=/t20/e260/a2009/10/
    &file=pcaxismun16.px&type=&L=0
17. Instituto Nacional de Estadística,
    http://www.ine.es/prodyser/pubweb/espcif/terr10.pdf
18. Jessop, B.: The dynamics of partnership and governance failure. In: Stoker, G. (ed.) The New Politics of Local Governance in Britain. Oxford University Press, Oxford (1999)
19. Jones, O., Little, J.: Rural Challenges (s): partnership and new rural governance. J. Rural Stud. 16, 171–183 (2000)
20. Klsnerman, N.: Comunidad. Humanitas, Buenos Aires (1986)
21. Kovach, I.: LEADER, a new social order, and the Central and East-European countries. Sociol. Ruralis. 40, 181–189 (2000)
22. Katona Kovacs, J., Fieldsend, A.F., Alderson, M., Szabo, G.: Human Factors and Social Factors stimulating endogenous growth as the LEADER Programme in Hungary. In: Florianczyk, Z., Czapiewski, K.L. (eds.) Stimulating Factors Endogenous Rural Development, Rural Areas and Development (vol. 4), National Research Institute, Institute of Geography and Spatial Organization, Polish Academy of Sciences, Warsaw (2006)
23. Lindeman, E.: The Community. An introduction to the study of community leadership and organization. Association Press, New York (1921)
24. Lowndes, V., Sullivan, H.: Like a horse and carriage or a fish on a bicycle: how well do local partnerships and public participation go together? Local Gov. Stud. 30, 51–73 (2004)
25. Hudson, R.: New geographies and forms of work and Unemployment and public policy innovation in Europe. Tijdschr. Econ. Soc. Ge. 93, 316–335 (2002)
26. MacKinnon, D.: Rural local governance and Involvement: Assessing state - community relations in the Scottish Highlands. J. Rural Stud. 18, 307–324 (2002)

27. Ministerio de Agricultura, Pesca y Alimentación: El Libro Blanco de la Agricultura y el Medio Ambiente(vol. 3, cap.4.8). Spanish Ministry of Agriculture, Fisheries and Food, Spain (2003)
28. Ministerio de Medio Ambiente, Rural y Marino, http://www.mapa.es/es/desarrollo/pags/Ley/ley.htm
29. Murdoch, J., Abram, S.: Defining the limits of community governance. J. Rural Stud. 14, 41–50 (1998)
30. Pettit, W.: Some Prognostications in the Field of Community Work. In: National Conference of Social Work at the Fifty-Second Annual Session Held in Denver, Colorado. University of Chicago Press, Chicago (1925)
31. Preston, R., Arthur, L.: Knowledge societies and planetary cultures: The Changing Nature of consultancy in human development. International Journal of Education 17, 3–12 (1997)
32. Porzecanski, T.: Desarrollo de comunidades y subculturas. Humanitas, Buenos Aires (1983)
33. Ray, C.: Neo-endogenous rural development in the EU. In: Cloke, P., Marsden, T., Mooney, P. (eds.) Handbook of Rural Studies. Sage, London (2005)
34. Rezsohazy, R.: El desarrollo comunitario. Narcea, Madrid (1988)
35. Rhodes, R.: The new governance: Governing Without Government. Political Studies 44, 652–667 (1996)
36. Roseland, M.: Sustainable community development: Integrating Environmental, Economic, and Social Objectives. Prog. Plann. 54, 73–132 (2000)
37. Sanderson, D., Polson, A.: Rural community organization. John Wiley & Sons, New York (1939)
38. Schejtman, A., Berdegué, J.: Desarrollo territorial rural. Debates y Temas Rurales 1, 7–46 (2004)
39. Shucksmith, M.: Endogenous Development, social capital and social inclusion: perspectives from LEADER in the UK. Sociol. Ruralis. 40, 208–218 (2000)
40. Storey, D.: Issues of integration, participation and empowerment in rural development: the case of LEADER in the Republic of Ireland. J. Rural Stud. 15, 307–315 (1999)
41. Unión de Centros de Animación Rural. Rev. Renov. Rural. 21, 31–32 (1991)
42. Ward, N., McNicholas, K.: Reconfiguring Rural Development in the UK: Objective 5b and the new rural governance. J. Rural Stud. 14, 27–39 (1998)
43. Ware, C.: Estudio de la Comunidad. Unión Panamericana, Washington DC (1949)
44. Westholm, E.: Exploring the role of rural partnership. In: Westholm, E., Moseley, M., Stenlas, N. (eds.) Local Partnerships and Rural Development in Europe: a Literature Review of Practice and Theory, Dalarna Research Institute, Falun (1999)
45. Williams, C.C.: Harnessing social capital: some lessons from rural England. Local Government Studies 29, 75–90 (2003)
46. Woods, M.: Advocating rurality? Changing the position of rural local government. J. Rural Stud. 14, 13–26 (1998)

Travel Health and Health Tourism: A Perspective of the Subject of Tourism

Jian Li[1,*], Huimei Liu[2], Jing Chen[1], Qunhui Xue[1], and Yafang Bao[1]

[1] School of Tourism & Health, Zhejiang A&F University, Lin'an, 311300 Zhejiang, China
[2] School of International Studies, Zhejiang University, Hangzhou, 310058 Zhejiang, China
leonjian08@yahoo.com

Abstract. The emphasis on travel health and health tourism shows a historic progress in tourism, which is the focus of tourism development under the post-modern society and post-tourism era, and as well as the mirror of the idea of Humanism in tourism. When the forms of tourism evolve from traditional ones, such as sightseeing tour and cultural tour, to health tourism, it pays more attention to both physical and mental health in the traveling, which shows the development in tourism, basing on the change from considering economic benefits simply to giving consideration to social benefits, ecological benefits, and human health. Travel health and health tourism are defined. The relationship between them are discussed and measures and suggestions to achieve them are also proposed.

Keywords: Tourism Management, Health tourism, Travel health.

1 Introduction

Hippocrates, an ancient Greek doctor, father of medicine, once said that the sunshine, air, water and sports were the source of life and health. According to this unsophisticated but wise theory, travel is the best way for man to achieve a state of health for that travel not only enables people to have more exposure to the sunlight and air, but also make them be closer to their soul. Our soul is unconsciously isolated from us by the trivial daily life. Health and tourism has been the basic human needs and the combination of the two is a new concept namely health tourism advocated by many people nowadays.

1.1 The Definition of Travel Health

What is travel health? In broad sense, travel health includes the health of the tourist, tourism resources, environment and tourism service providers in a broad sense; however, it refers to the health of the tourist in a narrow sense, including physical and mental health, specifically means that the physical and psychological function of the

---

* Corresponding author.

Q. Zhou (Ed.): ISAEBD 2011, Part I, CCIS 208, pp. 56–63, 2011.

tourists could be optimized to varying degrees(Tao,2001). In narrow sense, travel health particularly refers to the health of the travelers based on the perspective of the subject of tourism in this study.

From an ecological perspective, travel health refers to a higher level of dynamic equilibrium achieved from the progress of the exchange of complex material, energy and information between the micro-ecosystems of tourists and other natural and social ecosystems. This dynamic equilibrium has many variables or effect elements, including the influence of tourism resources and environment, the achievement of tourism motivation, the satisfaction of tourism demands, the settlement of conflicts and disputes, the service quality of tourism service providers and so on. Any changes of these variables will affect the value of the Function—travel health.

1.2 The Definition of Health Tourism

What is health tourism? "Health tourism is that all aspects of the journey, experience and places of residence must be conducive to maintaining or improving health status. Tourists need special hotels, professional advice on health and personalized service. Travelers also require for all the services that could improve their physical and mental health, including fitness, beauty, nutrition diet, relaxation, temperament refinement, spirit relaxation and mediation, and so on " (Cited from Wang & Gao, 2007).

Health tourism can be literally understood as "beneficial to health". However, "beneficial to health" wholly or systemically depends on travel environment, tourism resources and tourism products, service management process, promotion and application of academic researches of travel health and travel behavior, which all contribute to health(Wang,& Gao, 2007). In the appealing for health tourism, the object, media, subject of tourism all play an important role, and are interplaying with each other to realize the optimal function. Due to the limitation of the space, this paper only examines "tourism behavior which is beneficial to health" from the perspective of subject of tourism. The tourism behavior include the preparations, role positioning, screening of health tourism products, safe and security awareness and rational consumption etc.

2 Relationship between Travel Health and Health Tourism

Travel health is the objective and the guiding principle while health tourism is the means and ways. A logical connection exists between them.

Health tourism is one of important ways to realize travel health. Basing on the perspective of the subject of tourism, tourists are the biggest beneficiaries in the competition among the tourism object, media and the main tourist; meanwhile, the tourist is not passive recipient but active participant. As one of important subjects in the realization of travel health, tourist's travel behavior, which is in accord with travel health, to some extent, has more important and direct decisional significance. Their behavior not only contributes to travel health, but also indirectly dedicates to travel health by supporting coordination action and adjustment of active travel health behavior of the tourism object and media. Like the narrow sense of travel health mentioned above, tourist's health tourism certainly has profound economic and social culture background, touching upon travel consumption ethics of tourist, attitude, motivation, knowledge, psychological expectation, social communication skills and so on. The author believes that health tourism is one important way of realizing travel health.

2.1 Pre-travel Healthy Preparation

Pre-preparations like psychological preparation, knowledge preparation, skill preparation and material preparation are the booster of travel health and also the alleviant or detergent for destructive elements of travel health. For instance, in psychological preparation tourists should make an appropriate foreseen on causes of health problems (including the relatively inconvenience in travel life compared to family life) or health impact factors (resources and environment impact, etc.), tourism demand, and make a low-key psychological adjustment with the natural environment, human environment, service facilities and appropriate material and mental provider, hence the tourists can avoid the disappointment, frustration, anxiety, and tension caused by the discrepancy between high expectation and the reality, thus reduce the psychological harm, which will result in hurt in their body physiology, caused by the artificial defects of the tourism service.

In knowledge preparation, tourists get some prior knowledge about safety, health, specific areas (spots) and security, health-related information (such as weather, natural disaster, social order, etc.) and etiquette especially the knowledge of custom or religious taboo so that they could take appropriate measures for safety and health protection or way of communication and can try their best to avoid the security incidents and the arising of health problems or indirect health problem caused by culture shock.

In skill preparation, tourists take prior learning of related skills for trauma emergent treatment (such as fracture or snake bites, etc.) and sudden illness so that they could timely take proper handling to prevent the aggravation of illness or expansion of loss upon the occurring of emergent situation.

In material preparation, travelers could prepare some relevant daily backup medicine (for instance, Band-aid, etc.), emergent medicines (for example, Instant Cardio-Reliever Pill) and escape apparatus (for instance, the compass, etc.) for a rainy day use(Ye ,2005).

2.2 The Orientation of Role, Mood and Behavior

In role-orientation, tourists make a healthy role-orientation in economy (in the meantime as the consumer of travel products, service recipient, participant in the process of consumption, partner, right beneficiary and obligation undertaker), culture (at the same time as the experience of foreign culture and the disseminator and protector of tourism source culture) and environment (beneficiary of beautiful environment and protector of ecological environment) so that they will give more coordinated actions and ethical concerns and then reduce the incidence of complain and complaints.

In emotion role-orientation, tourists make emotion role-orientation in consumer objects (tourism products and related resources) and service providers, consumer partner, the natural and cultural environment of consumption place and creating relationship of equality, friendship, love, praise and thanksgiving, therefore they will be more welcomed and receive more friendly service and gain emotional experience of more real and more beneficial to health.

In behavior-orientation, tourists will easily change in identity, feeling and needs because of the off-site of travel areas and the temporary of travel time hence the tourists easily get rid of constraints from their identity or occupation, morality and manner and the "supervision" of law and temporary "vacuum" caused by the lack of supervision of law. Therefore, tourists should strengthen self-discipline and maintain rationality and locate the above role-orientation and emotion-orientation to consciously resist the erosion of consumerism, prevent the loose of duty restriction and the explicit of possession sense and inhibit the indulgent behavior caused from "reverse travel health".

2.3 Priority Selection of Strong Health Orientation Tourism Products

Travel and health has a natural coupling relationship. Ordinary journeys are all useful for spirit relaxation, regulating of physical and mental health and eliminating the sub-health status. However, through comparison, strong health orientation tourism products have more direct effect. The world strong health orientation elements range from the previous four S—sun, sands, sea and sex to the five S— sun, sands, sea, spa and sport. Among them the spa tourism and sport tourism become the favorite of health tourism. The improvement contains not only ethical advancement but importantly connotation variety. Health tourism products exceed the range of the five S motioned above. There are major health tourism products like healing tour, leisure vacation, forest travel, sport journey (low risk) and religious tourism at the present time. Some are endowed with Chinese characteristics health care elements. For example, some healing tour and leisure vacation are furnished with traditional Chinese acupuncture, massage, herbs and other services. And the Chinese traditional martial arts—Tai chi quan (a kind of traditional Chinese shadowboxing) is combined into the sport journey. The Chinese local religion—Taoism is poured in the forest travel to make the tourist experience the enjoyment of "harmony between man and nature", enjoy the comfort of returning to nature, returning to the "spirit home" and uneasiness relieving of body and mind. The religious philosophy is added into the religious tourism to experience new feeling, clean up worries and expand thought with an aim of remolding the confidence of life or gaining wisdom, by utilizing the geographical and environmental advantages like ancient trees, musical bells and drums and deep and distant artistic conception of the Taoist temple.

2.4 Maintaining Safety and Health Awareness and Keeping Rationality and Self-discipline in Behavior

Safety incidents are closely related to health issues, inappropriate disposal will be against the achievement of travel health. Safety consciousness makes for preventing incidents from happening and health awareness is in favor of taking precautions against health problems. Then keeping rationality in behavior and strengthening self-discipline conducive to calling for safety and health consciousness and building mental line of defense when coming across alluring and impulsion in order to guarantee the process and result of the behavior apart from the occurring of incidents and health troubles. In the dominance of the above consciousness, according to their physical condition, tourists could make rational choices of travel places and the mode and intensity of tourism activities (tourists who have altitude stress should be cautious in choosing high altitude areas (Tibet for example), travelers who get frail and just recover from dangerous illness and woman tourists who are in menstrual period should choose tourism activities of slow pace and low intensity); tourists keep self-discipline in accordance with the situation of the visiting areas (for instance, be cautious against animal scratching and bite because of teasing the poultry when visiting the countryside);travelers choose the varieties and the hot and soul degree or salty degree according to their body condition and food taboo (diabetes mellitus tourists should avoid sugary food or high sugar products); giving alerts of safety and persuasion of dangerous behavior to traveler accompanist (for example, parents who take nonage children together should strengthen the supervision of them according to their mental development); the accomplish of all the above factors could guarantee the travel health and put an end to incidents and health problems or annihilate them in bud（Wang,& Gao,2007）.

2.5 Be Careful about High-Risk Leisure Activities

Adventure sports tourism, concerning outdoor entertainment and leisure tourism and stimulating activities (such as bungee jumping, forest hiking, pick up trash along the climbing, roller coaster, etc.). Through these sports tourism, you can keep fit, train your perseverance and improve mind, enhance physiological psychological functions. But compared with common leisure activities, the above projects require a higher level of professional skills. Certainly, we should also consider the probability of accidents. Moreover, the slightest mistake you make in your traveling will lead to exercise injury physically and mentally, and even cause personal injury and, even death. In fact, the above-mentioned activities of the "experience" significance are much greater than the "health" of meaning. In order to prevent the movement of trauma, we should promote some fitness tourism activities which have low risk and be beneficial to people's life (such as leisure and tourism, forest bath, walking in the woods, etc). And you also should select the high-risk activities carefully. Even if you have selected the latter you should consider your age, health status and physical condition. And then choose the activities which have appropriate form and intensity. Furthermore, you should operate these activities strictly accordance with safety regulation to reduce the risk of travel safety and health risks（Zhou, Song & Zhou,2005）.

2.6 Impact from Other Health Tourism Travelers

Health tourism of tourists not only directly contribute to physical and mental health of tourists themselves but also improve travel quality indirectly through coordinating with tourism providers. For example, travelers can resist or refuse overloaded travel arrangement by tourism corporations and the action of forcibly using unsafe tour facilities so as to avoid safety accidents or health problems.

3   The Establishing of Scientific Health Tourism System

3.1   The Establishment of Healthy and Safe Destination

The base of the project "healthy and safe destination" should cover the following elements:Healthy and safe image-building in the tourism image orientation; the strategy of healthy and safe objective in tourism management system; tourism reception and operating facilities in the healthy and safe protection system; the creation and promotion strategy of the concept of healthy and safe of the operator and employee of tourism management; convenient inquiry system of healthy and safe consulting; opening up of "healthy and safe destination" together with construction and promotion friendly proposal; special fund plan for construction of "healthy and safe destination" (Shi, 2008).

3.2   Health Tourism Should Dominate in Tourism Programming

The health of tourist and health of environment are the major goal of developing tourism industry and the health tourism plan combine the three and realize collaborative development of the three. The health tourism plan guarantees the fundamental interests of the tourists and also meets the market need. A truly healthy and vitalized health tourism program should achieve perfect unity of ecological benefit, economic benefit and health benefit.

A healthy design of tourism development programming: strictly controlling the capacity of tourism areas; reasonable arrange of space capacity; usage of landscape ecology; increasing natural, open and flowing rest space and reducing artificial, closed and crowed facility areas, usage of healthy and hygiene elements.

An appropriate set up of health tourism products: ecological health care in elderly market, sport and leisure in middle age market; adventure and camp in teenage market and self-driving tour in white collar are becoming the favorite products for many people.

3.3   The Development Mode of Health Tourism

Health management pattern: it is based on the health maintenance plan, which has realized the perfect combination of "the health safeguard" and "the health management". Introducing the health management pattern into the development of the healthy leisure traveling, the developer who has no clinic service can help visitors in some scenic spots or traveling place through internet. And those will help the visitors to complete for a registered doctor, rehabilitation and a series of the overall health administration—the new pattern of "IT + health+ travel", which makes reasonable arrangements for tourist's daily life by the organization of network platform and the member system. And it will provide their nutritious meals in the distribution and health, sports, fitness for the series of activities according to need, which will promote health for tourists.

The development of health management model provide model for preserving one's health tourism destination and tourist attractions. It has coordination with insurance companies, travel agencies and medical institutions. The specific operation includes cooperation with the medical health insurance package, overall health management, which could make the tourism impact on human body and mind and offer better tourism projects.

Medical Tourism Model: Medical tourism is a new type of preserving one's health through the combination of high-quality health care and rehabilitation recreation tourism development pattern. It requires certain medical conditions and medical technology as a support; it is a way of travel , in addition to a certain amount and higher level medical staff, it also needs guide service of medical professional knowledge and skills; it could provide tourism train services of transport, accommodation, medical checks and sightseeing for foreign tourists. At present time, Thailand, India and Korea offer the kind of tourism service which makes medical tourism attract a growing number of foreign tourists flock to these countries and meanwhile bring them considerable economic benefits.

Health club model: taking the form of VIP or selling consumer cards and relying on main tourism resources and products, assembling a series of preserving one's health tourism and recreation tourism, especially preserving one's health tourism to an entire development pattern. This development model can use a tourist destination as a base, integrating with do-it-yourself tour and by using the flexible assembling of tourism projects and packaging style, extends to the surrounding areas (spots), thereby expanding the geographical space of fitness and recreation activities and form diversified and attractive tourism products.

3.4 Training of Tourism Practitioners

Tourism practitioners, whether tour guide, hotel staff or salesman of tourism goods should master relevant knowledge and service skills. The basic knowledge and skill that the health tourism talents need to acquire contains the following: rational combination of diet including diet match and tonic diet, according to the physical needs of tourists; the medical knowledge of common incidents of tourists, for example, the treatment of heat stroke, carsickness, bleeding and fractures; know well with the improvement effect of tourism programs for physical health, reasonable arrangement of the tourism schedule, giving directions of suitable tourism programs to the tourists according to their physical condition, especially the elderly tourists; know well with the medical function of tourism goods and give tourists suitable recommend of goods and fine communication skills, grasping the psychological activity of the tourists and conducting them to keep good mood.

3.5 Promotion of Tourism Products

Apart from the superior resources, ecological environment and cultural practices of national, regional and school district, the promotion of tourism products should be integrated in the education of the tourists.

Acknowledgements. This study was supported by the Team Program of Young Researchers for Innovation of Zhejiang Agriculture & Forestry University (No.2009RC10), the National Social Science Research Funds (No.10BGL047),and Zhejiang Province Social Science Planning Research Funds (10GYD70YB).

References

1. Lan, S.:Speeding the establishment of healthy and safe tourism destinations, and Creating the image of China being " healthy and safe tourism country, China Tourism News paper (June 16, 2008)
2. Tao, H.: New Introduction of Tourism Studies. Tourism Education Press, Beijing (2001)
3. Wang, X.: Guide for Tourism Industsry Programming. Chinese Tourism Press, Beijing (2000)
4. Wang, Y., Gao, Y.: Concept, Types and Development Expecations of Health Tourism. Journal of Guilin Institute of Tourism 6, 803–805 (2007)
5. Ye, Y.: Nursing Implementation of Special Care Ward in Tourism Areas. Nanfang Journal of Nursing 12(7), 37–38 (2005)
6. Zhou, Y., Song, H., Zhou, K.: Studies on the Development Strategy of Australia Sports Tourism. Journal of Sports Culture 20(1), 24–25 (2005)

Probing and Philosophizing about Religion

Weiwei Zhao

Shandong University of Technology, Shandong, 255049, China
WeiweiZhao2011@126.com

Abstract. In the modern multilateral society, many traditional concepts are being destroyed, re-established, or are being lost or replaced. Confronting with life pressure and life itself, modern people in material luxuries still can't escape from occasional perturbations, contradictions or other spiritual crises commonly existing nowadays. Since ancient time, religion has been playing the role of salvation and comforting human minds, nevertheless, while speculating on life, religion is apt to self-deception and escape. Based on the above opinions, and from the perspectives of philosophy and sociology, this paper probed respectively religion's root cause, religion's necessity as well as religion's limitations, pointing out that though religion bears wisdom and beauty, more valuable is human identity together with worldly life itself, where lies the final crux of happiness.

Keywords: religion, function, value.

1 The Heavenly Religion

So many people presume to know religion or deities that it is impossible to take up this subject without exposing oneself to attack as sacrilegious by some and as a prophet by others. We human creatures, who don't know the human world completely, presume to know the almighty religion or deities!

Yet "no philosophy of life is complete, no conception of human's spiritual life is adequate" (Lin Yutang, 2005:401). In fact, the negligible humankind's imagination is so boundless that it set foot not only in beautiful tales but in the unpredictable religion. Human is actually an incorrigible animist, interpreting all things anthropomorphically; he personifies and dramatizes nature, and fills it with a cloud of deities. Then, what on earth enabled humankind's imagination radiate to that supernatural and the mysterious field?

1.1 Common People's Desire

Schopenhauer has ever said, as experience begins to coordinate itself into wisdom, brain and body begin to decay. "Everything lingers for but a moment, and hastens on to death." (The World as Will and as Idea, II, 454) He considers that fear of death is the beginning of philosophy, and the final cause of religion. Pessimistic of course is his philosophy, while as tiny living things on earth, human beings naturally desire long life

Q. Zhou (Ed.): ISAEBD 2011, Part I, CCIS 208, pp. 64–69, 2011.

and immortality, but it seems unpractical, so besides fears and sighs, they looked foreword to some thing which can weaken their fear of death and fulfill their dream of immortality; furthermore though mankind master the earth, mankind can't master their own fates, they have too many desires, so they need an imaginary super power to serve them, to satisfy their innumerable desires, thus religion appeared. But surprisingly, from master to slave, mankind as a whole knelt down before the deities created by themselves...and they begin to pray.

Usually religion begins with thinking, so wisdom and sheep-following intersect within. For example, Buddhism summarizes wisely that there are four miseries in human life: old age, diseases, death and life itself, thus, as a fact, human's full and free exercise of his or her natural ability has to be limited. Nevertheless, in further thinking, most of human's suffering actually lies in human's own retrospect or anticipation; pain itself is brief. How much more suffering is caused by the thought of death than by death itself!

1.2 Inferior People's Dream

Simultaneously, Santayana thinks, with Lucretius, that it was fear which first made the gods. Faith in the supernatural is a desperate bet made by human at the lowest ebb of his fortunes. Since the beginning of human society, primary communism only flashed, society is apt to classify into different ranks, and it's a common scene that in fighting the exploiting class, often, the oppressed failed, their hope disillusioned, they didn't know what to do, so they had to look forward to next life for a better life, so the utopia of religion arises. Kale Marx had ever pointed out that religion is a kind of self-feeling of some people, who haven't found their "self" or "ego" or lost it again, namely religion is the consciousness of those who haven't taken their own fates under control, and is the alienation of their self-feeling. "Religion is the opium of people"(The collection of Karl Marx, I, People's Press,1972:1), he said sharply. Then to the oppressed people, perhaps what religion plays is but a lamentable role of anesthetic.

The heavenly religion knitted the world people a visionary paradise, where they can find what they dreamed in spirit mostly, they needn't fear death any more, for even religion can't ensure them immortality, they can console themselves that if they lived religiously and morally, they would be permitted to go to their Heavenly Father when died, and also in this way their spirits would be saved.

2 The Terrestrial Religion

Religion in air is as beautiful as children tales, heaven, angles, auspicious clouds...all arouses people's desire to fly away from the worldly miseries and worries. So we say, when Westerners are depressed, they turn to God; when Indians are depressed, they turn to Buddha; when Arabs are depressed, they turn to Allah ...since the beginning of human history, religion has been playing the role of salvation and consolation, nevertheless, has the paradise promised by religion appeared on earth? Has religion brought the world real blesses and happiness?

2.1 Puppet in Politics

When heavenly religion befell the world, its kind tenets changed into mechanical doctrines and rituals, and in stead of granting the weak hopes, religion is most often utilized to serve certain secular powers. Thus, in dealing with affairs of mankind, religion lost its ever charming hues in heaven.

In the materialist view, supernatural phenomenon is imaginary, only the physical world is real. The 19th century philosopher Ludwig Feuerbach (1804-1972) thinks that there is no supernatural beings, gods are only imaginary shadows projected, are the target reflections of human fears and desires. So Marx presented: "people created religion, rather than religion created people...religious world is a reflection of the real world...religion is sighs of the oppressed, is the gentleness of cruel world..." Accordingly, religion is actually invented or at least is applied to manipulate people, especially of their spirits. For thousands of years, how many tragedies have been created with the name of religion? How many bloody wars are lunched because of religious conflicts? All kinds of religious authorities claimed that they have mastered the absolute truth, and utilized it as a weapon to acquire social and political rights, even attributed poor people's sufferings to mistakes of their previous life. Such interpretation and application of religion not only restrained social help toward these people but enslaved them as prey and victim of the exploiting class. As a political puppet, terrestrial religion has deviated from its original intention as human's mental shelter, thus Marx asserted: "In order to access people the real happiness, we must give them the abolition of those illusory pleasures from religion."

2.2 Tool in Economy

While religion is serving politics, economic benefits will certainly accompany and gather to various religious communities and to most of the social citizens, then as a kind of sacrament, can religon deny itself as a tool in economy? Take Judaism, the pre-Christianity as an example, which not only killed its own prophets, such as the Baptist St. John and Jesus, but, during the course, it is economic interests instead of religious piety played the decisive role.

For many centuries, Jerusalem has always been a monopoly as the religious center, and in Jesus' period, this position naturally brought most of the residents enormous benefits, and the permanent success is based on the residents' obeying the antique laws from Moses. Hence, almost all the local citizens depended on "holy temple" to make a living, which including the few economic and political aristocrats—the class of flaman, and their assistants, and further down to common servants (who benefited from cleaning the "holy temple"), to coin-exchanging merchants, to bosses of restaurants and hotels (who offered board and lodging to innumerable pilgrims), and so on. While, Jesus the Christ missionized to the citizens: love God, love all people and God's spirit can be offered a sacrifice everywhere, not only in Jerusalem! Unintentionally, but imagine if Jesus serman takes effect, what will happen to Jerusalem? To flaman, to servants, to bosses and to all the others relevant? Especially to the Pharisees, who hated Jesus the most? So Jesus was sentenced to death just like St. John was killed before almost for the same reason.

Jesus is died, but human isn't saved, or in other word, human that time is indifferent to Jesus' blood. So we can infer thet it is the power of religion, the right of medicine and the effect of law together murdered Jesus, for he dare challeng Moses' authority and threatened Jerusalem's economic interests, for he cured patients with miracles, and also for he initiated political turbulence.

3 The Value of Religion

So many disadvantages and limitations are mentioncd above, while as an important part of human civilization, religion is anyhow a fashion of mankind's holding the world, and mankind, with the help of religion, realized their childish dreams of transcending themselves and transcending their secular lives.

3.1 Transcending Oneself

Religion is super mundane, while it is a remarkable phenomenon that human beings everywhere have had religions; How can we understand mankind if we do not understand religion? "such studies would bring the skeptic face to face with the mystery and pathos of mortal existence. They would make him understand why religion is so profoundly moving and in a sense so profoundly just." (Santayana, In religion, New York, 1913; p.4.)

Philosophers are most often rational and scientific, but even in modern time, not few philosophers and scientists approve religion and object human's deviation from religious belief, why? Santayana (1863-1952) the delicate and romantic Spanish-born American philosopher thinks that a world quiet divested of deity is a cold and uncomfortable home. He asked himself like this: "Why has man's conscience in the end invariably rebelled against naturalism and reverted in some form or other to a cultus of the unseen?" Perhaps "because the soul is akin to the eternal and ideal"; it is not content with that which is, and yearns for a better life; it is saddened by the thought of death, and clings to the hope of some power that may make it permanent amid the surrounding flux. But Santayana concludes bluntly: "I believe there is nothing immortal...Not doubt the spirit and energy of the world is what is acting in us, as the sea is what rises in every little wave; but it passes through us; and cry out as we may, it will move on. Our privilege is to have perceived it as it moved." (Scepticism And Animal Faith, p237 and 271; Reason in Common Sense, p189; Winds of Doctrine, p199.) Splendid of the philosopher's statement! The reason for why we human beings should live a decent human life is simply because we are decent human beings! Francisco Bacon also claimed that human beings are not real walking beasts but immortal spirits, human need fight against his or her greed, envy and evil, but in nature, human looks forward to loftiness and self-transcending.

3.2 Perfecting Moral

From the perspective of functionalism, owner of the planet, but because of human's individualism and monophobia, human lacks self-confidence, they need a more powerful existence to pray, to obey and to legislate for them.. According to the French sociologist Emile Durkeim (1858-1917), religion can be interpreted as a social cohesion and to him, religion is the symbol and consolidation of social order, which can possibly serve as human's moral reference.

Nowadays, this opinion is still available, for modern people seemingly are enjoying an uncomaparble material banquet, but they are not as happy as expected, whose alien spirits are calling for help, what is the help? Human morals? So many moral principles have been overturned; Mankind itself? Human seems wandering himself in puzzle, thus more and more people go back to turn to religion, something they had denied long ago. In the Is God a Virus? Published in 1995, the author John Bowker declares: "religion is an organized system to fulfill biological demands, is for the aim of co-existence to assemble people and offers them a living meaning." Can religion be so all-round, even"…offers them a living meaning"? I suspect.

At all times and in all over the world, moral's fall is not rare, and people racked their brains to find ways to save it, but, so often, people feel incompetent, and have to resort to religion. But why are human morals apt to fall? Aren't human morals actively established by human themselves? Plato's opinion is referential: If everyone is simple and honest, justice is an easy thing, but human is easily greedy, luxurious and ambitious, they love strife, every species "fights for the matter, space, and time of the other." Then how to persuade them to be reasonable and useful? By police baton? That is an annoying method and wastes money. He said there is a cleverer way of attaching a punishment from supernatural authority to social citizens, and place this supernatural authority above social morals, so religion becomes absolutely necessary. Montesquieu, while exposing religion's hypocrisy in The spirit of laws (Esprit des Lois, 8, The Commercial Press), considers that even if a religion is hypocritical, it is still the possibly best guarantee to make people honest and upright, and he intends that religion is always the optimal humanity assurance.

By all means, religion endowed the world external powerful deities, especially to the religious followers, the deities can comfort their spirits and reward or punish them according to their degrees of following social norms. The caused effect is not bad, but only stops here of religion's guiding human mind. Doctor Lin Yutang stated in The Importance of Living that the trouble with orthodox religion is that, in its process of historical development, it got mixed up with a number of things strictly outside religion's moral realm—physics, geology, astronomy, criminology... If it had confined itself to the realm of the moral conscience, it would be more acknowledged and welcomed.

In fact, just like what shows in the reasons for remaining even creating God advocated by those Enlightenment thinkers, human beings are not fooled by religion but unfortunately ruled by religion.

4 The Waning of Religion

Presuming a sovereign power, and following it in life completely, which means religion. Is it a nature that human desires to be ruled? With science's advancing, world has change a lot from that religion-breeding era, and mankind is sane enough that the neutral cosmos is neither with us nor against us; it is but raw material in our hands, and can be heaven or hell according to what we are. Religion is but a tale.

Besides, when mere creeds or ceremonies usurp priority over moral excellence as a test of religion, religion has disappeared and divided, which are united by devotion to the common moral law. It was to establish such a community that Christ lived and died; it was this real church which he held up in contrast to the ecclesiasticism of the Pharisees. But another ecclesiasticism has almost overwhelmed this noble conception. "Christ has brought the kingdom of God nearer to earth; but he has been misunderstood ; and in place of God's kingdom the kingdom of the priest has been established among us." (Quoted in Chamberlain, Immanuel Kant; vol. i.p.510) Creed and ritual have again replaced the good life; And instead of men being bound together by religion, they are divided into a thousand sects. Again, miracles cannot prove a religion, for we can never quite rely on the testimony which supports them; and prayer is useless if it aims at a suspension of the natural laws that hold for all experience. Finally, the nadir of perversion is reached when the church becomes and instrument in the hands of a reactionary government; when the clergy, whose function it is to console and guide a harassed humanity with religious faith and hope and charity, are made the tools of theological obscurantism and political oppression.

5 Conclusion

If human society indeed need a religion, according to Albert Einstein, it should be a spiritual support, a mental freedom and a loftiness of interests, which seeks not God nor natural deities but a rational-based perception, meditation and belief to the significance of human's living in the world, namely religion is mere the synonym of holy pursuit and holy ideal, "this religion" is not "that religion" again.

Kant said: "every man is to be respected as an absolute end in himself; and it is a crime against the dignity that belongs to him as a human being, to use him as a mere means for some external purpose." (Quoted in Paulsen, Immanuel Kant;.p.340) There are no gods, no need to worry about next life or spirit salvation, there is only human self or life itself, which is also a "religion", if you regard self-sublime and dependable.

References

1. Rousseau, J.-J.: The Social Contract. Wordsworth Editions Limited (2007)
2. Marx, K.: The collection of Karl Marx, I. People's Press (1972)
3. Durant, W.: The Story of Philosophy. Siman and Struster Inc. Press, New York (2006)
4. Shengnian, Y.: Western Culture:In Intruduction. Shanhai Foreigh Language Education Press, Shanghai (2005)

Study on Dynamic Efficiency of Agricultural Finance Projects under the New Countryside Background— Taking Henan Province as Example[*]

Peng Wang[1], Yinsheng Yang[1], and Liying Zhang[2]

[1] College of Biological and Agricultural Engineering, Jilin University, Changchun 130025
[2] College of Economics and Management, East China Institute of Technology, Fuzhou 344000
wp@cust.edu.cn, yys@jlu.edu.cn, zhangliying@ecit.cn

Abstract. Agricultural finance projects are the primary source of constructing new socialist countryside, and utilizing efficiency of the financial fund plays a prominent role for expediting construction of new socialist countryside. Taking 18 cities in Henan province as an example, the author constructed index system which consisted of input and output indexes according to the objectives of new countryside construction, adopted data envelopment analysis（DEA） and Malmquist index to measure the scale efficiency, technology efficiency and the changes of agricultural finance projects. In order to establish the sample for learning in the province, the author ranked for integrated efficiency of each city.

Keywords: New countryside background, Agricultural finance projects, Dynamic efficiency, Data Envelopment analysis (DEA), Malmquist index.

1 Introduction

China is a large nation for agriculture, the growth or decline of agriculture plays direct impact which is driving or inhibiting national economy. And it is easily influenced by the force of nature, in order to the importance and inferiority of agriculture, it always under support and regulation of government. The major historic task of building new socialist countryside in the "11th five-year plan" period was put in the No 1 central document in 2006 clearly, and it was emphasized in the third Plenary Session of the 17th Communist Party of China Central Committee as a strategic task. Therefore, the construction of socialist new countryside has become urgent need for the new development of a nation, the common aspiration of people across the country, and an important theme of harmonious development. Agricultural finance projects are the primary source of constructing new socialist countryside, and it plays strongly leading role. Therefore, the utilizing efficiency of the financial fund plays a prominent role for expediting construction of new socialist countryside.

---

[*] This work is supported by Science and Technology Department Research Project of Henan Province. (No.102400450031).

Q. Zhou (Ed.): ISAEBD 2011, Part I, CCIS 208, pp. 70–76, 2011.
© Springer-Verlag Berlin Heidelberg 2011

2 Theoretical Analyses on Efficiency of Agricultural Finance Projects under the New Countryside Background

Efficiency and Productivity are usually linked; their investigation is the relation between input and output, and its basic goal orientation is to obtain more utility with less investment. The government financial support is the key factor for countryside development, according to the view of economics, although the investment subject of government does not keep goods, the maximization utility is still its keeping goal. In order to achieve this goal, the government must keep funds to support agriculture development in all aspects, and implements the overall supervision and macro-control management, so as to make the limited funds to attain greater using effect. The efficiency of agricultural finance projects under the new countryside background is relatively efficiency, that is, the author chose 18 cities in Henan as samples, they are similar and homogeneous, the city in the samples of which had the best utilizing efficiency in the financial fund (its efficiency value is 1) as a standard, the rest samples are compared to it, the city which is nearest to the standard, the relative efficiency of using financial support funds is higher, instead, it is lower.

Efficiency improvement of agricultural finance projects in essence is that the government attains the more effective configured through technical progress or improvement measures, which reflects the capability of input-output and sustainable development. Study on dynamic efficiency of agricultural finance projects under the new countryside background, the choice of 2005 - 2009 time sequence data was to analyze the change about efficiency of agricultural finance projects in 18 cities of Henan province, first of all, the author analyzed efficiency change of agricultural finance projects in 18 cities of Henan province in the year of 2005-2006 in which the "new socialist countryside building" was brought forward hardly, and then analyzed efficiency change of agricultural finance projects in 18 cities of Henan province from the year 2006 to nowadays.

3 Model Constructing on Efficiency Evaluation of Agricultural Finance Projects under the New Countryside Background

3.1 Data Envelopment Analysis for Evaluating Basic Efficiency

Data Envelopment Analysis (DEA) was brought forward by Charnes, Cooper and Rhodes [1], which primarily builds the efficient production frontier by a linear programming, relative efficiency of the other Decision Making Unit(DMU) is attained by comparing with efficient production frontier.

Assume that there are n DMUs, and each DMU has m kinds of input indexes and s kinds of output indexes, which can be denoted respectively as follows:

$$X_j = (x_{1j}, x_{2j}, ..., x_{mj})^T \quad Y_j = (y_{1j}, y_{2j}, ..., y_{sj})^T, \quad j = 1, 2, ...n.$$

DEA model based on input-orientation under the condition of constant returns to scale is showed as follows:

$$\begin{cases} min_{\theta,\lambda}\theta \\ s.t - y_i + Y\lambda \geq 0 \\ \quad \theta_{x_i} - X\lambda \geq 0 \\ \quad e\lambda = 1, \lambda > 0 \end{cases}$$

Total inputs and outputs of all DMUs, e is an identity matrix. The constraint condition $e\lambda = 1$can ensure that the frontier is convex; it means variable returns to scale. The value of θ is the efficient value of the i_{th} DMU, if $\theta=1$, then we can say that the DMU with perfect technical efficiency, if not, it proves that the DMU is under production frontier with efficiency loss of $1-\theta$. Banker, Charnes and Cooper change the hypothesis from constant returns to scale to variable returns to scale, C^2R model was developed into BCC model [2]. BCC model which separate purely technical efficiency and scale efficiency can measure whether the DMUs are on the state of best production scale under certain production technique. The scale efficiency value of each DMU can be attained by the division which between the value of technical efficiency of C^2R model and the value of pure technical efficiency of BCC model.

3.2 Malmquist Index for Evaluating Efficiency Advancing

Malmquist index was brought forward by Sten Malmquist, who is the economist and statistician of Sweden in 1953.The new measuring index was used to analyze the moving of consumption on the indifference curve. Malmquist index in the early was usually used in the research area of consumer conduct, and then was used to analyze input and output, was used for evaluating the dynamic changes in production efficiency in some business and productivity trends of a region especially.

In order to measuring dynamic efficiency of agricultural finance projects in Henan province, the author chose the Malmquist index model. The method form dynamic evaluating system between several production frontiers in different years, which not only reflects the efficiency of DMU compares to production frontier, but also can reflect technical change and technical efficiency change. Caves,et al(1982) [3] used index meanings which analyzes consumption change in different period into production efficiency firstly, Fare,et al(1994) constructed Malmquist index for force change which was used to review the change of production efficiency between the continue periods. If there are t and t+1 periods to be observed.

And under the constant returns to scale, the author adopted the input-orientation model of DEA. For each period t (t=1,2,...,n), the eventual aggregate was denoted as the follow function F_t which contained input vector $X_t \in R_+^N$ and output vector $Y_t \in R_+^M$:

$$F_t = \{(X_t, Y_t) : X_t \Rightarrow Y_t\} \tag{1}$$

Malmquist index model is constructed by four distance functions which are input-orientation. The distance functions in t and t+1 period is showed as F_t and F_{t+1} :

$$D_t(X_t, Y_t) = \sup\{\theta : (X_t / \theta, Y_t) \in F_t\} = (\inf\{\theta : (\theta X_t, Y_t) \in F_t\})^{-1} \tag{2}$$

$$D_{t+1}(X_{t+1}, Y_{t+1}) = \sup\{\theta : (X_{t+1}/\theta, Y_{t+1}) \in F_{t+1}\} = (\inf\{\theta : (\theta X_{t+1}, Y_{t+1}) \in F_{t+1}\})^{-1} \quad (3)$$

Distance functions show the distance from observation point to frontier of t period, it is used to define the count down of input reduce maximum under certain inputs, therefore $D_t(X_t, Y_t) \geq 1$. The mix distance functions in the next periods are showed as follows:

$$D_t(X_{t+1}, Y_{t+1}) = \sup\{\theta : (X_{t+1}/\theta, Y_{t+1}) \in F_t\} = (\inf\{\theta : (\theta X_{t+1}, Y_t) \in F_t\})^{-1} \quad (4)$$

$$D_{t+1}(X_t, Y_t) = \sup\{\theta : (X_t/\theta, Y_t) \in F_{t+1}\} = (\inf\{\theta : (\theta X_t, Y_t) \in F_{t+1}\})^{-1} \quad (5)$$

Distance functions $D_t(X_{t+1}, Y_{t+1})$ that is link with technique condition of t period make (X_{t+1}, Y_{t+1}) to realize input reduce maximum under feasible condition, and distance functions $D_{t+1}(X_t, Y_t)$ that is link with technique condition of t+1 period make (X_t, Y_t) to realize input reduce maximum under feasible condition, the function of malmquist index is defined:

$$Mal = \left[\frac{D_{t+1}(x_{t+1}, y_{t+1})}{D_{t+1}(x_t, y_t)} \times \frac{D_t(x_{t+1}, y_{t+1})}{D_t(x_t, y_t)} \right]^{1/2} \quad (6)$$

According to the analysis of Fare.et al (1994) [4], Malmquist index about production efficiency is disassembled the product of technical efficiency change (effch) and technical change (techch), and then technical efficiency is further disassembled the change of pure technical efficiency and scale efficiency. It is shown as follows:

$$Mal = \frac{S_t(x_t, y_t)}{S_t(x_{t+1}, y_{t+1})} \times \frac{D_t(x_{t+1}, y_{t+1}/VRS)}{D_t(x_t, y_t/VRS)}$$
$$\times \left[\frac{D_t(x_{t+1}, y_{t+1})}{D_{t+1}(x_{t+1}, y_{t+1})} \times \frac{D_t(x_t, y_t)}{D_{t+1}(x_t, y_t)} \right] \quad (7)$$

The change of total factor productivity (TFP) is disassembled the change of scale efficiency, pure technical efficiency and technique. In the formula (7), the first item is scale efficiency change (Sech), the second item is pure technical efficiency change (Pech), the third item is technique change (Techch), and the product of the first and the second items is technical efficiency change (Effch). If the scale efficiency change is bigger than 1, it means that the change of input factors improve scale efficiency from t to t+1 period, if the pure technical efficiency change is bigger than 1, it means that the improvement of management enhance efficiency, if the technique change is bigger than 1, it means realizing technique advancement, if the change of total factor productivity (TFPch) is bigger than 1, it means that productivity has been improved. In the other way round, if the index value is referred above, it means that corresponding efficiency has been descended.

3.3 Index System for Evaluating Efficiency of Agricultural Finance Projects under the New Countryside Background

The building of new socialist countryside is an arduous and long-term task, which relates to an abroad area and contains agricultural production, farmer living, farm education, medical sanitation, society guarantee, village feature and democracy management and so on. And in the nowadays, more and more scholars take interested in the research about new socialist countryside. Therefore, when measuring the efficiency of agricultural finance projects in Henan province, the author combined 20 word counts which was brought forward by centre government in 2006, that is "growth of production, well-to-do life, civilized countryside atmosphere, neat rural face, democratic administration", on the foundation of proposing foregoing research, the author constructed the index system for evaluating efficiency of agricultural finance projects, during optimizing the index system, the author filtrated the input vectors and output vectors. The index system which has been optimized for evaluating efficiency of agricultural finance projects was shown as follows:

Table 1. Index system for evaluating efficiency of agricultural finance projects under the new countryside background

Classify	Basic demand	Main index
production	Advancing general ability	1. financial supporting for countryside production 2. consuming mechanism of each hectare 3.each unit yield of foodstuff
life	Promoting sustain addition of income	4. collaborating medicine scope 5.using electricity of each farmer 6. Engel's Coefficient 7.income of each farmer
Education medicine rural face democratic	Improving stuff of farmers Enhancing programming	8. medicinal workers of one thousand farmers 9.capital asserts of each middle school students 10.ratio of grading road 11.fulfil ratio of farmer· voting 12.opening ratio of governmental management

3.4 The Data Source for Evaluating Efficiency of Agricultural Finance Projects

There are 18cities that contain Zhengzhou, Luoyang, Kaifeng and so on from 2005-2009 sequence data was used to evaluate the efficiency change of agricultural finance projects in Henan province, The total data was from Statistics government of Henan province, Statistics reports, 2005-2009<Henan province yearbook of agricultural statistics>.

4   Demonstration Analyses

4.1 The Basic Efficiency of Agricultural Finance Projects in Henan Province

From the table 2 above, the efficiency of agricultural finance projects in 8 cities are efficient, they are Zhengzhou, Kaifeng, Jiaozuo and so on, they are can be the benchmarks for other cities to learn. The efficiency of other cities were in the interval 0.8183-0.991, that illuminated that efficiency of agricultural finance projects in the cities was not efficient, there must be some resource waste, thereinto, according to efficiency, Pingdingshan ranked the last, there must be some problems on technique and scale to be solute, the other not efficient cities as Pingdingshan should learn to the efficient cities in order to realize useful using of agricultural finance projects.

Table 2. Basic efficiency of agricultural finance projects in Henan province

Region	C^2R efficiency	BCC efficiency	Rank	Region	C^2R efficiency	BCC efficiency	Rank
Zhengzhou	1.000	1.000	1	Xuchang	1.000	1.000	1
Kaifeng	1.000	1.000	1	Luohe	1.000	1.000	1
Luoyang	0.943	1.000	12	Sanmenxia	0.979	0.991	10
Pingdingshan	0.813	0.828	18	Nanyang	1.000	1.000	1
Anyang	1.000	1.000	1	Shangqiu	0.880	0.950	15
Hebi	0.960	1.000	11	Xinyang	1.000	1.000	1
Xinxiang	0.897	0.906	16	Zhoukou	0.967	0.967	13
Jiaozuo	1.000	1.000	1	Zhumadian	0.980	1.000	9
Puyang	0.830	0.970	17	Jiyuan	0.910	0.970	14

4.2 Efficiency Change of Agricultural Finance Projects in Henan Province

Measuring efficiency of Malmquist index was further decomposed efficiency change and technique change, according to the efficiency change value, we can estimate that the efficiency of agricultural finance projects was amendatory or exasperate.

It showed that: (1) Efficiency of agricultural finance projects in Henan province has a steady increasing; it shows that each city try to close with frontier under the

Table 3. Efficiency change of agricultural finance projects in Henan province

R	2005-2006			2006-2007			2007-2008			2008-2009		
	TC	TEC	TFP	TC	TEC	TFP	TC	TEC	TFP	TC	TEC	TFP
1	1.25	1.05	1.45	1.03	1.05	1.02	1.05	1.04	1.11	1.14	1.05	1.19
2	1.08	1.05	1.05	0.79	1.09	0.77	0.97	1.09	0.99	0.99	1.00	0.96
3	1.13	1.06	1.45	0.99	1.05	1.03	0.97	1.04	1.02	1.6	1.09	1.16
4	1.13	1.07	1.10	0.82	1.03	0.84	1.013	0.94	0.87	0.98	1.06	0.98
5	1.07	1.04	1.19	0.81	1.08	0.83	0.92	1.09	1.01	1.05	1.03	0.96
6	0.90	1.06	1.03	0.64	1.07	0.63	1.08	1.06	1.10	1.09	1.08	1.09
7	1.02	0.95	1.18	0.93	1.18	1.05	1.13	1.03	1.08	1.15	1.04	1.10
8	1.12	1.07	1.27	0.92	1.09	0.92	0.96	1.09	0.96	1.06	1.09	1.05
9	0.90	1.07	1.07	0.79	1.07	0.79	1.15	1.09	1.15	1.01	1.06	1.01
10	0.84	1.06	1.23	1.05	1.09	1.02	1.01	1.06	1.03	1.04	1.06	1.06
11	0.82	1.06	1.03	0.64	1.07	0.63	1.08	1.06	1.10	1.09	1.08	1.09
12	1.09	1.03	1.21	0.78	1.00	0.78	0.86	1.05	0.81	0.94	1.03	0.93
13	1.06	1.00	1.31	0.97	1.09	1.03	1.09	1.05	1.09	1.02	0.96	0.92
14	0.82	0.98	1.32	1.09	1.06	1.12	1.08	1.03	1.11	1.11	1.02	1.17

Table 3. (*continued*)

15	1.06	1.06	1.26	0.96	1.03	0.96	0.99	1.06	0.96	1.09	1.05	1.13
16	1.17	1.07	1.2	0.88	1.06	0.92	0.97	1.07	0.94	1.02	1.05	1.04
17	1.08	1.09	1.25	1.02	1.05	0.99	1.11	1.04	1.08	0.99	1.05	0.95
18	1.04	1.04	1.21	0.68	1.08	0.68	0.84	1.04	0.87	1.11	1.04	1.10
M	1.02	1.05	1.23	0.88	1.07	0.89	1.02	1.05	1.01	1.06	1.05	1.05

1-Zhengzhou, 2-Kaifeng, 3-Luoyang, 4-Pingdingshan, 5-Anyang, 6-Hebi, 7-Xinxiang, 8-Jiaozuo, 9-Puyang, 10-Xuchang, 11-Luohe, 12-Sanmenxia, 13-Nanyang, 14-Shangqiu,15-Xinyang, 16-Zhoukou, 17-Zhumadian, 18-Jiyuan, R- Region, M- Means

guiding government policy, but technique frontier is still the weak spot of agricultural finance projects; (2) From the total factor productivity, in the 18 cities, there are only 5 cities whose efficiency value is smaller than 0.8, and most efficiency value is bigger than 1, it is shows that each city in Henan province has a advancing direction in agricultural finance projects during 2005-2009; (3) The change efficiency of *TC*, *TEC*,and *TFP* in 2005-2006 are higher than the other years, it is shows that there was efficiency advancing after the new socialist countryside.

5   Conclusion

Through constructing efficiency model of agricultural finance projects, and adopting DEA and Malmquist index, we analyzed the efficiency of agricultural finance projects in the year 2005-2009, DEA- Malmquist index is an available method for analyzing efficiency evaluation and change. There are 8 cities in technique and scale efficient status, they are the benchmarks to the other cities; under the new socialist countryside background, agricultural finance projects in Henan province is improving gradually, but technique frontier is still the weak spot of agricultural finance projects, in order to promoting the efficient using of agricultural finance projects it needs, the learning between cities and the management of local government are necessary.

References

1. Charns, A., Cooper, W.W., Rhodes, E.: Measuring the Efficiency of Decision Making Units. European Journal of Operational Research 6, 429–444 (1978)
2. Banker, R.D., Charns, A., Cooper, W.W.: Some Models for Estimating Technical and Scale Inefficiencies in Data Envelopment Analysis. Management Science 30 (1984)
3. Caves, D.W., Christensen, L.R., Diewert, W.E.: The economic theory of index numbers and the measurement of input, output, and productivity. Econometrica 50, 1393–1414 (1982)
4. Fare, R., Grosskopf, S., Norris, M., Zhang, Z.: Productivity growth, technical progress and efficiency Change in Industrialized Countries. The American Economic Review 84, 66–83 (1994)

Research of Real Estate Bubble Measurements Based on Ramsey Model – A Case Study of Nanning in China

Xiekui Zhang and Defu Wu

Business School of Guangxi University, Nanning, Guangxi 530004, China
gxzxk@126.com, wudeful@163.com

Abstract. Real estate bubble has become one of the serious problems that influence the economy sustainable development in our country. This paper employs Ramsey model to make measurement analysis on real estate bubbles in Nanning real estate market, and then we find there are varying degree real estate bubbles in the year of 2004, 2007 and 2008 in Nanning city of China. Meanwhile, according to the measurement results, we have put forward some effective measures to avoid the appearance of real estate bubbles.

Keywords: Ramsey model, Measurement analysis, Real estate bubble.

1 Introduction

Recently, there have been many primelots in Beijing, Shanghai and some other places, this has stated a heat discussion about real estate bubbles again. At 5 December 2009, two state-owned construction lands about 208 acres in Liusha peninsula of Nanning city have got an auction price of two billion, four hundred and seventy million RMB. The high land price would make real estate bubbles easily. Real estate bubble is a form of real estate economic fluctuation, and then the bubbles would intensify the fluctuation. Real estate bubble is a social economic phenomenon, occurs in those countries which own a big population but few lands, and economy develops fast. This phenomenon would appear when conditions are ready, and then it would seriously influence all aspects of nation economy and social development. There is no doubt that we should make great efforts to our real estate industry, but it is also very necessary to take reasonable measurement methods to make early warning of real estate bubbles, in this way to ensure sustainable development of real estate industry. This paper uses Ramsey model to make measurement analyses of real estate bubbles in Nanning city, and then puts forward effective measures to avoid appearance of real estate bubbles.

2 Theoretical Bases of Real Estate Bubble Measurements

The intension of real estate bubble is that the price of real estate goes against its basic value in the long term, that is to say, the actual price of real estate goes against its basic value. If we want to measure real estate bubbles, we should get the basic value and actual price. The formula is this: bi=(pi-ji) Among this, bi refers to real estate bubble

Q. Zhou (Ed.): ISAEBD 2011, Part I, CCIS 208, pp. 77–83, 2011.
© Springer-Verlag Berlin Heidelberg 2011

measurements, pi refers to market price of real estate property, and ji refers to basic value of real estate property. We can acquire the actual price of real estate from statistical data, but it is very difficult to get basic value of real estate property with this method. For that we should ensure property income of all terms in the future, if we want to make sure the basic value. On the contrary, we cannot get accurate basic value, for this income is determined by people's expectation to the future. So, we take Ramsey model to calculate basic value of real estate property.

3 Ramsey Model

Ramsey model is a kind of growth model in macroeconomics, and its assumption is harsh. The first assumption is this: the whole economic system is made by two parts, they are family and company. The family part does not make any products, and buy all things from market. On the contrary, the company part does not consume products, its commercials are all for sale, to make income by selling the products. The second assumption is this: labor will increase as population increases, the relation between total amount and quantity per capita is Xt=xten. In this condition, we can get this: Nt =ent. In our real life, output can not only be used as assumption, but also can be used to be investment. In the condition that the profit scale is invariable, we can get output per capita formula: f(kt)=ct+dkt/dt+nkt, according to this: Yt=f(Kt,Nt)=Ct+dkt/dt. The result is margin output rate of property in the optimal and stable equilibrium state of economy would be equal to the sum of growth rate "n" and time preference "θ", that is: f'(kt)=θ+n. At this time, labor needs and property needs are matched, this makes output to the optimal state, also the economy runs in an uttermost equilibrium way. We could make out basic value of required property, if technical specification is fixed, that is basic value j= f'(kt)=θ+n. Then only to make clear how much the property value surpasses basic value, we can know the property bubble measurements. According to these thoughts, we can make empirical analysis to see whether there exist bubbles in Nanning real estate market.

4 The Measurements of Real Estate Bubbles in Nanning from 2003 to 2008

4.1 Ascertaining Basic Value of Real Estate Property

The property would be easily influenced by inflation in the real life, so we should eliminate the impact of inflation β, then to make the basic value of property. The basic value of real estate property can be showed like this: j= f'(kt)=θ-β+n. From this formula, we know that three aspects form basic value of property. The first one is consumers' psychological factor, it relates with people's income and their expectation to the future, and equals to rate θ. The second one is inflation β, the higher of the inflation, the lower of the basic value of property. The third one is population growth rate n, if the number is big, it shows the labor growth rate is big, and the value of property is big.

In practical analysis, population growth rate and inflation rate are easy to obtain, for there are complete statistical data in real life. On the contrary, to confirm the rate is complicated, for there are many kinds of rate in our life. We choose these two kinds of rate here, the first one is one-year deposit rate. From this deposit rate, we can get the minimum basic value of property. The second one is the asset lending rate, bigger than 5 years, we can get the maximum basic value of property through this lending rate. When real estate value between the maximum and minimum, there are no real estate bubbles. When real estate value smaller than the minimum, we know the real estate value is underestimated. When real estate value higher than the maximum, we know there are real estate bubbles, the bigger of the surpassed number, the more of real estate bubbles. According to the figure 1, we can get the running range of real estates' basic value of Nanning city from 2003 to 2008.

4.2 Ascertaining Practical Price of Real Estate Property in Nanning City

How to ensure practical price of real estate property in Nanning is a problem. To make comparability between practical price and basic value in real estate demonstration analysis, and own the same scope of statistics, we choose the change rate of price index in Nanning real estate assets as its yearly yield rate, and this is practical price. For it is convenient to collect data, we choose the narrow meaning of real estate concept, that is to make real estate bubble measurements with the representative of commercial residential building of Nanning real estate.

4.3 Real Estate Bubble Measurements Analysis of Nanning City Based on Ramsey Model

If we have got the basic value and real price of real estate assets, we can make real estate bubble measurements of Nanning city from 2003 to 2008, according to the formula bi=(pi-ji) /ji. Meanwhile, we can get the results in table 1 and the expression in figure 2 by Ramsey model.

We can use Ramsey model to get real estate bubble measurements table and figure in Nanning city. When the growth rate of real estate's price between the maximum interest return rate and the minimum interest return rate, which is the running range of basic value, we consider there is no real estate bubble. When the growth rate of real estate's price is lower than minimum interest return rate, we consider the basic value is underestimated. When the growth rate of real estate's price is higher than maximum interest return rate, we consider there are real estate bubbles. The bigger of the surpassed number, the more of the real estate bubbles.

In 2003, the growth rate of commercial buildings' price is negative 5.2%, and the minimum interest return rate and maximum interest return rate are 2.12 and 5.63, we consider real estate value is underestimated. Real estate value in 2005 is also underestimated. As we can see that in the year of 2004, 2006, 2007 and 2008, there are real estate bubbles. Especially in 2004, as the growth rate of real estate's price is 22.92%, but the maximum interest return rate is 2.6%, surpassed by 20.32%, there are serious real estate bubbles. In 2007, the growth rate of real estate's price is 18.48%, but the maximum interest return rate is 4.23%, surpassed by 14.25%. We can also know there are little even can be neglected real estate bubbles in 2006. In 2008, the result that is measured by Ramsey model is small, we consider there are real estate bubbles. The model take many factors about one-year term deposit rate and five-year term lending rate, but they are reduced under state macro-control, so the maximum interest return rate and minimum interest rate are lower than the corresponding period., then causes real estate bubbles.

5 Effective Measures to Avoid Real Estate Bubbles

The key points to avoid real estate bubbles are as follows, according to the essence of real estate bubbles. The first one is how to control the real price of real estate, and the second one is how to ensure the basic price precisely.

5.1 About Controlling the Real Market Price of Real Estate

There are so many factors can influence market price of real estate. Such as geographical position, natural environment, environment around the real estate, population, price level, people's income, economic development stage, economic cycle, monetary policy, tax policy, fiscal policy, land policy, urban plan, urbanization level, the changes of family scale, the way of purchasing and financing the house, external finance, capital market, development degree of second-hand house market and so on. Among these factors, even state macro-control can do nothing to the geography position and environment factors. Therefore, we should do as the following to control real estate's price to avoid real estate bubbles.

5.1.1 Land Policy of Real Estate
Presently, we take the tender, auction and listing to make land lending, this is fair, with respect to land lease by mutual agreement. The shortcoming by auctioning is land price would be high, and causes prime lots. High price lands are usually used to construct high-grade buildings and villas, and this causes the supply of high-grade buildings is more than needed, the common buildings are more needed than supply. More high-grade houses would make the whole real estate's price high, and then real estate bubbles appear. Therefore, to land policy, the government should pay more attention to supply structure of land lending, improve the supply ratio of economically affordable houses and low-rent houses. Just in this way to cut down speculation and avoid the appearance of real estate bubbles.

5.1.2 Tax Policy of Real Estate
In our country, the real estate tax mainly emphasizes turnover tax and neglects value-added taxation to the retain link, and then this would cause unreasonable phenomenon in real estate market. Many people cannot buy their own house, for the high house price. At the same time, to keep a house would cost little, this leads to the house leave-unused. Therefore, to levy property tax in retain link would restrain the speculation, then could reduce the real estate bubbles. What is more, to levy value-added taxation in real estate transactions, this also can reduce bubbles. If people take real estate market as investment market, they should take value-added taxation without saying. Because most house-buyer buy house as their own living place, they

would not sell the houses quickly after they buy it. In this way, to levy real estate transaction tax would not hurt the real needs and could reduce the possibility to make real estate bubbles. We should levy sum business taxation from the houses which are used by the owners less than five years, take property tax an so on to effectively stabilize real estate market, control speculation, and effectively manage the house prices. In these ways to make real price of real estate close to basic price and avoid the appearance of real estate bubbles.

5.1.3 Perfecting Financial Credit Policy of Real Estate

The most important aim to perfect financial credit policy in real estate is to prevent real estate bubbles to strike banking system. Firstly, we should increase or control the down payment of mortgage loan. The risk of bank mortgage is small, when the mortgage payment is high. Meanwhile, when we increase mortgage payment, it can decrease the capital turnover which is used for speculation, and then to control speculation in real estate. Secondly, if there are many speculation activities, we can carry out different mortgage loan rate to the people who goes to buy a second house. Thirdly, if there are many speculation activities, we can forbid forward delivery housing transaction or transfer.

5.1.4 Completing Market Structure of Real Estate

Real estate market includes the first grade land market, the second grade land market and the third grade second-hand transaction market. The development of real estate market goes like ladder-frame. We should lead people's grades consumption, enlarge market needs of second-hand houses, and link the second and third grade market. Meanwhile, to lower the tax standard and transaction condition of second-hand house transaction, simplify transaction procedure and promote mortgage of second-hand houses, and then to regulate house medium.

5.2 About Ascertaining the Basic Price of Real Estate

After controlling the real market price of real estate, we should ascertain basic prices of real estate objectively and reasonably. There are some factors not only impact the real price of real estate, but also influence basic price of real estate, such as price level, monetary policy, population and so on. These factors are the three variable ones which can impact basic price of real estate, they are θ, β, n, we have mentioned them in using Ramsey model to confirm basic value of real estate. Therefore, we should ascertain basic price of real estate objectively and reasonably from these factors which can influence basic price of real estate, and then to avoid the appearance of real estate bubbles.

5.2.1 Information Policy of Real Estate

We have mentioned that, to make sure the basic value of real estate should firstly solve people expectation problem. Therefore, government should lead people to anticipate house price reasonably, solve the unsymmetrical problem of basic information in house price. The authorities improve transparency of house cost through all channels, punish these real estate developers who use fake and exaggerated information to make profit. To real estate enterprises, government should take information announcement policy, and establish special organization to supervise real estate cost, to supply object and accurate house price information to house-buyer as much as possible. In this way, the government can lead peoples' expectations reasonably.

5.2.2 Mortgage Rate Policy of Real Estate

The we have mentioned before is not only related with people's expectation, but also related to rate. Therefore, when the government improves mortgage rate, it would hit speculation needs in real estate effectively. Such as the authorities take high rate to high-grade buildings, villas and the people who is to buy a second house. This method could stabilize house price and make real price of real estate close to its basic price. We should also know the rate-increase must not be too much, if not, it would suppress the real needs. At the same time, pay more attention to some details, such as when we improve rate, it would make obvious effect to house-buyers, but it would be a long time to suppress the rising of house price.

5.2.3 Inflation Controlling

We have mentioned that basic value of real estate relates with inflation, when inflation is more serious, its influences to capital value is more serious. Real estate has double attribute, one is as common product and the other one is as investment product. Generally, when house is as common product, the house price would rise as the price level improving, name house price would go up, not down. When inflation rate is higher than the growth of house price, then real house price decreased. When inflation rate is high during some period, it would make house price go up. Therefore, we should control inflation, according to the formula $j = f'(k_t) = \theta - \beta + n$, the basic value of real estate would go up and this would lighten real estate bubble level.

5.2.4 Population Controlling

According to the basic value formula $j = f'(k_t) = \theta - \beta + n$, which is made by Ramsey model. We know basic value of real estate relates with population growth n, when the number is big, it shows labor growth rate is big and capital value is big. When there is a big population in one area, there must be more real needs to houses. This can avoid the real estate bubble problem, which are caused by lack of effective needs and high house price. To a city, it should promote urbanization and regulate industry structure reasonably, then make reasonable growth of urban population. This measure not only avoids appearance of real estate bubbles, but also prevents some urban problems which would be caused by population expansion.

6 Conclusion

This paper goes from the essence of real estate bubbles and uses Ramsey model to ascertain basic value of real estate in Nanning city. Ramsey model makes science standard for confirming real estate value and uses the maximum basic value and minimum basic value as early warning to measure real estate bubbles, so this supplies a good thought to state macro-control and has well operability. Otherwise, Ramsey model also has some weaknesses, such as there is a distance between its assumption and real economic state. In real life, there are not only complete competition market and two-sector economy. Meanwhile, because of space limitations, the researches of measures to avoid real estate bubbles need further analysis.

Acknowledgements. The authors thank the National Planning Office of Philosophy and Social Science for providing research grant (Project No. 10XJY0018) and Philosophy and Social Science department of Guangxi Zhuang Autonomous Region for providing research grant of "Eleventh Five-Year Plan" project (Project No. 08BJL001) and Region Education department of Guangxi Zhuang Autonomous Region for providing research grant (Project No. 200702MS148).

References

1. Wang, X.: Researches on China real estate bubble measurements. Modernization Economic Discussion (08) (2005)
2. Li, M.: Researches on China real estate bubbles. China Financial Publishing House, Beijing (2007)
3. Xu, D.: Houscing price and bubble economy. China Machine Press, Beijing (2006)
4. Ye, J., Sun, X.: Real estate marketing. Capital University of Economics and Business Press, Beijing (2006)
5. Zhang, X., Wei, W.: Researches of government's response behavior under macro-control policy of real estate. Journal of Guangxi University for Nationalities (Philosophy, Social and Science Edition) (02) (2009)

Empirical Research on Housing Condition of Rural Migrant Workers – A Case Study of Nanning in China

Xiekui Zhang, Jing Zhang, Ruoxi Liu, and Ming Xie

Business school, Guangxi University, Nanning, Guangxi, 530004, China
gxzxk@126.com

Abstract. Rural migrant workers have made great contributions to the industrialization and urbanization of our country, but they get unequal treatment to the urban residents, especially in housing security. This paper makes sample investigation of housing condition of Nanning urban migrant workers, by this, we find their housing condition are poor, and they are not able to apply for low-rent housing or buy affordable housing, even government pays little attention to their housing security. We suggest making suitable housing security system to urban migrant workers, make clear detail standards of low-rent and affordable housing for urban migrant workers, and make efforts to provide urban migrant worker apartments. What is the important thing is that the government should be in charge of supplying indemnificatory apartments.

Keywords: urban migrant workers, housing security, urbanization.

Along with the fast development of industrialization and urbanization, more and more urban migrant workers pour into city. They have made great contributions to the city development, but they don't get the equal treatment to urban citizens, especially to housing security. This problem connects with the harmony and stability of society development between urban and rural areas in China. As China - ASEAN Expo permanently settled in Guangxi Nanning, and Guangxi Beibu Gulf Economic Zone Development Plan is brought to national strategy, Nanning has become the core of Beibu gulf economic zone and a regional international city. In order to make clear the housing condition of urban migrant workers, the author makes sample investigation of their housing condition. The objects of this investigation are the migrant workers, who are working in the city but their registered residences are still in rural area. We totally give out 200 questionnaires and get 190 valid questionnaires.

1 Sample Analysis of Current Housing Situation of Urban Migrant Workers

1.1 Composition Situation of the Samples

(1) In the gender composition, the male and female take average ratio. Among the 190 samples, male samples are 88, take 46.30% of the sum number. The female samples are 102, take 53.70% of the total number.

Q. Zhou (Ed.): ISAEBD 2011, Part I, CCIS 208, pp. 84–91, 2011.

(2) In age distribution, the young adults which are full of energy take the main part. Among the valid 190 samples, people age from 18-25 are 52, take 27.4% of the number, the age from 26-35 are 34, take 17.9% of the number, and people age from 36-45 are 45, take 23.7% of the number. In other words, the samples of people who are in young adult phrase (age from 18-45) take 68.9% of the total number.

(3) In education degree, most of the people have poor education. Among the migrant workers who are under the investigation, the people who have never received education is 8, take 4.2% of the total number, people whose education degree is primary school are 31, take 16.3% of the sum number. People's education degree is middle school are 40, take 21.1% of the number, people whose education degree is technical school or above are 35, take 18.4% of the number, people whose education is above junior college and college are 12, take 6.3% of the whole number. As a whole, people whose education degree is above higher school take 45.8% of the total number.

(4) In working area distribution. Among the 190 samples, people who work in restaurant and food service are 22, take 11.6% of the total number, porters are 16, take 8.4% of the total number, and housekeepers are 14, take 7.4% of the total number. Anymore, people who work in construction industry are 18, take 9.5% of the total number, sanitation workers are 4, take 2.1% of the total number, drivers are 12, take 6.3% of the number, security guards are 7, take 3.7% of the number, carpenters are 10, take 5.3% of the number, self-employed men are 31, take 16.3% of the number, and people in other working areas are 55, take 28.9% of the total number.

(5) In occupation composition, there is no obvious changes of occupation and working position. Among the 190 samples, who have temporary job are 75, only take 39.5% of the number, who have stable job are 115, take 60.5% of the number, and 72.21% of the urban migrant workers sign labor contract with their employers. There are 125 people who don't often change working city, take 65.8% of the number, 65 people who always change their working city, take 34.2% of the total number. In this way, we can make conclusion that Nanning urban migrant workers have area stability when they choose jobs, so it is more important to solve their hosing problems.

(6) Urban migrant workers pay more attention to housing security than their salary. Among 190 samples, 76 people choose better living condition when asked what can cause them to change working city, take 40.0% of the number. Their second focus is salary condition, 70 people pay attention to it, take 36.8% of the number. Otherwise, 60% of them think they would consider housing problems when changing their working city.

(7) To salary, urban migrant worker almost have low income. Among 190 samples, those whose income is 10 to 30 thousand are 136 samples, and this is almost the same salary as city workers, take 71.6% of the number. Meanwhile, the questionnaires show the workers' salary are mainly spent in daily consumptions (take 49.76% of the total number), and then is the children education (take 27.89% of the number). There are few workers spend salary to housing, only take 8.95% of the total samples.

1.2 Current Housing Situation of Migrant Workers

(1) Housing types are various, the migrant workers most live in rent houses and hardly buy houses in city

Among the 190 samples, there are 52 people live in collective dormitory, take 27.4% of the total number, there are 87 samples live in rent house, take 45.8% of the total number, there are 22 people live in countrymen or relatives' house, take 11.6%. What should be pointed out is that there are 29 people who have bought their own houses in the city, take 15.3% of the total number.

(2)General satisfaction of house conditions

This survey goes from four aspects, as safety and health condition, facilities and environment to investigate the housing condition satisfaction of urban migrant worker. During the investigation, there are 104 people consider current housing safety conditions are general or good, take 54.7% of the total number, 79 people think housing condition is general, take 41.6% of the total number, 7 persons consider condition is poor, take 3.7% of the total number. There are 93 people regard health condition is good or general, take 48.9% of the number, 79 people think condition is general, take 41.6% of the number, only 10 persons consider condition is poor, take 5.3% of the number. There are 83 people consider supporting facilities is general or good, take 43.7% of the total number, 86 people think it is general, take 45.3% of the number, only 21 people think it is poor, take 11.1% of the number. There are 78 people consider peripheral environment is general or good, take 41.1% of the number, 87 people think it is general, take 45.8% of the number, and 25 people consider it is poor, take 13.2% of the total sum.

(3)Strong desire to change housing condition

When asked whether they are willing to spend money on improving housing condition, 63.7% of them say yes. Otherwise, the urban migrant workers' desires to live in Nanning are strong, 57.9% of them hope to stay here, and 61.6% of them hope to buy their own houses in Nanning. Meanwhile, there are 45.8% of them intend to get city registered permanent residence by using land tenure of their own homeland.

(4) Housing rent is reasonable, but it still does not reach the expectation of urban migrant workers

Among the 190 samples, there are 48.95% people show the housing consumption takes not half of their income, 24.74% of them consider the rent is only the small portion of their income, 12.11% of them don't spend money on housing, and only 8.95% of them consider the housing spent take the most part of their consumptions. However, 36.32% of them regard the main factor of choosing rent housing is rent price, 41.05% of them hope rent price could be lower to improve housing condition.

2 Main Problems of Current Urban Migrant Workers' Hosing Security

2.1 The Related Government Departments Lack Attention of Urban Migrant Workers' Housing Security Problems

In order to make clear current housing security system of Nanning migrant workers, the author go to human resource bureau, social security bureau, house property bureau, statistics bureau, survey team and other related government departments. Otherwise, people in these departments all don't know the housing condition of urban migrant workers and regard they don't in charge of this, and they even lack basic data and statistics of this problem.

2.2 Poor Housing Condition of Urban Migrant Workers

In order to understand urban migrant workers' housing condition, the author makes investigation of some construction sites in Defu and Xinwu village of Jiangnan area, urban migrant workers' dormitory of Nanning light rail construction team and some other building sites. The rent housings' health and safety condition is general, and they usually have independent toilet and kitchen. For the houses exist many years, the problems of aging circuit and obsolete facilities are serious. The whole families of urban migrant workers live in a single room, which lack privacy and are inconvenient for conjugal life. For the collective dormitory, such as the migrant workers' dormitory of Nanning light rail construction site, about 30 people of men and women live in a 40 square-meter room, the basic facilities such as iron bedsteads, toilet and kitchen are shared.

2.3 Housing Problems Impact Work Commuting

Urban migrant workers always choose isolate villages and suburbs to live, for saving consumption in housing. However, where the migrant workers gathered in working place, such as housekeeping, catering, building industry, are mostly distributed in noble residential and central business district, and there is a long distance to their living places. In addition, for recent road traffic transformation is frequent in Nanning, there are always rush traffic jams, and many migrant workers often need three to four hours in commuting. As 26.32% of them show they would choose the near place to work for improving housing condition, this number is just secondary to lower housing rent. What is more, urban migrant workers are engaged in physical work, labor intensity is big, and their commuting costs energy, for long term, these will cause serious health problems.

2.4 It Is Hard for Urban Migrant Workers to Buy Indemnificatory Apartments

Nanning belongs to western area. It is undeveloped areas, though developing fast in recent years, but urban worker' income level is low, and migrant worker's income is low too. Nanning per capita disposable for people in city and town is 16254 yuan in 2009, but in April 2010, the average house price is 6157 yuan. It is obvious that urban migrant workers' desire on its own power to purchase indemnificatory apartments is difficult.

3   Government Should Be in Charge of Providing Indemnificatory Apartments for Urban Migrant Workers

3.1   Make Clear the Responsibility Subject and Attach High Attention to Migrant Workers' Housing Security Problem

At present, the main implementation of migrant workers' housing security, supervising and regulation subjects in government departments are unclear. It should seriously divide related responsibilities in government and make clear the scope of their department functions and work division, only in these ways can effectively resolve the housing problems of migrant workers. Obviously, it should consider establishing specialized agency to ensure housing rights of migrant workers, when the conditions are prepared.

3.2   Establish and Perfect Housing Security Model of Urban Migrant Workers

Chongqing province tries to utilize and rebuild the unused and vacant buildings in city, unoccupied houses in labor market and the unused houses of enterprises to supply departments for migrant workers in 1997. Their strict management and high quality services make more and more "Bangbang Department" in Chongqing, and the scale unceasingly expands. [3] There are already 36 buildings of "migrant workers' department" in the main city area of Chongqing in 2007, and this provides low-rent houses to 1.3 million migrant workers. Why do urban migrant workers prefer Chongqing "Bangbang department" are two reasons: the first is low rent, one bed one yuan one day, this is the acceptable and affordable rent to migrant workers. The second is the rent model if flexible, and low application qualities for living. This accords with the actual situation of urban migrant workers, for the migrant workers who are law-abiding and have temporary residence permit in Chongqing south distract can apply for this. The dispersions of Chongqing migrant workers' apartments save the urban migrant workers much time and traffic consumptions, so the occupancy rate is as high as 95%.

Nanning migrant workers have decentralized distribution, and their residence is far away from their work place, these cause serious commute problems. Chongqing "Bangbang Department" supplies good reference to solve housing supply of urban migrant workers. Because the limited financial power of Nanning, it should build its own characteristics when referring to Chongqing "Bangbang Department" model. For example, Nanning city area is smaller than Chongqing, migrant worker departments should only distribute around the center commercial district, and this can solve most problems about commute. There is no need to build migrant worker departments in center commercial area, and this can also lighten government financial burden.

3.3   Establish Pyramid Housing System of Migrant Workers

For the economic limitations of Nanning, it is impossible to build large-scale public rent houses for migrant workers. Therefore, it must be according to different types of housing needs of migrant workers to make concrete analysis, then gradually to solve housing problems. Migrant workers can get houses in these three types: the employing units provide (including shed, collective dormitory, etc.), rent houses (including the low-rent, affordable commodity housing, etc.), buying houses (including affordable housing, affordable commodity house, etc.). Migrant workers who are at the bottom pyramid get houses by employing units to provide houses, this part of migrant workers is mainly engaged in construction, portaging and which are required a lot of physical activity work, namely low technical content position. Therefore, the government and the employing unit should make concerted efforts to encourage enterprises to provide standard dormitory for migrant workers. Migrant workers at the middle-level pyramid obtain houses by renting houses. For this part for migrant workers, the government's focus should be on building low-rent housing and ensure it would really benefit migrant workers, then to establish perfect information platform and broaden channels for them to get housing information. Migrant workers on the top pyramid by buying houses to get their own houses, and for this part of migrant workers, government should build more affordable houses. [4]

3.4 Utilize and Rebuild The Unused and Vacant Buildings in City, Unoccupied Houses in Labor Market and the Unused Houses of Enterprises to Supply Departments for Urban Migrant Workers, and the Department Facilities Should Be According to the Real Condition of Migrant Workers, Not Only to Pursue Perfect Facilities

Such as the housing to single migrant workers should mainly be collective dormitory and make low standard principle of its safety and health condition. Firstly, the residential safety should be ensured. Migrant workers housing should pass safety and quality detection to eliminate hidden dangers. At least to ensure cold resistant, sunstroke prevention, windbreak and surrounding public security is good, and they would not suffer crime scoundrels. Secondly, ensure residential health. The enterprise which have power should recruit specialized cleaning personnel to do external environment cleaning of migrant workers' housing, no power enterprises could use incentive means to encourage migrant workers and their families to do cleaning. Strengthen the propaganda, to remind migrant workers pay attention to hygiene and improve personal hygiene quality. Thirdly, secure basic living facilities. To regulate per capita residential area, the lowest stipulated minimum hutches, and per capita used several essential water, electricity, and heat preservation, cold resistant and other facilities.

For the migrant workers who have family should be provided with single or one-bedroom (less than 30 square meters) room. It should be equipped with toilet, kitchen, and basic water and electricity living facilities, but not need big area, good facilities, and these would lead to high occupancy. There should be versatile housing resources for migrant workers to choose, for example, some single rooms need to use a public toilet or kitchen, and the rent is lower, some other single rooms with toilet and kitchen facilities. Migrant workers can choose different types of housing, according to their own conditions and expectations. The housing sites should be close to migrant workers' working area in geography aspect.

3.5 Make Clear Specific Standards of Urban Migrant Workers to Apply for Low-Rent Housings or Buy Affordable Housings

Urban migrant workers should enjoy housing security, for they have made great contributions to the city construction. The fact is migrant workers have no fixed working place, not the same as the stable city workers, and western area city's financial is limited, it can not solve the housing security problems of city citizens and migrant workers in one time. In the current housing security system of Nanning, to apply for the low-rent or affordable housing needs registered households, this is not fair and in long-term would be the barrier of Nanning economy development. It should enlarge application qualification, according to the comprehensive assessment of the applicant's qualifications to decide whether they are qualified to apply for low-rent housing or buy affordable housing, not to use the registered households as the limited qualification and contuse the enthusiasm of urban migrant workers.

3.6 Regulate Housing Rent Market and Secure Migrant Workers' Housing Right

At present, migrant workers mainly solve housing problem by rent housings. For the rent price is regulated by market, migrant workers have rights to choose and it is a relatively reasonable way to solve housing problem. Government should strengthen supervision, regulate rent market and eliminate the rent hype, mess charges and fraud tenant behaviors. In these ways to secure the rent can be stable and at an acceptable level. Meanwhile, to check the safety quality of rent houses is necessary, in this way to eliminate hidden dangers and clear out some old houses that are unsuitable for living. In addition, it should cultivate migrant workers' own contract and right protection consciousness to secure the right after they live in the houses.

4 Conclusions

Urban migrant workers have made great contributions to industrialization and urbanization of our country, but they do not enjoy the equal social security benefits as city workers, especially to the housing security. This paper by using sample investigation of housing security of Nanning migrant workers finds the housing conditions of urban migrant workers are generally poor. They have difficulties in applying for low-rent housing or buying affordable housing, and there still lack government's attention to urban migrant workers' housing problems.

It is suggested to establish suitable housing security system for urban migrant workers, make clear the specified standard of migrant workers to apply for low-rent or buy affordable housing, and utilize and rebuild the unused and vacant buildings in city, the unoccupied labor market houses, and the unused housing of enterprises for providing migrant workers' departments. Meanwhile, regulate rent-housing market and secure the housing rights of migrant workers. This paper specifically points out that the government should be in charge of housing security of migrant workers.

Acknowledgements. The authors gratefully thank national student innovative experiment plan to offer research grant (Project No. 091059325) and Philosophy and Social Science department of Guangxi Zhuang Autonomous Region for providing research grant of "Eleventh Five-Year Plan" project (Project No. 08BJL001).

References

1. Zhang, X., et al.: The research on sustainable development of city group in Guangxi Beibu Gulf Economic Zone. China Financial and Economic Publishing House, Beijing (2009)
2. Zhang, X., et al.: The research on sustainable development suggestions of city group in Guangxi Beibu Gulf Economic Zone. China Soft Science (5) (2009)
3. Yu, J., Zhu, J.: Bangbang Department": The urban family of migrant workers in mountain city – Chongqing. People's Daily (June 12, 2005)
4. Zhou, Y., Wei, G., Wang, L., Liu, Y.: Constructing "pyramid" migrant workers housing model – Based on Hefei migrant workers housing problem investigation and study. Journal of Labor Safeguard World (9) (2009)

Evolution of Paper Industry

Shaoni Zhou and Chunling Shi

School of Economics and Management of Beijing Jiaotong University. Beijing, China
Shichunling_1989@yahoo.com.cn

Abstract. In recent years, development of the global paper industry is quite fast, so the research on China paper industry is becoming much-needed. From the angle of Kearney's industrial evolution theory, this paper analyzes indicators such as CR3 of the global paper industry and focuses on the development modes of 20 global paper firms, and determines the global paper industry is in the scale stage of Kearney's theory and China paper industry needs to accelerate the pace of horizontal mergers and acquisitions to improve their market share.

Keywords: Paper industry, Industrial Evolution, Kearney, scale, industrial chain.

1 Introduction

As a competitive industry, the global paper industry's development is quite fast in recent years, and the growth of the China paper firms attracts people's attention for its rapid rise in the world. In this backdrop, large numbers of foreign investment is pouring into China to seek opportunities, and Chinese enterprises also expand themselves. A large number of mergers and acquisitions occur, and some enterprises also turn to the overseas market.

In this international situation, how should China paper firms develop? o expand in scale as soon as possible, or take a comprehensive advance of the whole industrial chain?From the perspective of industrial evolution, this paper attempts to determine the evolution stage of China paper industry according to the analysis of the world's leading paper enterprises' history and then provide some useful references to China paper enterprises.

2 Introduction on Kearney's Industrial Evolution Theory

Industrial evolution theory, also known as industry life cycle, starts after 1980s from product life cycle theory. Among the many theories of industrial evolution, the industrial evolution proposed by some experts from A.T. Kearney in 2002 is based on firm mergers and acquisitions which is treated as the major logic of industrial evolution.

According to Kearney's industrial evolution theory, all industries follow the same path to achieve integration. An industry from the beginning runs along the curve of industrial evolution, which is divided into the start-up stage, the scale stage, the gathering stage and the balance and alliance stage. Industries are developing in the evolution of mergers, and each stage indicates special strategic and operational elements. Understanding and following these elements can help enterprises define their positions and benefit for their development. On the contrary, to neglect these points will destroy the business.

Typically, there are a small number of enterprises in the start-up stage of industrial evolution. The first mergers begin to appear in this stage, and the M&A trades are small and mainly horizontal. In the early scale stage, the number of enterprises reaches the maximum. Enterprises begin to expand their business sphere through acquisition of their competitors and thus a large number of mergers and acquisitions occur. And in order to participate in global competition, cross-border mergers and acquisitions begin to happen. In the gathering stage, enterprises turn their eyes from speed to quality. Reduction in the number of enterprises reduces opportunities of mergers and acquisitions, but the ultra-large-scale mergers and acquisitions take place. In the balance and alliance stage, as the industry has been fully integrated, only a few enterprises are in a dominant position in the industry, and mergers and acquisitions within the industry is not important industrial characteristics any more. Enterprises turn to merger some companies in the start-up stage to enter new industries.

Kearney experts' study suggests that long-term success depends on the upstream along the curve of industrial evolution. The key factor is the speed of acquisition when enterprises run along the curve of industrial evolution. Enterprises with low speed will eventually become targets and disappear from the curve.Therefore, we can predict the evolution and even predict mergers and splits through the curve of industrial evolution. What's more, there is a significant correlation between the stage of industrial evolution and the success rate of mergers and acquisitions.So enterprises can treat the curve of industrial evolution as tools to strengthen the strategy of mergers and acquisitions and coordinate the integration.

3 Basic Analysis of the Global Paper Industry Evolution

3.1 Data Source

At present, PPI (Pulp and Paper International) gives us the most authoritative statistics and ranks of global paper enterprises. So this paper directly uses the ranks of global paper enterprises in 1992-2008 given by PPI to analyze the evolution of paper industrial structure.

PPI counts out the data of the pulp, paper and their processing of all paper enterprises, and then rank them based on the turnover of this part. Based on the above, it also gives statistics of market pulp production (different from pulp production), paper and paperboard production, quantity of company employees and other information.

In this section, based primarily on CR3 indicators and supported by the relationship between production and turnover, paper will use Kearney's theory of industrial evolution to judge the evolution stage of the paper industry and then provide suggestion for China paper enterprises' development.

3.2   Analysis and Judgment about the Evolution of Global Paper Industry

Kearney's industrial evolution stage is judged based on CR3 indicator which reflects the industrial concentration. Lack of the data of global turnover, calculation of the market concentration in this section is only in accordance with the production of paper and paperboard. That is, this paper selects the top 3 companies of paper and paperboard production from the top 30 companies in PPI and calculates their market share of paper and paperboard production. The result of statistics is shown in Table 1 (complete data, including 1992-1994, 1999-2008 years).

Table 1. Production concentration of paper and paperboard based on the rank in PPI (%)

item	2008	2007	2006	2005	2004	2003	2002
CR3(production)	10	10	10	11	11	11	12
item	2001	2000	1999	1994	1993	1992	
CR3(production)	13	12	10	7	8	8	

Data source: Statistical processing based on historical data from PPI.

The evolution of CR3 ranked on the basis of production from 1992 to 2008 is shown in Figure 1.

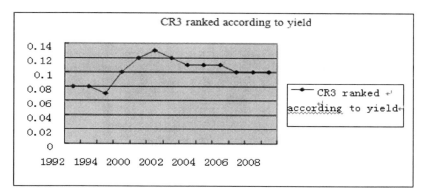

Fig. 1. The evolution of paper industrial concentration from 1992 to 2008

As can be seen from PPI's statistics, over the past 17 years, CR3 of paper industry ranked on the basis of production is around 10%, which means relatively low industrial concentration, but the degree of concentration of this century has increased over the last century.

What's more, we can determine the stage of industrial evolution auxiliary according to the change in the production and turnover of the global top-ranking companies. From the data of the top-ranking companies in recent years, we can see the production of paper has declined because of the current decline in the capacity of the market. However, the turnover increases year after year. This is mainly because these companies had adjusted their industrial structure in recent years and reduced their production to stabilize the market prices.

According to Kearney's judgment about the stage of industrial evolution, the level of the global paper industrial concentration has began increasing after a lower lever. The current CR3 is about 0.1 and production falls, but turnover rises. Basically judging from this, the global paper industry is in the early stage of scale. Based on the law of industrial evolution, the paper industry will be further integrated through mergers and acquisitions, etc., to improve concentration and achieve scale.

3.3 Analysis of Forest, Pulp and Paper Integration Strategy in Global Paper Industry

Paper industrial chain includes the purchase of land, planting trees, pulp and papermaking and other sectors, namely, the complete production process of paper making, is planting fast-growing forests in the land , fast-growing forest into pulp and then pulp into paper. According to the saying of paper industry, people who have forests and pulp will succeed. Pulp is resource-based products and it's the core of paper industrial chain. Forest, pulp and paper integration strategy has been proposed since 1990's in China. Has the pattern of vertical development in industrial chain been used by large international paper enterprises? This section will be devoted to the analysis of this question.

(1) The situation of pulp production of large international paper enterprises
Typically, the return of pulp industry is higher than the return of paper industry. However, the price of pulp is more volatility. As the international paper enterprises rarely directly disclose their total production of pulp, we can only get part of the enterprises' market pulp production. Then, this paper will make a brief analysis of paper industrial situation based on the market pulp supply of top-ranking enterprises.

The situation that the top 30 paper enterprises supply market pulp from 1992 to 2008 is shown in Table 2.

As can be seen from the table, about 63% (199/314) of the top 30 enterprises can not only satisfy their own needs for pulp, but also provide market pulp.

What's more, Table 2 shows that the global top-ranking enterprises also provide very little market pulp. Market pulp supplied by the top 30 enterprises over years only account for about 5% of the total pulp production, indicating that needs for pulp of most enterprises should be met by themselves and enterprises pulp mostly for their own needs. The cost of pulp is a tremendous impact on the total cost of papermaking and the price of pulp is more volatility. Therefore, paper enterprises usually need to control the supply of their main raw material in order to control risk.

Table 2. The situation that the top 30 enterprises supply market pulp from 1992 to 2008

Item	2008	2007	2006	2005	2004	2003	2002
Proportion of enterprises with market pulp	13/24	15/24	15/24	14/23	19/27	16/26	15/25
Proportion of enterprises supplying market pulp	54%	63%	63%	61%	70%	62%	60%
Proportion of market pulp in pulp production	5.7%	4.8%	3.3%	4.0%	5.2%	5.2%	5.6%
Item	2001	2000	1999	1994	1993	1992	
Proportion of enterprises with market pulp	15/23	14/22	14/22	15/24	18/26	16/24	
Proportion of enterprises supplying market pulp	65%	64%	64%	63%	69%	67%	
Proportion of market pulp in pulp production	5.6%	5.0%	5.9%	5.6%	7.7%	—	

Data source: Statistical processing based on historical data from PPI.

(2) The situation of investment in forest of large international paper enterprises
After analysis about the top-ranking enterprises, this paper finds most enterprises own a large-scale forest exploitation rights. For example, International Paper (IP) is the largest paper and forest enterprise in the world whose business includes paper, packaging and forest products.. In 2007, Mondi Group owned or leased over 2850 acres of forest resources in low-cost areas in Russia and South Africa, which can supply 800 million cubic meters woods each year. In 2008, their forest resources reached more than 3750 acres and the annual supply of wood was up to 9.2 million cubic meters. Mondi Group can supply more than half of the wood needed for their own pulp production, and each year they supply a certain amount of market pulp.

4 Verification of Industrial Evolution by Development of the Major Paper Enterprises

4.1 Selection of the Major Paper Enterprises

This section will select some paper enterprises and analyze their development process to further verify the evolution stage of the global paper industry we previously discussed. The following principles will be based when selecting enterprises. Firstly, enterprises' PPI ranking is more forward so that this paper can provide reference for China paper industry through the analysis of their development process. Secondly, selected companies are listed companies because their data is available. In accordance with the above principles, this paper selects 20 paper enterprises and analysis their situation of production layout in the world from 2000 to 2010.

By collecting information from their Web site, annual reports and the RISI database, this paper analyzes these 20 firms' development modes, especially their acquisition, single venture, joint venture, sale and closure matters, to understand international enterprises' development modes and directions.

4.2 Development Modes of Major Paper Enterprises

After analyzing these enterprises' development modes, this paper classifies them into five categories, that is acquisition, single venture, joint venture, sale (including reducing shares and asset divestiture) and closure, of which the first three types of development will bring increased investment and expansion of the scale, and the last two types will directly lead to contraction of the scale and alignment.The above 20 enterprises' development means from 2000 to 2010 are shown in Table 3.

Table 3. Font sizes of headings. Table captions should always be positioned *above* the tables.

Development means	Acquisition	Single venture	Joint venture	Sale	Closure
Times	165	25	26	111	5

Data source: Statistical processing based on information from enterprises' website, annual reports and RISI database

As can be seen from the above table, there were 332 major events (events whose complete information can be collected) during nearly 11 years of development history. The acquisition occurred most often, 165 times, followed by sale of the business, and they both belong to mergers and acquisitions. That is, mergers and acquisitions is not only important factor of global paper industry's restructure and development, but also the main reason for changes of enterprises rankings.

4.3 Development Directions of Major Paper Enterprises

As we talked earlier, paper enterprises mostly adopt paper, pulp and paper integration strategy. In this part, paper will deal with the above 20 enterprises' integration data of different segments in the industrial chain.

In these 20 paper enterprises, there were 278 paper-related business restructure, of which enterprises increased paper products production 156 times, reduced paper products production 56 times, increased pulp production (including waste pulp production) 16 times, but also reduced pulp production 9 times, purchased forest resources 18 times, and reduced forest resources up to 23 times.

As can be seen from the above statistics, international paper enterprises are currently restructuring mainly by some companies of paper products subdivided to expand the scale to obtain economies of scale. However, it is not obvious to restructure based on the strategy of forest, pulp, paper integration, especially to increase pulp production and forest resources.

The judgment is verified that enterprises should mainly depend on horizontal mergers and acquisitions to expand their scale and seize the market in the scale stage of industrial evolution by the major paper enterprises' development process.

5 Conclusions and Recommendations

As we can see from the above study, the global paper industry is in the scale stage of Kearney's industrial evolution theory. Paper enterprises are expanding their scale through a large number of mergers and acquisitions of their competitors. According to the law of industrial evolution, China paper industry should speed up horizontal mergers and acquisitions and expand their market share to compete with international enterprises in the limited market.

Slightly different from international paper enterprises, overseas development is not the best choice for China paper enterprises because China is now the largest country in paper demands. Since China is a country relatively lack of forest resources, it's impossible for paper enterprises to ignore the control of resources when they want to improve market share of paper and paperboard. Therefore, China paper enterprises should emphasize the strategy of forest, pulp, paper integration and mainly try to get forest resources from overseas.On the one hand, paper industry can share the excess profits of forest and pulp industry through the integration strategy. On the other hand, the total profit of the whole industry chain can be relatively stable to reduce investors' risk after the strategy of forest, pulp, paper integration.

References

1. Gort, M., Steven, K.:Time Paths in the Diffusion of Product Innovations. The Economic Journal (1982)
2. Deans, G.K.: Winning the Merger Endgame: A Playbook for Profiting From Industry Consolidation. China Machine Press (2004)
3. Fan, C., Yuan, J.: Empirical Study on the mergers and acquisitions of industry in Growth, Maturity and Decline. China Industrial Economy (2002)
4. Kuang, S.: Overview of the world's paper industry. China Paper News Letter (2003-2008)

Basic Thinking of Video Editing

Yimei Cao

Media Institute of Henan University, 475001, Kaifeng, Henan, China
YimeiCao2011@126.com

Abstract. Science and technology is changing rapidly every day. And the image world is very colorful as well. Films and televisions play more and more important role in people's daily life. Besides, more and more digital and high technology elements are being introduced in the process of people's communication, expressing feelings, exchanging thinkings and aesthetic entertainment. As ass result, the contents of video editing are extending. Mastering the thinkings of video editing and making use of video editing skills will surely improve the appeal of video works and satisfy the consumption need of the audience.

Keywords: Video editing, TV editor, digital technology.

1 Introduction

Zhengyi Fu, who has ever edited for the video works of Mourning, Bosom Friend, Four Generations and Dream of Red Mansions, is honored as the first pair of scissors in China. He once concluded the functions of video editing with 20 words: shearing actions, avoiding false, transplantation borrowing, deceptive of the audience and cutting out the play. But how can we cut so that the video is more outstanding? The following tasks should be fulfilled.

2 Complere Paraphrasing

Video editing must serve the subject of the video. And at the same time, we should fully understand the works, consider the way of expressing and explain the central idea by camera lens. Editors should improve the films by contributing their talents. They should not only fully understand what the director wants to express, but they should also keep a clear and independent mind like the conductors. Even when they get a note or rhythm, they shouldn't change the music, but they can still have their own artistic processes. There are still differences in every show. Both editors and conductors should not be stickled, but should share the same desire to make agreement in conflicts so that better understanding is developed.

Preparing the editing outline is very essential. We should blueprint the works based on complete paraphrasing. What's more, we should make accurate plans for the whole and each part of the works. Bearing this in mind and being well-prepared, we can make sure the smoothness of the follow-up tasks.

Q. Zhou (Ed.): ISAEBD 2011, Part I, CCIS 208, pp. 99–104, 2011.
© Springer-Verlag Berlin Heidelberg 2011

3 Selecting Material

Selecting material is a time-consuming task. Editors should read more original information to be familiar with image material and sound material. They should also make use of the information, referring to its shot records and taking full advantage of the lens of these scattered and broken scenes. Making notes, analyzing and processing them reasonably, and organizing them methodically are also their tasks. At the same time, making editing plans and choosing scenes that can combine time with space, have special beauty and be more impressive are also their essential tasks. Selecting and rejecting material is to make creation purpose better function in the audience so that imagination is aroused, feelings are touched, thinkings are enlightened and significance is created.

4 Creating Rhythm

Just like respiration and pulse, everything in the world has its own regulation of movement and rhythm. And the rhythms cut by video editors are helpful means to infect the audience from their emotion. By adopting this method, we can make the audience excited and calm as well.[1] Rhythms can also guide the audience's attention and lead them to some specific atmosphere so as to produce more dramatic functions.

American film Mental Illness Sufferers which is also called Psycho was produced in 1960. In the film, there are two murder scenes. The first one leads to the miserable death of the heroine Marian. And the second one leads to the death of the detective Milton. In order to show the film to be a suspense film and achieve its shock effects, the director Hitchcock carefully arranged the scenes and focused on rendering so that the film was finished in 37 days. In the film, it takes about one minute to show the murder of Marian in the bathroom. Among this one minute, it takes 45 seconds to show the climax. Shooting this scene made up 7 days of the whole film. Today, it has been the classic example of video editing.

5 Temporal and Spatial Restructuring

Special temporal and spatial structures formed from video editing are the unique way of expressing ideas in the visual arts. Space is changing with the passing time, while time is roaming in the changing space. Such intuition, image and vividness that build the novels, dramas, music, drawings, sculptures and other arts cannot express the temporal and spatial states. Narrative and lyric works isn't limited to the time and space. And reproduction and expression are created by imagination.

Restructuring time and space is an important kind of means to create rhythms. Generally speaking, we divide time and space into real space, silver screen space and psychic space. Although many video works produce a kind of illusion of the reality to make the continuity, integrity and truth of time and space so that they no longer exist, the audience will still feel their own psychic space. In the film Battleship Potemkin, the director devoted five minutes and eighteen seconds and totally 137 scenes to the

---

[1] Refer to (Soviet Union) Pudovkin *Techniques of the Films*, China Film Press, 1957, Page 94.

full expression of the murder in Odessa Steps. In fact, there are only three floors in the Odessa Steps in Petersburg City. It can take less than half a minute to escape from it. However, it is expanded to five minutes. And it seems that the three floors would never end. In this way, the brutal suppression is deepened correspondingly.

There are many ways to express the time and space in video editing. They can be tight or extended, omitted or expanded, zoomed in or zoomed out, slowing down or speeding up, stopping or reversing or reproducing. Editors can break the routine and rationality to create a dream space. We can take advantage of skills of flashback or flash before to present the pass, the present and the future. We can change from different views, different space with the jumping of the thinking so that the audience can enjoy the world and experience the reincarnation in the limited two-dimensional screens and time. The magnificence of time and space is surely a feast for the eyes without doubt.

6 Audio-Visual Preparation

Here, audio-visual preparation refers to the special making of sounds and scenes in videos.

Visual and hearing are two big components of the video language. The coherence vocal cord can make a series of incoherence scenes run smoothly. The accompaniment of music can be used by grasping a montage paragraph to make it to be seen as an integrated whole. When one paragraph transits to another, the music will easily make us combine the two paragraphs if we hear the smooth and continuous sound. We will also feel it natural. The two are complementary and an integrated whole. We shouldn't just pay attention to the scenes and ignore the music. We should balance them instead so that artistic effects won't be damaged.

Scenes are made up of by video production and subtitles. And the sounds consist of voices, music and audio. The scenes are vivid and intuitive, while the voices are the main ways to tell stories and express ideas. The audio, on the other hand, shows the reality. And the music contributes to the expression of emotions. Video editors should know their advantages and disadvantages well. They should discuss with the director in advance about the development of sound score. Comprehensive use of various elements to complement each other and enhance the mood so that the central idea is manifested is very significant.

Recording consists of pre-recording, corresponding recording and post-dubbing. And the next is sound mixing which makes use of equipments such as computers and mixers to correspondingly mix several or several hundred tracks based on the well-edited scenes. Finally, it is the match of sounds and pictures.

7 Styles Shaping

It is the major task for video editors to shape the whole style. The styles of the video works, the characteristics of directors, the preference of the producers, and the

---

[2] Refer to (Britain) Karel Laiz Gavin Miller, *Film Editing Techniques*, China Film Press 1982, Page 330.

customs of different nations and countries all determine the final choice of the editing staff. Imaginary styles, documentary styles and experimental styles all have their own characteristics. For example, advertisements and MTV have the characteristics of brightness and smoothness. While documentary ones and newsreels have characteristics of objectiveness and realness. The human mind is more complicated. Some hold the concept of scheduling expression by long lens; some are particular about the montage in lens clips; some direct the films to entertain the audience; and some only want to express their own ideas. Films in India and Pakistan take advantage of many songs and dances. In Hero, directed by Yimou Zhang, swords and flame on the water and in the bamboo forest, the flying snows all make the scenes bright and Chinese-stylish. And the costume of Yanglin Hu is so elegant and graceful that we can see the Chinese style and Zhang's unique way of directing.

Video editing should base on complete paraphrasing and the clipping tone. Some works are harmonious like the works directed by Abbas Kiarostami. Some works will add some rhythms and conflicts based on the whole integrity to create specific functions and express the central ideas. Rashomon directed by Akira Kurosawa in 1950, is a film contradicting the principle of editing direction consistence on purpose. For example, the scene that the woodcutter carries an ax into the forest connects two shots from the completely contrary way. The audiences feel confused at once. And this indicates the confusing and contradictions of the case, which attracts the audience's attention.

Editing seems easy, but it is much easier to say than to do, especially to create bright styles. Excellent works will always convey the perceptual characteristics of art. Some of them are grand and vehement; some are bitter; some are plain and simple; some are romantic and poetic; some are avant-graded, some miserable, some wide, and some subtly deep. The image world is so colorful that it is like a mirror, refracting the wonderful society.

8 Mishap Correcting

The mishap in video editing includes logical disorders, conceptual confusion and basic technical errors.

8.1 Inappropriate Arrangement of Dialogues and Plots, not Matching Characteristics of People at That Specific Time

There is one scene in the TV series Young Justice Bao, acted by Jie Zhou in 2000 that the emperor tests Justice Bao. The emperor says the first half of the couplet and asks him to say the second half. And Bao says the answer without hesitation. And the famous couplet is supposed to be Donglin's in Ming Dynasty. But now it turns out to be between the emperor and Bao. What's more, House of Flying Dragons directed by Yimou Zhang in 2004 attracted much confusion in spite of its magnificence. Regardless of the costume, appliance and weapons used in the film that are not accustomed to the late Tang Dynasty, the soulful confession between Sergeant Liu and the young girl when they meet is logically disordered. He says that during the three years, he is alone and misses her every second. From what he says, we can see that the director pays more attention to the style and neglects the contents, making the screen outweigh the plots and the scenes outweigh the logic. The film makers once said that if you didn't cry after seeing the film, you can come to find us. Actually, the words like Brother, You can love him but you cannot go with him, and so on or the pursuit of beautiful scenes all makes the audience laugh and feel unbelievable. For example, two sergeants fight from fall to the snowing winter. The Young girl can always be back from the dead after attacking by the flying. In Chongqing Youth Daily, Lin Cai says that Yimou Zhang is just like the child who cries the wolves have come by regarding the audience as mentally handicapped, making the same person come to life three times.

8.2 Pay More Attention to the Relations between People, Movement Direction, View Matches, Camera Matches and Lens Goof

Some lens goofs appear obviously in some video works. For example, the band-aid on the right hand of the heroine when she is hurt turns out to be on the left hand. Some newspapers are flying in the sky and there are poles and aircrafts seen in the streets of the ancient historical dramas. Someone has done a research showing that there are 571 errors in three series of Lord of the Rings. For example, the black knight stands near the river to pull out the sword from the left hand to fight against the Elf Princess. But a while later, the sword turns out to be in the right hand. The barefoot Hobbit Vlado wears something when he falls from the snow mountain. Another scene in Pandora's Box of Westward Journey is also an example. When the first master saw the second master walk up-side-down, he made a mistake and thought him to be the spider. And he hacked him with an ax. The ax with curved handle turned straight in a very short time.

Focus false, false light effects, subtitles or commentary or broadcast errors are all mishaps of the works. Editors and other staff should report the problem during the work's production so that the problem can be solved in time. It is better to solve the problem at site to avoid some troubles occurring in the following parts of the film. For the mishaps that have appeared, the editors should try their best to correct them. They can also delete the part or do it again. Making up for the false is a very important part in video editing.

9 Overall Repairing

Editing can be divided into several steps of rough cut, fine cut, detail cut and comprehensive cut. Some works are urgent so they adopt the method of rough cut, like TV shows where there are many rough places. They can't compare with films that are finely crafted. Overall repairing should implement in every period of video editing. Therefore, editors should think over and over again during the process. They should also think about the appropriateness of their works.

After being finely created, sounds and scenes are finally mixed. Now, overall examination is required. Video editors should see every part thoroughly from the viewpoint of audience and the overall requirements of the works in spite of their preferences.

There is no doubt that a wonderful piece of work can't come out easily. It is the result of people in the stage and those who are not. Video editors should bear this final task in mind, making the scattered verses to be exciting chapters.

Film editors and TV editors are directors of video clips. They have the right to command and dispatch. Different editing can make different possibilities of the works. Video editors should be like directors having their editing thinking and knowing how to direct arts. They should always regard their material and accomplish the purpose of the works as directors do. What's more, they should discover the value and significance of the material available, using appropriate scenes to interpret the director's central ideas, gathering different people's wisdom and making efforts to make successful works.

References

1. Karel, L., Miller, G.: Video Editing Techniques. China Film Press (1982) (Britain)
2. Kracauer, S.: The Nature of Films—the Rehabilitation of Physical Reality. China Film Press (1982) (Germany)
3. Fu, Z.: Art of Editors in Video Editing. Beijing Broadcasting Institute Press (2004) (China)
4. Bobuke, L.R., Wu, H. (tran.): Elements in Films. China Film Press (1986) (America)

Mismatches in College Students' Career Awareness and the Cultivation Strategies

Honglin Peng[1], Xiumin Zeng[2], Qiuyue Sun[3], and Wanqiu Cui[4]

[1] School of Arts, [2] Department of Ideological and Political Education,
[3] School of Foreign Languages, [4] School of Education
Hebei Normal University of Science and Technology, Qinhuangdao, Hebei, China
HonglinPeng2011@126.com

Abstract. With increasingly tough competition, college students are confronted with severe employment situation, while the improper career awareness is one of the causes for their difficulties in getting jobs. By the analysis of the mismatches in college students' career awareness, the author proposes the methods and strategies in developing their career awareness.

Keywords: college students, career awareness, mismatch, cultivation, strategy.

1 Introduction

Career awareness refers to the career knowledge, understanding, emotions and attitudes formed by the people engaged in certain occupational environment, which is the integration of mental qualities and ideological qualities. Career awareness is the reflection over a series of issues such as career goal, the path, ethics, capabilities, faith and its development, with career knowledge as the basis and the rational knowledge about career values as the core. College students' career awareness is the mental activities they have over the job issue, including the assessment of their own situation, and the expectations and wishes about future career. To a large extent career awareness influences college students' attitudes and ways in choosing their jobs.

2 Structural Elements of College Students' Career Awareness

2.1 Career Values

Career values are the sum of concept, position and attitude that a job-holder holds towards the job, in other words, the sum of his professional ethics, awareness, responsibilities, emotions, wills, attitudes and disciplines. College students' career values, an important component of their value system, are their general understanding about occupational assessment, choice of career, and career value orientation, which reflect the relation between occupational requirement and its social nature. It plays an important instructive role in college students' future career.

Q. Zhou (Ed.): ISAEBD 2011, Part I, CCIS 208, pp. 105–109, 2011.

2.2 Career Orientations

By career orientation, it means that college students will consider what social position they will put themselves in. It is the concrete manifestation and employment of their values in making career choices, and also the orientation of personal values, which shows the consideration over working region, occupation and standards in choosing jobs. Different career orientations suggest different career choices, and to some extent determine their life paths.

2.3 Career Ambition

Career ambition refers to people's dreams and pursuits for their future job, the desirable working department and achievement. It reflects their pursuits and desire to advance, and also gives expression to their ideals of life. It provides the drive and direction in the attainment of ideals of life. In view of this, career ambition is the base on which college students attain all of their life goals, and the beginning of their endeavor to fulfill great social ambitions.

2.4 Awareness of Career Risks

Risk means the uncertainty of the impacts, positive or negative, which career choices may have on the people. Career risks have the following five types: career survival risk, risk of going with the tide, occupational risk, job-hopping and structural unemployment.

2.5 Awareness of Carrer Adjustment

Adjustment, or mental adjustment, is a process of transforming or expanding the original cognitive structure to adapt to the new situation. College student will inevitably meet difficulties, setbacks and conflicts. They should adjust the career awareness in accordance with their personal development and situational requirements in order to develop their potentials to the maximum, resolve the difficulties and find out the optimal ways of fulfilling their career ambitions and goals.

3 Mismatches of College Students' Career Awareness

3.1 Mismatch between Career Values and Social Demands

With social reform in our country going on in all aspects, college students' career values have also gone through changes. First, career value shifts from society-oriented to individual-oriented. College students have more independence and options in job hunting, stressing on the realization of personal values. However, social demands should be met in the first place while most of them are unable to balance goals of the individual and the demands of society. Second, assessment criteria of career values tend to be realistic and concrete, turning from the original abstract idealism to pragmatism under market economy. Career values change to the type of economic values characterized with going after the maximum economic income and the type of personal values which emphasize on the realization of personal values. College students attach equal importance to the material and the spiritual, the benefits and the ideals. Third, the goals of career values turn from idealistic to realistic with a short-term and utilitarian tendency. College students shift the career goals from the social position and fame to practical interests. In choosing jobs, they always lack long-term strategic thinking and life orientation, but pay more attention to short- term interests, concerned with their own interests and achievements.

3.2 Mismatch between Job-Choosing Criteria and Career Orientation

In general, college student should choose the job which is their favorite, he is good at, and meets the demands of market. However, under the market economy college students' job choosing and their values tend to be utilitarian. They have two main criteria in choosing jobs, highly paid and advantageous to personal development. The survey shows they pay more attention to utilitarian standard than career development and social contribution. This utilitarian tendency will bring about obvious negative impacts. On one hand, it will lead to the blindness and short-sightedness of career ambitions. Driven by economic interests, some college students go after those highly-paid jobs, but ignore realistic employment conditions and their own long-term goals, hold an expectation beyond the realities, even give up their specialties, interests or ambitions. This will affect both smooth choice of career and its long-term healthy development. On the other hand, with utilitarian tendency, college students will aim at personal interests and values, but have weak sense of social responsibilities and show extreme individualism. Thus, some students will put the fulfillment of personal values as the priority without considering the national and social needs. Some only care about their personal values and material gains when their long-term goals clash with social goals. Moreover, utilitarian tendency of college students' career values result in the regional oversupply of professionals, which is the concentration of graduates in the hot jobs and highly-paid occupations in big cities. Meanwhile, there is the lack of professionals in the remote areas and arduous conditions. Hence, the imbalanced distribution of professionals gives rise to the devaluation of educational achievements and human resources, which also becomes one of the direct causes of college students' unemployment.

3.3 Mismatch between Career Values and Social Realities

At present, many college students always make less objective assessment of themselves, with big gap between job goals and social demands, and personal values divorced form objective realities and subjective condition, going after the jobs beyond one's qualities and capabilities. They seldom consider if the jobs suit them and if their expectations accord with realities, but with the only aim of short-term benefits. So, many would long for the comfortable working conditions in big cities, highly- paid jobs or prestige rather than go to practice in the arduous conditions of underdeveloped regions. Some dream of reaching the goals in one leap without rationally thinking about the distance between ideality and reality, and whether their career goals are good for personal development. Consequently, there appears the conflict between idealities and realities, together with the increasingly difficult employment situation arising from the disconnection between job goals and social demands. College students' high career expectations reflect their over-emphasis on material benefits, ignorance of social value, and pragmatism of their career ambitions.

3.4 Crowd Mentality and Career Risks

People who follow the crowd are inclined to be influenced by others in choosing jobs. Instead of thinking what they really want, they will choose what the others select. They are guided by others' behavior, hoping to copy others' career paths to success. In choosing a job, their standards are its popularity and the pay. They can even give up their strong points and make use of their weak points. They go with the crowd, forgetting what they really want deep down. They earn many certificates, take part in quite a number of training programs, send a lot of applications and then rashly find a similar job as the others. But before long they discover it is not what they want, and then they have to start all over again, which lead to more career risks.

3.5 Career Security and Career Adjustment

College students more emphasize on job security, for which they give up the dream of striking out on their own or neglecting their long-term goals. Many consider themselves as a generation of carving out. However, when they really come to choose jobs, they consider more about the pay, the insurance, the welfare and the stability, lacking sufficient awareness of career adjustment, which will affect the healthy development of their career in the long terms. When the job turns out to be unsatisfactory or they meet setbacks, they would turn to the family and friends rather than make full use f their advantages to resolve the difficulties and find out optimal ways to achieve their goals.

4   Strategies in Developing College Students' Career Awareness

4.1 Carrying Career Guidance through the Whole Span of College Life

College students' choice of jobs not only affects this social group's thoughts and behaviors but also the nation's economic and social development, so higher learning institutes must promote career guidance in all aspects. The objects of guidance include all the students, from the freshmen to the senior. As a matter of fact, one year is not enough for students to conceive their future. To develop the career -choosing concept is a gradual process. More often than not, students need several years to prepare and then make the decision, whether enter the work, further the study or go abroad. Therefore the higher learning institutes should change traditional mode of career guidance, and carry it through the whole span of college study. The contents of career guidance should include lectures on employment policies, job-hunting skills, career design and other relevant works, such as improving the working mechanism of career guidance, enhancing the theoretical study of career choice and design, establishing specialized career consulting agencies.

4.2 Guiding the College Students to Be Based on Realities, Set Correct Orientation, Make Reasonable Job Choices and Be Brave to Strike Out on Their Own

The higher learning institutes should further enhance the education on career ambition, career ethics and occupational values orientation, guiding the students to be based on realistic situations and social realities, correctly handle the relations among the nation, the collective, and the individual, to set proper orientation and career goals. They are not expected to aim to high or blindly vie with others who are better off than themselves in order not to make wrong decisions due to high expectations. The students should become aware that the aim of getting employed is not to find a highly-paid job and live a comfortable life, but to seek an opportunity and stage to practice themselves. They can not merely aim to achieve the goal in one leap and get it done once and for all, but to constantly study and advance. They can not just aim to achieve personal success and big fortune, but to earn the benefits based on creating values and fortunes for the society and the others. Meanwhile, the higher learning institutes should improve the employment information network, and increase both the quantity and quality of the recruitments held on campus to facilitate the college students' employment. In view of their stronger wish of striking out on their own, the whole society should encourage them to do so. However, the environment is not satisfactory for carving out. Therefore, not only should the government and the society make joint efforts in creating favorable conditions for them, but the higher learning institutes should promote the education on enterprising spirits and capabilities and offer assistance in their power.

4.3 Promoting Mental Health Education and Counseling Activities, Offering the Students the Assisstance in Facing the Job Hunting Positively and Optimistically

In job hunting, some college students have the negative mentality such as striving to keep up with others, going with the crowd, peacockery, frustration, anxiety and sense of inferiority. Thus, mental health education and counseling activities should be provided to make them face the reality, be brave to compete, unafraid of frustrations, look into the future, and handle the job hunting positively and optimistically. The higher learning institutes can do the mental tests related with job-hunting or social adaptability test on the students, leading them to have an objective understanding of themselves and to analyze their merits and weaknesses. The students should improve personal qualities and the abilities to adapt to the society and form the concept of life-long education so that the professionals will be reasonably distributed and job-hunting decisions will be scientifically made. For the students who do not have proper mentality, they should be given more attention, more instruction and counseling to make mental adjustments and go through the tough competition smoothly.

References

1. Jin, W., Xia, S.: The Survey on College Students' Career Awareness and Cultivation Strategies. Vocational Education Research (09) (2009)
2. Rongsheng, H.: The Study on the Creativity of Ideological Education of 21st Century College Students (July 2001)

Investigation and Analysis of Teacher's Questioning-Answering Behavior in College English Teaching

Yan Zhang

Li Ren School, Yanshan University, 438, Hebei Avenue,
066004 Qin Huangdao City, Hebei Province, China
zhangyandragon@yahoo.com

Abstract. Adopting the method of natural investigation, the paper selects as samples videos of national level exquisite courses from six different universities. It analyzes and discusses the data in four aspects: initiation of the questioning, waiting of the answering, distribbution of the answering, response of the answering. The result of research conveys that effective questioning-answering behavior in the teaching is helpful to encourage and direct students to participate in the communicative activities, and it is beneficial for language acquisition. The this paper draws some implicaitons for teachers to improve skills of questioning-answering behavior in college English teaching.

Keywords: questioning-answering behavior, national level exquisite courses, language acquisition.

1 Introduction

Questioning-answering behavior has played more and more improtant role in teaching under the learner-centered pedagogic notion at present. There are some advantages of questoning-answering behavior as follows: firstly, teacher can induce the students to participate in teaching and improve students' practical ability; secondly, it could provide some clues for the students, the learners can focus on some specific informations so that it is beneficial for the students to analyze the key points; thirdly, questoning behavior also can offer the students some chances of practice and feedback, then the teacher and the learners could take part in interactive communicative activity together. Therefore, questoning-answering behavior is the most common teaching manner, it is the most important part of teacher's discourses as well.

This paper takes national level exquisite courses for samples to research questioning-answering behavior in the college English classroom teaching, the reasons as below: First, it is accessible the videos of national level exquisite courses online. Then, exquisite courses can present the highest level of one course and reflect the latest teaching achivment of this field. Finally, the teachers of exquisite courses are experienced at the universities and they are the good examples of other teachers. For these reasons, this paper takes national level exquisite courses for samples to investigate and analyse the questioning-answering behavior of college English

Q. Zhou (Ed.): ISAEBD 2011, Part I, CCIS 208, pp. 110–116, 2011.
© Springer-Verlag Berlin Heidelberg 2011

classroom teaching, so that we can draw on the teaching experience of exquisite courses, which contributes to enhance English teaching.

2 Theories of Questioning-Answering Behavior

The questioning-answering behavior is one kind of interactive movement that is a series of ordered behavioral chain. As a result, questioning-answering behavioral chain is the basic unit to analyse the questioning-answering behavior, and the point lies in fixing the chain junction. The forerunner of this thoery is Bellack (1966) who considered that there are four chain junctions of the questioning-answering behavior. The first is structuring which refers to the teacher puts forward the topic that will be discussed; the second is soliciting which implies the teacher induces one answer or more students to advance the questions; the third is responding that means students respond the questions; the last one is reacting that gets at the teacher feedbacks the students' answers. Bellack discovers that the prorate of the former four parts is 10%,30%,30%,30%, in which the teacher's discourses are mostly soliciting, reacting, meanwhile the students' discourses are mainly responding.[1] During the practical teaching, one or twe chain junctions are likely to be omitted, but the teacher's soliciting and the students' responding are indispensable.

3 Rresearch Design

3.1 Research Question

This research takes national level exquisite courses for examples to explore the following aspects of questioning-answering behavior between the teacher and the students in college English teaching:1)the teacher's patterns of questioning; 2) the teacher's waiting time after questioning; 3) the teacher's ways and extent of questioning; 4) the teacher's responses toward the students' answering.

3.2 Research Methods and Samples

Adopting the method of natural investigation, the paper selects as samples videos of national level exquisite courses from six different universities. Because the samples are from different key institutes of higher learning: Tsinghua University, Fudan University, Huazhong University of Science and Technology, Beijing Jiaotong University, Chongqing University, Central China Normal University, so they are representative samples.

3.3 Data Collection and Analysis

It observes and records national level exquisite courses repeatedly and converts them to words, on that basis this paper collects and analyses the questioning-answering behavior between the teacher and the students, consequently the data are acquired. Because the aim of this research is to acquaint the features of questioning-answering behavior at college English classroom teaching., this paper does not adopt complex statistical method and just figures out the data and proportion of variable terms.

4 Results and Discussions

4.1 The Teacher's Patterns of Questioning

The questioning-answering behavior plays an improtant role in teaching, which has been the center of attention at the language teaching research(Nunan 1991:192).[2] Questioning not only can promote the students to participate in communication, but also encourage the students to adjust their languages that become more intelligible(Richards &Lockhart 1996:185).[3] According to the various degree of participation and the power of questioning, there are two kinds of expression in questioning-answering behavior. They are two types of beahivor: interrogating and communicative questioning-answering behavior, or displaying and participative questioning-answering behavior. Though they are two kinds of patterns, in principle they are similar. The teacher almost controls the procedure and direction of the questioning-answering behavior in interrogating or displaying questioning-answering behavior, the questioner has already known the answer. Meanwhile, the teacher could examine how well the student master the content or lead the students to follow procedure that the teacher has planed by frequent questioning.[4]

Table 1. Interrogating and Communicative Questioning-Answering Behavior

Teacher	Interrogating		Communicative		Sum
	Num.	%	Num.	%	Num.
T1	10	50	10	50	20
T2	17	53	15	47	32
T3	13	46	15	54	28
T4	18	58	13	42	31
T5	3	11	24	89	27
T6	7	43	9	57	16
Mean		44		56	

As shown in the table 1, the data display that there are four teachers who adopt communicative questioning-answering behavior over half of the total number, and other two teachers are slightly lower 50%, but above 40%. As a whole, the percentage of communicative questioning-answering behavior is 56% of the tatol. (1986)Brock's research shows that communicative questioning-answering behavior could increase the learner's linguistic output, which promotes language acquisition.[5] Communicative questioning-answering behavior between the teacher and the students can inspire the students enthusiasm and make the dialogues interactive in the classroom teaching. In table 1, the data reveal that the percentage of interrogating questioning-answering behavior is 44% of the total, it is lower slightly than proportion of communicative questioning-answering behavior. Because it is helpful for students to understand the content, meanwhile it is beneficial to focus the students' attention on related questions. Therefore, the teacher should arrange the ratio of the two patterns reasonably according to the teaching instructional objectives in the practical teaching.

4.2 The Teacher's WaitingTime after Questioning

It refers to the time that the teacher has been waiting for the students to answer the question, which has great influence in teaching. According to survey, the time that the teacher is waiting after asking question is within 3 seconds, usually less than 1 second. Some researchers find that when the waiting time increases to 3-5 seconds, there are more students taking part in teaching activities, thus the teaching is effective.(Rowe1974&1986)[6]

The data in the table 2 reflect that the mean of the teacher's waiting time is 4.82 seconds, which indicates that the teachers are patient to wait for students to answer the questions. They pay attention to provide more chances for students to think the question, and offer comfortable classroom dynamics for students to contemplate the issue, consequently the teaching is satisfactory.

Table 2. The Teacher's WaitingTime after Questioning

Teacher	Mean Time	The Longest Time	The Shortest Time
T1	4.3 "	90 "	1 "
T2	4.9 "	120 "	1 "
T3	5.3 "	110 "	1 "
T4	4.7 "	118 "	1 "
T5	4.1 "	85 "	1 "
T6	5.6 "	106 "	1 "
Grand mean	4.82 "		

4.3 The Teacher's Ways and Extent of Questioning

The Teacher's Ways of Questioning. On the basis of the observation, there are four ways that the students are to answer the issues in college English teaching such as: willing answering, collective answering, assigned answering, answered by oneself.[7] Willing answering conduces to foster the students' affective component and avoids the awkward situation when the student doesn't know how to answer the question as well. Then, the student has more choices during the communicative process, it makes the conversation more active. Assigned answering helps to cultivate the introverted students' language competence, which also takes account of equal opportunity for all. However,if it is excessive to adopt assigned answering, it is hard to motivate learner's passion, at the same time the students will be passive in the calssroom. Sometimes to use collective answering is to make for active atmosphere in the teaching.

Table 3. The Teacher's Ways of Questioning

Teacher	Willing Answering		Collective Answering		Assigned Answering		Answered by Oneself		Sum
	Num.	%	Num.	%	Num.	%	Num.	%	Num.
T1	4	20	0	0	16	80	0	0	20
T2	10	31	5	16	16	50	1	3	32
T3	10	36	4	14	13	46	1	4	28
T4	18	58	2	7	11	35	0	0	31
T5	19	70	3	14	5	16	0	0	27
T6	7	44	1	9	6	38	1	9	16
Mean		43		10		44		3	

The figures in the table 3 show that the percentage of the willing answering is 43% in total, assigned answering is 44% in total. Compared with other patterns, these two kinds of answering have a higher percentage. The willing answering can arouse learning passion and the learner's initiative, while the students who are willing to answer the question are a few. In addition, the other students' answering chances are difficult to guarantee. Hence, the experienced teacher could combine different answering ways, so that it can consider the equal opportunities of the students who have different knowledge base and distinct personality, which could encourage students to participate in teaching activities well.

The Teacher's Extent of Questioning. The related researches discover that the more extensive the extent is, the better teaching result is. The researcher had compared asking one student to answer question with ask all students to respond the topic, the latter is better with which the students are satisfied.[8]

As seen from the table 4, it is balanced that the six teachers distribute the chances of answering question. The chance that the students respond the question who are in the front row is 24% in total, The chance that the students answer the question who are in the back row is 22% in total, The chance that the students reply the question who are in the middle row is 27% in total, the chances of the left and right side row

Table 4. The Teacher's Extent of Questioning

Teacher	Front Row		Back Row		Middle Row		Left Side		Right Side		Sum
	Num.	%	Num.	%	Num.	%	Num.	%	Num.	%	Num.
T1	5	25	3	15	4	20	4	20	4	20	20
T2	5	19	7	27	7	27	3	12	4	15	26
T3	5	22	5	22	6	26	3	13	4	17	23
T4	7	24	5	17	8	28	5	17	4	14	29
T5	6	25	5	21	8	33	3	13	2	8	24
T6	4	29	3	21	4	29	2	14	1	7	14
Mean		24		22		27		13		14	

are lower slightly, 13% and 14% respectively. In general, it is wide that the six teachers assign extent of questioning, which indicates that they give consideration to studnents' equal opportunity and make sure most students can involve in classroom behavior. This is corresponding to the result of research.

4.4   The Teacher's Responses toward the Students' Answering

The other important part of questioning-answering behavior is that teacher responds the students' answering.[9] Teacher's distinct responses affect the students' psychology differently. This research mainly analyses the teacher's responses toward the students' answering as follows: the positive feedback, such as praise and comment so on; the negative feedback, as criticizing and scolding etc; the redirecting refers to different students answer the same question; the probing is to ask the student further with the same topic, if the student didn't answer the question correctly, the teacher would use related topic to replace the issue or divide the topic into some simple questions and come up with helpful clues. A large number of researches indicate that if the teacher gives positive feedback, the learners know that they complete the task correctly, and it can inspire their learning motivation. Consequently, positive feedback is better than negative feedback to improve learner's behavior.(Nunan,1991:104) But the gross praises, such as "Good", "Very Good"so on, are excessive, which can not lead great effect of teaching.(Brophy,1981;Nunan,1991)[10].

Table 5. The Teacher's Responses Toward the Students' Answering

Teacher	Positive Feedback		Negative Feedback		Redirecting		Probing		Sum
	Num.	%	Num.	%	Num.	%	Num.	%	Num.
T1	17	85	0	0	3	15	0	0	20
T2	22	71	0	0	0	0	9	29	31
T3	16	60	0	0	2	7	9	3	27
T4	29	84	0	0	1	3	1	3	31
T5	23	85	0	0	1	4	3	11	27
T6	12	80	0	0	1	7	2	13	15
Mean		79		0		6		15	

The data in table 5 show that the percentage of positive feedback is 79% in total, there is not negative feedback, the percentage of the redirecting is 6% in total, and the probing is 15%. It states clearly that the six teachers are good at applying positive feedback which is beneficial to enhance the learners' confidence, raise the students' learning interesting, extend their thinking. Even though the student's answer is not accurate, the teacher can affirm the viewpoints that are closed to correct answer. Then probing the student, the teacher offers clues to answerer or paraphrases the issue. The probing contributes to concentrate students' attention on learning activities and also arouse the students' learning initiative. Thereby, the teacher should put forward the questions that are within the student's ability according to learner's real competence.

5 Conclusions

The questioning-answering behavior is the most useful communicative way between the teacher and the students in the college English teaching, it constitutes the majority in teacher's classroom discourse, which plays a vital role in leading the students to participate in classroom activitiies actively. This paper analyses the experienced teachers who insturct English exquisite courses, on this ground we can draw the available conclusions as below. Firstly, the teacher should combine interrogating and communicative questioning-answering behavior to improve the effect of teaching. Secondly, the teacher must be patient with waiting for the students to answer the question in the light of the situation, and it is sound to encourage them bring forward doubts. Thirdly, the instructor ought to ensure every student enjoys equal opportunity, thus it could motivate their learning passion. Fuorthly, The teacher's response that is to the students' answering should be flexible in line with learners' answers. Meanwhile, the teacher is supposed to make good use of the positive feedback to strengthen the students' confidence and enhance their learning interesting.

References

1. Bellack, A.A., Kliebard, H.M., Hyman, R.J., Smith, F.L.: The Language of the Classroom. Teachers College Press, New York (1966)
2. Nunan, D.: Language Teaching Methodology: A Textbook for Teachers. Prentice Hall Inc., Englewood Cliffs (1991)
3. Richards, J., Lockhart, C.: Reflective Teaching in Second Language Classrooms. Cambridge University Press, Cambridge (1996)
4. Shi, L., Cui, Y.: Teaching Theory: Teaching Principles, Strategies,and Researches. East China Normal University Press, Shanghai (2002)
5. Brock, C.: The effect of referential questions on ESL classroom discourse. J. TESOL Quarterly 20 (1986)
6. Rowe, M.B.: Pausing Phenomena: influence on the quality of instruction. Psycholinguistic Research 3, 203–224 (1974)
7. Zhao, X.: The Investigation and Analysis on Teacher's Discourse of College English Reading Class. Foreign Language Word 2, 17–22 (1988)
8. Xing, Z., Yun, Z.: The Investigation and Analysis on Teacher's Discourse of College English Teaching. Foreign Language Teaching and Research 34, 59–68 (2002)
9. Brophy, J.: Teacher praise: A functional analysis. Review of Educational Research 51 (1981)

Empirical Analysis on Co-integration Relationship between Tertiary Industry and Urbanization in Jiangxi Province

Da-lin Wang and Xiang-qing Zheng

School of Economy and Management, Nanchang University,
Nanchang 330031, P.R. China
autobot@163.com

Abstract. According to co-integration test and Granger test to the interaction between tertiary industry and urbanization, we defined the long-term equilibrium as tertiary industry index growing about 0.2875 while urbanization increasing 1 percent; mean while, an unidirectional Causal relationship between tertiary industry and urbanization has been revealed, the increase of urbanization significantly promoted the development of tertiary industry, while the tertiary industry did not have significant impact to urbanization.

Keywords: Jiangxi Province, urbanization, tertiary industry, co-integration test, Granger test.

1 Introduction

In modern society, urbanization and tertiary industry related and interacted significantly. On one hand, urbanization means mass service needs which may stimulate and promote tertiary industry greatly; on the other hand, tertiary industry, by attracting large labor forces into urban area, promotes and improves urbanization. The interaction and promotion effects between urbanization and tertiary industry in different urbanizing stages are distinct. Generally, in the expanding stage, urbanization relatively promotes tertiary industry more; but in the stable stage, this relationship would be reversed. So different key points and directions of policies should be taken according to the stages.

Since 1978, both urbanization and tertiary industry grew rapidly in Jiangxi Province. In 2009, non-agricultural population and the urban population are 27.18% and 43.18% to the total, 12.74% and 26.43% higher than the figures of 1978; at the mean time, tertiary industry output, increased from 1.774 billion Yuan in 1978 to 263.707 billion Yuan in 2009, grew 148.65 times, and its proportion in GDP increased from 20.4% to 34.4%. Based on the developments of urbanization and tertiary industry, we are aimed to do empirical analysis of the interaction and provide decision making references by using co-integration test and Granger test.

Q. Zhou (Ed.): ISAEBD 2011, Part I, CCIS 208, pp. 117–122, 2011.
© Springer-Verlag Berlin Heidelberg 2011

2 Empirical Analysis

2.1 Index Choice and Definition

Due to the unique situation in our country, the urbanization index based on demography, in other word the proportion of urban population, made the urbanization level highly overestimated, while the non-agricultural population is an underestimated urbanization level index as well. Because of the floating population, time series of urban population is disturbed and not co-integrated; time series of non-agricultural population, however being underestimated urbanization level, eliminated interferences and clearly reflected the process of rural population transforming into urban population. Therefore, this paper measured urbanization level with non-agricultural population, which is expressed by X, and the underestimation will not disturb our study. The tertiary industry index was calculated like this: we took the year of 1989 as the base period, and the tertiary output of this year was assumed as 100, then we calculated the indexes from 1989 to 2009, expressed by Y; the logarithm of Y eliminated heteroscedasticity and guaranteed unchanged statistical characteristics. So LNY is the tertiary industry index we used.

Table 1. Urbanization levels and tertiary industry indexes over the years

Year	X (%)	Y	LNY
1989	18.50	100.0000	4.60517
1990	18.59	116.2518	4.755759
1991	18.70	124.0215	4.820455
1992	18.93	155.5002	5.046647
1993	19.17	189.2331	5.24298
1994	19.65	288.5114	5.664735
1995	20.25	381.9912	5.945398
1996	20.52	496.7593	6.208106
1997	20.86	567.8378	6.341836
1998	21.18	645.3978	6.469867
1999	21.43	722.3328	6.582486
2000	22.68	797.6282	6.681643
2001	23.33	860.4782	6.757488
2002	24.06	939.7073	6.845568
2003	24.95	1018.1355	6.925728
2004	26.13	1160.0780	7.056243
2005	26.28	1378.1552	7.228501
2006	26.75	1503.8066	7.315755
2007	26.70	1711.6250	7.445198
2008	27.25	1957.1204	7.579229
2009	27.18	2538.4088	7.839293

2.2 Unit Root Test

As making co-integration tests on data should be on the premise that the time series data must be stable, therefore, we first carry out ADF test on time series X and LNY by use of Eviews6.0, getting the following results:

Table 2. ADF Test Results of the Time Series

Serial Variable	Test Type (C T K)	ADF Statistical Value	Critical Value at the 1%/5%/10% Level	Conclusion
X	C T 0	- 3.062097	-4.532598/- 3.673616/ -3.277364	Unstable
LNY	C T 0	- 2.236689	-4.532598/- 3.673616/ -3.277364	Unstable
DDX	C T 0	- 7.630097	-3.857386/- 3.040391/ -2.660551	Stable
DDLNY	C T 0	- 5.755904	-3.857386/- 3.040391/ -2.660551	Stable

C, T, K represents the intercept, the time trend, and the lag period of ADF test respectively, and DDX and DDLNY are the second-order difference of the time series X and Y respectively.

Seen from Table 2, in the ADF unit root test, the ADF statistic of the time series X and LNY are greater than the critical value at the 1%/5%/10% level, so we accept the original hypothesis, that is, time series have unit root and it is not stable; the ADF statistic of the DDX and DDLNY is less than the critical value at the 1%/5%/10% level, so we reject the original hypothesis, that is, there doesn't exist unit root and time series is stable. This shows that both X and LNY are second-order integration series, meeting the same order and unit root condition for co-integration analysis, so the next step test can be carried out.

2.3 Co-integration Test

Co-integration test approach used in this paper is Engle-Granger test approach (or E-G two-step method). Its main steps are as follows: first, estimating $LNY_t = b_1 aX_t + U_t$ by using ordinary least squares or OLS approach, getting estimating equations and the error term U^; second, making ADF test on error term, if the error term is 0-order integration, or, I (0), it shows that the error term is stable and the original two time series are co integrated, otherwise, the error term is not stable, there may be false return phenomenon, and the original series does not exist long-run equilibrium.

By using LS method we get the estimated equation of LNY and X, namely, Y=-0.126577906108+0.287506015828*X, the determination coefficient of which after adjustment is 0.877327, indicating a higher goodness of fit. Specifically, the AIC value and SC value are 0.807609 and 0.907087 respectively, both of which are small, while the DW value is 0.209413, smaller than the goodness of fit value, so there may exist false regression, needing to make stability test on residual series. Through the residuals of Eviews we can get residual series, and by means of processing the residual U^ through ADF we get the following results:

Table 3. ADF Test Results of U^

Serial Variable	Test Type (C T K)	ADF Statistical Value	Critical Value at the 1%/5%/10% Level	Conclusion
U ˆ	*0 0 4*	*-4.18034*	*-2.717511/-1.964418/-1.605603*	*Stable*

The above results show that the ADF statistics of residual sequence is -4.180340, smaller than the critical value at the 1% / 5% / 10% level, so we can reject the original hypothesis, believing U^ doesn't have unit root and it is a stable series. Thereby, we believe X and LNY are co-integrated and there exists long-run equilibrium relationship between them, that is, when the level of urbanization increases by 1 percentage point, the tertiary industry index will increase by 0.287506015828.

2.4 Granger Causality Test

In order to study the causality between urbanization and tertiary industry of Jiangxi Province, this paper adopts Granger causality test. Its basic idea is as follows: If changes of Y are caused by changes of X, X should be helpful to predict Y, namely in the regression of Y on the past values of Y, the increase in the past value of X as an independent variable should significantly increase the explanatory ability of the regression. The basic process to test whether X is the reason to cause Y changing is as follows:

(1) Taking "X is not a reason for Y changing" as the original hypothesis;
(2) Making regressions on the lagged values of Y to Y and Y to X, and establishing regression model without restriction:

$$y_t = \sum_{t=1}^{m} a_i y_{t-i} + \sum_{t=1}^{m} b_i x_{t-i} + u_t$$

(3) Only making regressions on the lagged values of Y to Y, and establishing regression model with restriction:

$$y_t = \sum_{t=1}^{m} a_i y_{t-i} + u_t$$

(4) Calculating F statistics with the residual sum of squares of regression model and testing whether the regression coefficients b1, b2 ,..., bm are not significantly equal to zero at the same time. If it is, then refuse the original hypothesis of "X is not a reason for Y changing", that is, X is the reason for Y changing, showing that there exists causality between X and Y. Similarly, whether Y is the reason for X can be tested.

In order to obtain the optimal lag order of the Granger causality test, we apply distributed lag model (PDL) approach. Specifically, firstly take the maximum lag order as the 1 / 4 of the sample number, that is 5, then by applying PDL approach we can get the different AIC, SC, and R2 values under different lag orders. Analysis results by Eviews are as follows:

When the lag is 1, AIC = 0.767215, SC = 0.916574, R2 = 0.885785
When the lag is 2, AIC = 0.627471, SC = 0.776593, R2 = 0.886457
When the lag is 3, AIC = 0.389020, SC = 0.537415, R2 = 0.891922
When the lag is 4, AIC = 0.033958, SC = 0.180995, R2 = 0.905861
When the lag is 5, AIC =- 0.748643, SC =- 0.603783, R2 = 0.943475

Seen from the above, when the lag order is 5, AIC and SC values reach the minimum and their goodness of fit is the highest, therefore, we carry out Granger causality test to time series X and LNY with the lag order 5, getting results as follows:

Original Hypothesis:	P	F Statistical Value	Confidence Value.
X is not the Granger reason for LNY	5	*8.94986*	*0.0156*
LNY is not the Granger reason for X		*1.97410*	*0.2367*

This indicates that at the 5% confidence level, chance of making mistakes by refusing the hypothesis of "X is not the Granger reason for LNY" is 1.56%, so we should reject the original hypothesis, that is, the urbanization rate X is the Granger reason for the tertiary industry index LNY; as for the original hypothesis of "LNY is not the Granger reason for X", because chance of making mistakes by rejecting it is 23.67%, so we cannot determine whether LNY is the Granger reason for X at the 5% confidence level.

3 Conclusions

In summary, the following conclusions can be drawn:

First, there exists long-term stable equilibrium relationship between urbanization and the tertiary industry of Jiangxi Province, that is, when the level of urbanization increases by 1 percentage point, the tertiary industry index will increase by 0.287506015828, and any fluctuations in the short term will tend toward equilibrium in the long run. This indicates that urbanization plays a strong role in promoting the development of the tertiary industry in Jiangxi, and accelerating the process of urbanization is still an important engine to promote the development of tertiary industry and the economic growth in Jiangxi Province.

Second, there exists third one-way causality between urbanization and the tertiary industry of Jiangxi Province, that is, raising the level of urbanization has a significant effect on driving the development of tertiary industry, while the counteraction of the tertiary industry is not so obvious. This shows that the development of urbanization in Jiangxi is mainly due to the strong impetus of the secondary industry or industrialization, while the development of tertiary industry is seriously lagging behind, not matching the process of urbanization. Therefore, strengthening the guidance and support to the tertiary industry and further accelerating the development of tertiary industry is not only an important way to accelerate economic growth and industrial restructuring, but also a significant force to further promote the process, function and quality of urbanization in Jiangxi Province.

References

1. Ke, C., Naihua, G.: Dialectical Thinking on Coordinated Development of Urbanization and the Tertiary Industry. South China Economy (4) (2002)
2. Rongsheng, P.: Empirical Analysis of the Relationship between the Tertiary Industry Development and Urbanization. Inquiry into Economic Issues (10) (2006)
3. Qinjun, D.: An analysis of promoting of tertiary industry to urbanization. Urban Studies 5 (2005)
4. Liu, P., Zeng, S.: On relations between the tertiary industry and urbanization. Journal of Hunan Business College (7) (2003)
5. Hanhui, L., Jun, H.: The Empirical Study on Co-integration between Tertiary Industry and Urbanization of Guangdong Province. Journal of South China Normal University (11) (2009)
6. Tiemei, G.: Econometric Analysis and Modeling–EViews Applications and Examples, 2nd edn. Tsinghua University Press, Beijing (2009)

Innovation within Romanian SMEs

Simona-Clara Barsan[1], Mihaela-Georgia Sima[2], and Dan Savescu[3]

[1] Research Institute for Analytical Instrumentation, Technology Transfer Centre,
ICIA CENTI Cluj-Napoca, Romania
simonaclara_barsan@yahoo.com
[2] Bucharest Chamber of Commerce and Industry, Technology Transfer Centre, Romania
georgiasima@yahoo.com
[3] Faculty of Product Design and Environment, Transylvania University of Braşov, Romania
dsavescu@unitbv.ro

Abstract. The paper presents the main results of a study made within Romanian SMEs regarding the innovation potential and achievements in that area, taking into consideration several factors that influence this process. It starts with the basic notions, such as innovation and innovation expenditure. Then, the Romanian RDI system is presented, in order to shortly explain the context the companies function within and how the crises affected this system. A brief framing in the international context was also considered necessary, since ranking Romania provides a relevant picture. Conclusions reveal the tangible reality of innovation in the country, the obstacles and the solutions one could suggest in an economic crises period, in order to keep innovation from becoming a hard obtained past good.

Keywords: SMEs, financing programs, innovation.

1 Introduction

The goal of a business is to create a client. The business company has only two basic functions: marketing and innovation. These two produce results, the rest is only cost - after Peter Druker.

For SMEs, innovation is the main instrument of development. Whether we are talking about developing new products or services or about identification of the most efficient already existing accomplishment methods, innovation brings added value to every organization. At the same time, it allows to maintain or improve its market share.

2 Theoretic Notions

Innovation represents an activity from which it results a new or significantly improved product (good or service) which is launched on the market, or the introduction of a new or significantly improved process in its own unit.

Innovation relies on the results of a new technology, of technological development, of new combinations of existent technologies or on using other knowledge obtained.

Q. Zhou (Ed.): ISAEBD 2011, Part I, CCIS 208, pp. 123–126, 2011.
© Springer-Verlag Berlin Heidelberg 2011

The process of innovation consists of [4]: collecting ideas; ranking, depositing and classification of them; combination and selection; obtaining finances for the materialization of the selected ideas; the realization and testing of the prototype; the correction of the prototype; promoting the new product; fabrication and sale; the evaluation of the costs ratio for production and income; the correction of errors and reloading of innovation cycle.

The innovation process, regarded as a company long term risky investment, requires a sustained management effort dedicated to this sector.

Innovation expenditure [1] comprises both expenditure for finalized innovation activities, as well as those for on-going or abandoned innovation activities. The main components of expenditure for innovation activity are: internal and external research – development; machinery, equipment and software acquisition; other external knowledge (licenses, patents, know-how).

3 Case Study

3.1 The Situation of RDI System at Romanian Level

The national RDI system [3] is made out of: 264 R&D public units and institutions, out of which 168 R&D units of national interest: 46 R&D national institutes, 56 accredited public universities, 66 institutes and research centers of the Romanian Academy (52 institutes and 14 research centers), 17 agricultural institutes and R&D centers and 51 agricultural R&D stations in subordination of the Academy of Agricultural and Forestry Sciences "Gheorghe Ionescu-Sisesti" (AAFS).

> ➢ Approx. 2000 units with R&D activity, out of which 850 in the private sector;
> ➢ Specialized employees in a large range of approximately 50 scientific and technological fields, which comprise domains of leading technologies (ex.: information and communication technology, medicine, aeronautics). Still, there is a significant proportion (over 40%) of the researchers belonging to technical and engineering sciences;
> ➢ A network of specialized institutions for technology transfer and innovation, made of 54 specific entities (technology transfer centers, technological information centers, technological and business incubators), as well as 4 scientific and technological parks.

In 2009, the economic crisis affected deeply the research field in Romania as well, the financing provided through the national programs being thus significantly reduced, namely 27.6 % decrease as compared to the previous year.

An unwished consequence of reducing the public financing in the R&D field was the decrease of the number of the research employees with higher education.

The capacity of system to attract young graduates with superior performances was in decrease, being unable to counter the exodus of young people towards more developed countries or towards better paid sectors.

The decrease of the public funds allocated for research determined two synchronous trends regarding the expenses in the private sector: an increase of the economic operators' interest for accessing European funds and a significant decrease of the own funds invested by the economic operators in research projects.

The increase of the innovative enterprises share represents rather an inertial effect, a consequence of the structural reforms and of the direct foreign investments.

The „*European Innovation Scoreboard*" Report (EIS) [10] on year 2009 showed substantial progress of the EU countries, Romania included, regarding the performance in the innovation field. Though, Romania was ranked 25 of 27.

Although most indexes indicate values that are significantly small for Romania, as compared with the EU 27 average [8], the dynamics of some of them, as well as the F&S one, pointed towards a gaps catching-up trajectory. In the economic difficulties context of year 2009, this pointing was at least threatened and, for not being compromised, severe corrective measures were taken, such as growing the economic competitiveness through research and innovation.

The effect of these measures was the important number of research projects implemented, that led to the improvement of the innovation level [6].

3.2 Innovation within Private Companies

To determine the specific of Romania from the innovation view point, between July 2010 and January 2011, a survey was made within the 850 research units from the private sector, plus a number of 1472 SMEs, that tend to classify themselves as innovative ones within the near future (their investment level in research is almost 3% of the turnover). The results have shown that 89.6% of them consider that innovation is compulsory for maintaining their competitiveness.

Product-service innovation has been reported in 82.7% of the cases, process-technology innovation in 54.3%, organizational innovation in 42% and marketing innovation in 69.7% (especially due to the crises and lack of sales).

Out of all the active innovative enterprises, 548 (21%) are in Bucharest – Ilfov Region and the innovation expenditure for the area is 41.7% of national innovation expenditure. 72.57% are destined to licenses and patents.

The research proved that Bucharest – Ilfov Region has the highest development rank compared to the national average at all levels, offering the biggest opportunities of investment and development [3], [6].

In the same time, Bucharest – Ilfov Region is considered as the centre of research and innovation activities from Romania.

The analyzed innovation factors were: the potential of innovation management; the potential of creating knowledge; innovation capacity; innovative activities' performance; intellectual property.

The percentage in all cases is a "plus half", indicating the real preoccupation and potential of the SMEs for this field. If we were to analyze the correlation between factors, then knowledge creation (87.5%), together with management system (76.7%), provides the company the potential of "open market". The innovation capacity is 75% and reflects into a 51.9% of activities' performance. The final result is a 64.4% intellectual property capital.

There have been identified five activity sectors with high innovation potential: precision mechanics, IT&C, electronics, plastics and construction [9]. To these, the authors add the intensive knowledge-based services sector.

4   Conclusions

The potential exists, it even produces, as one could see from the research results, but the environment is totally unfavourable to evolution. Through active involvement of the entitled institutions, pro-business measurements, the impact of the present economic crises can be attenuated.

It is predictable that some economic sectors would recover slower than others, but they finally will. The soul facilitation to founding programs accessing, through innovation and technological transfer network, will provide a part of innovation destined necessary founds. Providing training for those who can and wish to access, these founds give companies two benefits [11]: the possibility of achieving their objective and knowledge enriched personal.

We hope that all of these, together with a good publicity, will constitute pylons for SMEs to sustain on and evolve, keep the innovation reality tangible and furthermore, help the local and national economy grow.

References

1. Bănacu, S.C.: Active necorporale, proprietăți intelectuale. EdituraTehnică Economică, București (2005)
2. Dan, D.M.: Managementul schimbarii si inovarii - Elemente fundamentale, Editura Universitara (2009)
3. National Development Program, Report (2010)
4. WIPO. Why is Intellectual Property Relevant to Your SME. WIPO report (2007)
5. Ordonanța nr. 57 din 16 august 2002 privind cercetarea științifică și dezvoltarea tehnică logică aprobată cu modificări și completări prin Legea nr. 324/2003 cu modificările ulterioare și modificată cu Ordonanța nr. 38/2004
6. Politicile guvernamentale pentru cercetare, dezvoltare si inovare in Romania (2010)
7. http://iri.jrc.ec.europa.eu/reports.htm
8. http://ec.europa.eu/research/innovation-union/index_en.cfm
9. http://www.proinno-europe.eu/metrics
10. European Innovation Scoreboard Report (2009)
11. IEEE-USA Webinar "Creative Thinking and Innovation",
    http://www.ieeeusa.org/careers/innovation/

Studying Romanian SMEs

Mihaela-Georgia Sima[1], Simona-Clara Barsan[2], and Dan Savescu[3]

[1] Bucharest Chamber of Commerce and Industry, Technology Transfer Centre, Romania
georgiasima@yahoo.com
[2] Research Institute for Analytical Instrumentation, Technology Transfer Centre,
ICIA CENTI Cluj-Napoca, Romania
simonaclara_barsan@yahoo.com
[3] Faculty of Product Design and Environment, Transilvania University of Braşov, Romania
dsavescu@unitbv.ro

Abstract. The paper presents the main results of a study made in collaboration, at the level of Romanian SMEs, in 3 different macro-economic regions. It was made within a doctoral research program and became the object of an intermediary PhD report. It emphasizes the main issues SMEs deal with today, the most powerful negative impact factors, as well as those with minimum impact. It continues with a detailed description of financing sources, to finally reach to a part of the provided solutions, in order to fix those problems and improve their management system.

Keywords: SMEs, factors, funds, management, innovation.

1 Introduction

Romania's economy is dominated by SMEs. Their evolution is conditioned by the economic, politic and social context in which they live and act. If until recently, their evolution and performance were predictable with the help of realistic estimation and professional management, leading to worthwhile results, in today's economy, due to the world economic crises, these estimations are hard to make. This imposes changes at internal level [1], concerning the management system as well as support measures from the local and central administration, government and especially the access to financing programs that could sustain these SMEs and furthermore the Romanian economy.

2 The Role and the Importance of SMEs

SMEs contribute to achieving fundamental objectives of any national economy due to the followings:

> ➤ flexible structure that confers a high capacity of adaptability to economic fluctuations [2];

Q. Zhou (Ed.): ISAEBD 2011, Part I, CCIS 208, pp. 127–130, 2011.
© Springer-Verlag Berlin Heidelberg 2011

> they can be easily integrated into an industrial network that contributes to the economic development of the region, to the reducing of unemployment and the growth of living standards;
> their small size contributes to avoiding excessive bureaucracy and dehumanization;
> SMEs form, at individual level, an ensemble easier to control and lead, favoring innovation and being a proper place for learning for its employees;
> they stimulate competition, being sub-contractors to large companies;
> they fabricate products and deliver services efficiently.

3 Case Study

In order to determine the main problems SMEs face with and to provide the best possible solutions, one has carried out a study upon the companies from 3 Macro-Regions of Romania [7], within a common project of a Business Incubator (ITA-Pro-Energ, Brasov) and 2 Technology Transfer Centers (CTT-CCIB, Bucharest and ICIA-CENTI, Cluj Napoca) [3].

3.1 Main Issues

The major negative influences: the legal frame (65%), social climate, as well as the politics of International Monetary Found and World Bank (19.3%); minimum negative impacts: privatization (2.13%) and interethnic tensions (1.19%).
  Other issues:

> over half of SMEs function based on own resources (60%), while as 17% go to banks for loans and 8% access other sources;
> the restrain of the activity and the diminution of large companies' production; the payment of suppliers, difficulties in contracting credits and closing the financial year with losses;
> unfit and improperly prepared management [4];
> marketing deficiency;
> difficulties in personal recruitment;
> disadvantageous salary package, as compared to large companies;
> instability.

The consequences of bankruptcy are manifested at:

- material level;
- psychological level: usually, an employer that suffered a bankruptcy will not start a new business so soon;
- social level: jobs reduction, the disappearance of certain products from the market.

In the SWOT analysis made, **"S"** refers to innovation orientation and quality services (49% of answers).

The Romanian labour market is made out of qualified labour force. The effect could be stronger if proper training were provided. This should be permanent, implicating universities, research and companies partnership, so that the results would correspond to the continuous changing needs of companies and market demands. That would lead to maintaining the competitive advantage and obtain profit.

"**W**" (weaknesses) or the main obstacles in carrying on innovative activities were personal fluctuation and material resources. If the personal fluctuation problem can be solved through an elaborated and constant retentions program, based on proper motivation, the lack of material resources (30% of companies mentioned this factor) will detain companies from making investments in innovative activities (21% of companies mentioned raised costs as an obstacle in achieving innovation). The major capital source comes from their income (80%), credits (29%) and other unmentioned sources. The financing from public founds (budgetary) proved to be insufficient and more than that, hard to obtain (72% of companies declared the programs accessing procedure difficult).

3.2 Solutions

> ➢ intensifying the contacts between Government, social partners, national bank and other factors that can contribute to defining a coherent politic for the field;
> ➢ financing for SMEs: a global loan, contracted by Ministry of Public Finances from Investment European Bank (BEI).

Business incubators, seen as economic labs, offer assistance and contribute to the stimulation and cultivation of the entrepreneurial spirit; allow exchange of ideas, training and perfecting courses, programs for managers and employees; offer free assistance and smoothen the contact with banks and partners.

Consultancy agencies offer support for SMEs in: testing entrepreneurial skills; business plan elaboration; training courses in business; offer basic information for business start up.

SMEs access to financing programs can be achieved through national innovation and technological transfer network (the list is available at www.ccib.ro/ctt). This will assure a part of the necessary funds for a coherent basic activity, innovation and competitiveness level maintaining.

4 Conclusions

Identifying opportunities generated by the present crises period is an important issue. Possible options are:

> ➢ rethinking the management system, implementing a professional one based mostly on intellectual capital instead of industrial production;
> ➢ development or business reorientation towards more profitable activity fields [5];

> ➤ gaining advantages as a result of a weaker competitiveness of companies or smaller prices for equipments or raw materials;
> ➤ strengthen the present client portfolio;
> ➤ quit raising the turnover currently and build objectives related to possible acquisitions or mergers;
> ➤ reducing costs generated by suppliers or different administrative expenditures;
> ➤ accessing financing programs, in order to obtain the necessary capital infusion[6].

Through training of persons who want and can access financing programs two important things can be carried out: achieving the objectives and increasing the professional competence of employees.

The support of the environment is important and, when we speak of environment, we refer to the economic field, local and central authorities, present legislation and especially to the promotion of fiscal relaxation politics sustained by the Central Bank of Romania.

These are some of the real possibilities of the Romanian society to combat the impact of economic crises in a slower, but sure rhythm, aiming to definitely positive results.

References

1. Bârsan, S.C., Sima, M.G.: Inovarea şi transferul tehnologic-instrumente de aliniere a IMM-urilor la cerinţele economiei de piaţă. In: Interferenţe Economico-Sociale la Frontiera Inovării, pp. 51–62. IRECSON Press, Bucharest (2008)
2. Nicolescu, O., Verboncu, I.: Management. Economic Press, Bucharest (1999)
3. http://www.ccib.ro/ctt
4. http://www.cnipmmr.ro
5. http://www.mimmc.ro
6. European Comission, Report: Internationalisation of European SMEs (2010)
7. Sima, M.G.: Contribution to SMEs management, PhD Intermediary Paper (2010)

Research on the Marketing Strategies of Energy Service Industry in China Based on Industry Life Cycle

Xiaoping Tian

School of Management, Tianjin University of Commerce, Tianjin, PR of China
tianxp8@sina.com

Abstract. The past few years have seen a rapid expansion of energy service industry penetrating into China's economy and starting to play an important role in achieving China's goal in energy conservation. Based on the industry life cycle theory, the paper studies the energy service industry's life cycle in China and draws the conclusion that China's energy service industry is currently in the growth stage. And according to the relationship between the industry life cycle and the marketing strategies, the paper puts forward the marketing strategies of energy service industry in China.

Keywords: energy service company (ESCO), industry life cycle, marketing strategy.

1 Introduction

China's economy is among the most energy-intensive ones in the world. China's CO2 emissions have risen from 1.4% of the global total since the foundation of the country to 20% at the beginning of the 21st century [1]. In order to achieve the binding target of 20% reduction of energy consumption per GDP regulated in the 11th Five-Year Plan, China needs to significantly raise the energy efficiency of its economy. The Chinese government is developing a policy framework to encourage the use of energy service companies and energy performance contracting as the catalyst to stimulate the market for energy efficiency services. Given the size of the energy and economic system of China, a 20% reduction in energy intensity implies a large market potential for energy service companies to realize.

Energy Service Companies (ESCOs) are usually differentiated from other firms that offer energy efficiency improvement or energy services, such as consulting firms and equipment contractors, by the concept of performance- based contracting, which means that the ESCO's payment is directly linked to the amount of energy saved (in physical or monetary terms). Energy services may include for instance energy audits, energy management, energy or equipment supply, provision of services such as space heating [2]. They usually offer the following services: they develop, design, and finance energy efficiency projects; install and maintain the energy efficiency equipment involved; measure, monitor, and verify the project's energy savings; and assume the risk involved in the expected amount of energy savings. Energy Performance Contracting (EPC) can be defined as 'a form of 'creative financing' for

Q. Zhou (Ed.): ISAEBD 2011, Part I, CCIS 208, pp. 131–137, 2011.
© Springer-Verlag Berlin Heidelberg 2011

capital improvement which allows the funding of energy efficiency upgrades from cost reductions'.

The reason energy service companies can provide energy services at lower cost than in-house energy management is that they combine economies of scale with the discipline of market incentives [3]. The ESCO concept appeared for the first time in Europe more than 100 years ago [4]. In the United States, ESCOs emerged in the 1970s, after the oil crisis which led to increasing energy prices. Today, the ESCO concept has spread with varying success to most industrialized countries, to several economies in transition and to the biggest developing countries.

2   The Industry Life Cycle and Marketing Strategies during the Industry Life Cycle

The life-cycle concept is an appropriate description of what happens to industries over time. The industry life cycle contains the four stages of introduction, growth, maturity, and decline. Depending on the stage of the industry life cycle, the marketing strategies should vary to meet the changing conditions.

In the introduction stage, the public is not aware of the industry and does not know what benefits it offers them. Product strategy is focused on introducing one model. Since the public is unaware of the product, to offer more models could confuse them as they learn the purpose of the product. The promotion efforts concentrate on informing the public of the product benefits and the company producing the product. And the company can use a skimming pricing strategy; that is, a very high price for the new product. Since there are few purchasers in the introduction stage, the distribution does not need to be widespread.

In the growth stage, the increasing sales result in the emergence of profits rather than losses. During the early part of the growth stage, the company can continue its product policy of offering one basic model. The original company will need to offer more models. And the market leader should switch to a persuasive promotion policy. As the competition enters the market, prices should be lowered so that sales can continue to grow, and the competition kept at bay. In a growing market, the company must increase its product distribution to maintain its leadership in the market.

During the maturity stage, the original company must continue differentiating their models so that the market is aware of the differences in the company's products and the competitors' products. The promotion strategy focus is on continuing the persuasion tactics started during the growth stage. The purpose of persuasion is to position the product to the market, which involves creating an image for a product. A cost and a price advantage over competitors in this stage are significant competitive advantages. The absence of a company's product in a particular location may result in lost sales during the maturity period. So the widespread distribution is essential.

During the decline stage, the product strategy now becomes one of reducing the number of models offered. The company now focuses its attention on the costs and profitability of the remaining models. The promotion efforts also include an examination of costs. Only the minimal amount of promotion necessary to keep the product selling is done. Consequently, the promotion effort shifts to reminder promotion. Products' prices are also kept as low as possible during the decline stage.

The declining sales may not justify the widespread distribution reached during the maturity stage. Only those areas or markets that are still profitable should be covered, and the unprofitable distribution outlets eliminated.

3   Analysis of Energy Service Industry's Life Cycle in China

According to the industry life cycle theory, the development course of China's energy service industry can be divided into the following two stages:

3.1   The Introduction Stage (1997-2006)

The introduction stage of China's energy service industry is from 1997 to 2006. Energy service industry in China started with the support of GEF (Global Environment Facility) and World Bank. From 1992 to 1994, GEF and World Bank conducted a research named China Issues and Options in Greenhouse Gas Emissions Control. And from December, 1998, the full scale project to introduce and raise ESCO started. The "China Energy Efficiency Project" consists of 2 phases, and the first phase was conducted from 1998 to 2003, and the second phase has been conducted from 2003.

The First Phase of China Energy Efficiency Project
China's first three ESCOs were created as new companies in 1997, in Beijing Municipality, Shandong Province and Liaoning Province. Startup was supported with European Commission and GEF grant assistance, and a World Bank loan was provided to help finance growth, through the China Energy Conservation Project. These three companies successfully pioneered the business beginning in 1998, adapting the energy performance contracting concept to the Chinese market.

The financial support from World Bank, GEF and other international organizations is applied to establishing and operating the pilot ESCOs, and to helping the ESCO market formation. 5 million USD out of 22 million USD from GEF and 1 million Euros out of 4 million Euros from EU are granted to each pilot ESCOs as reserve (cannot be cast into the capital), and a ceiling on loans of 21 million USD is settled for each by World Bank. 475 businesses were conducted in the first phase and the total investment amount was cumulatively 1 billion 330 million Yuan (about 160 million USD). And consequently, they have realized 1.51 million tce (tons of carbon equivalent) per year as cumulative energy efficiency effect, and 1.45 million tons of carbon per year as carbon dioxide reduction effect [5].

The Second Phase of China Energy Efficiency Project
The second phase of the project was implemented through enhancing the capacity of China's ESCOs by providing strong loan guarantees to ESCOs as well as the establishment of the Chinese EMCA (EMCA: China Energy Conservation Service Industry Association).

According to the investigation of EMCA, the investment to the ESCO business has rapidly increased since 2003 out of the whole energy efficiency investment. In 2006, it has expanded to 6 billion 330 million Yuan and the business by the performance contract has also grown to 1 billion 892 million Yuan (Table 1). This is approximately the same level as that of the ESCO business in Japan. As a result, the energy efficiency effect in 2006 on a sole fiscal year basis has realized 4.16 million tce per year from the whole energy efficiency investment, and 2.69 million tce per year from the business by the performance contract [5].

Overall, based on GEF investment, by the end of 2006, 1426 projects had been completed. The foreign ESCOs, especially those from the USA and Europe, are starting to open subsidiaries in China [6]. One of the key features of the foreign ESCOs is that they often come with energy efficient technologies and are willing to operate the project as a coowner in order to maximize their interests.

Table 1. Changes in Chinese Energy Efficiency Investment over Time

Year	Energy Efficiency Investment (100 Million Yuan)	EPC Investment (100 Million Yuan)
2003	11.48	8.51
2004	21.27	10.98
2005	30.60	13.10
2006	63.30	18.92
2007	114.60	65.50
2008	253.20	116.40
2009	360.37	195.32

3.2 The Growth Stage (2007-)

The growth stage of China's energy service industry is from 2007. According to EMCA's survey, more than 70% of the energy services companies in China changed from "chase the project to do" to "select the project to do" in 2006. There were significantly more opportunities in ESCO market. At the end of 2007, EMCA had 308 members, of which 185 were classified as ESCOs. Table 2 shows the rapid growth of both the Association's membership and the number of operating ESCOs in China. At the end of 2009, EMCA had 450 members, and the number of operating ESCOs rose to 502.

Table 2. The Evolution of ESCOs in China

Year	Number of ESCO	Number of EMCA Member
1998	3	0
2004	60	89
2005	106	158
2007	185	308
2008	386	385
2009	502	450

As of 2008, China had the largest ESCO industry in the developing world in terms of total investment [7]. In 2009, the whole energy efficiency investment has expanded to 36 billion 37 million Yuan and the business by the performance contract has also grown to 19 billion 532 million Yuan (Table 1). Estimated energy savings from 2009 energy performance contract investments total about 17.58 million tons of standard coal equivalent. And associated carbon dioxide emissions reductions from 2009 investments alone total about 11.34 million tons of carbon [8].

4 The Marketing Strategies of Energy Service Industry in China

From the above analysis, we can draw the conclusion that China's energy service industry is currently in the growth stage of the industry life cycle, with huge growth potential. According to the relationship between the industry life cycle and the marketing strategies, the following marketing strategies should be taken to foster the development of energy service industry in China.

4.1 To Increase Dissemination of Knowledge about Energy Efficiency, and Build Up Awareness of Energy Conversation and Promote EPC

The energy service industry in China is still an emerging industry. Due to the lack of propaganda, the clients are unfamiliar with energy services, which is a serious impediment for the development of energy service market. EPC is a primary model for energy services. The contract of EPC covers the standards and the effects of energy efficiency, and many other contents, so the clients are difficult to grasp. Therefore, China's ESCOs should take various measures to educe clients' awareness of energy conservation, and make use of knowledge marketing to improve the level of potential clients' energy conservation knowledge, to make up for the deficiency for the clients to professional energy conservation knowledge, and arouse clients' demands for energy services.

4.2 To Manage Clients' Credit Risk

Risk management on clients' creditworthiness is deemed as the top challenge for Chinese ESCOs. Good practice in managing clients' credibility becomes crucial for the success of ESCOs. It was found out that the prevailing practice of EPC in the market goes in the form of shared-savings in which the majority of cost savings in the first 1-3 years goes to the ESCO involved and all the savings belong to the customer afterwards [9]. The exact duration of the contract will then depend on the level of energy savings achieved: the greater the savings, the shorter the contract. In such arrangement it becomes easier for the ESCO to manage the risks associated with customers' willingness to comply with the contracts.

It is very important for an ESCO to apply a tailored project strategy to manage risks related to clients' credit. Example measures include a guarantee contract, which enables the ESCO to claim part of the clients' equity when the client ends up breaking the contract. The involvement of a third party financing guarantee institution can be another solution because such an organization often has its own resources and connections to force the clients to comply with the ESCO contracts.

4.3 To Enforce the Marketing Idea Innovations

China's ESCOs should enforce the following marketing idea innovations:

The Brand Marketing of Energy Service
With the development of China's energy service market, the heterogeneity degrees of energy conservation technologies will be gradually reduced, so ESCOs in China should implement brand marketing actively, to establish widely recognized brands through their excellent services, and form their core resources for the long-term development. At present, the competition among China's energy service market is diversified. However, with the continuous progress of energy conservation jobs, the existing energy conservation technologies will be improved and widely promoted, the stability of energy conservation products' performance will be enhanced, and the measures of energy conservation will also change from simple alternative products to the comprehensive energy conservation Solution. Some ESCOs in China have begun to focus on brand marketing, and a small number of star companies have emerged. Within less than a decade years, some ESCOs have become the industry leaders with annual output value of more than a hundred million or even a billion Yuan.

The Cultural Marketing of Energy Service
Cultural marketing is to carry out marketing jobs with the power of culture. Cultural marketing takes the products as the carrier of culture and get into consumers' awareness through market exchange, which reflects various cultural elements of consumers' material and spiritual pursuit, to some extent. Energy services are based on "green culture" that human beings and nature should develop in concordance, which require to improve energy efficiency and reduce greenhouse gas emissions. Therefore, China's ESCOs should make full use of the notion of "green culture", emphasize their social responsibility, and actively promote the development of "green culture" concept, so that energy conservation can become a way of living and the core of "green culture ".

The On-line Marketing of Energy Service
On-line marketing is a new way of marketing based on Internet. It achieves marketing objectives through the interactive influences between digital information and online media. Currently China's ESCOs have not yet take full use of the power of the Internet. Only a small number of ESCOs could be queried on the Internet, and the Internet pages of these companies are mainly on the status of the industry development, the introduction of the companies, and etc. Therefore, China's ESCOs should be active in on-line marketing, and take Internet as the integration an effective platform to integrate the client resources, promote energy conservation products and provide online assessment and consultation of energy conservation.

4.4 To Expand Industry Scale with the Power of Large Enterprises

In the developed countries, ESCOs are usually developed from relevant departments of large enterprises, such as Shell, BP, and etc. They have obvious advantages in brand, strength and technologies, coupled with good legal environment. So energy service industry in those countries is growing very well. To accelerate development, China's energy service industry should also make use of the power of large enterprises. If large enterprises participate in energy service industry, they can not only enhance the overall size and the competency of industry, but also promote the overall development of industry. Second, with large enterprises' financial strength and brand influence, the financial bottlenecks, technological innovation, market base and other problems that SMEs have faced with can all be solved. Central state-owned enterprises in China should consider the task of expanding the EPC as important work, promptly concentrate manpower, material resources, and funds on the work system of expanding the EPC, and act as the main force to expand the EPC.

References

1. Diana, U.V., Sonja, K., Liang, C., Benigna, K., Gireesh, G.N., Gamze, C.: An Assessment of on Energy Service Companies (ESCOs) Worldwide. WEC ADEME Project on Energy Efficiency Policies (2007)
2. Bertoldi, P., Rezessy, S.: Energy Service Companies in Europe Status Report 2005. Ispra, Italy: European Commission DG Joint Research Center (2005)
3. Sorrell, S., Schleich, J., O'Malley, E., Scott, S.: The Economics of Energy Efficiency: Barriers to Cost-Effective Investment, Edward Elgar, Cheltenham (2004)
4. Bertoldi, P., Hinnells, M., Rezessy, S.: Liberating the Power of Energy Services and ESCOs for the Residential Sector in a Liberalised Energy Market. Paper Presented at the EEDAL Conference, London (June 21-23, 2006)
5. Nakagami, H., Murakoshi, C.: Recent Activities of ESCO Industry in Japan, China and Thailand. The Yellow Sea Rim International Exchange Meeting on Building Environment and Energy, Kumamoto, Japan (January 2009)
6. Zhao, M.: EMCA and ESCO Industry Development in China. Presented at CTI Industry Joint Seminar: Successful Cases of Technology Transfer in Asian Countries, New Delhi, India (March 2007)
7. Taylor, R.P., Govindarajalu, C., Levin, J., Meyer, A.S., Ward, W.A.: Financing Energy Efficiency: Lessons from Brazil, China, India and Beyond. The World Bank, Washington D.C(2008)
8. EMCA (China Energy Conservation Service Industry Association).: China's Energy Service Industry Survey 2009. China (2010)
9. Wang, S. M.: Energy Performance Contracting in China. Presentation at the 2006 Conference on Energy Conservation in Buildings, Energy Performance Contracting and Financial Guarantee for Energy Efficiency Projects, Beijing, China (July 25-26, 2006)

Analyses Based on the Notes to Cash Flow Statement

Wenyan Fan

School of Business, Jianghan University, Wuhan, Hubei Province, 430000, China
WenyanFan2011@126.com

Abstract. The related information disclosing from the schedule of the cash flow statement is not less than that in the cash flow statement. Digging into the notes of the cash flow statement and analyzing the articulation among others statements, we can obtain more useful information so that we have made the right judgment of the financial statement of enterprises especially those list companies. In that case, information users are not misled.

Keywords: Cash Flow Statement, Notes, Adjustment.

1   Introduction

Cash flow statement is a kind of financial statement reflecting the inflow and outflow of the cash or its equivalent. Different items of the cash flow statement are divided according to the needs of different industries and different enterprises. Cash flow statement consists of two parts—the main table and the schedule (i.e. supplementary information). The disclosure of the schedule is two-fold. First, the enterprises provide more information of the enterprise's major investment and financial activities to information users. Second, enterprises disclose the quantity of net cash flow from operating activities in indirect way. And at the same time, they also make the situation of the net increase in cash and cash equivalents and the balance sheet be articulated. Going deep into the notes to the cash flow statement and analyzing it with the other statements, we can dig more useful information so that we can make correct decision of the quality of some financial statements from the enterprises, especially list companies.

2   Analyses of the Project—Adjusting Net Profit to Cash Flow from Operating Activities

The main purpose of this part is to adjust the net profit to be the cash flow from operating activities in an indirect way so as to make the articulation of net cash flow from operating activities. What's more signficant, we can obtain a lot of useful information at the same time.

Q. Zhou (Ed.): ISAEBD 2011, Part I, CCIS 208, pp. 138–143, 2011.

2.1 Impairment of Assets

This item—impairment of assets can reflect the actual provision of asset impairment of each item of the enterprises in specific period of time. It includes provision for bad debts, inventories, impairment of held-to-maturity investments, impairment of fixed assets, impairment of intangible assets, impairment of production of biological assets, impairment of oil and gas assets and so on. The above impairments all belong to the situation of having affected the net profit but not involving cash. Therefore, we should adjust appropriately based on the net profit. The impairment of assets can be filled in according to the management fees, investment incomes, operating expenses and so on. Provision for asset impairment will make more expenses, less profits and the value of fixed assets to be virtual reduction. Impairment of assets has great influence on the current profits and the income taxes.

According to No. 17 of the newly established standard— No. 8 Accounting Standards for Enterprises—Impairment of Assets, when impairment loss is recognized, it can't be reversed in future accounting periods. From the actual operation of the enterprise accounting in China, impairment of assets has often been the tool for many enterprises to manipulate profits. Because the old practice of enterprise accounting allows enterprises to gradually reverse the impairment of assets after two or three years, the situations of manipulating profits will happen once in a while. When listed companies suffer from losses in the last three fiscal years, their shares will be suspended from trading, i.e. PT or delisting. Therefore, some companies with poor operating results tend to take advantage of the vulnerability of the accounting system and the related laws, over-withdrawing the false impairment of assets in the year that is expected to suffer greater losses and then gradually reversing the impairment of assets in the following two or three years. This old trick is played over and over again after two or three years so that the loss years are intervals, which can avoid PT or delisting. This tactic happens frequently. And it brings very complicated situations for the management of listed companies in China. It can be seen in recent years when reversal of impairment of assets affects to some companies. In the long run, the regulation on the impairment of assets in the new standard will stop some enterprises from manipulating profits to some extent. The equity method of accounting for long-term equity investment, fixed assets, construction in progress and intangible assets are major items for provision for impairment of assets of many enterprises. There is great manipulating space in the old regulation, because it is still unclear about the judgment on whether there has been impaired, the amount of impairment and so on. This provides means for enterprises to manipulate profits. The new regulation, on the other hand, is clearer about the judgment on the signs of impairment of assets and the measurement of the reversible amount is more practical in operation and has more guidance. The new standard expressly prohibits the four items of reversal of the impairment of assets, which significantly reduces the space of the earnings management of enterprises for impairment of assets. What's more, it is also good for the improvement of the accounting information quality of listed companies.

2.2   Analyses of Adjustment on Depreciation of Fixed Assets

When calculating the depreciation of fixed assets, we should include management fees and manufacturing costs respectively. Management fees belong to expenses for the period which are offset by the current profit. While manufacturing costs belong to the operating costs, which are also offset by the current profit. All these provisions for depreciation are not involved with outflow of funds in the current period. On the contrary, it is the write-off of monetary funds outflow in prior periods in current period. When the depreciation of fixed assets has no influence on the net profit, depreciation of this part will be surely shown in the manufacturing costs, production costs and the increase of ending balance in finished products. Manufacturing costs, production costs and finished products all belong to inventories. Therefore, tight programming has been set in the notes on the cash flow statement. That is, any increase in inventory at end of year, it must be based on the reduction in net profit. If depreciation of fixed assets does exist and not influence the net profit, the note should be added under the item of depreciation of fixed assets. And this part should be reduced in the inventory immediately. In this way, adjustment on the outflow of cash in operating activities of depreciation of fixed assets based on net profit is more integrated. However, the sales, rejection, damage and foreign investment of fixed assets within the year can be adjusted simply by the difference between the ending balance of accumulated depreciation and beginning balance listed in the balance sheet. We should analyze the accumulated depreciation account, excluding the impacts of non-provision depreciation. Besides, comparison of the adjustment of depreciation of fixed assets and the beginning balance of fixed assets in the balance sheet as well as the significant accounting policies for fixed assets classification policy should be made. In this way, we can have clearer judgment on the actual implementation of the fixed assets depreciation policy. And we can easily find out the behavior of some enterprises that reducing the depreciation rate to manipulate profits.

2.3   Analyses of Adjustment on Amortization of Intangible Assets

The reason for the adjustment of this item is that amortization of intangible assets is included in the management fees. Any involvement of amortization of intangible assets in the management fees belongs to non-operating activities. It does not involve with cash and should be added in the net profit. The amount of amortization of intangible assets can be compared with the difference of ending balance and beginning balance in the item of intangible assets in the balance sheet as well as the significant accounting policies for amortization of intangible assets policy. In this way, we can have clearer judgment on the actual implementation of the amortization policy. When there is no change of intangible assets during the current accounting period, but the amount of amortization of intangible assets shown in the notes on the cash flow statement is much higher than that of the difference between the ending balance and beginning balance of the intangible assets in the balance sheet, and we calculate actual amortization rate by comparing the amount of amortization of intangible assets in the notes with the beginning balance of intangible assets, we can easily find out whether the amortization of intangible assets is correct or not. Besides, we can find out the inflated profits, amortization of intangible assets in the fictional notes and patchwork of net cash flow from operating activities of some enterprises.

2.4 Analyses on Disposal of Loss and Profit of Fixed Assets, Intangible Assets and Other Long-Term Assets

This item can be filled in with the operating income, operating expenses and their related details. Firstly, there is one point worthy of pointing out. That is, the content of this item only consists of the sales and damage of fixed assets. Any rejection of fixed assets will be shown specifically in the item of loss on disposal of fixed assets. The situation above is shown by increases of the operating incomes. And the disposal of fixed assets, intangible assets and other long-term assets don't belong to operating activities. But they all have influences on the net profit. Therefore, they should be adjusted on basis of the net profit. The reason is that for disposal of loss and profit, it will result in adding in the operating expenses or incomes account from the disposal of fixed assets account, which is brought into the profit and loss system and has influence on the net profit. However, the operating losses and profits are irrelevant to the outflow of currency funds, but are relevant to the decrease of fixed assets. Therefore, adjustment should be made on this part. Incomes should increase from the net profit, while losses should decrease from the net profit. The loss of disposal of intangible assets will have impact on the net profit by being added into the account of other operating expenses. Because the loss of other disposal of long-term assets is calculated into the account of operating incomes and expenses, it should be adjusted to show actual situation of cash flows of the enterprises.

3 Analyses of the Item—Major Investment and Financial Activities Not Involved with Cash

Major investment and financial activities not involved with cash release the information that they influence assets and liabilities in a certain period of time but not forming the flow of cash of all investment and financial activities. These investment and financial activities have great influence on the cash flows in the following periods of time. And the investment and financial activities not involved with cash are debt into capital, convertible bonds that are due within one year and fixed assets under finance leases.

Debt into capital refers to that the debtors convert their debts into capital, and at the same time, debtors restructure their debts into equity. It reflects the amount of capital converted. But that the debtors convert the bonds into capital according to the agreement belongs to normal situation, which can be regarded as debt restructuring. Debt into capital for corporation limited is to turn debts into shares. But for other enterprises, it is to turn debts into paid-in capital. The result of debt into capital is that the debtors will receive more shares or paid-in capitals and the creditors will have additional equity. Debt restructuring is the restructure of statements, which is an important way of financial operation in enterprises. It is also the common management tool for modern CEO and CFO in enterprises. In practice, debt restructuring has been the basis of implementation of assets and capital operation. For enterprises with financial difficulties, their management to survive is essential. We should prevent the loss of state-owned assets and the fictitious profits by debts restructuring.

Convertible bonds that are due within one year can be distinguished from two angles. Widely speaking, it can be referred to as any other convertible corporate debt securities. Narrowly speaking, it can be referred to as any convertible corporate bonds of equity shares and rights, for example, the Japanese right to buy stocks with convertible bonds. Countries like China and Japan adopt the narrow concept. Convertible bonds have characteristics of safety and speculative. It can be the long-term capital raised by the enterprises. What's more, it can attract investors. Practices prove that enterprises can transfer risks by convertible bonds. On one hand, on basis of the confirmation of debt financing decision, it can help enterprises to choose the most appropriate level of risk in operating activities. On the other hand, on basis of the confirmation of project decision, it can help enterprises to decide the financing scale and conversion ratio so that ultimate realization of the management and financing decision are matched.

Fixed assets under finance leases reflect the company's fixed assets financed by the leasing the minimum lease payments included in addition to interest charges should be phased unrecognized net financing charges. Enterprises take advantage of this method to lease fixed assets. Although the ownership of the assets belongs to lessor during the lease period, the leasing companies still enjoy the main profits from the leased assets in reality due to the reason that assets' lease period basically includes the effectively useful life of assets. Of course, enterprises also assume the related risks. Therefore, enterprises should record the finance lease assets as a fixed asset. Besides, related liabilities should be confirmed. Enterprises should also adopt the consistent depreciation policy as that of the other depreciable assets. During the lease period, the value of finance lease of fixed assets should be calcuted by way of depreciation and the unrecognized financing amortization cost should be recorded in the effective interest method amortizing the profits and losses or the financial expenses. Therefore, the total amount of profit and loss should be the sum the two. And the formula is: the fair value of the leased asset or the present value of minimum lease payments+ initial direct costs+ the difference between the minimum lease payments and fixed assets recorded.

4   Analyses of Net Changes on Cash and Cash Equivalents

The net changes on cash and cash equivalents reflect the net increase or net decrease after the ending balance of cash and cash equivalents deducting the beginning balance. It is the supplement of the item—net increase of cash and cash equivalents in the cash flow statement. The number shown here must match the one shown in the main table of cash flow statement, which reflects close relationship between the cash flow statement and the balance sheet.

References

1. Yin, C.: Research of Accounting Assets Impairment Popular Business (Investment Edition), vol. (6) (2009)
2. Middle-level Accounting Practice China Financial and Economic Publishing House (December 2008); Edited by Finance Ministry Accounting Qualification Assessment Centre
3. Accounting Standards Interpretation Edited by Finance Ministry Accounting Division (April 2007)

Teaching Examples and Pedagogy Methods of *Mechanical Drafting* Based on Behaviorism Teaching Theory

Zhongwei Liang[1,2,3,*], Chunliang Zhang[1], Sikun You[1], and Hongguang Deng[1]

[1] School of Mechanical & Electrical Engineering, Guangzhou University,
Guangzhou, 510006, P.R. China
lzwstalin@126.com,
{Zcl,Ysk,Dhg}@gzhu.edu.cn
[2] School of Mechanical & Automotive Engineering, South China University of Technology.
Guangzhou, 510640, P.R. China
[3] National Engineering Research Center of Near-Net-Shape Forming for Metallic Materials,
South China University of Technology. Guangzhou,
510640, P.R. China

Abstract. Behaviorism teaching theory is a pedagogy method which derived from human's exchange- behavior characteristics, such as opinion exchange, information transition and mutual interaction; it aims at the cultivation of student's engineering teamwork consciousness and cooperative practice ability. The principle of mechanical drafting-statistic in plastic molding machine's mechanical drafting-system is used as an example, behaviorism teaching theory is penetrated into the whole teaching process of *mechanical drafting*, thus example organization, pedagogy method and teaching content are investigated and improved. Practical experiment proves that the implementation of Behaviorism teaching theory entails a good teaching result; a new developing thought and effort direction are advanced for the practice of engineering education.

Keywords: Behaviorism teaching theory, Mechanical drafting, Teaching example, Pedagogy method.

1 Introduction

The mutual influence process among people for the purpose of exchanging idea and transmitting information is emphasized by Behaviorism teaching theory. The key point proposed by the present behaviorism teaching theory lies in the interactive property which is necessary for lecturing and developing of students' engineering practice ability [1]. Since the goal of language is transmitting information and instructing knowledge, thus the interactive study among students should be emphasized and encouraged in engineering knowledge's learning. Through interactive studying students can benefit from each other and develop the communicating and team working capability gradually. Teachers could actively use various channels to

---

* Corresponding author.

Q. Zhou (Ed.): ISAEBD 2011, Part I, CCIS 208, pp. 144–148, 2011.

help students developing their habit of coordinating ability. The theory of behaviorism is practiced through studying and investigating, students can inspire their inherent motivation of study when they interested in some certain knowledge.

The manner and process of learning technology lies greatly in the means of interactive cognitive to exchange information. Thus class instructing should be "interactive", and student's capabilities in practice, teamwork and project developing are overemphasized by Behaviorism teaching theory. But in the traditional teaching, the basic theory and class instructing are unilateral emphasized, which leads to the disconnection between teaching and case practice, thus the cultivation and development of student's practice ability have been seriously restricted. Only by practicing Behaviorism teaching theory, students' professional knowledge, team cooperation ability, professional attitudes can be cultivated systematically, a better adaptive capacity for enterprise and society in the area of engineering talent's quality requirements can also be established [2, 3]. The introduction of behaviorism pedagogy in professional curriculum, and the strengthening of student's studying ability have become a prominent difficulty needs to be solved urgently.

2 Investigation and Practice of Pedagogy Method

Mechanical drafting is a professional and practical course which covers different subject fields such as physical science, control theory and information science. The content of teaching should be focus on the latest scientific and technological achievements in *Mechanical drafting,* it is necessary that students pursuit for the course by solving engineering problems. The capability cultivation of independent innovation, interpersonal communication and inter-operability is regarded as the teaching goal; practical cases are adopted as the teaching means for the development of professional skills and engineering ability [4].

Mechanical drafting system in a compression molding machine is regarded as the examples for class teaching, and behaviorism pedagogy is penetrated into the whole teaching process. Lecture is conducted on the basis of classroom discussion, research and analysis, case practice, etc. The adoption of teaching cases and specific arrangement of pedagogy method in behaviorism background are introduced.

(1) Classroom discussion emphasizes on the grasp and inspiration of professional knowledge, its content is characterized by the concept of statistic in compression molding machine mechanical drafting system, the teaching object is defined as the studying of mechanical drafting-statistic, dynamics and pressure loss's calculation, thus grasping the calculating method of flow rate and flow velocity, thus providing bases for the analysis of mechanical drafting unit's construction and mechanical drafting circuit. Teachers are offered the leading role in the class process.

Firstly the main principle and classification of mechanical drafting are explained in detail by teacher, and then an experiment of static fluid's analysis is conducted. Students are required to grasp mechanical drafting' theoretical feature and understand its working process. Simultaneously the students are required to answer many questions on the concept of mechanical drafting and specific details, e.g., why mechanical drafting should be studied? Which method should be used for analyzing mechanical drafting in a certain condition? How about the specific requirement? How to select a model of mechanical drafting in a practical mechanical drafting application and how about the practical process? What principles should be followed? All these questions facilitate the teacher's seeking for the practical situation of student's knowledge- understanding, and they also prompt the student's thinking in class and preparing for following case discussion.

After the instruction of basic concepts is completed the students are separated into several studying groups, the case questions of teacher and predetermined tasks are discussed and conceived in each group respectively. The topics of discussion are around the principle of mechanical drafting, the mechanics properties of static fluid, the statistic mechanism, implementation tool, working medium, etc. Each group should reach their own consensus and the discussion conclusions are recorded in detail and submitted after the class is finished [5].   Case analysis is strictly implemented in the teaching process, the tasks and problem-oriented teaching are proceed with a schematic diagram of mechanical drafting system, the research problem is assigned and an analysis report or evaluating paper should be accomplished and submitted in 90 minutes. The studying process is conducted in a competing form by paper writing or group discussion, which leads to the maximum developing of student's cognitive power and creative capability.

Furthermore, a student representative from each study group is requested for stating their basic viewpoints, and the debating can take place when other groups have their respective viewpoints. During this process it is the teacher's responsibility that the discussion should be guided and student's initiative should be fully promoted. Thus the whole process of class discussion is achieved [6].

(2) The extracurricular research project requires the students prepare for the case example and self-directed learning by themselves. It is obligatory that students should possess the knowledge foundation needed before the extracurricular case analyzing. This task will be more detailed and complex than the traditional classroom discussion, for students accomplish the research object spontaneously, this process offer the dominant position to the students [7].

Teacher provides the relative information of mechanical drafting system in compression molding machine, and introduces some technical expanding problems for discussion. E.g. what position should be offered to statistic theory during the process of analyzing mechanical drafting system? What influence is exerted by statistic theory on mechanical drafting? Following difficult points are studied carefully: How about the distributing discipline of mechanical pressure?   Liquid pressure effect on the water plane, fluid's relative balance, etc. Furthermore; some key questions on the research methods and implementing tools need to be considered in detail: the Statistic mechanism, working theory of mechanical drafting system, the analyzing methods of mechanical drafting, the requirements of mechanical drafting system's performance index, the evaluating methods of mechanical drafting' working performance, etc. Students arrange the time and place spontaneously to realize the research process, discussion and analysis on the case examples, the monitoring system of mechanical drafting can be used as the auxiliary means to study the perceptual knowledge, the performance analysis and evaluation report are introduced for guiding the student's observation in mechanical drafting' working process and inspiration of the control principle's research. The study process should be recorded in detail [8].

At the next class the learning results of each group will be introduced and detailed described to other groups, after the introduction is finished everyone can discusses and inquires [9], for instance, how to use a basic monitoring instrument for detecting the index of mechanical drafting? How to coordinate their respective movement? What result can be gotten when the efficiency experiment is conducted on some key features? And so on.

(3) The analysis of a practical case is a new teaching step and pedagogy method by which the grouped students select the appropriate example for studying and practicing by themselves. With the accumulated knowledge obtained by the first two cases, the capability of independent analysis is established by students, and through the group discussion and classroom debate the preliminary conception and design of the whole mechanical drafting system in a compression molding machine are obtained. The specific content mainly covers the structure and composition in several kinds of the valves: the research content of mechanical drafting, the characteristics of mechanical pressure, and the fluid equilibrium differential equation, the distributing principle of mechanical pressure, and the benchmark and metric unit of pressure calculation. Through practical operation students can learn their basic operation principle and classification, grasp their respective construction, and understand their working process and mutual comparison in performance characteristics. The practice process will lead the students to study the construction of mechanical drafting system, inspire their comprehension, thus the discussing conclusion can be reached after the student's independent research. The whole process is characterized by the case evaluation and the student's participation, the teacher is only regarded as an academic advisor, he gives a necessary advice only when the practical difficulties exist. On the other hand, the teacher can also put forward some technical requirements during the development of a practical control system, which let the system developed be more practical and feasible [10].

Finally the evaluation of student's learning is conducted based on his performance result, finished effect and teamwork collaboration during the development of a practical project. The assessment methods can be classified into record, report or mutual score. In a unit test, the students are required to submit a summary report on the topic of mechanical drafting system's performance and mechanical drafting' model construction, and comment on their working property or application environment. (Ten questions will be installed; the difficulty will be span in low, medium and high); or the students be required to observe the working process of different kinds of mechanical drafting control valves in detail, submit a sketches of their respective working principle, and made an analysis reports on mechanical drafting' working performance.

3   Conclusions

The behaviorism teaching practice in *Mechanical drafting* proves that a positive and effective result can be obtained by the pedagogy method based on practice capability and teamwork collaboration. The reasonable adoption and arrangement of the teaching case of the control valves in mechanical drafting molding machine promote the cultivation of student's comprehensive ability. In the teaching practice, the pedagogy method and learning organization are improved and optimized continuously through extensive assessing and scientific evaluating; finally the goal of fully mobilizing students' learning initiative and developing their practical ability by Behaviorism teaching theory is reached.

Acknowledgements. Thanks the support from National Feature Specialty Construction Project (TS2479); National Education Scientific Planning Project (CIA090110); Guangzhou Higher School Education Teaching Reform Research Projects (2009, No.7); Excellent Talent Project of Guangdong's Colleges and Universities (LYM09110) and Research Project of Guangzhou University (10A068).

References

1. Connell, M.W., Sheridan, K., Gardner, H.: On Abilities and Domains. In: Sternberg, R.J., Grigorenko, E.L. (eds.) The Psychology of Abilities, Competencies, and Expertise, ch. 5, pp. 126–155. Cambridge University Press, Cambridge (2003)
2. Chi, M.T.H.: Two Approaches to the Study of Experts' Characteristics. In: Ericsson, K.A., Charness, N., Feltovich, P.J., Hoffman, R.R. (eds.) The Cambridge Handbook of Expertise and Performance, ch. 2. Cambridge University Press, Cambridge (2006) (2007)
3. Mayer, R.E.: What Causes Individual Differences in Cognitive Performance? In: Sternberg, R.J., Grigorenko, E.L. (eds.) The Psychology of Abilities, Competencies, and Expertise, ch. 10, p. 265. Cambridge University Press, Cambridge (1999) (2003)
4. Feltovich, P.J., Prietula, M.J., Ericsson, K.A.: Studies of Expertise from Psychological Perspectives. In: Ericsson, K.A., Charness, N., Feltovich, P.J., Hoffman, R.R. (eds.) The Cambridge Handbook of Expertise and Performance, ch. 4, p. 47. Cambridge University Press, Cambridge (2006) (2001)
5. American Society of Mechanical Engineers, Society Policy Ethic (2002), http://files.asme.org/ASMEORG/Governance/3675.pdf (Revised on November 5, 2006)
6. Li, J.: Research on behaviorism pedagogy theory. Chinese Adult Education 2009(15), 116–117 (2007)
7. Seering, W.: Redefining Engineering, MIT Faculty Newsletter (2003)
8. Feltovich, P.J., Prietula, M.J., Ericsson, K.A.: behaviorism Initiative. behaviorism Initiative Homepage (2006), http://www.behaviorism.org/
9. Gu, P., Lu, X., Xiong, G., Li, S., Shen, M.: The development of design directed engineering curriculum based on the behaviorism frame work. In: World Transactions on Engineering and Technology Education, pp. 267–270. IEEE Press, New York (2006)
10. Bloom, B.S.: Taxonomy of Educational Objectives. Hand books I: The Cognitive Domain. David McKay Co. Inc., New York (2008) (1956)

Empirical Study on the Contribution of Infrastructure to the Coordinated Development between Urban and Rural Areas: Case Study on Country Road Projects

Shijie Jiang[1], Liyin Shen[2], and Li Zhou[3]

[1] Chongqing University of Science and Technology, 401331, Chongqing, China
cqaj@163.com
[2] The Hong Kong Polytechnic University, HongKong, China
bsshen@inet.polyu.edu.hk
[3] Sichuan International Studies University, 400031, Chongqing, China
Fish_zl@hotmail.com

Abstract. This paper makes an empirical study using the data from projects of Chongqing Urban-Rural Infrastructure Coordination Demonstration Program. The results of the study indicate that the contribution of infrastructures to urban-rural coordination increases with the growing equity of investment, and infrastructure plays a significant role in closing the urban-rural gap and gradually achieving the urban-rural coordination. Therefore, conclusion is made that the infrastructure investment between town and country should be balanced in a manner that is "equity-oriented and efficiency-emphasized" in order to attain the strategic goal of urban-rural coordination and promote social justice.

Keywords: Infrastructure, Urban-rural coordination, Contribution, Empirical study, Country Road Projects.

1   Introduction

Infrastructure not only plays an important role in the social and economic activities of a country, a developing country in particular, but also makes an indispensable contribution to the urban-rural coordinated development in a country or region. As the existing evaluation models are found not able to effectively assess or scale the contribution of infrastructure to urban-rural coordination, it is necessary and imperative to establish a practical and applicable model to evaluate the infrastructure contribution to urban-rural coordination.

The research team has made three rounds of questionnaire survey for comparison and determination of the weights and reference values of evaluation indicators, [1] based on the empirical data collected from Chongqing urban-rural coordination infrastructure development demonstration program and information acquired from related statistical yearbook (manual), specifications, standards and other research findings. [2-4]Further, the team has established a model to assess the infrastructure contribution to urban-rural coordination on the basis of the existing evaluation models in this connection, and derived evaluation formula to calculate the contribution of

Q. Zhou (Ed.): ISAEBD 2011, Part I, CCIS 208, pp. 149–155, 2011.
© Springer-Verlag Berlin Heidelberg 2011

country road infrastructure to the urban-rural coordination. This is a significant instrument and reference for the quantitative analysis of infrastructure contribution to urban-rural coordination.

Nevertheless, the evaluation model for infrastructure contribution to urban-rural coordination should be empirically proved for its reliability and feasibility. Chongqing, a "National Pilot Zone of Comprehensive Concerted Reforms for Urban/Rural Coordination" approved and established by the National Development and Reform Commission in June 2007, launched the Chongqing Urban-Rural Infrastructure Coordination Demonstration Program (hereinafter referred to as "Demonstration Program") under the loan of the Asian Development Bank in 2008. The samples and cases for empirical analysis in this paper are mostly from country road projects of this program.

2 Empirical Study

2.1 Evaluation Model and Standards

According to the conclusions of Research on Evaluation Model for Infrastructure Contribution to Urban-Rural Coordination, Y is the contribution of infrastructure to urban-rural coordination, whilst X_{ij}, representing an evaluation index, remains unchanged. The following is the formula and evaluation standards:

2.1.1 The Model of Country Road Project

$$Y=\alpha*\{0.4*[0.27*(X_{11}/7.27-1)+0.24*(X_{15}/15.8-1)+0.22*(X_{16}/25461.5-1)+0.27*(X_{17}/5.74-1)]+0.34*[0.2*(X_{21}/1.97-1)+0.27*(1-X_{22}/42.16)+0.2*(X_{26}/6.1-1)+0.17*(X_{27}/0.73-1)+0.16*(1-X_{28}/0.41)]+0.26*[0.21*(1-X_{34}/0.63)+0.3*(1-X_{35}/0.3)+0.22*(X_{36}/0.54-1)+0.27*(X_{37}/4.71-1)]\}+(1-\alpha)*\{0.44*(1-X_{43}/10.92)+0.32*[0.46*(1-X_{51}/22.57)+0.54*(1-X_{55}/7.48)]+0.24*[0.34*(1-X_{61}/0.59)+0.39*(1-X_{62}/0.08)+0.27*(1-X_{63}/2.1)]\}$$

(1)

In this formula, the weight of an efficiency indicator is α, and the weight of an equity indicator will be $1-\alpha$, where $0 \leq \alpha \leq 1$.

2.1.2 Evaluation Criteria

When $Y \geq 0$, the project is acceptable. Specifically speaking, when the value of Y is above zero, the infrastructure contribution to urban-rural coordination is positive, which means it is beneficial to narrowing the urban-rural gap; when the value of Y is zero, the infrastructure contribution to urban-rural coordination is nil, which means the urban-rural gap remains unchanged.

When $Y < 0$, the project is unacceptable, because the infrastructure contribution to urban-rural coordination is negative, leading to the urban-rural gap widened.

With the above model formula and evaluation criteria, Chongqing urban-rural coordination infrastructure development demonstration program or other infrastructures, country road projects particularly, to be executed for the purpose of urban-rural coordination, can be evaluated and quantified with regard to their contribution to the urban-rural coordinated development, because their degree of contribution may be calculated through expert judgments and indicators.

2.2 The Principle in Value-Taking for α

With economic growth in the west, the theory of equality and efficiency has gone through three major stages: from the end of 19th century to early 20th century, welfare economics represented by "economic interventionism", "neo-classic synthesis" and "welfare economic school" advocated "the priority of equality"; following World War II, scholars, mainly those believing in economic liberalism, promoted "the priority of efficiency" and free market mechanism as a countermeasure against "efficiency crisis" emerging from the western countries. Since early 1970s, economists, represented by Arthur M. Okun, put forward a theory of alternation between equality and efficiency, arguing that both equality and efficiency have their own merits and should be integrated in the full play of market mechanism. [5]

The real intention of China's policy of coordinated urban and rural development is to provide urban and rural residents with equal opportunities for development, facilitate an appropriate flow and optimized allocation of resources, strengthen the role of city in leading rural development and the role of rural areas in stimulating urban growth and ultimately narrow the gap between urban areas and rural districts. In this way, both urban and rural community, as well as their economy, can be put into a balanced, sustainable and coordinated track. [6]

Based on the experience from developed countries, the infrastructure investment distribution among regions (highway construction, for instance) largely follows three principles: equality, efficiency and neutrality. The gap of development between cities and villages is a factor to be considered in the first instance when China formulates policies for the infrastructure investment distribution among regions. Since the issue of urban-rural dual structure has become prominent, infrastructure investment should have a full play in its role as an economic policy to bridge the income gap among regions. Therefore, a policy demonstrating that "equality is predominant and efficiency is important" should be set down. [7]

Although α represents the weight of efficiency indices, equity is an indispensable component of the model in terms of model structure and the connotation of urban-rural coordination. This is the principle to be followed as far as possible when value is assigned to α to evaluate the contribution of Demonstration Program or other infrastructure to urban-rural coordination.

2.3 The Result of Evaluation

The values of project indices need to be applied to corresponding formula to verify the contribution of the Demonstration Program to urban-rural coordination. Besides, α is a continuous variable ($0 \leq \alpha \leq 1$). For convenience of calculation, it is assumed that α is one of the discrete values between [0, 1] at an interval of 0.1. Then, the contribution of projects of the Demonstration Program can be acquired by taking different value of α (see Table 1).

Table 1. The table of the contribution value of the country road project

District	Project site	α=0.0	α=0.1	α=0.2	α=0.3	α=0.4	α=0.5	α=0.6	α=0.7	α=0.8	α=0.9	α=1.0
Chengkou	Chengguan road	0.21	0.21	0.21	0.21	0.20	0.20	0.20	0.20	0.19	0.19	0.19
	Caotang	0.21	0.18	0.15	0.12	0.09	0.05	0.02	-0.01	-0.04	-0.08	-0.11
Fengjie	Hongtu	0.21	0.18	0.15	0.12	0.09	0.06	0.03	-0.01	-0.04	-0.07	-0.10
	Qinglong	0.21	0.18	0.16	0.13	0.10	0.07	0.04	0.01	-0.02	-0.05	-0.08
	Tuxiang	0.21	0.18	0.15	0.12	0.09	0.06	0.03	0.00	-0.03	-0.07	-0.10
Fuling	Baisheng	0.21	0.18	0.16	0.13	0.10	0.07	0.04	0.01	-0.02	-0.05	-0.08
	Wubai road	0.21	0.20	0.19	0.17	0.16	0.14	0.13	0.11	0.10	0.09	0.07
Qianjiang	Houhuang road	0.21	0.19	0.18	0.16	0.14	0.12	0.10	0.08	0.06	0.04	0.02
	Baiquan	0.21	0.18	0.15	0.12	0.08	0.05	0.02	-0.01	-0.05	-0.08	-0.11
	Baishui	0.21	0.18	0.15	0.12	0.09	0.06	0.03	-0.01	-0.04	-0.07	-0.10
Wushan	Hongmiao	0.21	0.18	0.15	0.12	0.09	0.06	0.02	-0.01	-0.04	-0.07	-0.10
	Shili	0.21	0.18	0.14	0.11	0.07	0.04	0.00	-0.03	-0.07	-0.10	-0.14
	Xiping	0.21	0.18	0.15	0.12	0.09	0.06	0.03	0.00	-0.03	-0.06	-0.09
Xiushan	Meiyun road	0.21	0.21	0.20	0.20	0.19	0.19	0.18	0.18	0.17	0.17	0.16
	Ganhuo road	0.21	0.20	0.18	0.17	0.15	0.14	0.12	0.11	0.09	0.08	0.06
Youyang	Heimao road	0.21	0.18	0.15	0.12	0.09	0.05	0.02	-0.01	-0.04	-0.08	-0.11
	Shuiyao road	0.21	0.18	0.14	0.11	0.08	0.04	0.01	-0.03	-0.06	-0.10	-0.13
	Nixi	0.21	0.18	0.14	0.10	0.06	0.03	-0.01	-0.05	-0.09	-0.12	-0.16
Yunyang	Nongba	0.21	0.18	0.15	0.12	0.09	0.06	0.03	0.00	-0.03	-0.06	-0.09
	Yanglu	0.21	0.18	0.14	0.11	0.07	0.04	0.01	-0.03	-0.06	-0.10	-0.13
	Yaoqing road	0.21	0.18	0.15	0.12	0.09	0.07	0.04	0.01	-0.02	-0.05	-0.08

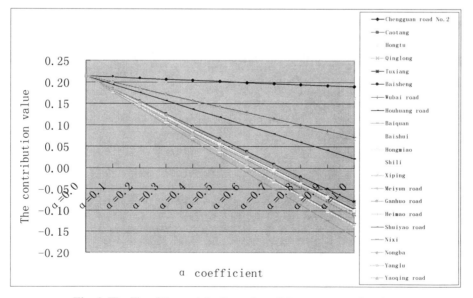

Fig. 1. The Fig of the contribution value of the country road project

In addition to the above, diagram is a visually clearer way to display the extent and trend of the contribution of projects to urban-rural coordination while α is changing (see Fig. 1 for details).

The above-mentioned figures show that under the principle of being "equity-oriented, efficiency-emphasized", the weight of efficiency indices α is ≤ 0.5 and the contribution Y of each water supply project in the Demonstration Program is above zero, indicating the project is acceptable; in other words, the contribution of Chongqing Urban-Rural Infrastructure Coordination Demonstration Program is positive and beneficial to narrowing the urban-rural gap.

3 Discussion

3.1 The Relation between α and Contribution

The definition of α is very clear, i.e. the weight of efficiency indices, and besides $0 \leq \alpha \leq 1$. Seeing from the aforesaid figures, we will find the contributions of all country road projects are all monotone decreasing with the increase of α within [0, 1]. This shows that α is in inverse proportion to the contribution, i.e. the infrastructure contribution to urban-rural coordination will reduce, even below zero for some projects, as the weight of efficiency index increases and weight of equity index decreases. It is therefore concluded that overemphasis on efficiency and negligence of equity will fail to contribute to urban-rural coordination; and what's worse the urban-rural gap is to be enlarged.

3.2 Evaluation of the Significance of the Model

Further explanation can be found from this empirical study on the evaluation model that infrastructure contribution to urban-rural coordination is mainly reflected by both equity and efficiency, regardless of the value of α (except when $\alpha=0$, the contribution is only from equity and when $\alpha=1$, the contribution is only from efficiency). Moreover, the results of verification for projects also show that the infrastructure's role in the social and economic activities of a country and its contribution to the regional urban-rural coordination are not only reflected by efficiency, but more importantly, by the equity.

3.3 Applicability and Reliability of Evaluation Model

The applicability and reliability of the evaluation model have been approved by the above verification for all country road projects of the Demonstration Program. Nevertheless, as Chongqing Urban-Rural Coordination Infrastructure Development Demonstration Program is limited in number, scale, type and location, the evaluation model derived from the Program is also confined in its application. Likewise, the reliability of the model, relying on the trueness and accuracy of project and statistical data, is also dependent on the professional and objective judgment of experts and the continuous improvement in practice. Therefore, it is beneficial exploration and attempt to establish a model for evaluating infrastructure contribution to urban-rural coordination; and this model is relevant and reliable for quantitative evaluation and measurement of the contribution.

4 Conclusion

It is the result of the study that the infrastructure contribution to urban-rural coordination will decrease with the growing weight of efficiency indices, indicating the upward trend of urban-rural gap when efficiency is overemphasized and equity is neglected during infrastructure investment. The gap of development between cities and villages is a factor to be considered in the first instance when China formulates policies for the infrastructure investment distribution among regions. The infrastructure investment should be focused on rural areas, especially for the cities in middle or western China, such as Chongqing, where the problem of dual urban-rural structure is remarkable and the urban-rural gap is large.

Besides, the majority of the projects reach a similar conclusion that the infrastructure contribution to urban-rural coordination will constantly increase when the weight of efficiency indices gets lower and the weight of equity indices grows up, until it reaches the maximum when the former is reduced to zero and the latter is 1. Therefore, the problem of dual rural-urban structure currently faced by Chongqing will be alleviated by using infrastructure investment as an economic tool to bridge the urban-rural gap and gradually attain the goal of coordinated development. On the other hand, the contribution of the infrastructure increases as the weight of equity indices (i.e. the equity of investment) grows.

Thus derived the central tenet of urban-rural coordinated development and reform of Chongqing-----social justice and equity shall be promoted in parallel with economic growth. In other words, the urban and rural residents are entitled to equal opportunities for development, the overall planning should be made to cover both the town and the countryside, the policies should be adjusted where residence registration, land, social security, etc. are concerned, the resources (such as investment into country road, water supply to small towns) should be allocated, and incessant efforts should be put into the interaction of urban and rural areas, so that the urban-rural gap may be narrowed and the social and economic development may be balanced, sustained and coordinated.

Finally, the methods and practices of study in this subject will serve as a good reference to other similar researches on the infrastructure contribution to urban-rural coordination.

Acknowledgment. I am deeply indebted to the doctor and the professor fund of Chongqing University of Science and Technology for its sponsorship (CK2010B19).

References

1. Jiang, S.J., Shen, L.Y.: Research on Relatively Important Indicator Extraction by means of PCA. In: The International Conference on E-Business and E-Government, ICEE 2010, pp. 4426–4429 (2010)
2. National Development and Reform Commission, Economic Evaluation Method and Parameter of Construction Projects, 3rd edn. China Planning Press (2006)
3. Standard and norm institute of the Ministry of Construction, Economic Evaluation Cases of Construction Project. China Planning Press (2006)
4. China International Engineering Consulting Corporation, Social Evaluation Guidance for Investment Projects in China—Projects Financed by the World Bank and Asian Development Bank. China Planning Press (2004)
5. Huang, L., Wei, X.: The Evolution of Fairness and Efficiency Theory in the West. Northern Economy 12, 64–65 (2007)
6. Ma, Y.: Building of Villages and Towns under Coordinated Urban and Rural Development: Abroad Experience and China to Go. Special Zone Economy, 41–43 (May 2006)
7. Liu, M.: To Explore the Effectiveness of Infrastructure Investment in Urban and Rural Areas. Journal of Nanjing Party Institute of CPC and Nanjing Administration Institute 3, 32–36 (2007)

Study on the Countermeasures for the Development of Heilongjiang Service Outsourcing Industry

Xueli Yang

College of Economics & Management
Heilongjiang Bayi Agricultural University
Daqing, China
Yangxueli1130@163.com

Abstract. The service outsourcing is a green industry in the real sense. To develop service outsourcing vigorously can help to optimize industrial structure in Heilongjiang province, change the growth mode of trade, and has a great significance for accelerating the economic structure adjustment and realizing the economic sustainable development. This article studies the present situation and features of the development of Heilongjiang service outsourcing through the investigation of the development situation of Heilongjiang service outsourcing and analyzes the environment for Heilongjiang province to development service outsourcing industry, through qualitative and quantitative analysis of Heilongjiang service outsourcing industry, the writer puts forward that our province should perfect related policy system in developing service outsourcing industry, increase greatly support intensity of force in funds, strengthen the support to key enterprises and increase the service outsourcing talents cultivation, develop characteristic outsourcing, and enhance the competitiveness of service outsourcing enterprise, etc.

Keywords: service outsourcing, evaluation system, solving countermeasures.

1 Introduction

With the acceleration process of global economic integration, the application and development of Internet and modern communications technology, service outsourcing gets developed rapidly with its advantages of low cost and high efficiency service. UNCTAD estimates that the expected international service outsourcing market growth will reach to $1.2 trillion in 2010. In recent years, multinational enterprises have gradually turned more business to China, and through outsourcing to reduce supply chain cost, our government has also taken active support policies, and promoted the development of China's service outsourcing industry. The current service outsourcing has brought 600 thousand jobs and later will add 250 thousand jobs every year. Heilongjiang province pays great attention to the development of service outsourcing, software and service outsourcing enterprises reach 320 in the whole province in 2009, the output value of service outsourcing industry has been over 100 million Yuan, the number of employees is more than 30 thousand.

Q. Zhou (Ed.): ISAEBD 2011, Part I, CCIS 208, pp. 156–162, 2011.

2 Heilongjiang Service Outsourcing Evaluation Index System Structure

The major factors that influence the development of service outsourcing industry are: policy services, social cultural environment, human resource and skills, economic development environment etc. Through the analysis of these factors, we may safely draw the Heilongjiang service outsourcing evaluation index system, as is shown in table 1.

Table 1. Heilongjiang service outsourcing evaluation index system

First-class index	Second-class index	Third-class index
Heilongjiang service outsourcing industry comprehensive factors (A)	Policy services (B1)	Industry positioning (C11)
		Legal environment (institutional policy) (C12)
		Tax policy (preferential tax measures) (C13)
		Infrastructure investment subsidies (C14)
	Social cultural environment (B2)	Cultural compatibility (C21)
		Intellectual property protection (C22)
		Work attitude and behavior (C23)
	Human resource and skills (B3)	Experience and quality of distance service(C31)
		Personnel quality and knowledge structure (C32)
		Education and language (C33)
		Loss risk (human resources endowment and cost) (C34)
	Economic environment (B4)	Economic development level (C41)
		Consumption level (C42)
		Industrial structure (C43)
		Materials endowment (C44)

(1) To establish judgment rules. According to the experts' advice, we adopt 9 level grade difference method for binary comparison, we provide:

when the extreme importance to B_i compared with B_j, B_{ij} =9;

when the more importance to B_i compared with B_j, B_{ij} =7;

when the obvious importance to B_i compared with B_j, B_{ij} =5;

when the slightly more importance to B_i compared with B_j, B_{ij} =3;

when the equally importance to B_i compared with B_j, B_{ij} =1.

Among which B_{ij} and B_{ji} have the mutual reciprocal relationship. And 2, 4, 6 and 8 are among the above estimation value.

（2）To establish judgment matrix(Table 2——Table 6), and input to V0.5.2 software yaahp, calculates the results are as follows.

Table 2. Rule layer Judgment Matrix

	B1	B2	B3	B4	Weight(W)
B1	1	7	5	5	w_1(0.6239)
B2	1/7	1	1/5	1/5	w_2(0.0487)
B3	1/5	5	1	3	w_3(0.2189)
B4	1/5	5	1/3	1	w_4(0.1085)

Note: C.R=0.063<0.1. CI=0.0569 l_{max} =4.1708

Table 3. B1-C Judgment Matrix

	C11	C12	B13	B14	Weight
C11	1	4	5	7	W_{11}(0.6320)
C12	1/4	1	2	1	W_{12}(0.1490)
C13	1/5	1/2	1	1/2	W_{13}(0.0860)
C14	1/7	1	2	1	W_{14}(0.1329)

Note: C.R=0.042<0.1. CI=0.038 l_{max} =4.1013

Table 4. B2—C Judgment Matrix

B2	C21	C22	C23	Weight
C21	1	3	5	W_{21}(0.6370)
C22	1/3	1	3	W_{22}(0.2583)
C23	1/5	1/3	1	W_{23}(0.1047)

Note: C.R=0.033<0.1. CI=0.019 l_{max} =3.0385

Table 5. B3—C Judgment Matrix

B3	C31	C32	C33	C34	Weight
C31	1	3	5	3	W_{31}(0.5048)
C32	1/3	1	3	1/3	W_{32}(0.1430)
C33	1/5	1/3	1	1/5	W_{33}(0.064)
C34	1/3	3	5	1	W_{34}(0.2876)

Note: C.R=0.07<0.1. CI=0.066 l_{max} =4.1981

Table 6. B4—C Judgment Matrix

B4	C41	C42	C43	C44	Weight
C41	1	1/3	1/9	1/2	W_{41} (0.0620)
C42	3	1	1/5	2	W_{42} (0.1761)
C43	9	5	1	5	W_{43} (0.6510)
C44	2	1/2	1/5	1	W_{44} (0.1108)

Note: C.R=0.02<0.1.   CI=0.017 l_{max} =4.053

Table 7. Total sorting of the influencing factors

Influencing factors	W				Wsum
	W_1 (0.6239)	W_2 (0.0487)	W_3 (0.2189)	W_4 (0.1085)	
C_{11}	W_{11} (0.632)				0.3943
C_{12}	W_{12} (0.149)				0.0930
C_{13}	W_{13} (0.086)				0.0540
C_{14}	W_{14} (0.1329)				0.0829
C_{21}		W_{21} (0.6370)			0.0310
C_{22}		W_{22} (0.2583)			0.0126
C_{23}		W_{23} (0.1047)			0.0050
C_{31}			W_{31} (0.5048)		0.1105
C_{32}			W_{32} (0.1430)		0.0313
C_{33}			W_{33} (0.0640)		0.0140
C_{34}			W_{34} (0.2876)		0.0630
C_{41}				W_{41} (0.0620)	0.0067
C_{42}				W_{42} (0.1761)	0.0191
C_{43}				W_{43} (0.6510)	0.0706
C_{44}				W_{44} (0.1108)	0.0120

Above judgment matrixes have better satisfied the single sorting consistency inspection, and then we will carry on the total ordering and one-time inspection, its one-time inspection is as follows:

$$CR = W_1(CI)_1 + W_2(CI)_2 + W_3(CI)_3 + W_4(CI)_4 \Big/ W_1(RI)_1 +$$

$$W_2(RI)_2 + W_3(RI)_3 + W_4(RI)_4 = 0.08 < 0.1,$$

total sorting inspection conform to test and verification.

Through the analysis towards the above factors, we can conclude influencing factors weights that influence the Heilongjiang service outsourcing. (as show in table 7.) First, seen from rule layer influencing weight proportion, policy service makes the greatest contribution to service outsourcing factors, accounting for 62.39%; followed by human resources factor; then the economic environment and the social cultural environment. Second, seen from the program layer influencing factors, the government's industry positioning makes the greatest contribution to the total goal, the government should emphasize its industry positioning while strengthening policy service. The second influencing factor is the experience and quality of distance service, which belongs to human resources influencing factors category, in order to improve the human resources factor weight on the general objective, to improve distance service quality should be primarily considered, to cultivate numbers of experienced outsourcing service personnel, and emphasize the personnel's experience and skill education in the human resources construction process.

3   Countermeasures to Develop Service Outsourcing Industry in Heilongjiang

3.1   Perfect Related Policy System

Service outsourcing as an important part of modern service industry, the governments and departments at various levels need to adjust the thought, update the conception, and pay full attention to various work related with service outsourcing industry development. Practice proves that industrial policies have a strong supporting function on industrial development, so governments at various levels, various functional departments and related enterprises should cooperate and promote it together, to develop the service outsourcing industry around the economic revitalization and industry upgrade in our province.

3.2   Increase Capital Support

Set up a special fund for the development of service outsourcing industry, earmark a fund for its specified purposes only, and improve support service outsourcing enterprise development fund proportion as far as possible in the expenditure structure of foreign funds in our province. Offer certain fund subsidies to patent application fee or patent information retrieval fee of the service outsourcing enterprises; and give certain financial support to patent project of service outsourcing enterprises in accordance with Heilongjiang patent technology industrial capital support conditions.

Increase attracting investments dynamics in a way of multi-channel, many measures, and expand the market, develop the service outsourcing industry special investment promotion activities, and cultivate service outsourcing enterprises.

3.3 Cultivate Professional Talents

Service outsourcing industry needs "pyramid" structure of talents with both high-end talent and a high quality of basic-level practitioners, to adapt to the service outsourcing industry personnel demand, we must strive to resolve actual problems such as talent shortage, talent cultivation and the disconnected with actual demand of enterprise employing, actively implement outsourcing talent cultivation project and cultivate high-quality and practical talents who can meet international standards for service outsourcing enterprises.

3.4 Implement the Brand Strategy

Encourage service outsourcing enterprises to develop independent brand construction, cultivate and develop the export famous brand and intensify protection efforts to brand products, give appropriate protection to certain popular service outsourcing enterprise brands, and develop international market with brand products. Make "Heilongjiang service" be known in service outsourcing market both at home and abroad. Increase company strength of the service outsourcing enterprises, enrich the connotation of the brand, strengthen the brand value, and also maintain the whole image of Heilongjiang brand, formulate Heilongjiang outsourcing brand strategy, set foreign propaganda target, unveil specific measures, encourage brand enterprise listing and financing and increase its ability to exploit market, encourage the brand enterprise to establish the cooperation relations with leading multinational company and form a joint venture to gain international customer resources. Establish authority BBS of the provincial and municipal level service outsourcing, build important platform for execution of brand strategy, and establish brand image. Expand brand scale, broaden the ability to pay, and promote brand popularity and international recognition of Heilongjiang service outsourcing.

3.5 Enhance Service Consciousness

The development of Heilongjiang service industry is relatively slow, some service outsourcing enterprises lacking service experience, and the service consciousness is relatively weak, can't grasp the customer psychology correctly, and then cause customers' dissatisfaction. In view of this situation, it is necessary to start from the service concept of the service outsourcing enterprise in our province, to change the competition strategy solely depended on low price in the past, let promoting service level and enhancing service quality be the law code for enterprises to improve the competitiveness. Continuously change enterprise management concepts, improve the service consciousness, increase the service efforts, and make it really start from the customers' demand, strengthen cooperation and communication with customers, and provide "customization" service for the customers according to their needs. Have periodic investigation, statistics, arrangement and analysis for customers' satisfaction, and constantly adjust the thought, innovate methods, provide more nuanced services for customers, improve service skills while improving service consciousness of service outsourcing enterprise, guarantee the quality of service, and enhance the competitiveness of enterprises.

4 Conclusion

Developing service outsourcing industry is the effective way for Heilongjiang to accelerate information industry development, optimize the industrial structure adjustment, and take a new road to industrialization. To accelerate the development of Heilongjiang service outsourcing industry, we should start from developing environment, promoting enterprises' competitiveness and integrating industrial resources to play conglomeration effect. In the aspect of optimizing the environment, we should perfect policy system of the service outsourcing industry development, strengthen capital support intensity of the service outsourcing industry, utilize the capital positively and effectively; In the aspect of promoting service outsourcing enterprise competitiveness, we should improve the service consciousness and the market maturity, drive the service outsourcing industry development, enhance the talent cultivation, comprehensive development, key support and implement brand strategies; In the aspect of integrating industrial resources, we should increase the service outsourcing base and demonstration construction, promote the whole industry development with characteristics business, create public information platform, implement co-construction mechanism among government, society and enterprises.

References

1. Michael, C.: The Outsourcing Resolution. Kaplan Business 9 (2004)
2. Grossman, G.M., Helpman, E.: Outsourcing in a Global Economy (2008)
3. Sen, R., Shahidul Islam, M.: Southeast Aisa in the Global Wave of Outsourcing: Trends, Opportunities, and Challenges. Around Southeast Asia 4, 23–25 (2005)
4. Mann, C.L.: Globalization of IT Service and White Collar Jobs: The Next Wave of Productivity Growth. International Economics Policy Briefs. Institute of International Economics, 3–11 (2004)
5. Baily, M.N., Lawrence, R. (2005). What Happened to the Great US Job Machine? The Role of Trade and Offshoring. Brookings Paper on Economic Activity (2005)
6. Jolanda, S., Hessels, A.: Innovation and international involvement of Dutch SMEs. International Journal of Entrepreneurship & Small Business 4(3), 53–54 (2007)
7. Welch, L.S.: Foreign operation methods: theory, analysis, strategy, pp. 30–32. Edward Elgar, USA (2007)

Social Welfare, Crisis, Health, Education, Financial Resources and Tracks to Return

Antonio Bazarra-Fernández

A Coruña University Hospital Trust
C/ Amparo Lopez Jean 13 4° A
15174 Culleredo, La Coruña, Spain
abazarra@udc.es

Abstract. The western and the eastern man have the same intrinsic dignity. Whatever happens in the world, somehow it is always good because it gives us the chance to learn a lesson. Meanwhile world's richest countries are mired in one deep crisis. There is a crisis in the National Health Service (NHS). The publication of the Health and Social Care Bill last week heralds dramatic changes for the NHS, which will affect the public health and social cares that are provided in the UK. The emerging economies are growing due not only to increased adoption of medical devices owing to increased health awareness, but these nations are also lucrative investment regions for multinational medical device companies to offshore business operations and production. If universal health coverage is not a political issue across the country, it is because historically speaking, the idea of political rights is more established than social rights It is not known where is the issue and where is the solution to this big and bewildering succession of events.

Keywords: Social Welfare, Health, Crisis, Resources, Education.

1 Introduction

Whatever happens in the world, somehow it is always good because it gives us the chance to learn a lesson, if we have enough humility to acknowledge our shortcomings in relation to life, health, social welfare and financial resources necessary that are required for it. "Mediocrity, perhaps, is to stand before the greatness and not realize", *Gilbert Keith Chesterton.*

When man is able to set aside cynicism, to avoid certain perspectives that hide the reality in a voluntary or involuntary way, to recognize who he really is, what he wants where he goes, and be aware of the Tucson Effect: heal, not hurt. When he is aware of his ignorance it is when he is ready to learn and then be able to accept that human life has a price. That price is a common measure for all. This measure is existing financial resources. In other words more vulgar that measure is money. Hence we often find situations like these.

Q. Zhou (Ed.): ISAEBD 2011, Part I, CCIS 208, pp. 163–169, 2011.
© Springer-Verlag Berlin Heidelberg 2011

2   Items

In this paper we consider two situations that are the extremes of the current global crisis and its induced contagion effects that have caused disruptions and extreme volatility in global financial markets and increased rates of default and bankruptcy and have already driven more than 50 million people into extreme poverty, particularly women and children. In the midst of the economic and financial bonfire of the vanities, which continues to smolder around us, it becomes even more difficult to consider the condition of extreme hardship of the poor and the people without means of subsistence who reside in distant 'exotic' lands. The financial crisis has a strong effect on people living in extreme poverty and the enjoyment of their human rights. Developing countries face especially serious consequences, as the financial and economic crisis turns into a human and development calamity. The crisis and the need for a strong multilateral response further highlight the relevance of ensuring enhanced voice and participation of developing and transition countries. The crisis offers an opportunity to move beyond the restructuring of the global financial and monetary systems.

2.1   The World's Richest Countries Are in Crisis

The U.S. Food and Drug Administration today approved denosumab (Prolia), an injectable treatment for postmenopausal women with osteoporosis who are at high risk for fractures(1) June 1 2010.

Once a medicine has been granted a Community marketing authorisation by the European Commission, the European Medicines Agency published a full scientific assessment report called a European Public Assessment Report (EPAR)(2) that approved the drug on 28th May 2010. This EPAR was last updated on 23/06/2010. This approval does not immediately make that the drug would be available in every European country because those decisions are made by individual nations, but approval by EMEA is a necessary first step before a new drug can be made available anywhere in Europe. The U.K.'s National Institute for Health and Clinical Excellence, or NICE, Wednesday the 27th of October 2010 said that recommended the Amgen's (AMGN) osteoporosis drug denosumab would be made routinely available on the publicly funded National Health Service for the postmenopausal patients who are at increased risk of osteoporotic bone fractures.

Spanish Agency of Medicines and Health Products (AEMPS) Medicines Online Information Center says: denosumab is not in the market(3), January 31 2011.

2.2   The Emerging Countries

So, Mother Nature has not made us all equal. In spite of that it is something other than human dignity which are the same for everyone. "The greatest wisdom that there is it is to know oneself", Galileo Galilei. We know it's within us. We know we want to be the best we can be to each and every one of men.

The emerging economies are not only growing due to increased adoption of medical devices owing to increased health awareness, but these nations are also lucrative investment regions for multinational medical device companies to offshore business operations and production. We can read in The Lancet: India: Towards Universal Health Coverage. Published January 11, 2011. The latest Lancet Series of papers on India's path to full health coverage reveals that a failing health system is perhaps India's greatest predicament. The papers in this Series reveal the full extent of opportunities and difficulties in Indian healthcare, by examining infectious and chronic diseases, availability of treatments and doctors, and the infrastructure to bring about universal health care by 2020(4).

India rightly brands itself incredible. The country's remarkable political, economic, and cultural transformation over the past half century has made it a geopolitical force almost equal to that of China(5).

In India, despite improvements in access to health care, inequalities are related to socioeconomic status, geography, and gender, and are compounded by high out-of-pocket expenditures, with more than three-quarters of the increasing financial burden of health care being met by households. Health-care expenditures exacerbate poverty, with about 39 million additional people falling into poverty every year as a result of such expenditures. We identify key challenges for the achievement of equity in service provision, and equity in financing and financial risk protection in India(6). If universal health coverage is not a political issue across the country, it is because historically speaking, the idea of political rights is more established in India than social rights.

India has a severe shortage of human resources for health. It has a shortage of qualified health workers and the workforce is concentrated in urban areas. Bringing qualified health workers to rural, remote, and underserved areas is very challenging. Many Indians, especially those living in rural areas, receive care from unqualified health providers. The migration of qualified allopathic doctors and nurses is substantial and further strains the system. Nurses do not have much authority or say within the health system, and the resources to train them are still inadequate. Little attention is paid during medical education to the medical and public health needs of the population, and the rapid privatisation of medical and nursing education has implications for its quality and governance(7). But India is going towards universal health coverage.

2.3 Learning from Others

"Is there anyone, in the five parts of India, who does not admire China?" asked Yi Jing in the 7th century, on returning to China after being in India for 10 years.

But comparison of China with India was not only a common pastime then, it gets a lot of attention today. And rightly so.

What, however, goes wrong in the current obsession with the India—China comparison is not the relevance of comparing China with India, but the field that is chosen for comparison.

In our times, China went towards a massive expansion of public health care shortly after the revolution. Through a governmental commitment, China came close to have universal coverage(8).

3 The Social and Economic Dangers of the Western World

It has now been almost a decade since the UK Science Media Centre (SMC) was created, after a UK House of Lords committee concluded that scientists in the country were not engaging effectively with the media. Its remit: to ensure scientists take part in media stories about science, rather than complaining about inaccurate or sensationalist coverage. Since then, the UK centre, directed by communications expert Fiona Fox, has been deemed a success by scientists and journalists alike, and sister SMCs have been set up in Australia, New Zealand, Canada, and Japan, with Denmark expected to launch in 2011(9).

There is a crisis in the National Health Service (NHS). The publication of the Health and Social Care Bill last week heralds dramatic changes for the NHS, which will affect the way public health and social care are provided in the UK. Those changes alone will have huge impact, but it is the formation of an NHS Commissioning Board, and commissioning consortia, that will once and for all remove the word "national" from the health service in England. The result, due to come into force in 2013, will be the catastrophic break up of the NHS(10).

This in turn is responded that is simply wrong to say that our reforms were not trailed before the election; contrary to your claim, the Conservative manifesto did propose.

GP-led commissioning and an independent NHS board to oversee commissioning. The Liberal Democrat manifesto proposed the abolition of strategic health authorities, increased competition, and stronger local democratic input in the NHS—all policies which have been taken forward in our plans. (11)

4 The Man as a Being Worthy

Every one is worthy but not each person is worth in the same way or equally worth to the various situations that may occur in social life in which the man is immersed. Any person with a normal mental factor could realize the evidence of the facts found in the day to day.

The same applies to countries. At present, some countries are the first and the dominating. In the future they will no longer. Then other countries that could even be the last and the dominated will became the first countries and key by value. And it has always been so, over the centuries.

And following this line of thought we can get to situations that have no relation with social welfare or health. And speaking of health could lead us to understand what is the proper functioning of a government in relation to the population that leads to one viable or not viable society.

The lack of health often is managed in a hospital. Running a hospital is similar to an enterprise, albeit more uncoordinated. Companies can be very small or very large. A state is something like a big company with its entire legal framework.

If a hospital goes wrong it will impact more on the weaker it is the patient. If a company goes wrong is going to impact more on the worker. And if a government goes wrong it will impact more on the citizens who make up that society badly governed.

5 The Man and Legislation

The western and the eastern man have the same intrinsic dignity. But the Eastern man does not have the same value?. Or it is that we must learn from them?. They are more or less worth?. What is the value?. It's the money? Adaptability?. Why the West is reeling with a financial crisis when the finances of the East rise year after year. We are facing a cyclical change in history? . Or we have a tangled social legislation, which could not defend society?. So, as examples we have the following ones: "complete regulatory collapse" allowed Philadelphia physician, to illegally abort third-trimester fetuses, sever the spinal cords of babies aborted alive with scissors, and leave a trail of injured and dead female patients in his wake over several decades, according to a grand jury report on a case that has shocked the nation.

The Pennsylvania grand jury, which released its findings last week, said it was shocked not only by the medical "mayhem" but also by a pattern of "official neglect" that extended from the state medical board to physicians at Philadelphia hospitals who treated their patients for perforated bowels and uteruses. Plenty of agencies and individuals saw numerous signs of something gone terribly wrong but failed to intervene.

Much of the grand jury's reproof was reserved for the state Department of Health (DOH), which was responsible for overseeing abortion clinics. The DOH first approved the clinic, grandly called the Women's Medical Society, to perform abortions in December 1979 after a site inspection.

This week's decision by federal district Judge Roger Vinson in Pensacola, Florida, declaring the Affordable Care Act (ACA) unconstitutional is far and away the most prominent decision issued to date in this ongoing litigation. Because this lawsuit involves about half the states, it has received the most attention. But it is only one of about two dozen legal challenges across the country. Two other federal judges (in Detroit and in Lynchburg, Virginia) have upheld the law, and one other (in Richmond, Virginia) sided with Judge Vinson on the unconstitutionality of the individual mandate to obtain health insurance(12). Of the remaining suits, more than half have been dismissed on procedural grounds, and the rest await an initial decision.

Despite the heated rhetoric in Congress about repealing and replacing the Affordable Care Act (ACA), there is a dearth of productive ideas for improving on the legislation. As a Democratic U.S. representative from Washington State, I supported the ACA, but I believe that there remain essential areas of concern that must be addressed long before 2014, when 32 million newly insured Americans will join our health care system. Our foremost task this year must be to develop a strategy to ensure the sustainability of our primary care system.

The House voted 245 to 189 to repeal the healthcare reform law known as the Affordable Care Act (ACA).

Republicans who took control of the House in last year's mid-term elections voted unanimously to erase the ACA. Three Democrats rounded out the ranks of repeal supporters.

The ACA passed both the House and Senate last year without a single GOP vote.

The facts are in dispute all around. Democrats counter that the ACA will create jobs both in the healthcare industry and the country at large, as well as reduce the deficit.

On the other side of the law is the education. The provision of education in all circumstances is a fundamental principle. The crisis in public education is well known. High dropout rates, low test scores, deficits in reading, math, and history, and inarticulate young people who do not read books are so frequently reported in the news that we have almost come to expect bad news about education. More educators are agreeing that the natural path of online and brick-and-mortar learning is to continue to blur until their separation becomes almost indecipherable. All governments say they are committed to Education for all but fail to tackle persistent inequalities based on wealth, location, gender, race, ethnicity, language and disability.

Education reforms are not reducing inequalities. Often governments have a poverty plan and an education plan and no bridge between them. Education has to be integrated into a wider poverty reduction strategy. Governments around the world have been called on to provide financial assistance to banks whose problems have arisen directly from their blindness and greed for profits.

Transacting members need to know how cooperatives are different from ordinary companies and challenge boards and executives who claim falsely that the only difference is who owns the shares or that there is no alternative to demutualisation or that by unlocking the value of the shares members will benefit.

Likewise, education and training are linked and so we have computer science is driving an economic and Cultural Revolution across the planet Earth. Sometimes it does not work. One argument heard as to why this is happening? is that educators assume computer science is being included in science, technology, engineering and math initiatives, when it actually isn't. Another may be that many students are misinformed and therefore disinterested about the type of jobs a computer science background can lead to.

And other leaders will emerge from this flawed society that will close a circle of follies. It is followed that the process must be reversed (13). Education is needed (14) since the beginning of life and this should continue during all that time (15). We are only human after all. A commitment to political education and social ethics is necessary for everyone in the world and it is to come. Because otherwise, the people will rise up and demand what belongs to, it is the dignity of personhood. We are currently looking at different uprisings in different countries which should not take place if dignity was respected. Leaders of the Egyptian democracy movement vowed to escalate their pressure for the resignation of President Hosni Mubarak, even as his government portrayed itself as already in the midst of American-approved negotiations to end the uprising. The government announced that the transition had begun with a meeting between Vice President and two representatives of the Muslim Brotherhood, the outlawed Islamist group the Egyptian government has sought to repress for many years as a threat to stability.

As protesters in Tahrir Square faced off against pro-government forces, they drew a lesson from their counterparts in Tunisia: "Advice to the youth of Egypt: Put vinegar or onion under your scarf for tear gas."

The exchange on Facebook was part of a remarkable two-year collaboration that has given birth to a new force in the Arab world, a pan-Arab youth movement dedicated to spreading democracy in a region without it. Young Egyptian and Tunisian activists brainstormed on the use of technology to evade surveillance, commiserated about torture and traded practical tips on how to stand up to rubber bullets and organize barricades.

All this should be with a lot of alertness and prudence in this hazardous situation so that there is no winners or losers, gaining in education and dignity, aiming a commitment to political education and social ethics and so also health to arrive for every one in the world.

References

1. Retrieved from
   http://www.fda.gov/NewsEvents/Newsroom/PressAnnouncements/ucm214150.htm
2. Retrieved from
   http://www.ema.europa.eu/ema/index.jsp?curl=pages/medicines/landing/epar_search.jsp&murl=menus/medicines/medicines.jsp&mid=WC0b01ac058001d125&jsenabled=true
3. Retrieved from https://sinaem4.agemed.es/consaem/fichasTecnicas.do?metodo=buscar
4. Jacob John, T., Dandona, L., Sharma, V.P., Manish Kakkar, M.: Continuing challenge of infectious diseases in India. Lancet 377(9761), 252–269 (2011)
5. Horton, R., Dasa, P.: Indian health: the path from crisis to progress. Lancet 377(9761), 181–183 (2011)
6. Balarajan, Y., Selvaraj, S., Subramanian, S.V.: Health care and equity in India. Lancet (2011), doi:10.1016/S0140-6736(10)61894-6
7. Rao, M., Rao, K.D., Shiva Kumar, A.K., Chatterjee, M., Sundararaman, T.: Human resources for health in India. Lancet 377(9765), 587–598 (2011)
8. Sen, A.: Learning from others. Lancet 377(9761), 200–201 (2011)
9. Kirby, T.: Science Media Centres go global. Lancet 377(9762), 285 (2011)
10. The end of our National Health Service. Lancet 377(9763), 353 (2011), doi:10.1016/S0140-6736(11)60110-4
11. Howe, L.: The end of the National Health Service? Lancet 377(9765), 551 (2011)
12. Hall, M.A.: Health care reform–what went wrong on the way to the courthouse. N. Engl. J. Med. 364(4), 295–297 (2011)
13. Robert, F., Leibenluft, J.D.: ACOs and the Enforcement of Fraud, Abuse, and Antitrust Laws. N. Engl. J. Med. 364, 99–101 (2011)
14. Office of Inspector General, Office of Evaluation and Inspections. Medicare and Medicaid fraud and abuse training in medical education (October 2010), Retrieved from http://www.oig.hhs.gov/oei/reports/OEI-01-10-00140.pdf
15. Taitsman, J.K.: Educating Physicians to Prevent Fraud, Waste, and Abuse. N. Engl. J. Med. 364, 102–103 (2011)

Goals and Principles of Software Engineering

Xiaogang Zhu[1] and Huaiming Zhao[2]

[1] Nanchang University, 330000, Jiangxi, China
[2] Jiangxi Industry Polytechnic College, 330000, Jiangxi, China
XiaogangZhu2011@126.com

Abstract. As computers have been used more and more widely in the information era, and more and more people have been aware of the value of them, software engineering came to being inevitably. Various kinds of software engineering are the targets of project development. However, the whole operation process of software is not as easy as what you imagine. In order to create more use and economic values, following the goals and principles of software engineering development strictly is of vital importance. This essay focuses on analyses of the goals and principles of software engineering development.

Keywords: software engineering, development, goals, principles.

1 Software Services Targets—Users

People's income level has been improved with the development of social economy. Computers become more and more common in people's daily life. During this process, many related products are developed to satisfy various demands from different users. It can lead a new industry and create more economic values. The development of software engineering should be user-based.

1.1 Master User Information

Market demand is the fundamental direction of software development enterprises. Profit can only be made when the software is user-based. Nowadays, many kinds of software such as downloading, antivirus, browsing and games are all available in the market. So user research is necessary before the development of new software to catch actual market information. What's more, deep analyses of the users are of great help to the development of new software.

1.2 Encourage Users to Participate

Software engineering is a technology-based industry while at the same time user-based. Modern software design promotes the idea that users should be "put into" the software and vote for product representative to provide more suggestion. Enterprises can select user representatives from antivirus, music and videos to get to know the actual need of them, for example.

Q. Zhou (Ed.): ISAEBD 2011, Part I, CCIS 208, pp. 170–176, 2011.

1.3 Create User Groups

Quality is determined by professional. Software development requires professional knowledge. And the whole process of development needs professional theories and skills. We can create user groups from the elite in the industry to fulfill different tasks of development and take optimization measures to achieve upgrade processing of software products. Besides, users' feedback can also help to examine their shortcomings.

1.4 Ensure Customer Satisfaction

To make users choose some kind of software, quality counts, which can also help to win good reputation is the software market. In order to maximum the customer satisfaction, software developers should pay more attention to the quality to ensure practicability, reliability, safety and efficiency. Besides, some unique features such as automatic updates and regularly upgrading can also allow users to enjoy the software at different times.

2 Development Objectives Basis—"Theory"

As a branch of computer science, the development of software becomes various with its own unique features. While developing, we have to examine the final purpose in an objective way, which can ensure the process to be orderly. From a professional theory of viewpoint, goals we need to establish are as follows during the process of software engineering development.

2.1 Allow to Modify While Remain the Same

No software can be developed successfully in the first time. After completion much software must be used to simulate before putting to the market. The existing of unknowns requires software to be modified so that shortcomings are dealt with in time. However, the original structure of software should not be made complicated during the revision process, which is difficult to achieve.

2.2 Convenient Operation to Meet Customer Needs

Nowadays, electronic products change very fast in the market and the computer products are regularly updated, upgraded and transformed. Software is the internal operation tool of the computer system which can be used to draw, play music and videos. When developing the software, we have to keep in mind that it should adapt to the conditions of computer operation system. Program design and language code should match the user's operation system so that conflicts can be avoided.

2.3 Optimize Structure While Maintain Efficiency

Software developers must be familiar with the theories of software engineering. Otherwise, quality of software will be greatly reduced. Designers should improve and optimize the internal structure of software, not to be too simple, nor to be too difficult. Embedded computer system, for example, is usually used in the control of playing music, which can be referred to in Figure 1. If the internal design is unreasonable, the audio will fail when software system control is used.

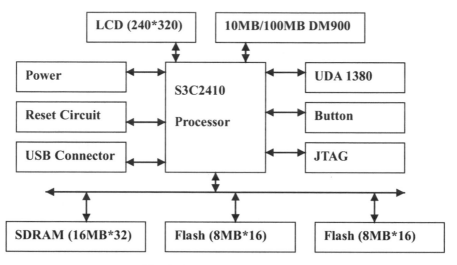

Fig. 1. Embedded System Control

2.4 Collaborative Operation and Mutual Compatible

Generally speaking, computer users will install more than one kind of software in the same computer, which requires higher compatibility. So software designers should consider comprehensively so that different software can be compatible and improve each other. For example, antivirus software and firewall both belong to tools that prevent computers from danger. Developers should make sure that there will be no conflicts between these two.

3 Key Objective—Use

The final purpose of software engineering development is to satisfy users' needs and make software plays an ideal role in our daily life. Besides knowing the objective theoretically, we have to focus on the practical application, regarding the objectives of software engineering development from different aspects. Objectives we need to pay attention to include the following.

3.1 Focus on Software and Improve Quality

Software is a one of the most common types encountered in software engineering. These components refer to independent modules in theory, function and operation. The biggest advantage of software is that it can be widely used in various occasions, which can also illustrate the value of its development. We must ensure its well structure, the accuracy of coding as well as the low cost of time or space so that quality can be improved.

3.2 Software Maintenance and Long-Term Usage

Maintenance is the essential feature of any software and it is also the most important objective of software engineering. Errors and failure will inevitably occur during the usage, which requires a platform to maintain it, where error correction and adjustment are available in time. Software maintenance can reduce the number of purchases and make long-term usage possible.

3.3 Portable Software Language

In order to meet the performance of computers and customers' need, we have to transfer the software from one computer to another, which require portable language that can adapt do different operation environment. For example, there are two versions of Microsoft Word—2003 and 2007. The former is used in lower operation systems, while the latter requires higher level system. When files of Word 2007 version can't be opened in lower level systems, software transplantation is necessary.

3.4 Follow Up Software Problems Regularly

Combining different structures of software and performance can add related tracking performance, which is the essential objective of the software development. Tracking software can trace detection of software. Once software operation fails, software tracking can determine the reasons as soon as possible and provide guides to help solve the problem. For example, we have to record the events and command signals when doing software testing to provide basis for later problem solving.

4 Concern of the Development Process—Principle

Principles of software engineering development should be followed throughout the design, development and management of the whole process. And de defined principles should take software, users and developers into account. Software engineering development will be much easier if basic principles are grasped. The author summarizes four principles based on long-term experience on software engineering.

4.1 Principle of Design

Designing is the preliminary work of software development. Only by using scientific way can we ensure smooth later work. During the design period, developers should consider both the software and the hardware, choosing the ones suitable for computer operation. Besides, developers should also analyze the compatibility of the software with other to avoid conflicts. (Figure 2)

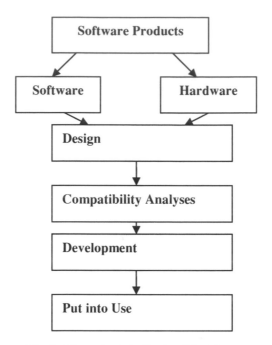

Fig. 2. Schematic of the Design Principle

4.2 Principle of Methodology

The choice of development ways can lead to two aspects of functions—software structure such as coding, programming and language and time consuming. If the method is adopted wrongly, complexity will be added to the software structure. Thus, various problems will occur. Besides, if the structure is too complex, it will take more time to sign and develop and it will be more difficult to modify. Whatever design or develop, choosing the right methodology can shorten the time devoted.

4.3 Principle of Cost

From the viewpoint of developers, the purpose on investment on hi-tech products is to get profit. This requires strict control of cost investment to avoid poor sales caused by cost. Firstly, structure should be simplified. Secondly, efficiency should be improved so that less staffs participate in the development of software engineering, which can prevent human resources, machinery and properties from overused.

4.4 Principle of Management

No rules, no standards. Good management can make good and smooth working environment possible. And the efficiency of software engineering management determines the efficient use of resources so that ideal operation value can be created and computer users' needs are meet. Software enterprises should build scientific management system to fulfill tasks of software development, while their staffs should clear development objectives.

5   Details Paid Attention to—Examination

Software engineering projects should be operated strictly and should pay attention to some details, which can ensure earlier development and use of the software. Recently, many developers neglect the details, thus many problems occur. The details need paying attention to are as follows.

5.1   Life Circle

For software engineering, its development time is limited while there are lots of tasks to be finished. Developers should pay more attention to the life circle of the products and try to extend their span, which can lay foundation for the next style and be more convenient to use and maintain the products. In this way, more users will be won.

5.2   Error Detection

According to the research, 67.4% of the errors occur before coding. If there is any modification at this period of time, cost will increase greatly. On the other hand, this manifests the importance of error detection. Software engineers should examine the tasks regularly and pay highly attention to the errors occurring before coding to reduce losses.

5.3   Technological Innovation

Users will upgrade the software after a period of time to meet their growing needs. Early stage of software development structure had developed to be technology target-oriented. Programming languages have developed from Generation 1 to Generation 4, which indicates the necessity of going the road of technological innovation that founds basis on higher level of software development.

5.4   Human Resources Strategy

Groups formed in enterprises should consist of talent from three aspects—professional, quality and ethics. Thus the R & D team is of high level, high efficiency and high standard. Streamlining the team can not only improve efficiency, but also prevent the project from being disclosed, which ensures the enterprises to act actively.

6   Conclusion

Software engineering is the outcome of the diversity of the social economy market. This new industry creates huge commercial value for enterprises and provides multi-performance for users. We should set up objectives based on facts and follow the principles mentioned above. Only by taking as many as aspects into consideration can we have more values created by software engineering.

References

1. Dong, S.: Software Quality and Management Reliability Research in Modern Software Engineering. Computer Learning 32(13), 53–55 (2009)
2. Jia, L.: Realization of Control Technology in Dynamic Structure Data Reports in VFP. Computer and Information Technology 11(6), 92–93 (2008)
3. Hu, L.: Software Quality Engineering and Technology Analyses in Market Economy System. Newspaper of Hebei Academy of Science 18(4), 29–31 (2009)
4. Wang, Y.: Analyses of Information Hiding Program of the C++ Header. Information Technology 9(2), 103–104 (2008)
5. Liu, W.: Development of the Systematic Software of Solid Rocket Motor Reliability Design. Computer Technology 27(19), 34–36 (2009)
6. Zhou, X.: Summary of Principles Needed during Software Engineering Development. Computer Engineering and Applications 30(12), 87–88 (2009)

An Empirical Study on Foreign Exchange Assets and Monetary Base Endogeneity of China Based on the Monetary Base Supply Structure

Shui Qing Yang[1], Peng Zhang[2], and Dong Wang[3]

[1] School of Economy and Trade, Hunan University
Changsha, China
[2] School of Property, Construction and Project Management, RMIT University
Melbourne, Australia
[3] Department of Civil Engineering, Qingdao Technological University Qindao College
Qing Dao, China
287019936@qq.com

Abstract. Based on the monetary base supply structure, the relationship between monetary base and its components from December 1999 to August 2010 of China are explored by cointegration analysis, Granger causality, VAR models and other methods. The results show that issuing notes and withdrawing re-lending financial institutions have been important means of hedging the increasing net foreign assets, net foreign assets is the main Granger cause of the changes in monetary base and China's current money supply is endogenous obvious. Therefore, the government should widen the RMB exchange rate floating space and promote RMB internationalization process, try to solve the problem of increasing foreign exchange assets fundamentally.

Keywords: Monetary Base Supply Structure; Foreign Exchange Assets; Monetary Endogeneity.

1 Introduction

Mundell-Fleming model showed that under the fixed exchange rate system, monetary authorities change the supply of monetary base passively to maintain a stable exchange rate, which could bring open economy's endogeneity to the money supply. [1][2] Nominal price stickiness cannot guarantee the adjustment of monetary policy on output and the effect on the real economy. [3] The endogeneity of money supply has been experimentally verified by various scholars in different ways. [3][4][5][6][7] This paper will draw on the previous researches to create a VAR model of money supply based on the monetary base supply structure. In addition, this model will be adopted to investigate the impact of huge foreign exchange assets on the gross monetary base and its components, under the current floating exchange rate regime in China, so as to provide a valuable reference for the policy maker of China.

Q. Zhou (Ed.): ISAEBD 2011, Part I, CCIS 208, pp. 177–183, 2011.
© Springer-Verlag Berlin Heidelberg 2011

2 Model and Data Collection

Theoretically, the monetary base reflects the central bank's liabilities. It could be directly controlled by the central bank. However, when a country's base money is put into circulation mainly passively, the country's money supply will be endogenous. According to the principle of assets equal liabilities, basic money supply structure could be divided into for aspects: net foreign assets (NFA), financial institutions re-lending (FRL), net claims of government debt, net (NCG) and other net assets (NEA). This will select the monetary base (MB) and its four components as indicators. The net foreign assets and financial institutions re-lending are the two main elements for China's monetary base release. Before 1994, money supply endogeneity mainly appeared as the financial institutions re-loaning is the main channel for releasing the base money. It could be caused by the "Contrary Forced Mechanism", which is the result of economy of shortage. With the openness of the Chinese economy, the net foreign assets has been instead of financial institutions re-lending and become the No.1 elements of base money since 2002. By the end of 2009, net foreign assets accounted for the monetary base as high as 127.63%. It indicates that money supply endogeneity shows new forms of presentation in an open economy. In order to maintain the RMB exchange rate stability, the NCG and FRL take the role of hedging the increase of net foreign assets to make the volume of base money depends on the foreign exchange market conditions.

The central bank balance sheet data is from the division of statistical inquiry of People's Bank of China. The total sample interval is the monthly data from December 1999 to August 2010. Since July 21, 2005, China began to implement a market-based, with reference to a basket of currencies, managed floating exchange rate system, in hence to establish a more flexible RMB exchange rate mechanism. In order to compare the difference of money supply channels between before and after the reform, the samples are divided into three intervals: from December 1999 to July 2005, from August 2005 to August 2010 and from December 1999 to August 2010. In this paper, the quantitative analysis software is EViews6.0.

Vector autoregression Model (VAR) is an econometric model used to capture the evolution and the interdependencies between multiple time series, generalizing the unvaried AR models. All the variables in a VAR are treated symmetrically by including for each variable an equation explaining its evolution based on its own lags and the lags of all the other variables in the model. Based on this feature, VAR models could be used as a theory-free method to estimate economic relationships, thus being an alternative to the "incredible identification restrictions" in structural models. [8] This paper will test the stability of MB, NFA, FRL, NCG and NEA by unit root test, cointegration test. After that, error correction model will be generated. In addition, Granger causality test will be adopted to determine the main elements of impacting the supply of base money, and distinguish the endogenous and exogenous variables of VAR model. Because the NEA for these three periods are all exogenous variables after testing, it does not need to use the lag order. Finally, the VAR model distinguishing endogenous and exogenous variables for these three periods could be generated as follows:

$$MB_t = c_1 + \sum_{i=1}^{k} \alpha_{1i} MB_{t-i} + \sum_{i=1}^{k} \beta_{1i} NFA_{t-i} + \sum_{i=1}^{k} \chi_{1i} FRA_{t-i} + \sum_{i=1}^{k} \delta_{1i} NCG_{t-i} + \phi_{11} NEA_{t-1} + \varepsilon_{1t} \quad (1)$$

$$NFA_t = c_2 + \sum_{i=1}^{k} \alpha_{2i} MB_{t-i} + \sum_{i=1}^{k} \beta_{2i} NFA_{t-i} + \sum_{i=1}^{k} \chi_{2i} FRA_{t-i} + \sum_{i=1}^{k} \delta_{2i} NCG_{t-i} + \phi_{21} NEA_{t-1} + \varepsilon_{2t} \quad (2)$$

$$FRA_t = c_3 + \sum_{i=1}^{k} \alpha_{3i} MB_{t-i} + \sum_{i=1}^{k} \beta_{3i} NFA_{t-i} + \sum_{i=1}^{k} \chi_{3i} FRA_{t-i} + \sum_{i=1}^{k} \delta_{3i} NCG_{t-i} + \phi_{31} NEA_{t-1} + \varepsilon_{3t} \quad (3)$$

$$NCG_t = c_4 + \sum_{i=1}^{k} \alpha_{4i} MB_{t-i} + \sum_{i=1}^{k} \beta_{4i} NFA_{t-i} + \sum_{i=1}^{k} \chi_{4i} FRA_{t-i} + \sum_{i=1}^{k} \delta_{4i} NCG_{t-i} + \phi_{41} NEA_{t-1} + \varepsilon_{4t} \quad (4)$$

3 Results and Findings

3.1 Cointegration Test and Error Correction Model

ADF test method is used to do unit root test for the five time series variables. The results showed that the ADF values of MB, NFA, FRL, NCG and NEA are all greater than the threshold of 5%. It means all of them are un-stabile. After the first order difference, the value of ADF is lower than the threshold of 5%. It means they are stabile. Therefore, these five variable is the first order entire single variable. According to the previous test results, five sequences entire single order are same. Therefore, the cointegration test could be used for them to determine whether the five non-stationary series have the long-term equilibrium relationship. Cointegration test results show that MB, NFA, FRL, NCG, and NEA have the long-term equilibrium relationship in these three periods. In addition, according to Granger theorem, first-order error correction model could be generated. And the results show that apart from coefficient of the error correction term from the first period does notpass the test of significance, all the others pass the test. The reason is that before the reform on RMB exchange rate, U.S. dollar is stared only, RMB exchange rate the lack of flexibility and the long time balance of market supply and demand is constrained by government. After the reform, these problems are solved in a certain extend.

All the coefficients of the error correction term are negative. It means all the models are in line with the reverse correction mechanism. The value of error correction term reflects the adjustment degree of deviation from the long-run equilibrium. When the short-term fluctuations deviate from the long-run equilibrium, in the second and third period, the errors of the non-equilibrium of NFA, FRL, NCG and NEA will adjust the MB's supply as the degree of 1.036 and 1.034.

Table 1. First order error correction model

Time	Error Correction Model	R^2	DW
1999.12 -2005.7	$\Delta MB_t = \Delta NFA_t + \Delta FRL_t + \Delta NCG_t + \Delta NEA_t - 0.0083ecm_{t-1}$ (0.0000) (0.0000) (0.0000) (0.0000) (0.6274)	1.0	2.87
2005.8 -2010.8	$\Delta MB_t = \Delta NFA_t + \Delta FRL_t + \Delta NCG_t + \Delta NEA_t - 1.036ecm_{t-1}$ (0.0000) (0.0000) (0.0000) (0.0000) (0.0000)	1.0	2.00
1999.12 -2010.8	$\Delta MB_t = \Delta NFA_t + \Delta FRL_t + \Delta NCG_t + \Delta NEA_t - 1.034ecm_{t-1}$ (0.0000) (0.0000) (0.0000) (0.0000) (0.0000)	1.0	1.99

Note: (•) is the P statistic

3.2 Granger Causality Test

Granger causality test could identify the impact between MB, NFA, FRL, NCG and NEA. Test results could be summarized as bellow.

Firstly, the net foreign assets are the main reason of the changes on the base money supply in the three periods. After the exchange rate reform in 2005, the percentage of net foreign assets in the base money supply increased continuously. And the significance of net foreign assets to the changes on the monetary base is improved. For example, when the significance level is 1%, Granger cause is the only reason that central bank net foreign assets cause the changes in base money. If Granger causality exists between variables, the causality transport phenomena could exist between these variables.

In addition, two-way Granger causality exists in these three periods between government net clams and net foreign assets. Due to the rapid increase of foreign exchange assets, Government issues central bank bills to hedge against the excess liquidity which is caused by the increase of foreign exchange reserves, and releases the endogenous stress of money supply. After that, the balance of the central bank bills will be accumulated continuously. And the proportion of account for the base money is increasing ceaselessly, which could increase its significance on the base money.

Furthermore, the net foreign exchange assets are the Granger reason of financial institutions re-loaning after the reform. And the government net claims is the Granger reason of financial institutions re-loaning before and after the reform. It means with the development of bills, the excess reserves of commercial banks are a significant increase. The financial institutions re-loaning is retracted in order to take back the base money, which reduce the percentage of financial institutions re-loaning in the base money and reduce the impact on base money as well.

Table 2. Results of Granger causality test

H0	1999.12-2005.7		2005.8-2010.8		1999.12-2010.8	
	F	P	F	P	F	P
NFA does not Granger Cause MB	4.760	0.012	8.255	0.001	10.64	5E-05
MB does not Granger Cause NFA	0.413	0.663	1.227	0.301	3.676	0.028
FRL does not Granger Cause MB	0.080	0.923	0.565	0.571	0.648	0.524
MB does not Granger Cause FRL	0.367	0.694	1.090	0.3434	0.199	0.819
NCG does not Granger Cause MB	10.56	0.000	3.242	0.046	7.214	0.001
MB does not Granger Cause NCG	5.117	0.009	0.061	0.940	1.810	0.168
NEA does not Granger Cause MB	0.608	0.548	0.565	0.571	1.988	0.141
MB does not Granger Cause NEA	4.006	0.024	2.143	0.127	2.150	0.121
NFA does not Granger Cause NCG	9.834	0.000	3.989	0.078	3.731	0.026
NCG does not Granger Cause NFA	3.617	0.033	5.182	0.008	14.62	2E-06
NFA does not Granger Cause FRL	1.211	0.305	3.316	0.043	0.344	0.709
FRL does not Granger Cause NFA	0.403	0.670	1.716	0.189	6.909	0.001
NCG does not Granger Cause FRL	2.468	0.094	3.712	0.030	1.487	0.230
FRL does not Granger Cause NCG	1.873	0.163	0.918	0.405	2.102	0.126

3.3 VAR Model

According to the time period, three VAR Models could be generated. Before and after the reform, the coefficients of MB (-1), NEA and NFA (-1) are Stable. And the impact of NFA (-1) on MB is greater than 0.6. It means foreign net assets impacts base money in a big extent, which is the same with the result of Granger causality test. However, after the reform, the coefficients of FRL (-1) and NCG (-1) changed significantly, which mainly reflected in the reduce of the impact of financial institutions re-loaning on base money. And the impact has changed from positive to negative. The negative impact of government net claims on base money was increasing at the same time. It shows that before the reform, base money increased dramatically after being negative impacted by financial institutions re-loaning. After the reform, financial institutions re-loaning takes part responsibility to hedge the increase of foreign net assets.

Before the reform, money base supply is mainly impacted by the financial institutions re-loaning and foreign net assets. After the reform, central bank expanded the scale of bills issued to hedge the increase of foreign net assets. The increase of the percentage of bills on base money makes its negative impact to base money get improved. However, from the long term perspective, with the bills to fall due, the new pressure of return of capital and the rising cost of bills issued will emerge. In this sense, it is not effective to issue bills for adjusting the base money. For the view of long term, the impact of bills issued on the base money will be neutral.

Expression of VAR Model from December 1999 to July 2005:

$$MB = 0.3215 * MB(-1) - 0.015 * NCG(-1) + 0.4550 * FRL(-1)$$
$$(0.1470) \qquad (0.1915) \qquad (0.1865)$$
$$[2.1865] \qquad [0.0780] \qquad [2.4402]$$
$$+ 0.6163 * NFA(-1) + 0.6325 * NEA + 4763.2$$
$$(0.1487) \qquad (0.0979) \quad (3225.5)$$
$$[4.1438] \qquad [4.7644] \quad [1.4798]$$

Expression of VAR Model from August 2005 to August 2010:

$$MB = 0.3054 * MB(-1) - 0.2908 * NCG(-1) - 0.1924 * FRL(-1)$$
$$(0.1485) \qquad (0.1528) \qquad (0.2985)$$
$$[2.0565] \qquad [1.9031] \qquad [-0.6445]$$
$$+ 0.6033 * NFA(-1) + 0.5549 * NEA + 24091.95$$
$$(0.1350) \qquad (0.1426) \qquad (8426.77)$$
$$[4.4683] \qquad [3.8930] \qquad [2.8590]$$

Expression of VAR Model from December 1999 to August 2010:

$$MB = 0.3271 * MB(-1) - 0.2963 * NCG(-1) + 0.2165 * FRL(-1)$$
$$(0.1006) \qquad (0.1048) \qquad (0.1375)$$
$$[3.2521] \qquad [2.8293] \qquad [1.5741]$$
$$+ 0.6073 * NFA(-1) + 0.5091 * NEA + 10162.6$$
$$(0.0933) \qquad (0.0930) \qquad (2847.3)$$
$$[6.5123] \qquad [5.4724] \qquad [3.5692]$$

Note: (•) is standard deviation. [•] is "t".

4 Conclusion and Suggestion

Based on the monetary base supply structure, this paper explores the relationship between monetary base and its components from December 1999 to August 2010 of China by adopting the Cointegration analysis, Granger causality, VAR models and other methods. The key findings are: Cointegration test results show that MB, NFA, FRL, NCG, and NEA have the long-term equilibrium relationship in these three periods; when the short-term fluctuations deviate from the long-run equilibrium, in the second and third period, the errors of the non-equilibrium of NFA, FRL, NCG and NEA will adjust the MB's supply; the net foreign assets is the main reason of the changes on the base money supply in the three periods; two-way Granger causality exists in these three periods between government net clams and net foreign assets between; with the development of bills, the excess reserves of commercial banks is a significant increase; the increase of the percentage of bills on base money makes its negative impact to base money get improved; and for the view of long term, the impact of bills issued on the base money will be neutral. According to the above, some suggestions could be summarized as bellow:

- Further expand the RMB exchange rate floating space and reduce the frequency of central bank intervention in the market;
- Increase the impact of market supply and demand on the exchange rate mechanism and give full play to commercial banks in the foreign exchange market;
- Increase the flexibility of exchange rate s to reduce the endogeneity of base money supply and improve the effectiveness of monetary policy;
- Expand the operation space of central bank open market operations tool, and the government bond market;
- Moderately open capital account and regulate the money multiplier;
- Reduce the incremental of foreign net assets by encourage Chinese companies invest in overseas and promote the internationalization process of RMB
- Abandon the target of base money supply and look for other target.

5   Future Research

This paper adopted VAR Model to investigate the impact of huge foreign exchange assets on the gross monetary base and its components, under the current floating exchange rate regime in China. Base money supply is also subject to other macroeconomic factors. The problems of keep base money supply active and reduce the impact of foreign exchange reserve on monetary policy need to be discussed deeply.

Acknowledgments. This paper is one of the initial results of the National Social Science Fund Project "The research on RMB exchange rate, trade surplus and the money supply"(09BJL043).

References

1. Mundell, R.A.: The Monetary Dynamics of International Adjustment under Fixed and Flexible Exchange Rates. Quarterly Journal of Economics 74, 227–257 (1960)
2. Fleming, J.M.: Domestic Financial Policies under Fixed and under Floating Exchange Rates. International Monetary Fund 9, 369–379 (1962)
3. Ireland, P.N.: Endogenous money or sticky prices? Journal of Monetary Economics 50, 1623–1648 (2003)
4. Wan, J.Q., Xu, T.: The Endogeneity of Money Supply and the Efficiency of Monetary Policy. Economic Research Journal 3, 40–45 (2001)
5. Yue, Y.D., Zhang, X.: Empirical Research on the Impact of Foreign Exchange Reserve on the Money Base in China. World Economy Study 1, 48–53 (2007)
6. Huang, X., Yu, D.: Study of the Endogencity of China's Money Supply in the Current International Monetary System. Journal of Zhongnan University of Economics and Law 4, 53–63 (2009)
7. Liu, Z.Z., Liang, J., Liu, B.: The Empirical Research on the Relationship between China's Trade Surplus and Money Supply after Foreign Exchange Rate System Reform. Tong Ji Yu Jue Ce 3, 117–120 (2010)
8. Enders, W.: Applied Econometric Time Series, 2nd edn. John Wiley & Sons, Chichester (2003)

The Research on the Effect of Farmers Employment Creation Based on Agriculture Industry Cluster

Yanrong Wang

School of Economic and Management, Anhui Agriculture University,
Hefei, Anhui, China
jxwyr@163.com

Abstract. Farmers employment is the key point to promote the sustainable economic development of China, and is an important foundation for building a harmonious society. The paper through theory and case method, from three perspective of the effect of agricultural production, farmers start their own businesses, non-agricultural employment, and using Agricultural Industrial Cluster in Anhui province as examples to illustrate the Agricultural industry cluster can solve the employment problems of farmers, and through analysis of case worth considering, proposing the corresponding countermeasures.

Keywords: Agricultural cluster, farmers employment, rural surplus labor.

1 Introduction

China is a large agricultural nation, the "three rural issues" is related to social stability, economic development and national prosperity, and the essential core of "three rural issues" is the farmer's employment problem. In 2008, agricultural practitioners of rural labor force in our country is about 2.965 billion people, rural surplus labor is roughly in 0.7 billion ~ 120 million[1] and farmers unemployment problem becomes more and more serious. Therefore, expanding China farmer's employment in multi-channel is demanding prompt solution, which not only has a decisive impact on our country's agricultural development, but also has the great significance for the smooth advancing the industrialization, the urbanization and modernization. However, how to solve farmers employment problem? It is a systematic project, needs social efforts and support from every field, the solution also shows diversity, this paper investigates the effect of agriculture industry cluster for the farmers' employment problem. At present, although there are a lot of research about industry cluster in domestic and overseas, they mainly concentrated in the concept, characteristics, classification of industrial cluster and analyzing countermeasures of developing industrial cluster, and mostly rest on industrial economic management and geography, etc, to explore, seldom put it in agricultural economy and rural development to study, while modern agricultural competition is

---

[1] Source: development research center of the state council, the office of peasant worker of the state council, the research of "peasant worker's working farmer's twelfth five-year development plan ".

Q. Zhou (Ed.): ISAEBD 2011, Part I, CCIS 208, pp. 184–190, 2011.

mainly rely on industrial clusters, and it is an inevitable trend for the agricultural management developing a higher level to promote the advantage agricultural processing enterprises to advantage agriculture and advantage region forming a cluster. Therefore, in this article, we insist on the latitude of scientific development outlook, research the development of agricultural industrial cluster to add way for promoting rural employment.

2 Literature Review

Agriculture industry cluster, as a new industrial spatial organization form, the cluster in space forms flexible network cooperation organisms containing farmers, enterprises, intermediary, market and government. Agricultural industrial cluster is an important channel to absorb rural employment, but at present, there are fewer circles about the influence of agricultural industrial cluster for farmers' employment in academic and the article is mainly about the following three aspects:

Through empirical analysis, proving the role of industrial cluster for farmers employment. For example, Su Yongzhao (2010) taking employment location entropy as index to judge the employment creation ability of industrial cluster, make the empirical analysis for the create employment effect of the main industry cluster in Jiangsu province, and the results showed that the all degree of the cluster in food manufacturing, agricultural and sideline food processing industry is reducing, effect of creating employment is down [1]; Shi Wen (2007) takes Guangdong province as an example, through data analysis method, analyzes the promoting function of industrial cluster for rural labor force transformation and employment [2]. This type of research certifies whether the industry cluster and labor employment existing relationships, but did not analyze how the industrial cluster creates jobs.

Through qualitative analysis, explaining employment creation and employment transfer effect of agricultural industrial cluster. For example, Huang Haiping (2009) from 7aspects, such as extending employment chains and so on, analyzed the employment creation effect of the agricultural industrial cluster, and puts forward some policy suggestions to solving rural labor employment [3]. Liu Yuqing (2008) in hebei province, as an example, this paper proposes the development of labor-intensive industries case group, low cost industrial cluster with special characteristics, private type industrial cluster enterprise to promote rural surplus labor employment [4]. Tan Jianxin (2008) thinks that agriculture industry cluster enterprise has higher Labor productivity, and then encourages other enterprises go to the local cluster to provide more job opportunities for local farmers, lift contractor employment, be helpful for the transfer of rural power [5]. This type of research is about the agricultural industry agglomeration and farmers' employment, but does not reflect the logical relationship between them lacking of argument.

This paper employs theories and cases method, from three perspectives: agricultural production driving effects, farmers self-employed and non-farm jobs. Taking Anhui province agriculture industry gathering area as an example, it explains that the agricultural industrial concentration can promote the solving of farmers employment problem, and pertinently put forward some suggestions about how does agricultural industrial agglomeration achieve rural employment better.

3 Analysis of Create Employment Effect

3.1 Agricultural Production Creating More Employment Opportunities

Leading enterprise promoting farmer production

Agricultural industrial cluster forming a pattern is leading enterprises prompting [6]. Giving full play to leading enterprises to exploit market, guide the production deepening processing, supporting service function, achieve integration of producing, processing, and selling, through "factory + base + farmer", "company + peasant household", ordering production mode, etc, bring farmers into agricultural production and processing system, and to establish good benefit coupling relationship farmers. Through the development of the agriculture leading enterprise, it greatly promotes solving the local farmer's employment problem, not only lets farmers obtain benefits of production links, but also can share profit of processing and circulation links, thus makes farmers richer.

Radiation driving effects of leading enterprise is obvious. By 2010, Anhui province formed many different types of leading enterprises prompting gathering area such as Huaibei food industry, Xuancheng poultry processing, Bozhou Chinese herbal medicine processing and so on, the leading enterprise promoting 40 million farmers' employment. Taking grain and oil processing industry agglomeration in Feidong city, Anhui province as example, this gathering area gather Anhui Yan Zhi Fang Food, Anhui Kaili Cereals, Oils and Foodstuffs, Anhui Yan Zhuang Grease and a number of provincial agriculture industry leading enterprises, implement pre-ordered agriculture, drive 150,000 farmers households, the farmers' average income increasing 3500 Yuan.

Brand effect driving farmers' production

The development of modern agriculture is inevitable the resource predominance in certain areas, market-oriented, industrial cluster from the resource advantage to industry and brand advantages. And when agricultural industrial agglomeration developing to a relatively mature degree, it can form agricultural geographic marks, namely the agricultural products mark with special geographical origin and of the reputation and quality related to the origin. According to statistics, when agricultural gain getting geographic marks, the market sale price will increase 20% to 30% generally in average. Therefore, agricultural geographic marks can not only improve the competitiveness of agricultural products, but also can promote farmers' planning enthusiasm and largely promote employment.

Take the pecan of Ningguo in Anhui province as an example, with registration of each pecan brand, such as "Zhanshi", "Yupan Mountain", and "Shan Li Ren" and so on, the pecan industry of Ningguo start the development road with normalization and industrialization. In 2009, "Ningguo pecan" formally applies to be the geographic marks and was classified as a national pilot demonstration projects by ministry of agriculture. The manufacturing district, ten towns, such as Nanji, Wanjia, Hule and so on, was protected by geographical mark, economic forest area of pecan, reaches 30 million acres, the annual output reaches 3.5 billion driving 3 million farmers families and solving the employment problem 1/3 peasant families.

3.2 Pushing Farmers Do Pioneering Work Independently

Founding modern agricultural enterprises

Due to the formation of agricultural industry cluster, it strengthened the cooperation with universities and institutes and founded many research institutes, it can form knowledge outflow and strengthen the absorption ability of farmer's in gathering area for the development of new varieties and breed and improving production efficiency. Therefore, agricultural industrial cluster not only can cultivate new-type farmers, but also can make a good number of farmers pioneering group with business passion. It not only solve the own development outlet problem farmer entrepreneur's better, but more effectively activate the rural economy.

To meet the returning rural migrant workers' demand of entrepreneurial field, it established originalities for migrant workers in the town with industrial concentration and more returning peasant workers in Anhui province. By 2010, the province it constructs 300 workers originalities, introduces more than 2000 agricultural production enterprise, drives 10 million people getting job in migrant workers campus, provides more opportunity and conditions for farmers to startup business in the whole province.

Extending industrial chain business

By extending agriculture industry chain, industrial cluster will combine each link and element constituted the agricultural industry to construct modern agriculture industry system. In the form of industrial cluster, the coverage of farmers' entrepreneur will be wider and wider; have already broken through the traditional breeding, more involved in industry, construction, catering services, traffic and transportation, and rural tourism. Farmers' entrepreneurial behavior not only produce good economic benefits, but also better solve the founders' own development outlet problem, also highlight the advantages and characteristics of agricultural industrial cluster.

Extending agriculture industry chain entrepreneurship can be classified into two categories, one is extending from upstream and downstream of agriculture industry, take the strawberry industrial agglomeration of Changfeng city in Anhui as an example, the local venture agricultural buys and concentrates local fresh strawberry, transports to Hefei, Huainan and other neighboring cities to make conversions of their own employment role. The other is extending from ordinary planting and breeding industry to characteristic agriculture, tourism agriculture, such as the tourism of "happy farmer's house", etc. For example, the town of Zipeng in Feixi city, as the core of farm tourism agriculture industry clusters, large quantities of farm households near the town were attracted to open hotel and successfully implement the change from farming to self-employed.

3.3 Increasing the Non-agricultural Employment Opportunities

The development of the processing of agricultural products

As mentioned above, the formation of the agricultural industrial agglomeration not only needs large-scale production of agricultural products and driving by leading enterprises, but also attracts a batch of farmers started agricultural processing enterprises and form processing industry clusters around the agricultural production. The agricultural products processing enterprise are most the labor-intensive enterprises which have great advantages for promoting employment, can absorb farmers labor transferred nearby their home, provide a large number of employment opportunities for workforce stopped in agricultural areas, and accelerate the developing pace of the new countryside construction.

The Dangshan city, as the national fruit non-polluted production demonstration county and the provincial fruit industrialization base, it has taken the accelerating agricultural transformation appreciation as the important measure to increase farmers' income and coordinate economic development of urban and rural in recent years. Through strengthening the leading enterprises and the construction of base, actively promoting the industrialized operation of agriculture, agricultural product processing has got rapid development, the processing of main agricultural products reaches 63%, annual sales income of agricultural product processing reaches 38.2 billion Yuan. At now, the county-wide has formed 46 agricultural industrialization bases, each of which has more than1,000 acres, 13 scale cultivation areas, 29 agriculture leading enterprises, expanding employment personnel about 20,000 people, which are all benefit from the driving of agricultural industrial cluster development.

The third industry's rising
The development of service trade must be supported by conditions of dense population and strong demand, and the production concentration brought by agricultural agglomeration and upstream and downstream consumer market linked up by processing enterprise's cluster, which will meet the need of the third industry development. Therefore, in the agricultural gathering zone, all kinds of commerce, logistics and service intermediary organization develop and rise subsequently and ceaselessly, which is favorable to drive the local and nearby farmers' employment.

Take the town of YejiIn in Anhui province as an example, it relies on the bamboo industrial agglomeration, constructs the bamboo industrial center, actively develops the bamboo processing and trade and logistics industry, reforms provincial Wanxi market and Dabie Moutain bamboo market, guides farmers to go to the city doing business and constructing market, inducts farmers doing market operation, relocates more than 30,000 farmers employment cumulatively.

4 Concluding

4.1 Taking Fostering Industry Leading Enterprises as the Key Point, Vigorously Develop Labor Intensive Processing of Agricultural Products

Development of agriculture industry cluster can not only confined within the production chain of agriculture, but should from overall Angle of agriculture industry, extend agriculture industry chain from both ends, realize the serialized service of agricultural production and the added value of deep agricultural products processing and guide related enterprise's concentration in order. At present, the important is extending line industry chain forward and actively developing processing of agricultural products. Around industrial agglomeration layout, it should cultivate industrialization of agriculture leading enterprise which can promote industrial agglomeration development and peasants' employment, along with the development of the processing of agricultural products, the ability of absorbing rural surplus labor force has been strengthened unceasingly. The agricultural products processing enterprise should establish long-effect mechanism of interests and risks sharing with local farmers, perfect the operation mode of "enterprise + farm households", foster typical case of big planting and breeding, prompt farmers to learn technique, foster high yield and high quality near the industrial agglomeration area, and guarantee stable sufficient raw material supply for agricultural products processing.

4.2 Vigorously Supporting Farmers Do Pioneering Work from Policy

The government's benefit farming policy should combine with the long-range planning and development stages of industrial agglomeration and ensure the sustainable development of local agricultural industry, thus reduce the influence from policy risk for farmers' entrepreneurs. The government policies should provide supports of services, capital, technology, etc, to the farmer are doing pioneering work in every link. Various kinds of factors of production support. Especially in a venture capital shortage problem, it should perfect microfinance system of farmers doing pioneering work, which can let the farmers obtain the relative powerful part of financial support on the foundation of self-owned and self-raised funds. It should strengthen the construction of industrial cluster's external environment, reduce the various administrative barriers, and simplify various formalities of handling affairs and approving. It should take the construction of rural migrant workers originalities as a long-term development strategy to grasp and conscientiously implement support policies such as tax cuts, plant site, funds allowance, etc, in farmers' originalities. And in census register, medical care and social safeguard, etc, it should provide policies consulting and facilitation measures and provide them with supporting of entrepreneurial information, policies consulting and enterprise reporting, etc.

4.3 Promoting Industrial Structural Optimization and Actively Developing the Non-agricultural Industries

Rural industry is single with agricultural dominated and industrial develops sporadically and service level is low. The development of industry cluster can be effective remedy the defect, achieve the benign interaction of rural industry, and help farmers obtain employment to greatest extend. It need to lay stress on investment of rural basic industrial facilities, must develop modern logistics simultaneously and improve network construction of electronic marketing in trade fair to provide convenience and fast sales channels and broad market for agricultural industrial cluster. Through all intermediary business cooperation organization, it can provide service of before, during and after producing to enhance the level of agricultural industrialization and farmers' organizational and to promote diversification development of rural economic structure, and drive the gathering of population, enterprise and resources in the industry agglomeration. Expanding the scale of floating population, promote the development of infrastructure and the third industry in concentration zone, perfect the industrial structure of rural area, which can lay the economic basis for the conversion of urbanization and can create conditions for the situ conversion of farmers from the agricultural population to the non-agricultural population.

4.4 Strengthening Training, Improving the Level of Rural Labor Quality and Reducing Employment Resistance

For the low level of rural surplus labor quality, the low level averaged education degree and low level skill and weak ability to adapt the job requirements in the present situation, it should vigorously strengthen rural basic education, match the development of industry cluster at the same time and vigorously develop agricultural technology training and professional skill training. Through the agricultural professional formed by industry agglomeration, it provides training opportunity for farmers to learn professional skills, combining the need of production and management of agricultural cluster enterprise, changes the traditional farmers into modern farmers who can become qualified even outstanding industrial workers. By increasing the farmers' training opportunities, it forms a reliable way of transferring the rural surplus labor and attracting farmers into town. Eventually, the mass work environment formed by industrial agglomeration will promote the employed self-management and self-improvement and lay the foundation of for farmers' employment.

References

1. Su, Y.: Empirical analysis of employment creation effect of Jiangsu provincial industrial cluster. Journal of Economic BBS 6, 77–80 (2010)
2. Shi, W.: The study of industrial cluster and labor employment expansion mechanism – with an example of Guangdong province. Journal of SAR Economy 3, 43–44 (2007)
3. Huang, H., Gong, X., Huang, B.: The study on employment creation effect of Agriculture industry cluster's. Journal of Agricultural Economy 4, 21–23 (2009)
4. Liu, Y.: The study of countermeasures on promoting surplus rural labor employment in Hebei. Journal of Economy and Management 2, 92–96 (2008)
5. Tan, J., Guo, J., Gu, W.: Study on Chinese agricultural industry cluster. Journal of Chinese Township Enterprise Accounting 8 (2006)
6. Wang, Y.: Development pattern of agricultural industrial cluster -—based on the study of feature agricultural products in Anhui. Journal of Anhui Agricultural University (social sciences) 1, 23–26 (2009)

Green Food Marketing Strategies Based on Consumer's Behavior Influencing Factors Analysis

Wenyi Hao

College of Economics & Management
Heilongjiang Bayi Agricultural University
Daqing, China
haowenyi2000@tom.com

Abstract. With the development of economy and the improvement of income level, green food's demand is growing, and consumer's consumption psychology and behavior are also have changed. For green food enterprise, only caught consumers' psychology and behavior characteristics, can the enterprise caught better opportunity in the competition. Based on the theory of consumer behavior, the green food consumption behavior is affectted by policies and legal factor, social and cultural factors, individual characteristics, marketing factors and so on. such factors are analyzed in this paper by using the analytical hierarchy process (AHP). According to the results of analysis, the paper proposed corresponding marketing strategy: greenfood enterprise should attach importance to cultivate more green food consumers, pay more attention to the promotion, enhance the brand consciousness, ensure the reasonable price etc.

Keywords: green food, consumer behavior, analytical hierarchy, marketing strategy.

1 Introduction

Green food is a kind of high quality food that following the principles of sustainable development and standard technological process, and Be allowed to use the green food symbol . In order to highlight such food from the good ecological environment and favorable environmental protection, hence named green food. China proposed developing the green food since 1990, and after tewnty years of development, China have developed many green foods including grain, vegetable, fruit, beverage, wine, eggs etc., and constructed a series of basic green food production systems and management systems. China's green food industy develops steadily toward industrialization and internationalization. Green foods' production and consumption are paid close attention by the government, enterprises and public, but it is no doubts that China's green food still exists many problems in the marketing practice presses.

Q. Zhou (Ed.): ISAEBD 2011, Part I, CCIS 208, pp. 191–197, 2011.
© Springer-Verlag Berlin Heidelberg 2011

2 Main Factors That Influence Consumer Behavior

The main factors are as follows:

(1)Social factors. Including social production capacity, the policies of the government, reference groups, social bracket and consumers' family members composition, etc.

(2)Culture factors. As a consumer, his or her behavior will be influenced by the customs, religious beliefs, values and aesthetic standard and other social culture factors.

(3)Individual factors.these factors mainly includes consumer's age, occupation, income and so on.

(4)The enterprise's marketing factors. These were the major influencing factors: product factors, price factors, channel factors and promotion factors.

3 Construction of Evaluation Index System

According to the descriptions above, we may easily draw a conclusion that the green food's consumption is influenced by various factors. In order to further the quantitative research, the author intends to analyze the problem by using the analytical hierarchy process (AHP). The author invited seven experts to discusse the problem, 4 scholars come from universities and research institutions and 3 come from green food enterprises. According to all the experts' opinions, the author constructs the green food consumption evaluation index system, as shown in Table 1.

Table 1. Green food consumption evaluation index system

First-class index	Second-class index	Third-class index
Green food consumption（A）	Social factors(B1)	Policies and laws (C11)
		Family members (C12)
		Reference groups (C13)
		Social bracket (C14)
	Culture factors (B2)	Religious beliefs (C21)
		Eating habits (C22)
		Consumption Concept (C23)
	Individual factors (B3)	Occupation (C31)
		Income (C32)
		Green food understanding degree (C33)
		New knowledge learning ability (C34)
	Marketing factors (B4)	Quality and production methods (C41)
		Packaging (C42)
		Brand (C43)
		Price (C44)
		Channel convenience degree (C45)
		Sales Promotion (C46)

(1) To establish judgment rules

According to the experts' advice, we adopt 9 level grade difference method for binary comparison, we provide:

When the extreme importance to B_i compared with B_j, B_{ij} =9; when the more importance to B_i compared with B_j, B_{ij} =7; when the obvious importance to B_i compared with B_j, B_{ij} =5; when the slightly more importance to B_i compared with B_j, B_{ij} =3; when the equally importance to B_i compared with B_j, B_{ij} =1. Among which B_{ij} and B_{ji} have the mutual reciprocal relationship. And 2, 4, 6 and 8 are among the above estimation value.

(2) To establish judgment matrix(Table 2——Table 6), and input to V0.5.2 software yaahp, calculates the results are as follows.

Table 2. Rule layer Judgment Matrix

A	B1	B2	B3	B4	Weight(W)
B1	1	1	1/3	1/7	W_1 (0.1517)
B2	1	1	1/3	1/7	W_2 (0.1517)
B3	3	3	1	1/2	W_3 (0.2630)
B4	7	7	2	1	W_4 (0.4336)

Note: C.R=0.0169<0.1; CI=0.0151; l_{max} =4.0452

Table 3. B1-C Judgment Matrix

B1	C11	C12	C13	C14	Weight(W)
C11	1	1/2	1/2	1	W_{11} (0.2244)
C12	2	1	2	2	W_{12} (0.2881)
C13	2	2	1	3	W_{13} (0.2741)
C14	1	1/2	1/3	1	W_{14} (0.2134)

Note:C.R=0.0056<0.1; CI=0.005; l_{max} =4.0150

Table 4. B2—C Judgment Matrix

B2	C21	C22	C23	Weight(W)
C21	1	3	1/3	W_{21} (0.3256)
C22	1/3	1	1/3	W_{22} (0.2494)
C23	3	3	1	W_{23} (0.4251)

Note:C.R=0.0171<0.1; CI=0.019; l_{max} =3.0178

Table 5. B3—C Judgment Matrix

B3	C31	C32	C33	C34	Weight(W)
C31	1	1/3	1/4	1/3	W_{31} (0.1726)
C32	3	1	1	1	W_{32} (0.2707)
C33	4	1	1	2	W_{33} (0.2992)
C34	3	1	1/2	1	W_{34} (0.2575)

Note:C.R=0.0019<0.1; CI=0.002; l_{max} =4.0050

Table 6. B4—C Judgment Matrix

B4	C41	C42	C43	C44	C45	C46	Weight(W)
C41	1	1/2	1/5	1	1/3	1/9	W_{41} (0.0963)
C42	2	1	1/3	1/2	1/2	1/4	W_{42} (0.1300)
C43	5	3	1	1	2	1/2	W_{43} (0.1940)
C44	1	2	1	1	2	1/2	W_{44} (0.1642)
C45	3	2	1/2	1/2	1	1/3	W_{45} (0.1536)
C46	9	4	2	2	3	1	W_{46} (0.2618)

Note:C.R=0.0224<0.1; CI=0.028; l_{max} =6.1408

Above judgment matrixes have better satisfied the single sorting consistency inspection, and then we will carry on the total ordering and one-time inspection, its one-time inspection is as follows:

$$CR = \frac{CI}{RI} = \frac{\sum_{j=1}^{m} a_j CI_j}{\sum_{j=1}^{m} a_j RI_j} = 0.0163 < 0.1$$

total sorting inspection conform to test and verification, total sorting of the influencing factors are as shown in table 7.

From rule layer influence weight scale, the enterprise marketing factors achieve the greatest contribution 43.36%; Secondly, Individual factors is 26.30%; thirdly, is the social and cultural factors, each account for 15.17%. Visible, green food enterprise's marketing strategy makes a significant influence.Meanwhile, individual factors also should consider as important factors. The enterprise should guide and help consumer to form green food consumption customs, so as to improve the green food's sales opportunity and quantity.

Judging from the program layer influence factors, enterprise's promotion, advertisement and person sales promotion make the greatest contribution. The second and fourth were the brand factor and price factor, to the enterprise, they are also controllable factors. Third is the consumers understanding of green food and intervention level, this suggests that enterprises and government departments should increase green food knowledge by more transmission and ads.

Table 7. Total sorting of the Green food consumption Influencing factors

Influencing factors	W				W_{sum}
	W_1 (0.1517)	W_2 (0.1517)	W_3 (0.2630)	W_4 (0.4336)	
C11	W_{11} (0.2244)				0.0340
C12	W_{12} (0.2881)				0.0437
C13	W_{13} (0.2741)				0.0416
C14	W_{14} (0.2134)				0.0324
C21		W_{21} (0.3256)			0.0494
C22		W_{22} (0.2494)			0.0378
C23		W_{23} (0.4251)			0.0645
C31			W_{31} (0.1726)		0.0454
C32			W_{32} (0.2707)		0.0712
C33			W_{33} (0.2992)		0.0787
C34			W_{34} (0.2575)		0.0677
C41				W_{41} (0.0963)	0.0418
C42				W_{42} (0.1300)	0.0564
C43				W_{43} (0.1940)	0.0841
C44				W_{44} (0.1642)	0.0712
C45				W_{45} (0.1536)	0.0666
C46				W_{46} (0.2618)	0.1135

4   Green Food Marketing Countermeasures and Strategies

Based on the analysis by using analytic hierarchy process(AHP), the green food enterprises should consider the following aspects in making marketing strategy.

4.1   Cultivate More Green Food Consumers

Green consumer refers to those who care about ecological environment, has reality and potential purchasing intention and purchasing power. According to the environmental concerned degree, foreign scholars divided people continuously from low to high: light green consumers, medium green consumers and dark green consumers. Enterprise should catch medium green consumers and dark green consumers, or through opinion leaders, with their powerful influence on other consumers, to change other consumers' green food consumption attitude and expand green food consumption scope and varieties unceasingly. Enterprise may establish green food exhibition, through the text pictures, physical example etc to show the green products developed technology to consumers.

4.2 Develop the Green Food Vigorously

Green food production is the foundation of its marketing strategy. Green food enterprises should control pesticide, fertilizer application, constantly improve green food cultivation technique, breeding techniques, processing technology, packaging technology, clearner production technology (such as using green packing in shipping sales process, etc), green storage etc, to avoid the product second-hand polluted. The country and Green food enterprises must set up the sustainability of green food production and development models.

4.3 Pay More Attention to the Promotion

Green food enterprises must enhance propaganda. Enterprise should carry out publicity and promotion especially carefully because sales promotion means diversification. Enterprises should not noly pay attention to highlight the characteristics of green food, but also pay attention to the product brand publicity. The relevant government departments should also intensify, by playing on environmental advertisement, documentary and so on to promote the green consumption knowledge popularization, to formed a kind of advocating green consumption of social atmosphere in the whole society, to make more and more consumers believe green consumption is healthy for himself and to formate green food positive consumption attitude.

4.4 Enhance the Brand Consciousness

Brand is the intangible asset and the most valuable fortune for enterprises. Green food enterprises must establish the brand concept by adopting the appropriate strategy to incorporating the brand concept into buying behaviors of customers and potential consumers. In the fierce competition, brand has become a kind of strategic assets and important source of core competitiveness. The key point to promote business strategy by the brand concept is the positive actions in favor of the brand establishment from senior managers, which will involve senior managers in the corporate strategy and understanding the importance of brand concept from the strategic viewpoints. Enterprises should carry out brand establishment, cultivate their famous brands and protect their brands at the same time. Furthermore, enterprises should enrich their brand content and improve the value of brands in order to expand and promote their brand popularity as well as brand recognition.

4.5 Determine Reasonable Prices

Generally speaking, the green food pricing should mainly be consider the following aspects: one is the cost factors, the foundation of price; the other is market factors, including the target market buyers' consumption psychology, purchasing behavior and purchasing ability; the third is competitive factors, including the market competition intense rate and the competitors' products price level. In the green food pricing strategies, the author thinks that the enterprise should adopt more psychology pricing strategies, including popularity pricing, habit pricing, soliciting pricing strategies and so on. So far, green food psychological demands mainly determined by the commodity type and purchasing motivation, so enterprises should fully consider these factors. Green product price may better than the green product price generally higher than 30% ~ 100%. Thus, using psychological pricing can bring the enterprise considerable economic benefit and more power to promote green foods.

5 Conclusion

According to consumers' behavior and other related theories, following the experts advice, the author build a green food consumption evaluation index system, and through the analysis of the influencing factors, the author concluded that green food enterprises should make great efforts to develop the green food, pay attention to cultivate more green food consumers, pay more attention to the sales promotion, strengthen brand awareness and determine reasonable prices. Meanwhile, the author believes that, the government and related departments play important roles in green food marketing too, the government should adjust green food product structure in macroscopically, cultivate and strengthen the leading enterprises and gradually improve the green food industrialization.

References

[1] Hawkins, D.I., Best, R.J., Coney, K.A.: Comsumer Behavior:Implications for marketing strategy. Irwin, Boston (1992)
[2] Loudon, D.L., Della Bitta, A.J.: Consumer Behavior. Mcgraw-hill, New York (1993)
[3] Guoqun, F.U.: Consumer Behavior. Higher Education Press (2005)
[4] Kotler, P.: Marketing Management, 16th edn. Prentice-Hall International Inc., Englewood Cliffs (2009)
[5] Horton, R.L.: Buyer Behavior: A Decision-making Approach. Charles E. Merril Publishing, Ohio (1984)

An Empirical Research on the DIC of Hubei Rape

Yunfei Chen[*] and Ying Huang

College of Economics & management, WHPU,
Wuhan 430023, China
hc1315@Sina.com

Abstract. While studies on DIC have been one of the hignlights in the academe in recent years, The empirical research on the DIC of Hubei rape, which has become the mainstay industry of "Hundred-Billion-Yuan" and the efficency-adding to agriculture & income-adding to farmers because of the largest planting especially the largest "Double-Low" planning area in China, becomes more and more important and is given in this paper. By the study that has not been done before, we know that Hubei rape owns high quality in itself and has its advantages and disadvantages in the DIC. According to these, we give the corresponding advices on Hubei rape industry.

Keywords: Hubie Rape Industry, DIC, An Empirical Research.

1 Introduction

Rape is one of the staple crops which is cultivated around the whole place in Hubei province, whose indexes as cultivated area, overall production and factor of merit, etc. have been in the first place for 14 years continuously in China. Take the overall production as an example, it is about 2,000,000 tons, which is about 1/6 of the country, and 1/18 of the world. Especially in the factor of merit, the 95% of the popularizing high rate of "Double-Low" rape makes Hubei the largest base of rape on this variety. Therefore, after economical analysis, professor Feng Zhongchao and related experts, as the representative of economists on national rape industrial systerm post, proposed to make rape industry into "Hundred-Billion-Yuan" industry, which will be the mainstay industry of efficency-adding to agriculture & income-adding to farmers[1].

Domestic industrial competitiveness (DIC) means the ability of competitiveness by comparison between industries or in the industries. The region is restricted inland, and the competitive objects are between the industries or in the same industry. Say the DIC of rape, it is the competitiveness between rape industry and other related industries as well as in the rape industry. Therefore, in order to realize the economical target of rape industry itself and to maintain the leading position in nationwide, it is necessary to make empirical analysis on DIC of Hubei rape among regions and between rape and other related crops.

---

[*] Foundation items: WHPU(08Y21).

Q. Zhou (Ed.): ISAEBD 2011, Part I, CCIS 208, pp. 198–202, 2011.
© Springer-Verlag Berlin Heidelberg 2011

2 Judgement System in DIC

The analysis of DIC relies on the establishment of judgement system firstly. This thesis applys the system structured by Chen Yunfei, Cai Xiaoyong and Niu Yanhong, etc [2] [3] (Figure 1) .

I grade	II grade	III grade
Between industries	Potential	Development Future
	Strength	Weight Market Share
In the industries	Revenue Opportunities Cost Strategies Resources Demands Supporting Industries Abilities of Knowledge Absorbing and Innovating	

Fig. 1. DIC Judgment System

3 An Empirical Analysis in DIC of Hubie Rape

3.1 The Rape Itself

Quality of rape mainly depends on its oil content and it's " Double-Low "(low erucic acid and low sulfur clucoside) or not. Takes the " Double-Low " as an example, the planting rate of it is 95%, which occupies 1/4 of the cultivated area in whole country, makes Hubei the first place for long in China.

3.2 In the Industries of Hubei Rape

According to the industrial judgement system, competitiveness in the industries is decided by such five elements as strategies, resources, demands, supporting industries and abilities of knowledge absorbing and innovating. From the aspects of strategies, supporting industries and abilities of knowledge absorbing and innovating, Hubei rape has its own superiority because it is a " Hundred-Billion-Yuan " industry which the province decided to build and Hubei owns such best manufacturing, processing and researching institutes as the Oil Crops Research Institute (OCRI) of the Chinese Academy of Agricultural Sciences (CAAS), Huazhong agricultural university (HZAU) and Wuhan Polytecnic University (WHPU) as well as the best rape science&technology popularizing organization in the nation. From the aspects of resources, Hubei is not so excellent comparing adjoining provinces like Jiangxi, Henan and Sichuan, etc [3]. About the demands, Hubei rape has many chances because the commercial demand is in net import situation with the increacing living standard of people in our country. Take the 2009 as an example, the importation of rapeseed in this year has passed 3,200,000 tons, which makes a new record.

3.3 Between Industries of Hubei Rape

By the industrial judgement system, we know that between industries of rape is combined by potential, strength, revenue and opportunities cost. While potential can be analysed from the development and future; strength should be analysed from weight and market share.

From Table 1 we could find that, from the aspect of potential, although rape is one of the supported industries in Hubei province, its developing speed, which is even in negative condition in 2005-2006 and 2010, is slower than that of GDP. From the aspect of strength, on the weight, rape is the second largest crop in gricultural area (more than 38%) only next to rice and the fourth largest crop in total production (more than 6% of the year-harvest planting and 60% of the summer-harvest planting) only after grain, cotton and vegetables in Hubei, on the market share, rape is not only in short supply and so with a large market place but also its production in Hubei is always listed on the first place in China. From the aspects of revenue and opportunities cost, rape is planted in winter in Hubei, its benefits is almost the whole because it does not reclaim land with other crops and thus with a very low opportunities cost. At present, although rape planting's profit of one acre is not stable, it can be an income somehow because of its making profit always.

4 Conclusion

From the above analysis, we can draw the following conclusion.

4.1 The Rape Itself

Rape planted in Hubei owns high quality because of its main " Double-Low " rapeseed whose oil is recognized as one of the most healthy edible vegetable oil to human body around the world. Take the nutritional value as an example, " Double-Low " rapeseed's content is only rank second for olive oil. Furthermore, the meals of rape is good protein resources with proper proportion of amino acid, most of which are necessary ones that human and animals could not compose naturally. Certainly, the " Double-Low " rape in Hubei should be improved to keep up with the advanced level such as Canada, etc.

The source of seeds is an important factor to influence rape quality. If there are too many seeds in a mess which causes flower planting and cross pollination, the quality of " Double-Low " rapeseeds would be fell directly. Rapeseed's special character like this should be taken into accounted by Hubei and make strict barrier. For example, Hubei could enlarge management power of seeds market, readjust seeds market in a large scale, strike the false and bad seeds according to the law, regulate seeds market order and stop popularize varieties of " Double-Low " rapeseeds which are such no longer super in production as those are examined backward, etc [4].

Table 1. Development of rape, Hubei and China(2005-2010)   Unit:ten thousand ton, %, Yuan/Mu.

Item / Year	Hubei				China		
	Production	Incresing rate	GDP increcing	Cost-profit	China	Hubie in China	Rank
2005	219.2	-6.8	11.4	30.51	1305.2	16.8	1
2006	191.8	-12.5	12.1	249.0	1096.6	17.5	1
2007	193.3	0.8	14.5	439.0	1057.3	18.3	1
2008	214.9	11.2	13.4	288.61	1055.3	20.4	1
2009	236.5	10.1	13.2	79.28	1300.0	18.2	1
2010	230.0	-2.8	14.0	108.83	1220.0	18.9	1

4.2 In the Industries of Hubei Rape

About the in the industries, rape in Hubei is not talented in resources oweing to the influence of material cost, which is comparatively related with weak supporting policies closely in Hubei in the rape production. To improve this situation, Hubei should take such policies as strengthening management power of compounded agricultural market and actively increasing input in the agricultural material subsidies, fine-seed subsidies and rape insurance, etc.

In the strategies, supporting industries and abilities of knowledge absorbing and innovating, rape in Hubei has a certain advantages. Hubei should practice "Hundred-Billion-Yuan" industry strategy as soon as possible. For example, Hubei could increase the power of science research and popularizing on rape, extende rape industrial train. At the same time, it is very necessary to promote the construction of rape trade and logistic center to make Hubei the industrial center of rape in whole country.

In the demands, under the market of short supply of nationwide, Hubei has relatively developing room in rape industry. The government should grasp this fine chance and develop production vigorously. The rape varieties of "Huayouza" & "Zhongyouza", etc. should be promoted actively because of their production of more than 110kg per unit acre and high oil content more than 41% [4].

4.3 Between Industries of Hubei Rape

About the between industries, as we have talked above, Hubei rape has relatively industrial potential under the circumstance of short supply in nationwide. Hubei should make a developing target, by which the value and volume of production could catch the developing speed of GDP annually.

In the strength, Hubei rape has a certain advantages in our country. The main problems may be in the low revenue with the almost no opportunities cost. The low revenue in Hubei may be due to two factors of high production cost and less fine & deep processing. To improve this situation, in the production cost, which is related to land process scale and production structure, Hubei should increase landing circulation and reduce the grain production rationally in northwest and east part of it to expand rape cultivation scale. In the fine & deep processing, Hubei should apply all kinds of technologies as biology, chemistry etc. to develop such new and high-added-value productions as natural plant Perborate, enriched albumen powder and biological diesel oil, etc [5].

References

1. Yi, M.: What a "Hundred-Biliion" industry from of Hubei Rape. [EB/OL]. Information Net of Hubei Agricuoture (2009), http://www.hbagri.gov.cn
2. Chen, Y., Cai, X.: Study on the Construction of Judgement System in DIC. Journal of Jiangsu Commercial 7 (2009)
3. Chen, Y., Niu, Y.: Study on the Construction of DIC Judgment System in Real Estate. In: Proceedings of CRIOCM 2009 International Symposium on Advancement of Construction Management and Real Estate, vol. 6 (October 2009)
4. Chen, Y.: An Empiriacl Analysis on Comparative Advantages of Hubei Rape. Journal of Wuhan Politechnic University 2 (2010)
5. Chen, Y.: Study on the Construction of Judgement System in DIC of Rural Products Processing Industry. Journal of Wuhan Politechnic University (2009) (Special on bussiness management of rural products processing)

Study on the Methods of Payment with Mergers & Acquisitions

Jing Zhang[1] and Yong'an Zhang[2]

[1] Economics and Management School, Beijing University of Technology, Beijing, China
Business and Management Scholl, Shandong Economic University, Jinan, China
[2] Economics and Management School, Beijing University of Technology, Beijing, China

Abstract. Selection of Methods of payment with Mergers & Acquisition (M&A), is the key of a successful M&A. Methods of payment includes cash payment, security payment and leveraged buyout. This paper studies the impacts of the selection of payment methods with M&A on the selection of financing methods with M&A. This paper also studies the influences of payment methods on the capital and controlling structures of the surviving purchasing companies, and the way in which payment methods affect the performance of M&A based on taxation factors and signal factors.

Keywords: methods of payment, methods of financing, capital structure, controlling structure, mergers & acquisitions.

1 Introduction

Payment with mergers & acquisitions is the last step of mergers & acquisitions, and the most important factor on the success of mergers & acquisitions. Selection of payment methods determines selection of financing methods. And different methods of payment exert different influences on the financial status, capital structure, and controlling structure of the surviving purchasing companies after the mergers & acquisition. Methods of payment also have effects on the performance of mergers & acquisitions.

This paper focus on the research on the impacts of payment methods with mergers & acquisitions on the selection of financing methods with mergers & acquisitions, the financial and capital structure, controlling structures of the purchasing companies, and performance with mergers & acquisitions. It is expected to provide helpful instructors for strategies and decisions with mergers & acquisitions.

2 Methods of Payment

Methods of payment with Mergers and Acquisitions refer to the resources and financial tools through which the purchasing companies acquire the ownership and controlling rights of the target companies. Payment methods with mergers & acquisitions includes: cash payment, security payment and leveraged buyout.

Q. Zhou (Ed.): ISAEBD 2011, Part I, CCIS 208, pp. 203–208, 2011.
© Springer-Verlag Berlin Heidelberg 2011

2.1 Cash Payment

Cash payment is a simple purchasing action, which means the purchasing corporation purchases a certain amount of assets or stocks from the target company by paying a certain amount of cash. It is the most popular payment method with mergers & acquisition on Chinese capital markets.

2.2 Security Payment

Security payment is the payment method under which the purchasing companies issue new securities in order to buy the stocks or assets of the target companies. It includes the following two forms:

2.2.1 Stock Payment

With stock payment, the purchasing companies issues new stocks to buy the stocks or assets of the target companies. Among which, the most popular form is stock exchange, which means the purchasing company pays the stocks of the purchasing company directly to the target company to buy out the stocks or assets of the target companies.

2.2.2 Bond Payment

With bond payment, the purchasing companies issues new corporate bonds to buy out the stocks or assets of the target companies. As a payment method with mergers & acquisitions, this type of bonds has to have relatively higher negotiability and credit rating.

2.3 Leveraged Buyout (LOB)

Leveraged buyout is a payment method with which the purchasing companies finance capitals with mergers & acquisitions through increasing debts. Under leveraged buyout, the purchasing companies take the assets or future operating cash flows of target companies as pledges in order to raise debts to finance capitals from investors, and then purchase the stocks and ownerships of target companies with cash payment. that's why some studies put LOB under cash payment. Compared with bond payment, leveraged buyout results in a higher capital cost, as regularly interest of bank loans is higher than corporate bonds.

3 Impacts of Methods of Payment on the Methods of Financing

Financing methods with mergers & acquisitions refer to the financing tools through which the purchasing companies raise capitals with mergers & acquisitions. Financing methods consist of two main channels, namely internal financing and external financing.

   Under internal financing, the purchasing companies use their retained revenues to pay the capitals with mergers & acquisitions to the target companies. Internal financing is usually corresponding to cash payment.

Under external financing, the purchasing companies raise capital with mergers & acquisitions through external channels. External financing consists of debt financing and equity financing. Debt financing means the purchasing companies borrow money from banks, or sell corporate bonds or bills to individual or organization investors to raise capitals. Purchasing bonds or bills from companies, individual or organization investors lend out money and become creditors of the companies, and accordingly acquire the guarantees from the companies to repay the principle and interest. Equity financing means the purchasing companies raise capital through enlarge their equity, for instance, issuing new stocks or increasing additional investment. Equity financing results in the diluted control rights of former investors.

Generally speaking, a specific payment method is corresponding to a specific financing method, in other words, there is a corresponding relation between payment methods and financing methods, which is listed as Table 1.

Table 1. Corresponding relation between payment methods and financing methods

	Internal Financing	External Financing	
		Debt Financing	Equity Financing
Cash Payment	X		
Stock Payment			X
Bond Payment		X	
LBO		X	

4   Impacts of Methods of Payment on the Capital Structure

Cash payment requires the purchasing company to pay out a large amount of cash, most of which comes from its retained revenue. Cash payment is the most simple payment method, and with a high-speed settlement and thorough ownership transferring. Based on Financing Sequence Theory, in case the purchasing company has enough retained revenue, cash payment should be its top-priority due to cash payment's lower capital cost and the fact that cash payment will not change the capital structure and controlling structure of the purchasing company , nor dilute its revenue on equity. Nevertheless, cash payment will exert great financial pressure on the purchasing company, and it will take the purchasing company a long time to recover these capital. After the cash paying with mergers & acquisitions, in case the purchasing company need a large amount of cash to deal with emergency, it will have to raise capital through some channels, such as, issuing bonds or stocks. In this situation, additional debts or equities will increase, capital structure will be affected, weighted average capital costs will be boosted, the company's financial risks will be increased. And as a result, the purchasing company's financial status and financial strength will be influenced negatively. So the purchasing company has to evaluate its financial status and predict future operation before it select cash payment as payment method with mergers & acquisitions.

In a mature capital markets, stock payment usually do not require a large amount of cash, as a result, it could avoid the pressure of large cash outflow, and decrease the risks with mergers and acquisitions to a certain level. Additionally, listed companies issue common stocks to the new shareholders, at the same time, their total capitals are increased, and their net assets are increased, therefore their debt rate are decreased, which will result in the enhanced performance of mergers and acquisitions. Anyway, issuing common stocks would change the elements of the firm's balance sheet, and change its related financial indexes, for instance, it likely increase the equities and decrease the revenue per unit of stocks.

With bond payment, capitals with mergers and acquisitions come from issuing corporate bonds. According to corrected MM theorem [1], compared with common stocks, raising money by corporate bonds are more inexpensive. As the interest of bonds are tax deductible, it could save financing costs and therefore increase the performance of mergers and acquisitions positively.

Finally, leveraged buyout just requires the purchasing company to pay a relatively small amount of Equity Funds In order to purchase the target company, therefore, it relieves the short-term financial pressure on the purchasing company. Whereas at the same time, leveraged buyout could increase its financial lever, and affects the purchasing company's capital structures and increases its financial risks. Also, this way increases the purchasing company's financing costs with mergers and acquisitions, and have it under a high pressure to pay off the borrowed money. Additionally, as there exists a high risk with leveraged buyout, the interest rate of capitals for leveraged buyout is relatively higher, which also enhances the cost of mergers and acquisitions. Under the high financial risks and pressure of paying off the loan, if it is badly run, the purchasing company would be possibly overwhelmed by the loans.

5   Impacts of Methods of Payment on the Controlling Structure

Under cash payment, the purchasing company buy-out with cash total rights of the target company from its former shareholders, who will lose their total ownerships of the target company after the mergers & acquisitions. And cash with mergers and acquisitions usually comes from the retained revenues of the purchasing company, instead of issuing stocks or bonds, in this situation, ownership won't be diluted at all, and stockholders of purchasing company won't lose their control to the new surviving company after mergers & acquisitions.

Additionally, cash payment thoroughly cut off the relationships of shareholders of the target company with the target company, so it simplifies the personnel arrangement. In this way, owners the purchasing company could freely deal with the target company according to the their wishes and the purchasing company' demands without the interferences from those former owners of the target company. Cash payment is the top-priority of major shareholders who are in the absolute controlling situation in the purchasing company.

Stock payment is a financing method as well as a payment method. As a payment method, the purchasing company pays the stocks of the purchasing company to the target company as the payment for mergers & acquisitions. as a financing payment, the purchasing company issues targeted stocks to the target company's shareholders, or issue common stocks to other individual or organization investors in order to finance capitals for mergers & acquisitions. Stock payment increases total stockholdings of the future company after mergers & acquisitions, and dilutes ownerships and controlling rights of the controlling shareholder. In case the purchasing company issues common stocks to other individual or organization investors, as these investors are relatively separate, the controlling situation of the purchasing company's controlling shareholders usually won't be challenged. While in case the purchasing company issues targeted stocks to the target company's shareholders, the major shareholders of the target may affect the controlling situation of the purchasing company's controlling shareholders. This is the reason why major controlling shareholders resist issuing targeted stocks to the former shareholders of the target company.

Under bond payment and leveraged buyout, capitals with mergers and acquisition actually come from liabilities of the purchasing company, the controlling structure of the purchasing company won't be affected.

6 Impacts of Methods of Payment on the Performance of Mergers & Acquisitions

Methods of payment on the performance of mergers & acquisitions result from two aspects which are taxation factors and signal factors.

6.1 Taxation Factors

Eckbo (1983) [2] states that companies could take advantages of mergers & acquisitions as tax shelters. He advances that shareholders of target company could postpone taxation payment and adopt substitutions of taxation items through stock payment, so stock payment benefits target corporations, while payment with cash would increase the sheltered depreciation amount of the purchasing company and accordingly improve the revenues of the purchasing company.

6.2 Signal Factors

First of all, various methods of payment deliver various signals about anticipation to values of the future company after mergers & acquisitions towards the potential investors on capital market. Cash payment delivers a signal that the target company is undervalued seriously by the market, therefore potential investors may anticipate that the value of the future company's stock will tend to increase. Oppositely, stock payment delivers an totally inverse signal and potential investors may anticipate in an inverse way. (Myers and Maijluf (1984) [3], Loughran and vijh (1997) [4], Rau and Vermaelen (1998)) [5]. Secondly, cash payment delivers a signal that the purchasing company possesses abundant amounts of operating cash flows, while stock payment, bond payment and leveraged buyout delivers a opposite signal. Finally, bond payment and leveraged buyout delivers a signal of superintendence and validation to the purchasing company from outsides. Bharadwaj and Shivdasani (2003) [6] discovered that, with leveraged buyout, if the required capital comes from bank loans, then the pronunciamento effects will be positive, the reason is that bank loans deliver a positive signal that the banks implement superintendence and validation to the purchasing company.

On realistic capital markets, impacts of methods of payment on the performance of mergers & acquisitions is complex, whether they have a positive or negative impacts depends on the status of the mergers & acquisitions market, financial and controlling status of purchasing companies and target companies.

A specific payment method may bring benefits to the purchasing company, at the same time, it may bring it various risks. Therefore, selection of payment methods is a series of complicated Chess Games about benefits. All-sided analyzing on the factors and processes leading to M&A risks and selecting payment methods on the principle of risk minimization are the keys of successful mergers & acquisitions.

References

1. Modigliani, F., Miller, M.: Corporate income taxes and the cost of capital: a correction. American Economic Review 53(3), 433–443 (1963)
2. Eekbo, B.E.: Horizontal Mergers, Collusion, and Stock Holder Wealth. Journal of Financial Economics 11, 241–273 (1983)
3. Myers Stewart, C., Majluf, N.: Corporate Financing and Investment Decisions when Firms have Information that Investors donot have. Journal of Financial Economies 13, 187 (1984)
4. Loughran, T., Vijh, A.M.: Do Long-term Shareholders Benefit from Corporate Acquisitions? Journal of Finance 52, 1765–1790 (1997)
5. Rau, R.P., Vermaelen, T.: Glamour, value and the post-acquisition performance of acquiring firms. Journal of Financial Economics 49, 223–253 (1998)
6. Bharadwaj, A., Shivdasani, A.: Valuation Effects of Balk Financing Acquisitions. Journal of Financial Economies 67, 113–148 (2003)

Research on the Correlation between Performance and Compensation of Executive and Staff in Agricultural Enterprises

Fayuan Wang[1] and Danwei Lin[2]

[1] College of Economics, Yangtze University, Jingzhou, Hubei, China 434025
wangfayuan315@sina.com
[2] Hansan Normal University, Chaozhou, Guangdong, China 521041
ldwgd@sina.cn

Abstract. In order to stimulate the activity of executive and staff in agricultural enterprises and improve management measures, we adopt semi-log weighted least square regression method to analyze the correlation between enterprise performance and compensation of executive and staff. Analysis results show that correlation between enterprise performance and the total and average compensation of senior executives, the highest executive's pay and staffs' average salaries is obvious. And the correlation rises quickly at first, then at a lower speed to a certain level, and even declines in the end. The increase of highest executive's pay can maximally improve enterprise performance. And increasing the total executive compensation can also enhance enterprise performance to a certain extent.

Keywords: Agricultural enterprise, compensation and performance, correlation.

1 Introduction

Management compensation incentive is often regarded as an important governance mechanism to alleviate agency problem. General meeting of shareholders elects board of directors who select the management staffs and determine their salaries, which is considered to be the basic model of running management incentives. In this mode, the board of directors control and decide executive compensation contracts and based on which they can set pay arrangements maximizing shareholder value [1]. In practice, executives can affect and even determine their salaries to a large extent [2]. Is there close correlation between enterprise performance and executive compensation? This will determine the way of board of directors to manage executive performance and clients' trust degree to agents.

Based on former studies, Bebchuk and Fried systematically proposed a managerial power theory for the design of executive compensation. They suggested that boards do not operate at arm's length in devising executive compensation arrangements. Rather, executives have power to influence their own pay, and they use that power to extract rents [3]. Betrand and Mullainathan also found that without the presence of large shareholders, CEO pay is accordance with luck rather than performance [4]. In

Q. Zhou (Ed.): ISAEBD 2011, Part I, CCIS 208, pp. 209–214, 2011.
© Springer-Verlag Berlin Heidelberg 2011

this study, we collect the cross-sectional data from the information released by listed companies. In addition, regression statistical method is adopted to analyze the impact of executive compensation and staff's average salary on enterprise performance. The analysis results can provide scientific evidences for boards of directors in listed company to determine executive compensation and staff's salary.

2   Related Work

There are numerous researches on the correlation between enterprise performance and executive compensation, but conclusions they obtained are quite different. In addition, researchers have not realized that there is also correlation between staff's salary and enterprise performance. Especially there are few researches on the correlation between performance and compensation of executive and staff in agricultural enterprises.

In [5], it was shown by multi-variable linear regression method that executive compensation in our country is positively related with enterprise scale. But there is no long consistent positive correlation between executive compensation and enterprise performance. The correlation between them is in general weak. Li et al in [6] also utilized linear regression model to analyze correlation. They found that managers' annual compensation in listed companies of our country does not rely on enterprise performance, but is closely related to enterprise scale. When managers hold certain stocks of their company, shareholder proportion has obvious impact on enterprise performance. In [7], Chen et al selected compensation as dependent variable and ROE as independent variable, adopted cross-sectional regression method and found that the decision of compensation is not closely related to enterprise performance. The performance of listed company with annual salary system is obviously better than that without annual salary system. In addition, they also pointed out that annual salary and shareholder proportion are both weakly related to performance, which indicates that annual salary and shareholder have certain incentive functions for increasing performance. Guo et al in [8] also adopted the method of linear regression and found that in industries with high competition, the increase of executive compensation is mainly influenced by the growth rate of earning per share (EPS). In highly competitive industries, the increase of executive compensation can bring the improvement of enterprise performance. But this correlation will fall with the decrease of competition degree. In industries with low competition and high monopoly, there is no relation between them. Lu proposed in [9] that sensitivity between compensation and profit is higher than that between compensation and deficit. Even in some enterprises, there is weak or no correlation between compensation and performance. Why is there so much difference between the conclusions obtained by different scholars? It was figured out in [10] that there is no obvious linear relation between executive compensation and enterprise performance in listed companies of our country. Therefore, the conclusions obtained from analysis based on linear models are quite different. Although currently the executive compensation system has not played great incentive role, it is still strongly related to enterprise performance. These different conclusions can still provide some inspirations for the research on correlation between executive compensation and enterprise performance.

3 Empirical Study

3.1 Materials and Methods

From the information released by listed companies, according to the industry standard classification of listed companies set by Securities Regulatory Commission, we collected the data of performance and executive compensation and staff's salary of 35 Chinese agricultural listed companies in 2009. In addition, we chose the rate of return on equity (ROE) as the indicator of enterprise performance, the total executive compensation, the average executive compensation, the highest executive's pay and staff's average salary as explanatory variables. In order to obtain the correlation between ROE and four explanatory variables, we adopted semi-log weighted least square regression method and utilized statistical software Eviews 4.0 to process data.

Table 1. Statistical features of performance and compensation of 35 listed agricultural companies in 2009

	Y	X1	X2	X3	X4
Mean	6.610857	189.4060	10.83171	30.38686	15074.05
Median	6.430000	145.4400	7.670000	18.96000	14820.51
Maximum	34.89000	782.1000	41.16000	148.5000	28563.54
Minimum	-64.85000	65.54000	3.500000	5.130000	8741.860
Std. Dev.	17.13077	152.7249	7.900123	30.55272	4309.045
Skewness	-1.960443	2.549079	2.256202	2.291959	0.787073
Kurtosis	10.19039	9.814303	8.698342	8.427927	3.923291
Jarque-Bera	97.81787	105.6212	77.04796	73.60893	4.856840
Probability	0.000000	0.000000	0.000000	0.000000	0.088176
Observations	35	35	35	35	35

The data of 35 listed agricultural companies is processed by Eviews4.0. Analysis results are shown in Table 1. It can be seen that the average ROE (Y) of these 35 companies is 6.61%, the highest and the lowest ROE are 34.89% and -64.85% respectively, the standard deviation is 17.13077%. In addition, the average total executive compensation (X1) is 1,894,060 yuan, the highest one is 7,821,000 yuan, the lowest one is 655,400 yuan and the standard deviation is 1,527,249 yuan. Furthermore, the average salary for the highest executive (X3) is 303,868 yuan, the highest and lowest ones are 1,485,000 yuan and 51,300 yuan, the standard deviation is 305,527 yuan. Finally, the staff's average salary (X4) is 15, 074 yuan, the highest one is 28,563 yuan, the lowest one is 8,741 yuan and the standard deviation is 4,309 yuan.

3.2 Model and Variable Analysis

Variable analysis. We select ROE as explained variable, and choose the total executive compensation (X1), the average executive compensation (X2), the highest executive's pay (X3) and staff's average salary (X4) as explanatory variables for mapping and modeling. The total and average executive compensation can reflect the overall annual salary level of the management in a company. In general, the highest executive of a company is the highest decision-maker and the salary level can reflect his own value to a certain extent, it can also reflect the highest executive's level of making decisions and contributions to the company. The staff's average salary can directly reflect the enterprise's acceptance to workers' performance and caring degree about workers, and can also reflect the benefits of enterprises indirectly. These four variables are strongly representative to be explanatory variables. The coordinate graphs about ROE (Y) and the total executive compensation (X1), the average executive compensation (X2), the highest executive's pay (X3) and staff's average salary (X4) show that each explanatory variable is non-linearly related with ROE. The enterprise performance increases with the increase of executive compensation and staff's average salary, and with the improvement of incentive mechanisms to staffs and managers. The rising trend will be weakened with the decrease of incentive effects. When the rising trend goes up to a certain extent, further increase of incentive does not necessarily lead to increase of performance, or even result in decline.

This phenomenon is typically due to marginal utility. Marginal utility indicates that if the consumption of other goods remains the same, the consumers' satisfaction degree to a particular commodity will decrease with the increase of that particular commodity [11]. In our study, in the initial stage of increasing compensation, executive's enthusiasm and passion rise highly, and their intelligence and wisdom come into play, thus the enterprise performance increases significantly. But when it reaches to a certain extent, the effect caused by the increase of executive compensation will decline, and as the intelligence and wisdom is limited, it shows a weak correlation or negative correlation between performance and executive compensation. According to the analysis results, it is seen that the majority of enterprises are in the cluster of positive effects of incentive mechanisms and only a small number of companies show a downward trend. It is because those few enterprises' ROE is very low or even negative but executive and staff are still needed to be paid.

Modeling and analysis. Taking heteroscedasticity into account, we adopt the method of semi-log weighted least square regression to analyze the impact of four explanatory variables on ROE. The results are shown as follows: (Statistic T is in the brackets)

$$\hat{y} = -20.7844 + 5.4724\ln(x1) \qquad R^2 = 0.9888 \quad F = 100.437 \quad n = 35 \tag{1}$$
$$(-7.6359) \quad (10.0218)$$

$$\hat{y} = -10.9513 + 8.1105\ln(x2) \qquad R^2 = 0.9353 \quad F = 400.7884 \quad n = 35 \tag{2}$$
$$(-14.6133) \quad (20.0197)$$

$$\hat{y} = -13.6028 + 6.5416\ln(x3) \qquad R^2 = 0.9983 \quad F = 1138.192 \quad n = 35 \tag{3}$$
$$(-16.9332) \quad (33.7371)$$

$$\hat{y} = -156.0251 + 16.9516 \ln(x4) \qquad R^2 = 0.9509 \quad F = 408.7466 \quad n = 35 \tag{4}$$
$$(-19.8033) \quad (20.2175)$$

The four equations above show that all the slope coefficients are in the level of 1%. It means the increases of executive compensation and staff's average salary have positive and obvious impact on the increase of ROE. Especially the increase of highest executive's pay has the greatest impact. The goodness of fit is as higher as 99.83%, which is followed by 98.88% affected by increase of the total executive compensation. The impact of executive's average compensation on ROE is the lowest. The goodness of fit is 93.53%. It demonstrates that enterprise performance mainly depends on the decisions and contributions of the highest executive, other executives have limited influence on ROE. Staff's salary is positively related with ROE, but its influence is not so critical, which is 95.09%.

4 Conclusion and Future Work

The relation between executive compensation and enterprise performance is not linear. The conclusions obtained from research based on linear relationship are inaccurate. Our study believes that the correlations between the total executive compensation, the average executive compensation, the highest executive's pay and staff's average salary and enterprise performance are obvious. And the correlation rises quickly at first, then at a lower speed to a certain level, and even declines in the end. It is due to the marginal utility of executive compensation and staff's salary on enterprise performance. However, the total executive compensation, the average executive compensation, the highest executive's pay and staff's average salary have different influences on the performance. In agricultural enterprises, the highest executive's pay has the greatest influence on the performance, the total executive compensation takes the second place, and staff's average salary is in the third, the average executive compensation has the lowest influence on enterprise performance.

Therefore, it is necessary to reform executive compensation system in agricultural enterprises. First, it needs to determine basic executive compensation in different levels. Based on that, it is required to establish performance related pay system, to fully utilize the incentive function of compensation in order to stimulate the activity of management. In addition, it can be supplemented to allow executives holding stocks. Particularly, it is quite important to select a good highest executive who will make decisions for enterprise and to establish scientific incentive mechanism and system, which is a critical factor for enterprise performance. Meanwhile, it is also needed to care about staff's salary, to fully exploit compensation incentive function and provide reasonable salary for staffs. As the cross-sectional data in our study is selected from 2009, we haven't analyzed the impact of increasing different employees' salary on enterprise performance. It can be obtained by analyzing the effect of different employees' salary change on the performance in different years in the future.

References

1. Lu, R.: Analysis of Managerial Power, Compensation and Performance Sensitivity (in Chinese). Contemporary Finance & Economics 7, 107–112 (2008)
2. Main, B.: Pay in the Boardroom Practices and Procedures. Personnel Review 22, 3–14 (1993)
3. Bebchuk, L.A., Fried, J.M., Walker, D.I.: Managerial Power and Rent Extraction in the Design of Executive Compensation. University of Chicago Law Review 69, 751–846 (2002)
4. Bertrand, M., Mullainathan, S.: Are CEOs Rewarded for Luck? The Ones without Principles are. The Quarterly Journal of Economics 116, 901–932 (2001)
5. Tang, J.: Study of Top Management Compensation and Performance in Listed Companies (in Chinese). Market Weekly. Disquisition Edition 12, 83 (2006)
6. Li, Z.: Incentive Mechanism and Enterprise Performance: an Empirical Study of Listed Companies (in Chinese). Accounting Research 1, 24–30 (2000)
7. Chen, X., Liu, S.: An Empirical Study on the Structural Difference among the Compensation of Managers in Chinese Public Companies (in Chinese). Economic Research Journal 8, 55–63 (2003)
8. Guo, X., Hu, Y.: Study of Correlation between Top Management Compensation and Performance based on Competition (in Chinese). Science & Technology Association Forum 3, 64 (2007)
9. Lu, R.: Managerial Power, Corporate Governance and Pay-Performance Sensitivity (in Chinese). Contemporary Finance & Economics 7, 112 (2008)
10. Zhu, Q., Peng, W.: The Study of the Correlation between Pay and Performance of Chinese Listed Companies. East China Economic Management 8, 116 (2008)
11. Li, Y.: Western Economics (in Chinese). Higher Education Press, Beijing (2000)

Social Welfare in China's Changing Society

Minjie Zhang

College of Public Administration, Zhejiang Gongshang University
Hangzhou 310018, China
chinaminjie@yahoo.com.cn

Abstract. This paper reviewed and addresses China's social welfare system from historic prospects. In previous six decades, China's social welfare experienced great changes, and Chinese people's living standard was improved, but the uncertainties of life in the rapidly changing social and economic realities in a changing society still create a need for the comfort and stability of the social security system.

Keywords: Social welfare, Social policy, Social security, China.

1 Introduction

China is a country has a written history of 4,000 years, its culture has had an extensive impact upon social welfare issues and the provision of assistance. After the establishment of the People's Republic of China in 1949, the new government focused more on social welfare. The new social welfare programs favored urban dwellers by giving them considerable welfare entitlements, whereas rural residents had to rely more on family care. Because this distribution system mainly covered part of the employees in state enterprises, it was call Unity (*danwei*) Welfare by Chinese scholars (Zhang M. 2001).

The contemporary Chinese social security system reform, which is a result and a part of the economic system reform, has had many achievements in recent years, and social welfare also achieved great progress; but the uncertainties of life in the rapidly changing social and economic realities of China create a need for the comfort and stability of the social security system. It seems that social welfare reform still facing a long way to go.

2 Development of Social Welfare in New China

During the early 1950s China's social security system was established, and it provided benefits for retirement, industrial injury, birth, illness, and death. In 1951 the first legislative enactment of social security, the Labor Insurance Regulations of the People's Republic of China, came into effect, and it provided benefits for birth, disease, injury, medical care, unemployment, retirement, and death internment.

Q. Zhou (Ed.): ISAEBD 2011, Part I, CCIS 208, pp. 215–221, 2011.
© Springer-Verlag Berlin Heidelberg 2011

However, this social security system was based on unit security. In China, the term unit originally referred to those urban dwellers with employment in a work organization, such as an economic enterprise, professional institute, government bureau, school, shop, and so forth. These work units were not only specialized organizations for different divisions of labor but were also providers of free, comprehensive, in-kind health, housing, and pension benefits designed to compensate for the low national standard wages. The state was responsible for arranging the employment of city and town dwellers. In principle, once an employee was hired, that person had a lifelong voucher to various welfare packages. Some large state-owned enterprises operated their own medical clinics, kindergartens, and schools. Employees cannot resign to work in another work unit. The social security system for these work units is described as 'small and comprehensive' or 'work unit managing society,' in terms of the comprehensiveness of the benefits. Without the work unit, Chinese society would not function properly. The social security system provides coverage for those working in state agencies and institutions, state-owned enterprises, and some collective enterprises. Workers in other collective enterprises, the self-employed, and farmers, which together comprise 70% of the population, have no social security coverage.

The social security system, based on work unit security, primarily covered government workers, and it was not administered in a unified way. All social security expenditures were funded by the state and state-owned enterprises. Chinese farmers and laborers outside this security system relied excessively on their children for security during accidents, calamities, and old age.

Obviously, Coverage of China's social welfare was small and unfair. Further more, during the 10 chaotic years of the Cultural Revolution, from1966 to 1976, and the social insurance work suffered serious setbacks as management agencies and trade unions were dissolved, social pooling from society for retirement expenses was cancelled, and social insurance was turned into enterprise insurance.

3   Social Welfare Reform: 1984 to 2000

In 1978 China began a new age of reform when it opened its doors to the world. The Communist Party of China explicitly pointed out that the basic target of the reform was establishment of a socialist market economic order. This breakthrough provided an important basis for establishing a new social welfare system that would be compatible with the development of the market economy, and that would guarantee citizens their livelihood rights.

While shortcomings of the social welfare system cited above could be traced back to the ineffective work unit security system, it was between 1984 and 1986 that this security system began to be regarded as an impediment to the market competitiveness of state-owned enterprises. The state-owned enterprises were regarded as having low economic productivity, and their employees were viewed as having low-work incentives. These conditions resulted in a mounting burden on production costs. To address these problems, the work unit security began to be dismantled in 1986 through a series of measures including the introduction of the contract worker system, bankruptcy law, open recruitment of labor, and the allowance of employee dismissal.

From 1987 to 1990, a somewhat expanded social security program went into effect across the country on the county, city, and provincial levels to cover industrial accidents and medical care. This program blazed the way for the expansion of the old-age security system and strengthened the ability of social security in general to take risks. Statistics show the direct expenditure on social security was 110.3 billion yuan in 1990. Meanwhile, 12.6 billion yuan of 11.4% of the total monies were paid to the rural population, and each recipient received 14 yuan. Payment to urban residents was nearly 30 times more than that to rural residents who actually make up more than 80 per cent of the country's population.

Government support for social welfare was demonstrated in its Work Report to the First Session of the Seventh National People's Congress in 1988 when Premier Li Peng promulgated the need to accelerate reform of the social security system, establish and perfect various social insurance systems, and gradually form a social security system unique to China.

In 1990, Premier Zhu Rongji noted that reforms of the housing system, insurance system, and medical system should be priorities for the next 10 years because they directly impact the well-being of the people. For the next two years, from 1991 to 1993, an overall social insurance reform focused on expanding its public provision program (Cao, 1995). On the one hand, the state paid 69.4 billion yuan in pensions in 1992, nearly 14 times the sum in 1982. In 1993, pension payments soared to 74 billion yuan, and of that sum, 22.2 billion yuan was paid to retirees in government institutions. On the other hand, reform promoted the following: individual workers could make contributions to their own old-age pensions, regulations managed all social welfare funds, and new social security legislation was passed. The target of social security reform was that the state financial department, institutions or companies, and employees all collaboratively fund the program.

Since 1994, as China's market-oriented economic reforms deepened, the urgent task to develop, standardize, and improve the social security system became most important. It was difficult to visualize and implement a unified, standardized, and perfect social security system. During this stage, the development of a social security system in China focused on providing security to enterprises by emphasizing the great importance of social insurance programs such as old age insurance, unemployment insurance, and medical care insurance. Determining the kind of social security system for the countryside was another important theme at this time. Policy Research Unit at Ministry of Civil Affairs (1997) clarified in its Guidelines for Developing a Rural Social Security System that the rural security system to be developed should consist mainly of: social relief, social old-age insurance, social welfare, care to servicemen with disabilities, care to family members of revolutionary martyrs and servicemen, social mutual aid and cooperative medical services, and a service network.

Reform of the social security system, which started in 1984, continues to move forward and is targeting to gradually expand social security coverage, to guarantee daily life needs and promote production, to establish a revenue generation system with contributions from the state, enterprises and individuals, to establish a social security management system, and to establish the social security system in rural areas while developing the rural economy (Zhang M. 2006).

There are two current trends in the social security system: one is the government's control over the economy is relaxing, and the urban residents are losing their price subsidies benefits for food and housing; another is the state enterprises are exposed to the market, unemployment is becoming a serious issue; therefore, the most urgent task in urban areas now is to establish a new, rational, and effective social security system to address possible poverty.

4 Current Developments in Social Welfare

The social welfare system is one of the basic aspects of China's socialist market economic system. Under this system the elderly are supported, patients with diseases are treated, workers suffering from industrial injury are given insurance, disaster survivors receive compensation, the unemployed are given relief, people with disabilities are properly placed, and the poor are provided with aid. Social welfare guarantees people essential life needs, ensures industrial and agricultural production, and therefore guarantees social stability. Social welfare is a safety net that also helps compensate for the limitations of the market economy. Furthermore, the social welfare distribution system regulates the income distribution of different groups in society. Laws and regulations protect the elderly, children, and people with disabilities, and the state and society have adopted measures to improve their livelihood, health, and participation in social development. In recent years, China's social welfare has developed into four parts: the aged, people with disabilities, children, and those with low-income.

4.1 Social Welfare for the Older People

Report presented by China National Committee on Aging shows that at the end of 2009, the number of China's elderly people reached 167 million, with 11 percent, or nearly 19 million, being 80 years old or above, and most of the 11 percent were wholly or partly unable to look after themselves. However, there is clearly a lack of family and social support for old people in both urban and rural areas. In light of these problems, the Chinese government has decided to make more efforts to improve the governmental elder care system (CNCOA, 2010).

China is establishing subsidy system for elder care services. Eligible elderly people will receive considerable government subsidies so they can be well cared for in rest homes or their own homes, and their living standards will not be lower than the average levels of local residents. In addition, residents over 80 years old will be entitled to a unified monthly old age allowance across China. A community basic care program is also establishing in all cities and towns, where the low-income senior citizens who are physically challenged or live alone could move to rest homes or enjoy home care services on government subsidies. All levels of government include services for elderly people in their social-economic development plans, gradually increase investments in services for elderly people, and encourage investments from all sectors of society. Enterprises, private entrepreneurs, and other investors have invested in and built welfare institutes. Recently, a social service system for elderly people was established as the result of campaign awareness describing their needs.

More elderly people now live at home due to state and collective run social welfare organizations that provide basic support.

4.2 Social Welfare for People with Disabilities

China currently has 83 million disabled people. The successful 2008 Beijing Paralympics promoted the work of organizations serving people with disabilities and demonstrated the Chinese people's unprecedented enthusiasm to help people with disabilities.

Nowadays, people with disabilities across China have received more income and better social welfare as well as public and rehabilitation services over the past five years. Government spending on programs for the disabled for the 2006-2011 periods more than doubled that of the previous five years. The increased funding went into improving vocational training and employment services for the disabled. The government has provided discounted loans worth 4 billion yuan since 2006 to help poor disabled persons in rural areas find work in the agriculture sector. This program lifted over six million disabled people out of poverty. Nearly 18 million disabled people in rural areas now earn more income through such job programs. In 2008, the government made a plan to renovate and build 1,160 special schools for the disabled in China's central and western areas, with 300 of them now completed. Concerning social welfare, nearly 95 percent of disabled people in rural areas were part of a health care insurance program and 2.38 million in urban areas received minimum subsistence allowances from the government by the same period.

4.3 Social Welfare for Children

China's children make up one fifth of the children in the world and 24% of the total population of China. Children are the future of the world and their well-being is an important part of the human life cycle.

Welfare homes play a special role in efforts to care for children. The welfare homes and some social welfare institutions care for orphans, who have lost their parents due to natural disasters or accidents or have been abandoned by their parents due to serious illness or severe mental or physical disabilities. Currently, about 20,000 children live in welfare institutions, and this accounts, for five per one hundred thousand adolescents in China.

Some children are unable to attend school due to poverty. According to a government document issued by the Information Office of the State Council of the People's Republic of China (1996), in the "Help-the-Poor Programs", governments at all levels have provided the assistance needed for children to attend school. Due to vigorous promotion by the government, people have been helping these children enjoy the fundamental right of an education. The state also provides comprehensive welfare for children, including education and planned immunizations. In addition, the state takes special care to ensure the livelihood, recovery, and education of children with special difficulties. Children with disabilities, orphans, and abandoned babies live in residential facilities and receive services.

According to report by National Working Committee on Children and Women under the State Council (2005), China has 192 special welfare institutions for children and 600 comprehensive welfare institutions with a children's department, accommodating a total of 54,000 orphans and children with disabilities. There are nearly 10,000 community services throughout China such as rehabilitation centers and training classes for orphans and children with disabilities such as mental retardation.

4.4 Social Welfare for Low-Income Groups

The poverty level was 785 yuan per person per year in 2008. According to the Ministry of Finance, the central government spent 276.16 billion yuan on social welfare and employment programs in 2008 a 19.9% increase over 2007 expenditures. This also increased the monthly subsidy to low-income households by 15 yuan for each urban citizen and 10 yuan for each rural resident in 2009. The government hopes to strengthen social welfare and health care by providing higher subsidies for the low-income people and a 10% increase in the basic retirement pension for enterprise retirees. Low-income subsidies in China vary by region, where a low-income citizens in Beijing can receive a monthly subsidy of 410 yuan while a farmer could receive 170 yuan a month.

Currently, most low-income people are workers laid off from state-owned enterprises, migrant workers living in cities, and farmers who lost their land due to industrialization or urbanization. Many employees were dismissed when their enterprises were restructured and their income, usually quite low, was fixed at their dismissal. This income amount was unlikely to change even after their former employers saw huge increases in revenue. Migrant workers are often under paid and usually not covered by employee insurance and subsidies. Many farmers who lost their farmland due to urbanization not only lost their source of stable income but were also not fairly compensated for their land. It is estimated that farmers usually received only 10% of all the revenues generated in land transference. If the government could grant a higher compensation to farmers for lost land and as a general matter initiate policies to prevent these several vulnerable groups from falling below the poverty line, the effect would be remarkable.

In 2010, the government will also raise the pension for enterprise retirees, improve treatment for those who enjoy special care as disabled former servicemen, and family members of revolutionary martyrs, and offer more affordable housing to middle- and low-income families. This will increase the supply of low-rent housing and affordable housing, and promote the rebuilding of shanty towns and substandard buildings in urban areas. In November 2008, the Ministry of Housing and Urban-Rural Development of China issued a plan to make available over two million low-rent houses and over four million economic houses for low-income workers in three years. In addition, there should be more than 2.2 million houses in slum areas.

5 Conclusion

In summary, during the last 100 years China has undergone a number of changes, including going from a government that did not provide social services to a government that is more concerned about the social welfare of its people, including vulnerable populations such as orphans and people with disabilities. The early exclusive social welfare unit security system that favored urban government employees has changed markedly to a social security system today that is more equitable, comprehensive, and broad-based in its revenue sources in the market economy.

An important feature of the social economic structure of China was the unity security system with its dualistic social structure separating the rural and urban people. Employment security, social insurance for old age, industrial injury, medicine and child bearing, and various subsidies were provided only for those urban staff and workers employed by the government and other state sectors. Beyond this were a few relief programs provided by the civil affairs departments of the government agencies. Farmers in some regions, especially in Southwest and Northwest China, are too poor to put much money into insurance funds such as old-age insurance, medical insurance, and industrial injury insurance. Therefore, it is important to hasten development of the farmers' old-age security and health security guide, actively explore in rural areas a basic security system suited to the socialist market economy system and the country's economic development level, and initiate a system to help vulnerable groups in society work and care for themselves.

Social security system reform, which is a result and a part of the economic system reform, has had many achievements in recent years. The unequal, employment-based, and mismanaged unity system has been transformed into a more equal, more comprehensive, and more economical contributory system in a market economy. However, the uncertainties of life in the rapidly changing social and economic realities of China create a need for the comfort and stability of the social security system.

Nowadays, family planning and change of lifestyles have reduced the function of the family as an insurance factor. All these issues depend on the improvement of the social security system and development of the insurance industry for solutions. So that it is imperative to develop a social welfare system embodying the principles of universality, fundamentality, and differentiated approaches in the context of China's realities.

References

Cao, M.: Provide insurance to more farmers. China Daily (1995-02/11)
China National Committee on Aging (CNCOA),
   http://www.cncaprc.gov.cn/en/info/618.html
Gao, S.Q., Chi, F.L.: China's Social Security System. Foreign Languages Press, Beijing (1996)
Qian, N.: Modern Social Welfare. Higher Education Press, Beijing (2004)
Shi, Z.X. (ed.): Report on China's Social Welfare and Social Progress. Social Sciences and Documents Publishing House, Beijing (2000)
Si, B.N. (ed.): Introduction to Social Security. Higher Education Press, Beijing (2004)
Wang, D.J. (ed.): The Reform and Development of Social Security System in China. Law Press, Beijing (2004)
William, H.W., Ronald, C.F.: Social Welfare in Today's World. Law Press, Beijing (2003)
Zhang, M.: The development of Chinese social work in the 20th century. Journal of Zhejiang Social Academy 2, 62–66 (2001)
Zhang, M.: Workfare policy and its revelation to China. Journal of Zhejiang Social Academy 4, 91–97 (2006)

The Puzzle of Lost Wallet Game: Challenge of Reciprocity Theory

Jianbiao Li and Yuliang Zhao

A901 MBA Building, Business School of Nankai Unversity,
94# Weijin Road, Nankai District, 300071 Tianjin, P.R. China
zhaoyuliang327@163.com

Abstract. The theory of reciprocity is one of main topics of behavioral economics and experimental economics in recent several decades. However, lost wallet game proposed by Dufwenberg and Gneezy in 2000 indicated that the reward behavior of wallet owner and the size of the outside option the wallet picker forgone are uncorrelated or weakly correlated. Servátka and Vadovič (2009) and Cox et al (2010) were trying to use the inequality of outside option and the saliency of outside option to the wallet loser to shed some light on the puzzle of lost wallet game, but their experiments hasn't solved the asymmetry between the wallet loser's reward behavior y and the outside option the wallet picker forgone. Therefore, the lost wallet game is still an open puzzle.

Keywords: puzzle of lost wallet game, reciprocity theory, inequality of outside option, saliency of outside option.

1 Reciprocity Theory

Reciprocity as a basic human interaction norm has played an important role in daily life. The idea that the subject of grace drip, given the smallest favor, as one of China's traditional culture, makes numerous examples that one is generous just because of the kindness of the one she or he interacted in china's long history. Adam Smith in his Theory of Moral Sentiments gave several reference to the thought of kindness is the parents of kindness. On the one hand, people tend to be generous to the ones who show kindness to him; on the other hand, people usually sacrifice a great deal to punish the ones that display unkind to him. The former is called positive reciprocity and the latter is called negative reciprocity by Rabin. In recent decades, [1][2][3][4][5] Behavioral economics and experimental economics have begun to focus on the phenomenon of reciprocity in the field and experimental environment and model the phenomenon of reciprocity in different game(Rabin(1993), Fehr and Schmidt (1999), Bolton and Ockenfels (2000), Charness and Rabin(2002), Li and Li(2009)),. People inspired by the reciprocity may be produced outcome that completely different from the model base on the pure self-interest assumption predicts. [6]-[11] Experimental economists and behavioral economist find a quiet number of phenomenon of reciprocity and the preference of reciprocity strongly

Q. Zhou (Ed.): ISAEBD 2011, Part I, CCIS 208, pp. 222–228, 2011.

influence the behavior of the subject in the lab in the ultimatum game, trust game, moonlighting game and gift exchange game (Guth, Schmittberger and Schwarze(1982), Berg, Dickhaut and McCabe (1995), Abbink, Irlenbusch and Renner(2000), Falk, Fehr and Fischbacher (2008), Fehr, Kirchsteiger and Riedl(1993),Fehr, Gachter and Kirchsteiger(1997)).

2 The Puzzle of Lost Wallet Game

[12] Lost wallet game was proposed by Dufwenberg and Gneezy, they supposed the following scenery: one finds a wallet which contains some cash and several certificates in the street and no one finds him. It is obvious that the cash is of value to both the owner and the picker of the wallet, but the certificate is no use to the picker. The finder can either keep the wallet or bring it to a nearby police office to wait for the owner to pick up and the police man will routinely write down the finder's name and in the subsequent time ask the owner to reward the finder some amount money that he consider appropriate.

The special instance of situation can be described by Fig.1. At stage 1, player 1 (picker) has two options: TAKE or LEAVE. If player 1 chooses TAKE, then he gets the value of cash x (x is an exogenously given parameter such that $0 < x < 20$), while player 2 (owner) get nothing. If player 1 chooses LEAVE, then player 2 specify y($0 \leq y \leq 20$) for player 1 and he get 20-y for himself. The subgame of player 2's move is a dictator game in essence. Apparently, the unique subgame perfect equilibrium of lost wallet game is (TAKE, y=0). However, it is an inefficient outcome that there is much space for Parato-superior, because both the players will be better off when the player 1 chooses Leave and player 2 gives player 1 a value of y more than x.

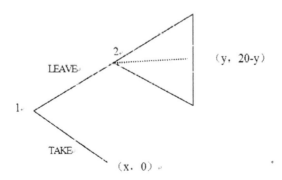

Fig. 1. Lost Wallet Game of Dufwenberg and Gneezy

There are five sessions in Dufwenberg and Gneezy's lost wallet game experiment, x was fixed at 3, 7, 10, 13, and 16 in every session respectively. 12 group participants were included in every experiment. Dufwenberg and Gneezy use strategy method to elicit player 2's decision, that is, they ask player 2 to make a decision y without knowing the player 1's decision, the player 2's decision works only player 1 chooses

LEAVE. In order to test reciprocity effect, they also conducted dictator game [1] experiments so that player 2's behavior can be compared with dictator's decision. If reciprocity effect works, then player 2 could be more generous than he or she would be as a dictator in dictator game. At the same times, to examine belief's influence on decision, two authors measured player 1's guess about y, which player 2 allocate him, as well as player 2's guess about what player 1's guess about y, and the reward is depend on the accuracy of guesses.

The outcome of lost wallet game experiment showed player 1's behavior fall short of prediction of pure self-interest model. In the experiment of x=4, 7, 10, 13,16, the percentage of player 1 who chooses LEAVE 100%, 50%, 66.7%, 33.3% and 8.3% respectively, even if some subject expect that player 2 will give him or her less than x. of course, less the subject who would like to show kindness, the bigger the outside option player 1 forgone. Player 2's behavior is inconsistent with reciprocity model. In the experiments of x=4, 7, 10, 13, 16, the average y that player 2 gives player 1 are 7.33, 4.83, 7.54, 6.12, 5.75 respectively. Nonparametric Wilcoxon test show that the hypothesis that y and x are uncorrelated is not rejected at the 5% significance level surprisingly. But they find the evidence that y is positively correlated with player 2's guess about player 1's guess about y. More surprisingly, in the two sessions dictator game experiments, the average of y that the dictator chooses is 6.08, which is of no significant difference from y that player 2 choose in the lost wallet game. In the same way, In the Dictator game, y is positively correlated with player 2's expectation of player 1's expectation of y. their explanation was that player 2 (or dictator) may be averse to letting player 1 down and then gives the player 1 a value of y more than their expectation of y.

[13] Brandts, Guth and Stiehler (2006) conducted three-player lost wallet game which adding the third party in addition to the picker and the owner of the wallet when they studying the granting allocation power. X, Y and Z share the wallet that totally maximum valued 12 tokens. First, X decides whether take the outside option which yields 3 or 6 tokens for himself and leave the other two players empty-handed or he wants the whole wallet to be divided by either Y or Z. when X gives up the outside option, Y or Z will be the allocator who divides wallet with the value of 12 tokens. And so the sum of the payoff of X, Y, Z is 12. To study the assigning distributive power's influence on the motivation effect, they designed two treatments: SA treatment which X selected allocator in case that X gives up the outside option and RA treatment which random device selected the allocator in case that X gives up outside option. In the SA treatment, both Y and Z were selected with the probability of 0.5.

Inspired by the model of Dufwenberg and Gneezy as well as by intuition, Brandts, Guth and Stiehler studied the way that allocator was selected affect distribution outcome as well as how the size of outside option influence the distribution outcome. In their 2(treatments) x3(sessions) x15(participants) experiments, there are 3 rounds in every session, the first two rounds the outside option was fixed at 3 tokens and the third round the outside option was equal to 6 tokes. Because magnitude of outside option amount to the potential loss of player X, they supposed that the

---

[1] That is one player decides how to divide some money between him and the other player, while the other player have no right to reject.

allocator would keep less for himself for the larger outside option than for the smaller one. However, experimental result did not provide any evidence for their hypothesis, higher outside option does not necessarily make the allocator keep less for himself. They think that counter-intuitive result may be as a result of inequity of outside option, which both outside options were left to player X and the other players get nothing. Therefore unfairness of outside option makes player X giving up of his outside option may be considered as responsibility rather than generosity and does not affect the allocator's following distributive behavior.

[14] Chaness, Haruvy and Sonsino(2007) explore the effects of social distance on reciprocity through lost wallet game experiment conducted over the internet on three continents, and in classroom laboratory of Israel and Spain, and in computer of two states—Texas and California. Although they reached the conclusion that many participants do have some regard for others, even when these others are distant and disembodied strangers and nearly 30% of all internet responders chose a profile in which y the owner of wallet chose increase with x the picker of wallet foregone. In fact, in the internet experiment, as for different levels of x, up to 48% of wallet picker chose a fixed y (36% of the subjects chosen y = 0, 13% of the subjects chose y=50, 9% of the subjects choose another fixed value). In the classroom laboratory and inter-state computer room, the percentage of subjects that chose a fixed y are up to 35% and 40% respectively. The percentage of y is weakly correlated with x in internet, classroom laboratory and computer room of inter-state are 28%, 43% and 33% respectively.

What on earth makes the reward behavior of wallet owner and the size of the outside option the wallet picker forgone are uncorrelated or weakly correlated? Is it inequality of outside option or the saliency of outside options to the wallet owner that make the wallet pickers are not sensitive to the forgone outside option?

3 Inequality of Outside Option and the Puzzle of Lost Wallet Game

To explore whether the inequality of outside option result into the puzzle of lost wallet game that Brandts, Guth and Stiehler proposed, [15] Servátka and Vadovič compared subject's behavior of equal outside option with the behavior of unequal outside option experimentally. If player 1 chooses IN, then player 2 can divide the surplus between himself and player 1. If player 1 decides OUT, then the outcome of outside option is (x_1, x_2), x_1 is the payoff of player 1 and x_2 is the payoff of player 2. In case that players care strongly about equality of payoffs then actions leading to equal outcomes may be considered more seriously than those leading to unequal outcomes. Based on the logic, it follows that if outside option payoffs are unequal then player 2 may not consider the payoff that player 1 forgone and makes just his own pecuniary payoffs into account. They argue that if ending the lost wallet game with equal outside option might make player 2 cares more about player 1 forgone payoff.

[15] Servátka and Vadovič use between-subject design and strategy method to implement experiments which consist of two treatments with equal outside option and unequal outside option at the University of Canterburey in New Zealand. In the

unequal outside option treatment, at first, player 1 receives 10 tokens and player 2 receives 0 tokens. If player 1 chooses IN, lost wallet game continues and then player 2 chooses how to split 20 tokens between him and player 1, that is, player 2 chooses to keep y for player 1 and keeps 20-y for himself. If player 1 chooses OUT, lost wallet game ends and player 1 gets 10 tokens and player 2 gets 0 tokens. The only difference between equal outside option treatment and unequal outside option treatment is that both players get 5 tokens when player chooses OUT in equal outside option while 10 and 0 in unequal ones. To avoid the mixed effect, the sum of outside option payoffs of two players are kept constant, that is, $x_1 + x_2 = 10$.

However, their experimental result did not provide evidence for Brandts, Guth and Stiehler's conjecture on player 2. Player 2 chose on average y=6.12 in the unequal outside option treatment while player 2 chose on average y=5.19 in the equal outside option treatment. 2-sided Wilcoxon rank-sum test showed that difference in player 2 in two treatments is not significant. Therefore, conclusion that inequality of outside option do not account for the behavior of player 2 in the lost wallet game is reached. Puzzle of lost wallet game is still an open mystery.

4   Saliency of Outside Option and the Puzzle of Lost Wallet Game

[16] According to psychological forward induction of Batigalli and Dufwenberg, player 2 behavior should be different across lost wallet game with different amounts of outside option, which is consistent with reciprocity theory. Player 1 giving up his outside option to some extent reveals that he has higher hopes and expects more from player 2. Therefore, in case that player 2 is guilt-averse, he will respond generous to player 1's belief and give more to player 1 at the case of higher outside option.

[17] Cox attempted to shed light on the puzzle of lost wallet game that outside option player 1 forgone do not affect player 2's reward behavior. They doubted uncorrelation between player 2's reward y and x player 1 forgone in lost wallet game and argued that the response y to x depend on the saliency of the magnitude of outside option to player 2, because he must be conscious about the size of his opponent giving up outside option when they make decision. They conjectured that Dufwenberg and Gneezy's original protocol may not have made the magnitude of outside option forgone by player 1 salient to player 2. Hence, they change Dufwenberg and Gneezy's original protocol from two perspectives. First, strategy method for player 2 was replaced by direct response method which is sequentially played. Second, instead of having players write down numbers representing their decision in Dufwenberg and Gneezy's experiments, they make players pass paper money certificates.

They used direct method and between-subject design to conduct 12 lost wallet game experiment sessions which consist of 112 group undergraduate participants at University of Canterbury in New Zealand. In the first stage, player 1 chooses to whether to keep a legal-size envelope containing 4(7) one-dollar certificates or whether to send it to an anonymously matched player 2. If player 1 keeps the envelope, the game will end and player 1 receives 4(7) New Zealand dollars (NZD) and player 2 receives a large manila envelope containing blank pieces of paper instead of one-dollar certificates and has no decision to make. If player 1 does not keep the envelope, the lost wallet game continues. Experimenter will pass a large manila envelope to player 2, which contains 4(7) one-dollar certificates in a legal-size envelope labeled "other's certificate", an empty legal-size envelope labeled "my certificates" and additional 16(13) one-dollar certificates. Player 2 then has to split 20 certificates between himself and player 1.

[18] It is the strategy method that Selten introduced to elicit decision in an experiment in 1967. As for whether it affect behavior of agents, [19] Brandts and Charness provide a good survey. But they did not give a fixed answer. It seems to return to specific context to answer this issue. In a similar experiment with lost wallet game, [20] Casari and Cason measure strategy method and direct response method's impact on agents' behavior in a simple trust game. Experimental result shows that strategy method did not change behavior of trustor, but lowers measured trustworthy behavior significantly. Trustee on average returned 12.6 in direct response method while they on average return only 7.4 in the strategy method. As for whether real money or paper money certificates as well as writing down numbers representing decision produce different outcome, there is no documentation referring to such issue so far.

Cox's experimental result showed that behavior of player 1 has no difference from Dufwenberg and Gneezy's. Surprisingly, the change of saliency of outside option to player 2 did not affect behavior of player 2. Player 2 returned 6.61 NZD on average in treatment of x=4, and returned 6.00 NZD on average in treatment of x=7. They speculate that no difference of player 2's behavior is as result of the same feasible set of player 2 in two treatments while in trust game trustee's feasible set is increased by player 1's sent behavior. Player 2 in lost wallet game only can split the fixed sum value "wallet". Saliency of outside option to player 2 did not account for the puzzle of lost wallet and positive reciprocity theory can't produce reasonable prediction.

5 Discussion

The uncorrelation or weak correlation between reward behavior of wallet owner and the size of the outside option the wallet picker gives up in the lost wallet game propose by Dufwenberg and Gneezy in 2000 challenges the reciprocity theory developing recent several decades. This paper surveyed the puzzle of lost wallet game propose by Dufwenberg and Gneezy and provided other evidence from other scholars' experiment, and then we track the following study. Servátka and Vadovič (2009) examine conjecture from Brandts that inequality of outside option may account for the asymmetry between reward behavior of wallet owner and the size of the outside option the wallet picker gives up. But the experimental result show that equality of outside option does not change the uncorrelation of x and y. Cox et al (2010) attempted to explain the puzzle of lost wallet game with the saliency of outside option to player 2. After using a direct response method for player 2 instead of strategy method and paper money certificate that passed between players instead of writing down numbers for decision, they still did not solve the asymmetry y that owner's reward behavior and x that the picker gives up. There is still a mysterious veil over the lost wallet game.

Acknowledgments. This paper is supported by Project (No. 70972086) of National Natural Science Foundation of China and Key Research Base for Humanity and Social Science Major Project of Chinese Ministry of Education (10JJD630002).

References

[1] Rabin, M.: Incorporating fairness into game theory and economics. American Economic Review 83(5), 1281–1302 (1993)

[2] Fehr, E., Schmidt, K.M.: A theory of fairness, competition and cooperation. Quarterly Journal of Economics 114(3), 817–868 (1999)

[3] Bolton, G.E., Ockenfels, A.: ERC: a theory of equity, reciprocity, and competition. American Economic Review 90(1), 166–193 (2000)

[4] Charness, G., Rabin, M.: Understanding social preferences with simple tests. Quarterly Journal of Economics 117(3), 817–869 (2002)

[5] Li, X., Li, J.: Reciprocity, trust and efficiency of governance. Nankia Economic Research 1, 101–121 (2009)

[6] Guth, W., Schmittberger, R., Schwarze, B.: An experimental analysis of ultimatium bargaining. Journal of Economic Behavior and Organization 3(4), 367–388 (1982)

[7] Berg, J., Dickhaut, J., McCabe, K.: Trust, reciprocity, and social history. Games and Economic Behavior 10(1), 122–142 (1995)

[8] Abbink, K., Irlenbusch, B., Renner, E.: The moonlighting game. Journal Economics Behaviror and Organization 42(2), 265–277 (2000)

[9] Falk, A., Fehr, E., Fischbacher, U.: Testing theories of fairness—Intentions matter. Game and Economics and Behavior 62(1), 287–304 (2008)

[10] Fehr, E., Kirchsteiger, G., Riedl, A.: Does fairness prevent market clearing? An experimental investment. Quarterly Journal of Economics 108(2), 437–459 (1993)

[11] Fehr, E., Gachter, S., Kirchsteiger, G.: Reciprocity as a Contract Enforcement Device: Experimental Evidence. Econometrica 65(4), 833–860 (1997)

[12] Dufwenberg, M., Gneezy, U.: Measuring beliefs in an experimental lost wallet game. Games and Economic Behavior 30(2), 163–182 (2000)

[13] Brandts, J., Güth, W., Stiehler, A.: I Want YOU! An experiment studying motivational effects when assigning distributive power. Labour Economics 13(1), 1–17 (2006)

[14] Charness, G., Haruvy, E., Sonsino, D.: Social distance and reciprocity: an internet experiment. Journal of Economics Behavior and Organization 63(1), 88–103 (2007)

[15] Servátka, M., Vadovič, R.: Unequal outside options in the lost wallet game. Economics Bulletin 29(4), 2870–2883 (2009)

[16] Battigalli, P., Dufwenberg, M.: Dynamic psychological games. Journal of Economic Theory 144(1), 1–35 (2009)

[17] Cox, J., Servátka, M., Vadovič, R.: Saliency of outside options in the lost wallet game. Experimental Economics 13(1), 66–74 (2010)

[18] Selten, R.: Die Strategiemethode zur Erforschung des eingeschränkt rationalen Verhaltens im Rahmen eines Oligopolexperiments. In: Sauermann, H. (ed.) Beiträge zur experimentellen Wirtschaftsforschung, pp. 136–168. Mohr, Tübingen (1967)

[19] Brandts, J., Charness, G.: The strategy verse the direct-response method: a survey of experimental comparisons, Working papers (2010)

[20] Casari, M., Cason, T.: The strategy method lowers measured trustworthy behavior. Economics Letters 103(3), 157–159

Quantificational Analysis of Reasons for Drain of High-Level Talents in Ningbo

Guo Tang

College of Science & Technology, Ningbo University, 315212 Ningbo, China
tangguo@nbu.edu.cn

Abstract. High-level talents are one of the most important resources in the era of knowledge economy. Drain of high-level talents in Ningbo may affect economic development of Ningbo and especially its competitiveness of science and technology. This thesis regards organizational factors, individual factors, and other factors as the main factors leading to drain of high-level talents in Ningbo, and this thesis determines weights of these factors by means of AHP. Among all factors affecting drain of high-level talents in Ningbo, weight of salary level and problem of immediate superior is the greatest, and influences of sense of individualism, organizational culture and housing factor are also worthy of consideration.

Keywords: Ningbo, high-level talents, drain.

1 Introduction of AHP

The Analytical Hierarchy Process (AHP) is a decision-aiding method developed by Saaty. It aims at quantifying relative priorities for a given set of alternatives on a ratio scale, based on the judgment of the decision-maker, and stresses the importance of the intuitive judgments of a decision-maker as well as the consistency of the comparison of alternatives in the decision-making process. Since a decision-maker bases judgments on knowledge and experience, then makes decisions accordingly, the AHP approach agrees well with the behavior of a decision-maker. The strength of this approach is that it organizes tangible and intangible factors in a systematic way, and provides a structured yet relatively simple solution to the decision-making problems. In addition, by breaking a problem down in a logical fashion from the large, descending in gradual steps, to the smaller and smaller, one is able to connect, through simple paired comparison judgments, the small to the large [1].

2 Cause of Drain of High-Level Talents in Ningbo

Along with arrival of knowledge economy, function of talent resource in development of economy and society is becoming more and more important, and talent resource is the first resource impelling social development. All competitions rely on competition for talents, as a result, competition for talents among enterprises, regions or nations

Q. Zhou (Ed.): ISAEBD 2011, Part I, CCIS 208, pp. 229–235, 2011.
© Springer-Verlag Berlin Heidelberg 2011

are becoming fiercer and fiercer. High-level talents are always the focus of scramble for talents. Ningbo needs great number of high-level talents to provide intellectual support for overall harmonious, sustainable development of society and economy, and if Ningbo wants to become an open and free port city with quantitative talents, it has to attract high-level talents of all trades and professions, and to prevent drain of high-level talents. Therefore, it's necessary to study causes of drain of high-level talents in Ningbo. Causes of drain of high-level are multilevel and complex, among the causes, various indices have different relative importance, it's difficult to determine weights of indices. The commonly used methods such as estimation by experience or experts determination are difficult to get the desired results. AHP can be used to raise accuracy of weights of various indices, credibility and validity in determining index weights can be increased by use of judgment metrics to check consistency.

The so-called high-level talents refers to talents who are in the leading position in a certain field and have made great contribution in this field or who function as pioneer or leading role in certain field. With regard to its scope of influence, high-level talents have nature of relativity, a nation, a region or an economic unit all has its own corresponding layer of high-level talents [2]. According to concrete situation of Ningbo, the research group defines high-level talents in Ningbo as those who have doctor's academic degree or who have senior professional title.

High flow rate of employees is always a difficult problem for an organization. Many scholars have studied factors affecting employees' flow from different aspects. Ham and Griffeth studied this problem and found some factors which are closely related to flow rate, including age, sex, family burden, job satisfactory magnitude, expectations for job, work performance, opportunities for promotion, incentive measures, difficulty of work and so on. David J. Kennedy and Mark D. Fulford pointed out that factors affecting employees' flow include distinct factors and indistinct factors, the former contains age, income, nature of job, desire for personal development, expectations for future prospect, attitude for shift of post and so on, the later includes sex, race, marriage condition, number of family member, educational background, office term of job, previous experience of job transfer. Jean Hiltrop put forward that factors affecting employees' flow involve job reward, challenge from work, training and promoting opportunities, social economic situation, arrangement of working hours, working responsibility, autonomous right in work, labor security and opportunities for professional development. Margaret A. Deery found out that besides reward, working expectation, corporate culture and lack of communication between the management and employees are also important factors that influence employees' flow [3]. In China, although people have studied some aspects in employees' flow, there are few conclusions which are generally applicable. The research group has sent out 300 questionnaires in Ningbo urban district titled as "Investigation on factors affecting drain of high-level talents in Ningbo", 276 questionnaires are withdrawn which account for 92% of all questionnaires sent out, and effective questionnaires are 214. The scale used in this thesis is obtained according to data from investigation. In the light of concrete situation in Ningbo, the research group divides causes of drain of high-level talents in Ningbo into three types, they are organizational factors, individual factors and other factors. Organizational factors mainly include salary level, organizational culture, training and immediate superior problem. Immediate superior problem means the personality and capacity and management style of immediate superior leading to drain of high-level talents. Individual factors mainly contain personal performance, individualism sense and uncertainty evasion sense. Individualism sense refers to individual attitude in dealing with relationship between individual and community. Individuals who have strong individualism sense are emotionally independent with their organization, their behavior within organization are self-orientated and they want their performance to be recognized by their organization, and they hope to be highly appreciated by their superiors, they pay great attention to opportunities and challenges, and they stress initiative insight and creation spirit, they prefer initiative management and dislike supervision and management from their leaders. Sense of uncertainty evasion means individual's attitude to uncertain position. Persons with strong sense of uncertainty evasion have strong anxiety, they worry about future and failure, they lack spirit of challenge, they dislike organizational transform, they prefer to work in the same organization till retirement, and they would choose familiar region to live and work in. These persons consider scale of organization very important in professional choice, they usually prefer large-sized organization. Other factors include social employment rate, housing and living environment.

3 Determining Weights of Causes for Drain of High-Level Talents

The system of reasons for drain of high-level talents in Ningbo includes three levels. The top level is reasons for drain of high-level talents in Ningbo (A); the intermediate level consists of organizational factors (B1), personal factors (B2) and other factors (B3); the lowest level includes ten indicators (C1-C10). The system of reasons for drain of high-level talents in Ningbo is shown in Table 1.

Table 1. System of reasons for drain of high-level talents in Ningbo

	Organizational factors (B1)	Salary level(C1)
		Training(C2)
		Organization culture(C3)
		Direct lead problem(C4)
Reasons for drain of high-level talents in Ningbo (A)	Personal factors (B2)	Personal preference(C5)
		Individualism consciousness(C6)
		Incertitude-avoiding consciousness (C7)
	Other factors (B3)	Unemployment rate(C8)
		Housing factor(C9)
		Environment(C10)

According to the importance of factors, we construct a set of pair-wise comparison matrices and calculate, the results are as follow:

3.1 Weights of Intermediate Level Indicators B1、B2、B3 Relative to Top Level Indicator A

We check the consistency of the pair-wise comparison matrix and the CR is acceptable because it does not exceed 0.10. The pair-wise comparison matrix is shown in table 2.

Table 2.

A	B1	B2	B3	Wi	
B1	1	3	4	0.614	λmax=3.074
B2	1/3	1	3	0.268	CI=0.037 RI=0.580
B3	1/4	1/3	1	0.117	CR=0.064

3.2 Weights of Lowest Level Indicators C1、C2、C3、C4 Relative to Intermediate Level Indicator B1

We check the consistency of the pair-wise comparison matrix and the CR is acceptable because it does not exceed 0.10. The pair-wise comparison matrix is shown in table 3.

Table 3.

B1	C1	C2	C3	C4	Wi	
C1	1	5	3	1	0.394	λmax= 4.004
C2、	1/5	1	1/2	1/5	0.075	CI=0.001 RI=0 .900
C3	1/3	2	1	1/3	0.137	CR=0 .001
C4	1	5	3	1	0.394	

3.3 Weights of Lowest Level Indicators C5、C6、C7 Relative to Intermediate Level Indicator B2

We check the consistency of the pair-wise comparison matrix and the CR is acceptable because it does not exceed 0.10. The pair-wise comparison matrix is shown in table 4.

Table 4.

B2	C5	C6	C7	Wi	
C5	1	1/7	1/4	0.075	λmax= 3.076
C6	7	1	4	0.696	CI=0 .038 RI=0 .580
C7	4	1/4	1	0.696	CR=0 .066

3.4   Weights of Lowest Level Indicators C8、 C9、 C10 Relative to Intermediate Level Indicator B3

We check the consistency of the pair-wise comparison matrix and the CR is acceptable because it does not exceed 0.10. The pair-wise comparison matrix is shown in table 5.

Table 5.

B3	C8	C9	C10	Wi	
C8	1	1/7	1/5	0.072	λmax= 3.065
C9	7	1	3	0.649	CI=0 .032 RI=0 .580
C10	5	1/3	1	0.279	CR=0 .055

According to the weights gained from above calculation, based on the calculating principle of AHP, we can get the overall sequence of weights of lowest level indicators relative to top level indicator A. We check the consistency of the pair-wise comparison matrix and the CR is acceptable because it does not exceed 0.10. The pair-wise comparison matrix is shown in table 6.

Table 6.

	B1 0.614	B2 0.268	B3 0.117	Overall ranking of C level (weight)
C1	0.394			0.242
C2	0.075			0.046
C3	0.137			0.084
C4	0.394			0.242
C5	0.075			0.020
C6		0.696		0.187
C7		0.696		0.061
C8			0.072	0.008
C9			0.649	0.076
C10			0.279	0.033
CI	0.001	0 .038	0 .032	CI=0 .018 RI=0 .777
CR	0 .001	0 .066	0 .055	CR=0 .023

4   Conclusions and Countermeasures

By applying AHP, the research group has gained weights of factors affecting drain of high-level talents in Ningbo.

Salary level C1 and immediate superior problem C4 have the greatest weight, both are 0.242. Whether Maslow's layers of need or Herzberg's double factors theory or Alderfer's ERG theory, all consider physiological need as the top layer need. Pursuit for maximum benefit is the rational choice for every "economic man", high-level talents are not exception. Individual income as the most important security for satisfying physiological need is the first consideration in high-level talents' choice of profession, and seek for higher income is an important cause for flow of knowledge workers. The organization where high-level talents are employed may be unaware of the market value of high-level talents because of lack of information, so the organization hasn't consider external competitiveness in determining salary treatment for high-level talents. In light of the phenomenon of drain of high-level talents because of asymmetric information, government of Ningbo should make effort in facilitating communication of information. Local government can provide to local employing units the information of treatment for high-level talents in various regions, thus local organizations can offer more reasonable salary to high-level talents. The famous American psychologist Lewin put forward that personal performance has a functional relationship with individual capacity, external conditions and environment. If an individual dwells in a disadvantageous environment, it's difficult for him to exert his wisdom and intelligence and get due achievement. Normally, an individual is powerless in the face of environment, the only means of change is to depart from the present environment and turn to work in a suitable environment. The famous American Gallop Co. has drawn the following three conclusions based on years of large quantities of investigation and research: (1) What employees enter into is the corporation, and what employees is their manager. (2) 75% employees resign because of their manager rather than their corporation. (3) Among the reasons of employees' resignation, 85% are controlled by employees' immediate superior. Therefore, organizations need to pay attention to not only to external competitiveness of salary but also to working environment of high-level talents, especially problem of immediate superior. Employing units need to train immediate superior of high-level talents in leadership skills and thus create a good working environment for high-level talents [4].

The weight of individualism sense (indicator C6) ranks the third, which indicates that individualism sense has great influence on drain of high-level talents. Generally, high-level talents have strong sense of individualism, employing units should grant their high-level talents sufficient freedom in working in order to increase their working satisfaction magnitude. For example, employing units can carry out system of elastic working hours for high-level talents. Additionally, employing units should establish a scientific performance evaluating system to know and survey employees' performance and to improve employees' performance and corporate management by means of feedback from results of performance evaluation. Furthermore, performance appraisal has incentive function, it can make high-level talents have sense of pride and increase their professional satisfaction. At last, results of performance appraisal are helpful for determination of employees' promotion, reward and punishment, allocation of benefits [5].

Attention should be paid to functions of organizational culture on lowering drain of high-level talents. Organizational culture is values recognized by all employees, it has strong cohesion and plays important role in stabilizing its personnel staff. Employing units should increase training of organizational core values and organizational systems for newly recruited personnel, so as to help high-level talents to understand organizational culture and increase their recognition of organizational core values. Periodical training or seminar should be conducted for high-level talents to enhance their understanding about organizational values.

Apart from the above, weight of housing factor ranks the fifth, which indicates that price of housing in Ningbo has affected drain of high-level talents to a certain degree. According to investigation made by State Statistic Bureau, in October 2007 the year-on-year growth of prices of newly-built housing in Ningbo is 19.1%, which is the highest increase in the nation then; in July 2009 the year-on-year growth of housing price in Ningbo is 4.3%,which is the second high in the nation; and the year-on-year growth of prices of newly-built housing in Ningbo is 6.8% in July 2009, the extent of price increase is also the highest in the nation. As the saying goes, only after settling down in a house can people work contentedly. In order to attract and retain high-level talents, government of Ningbo should adopt some measures against the constant increase of housing prices. Weight of other factors such as sense of uncertainty evasion C7, training C2, living environment C10, individual preference C5, and social employment rate C8 is relatively small, but we should also pay attention to these factors to prevent high-level talents from voting by feet and flowing out of Ningbo.

References

1. Saaty, T.L.: The Analytic Hierarchy Process. McGraw-Hill, New York (1980)
2. Ye, Z.: The Basic Principle of Talent. Blue Press, Peking (2005) (in Chinese)
3. Jiang, X.: The Management of Employee Flow. Shandong People Press, Shandong (2004) (in Chinese)
4. Wu, B.: Chinese Talent Flow. Peking People Press, Peking (2005) (in Chinese)
5. He, X.: Probe of drain of high-level talents in Ningbo. Forum of Science &Technology 1, 23–26 (2008)

China's Manufacturing Industry Structure Adjustment in the Context of Intro-product International Specialization

Xiuzhen Li

Shanghai Lixin University of Commerce
Shanghai, 201620, China
zhylixin@yahoo.cn

Abstract. China is mainly engaged in assembling and other low value-added assembling work in the international labor division system. In this study, a quantitative analysis on the situations of China's manufacturing industry in the intra-product international specialization is conducted based on the review of the related researches on the intra-product international specialization. The current situation of China's manufacturing industry in the intra-product international specialization system is described by means of regression analysis and it is suggested that several deep-seated problems existing in resource allocation should be addressed in China's industrial restructuring. For this purpose, it is necessary for China to make use of its comparative advantages continually, to actively participate in the international labor division, and to improve the accumulation of physical capital and human capital, so as to integrate into the intra-product international specialization, thus enhancing China's status in the international specialization.

Keywords: Intro-product International Specialization, Manufacturing industry, Industrial structure.

1 Introduction

Under the constraints of China's binary economic structure and resources per capita, China has no other choices but to take a new road to industrialization. During the construction of new industrialization, the construction of advanced manufacturing base is carried out throughout China. The connotation of the advanced manufacturing industry is summarized from the practices, i.e. the advanced manufacturing industry is not only characterized by the advanced product itself, but is also characterized by the advanced management and process as well as the comprehensive industrial competitiveness. However, China is currently located at the middle or lower reaches of the entire global chain of manufacturing industry, mainly engaged in assembling and other low value-added assembling work in the international specialization system. In this study, based on the conditions of the intra-product international specialization, issues on China's integration into economic globalization and those on the restructuring

Q. Zhou (Ed.): ISAEBD 2011, Part I, CCIS 208, pp. 236–242, 2011.

and upgrading of manufacturing industry on the new road to industrialization with Chinese characteristics are studied and explored.

2   Review on the Related Researches

The intra-product international specialization is gaining more and more importance in the international trade. In early studies, the production process was assumed to be the vertical two-stage structure and the pure intermediate products were produced at the upstream stage with the basic factors, which were combined with the basic factors at the downstream stage to produce the final products. Under the conditions that the intermediate and final products are tradable, Balassa (1965), Corden (1966) and Jones (1971) et al analyzed the effective protection and studied the effect of the tariff structure on resource allocation by using this structure. Grossman (1981) studied the trade protection required by the domestic content also with this method. Under the conditions that all products are assumed to be further processed at their final destinations prior to being consumed, Sanval and Jones (1982) analyzed the trade patterns and results of the intermediate products by using this structure. All the two-stage production structure can be summarized as the complete input-output model, in which the products can be both intermediate products and final products.

In the early1980s, Dixit and Grossman (1982) studied the influence of changes of factors resource and protection policy on the comparative advantages and resource allocation by extending the vertical two-stage structure into the vertical multi-stage structure. They proposed the concept of the multistage production, believing that the manufacturing process was composed of a series of continuous vertical stages and some additional values at each stage were added to the intermediate products of the previous stage to produce the semi-finished products of this stage, with the purpose of making preparations for the next stage. The production technology or factor intensity at each stage was different, and the comparative advantage determines the model of specialized labor division of each country at the production stage. Deardorff (1998) believed that the fragmentation of the production process referred to that the production process of product could be divided into two or more stages and the production of different stages would be finished in different locations so that the final products were produced. The fragmentation of the production process, also called infra-product specialization or outsourcing, could be realized domestically or between countries. The intro-product specialization itself is not a new phenomenon. In recent years, with the progress of technology, it has become increasingly feasible for the fragmented production activities to be coordinated between countries. It is the premise of the intro-product specialization that the production process of products can be fragmented technically. At the same time, with the continued improvement in the technology of transportation and communication, trade barriers decrease constantly. The cross-border intra-product international specialization finally comes true as a result of decreasing cost in trade and production coordination.

3 Analysis on the Status and Current Situation of China's Manufacturing Industry in the Intra-product International Specialization

3.1 Quantitative Analysis on the Situation of China's Manufacturing Industry in the Intra-product International Specialization

In terms of the measurement for intro-product specialization and trade, the intro-product trade value is approximately given through different calculation of diameter and methods generally using Input-Output Table in the existing research literatures. The typical cases are the methods proposed by Hummels, Ishii and Yi (2001).

According to the definition of the vertical specialization made by Hummels et al, three conditions are required to be met: (1) The production process of products consists of two or more consecutive stages; (2) during the production process, two or more countries provide the added value; (3) at least one country uses the imported inputs in the processing stage of products, and at the same time the products produced with the imported inputs must be partly used for export. In order to measure the trade activities induced by the vertical specialization, Hummels et al defined the basic equation for the vertical-specialization-based trade:

VS= (Value of the imported intermediate inputs / Total value of product)×Total export value

Accordingly, the vertical specialization trade value of Industry j can be expressed as follows:

$$VS_j = \frac{M_j^I}{Y_j} \cdot X_j = \frac{X_j}{Y_j} \cdot M_j^I. \tag{1}$$

Where $M_j^I = \sum_{i=1}^{n} M_{ij}$ represents the imported inputs of Industry j; M_{ij} represents the inputs provided by Industry j for importing the products from Industry i; VS_j represents the vertical specialization trade value of Industry j; X_j represents the export value of Industry j; Y_j represents the total output of Industry j; Industry $j = 1,2,.......n$ 。

Then, the computational equation for the proportion of vertical specialization of a country is as follows:

$$VSS = \frac{VS}{X} = \frac{1}{X} \sum_{j=1}^{n} VS_j = \frac{1}{X} \sum_{j=1}^{n} \sum_{i=1}^{n} \frac{X_j}{Y_j} M_{ij} \tag{2}$$

Where VSS represents the proportion of vertical specialization of a country and X represents the total export value of a country.

If $m_{ij} = \dfrac{M_{ij}}{Y_j}$, then the following equation can be obtained:

$$VSS = \frac{1}{X} \sum_{j=1}^{n} \sum_{i=1}^{n} m_{ij} X_j = \frac{1}{X} \mu A^M X^V . \tag{3}$$

Where $\mu = (1\,1...1)$; $A^M = \begin{pmatrix} m_{11}...m_{1n} \\ ...... \\ m_{n1}...m_{nn} \end{pmatrix}$ is the import coefficient

matrix; $X^V = \begin{pmatrix} X_1 \\ ... \\ X_n \end{pmatrix}$ is the export matrix of industry.

If the phenomenon that the imported products are processed for many times in the country is taken into consideration, it can be expressed with the complete consumption coefficient:

$$VSS = \frac{1}{X} \mu A^M (I - A^D)^{-1} X^V \tag{4}$$

$$VS^V = A^M (I - A^D)^{-1} X^V \tag{5}$$

Where I is n-order unit matrix; A^D is n-order domestic consumption coefficient matrix; $A^M + A^D = A$, where, A is n-order direct consumption coefficient matrix in the Input-Output Table; $VS^V = \begin{pmatrix} VS_1 \\ ... \\ VS_2 \end{pmatrix}$ represents the matrix of vertical specialization trade value of the industry.

Therefore, VSS value can be obtained by solving A^M matrix.

The Input-Output Table is drawn up once every five years in China. The change status of the proportion of vertical specialization of China's manufacturing industry during these two years is calculated and compared by using China's Input-Output Table in 1997 and in 2002. Then the vertical specialization trade value during 1997-2001 is calculated according to the import coefficient matrix in 1997 and that during 2002-2006 is also calculated according to the import coefficient matrix in 2002. As a result, the status of the development and changes of China's manufacturing industry in the intro-product specialization and trade during 1997-2006 can be obtained.

According to the calculation results, it is clear that the proportion of vertical specialization of China's manufacturing industries took on the rising trend to varying degrees by comparing the proportion of vertical specialization value in 1997 and 2002. Therefore, the total proportion of vertical specialization of the manufacturing industry also rose from 14.88% in 1997 to 19.92% in 2002. Just in five years, the proportion of vertical specialization of China's manufacturing industry had risen by 5.04 percentage points, which indicated that the extent of the manufacturing industry participating in the intra-product international specialization rapidly deepened. However, the difference in the proportion of vertical specialization of China's manufacturing industries was enormous, which reflected that the degree of participation in the intra-product international specialization varied for different industries. The sequencing order of the proportion of vertical specialization for China's manufacturing industries in these two years underwent little changes. The industries with a relatively high proportion of vertical specialization in the decreasing order included: communications equipment, computers and other manufacturing industries in electronic equipments, manufacturing industries in instruments and cultural and office machinery, petroleum processing, coking and processing industry in nuclear fuels, electric, machinery and equipment manufacturing industry. Among them, the proportions of vertical specialization of communications equipments, computers and other electronic equipments manufacturing industries were at the top of the list in these two years, reaching 28.53% and 3 7.20%, respectively, far higher than the average level of proportion of vertical specialization of the manufacturing industry.

3.2 The Current Situation of China's Manufacturing Industry in the Intra-product International Specialization

China's participation in the intra-product international specialization deepens, which is conducive to strengthen the connection between China's manufacturing industry and the world's economy, by means of which the development of related domestic industries can be promoted. However, the participation of China's manufacturing industry in the intra-product international specialization is still at the low processing degree and low value-added stage without effectively promoting the competitiveness of the industry. The characteristics of low processing degree and low value-added for the participation of China's manufacturing industry in the intra-product specialization can be inspected through the relationship between the vertical specialization and the industrial profit rate. The functions to be tested are built as follows:

$$P_j' = \beta_0 + \beta_1 VSS_j + \varepsilon_j . \qquad (6)$$

Where j= year 1997 and year 2002; ε_j is random disturbance item; P_j' is profit index; VSS_j is vertical specialization index. The calculation results are as follows:

For year 2002: $P_{2002}' = 0.247 - 0.347\beta_1 \quad R^2 = 0.32$

For year 1997: $P_{1997}' = 0.2147 - 0.181\beta_1 \quad R^2 = 0.06$

Where only the coefficient, -0.181, in year 1997 did not pass t test.

The results showed that the vertical specialization degree of China's manufacturing industry and the profit rate manifested a negative correlation. The profit rate of industries with relatively high degree of vertical specialization was relatively low, which basically indicated that China's manufacturing industry is still at the low processing degree and low value-added stage in the participation in the intra-product specialization. Although the vertical specialization of China's manufacturing industry mostly occurred in the industries with more intensive capital from the perspective of the capital intensity degree of domestic manufacturing industry, China still took advantages of labor factors in participating in the intra-product international specialization, if judged from the perspective of the capital intensity degree of manufacturing industry worldwide, combined with the characteristics of low processing degree and low added value.

4 Conclusions and Enlightenments

China's manufacturing industry in participating in the intra-product international specialization is developing in breadth and depth in the context of the increasing degree of China's opening-up and economic globalization, which will have a profound impact on the upgrading of the industrial structure of China's manufacturing industry. China's manufacturing industry has been rapidly developed since the reform and opening-up and its scale of surplus accumulation also has reached a certain level, thus laying a foundation for improving the factor resources for the manufacturing industry. From the perspective of market economic operation, it is necessary to solve some deep-seated problems existing in resource allocation for China's industrial restructuring under in the context of China's opening-up. Only by this means can a good foundation be laid for China's economic development. First, comparative advantage should be made use of continuously in combination with the active participation in the intra-product international specialization, including the active attraction of foreign capital or encouragement of the development of relatively more capital (technology)-intensive industries; second, the accumulation situation of physical capital and human capital should be improved and the investment of production factors should be focused on the general projects in all industries such as basic education and scientific researches; third, China should integrate into the intra-product international specialization and increase its status so as to realize the upgrading from labor-intensive industries to capital and technology-intensive industries.

Acknowledgements. I am grateful to be sponsored by the projects of "Shanghai Planned Subjects on Philosophy and Social Sciences" (Number:2010BJL001) and Leading Academic Discipline Project of Shanghai Municipal Education Commission (Number:J51702).

242   X. Li

References

1. Arndt, S.W.: Globalization and the open economy. North American Journal of Economic: and Finance 8, 71–79 (1997)
2. Balassa, B.: Tariff protection in industrial countries: An evaluation. Journal of Political Economy 73, 573–594 (1965)
3. Corden, W.M.: The structure of a tariff system and the effective protective rate. Journal of Political Economy 74, 221–237 (1966)
4. Dixit, A.K., Grossman, G.M.: Trade and protection with multistage production. Review of Economic Studies 49, 583–594 (1982)
5. Grossman, G.M.: The theory of domestic content protection and content preferences. Quarterly Journal of Economics 96, 583–603 (1981)
6. Helpman, E.: Trade, FDI and the organization of firms. NBER Working Paper. 12091(2006)
7. Jones, R.W.: Effective protection and substitution. Journal of International Economics 1, 59–81 (1971)
8. Sanyal, K., Jones, R.W.: The theory of trade in middle products. American Economic Review 1, 16–31 (1982)
9. Wen, T.: Theory of Intra-Product Trade. Economic Science Press, Beijing (2006) (in Chinese)

The Evaluation Model of Bank's Assets Quality Based on G1 and Mean-Square Deviation Methods and Its Empirical Research[*]

Yanping Liu and Leilei Qu

Faculty of Management and Economics Dalian
University of Technology,
Dalian, China

Abstract. In order to improve the accuracy of evaluation of banks' assets quality, this paper constructed a comprehensive evaluation index system of asset quality, determined the optimal weights of indicators by combining G1 method with the mean-square deviation method, and then established a comprehensive evaluation model of asset quality, lastly empirically analyzed the levels of nine commercial banks' assets quality. The contribution lies in three aspects. Firstly, selecting the index of return on total asset to enrich the existing index system. Secondly, rejecting the virtually increased assets because of accounting matching principle and capitalization expenses to raise the authenticity of assets quality. Thirdly, evaluating the banks' assets quality by combining objective weight and subjective weight, which could avoid the disadvantage of objective weight, which can not reflect expert experience and subjective weight. Meanwhile the paper provides an effective evaluation method of assets quality for commercial banks.

Keywords: Asset quality, commercial bank, G1, mean-square deviation, evaluation.

1 Introduction

Financial assets is the physical infrastructure of commercial banks relying for existence and making profit. The level of the assets quality decides the existence condition and the capability of making the profit of the business. Financial crisis has brought about unprecedented challenges for our financial industries. All kinds of risks (market risk, credit risk, and operation risk) turn worse day by day, and the capital gap increases significantly. Consequently, the evaluation studies on bank's assets quality are important to the development and management of banks.

In recent years, domestic and international academics have done a great deal of researches on the evaluation of banks' assets quality, the main research fruits follow:

[*] Fund Projects: Supported by Social Science Founds for Youth of Ministry of Education of China(09YJC790024); Supported by the Fundamental Research Funds for the Central Universities (DUT10ZD107, DUT10RW107).

Q. Zhou (Ed.): ISAEBD 2011, Part I, CCIS 208, pp. 243–249, 2011.
© Springer-Verlag Berlin Heidelberg 2011

The last few years foreign scholars are mainly studying on the relationship between the banks' assets quality and credit risk or scale economies of banks. David Bemstein (1996) [1] carried on a research of commercial banks' assets quality and scale economic, discovering that there was a direct or indirect relationship betweem loan quality and scale operation:the worse the banks' assets quality was, the cost was higher, but this relationship was not very obvious. Besides,in David Bemstein's research he presented that there was a scale effect when the total assets of banks over 55,000,000,000 dollars. The banks who had low bad loan ratio could reduced their average costs by expanding scales, while the banks with high bad loan ratio could't adopt this method. Chris Downing, Dwight Jaffee, Nancy Wallace (2006) [2] pointed out that there was a close connection between the level of indivisible asset quality and whether selling the assets to the special purpose organization, and discovered that selling the indivisible asset to special purpose organizations will reduce the quality of assets seriously.

Nian Yang(2002) [3]considered the financial statement of loan corporation as a point of departure, and evaluated the commercial banks' assets quality with the method of AltmanZ.Cunjing Zhang etc(2006) [4] put forward three basic featureses of assets quality: existence, effectiveness and availability, and created the evaluation system of assets quality based on the three basic featureses. Cuichun Wang etc(2009) [5] studied the relativity of city commercial banks' assets quality and managerial performance, and came to a conclusion that the two factors had remarkable positive correlation.

There are two questions of the exsiting studies on banks' assets quality : Firstly, evaluating the quality of the banks with individual or a few indicators .Secondly, lacking a reasonable index system of evaluation, so the results of evaluations are not real and effective, which goes against the advance of banks' assets quality.

Contraposing the above two questions, this paper selectes the high frequency indicators that could reflect banks' assets quality to construct a reasonable index system through referring relevant authoritative literature both of home and abroad, and combines the G1 method with the mean-square deviation method to smooth the difference of objective weight and subjective weight in order to improve the rationality of the evaluation.

2   Establishing the Index System

The selection of original indices: The paper makes reference to the the main indicators that the CAMELS rating system weighs the assets quality the important index of Moody Corp and Standard and Poor's Corp, and other key indicators proposed by famous scholars in the process of selecting index to reflect the level of commercial banks' assets quality fully. Considering the rentability of assets, this paper adds return on total asset[6] to the exsiting index system, the higher the index value is, the higher the level of assets income is, the higher the assets quality is. In addition , because of the authenticity character of assets qulity ,the paper rejects the virtually increased assets because of accounting matching principle and capitalization expenses (for example:long term deferred assets, deferredexpense and equity investment difference etc), and the bubble assets caused by whitewashing accounting statement

[4]. Lastly this paper establishs auditions index system containing the following 13 indicators:the biggest clients loan ratio, the biggest ten clients loan ratio, toxic assets, non-performing loans ratio, deposit ratio, overdue loans, asset growth rate, loan growth, loan losses, credit loans to total assets ratio, guaranteed total assets scale, cover ratio, return on total asset etc.

The establishment of the index system : The first step,do correlation analysis for auditions indicators, and then pick and get rid of the indicators having remarkable correlation (the correlation is higer than 0.9), so as to avoid the repeatability of information. The second step, reserve all effective indexes in order to ensure the integrity of the index information. The last step, establish index system containing the following nine indicators: the biggest clients loan ratio, the biggest ten clients loan ratio, non-performing loans ratio, deposit ratio, asset growth rate, loan growth, loan losses, cover ratio, return on total asset.

3 Model Principle and Construction

3.1 The Method of G1 for Indicators Weights

The G1 method, also calls order relation analysis, is a kind of method that need't to structure judgment matrix and to validate the consistency. This method is simple, intuitive and applicated easily.The basic principle and steps of G1 method:

(1) Determine ordering relationship of the indictors [8]
(2) Give comparative judgment of relative importance of every two indices
(3) Calculate the weight coefficient . If the rational voluation of r_k given by the experts satisfy the conditions $r_{k-1} \succ \dfrac{1}{r_k}$, then the weight ω_m is:

$$\omega_m = (1 + \sum_{k=2}^{m} \prod_{i=k}^{m} r_i)^{-1} \tag{1}$$

and $\omega_{k-1} = r_k \omega_k$,   k=m,m-1,...3,2.

3.2 The Method of Mean-Square Deviation for Indicators Weights

The mean-square deviation is an objective method for weights.The method reflects the importance of the indictors according to the difference of the same index. There are transparency, reproducibility but no subjective color in the evaluation process.The main steps of this method:

$$\omega_i = \dfrac{s_j}{\sum_{k=1}^{m} s_k} \qquad j=1,2,...m \tag{2}$$

$$s_j^2 = \frac{1}{n}\sum_{i=1}^{n}(\chi_{ij} - \overline{\chi}_j)^2$$

and $\qquad\qquad\qquad\qquad\qquad\qquad$ j=1,2,...m $\qquad$ (3)

$$\overline{\chi}_j = \frac{1}{n}\sum_{i=1}^{n}\chi_{ij}$$

and $\qquad\qquad\qquad\qquad\qquad\qquad$ j=1,2,...,m $\qquad$ (4)

3.3 "Addition" Integration Method for Weights

This method can integrate both subjective and objective information in the process of determining the weights,its principle as follows:

(1)Assuming that p_i, q_j are the index weight coefficient generated based on "difference driven" and "function driver principle respectively respectively,so:

$$\omega_j = k_1 p_j + k_2 q_j \qquad j=1,2,...m \qquad (5)$$

(2)In formula (5), k_1, k_2 are undetermined coefficients,and satisfy the conditions: $k_1^2 + k_2^2 = 1$, and $k_1 \succ 0, k_2 \succ 0$

(3)Apply the theory of "Lagrange conditional extreme value",we can get :

$$k_1 = \frac{\sum_{i=1}^{n}\sum_{j=1}^{m}p_j\chi_{ij}}{\sqrt{(\sum_{i=1}^{n}\sum_{j=1}^{m}p_j\chi_{ij})^2 + (\sum_{i=1}^{n}\sum_{j=1}^{m}q_j\chi_{ij})^2}}$$

$$\qquad (6)$$

$$k_2 = \frac{\sum_{i=1}^{n}\sum_{j=1}^{m}q_j\chi_{ij}}{\sqrt{(\sum_{i=1}^{n}\sum_{j=1}^{m}p_j\chi_{ij})^2 + (\sum_{i=1}^{n}\sum_{j=1}^{m}q_j\chi_{ij})^2}}$$

$$\qquad (7)$$

4   The Contribution of This Paper

Firstly,selecting the index of return on total asset to enrich existing index system.

Secondly, rejecting the virtually increased assets because of accounting matching principle and capitalization expenses to raise the authenticity of assets quality data.

Thirdly, evaluate the asset quality of commercial banks by combining objective weight with subjective weight, which could avoid the two disadvantages of objective weight, which can not reflect expert experience and subjective weight, which can not reflect the change of objective conditions.

5   Empirical Analysis

This paper choses the data of the nine large-scale commercial banks in 2008 and the date of a huge commercial bank from 2004 to 2009. Because of unfair measure caused by the difference of the dimension and magnitude of indices, the paper standardizes the original data to reflect the real situation. Table 1 is the standardized data of the nine commercial banks after the establishing the index system.

Table 1. Standardized data of the nine commercial banks

	x1	x2	x3	x4	x5	x6	x7	x8	x9
s1	0.116	0.131	0.160	0.123	0.121	0.168	0.156	0.115	0.033
s2	0.077	0.086	0.129	0.094	0.061	0.107	0.075	0.099	0.002
s3	0.160	0.143	0.243	0.085	0.158	0.167	0.069	0.048	0.129
s4	0.141	0.135	0.062	0.113	0.001	0.002	0.002	0.170	0.219
s5	0.119	0.115	0.067	0.125	0.072	0.093	0.114	0.114	0.242
s6	0.078	0.102	0.068	0.121	0.212	0.118	0.163	0.147	0.062
s7	0.097	0.087	0.124	0.099	0.071	0.171	0.125	0.100	0.234
s8	0.112	0.113	0.038	0.132	0.170	0.042	0.173	0.080	0.009
s9	0.101	0.089	0.108	0.107	0.134	0.132	0.124	0.127	0.070

In table 1, x1,x2,...x9 represent the biggest clients loan ratio, the biggest ten clients loan ratio , non-performing loans ratio, deposit ratio, asset growth rate, loan growth, loan losses, cover ratio, return on total asset respectively. s1,s2,...s9 represent nine commercial banks respectively.

5.1   The Steps of G1 Method for Weights

(1) Experts sort the nine indicators according to the influence on assets quality,and then determine the order,the result is: $X_8 \succ X_9 \succ X_1 \succ X_2 \succ X_4 \succ X_6 \succ X_7 \succ X_5$

(2)The experts scored adjacent two indicators: $r_2 =1.27$, $r_3 =1.18$, $r_4 =1.22$, $r_5 =1.13$, $r_6 =1.07$, $r_7 =1.07$, $r_8 =1.08$, $r_9 =1.08$

(3)Put the data of the second step into the formula (1),we can get all the indicators weights: $\omega_{11} =0.105$, $\omega_{12} =0.102$, $\omega_{13} =0.202$, $\omega_{14} =0.085$, $\omega_{15} =0.067$, $\omega_{16} =0.073$, $\omega_{17} =0.079$, $\omega_{18} =0.156$, $\omega_{19} =0.131$

5.2   The Method of Mean-Square Deviation for Indictors Weights

Put the data of table1 into the formula (4),(3),(2),we can get: $\omega_{21} =0.062$, $\omega_{22} =0.050$, $\omega_{23} =0.143$, $\omega_{24} =0.036$, $\omega_{25} =0.147$, $\omega_{26} =0.134$, $\omega_{27} =0.125$, $\omega_{28} =0.081$, $\omega_{29} =0.223$

5.3 "Addition"Integration Method for Weights

(1) Put the weights determined by G1 method and mean-square deviation method into formula (5) respectively,according to the constraint condition and formula (6), formula (7),we can get : $k_1 = 0.703$, $k_2 = 0.711$, the contribution on the two kinds of methods determine the weights is almost equal.

(2) The ultimate index weights

$$\omega_{31} = 0.083, \quad \omega_{32} = 0.076, \quad \omega_{33} = 0.173, \quad \omega_{34} = 0.061, \quad \omega_{35} = 0.107,$$

$$\omega_{36} = 0.103, \quad \omega_{37} = 0.102, \quad \omega_{38} = 0.119, \quad \omega_{39} = 0.1774$$

Table 2. The score and sorting of asset quality based on the above three methods

	G1 method		Mean- square deviation method		"Addition"integration method	
	score	sorting	score	sorting	score	sorting
s1	-0.0167343	7	-0.000572	7	-0.008653	7
s2	-0.0167761	8	-0.011593	9	-0.014184	8
s3	-0.0446948	9	-0.006545	8	-0.02562	9
s4	0.02385779	3	0.0426292	3	0.0332435	3
s5	0.02947878	1	0.0575039	1	0.0434913	1
s6	0.02744288	2	0.0460999	2	0.0367714	2
s7	0.01271834	5	0.0388098	4	0.0257641	4
s8	0.01585473	4	0.0361327	5	0.0259937	5
s9	0.00579251	6	0.0210683	6	0.0134304	6

From the above empirical results,we can find that:

(1) The evaluation result based on G1 method is different from that based on the mean-square deviation method.But the scores based on the two different methods of four banks are same,which proves that the data acquisition and evaluation method are reasonable.

(2) Compared "Addition"integration method with the G1 method , the scores based on the two different methods of six banks are same,while compared "Addition"integration method with the mean-square deviation method,the scores of seven banks are identical. The method combining objective weight and subjective weight could embody the advantages of both the G1 method and the mean-square deviation method, and at the same time smooth the difference from the two methods.

6 Suggestions

(1) Commercial Banks should't evaluate their assets quality with individual or a few indicators(such as: non-performing loans ratio, loan losses, cover ratio), the right way is that considering other important indicators in order to avoid evaluating one-sidedly and lacking of important informations.

(2) Commercial Banks should disperse all kinds of risks and prevent the loans to be over-concentrated, or else the banks will face huge risk if the industries and groups cannot pay off the banks loans in time,then the asset quality of banks decreases dramatically.

Acknowledgments. Many people have done invaluable contributions to this research. I would like to express my deeply gratitude to my sponsors "Social Science Founds for Youth of Ministry of Education of China" (09YJC790024) and "the Fundamental Research Funds for the Central Universities" (DUT10ZD107, DUT10RW107).

References

1. Lingning, G., Yanling, W.: The Reviewe of Quality Assets and Capital Structure Research
2. Downing, C., Jaffee, D., Wallace, N.: Asset Indivisibility, Security Design and Asset Quality J. (June 5 (2006)
3. Nian, Y., Altman, Z.: Value Method in The Application of The Evaluation of The Banks' Assets Quality (2002)
4. Zhang, J., Xu, W.: The Empirical Analysis of The Evaluation of China's Listed Companies' Asset Quality. Accounting Monthly (July 2006)
5. Wang, C., Liu, G.: Study on The Correlation of The City Commercial Bank Asset Quality and Management Performance. Technology and Management (May 2009)
6. Xu, H., Wang, Y.: Study on The Index System of The Evaluation of The Asset Quality. Economic and Management Research, 117–121 (May 2009)
7. The Chinese Banking Regulatory Commission, The Risk Rating System of Joint-stock Commercial Bank (Interim) (February 2004),
   http://www.fsi.com.cn/policy200/rules202/202_0402/
   202_04022301.htm
8. Guo, Y.: Comprehensive Evaluation Theory, Method and Application, pp. 46–47. Science Press, Beijing (2008)

Diamond Model of National Economic Competitive Advantage Based on National Economic Security

Siyi Qin and Genhua Hu

School of Economics, Guangdong University of Business Studies,
Guangzhou, China
qinsiyi2006@163.com, garyuser@hotmail.com

Abstract. This paper firstly analyzes China's national economic competitive advantage (NECA) using method of principal components analysis. The result presents that the level of Chinese economic competitive advantage is low but increases continuously. Based on empirical study, it builds a Diamond Model of National Economic Competitive Advantage based on national economic security and regards factors of external risk, economic performance, motivation for growth and low-carbon as the basic elements. To ensure that the Diamond Model of National Economic Competitive Advantage works well and upgrade national economic security, it could take the paths formed in the Diamond Model into consideration.

Keywords: National economic security, national economic competitive advantage, diamond model.

1 Introduction

The concept of security has evolved to an untraditional and complex concept since formation of new international politics. During the Cold War, many nations regarded political security and military security as national security strategies, especially the United States and the Soviet Union. That economic competition heats gradually guides all nations to adjust their national security strategies for upgrading economic security. In 1980, Japanese government issued Report of National Comprehensive Security, which was the first official report referring economic security and listed economic security in component elements of national security strategy. American Clinton Government integrated economic security into national security strategy for the first time and put economic security on the top priority of foreign strategies in 1993. Russia firstly declared national economic security strategy and unveiled them in 1996 which emphasized the primary of economic security in national security.

Nowadays, economy has become a significant factor for national power strengthening, social steadiness and national security achievement. Therefore, research on national economic competitive advantage is feasible.

Q. Zhou (Ed.): ISAEBD 2011, Part I, CCIS 208, pp. 250–257, 2011.
© Springer-Verlag Berlin Heidelberg 2011

2 Literature Review

National economic security is a hot topic all the time. There exists different comprehension to it but without an authorized definition so far. Gilpin (1987) [1] defines national economic security as economic competitiveness and relevant international political standing and capability brought from economic competitiveness. However, Charles and Neu (2001)[2] suggest that economic security can protect economic interests when a nation faces the events which could threat economic interest or hinder economic running, and economic security endows a nation with the capability of national economic environment which is in accordance with itself interests.

It was Brown's Prophecy in 1994 that Chinese scholars began to realize the issue of national economic security. Zhao, Xu and Xing (1994) [3] propose that national economic security is economic competitiveness, capability of resisting interference, threat and aggressiveness at home and abroad, and internal and external environment for economic development of a nation. However, the factors influencing national economic security have changed dynamically as the development of the world economy. Therefore, it should synthetically take both era background and developmental stage into consideration when we perceive the meaning of national economic security of China. Zhang (2007) [4] proposes, national economic security is a capability of overcoming crisis and a stable but orderly state when a nation fulfills its economic and managerial function; Liu (2010) [5] suggests, national economic security is a state that the economic development and interests of a sovereignty are immune to threat or destroy from the factors at home and abroad in an open system.

In 2007, American subprime crisis broke out which remained people of rethinking about national economic security further. How to guarantee national economic security becomes the key of research. Porter (1990) [6] advances the theory of Competitive Advantage of Nations and proposes whether a nation can obtain economic competitive advantage in the international competition is the fundamental element to determinate prosperity or recession for a nation. Stigliz and Walsh (2002) [7] review the developmental process of economic growth achievement and competitive advantage of nations upgrade firstly, then address the concept of absolute advantage and regard technology innovation as a nation's competitive advantage; Harrison (2005) [8] elaborates the elements of international competitiveness for a nation and builds the TFP-Competitive Advantage Model to measure the level of competitiveness; Uchida and Cook (2005) [9] study the transformation of competitive advantage in East Asian nations from the viewpoint of technological and trade specialization; Grilo and Koopman (2006) [10] analyze the strategies of strengthening European Union's competitiveness from the aspects of productivity and microeconomic reforms, and hold that living standard is the most meaningful index to measure competitiveness; Stone and Ranchhod (2006) [11] build a Quantitative Model of Competitiveness Advantage of a Nation Determination based on Porter's Diamond Model and analyze the competitiveness advantage of nations in the UK, USA and BRIC nations using a quantitative model. However, Smit (2010) [12] suggests that Porter's Diamond framework isn't a new theory but a theory framework.

Although there are some arguments about Porter's Diamond Model, relevant studies in China are still made based on Porter's model. Here we build a Diamond

Model of National Economic Competitive Advantage in China based on national economic security in the Porter's theoretical framework, for win-win purpose of upgrading National Economic Competitive Advantage and guaranteeing national economic security.

3 Empirical Results and Building a Diamond Model

3.1 Analysis Based on Competitive Advantage

Traditionally, there mainly exist three indices to measure competitive advantage, i.e. international market share, trade competitiveness and market penetration rate. Here we measure national economic competitive advantage in China applying the index of trade competitiveness. As a relative representation, index of trade competitiveness casts the impacts from economic expansion and inflation. Trade competitiveness index, i.e. Index of Normalized Trade Balance (NTB), indicates international competitiveness and market positioning of products. It is defined on [-1, 1] and the larger is the value, the stronger is the competitiveness advantage.

Figure 1 presents the yearly competitive advantage in China from 1990~2009. The resources are from China Statistics Yearbook (1991~2010). Generally speaking, the products have strong international competitive advantage when NTB index is larger than 0.3. Figure 1 indicates that the NTB index ranges from -0.062 to 0.134, which has exhibited feeblish competitive advantage for Chinese products. Besides, in all target samples, the value of index is negative and equals to -0.062 in 1993. The following reasons may serve as this state. Firstly, make plan of economic incentive. After 1991~1992 recession, the government vigorously enforced the plan of economic incentive to develop economy for demand increase. Secondly, promote the method of market-oriented development. China's economy grew fast because the method of market-oriented development was promoted and strengthened domestic purchasing power. Thirdly, largely import raw materials and mechanical devices in short supply. Import volume was larger than that of export for China's economy growth and economic structure optimization.

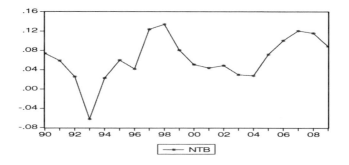

Fig. 1. Index of Normalized Trade Balance (NTB)

However, we suggest that there are some shortcomings to measure national economic competitive advantage using the index of NTB. Firstly, the index of NTB only takes external trade into consideration. In reality, some nations have a long-term foreign trade deficit, but their products take a large rate of market share in the international markets which still indicate strong international competitiveness, such as the United States. Secondly, there are many other factors influencing economic competitive advantage, such as political factors and military factors. Therefore, it should measure economic competitive advantage on the whole. Thirdly, this approach measures national economic competitive advantage without considering the framework of national economic security. Based on above analysis, we will present another viewpoint to measure national economic competitive advantage in China, which is in the framework of national economic security.

3.2 Analysis Based on National Economic Security

In this section, we choose some factors which may influence national economic competitive advantage in China based on national economic security and apply the method of factor analysis to measure the level of national economic competitive advantage in China based on national economic security. These factors are as follows: growth rate of GDP (X1), inflation rate (X2), unemployment rate (X3), growth rate of M1 (X4), ratio of dependence on foreign trade (X5), ratio of external debt (X6), rate of financial deficit (X7), growth rate of fixed assets (X8), balance of foreign exchange reserve (X9), growth rate of energy input per GDP (X10), high-tech-product-GDP ratio (X11), and national-defense-expenditure-GDP ratio (X12). Here, we only choose index X12 to measure the level of military security and haven't chosen any index to measure the level of political security for difficulty in quantification.

Table 1 shows partial results of total variance explained. The cumulative extraction sums of squared loadings for the first four components is 91.548%, therefore there are four main factors.

Table 1. Total Variance Explained (Partial)

Com-ponent	Initial Eigenvalues			Rotated Extraction Sums of Squared Loadings		
	Total	%of Variance	Cumulative%	Total	%of Variance	Cumulative%
1	4.425	40.229	40.229	4.247	38.611	38.611
2	3.154	28.669	68.898	2.201	20.010	58.621
3	1.366	12.418	81.316	2.038	18.531	77.152
4	1.125	10.232	91.548	1.584	14.396	91.548
5	0.433	3.937	95.485			

Extraction Method: Principal Component Analysis.

Table 2 reports the results of component matrix. Four main factors are as follows: the first main factor F1 is mainly determined by the five indices of X3, X5, X6, X9 and X11, named external risk factor with 38.611% of contribution ratio; the second

254   S. Qin and G. Hu

main factor F2 includes X1, X2 and X7, named economic performance factor with 20.01%; the third main factor F3 includes X4 and X8, named motivation for growth factor with 18.531%; the fourth main factor F4 includes X10 only, named low-carbon factor with 14.396%. Therefore, using weighted contribution ratio of four main factors, the value of comprehensive evaluation of national economic competitive advantage based on national economic security could be defined as:

$$Z = 0.38611F1 + 0.2001F2 + 0.18531F3 + 0.14396F4 \qquad (1)$$

Table 2. Component Matrix[a]

	Component					Component			
	1	2	3	4		1	2	3	4
X11	.967	-.039	-.194	.011	X7	-.285	-.702	.022	.590
X3	.942	-.068	-.105	.144	X2	-.522	.661	.344	.058
X9*	.854	.023	.192	-.329	X4	-.143	.083	.947	.000
X6	-.815	.088	-.238	.419	X8	.131	.468	.785	-.033
X5	.798	.529	-.209	.085	X10	-.012	-.008	.008	.959
X1	-.046	.866	.471	.024					

Extraction Method: Principal Component Analysis.   Rotation method: Varimax with Kaiser Normalization. a. Rotation converged in 7 iterations. *: Here it is normalized data of X9.

Table 3 displays the results of comprehensive evaluation of national economic competitive advantage based on national economic security from 1993 to 2009 using (1) and component score coefficient. Here we propose to divide the value of comprehensive evaluation into four classes enlightened by the idea of dividing the index of NTB, see Table 4. The larger is the value, the stronger is the national economic competitive advantage. Therefore, the value of comprehensive evaluation is very low but has been increasing since 1993. The largest value is 29.592 in 2009, indicating the strongest national economic competitive advantage.

Table 3. Comprehensive Evaluation

Year	Value	Year	Value	Year	Value
1993	9.990	1999	3.713	2005	16.420
1994	7.162	2000	5.370	2006	19.148
1995	4.694	2001	5.874	2007	23.331
1996	4.346	2002	8.065	2008	25.083
1997	3.769	2003	12.022	2009	29.592
1998	3.861	2004	14.391		

Table 4. Class of National Economic Competitive Advantage

Class	Low	Medium	High	Higher
Scope	0~30	30~ 60	60~ 85	85~100

3.3 Modeling National Economic Competitive Advantage Based on National Economic Security

In this part, we model National Economic Competitive Advantage (NECA) based on national economic security in the framework of Porter's Diamond model. In section 3.2, we have presented four main factors influencing national economic competitive advantage. Here we propose another two significant factors, i.e. military security and political security, and build a six-factor Diamond model of National Economic Competitive Advantage, see Figure 2.

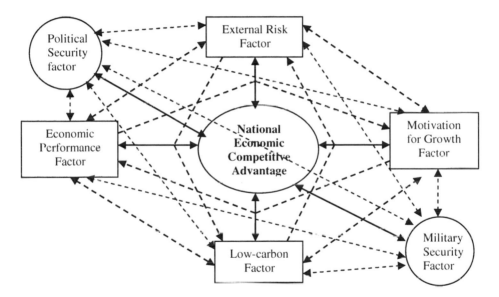

Fig. 2. Diamond Model of National Economic Competitive Advantage

   The above model includes double meanings: on the one hand, the level of national economic competitive advantage is determined by not only the absolute level of four main factors and degree of political security and military security, but also reciprocity among six factors in the diamond model; on the other, there exist six paths (solid lines with double arrows) formed between national economic competitive advantage and the other six factors respectively, i.e. NECA- external risk factor, NECA- economic performance factor, NECA- motivation for growth factor, NECA- low-carbon factor. All the paths are bidirectional, indicating that the level of NECA could be upgraded by the reciprocity among six factors while the level of six factors could also be improved by NECA. Therefore, national economic security could be guaranteed by the circulatory effects.

Based on above analysis, we build the econometric model of national economic competitive advantage based on national economic security. The expression is:

$$NECA_{i,t} = \alpha \cdot Z_{i,1t} + \beta \cdot Z_{i,2t} + \gamma \cdot Z_{i,3t} + \varepsilon_{i,t} \qquad (2)$$

where $NECA_{i,t}$ represents national economic competitive advantage; $Z_{i,1t}$, $Z_{i,2t}$ $Z_{i,3t}$ are comprehensive evaluation of four main factors, political security and military security, respectively; $\varepsilon_{i,t}$ is distracter. Besides, i and t represent nation and time respectively.

4 Conclusion and Outlook

This paper firstly analyzes economic competitive advantage for China using trade competitive advantage index. It shows that China has a weak economic competitive advantage. Then, it analyzes national economic competitive advantage (NECA) for China using the method of principal components analysis. The result indicates that the level of Chinese economic competitive advantage is low but increases continuously. Following the above study, we build a Diamond Model of National Economic Competitive Advantage based on national economic security for the first time and regard the factors of external risk, economic performance, motivation for growth and low-carbon as the basic elements. Besides, the factors of military security and political security are added as two significant elements in the model. To guarantee the Diamond Model works well and upgrade national economic security, it could be to take the six paths formed in the Diamond Model into consideration.

An open question is still the choice of indices based on national economic security. There are many indices influencing national economic competitive advantage based on national economic security which are proposed to be taken into consideration in the future. Besides, whether our model is good for application in any nation is still to be explored. If it was positive, we could do comparative analysis among different nations.

Acknowledgments. Our work is supported by grants from the General Program of Humanity and Social Science, Ministry of Education, China (No. 10YJAGJW012) and the Eleventh Five-year Planning Program of Guangdong Philosophy and Social Science (No. 09E-15).

References

1. Gilpin, R.: The Political Economy of International Relations. Princeton University Press, Princeton (1987)
2. Wolf, C., Neu, C.R.: The Economic Dimensions of National Security. In: RAND (1994)
3. Zhao, Y., Xu, H., Xing, G.: Risks Faced by Chinese Economy-Theory of National Economic security. Yunnan People's Publishing House (1994) (in Chinese)
4. Zhang, X.: Study of Legal Assurance System of National Economic Security. Chongqing Publishing House, Chongqing (2007) (in Chinese)

5. Liu, B.: Assurance and Risk Management of National Economic Security. China Economic Publishing House, Beijing (2010) (in Chinese)
6. Porter, M.E.: Competitive Advantage of Nations. The Free Press, New York (1990)
7. Joseph, E., Stiglitz, C.E.: Walsh: Economics, 3rd edn. W. W. Norton & Company (2002)
8. Ezeala Harrison, F.: On the Competing Notions of International Competitiveness. Advances in Competitiveness Research 13(1), 80–87 (2005)
9. Uchida, Y., Cook, P.: The Transformation of Competitive Advantage in East Asia: an Analysis of Technological and Trade Specialization. World Development 33(5), 701–728 (2005)
10. Grilo, I., Koopman, G.: Productivity and Microeconomic Reforms: Strengthening EU Competitiveness. Journal of Industry, Competition and Trade 6(2), 67–84 (2006)
11. Stone, H.B.J., Ranchhod, A.: Competitive Advantage of a Nation in the Global Arena: a Quantitative Advancement to Porter's Diamond Applied to the UK, USA and BRIC Nations. Strategic Change 15(16), 283–294 (2006)
12. Smit, A.J.: The Competitive Advantage of Nations: Is Porter's Diamond Framework a New Theory that Explains the International Competitiveness of Countries? Southern African Business Review 14(1), 105–130 (2010)

Application of Taylor Rules in China Based on
Neo-Keynesian Model

Xinxin Chang[1] and Guohua He[2]

[1] Department of finance, Wuhan University, Wuhan, China
changxinxin88@163.com
[2] Department of finance, Wuhan University, Wuhan, China
ghhe@whu.edu.cn

Abstract. This paper provides a dynamic neo-Keynesian model of open economy that can be used to analyze the impact of monetary policies including three kinds of Taylor rules in china. The economy is characterized by backward-looking and forward-looking variables. The main findings of the paper are that aggregate demand shocks have great influence on output, aggregate supply shocks or productivity shocks have great influence on inflation and all macroeconomic variables are affected very much by foreign monetary policy shocks. Moreover, first, the nominal interest Taylor rule is good for Chinese economic stabilization. Second, the open economy Taylor rule including foreign exchange rate and forward-looking variables is good for output increment.

Keywords: neo-Keynesian model, Taylor rules, monetary policy, forward-looking variables.

1 Introduction

Since the 1990s, the monetary policy of United States has already been adjusted to "interest rules" instead of "quantity rules". However, 20 years later, China still adjusts the macro economy through quantity rules by controlling monetary supply. The practice of the United States tells us the monetary supply is not only more and more difficult to definite, but also becoming less correlation with domestic economy. In short, the money supply is determined by many economic endogenous factors and difficult to control by central bank. Although China has not realized liberalization of interest rates which is the necessary condition for Taylor rules application, deregulation of interest rate becomes an inevitable choice along with the complete opening of China's economy. Therefore, the research on Taylor rule's applied question in China has important instruction meaning to the practice of Chinese monetary policy in future.

In recent years, many Chinese scholars employ Taylor rules to study the relationship of Chinese interest rate, inflation and output with a great deal of empirical tests. Xie and Luo (2002) carry on the examination of Taylor rules for the first time in china and the research shows that the Taylor rule is fit for Chinese

Q. Zhou (Ed.): ISAEBD 2011, Part I, CCIS 208, pp. 258–265, 2011.

monetary policy well, but it is a unstable interest rate rule. Liu (2003) compares the welfare effect of Taylor rule with other monetary policy rules based on a neo-Keynesian model in closed economy. It tells us Taylor rule can enhance social total welfare more than "Discretion" rule. Wang (2006) discovers the smooth interest rate Taylor rule can fit the movement of Chinese interest rate well, but it cannot contribute to the stabilization of output and commodities price. Li and Wang (2009) find Taylor rule is unstable in china through the method of historical analysis, policy response function method and cointegration test theory. Zhu (2010) discovers the smooth interest rate Taylor rule can not reduce the fluctuation of the macro economic variables. Zheng and Liu (2010) find linear Taylor rule has its limitation and a non-linear Taylor rule is better. Although the above researching results in Chinese raise great attention for the Taylor rule application, it doesn't have the Taylor rule implementation environment in China. Hence, all above empirical tests about China are not appropriate because of the ineffective data.

In order to avoid the problem of ineffective data, this paper adopts stochastic simulation to analyze the application of Taylor rules in China based on a dynamic neo-Keynesian model of open economy including backward-looking and forward-looking variables. The paper is organized as follows. Section 2 contains a development of the framework and the methodology about the neo-Keynesian model. Section 3 presents a description of different Taylor rules. Section 4 takes a stochastic simulation to analyze the application of Taylor rules in China with Matlab software. The final section summarizes the results and their implications for models of monetary policy.

2 Basic Model

Taking the model of Liu(2003) and Parrado(2004) as reference, this paper develops a comprehensive neo-Keynesian model including exchange rate, backward-looking and forward-looking variables. All variables are log-linearized around the steady state, which is expressed in lower-case letters.

2.1 Aggregate Demand Curve

$$x_t = (1-\mu)\alpha_1 x_{t-1} + \mu E_t x_{t+1} - \sigma(i_t - E_t \pi_{t+1} - r^*) - \gamma(E_t e_{t+1} - e_t) + \varepsilon_t^x \qquad (1)$$

Where x is output gap, μ is the impact factor of expected output gap, α_1 is coefficient of former output gap, t is time, σ is the consumption elasticity of substitution, E is expectation, i is home interest rate, r^* is interest rate around the steady state, π is inflation, γ is sensitivity of output to exchange rate, e is nominal exchange rate and ε_t^x is aggregate demand shock. Equation (1) represents a nontraditional IS curve that relates the output gap not only to the interest rate, but also to the prior output gap and the expected future output gap and nominal exchange rates. A nominal exchange rate's appreciation, the rise of expected inflation, the rise of the prior output gap and the expected future output gap would increase domestic current output. However, the rise of interest rate and the expected exchange rate would lead to the decline of current output.

2.2 Aggregate Supply Curve

$$\pi_t = (1-\omega)\beta_1\pi_{t-1} + \omega E_t\pi_{t+1} + kx_t + \phi e_t + \varepsilon_t^\pi \tag{2}$$

Where ω is responding factor of expected inflation, β_1 is the coefficient of prior period inflation, k is coefficient of current output, ϕ is coefficient of nominal exchange rate and ε_t^π is aggregate supply shocks or productivity shocks. Equation (2) represents a nontraditional Phillips curve. Current inflation is affected by prior period output gap and exchange rate. We also use the uncovered interest parity condition $e_t = E_t e_{t+1} + i_t^* - i_t$. Where i^* is foreign nominal interest rate. It relates the movements of the interest rate differentials to the expected variations in the nominal exchange rate. Just as Parrado (2004), $i_t^* = \rho_1 i_{t-1}^* + eq$, $\varepsilon_t^x = \rho_2\varepsilon_{t-1}^x + ed$ and $\varepsilon_t^\pi = \rho_3\varepsilon_{t-1}^\pi + es$ describe the evolution of foreign interest rate, domestic aggregate demand shock and domestic aggregate supply shock or productivity shock respectively. Where eq, ed and es are independent and identically distributed(i.i.d) shocks with zero mean and 0.01 variance.

3 Taylor Rules

Through the rational expectations model and empirical analysis of 7 industrial countries, Taylor (1993) finds the real interest rate is the only variable which is related with the price stability and the economic growth in the long term, called interest rules or Taylor rule. Taylor rule means to regulate the monetary policy by interest rate adjustment according to output gap and inflation which is advantageous to the stabilization of output and commodities prices. The Taylor rule has received the widespread attention and many scholars study and develop the basic Taylor rule.

3.1 Nominal Interest Rate Taylor Rule

$$i_t = \kappa_\pi\pi_t + \kappa_x x_t \tag{3}$$

Where κ_π and κ_x is the coefficient of inflation and output gap respectively. Because the real interest rate is not advantageous for the operation in the monetary policy practice, according to the Fischer equation, $I = r + \pi$, where I is nominal interest rate, the Taylor rule can transform to be equation (3) with log-linearizing.

3.2 Exchange Rate Taylor Rule

$$i_t = \kappa_\pi \pi_t + \kappa_x x_t + \kappa_e e_t \tag{4}$$

Where κ_e is the coefficient of exchange rate. Ball (1999) argues traditional Taylor rule is based on closed economy, but exchange rate Taylor rule can fit monetary policy well along with the deepening of globalization. He constructs money condition index (MCI), which is generated by weighting of interest rate and exchange rate, to replace interest rate index.

3.3 Smooth Interest Rate Taylor Rule with Forward-Looking Variables

$$i_t = \rho i_{t-1} + (1-\rho)(\kappa_\pi E\pi_{t+1} + \kappa_x x_t + \kappa_e e_t) \tag{5}$$

Woodford (1999) argues the traditional Taylor rule make the economy fluctuate a lot and lead to excessive response. After the adding of interest rate lag, the macro economy will be more stable. At the same time, Clarida, Gali and Gertler (2000) think the transmission monetary policy to economic variable exists a time lag, so they present the forward-looking interest rate rule which include the expected variables. In open economy, we can get Taylor rule of equation (5) through introducing the smooth interest rate factor with forward-looking variables.

4 Model Simulations

In order to compare the different effects of Taylor rules to aggregate demand shock, aggregate supply shock and foreign interest rate shock, this paper uses Matlab software to take stochastic simulation to analyze the application of three Taylor rules described in equation (3), (4) and (5) in China. The times and the periods of Monte Carlo simulation is 2100 and 25 respectively.

4.1 Parameter Values

The following parameter values are selected from traditional related literature about China monetary policy or neo-Keynesian model of open economy such as Liu (2003), Parrado (2004), Leitemo (2008) and Zhu (2010). Table 1 presents the values of 18 parameters and the contents in the brackets are their data resources respectively.

4.2 Aggregate Demand Shocks

Where x is output gap, pi is inflation, e is nominal exchange rate and i is home nominal interest rate in figure 1. And, taylor1, taylor2 and taylor3 represent three kinds of Taylor rules described in equation (3), (4) and (5) respectively. Figure 1 gives the response of output gap, inflation, exchange rate and home nominal interest rate to aggregate demand shocks.

Table 1. Parameter Values

parameter	value	parameter	value
μ	0.62(Liu, 2003)	ρ_1	0.8(Parrado, 2004)
σ	1(Leitemo,2008)	ρ_2	0.8(Parrado, 2004)
α_1	1.27(Liu, 2003)	ρ_3	0.8(Parrado, 2004)
β_1	1.02(Liu, 2003)	ω	0.68(Liu, 2003)
ϕ	0.05(Leitemo,2008)	k	0.27(Liu, 2003)
γ	0.45(Parrado, 2004)	r^*	4.01(Liu, 2003)
ρ	0.5(Parrado, 2004)	κ_π	1.01(Parrado, 2004)
κ_x	0.4(Zhu,2010)	κ_e	0.05(Zhu, 2010)

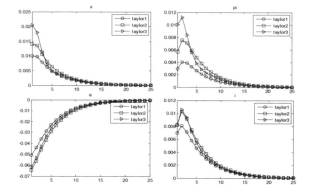

Fig. 1. Responses to Aggregate Demand Shocks

From the figure 1, we can know when the aggregate demand shocks occur, output, inflation and home nominal interest rate rise, but exchange rate declines. Then, all variables converge to steady state. Specifically speaking, in the output aspects, when the China Central Bank adopts taylor3, the influence of aggregate shock to output is biggest. The output gap would rise 2% in the beginning, but the speed of convergence is very quick. Using taylor1, the influence of aggregate shock to output is smallest. In the inflation aspects, the effect of taylor3 is also biggest and taylor1 is also smallest. Due to the expected inflation in the model, the inflation curve riser firstly and declines later. The aggregate demand shock changes the inflation expectation of households, so the inflation rises at the first period. In exchange rate aspects, the effect of taylor2 is biggest, exchange rate declines 6.5% after the shocks in the beginning. The effect of taylor2 is smallest. In nominal interest rate aspect, the effect of taylor1 is smallest. The effects of taylor2 and taylor3 are similar. In short, the fluctuation of output gap, inflation, exchange rate and home nominal interest rate is small to aggregate shock when the central bank adopts taylor1. In contrast, variance is big with taylor3.

4.3 Aggregate Supply Shocks

Figure 2 gives the responses of output gap, inflation, exchange rate and home nominal interest rate to aggregate supply shocks.

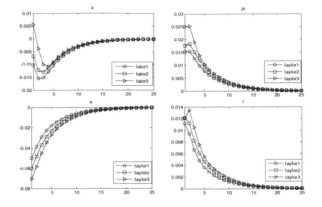

Fig. 2. Responses to Aggregate Supply Shocks

When the aggregate supply shocks occur, inflation and home nominal interest rate rise, while exchange rate declines. The change of output gap depends on the monetary policy. In the output aspects, if China central bank adopts taylor3, the output increases 0.5% at the first period. Then, it goes to be negative. If China central bank adopts taylor1 or taylor2, the output is negative all the time. In inflation aspects, the effect of taylor3 is biggest. The inflation increase 2.5% when the aggregate shocks occur. The effect of taylor1 is smallest. In exchange rate aspects, taylor3 also has the biggest influence. The exchange rate decline 7% when the shocks occur. In home nominal interest rate aspects, it raises when shocks occur and then decline all the time under the monetary policy of taylor1 and taylor2. However, when taking taylor3 it continues to go up at the first period and then decline because of expected inflation. Generally speaking, the effect of taylor3 is more severe.

4.4 Foreign Interest Rate Shocks

Figure 3 gives the responses of output gap, inflation, exchange rate and home nominal interest rate to foreign interest rate shocks.

In order to analyze the influence of foreign monetary policy to domestic economy, this paper adds the foreign interest shocks. The domestic inflation, exchange rate and home interest rate rise when the foreign interest rate shocks occur. However, the change of output is not consistent between short term and long term. In the output aspects, it responses biggest with the monetary policy of taylor3, increasing by 0.6%. But it goes to be negative from the third period. By comparison, the economy is more stable under taylor1 and taylor2. In the inflation aspects, the effect of taylor3 is

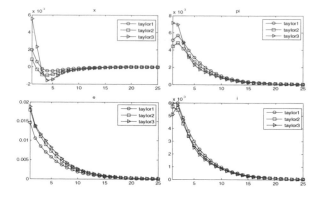

Fig. 3. Responses to Foreign Interest Rate Shocks

biggest to the foreign interest shocks. In the exchange rate aspects, the influences of taylor2 and taylor3 are similar. In home interest rate aspects, there is no striking difference among three kinds of Taylor rules.

5 Conclusions

Based on massive existing literature such as Liu (2003), Parrado (2004), Leitemo (2008), Zhu (2010) and so on, this paper provides a dynamic neo-Keynesian model of open economy that can be used to analyze the impact of monetary policy that considers three kinds of Taylor rules in china: nominal interest rate Taylor rule, exchange rate Taylor rule and smooth interest rate Taylor rule with forward-looking variables. According to Monte Carlo simulation method with Matlab software, we can draw following forth conclusions: first, it is better to increase output for China central bank to adopt smooth interest rate Taylor rule with forward-looking variables. This rule can make the output increase in a short time no matter which shocks occur. Because of the expected inflation added in the policy, the economy can adjust in advance. Second, the fluctuation of macro economy is smallest when using nominal interest rate Taylor rule. The effectiveness of monetary policy and stability of macro economy are both important. Although the smooth interest rate Taylor rule with forward-looking variables is more effective, the nominal interest rate Taylor rule is good for keeping economy stable. The reason is that it can reduce the times of monetary policy adjustment without expected variables. Third, the influence of aggregate demand shocks on output is most remarkable. In the market economy, the output is determined by demand which promotes economic development. Forth, the influence of aggregate supply shocks on domestic inflation is biggest. The aggregate supply shocks or productivity shocks can increase the average wage of labor which leads to the rising of inflation.

Generally speaking, the main findings are it's better for China central bank to use smooth interest rate Taylor rule with forward-looking variables to increase output and use nominal interest rate Taylor rule to keep macro economy stable. Although China has not realized liberalization of interest rates which is the necessary condition for

Taylor rules application and China central bank also plays dominant role in interest rate system, deregulation of interest rate becomes an inevitable choice for the complete opening of China's economy. For instance, the regulations of China inter-bank offered rates (CHIBOR), discount market interest rates and money market bond repurchase rates are released.

Acknowledgements. This topic is subsidized by project fund "Economic openness, the monetary policy validity and international monetary policy cooperation"([10YJA790066]) and supported by the Fundamental Research Fund for the Central Universities.

References

1. Ball, L.: Efficient Rules for Monetary Policy. International Finance 2(1), 63–83 (1999)
2. Clarida, R., Gali, J., Gertler, M.: Monetary Policy Rules and Macroeconomic Stability: Evidence and Some Theory. Quarterly Journal of Economics 115, 147–180 (2000)
3. Liu, B.: Choice and Implementation of the Optimal Monetary Policy Rules in China. Economic Research Journal 9, 3–13 (2003) (in Chinese)
4. Li, Q., Wang, Z.W.: Taylor rules and Chinese macroeconomic volatility: 1994–2006 empirical test. Economic Sciences 2, 9–22 (2009) (in Chinese)
5. Leitemo, K., Soderstrom, U.: Robust Monetary Policy in a Small Open Economy. Journal of Dynamics & Control 32, 3218–3252 (2008)
6. Parrado, E.: Inflation Target and Exchange Rate Rules in a Open Economy. R. IMF Working Paper 04/21 (2004)
7. Taylor, J.B.: Discretion versus Policy Rules in Practice. Carnegie-Rochester Conferences Series on Public Policy 39, 195–214 (1993)
8. Woodford, M.: Optimal Monetary Policy Inertia. R. NBER Working Paper No.7261 (1999)
9. Xie, P., Luo, X.: Taylor Rule and Its Empirical Test in China's Monetary Policy. Economic Research Journal 3, 3–12 (2002) (in Chinese)
10. Wang, J.G.: An Empirical Study On the Taylor Rule and China's Monetary Policy Reaction Function. The Journal of Quantitative and Technical Economics 1, 43–49 (2006) (in Chinese)
11. Zheng, T.G., Liu, J.J.: Taylor Rule with Regime Switching and Its Application to China's Monetary Policy. Economic Research Journal 9, 3–13 (2010) (in Chinese)
12. Zhu, L.F.: Optimal Monetary Policy Rules for an Open Economy. Wuhan University, Wuhan (2010) (in Chinese)

Financing Capacity Analysis of Real Estate Development Enterprises Based on DEA

Ning Liu, Xiaoqing Xu, and Yachen Liu

School of Management, Shenyang Jianzhu University,
110168 Shenyang, China
{72824146, qing_625450794, 47023704}@qq.com

Abstract. Fuzzy Data Envelopment Analysis (DEA) evaluation model in real estate enterprise financing capability have improved incomplete weight deficiency of information processing. Indices values were converted to trapezoid fuzzy numbers, then with incomplete information on indices weights as constraints, a fuzzy DEA model with outputs only and preference was established, and then by applying the α-cut approach, the model was transformed to a family of crisp DEA models and was solved. Experiments demonstrated the feasibility and applicability of the method.

Keywords: Financing capacity, Real estate Fuzzy Theory, Incomplete information, Data Envelopment Analysis.

1 Introduction

With China's rapid economic development, financing demand of real estate market is gradually increasing, multi-level and multi-channel financing to satisfy the demand for investment currently become a remarkable characteristic of real estate finance. Financing capacity plays a crucial role in structural reforms in facilitating an understanding of the behavior of real estate development enterprises. The research of financing capacity analysis of real estate development enterprises has become an important topic.

Some researches have applied Data Envelopment Analysis (DEA) to develop Financing of real estate, but none of these DEA studies have incorporated Financing capacity analysis. In this paper, we apply Data Envelopment Analysis- Analytic Hierarchy Process (DEA-AHP) methodology to analyze the Financing capacity analysis of real estate development enterprises. Fuzzy Data Envelopment Analysis (DEA) evaluation model in financing capacity analysis of real estate development enterprises have improved incomplete weight deficiency of information processing. Firstly, indices values were converted to trapezoid fuzzy numbers, then with incomplete information on indices weights as constraints, a fuzzy DEA model with outputs only and preference was established, and then by applying the α-cut approach, the model was transformed to a family of crisp DEA models and was solved. Experiments demonstrated the feasibility and applicability of the method.

Q. Zhou (Ed.): ISAEBD 2011, Part I, CCIS 208, pp. 266–272, 2011.

2 DEA –AHP Model

2.1 DEA and AHP

Data Envelopment Analysis (DEA) is a nonparametric method in operations research and economics for the estimation of production frontiers. It is used to empirically measure productive efficiency of decision making units. There are also parametric approaches which are used for the estimation of production frontiers (see Lovell & Schmidt 1988 for an early survey). One can also combine the relative strengths from each of these approaches in a hybrid method. Data Envelopment Analysis (DEA) is a Linear Programming methodology to measure the efficiency of multiple.

Comparing the relative efficiency of Decision Making Unit (DMU) through mathematical programming, DEA is the method that assesses efficiency of decision-making unit based on the concept of relative efficiency. Based on input and output data of comprehensive analysis, DEA can draw the efficiency of each DMU comprehensive quantitative indexes. Accordingly, the DMU classification ranking will determine effective (that is, relative efficiency of the highest) DMU, and point out other non-effective DMU on the causes and extent. [1][2] Now the representative DEA model, have model, FG model and ST model.

FG model is as follows:

$$P_{FG}^I = \begin{cases} \max(\mu^T Y_0 - \mu_0) \\ w^T X_j - \mu^T Y_j + \mu_0 \geq 0, j = 1,2,\cdots,n \\ w^T X_0 = 1 \\ w^T \geq 0, \mu \geq 0, \mu_0 \geq 0 \end{cases} \tag{1}$$

$$D_{FG}^I = \begin{cases} \min \theta \\ \sum_{j}^{n} X_j \lambda_j \leq \theta X_0, \\ \sum_{j=1}^{n} Y_0 \lambda_j \geq Y_0 \\ \sum_{j=1}^{n} \lambda_j \leq 1 \\ \lambda_j \geq 0, j = 1,2,\cdots,n, \theta \in E^1 \end{cases} \tag{2}$$

The relative answers may be:

$$T_{FG} = \left\{ (X,Y) \middle| \sum_{j=1}^{n} X_j \lambda_j \leq X, \sum_{j=1}^{n} Y_j \lambda_j \geq Y, \sum_{j=1}^{n} \lambda_j \leq 1, \lambda_j \geq 0, j = 1,\cdots n \right\}$$

D_{FG}^I has the other form:

$$\begin{cases} \min \theta, \\ \left(\theta X_0, Y_0\right) \in T_{FG} \end{cases} \tag{3}$$

FG model is chosen in this paper. FG model is one of DEA basic models, which is an ideal method that evaluates relatively effective technology for multiple inputs and multiple outputs decision-making units. It may involve the production set which is more than one set of convex set to meet convex, invalid and the smallest assumptions of justice system..

When we apply the AHP method to take the weights of criteria and alternatives, the decision maker should be consistent in the preference ratings. The equation below describes the process of taking the overall weights of alternatives.

$$\begin{pmatrix} \dfrac{w_1}{w_1} & \cdots & \dfrac{w_1}{w_n} \\ \vdots & \ddots & \vdots \\ \dfrac{w_n}{w_1} & \cdots & \dfrac{w_n}{w_n} \end{pmatrix} \begin{pmatrix} w \\ w_2 \\ \vdots \\ w_3 \end{pmatrix} = \begin{bmatrix} nw_1 \\ nw_2 \\ \vdots \\ nw_n \end{bmatrix} \Rightarrow AX = nX \tag{4}$$

Where a_{ij} represents the importance of alternative i over alternative j and a_{ik} represents the importance of alternative i over alternative k, $a_{ij}\ a_{jk}$ must be equal to a_{ik} that is an estimate of the ratio $\dfrac{w_i}{w_k}$ for the judgments.

2.2 Comprehensive Model

Each influence financing capability index as a unit, after pretreatment of fuzzy index (the higher the value, the more good, namely all indexes as output index as the basis, incomplete weight information of linear expression as constraint, establish only output index and contain preference information of the fuzzy DEA model, as follows:
(FG) :

$$\max \sum_{i=1}^{b} w_i r_{ik} = \tilde{E}_k, \ \sum_{i=1}^{b} w_i r_{ik} \leq 1, j = 1,2,\cdots,a , \ Cw \leq b \ w_i \geq 0 \tag{5}$$

Among above, the $\tilde{E}_k$ is model of optimal value, called the evaluation index proportion schemes k, $w = (w_1, w_2, \cdots, w_m)^T$ is said each index weight a group of variable, C is $n_1 \times m$ dimension of the coefficient matrix (n_1 is weight the constraint condition of number), $b = (b_1, b_2, \cdots, b_n)^T$ is the constant vector.

Model (FG), for a given incomplete weight information, just click on the parameters of the C and B values are properly set, can build constraint $Cw \leq b$ this model of index eliminate the influence of dimensional and orders of magnitude, the corresponding weights with practical meaning, eliminate the traditional fuzzy DEA model the weight coefficient is not practical meaning of defects.

2.3 Model Algorithm

Model (FG) is a not directly solving fuzzy mathematical programming. To facilitate the solution model (FG) in various fuzzy number, use their own α (($0 \leq \alpha \leq 1$) sets of interval the model (FG) has been written for:

(FG1):

$$\max \sum_{i=1}^{m} w_i \left[(r_{ik})_\alpha^L, (r_{ik})_\alpha^U \right] = \left(\tilde{E}_k \right)_\alpha$$

$$\sum_{i=1}^{m} w_i \left[(r_{ik})_\alpha^L, (r_{ik})_\alpha^U \right] \leq 1, j = 1, 2, \cdots, n \qquad (6)$$

$$Cw \leq b, \qquad w \geq 0$$

Among above:

$$\left(r_{ij} \right)_\alpha^L = \min \left\{ r_{ij} \middle| r_{ij} \in \mathrm{supp} (r_{ij}) \boxminus \mu_{r_{ij}} (r_{ij}) \geq \alpha \right\}$$

$$\left(r_{ij} \right)_\alpha^U = \max \left\{ r_{ij} \middle| r_{ij} \in \sup p (r_{ij}) \boxminus \mu_{r_{ij}} (r_{ij}) \geq \alpha \right\}$$

For any given α value, in its evaluation index $\left[(r_{ik})_\alpha^L, (r_{ik})_\alpha^U \right]$ sets interval α scope changes, its value but can small. Therefore, all evaluation indexes of any kind of portfolio corresponds to an evaluation results. In order to determine the model (FG) in the confidence level to α when the optimal solution of the change of scope, will model (FG1) is decomposed into pessimistic programming model and optimistic programming model. [3]

Pessimism model (P-FG):

$$\max \sum_{i=1}^{m} w_i (r_{ik})_\alpha^L = (E_k)_\alpha^L \quad \sum_{i=1}^{m} w_i (r_{ik})_\alpha^L \leq 1 \quad \sum_{i=1}^{m} w_i (r_{ik})_\alpha^U \leq 1, j = 1, 2, \cdots, n, j \neq k$$

$$Cw \leq b \quad w_i \geq 0 \qquad (7)$$

Optimistic model（O-FP）:

$$\max \sum_{i=1}^{m} w_i (r_{ik})_\alpha^U = (E_k)_\alpha^U \quad \sum_{i=1}^{m} w_i (r_{ik})_\alpha^L \leq 1 \quad \sum_{i=1}^{m} w_i (r_{ik})_\alpha^L \leq 1, j = 1, 2, \cdots, n, j \neq k$$

$$Cw \leq b \quad w_i \geq 0 \qquad (8)$$

Model (P-FG) and (O-FP) is deterministic linear programming model, which can be directly obtained solution, the optimal solution is and. and respectively representation model in the confidence level of when the objective function values of the minimum and maximum. In these two optimal solution for boundary constitute the interval number is k in namely for scheme for confidence level when interval of assessment index. For any, repeat solution (P-FG) model and(O-FG)model, piecing get all the scheme in the confidence level as when interval estimate index, based on this, judgment in the confidence level of each scheme for when of the pros and cons. Therefore, the algorithm can overall recognition and understanding each high-performance concrete proportion schemes of comprehensive attributes.

Table 1. Financing Capacity Analysis of Real Estate Development Enterprises' Indexes

INDEX NO.	Project development team governance structure	Political attention			Guarantee reliability	Income stability	Development scale
		R_s	R_m	R_w			
1(x_1)	190	27.0	39.0	48.0	920	optimal	295.17
2(x_2)	180	39.3	46.7	60.5	782	optimal	294.695
3(x_3)	170	37.5	42.0	49.5	1005	fine	300.06
4(x_4)	180	35.5	48.0	55.0	980	middle	301.595
5(x_5)	180	36.5	47.5	57.0	950	fine	304.05

Table 2. The Evaluation Index of Fuzzy Index

RATIO INDEX	x_1	x_2	x_3	x_4	x_5
Project development team governance structure	1,1,1,1	0.5,0.5,0.5,0.5	0,0,0,0	0.5,0.5,0.5,0.5	0.5,0.5,0.5,0.5
Political attention	0,0,0,0	0.86,0.86,0.86,0.86	0.33,0.33,0.33,0.33	1,1,1,1	0.94,0.94,0.94,0.94
Guarantee reliability	0.38,0.38,0.38,0.38	1,1,1,1	0,0,0,0	0.11,0.11,0.11,0.11 0.25,0.25,0.25,0.25	
Income stability	0.7,1.0,1.0,1.0	0.7,1.0,1.0,1.0	0,0.3,0.3,0.5	0.2,0.5,0.5, 0.8	0,0.3,0.3,0.5
Development scale	0.95,0.95,0.95,0.95	1,1,1,1	0.43,0.43,0.43,0.43 0.26,0.26,0.26,0.26 0,0,0,0		

Table 3. Based on The Results of The evolution of Weight Order Relation

	x_1	x_2	x_3	x_4	x_5
0.0	(0.5191,0.5491)	(0.8872,0.9172)	(0.2052,0.2552)	(0.4349,0.4949)	(0.3663,0.4163)
0.1	(0.5221,0.5491)	(0.8902,0.9172)	(0.2082,0.2532)	(0.4349,0.4949)	(0.3693,0.4143)
0.2	(0.5251,0.5491)	(0.8932,0.9172)	(0.2112,0.2512)	(0.4349,0.4949)	(0.3723,0.4123)
0.3	(0.5281,0.5491)	(0.8962,0.9172)	(0.2142,0.2492)	(0.4349,0.4949)	(0.3753,0.4103)
0.4	(0.5311,0.5491)	(0.8992,0.9172)	(0.2172,0.2472)	(0.4349,0.4949)	(0.3783,0.4083)
0.5	(0.5341,0.5491)	(0.90272,0.9172)	(0.2202,0.2452)	(0.4349,0.4949)	(0.3813,0.4063)
0.6	(0.5371,0.5491)	(0.9052,0.9172)	(0.2232,0.2432)	(0.4349,0.4949)	(0.3843,0.4043)
0.7	(0.5401,0.5491)	(0.9082,0.9172)	(0.2262,0.2412)	(0.4349,0.4949)	(0.3873,0.4023)
0.8	(0.5431,0.5491)	(0.9112,0.9172)	(0.2292,0.2392)	(0.4349,0.4949)	(0.3903,0.4003)
0.9	(0.5461,0.5491)	(0.9142,0.9172)	(0.2322,0.2372)	(0.4349,0.4949)	(0.3933,0.3983)
1.0	(0.5491,0.5491)	(0.9172,0.9172)	(0.2352,0.2352)	(0.4349,0.4949)	(0.3963,0.3963)

3 Case Analysis

3.1 Financing Capacity Analysis of Real Estate Development Enterprises' Indexes

According to the literature provided data, conduct concrete with scheme evaluation, each index data in table 1. [4]

3.2 Data Preprocessing

According to the table 1, quantified it as trapezoidal fuzzy number form, and the evaluation index of pretreatment method according to the standard treatment, the results as shown in TABLE 2. [5]

3.3 The Determination of Weight Vectors

These five kinds of indexes involved the Project development team governance structure, Political attention in engineering requirements within the permitted to engineering, less influence, but should not be ignored. And Guarantee reliability, Income stability, Development scale three index importance quite, so as to determine weight vectors, 0.27 for (0.09, 0.27, 0.1, 0.27). [6] By (0.09, 0.27, 0.27, 0.1, 0.27) knowable, five evaluation index, Guarantee reliability, Income stability, Development scale is equal and Project development team governance structure is the largest. For simplified sake, not consider the rest two indexes of the relative importance of relationship between, namely, known for weight information

$$w_2 = w_3 = w_5, w_2 - w_j \geq 0.15(j = 1,4) \quad \text{put} \quad w_2 = w_3 = w_5, w_2 - w_j \geq 0.15(j = 1,4) \quad \text{and}$$

$\sum_{i=1}^{5} w_i = 1$ get together with $Cw \leq b$, then get the evaluation model.

3.4 Financing Capacity Indexes Analysis

According to the above model and the weights of the order relation representation method, and separately calculated and five measures in different α confidence level under evaluation result, as shown in table 3.

From the table 3, for different α value, five measures based on the order relation of sorting and the weights of the sorting are exactly the same, all is $x_2 > x_1 > x_4 > x_5 > x_3$ As the evaluation result, the greater the scheme, so the better plan 2 is the optimum scheme, this result with literature [11] measure model using the obtained results consistent, proved the feasibility and effectiveness of this method. In addition, five measures based on order relation rank in the weights of the sorting identical also explain evaluation results of the confidence level α change not sensitive.

4   Conclusion

This paper applies a DEA method that is combined with AHP to jointly analyze Financing capacity analysis of real estate development enterprises several important conclusions are evident.. Based on the index, the index weight with incomplete information of Financing of real estate development enterprises problems, and puts forward the improved fuzzy DEA evaluation model. This model will first index convert dimensionless fuzzy number, and then, with the converted fuzzy number as the basis, incomplete weight information as constraint, and fuzzy DEA model was improved, and established based on the improved fuzzy DEA of concrete proportion schemes evaluation model, and gives the corresponding solving algorithm. In case analysis view of, also contains deterministic quantitative indices and qualitative index of the problem, respectively based on interval Numbers weight, ordering relationship weight two incomplete weight information as an example, the validity of this method. For other forms of evaluation indexes and incomplete weight information, solving process is similar.

Acknowledgement. This paper is supported by fund of Ministry of science research project (2009 - R3-2009).

References

1. Partanen, J., Lassila, J., Viljainen, S.: Analysis of the benchmarking results of the electricity distribution companies in Finland. In: IEEE Postgraduate Conference on Electric Power Systems, Budapest, Hungary (2002)
2. Tanurej, E.P.S.: Comparative Analysis of the Distribution Companies in the Establishment of Quality Targets in Terms of Continuity Indices. Master Dissertation, IEE/DET, Escola Federal de Engenharia de Itajubi - EFEI, Brazil (November 2000) (in Portuguese)
3. Zhang, M., Li, G., Yang, G.: With fuzzy triangular element of chance constraint DEA model. Journal of Mathematics of Practice and Cognition 34(2), 42–52 (2004)
4. Huang, S., He, S., Qiu, Q., Zhan, j.: Bay bridge main piers of SFRC four-pile caps high-performance concrete proportioning design. The Road, 224–225 (2007)
5. Liu, Y., Gao, X., Shen, Z.: Based on fuzzy data envelopment analysis of product design scheme evaluation research. Computer Integrated Manufacturing System, Stratigraphy 11, 2099–2104
6. HuiGe, X., ZhuoFu, W., GongLian, Y.: Based on DEA decision unit sorting method research. Journal of Systems Engineering and Electronics 11(31), 2648–2651 (2009)

Analysis of Infrastructure Investment Risks by VaR

Yachen Liu, Xiaoqing Xu, and Ning Liu

School of Management, Shenyang Jianzhu University,
110168 Shenyang, China
{47023704,qing_625450794,72824146}@qq.com

Abstract. This paper puts forward the VAR in the application of infrastructure construction investment risks. Firstly, infrastructure construction investment risk of the application of VAR in our country is necessary, and through VAR calculation methods including History Simulation method, Risk Metrics method, Monte Carlo method and Variance-covariance method we know how to use VAR for measuring risk in infrastructure construction. The paper mainly discuss Variance-covariance method to deal with infrastructure investment risk by concrete examples. At last, foreground of using VAR in infrastructure construction is analyzed and put forward a new calculation method CVAR.

Keywords: Infrastructure Construction, VAR, Investment.

1 Introduction

In recent years, there is an accumulating number of China's infrastructure construction, but for increasing responsibility government assumes or implementation that investors voluntarily resulted, the effect is not good. At present, the main method for government to build infrastructure project evaluation is NPV, IRR, and other conventional methods. On the circumstance of the uncertainty at the increasing development, the core of the traditional investment decision methods in the application scope with net present value (NPV) method is shrinking, but VAR is a kind of uncertainty environment of investment decision-making method, through the analysis of the advantage of an opportunity to create expectations of costs and benefits to decide whether to investment. But for larger environmental uncertainty, VAR appears more effective and scientific. Along with the development of VAR and its application in practice is more widely, VAR pricing method is used by some domestic scholars and industrial circles personage in infrastructure investment, infrastructure construction development, drug development, flexible manufacturing system, licenses and patents and other evaluation, at the same time, a large number of empirical research work is done for enterprise's actual investment evaluation and decision analysis providing a strong support. [1]

This paper puts forward the VAR in the application of infrastructure construction investment risks. Firstly, infrastructure construction investment risk of the application of VAR in our country is necessary, and through VAR calculation methods including History Simulation method, Risk Metrics method, Monte Carlo method and Variance-covariance method we know how to use VAR for measuring risk in infrastructure construction. The paper mainly discuss Variance-covariance method to

Q. Zhou (Ed.): ISAEBD 2011, Part I, CCIS 208, pp. 273–279, 2011.
© Springer-Verlag Berlin Heidelberg 2011

deal with infrastructure investment risk by concrete examples. At last, foreground of using VAR in infrastructure construction is analyzed and put forward a new calculation method CVAR(Conditional VAR).

2   VAR

VaR(Value at Risk) is a risk management concept firstly proposed by Morgan [2], and initially it is applied for the measurement and supervision of financial market risk.

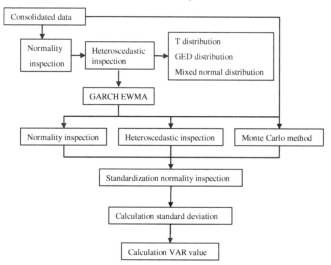

VaR means to point in normal market conditions, a project investment or portfolio in a given confidence level and determine the largest holding period of the expected losses. The principle of VaR is very simple, but its calculation is extremely complicated. To calculate the VaR must determine the risk probability distribution, in the normal circumstances, the probability distribution of different financial time series is not the same. [3] Most scholars have focused on the calculation of VaR to be more in line with the actual value of the investment risk, such as the case of VaR calculation of mixed-normal distribution [4,5] and extreme value distribution In China, many academics carry out research on the VaR calculation in a variety of different situations. Yu Suhong etc. verify the superiority of VaR calculated value with the SV model by the comparison with the VaR calculated values based on GARCH model [6]. Ye Wuyi etc. aim at the deficiency of the linear sub-site model with the certain reality to give a sub-threshold locus regression model and apply the model to the VaR   calculation. These scholars above merely measure the risk, and very few scholars have discussed how to make investment decision according to the result.

3   The Application of Infrastructure Investment Risks Base on VAR

3.1   The Necessity of VAR in Infrastructure Investment Risk

Now the analysis of infrastructure investment risk mainly with three ways: Balance analysis of profit and loss; Sensitivity analysis; Probability Analytic Method. But all three tactics have their limits. Balance analysis of profit and loss based on some assumptions basis such as keeping the price of something constant. Obviously it is of no use. Sensitivity analysis has only one risk-factor, other parameters keep maintained. In fact, the existence of correlation will make surface without significant factors through the high correlation with other factors to exert great influence on the benefit of the project, which is the main defects Sensitivity analysis. The probability analysis despite the introduction of scene, but with the probability of occurrence in this scenario analysis assumes that the future is discrete, and the situation of its risk factors and not a detailed analysis of this again with the facts. Using VAR this more precise measure risk index became infrastructure construction investment risk metric research of choice. [7]

There are two forms of infrastructure investment: Direct investment and indirect investment. Direct investment refers to infrastructure investment developers and financing, and actual themselves for infrastructure construction development. Indirect investment refers to infrastructure developers only for investment instead of making a infrastructure investment development, marked by investors who hit it big on the stock market. These two kinds of investment form leads to infrastructure construction investment risk using VAR decision-making process may have two different ways, indirect investment may directly apply mechanically VAR theory in the financial sector to the method, this paper mainly expounds the VAR theory in the use of infrastructure construction direct investment fields.

3.2 The Calculation of VaR

- History simulation method

History simulation method does not need the yields of infrastructure construction projects statistical distribution of any restrictions, but from the history of the sequence of yield of the samples. For instance, Select the past "n" year (quarterly and monthly) yields history samples. Using the infrastructure construction market yields to construct historical changes future investment projects the probability distribution of profit and loss. In a given confidence (such as 95%) conditions, the distribution function of frequency distribution of out to 5% of the loss, as a critical value, the VAR formulas as follows:

$$\text{VAR} = \omega_0 (\overline{R_P} \times \Delta t - R^*) \tag{1}$$

Among above, $\overline{R_P}$ is the sample rate of return of the mean, R^* is the rate of return of distribution at the obvious level α, ω_0 is the initializing investment, Δt is the infrastructure investment period.

- Risk Metrics [8]

Use Risk Metrics method to calculate the VAR value with two important parameters: Confidence Level $1 - \alpha$ and the infrastructure project period Δt. The former depends on decision-making risk preferences of degree and project funding surpluses, general value is 95% ~ 99%, while the latter is decided by the infrastructure project itself, its computation formula is: [9]

$$\text{VAR}=\omega_0(\text{E}(\text{R}_P)\times\Delta t - R^*) \tag{2}$$

Among above, R_P is a specific period (usually a year) infrastructure construction investments return rate. $\text{E}(\text{R}_P)$ is the expectations of infrastructure projects Δ t return, ω_0 is the initializing investment, R^* is the minimum rate of return of distribution at the confidence level 1-α, that is $P(R_P < R^*) = \alpha$.

When R_P obey the normal state distribution of logarithm with Δt, assuming:

$$R_P \sim N(E(R_P)\Delta t, \sigma_P^2\Delta t)$$

then lead to :

$$\text{VAR}=\omega_0 \times Z_\alpha \times \sigma_p \sqrt{\Delta t} \tag{3}$$

When R_P do not obey the normal state distribution of logarithm with Δt, assuming :

$$R_P \sim N(E(R_P)\Delta t, \sigma_P^2\Delta t)$$

then lead to :

$$\text{VAR}=\omega_0 \times Z_\alpha \times \frac{\sigma}{\sqrt{\Delta t}} \tag{4}$$

σ is the sale price fluctuations of infrastructure project of standard deviation, infrastructure investors can according to project sales price expectations and surrounding areas that dish selling price.
- Monte Carlo method [10]

Monte Carlo Simulation (MCS) is a random sampling or simulation experiment method widely applied to solve infrastructure construction investment decision-making over the past decade. The principle is to extract sample values which fit the activities duration distribution by generating a large mount of random numbers with certain probability distribution in the process of Monte Carlo Simulation, then take simulation calculation of decision-making on the basis of critical path, finally the project duration expectation and variance, which are important basis for decision-making of project activity duration, are obtained by making statistical calculation to the simulation results.
- Variance-covariance

Assuming that there are n kinds infrastructure construction assets, its return rate is $R_1, R_2, \cdots R_n$, their expectancy is $\overline{R_1}, \overline{R_2}, \cdots, \overline{R_n}$, Selection rate of return no less than R_0, standard deviation is $\sigma_1, \sigma_2, \cdots, \sigma_n$, and covariance of i kind of assets and j kind of assets is, Selection rate of return larger than R_0.

Set

$$I = [1, 2, \cdots, 1]^T$$
$$R = [R_1, R_2, \cdots, R_n]^T$$
$$\overline{R} = \left[\overline{R_1}, \overline{R_2}, \cdots \overline{R_n}\right]^T \tag{5}$$
$$\omega = [\omega_1, \omega_2, \cdots, \omega_n]^T$$

ω is a vector of optimal investment coefficient of proportionality and $\sum_{i=1}^{n} \omega_i = 1$, Q

is variance-covariance, so the expected value of portfolio $R_P = \sum_{i=1}^{n} \omega_i R_i$ is :

$$\overline{R_P} = \sum_{i=1}^{n} \omega_i \overline{R_i} = \omega^T \overline{R} \tag{6}$$

Variance is:

$$\sigma_P^2 = \sum_{i=1}^{n} \sum_{j=1}^{n} \omega_i \sigma_{ij} \omega_j = \omega^T Q \omega$$

Set X as a random variable, the expectation of X is E(X),

$$(X - EX)^- = \min(X - EX, 0)$$
$$(X - EX)^+ = man(X - EX, 0)$$

Assume X and Y as two random variable, and the variance-covariance of them is $COV(X,Y)$, $D(X)$ and $D(Y)$ is variance, $D^-(X), D^+(X), D^+(Y), D^-(Y)$ is semi-variance, combine the following formula:

$$\frac{D^-(X) \cdot D^-(Y) + \frac{1}{2} D^-(X) D^+(Y) + \frac{1}{2} D^+(X) D^-(Y)}{D(X) D(Y)}$$

with

$$\frac{D^+(X) + D^+(Y) + \frac{1}{2} D^-(X) D^+(Y) + \frac{1}{2} D^+(X) D^-(Y)}{D(X) D(Y)}$$

then   get $COV^-(X,Y)$ and $COV^+(X,Y)$,   then   called
$Q^- = \left[COV^-(R_i R_j)\right]_{n \times n}$, $Q^+ = \left[COV^+(R_i R_j)\right]_{n \times n}$ as semi- variance-covariance .

Use $\omega^T Q^- \omega$ to measure degree that $R_P < \overline{R_P}$, $\omega^T Q^+ \omega$ to measure degree that $R_P > \overline{R_P}$,lure risk coefficient ρ into function below:

$$f(\omega) = (1 - \rho) \omega^T Q^+ \omega - \rho \omega^T Q^- \omega \tag{7}$$

Investors bear ability determination according to their own specific investment projects.

$$\max f(\omega) = (1-\rho)\omega^T Q^+ \omega - \rho Q^- \omega$$

$$s.t. \begin{cases} R\omega^T \geq R_0 \\ \omega^T I = 1, \omega_i \geq 0 \\ \rho \in (0,1) \end{cases} \tag{8}$$

Set $R_f = \dfrac{\omega^T Q^+ \omega}{\omega^T Q^- \omega}$ as per-risk attached.

4 Case Analysis

Assuming that the infrastructure investor is faced with the portfolio decision-making problem of n kinds of residential, office, Sewage treatment plant, industrial for four categories. Their $R_1 = 0.1875, R_2 = 0.20, R_3 = 0.2625, R_4 = 0.1750$

$$Q = \begin{pmatrix} 0.0073 & -0.0017 & 0.1177 & 0.0021 \\ -0.0017 & 0.00117 & -0.0033 & -0.0008 \\ 0.0077 & -0.0033 & 0.00123 & 0.0054 \\ 0.0021 & -0.0008 & 0.0054 & 0.0042 \end{pmatrix}$$

Risk coefficient is $\rho = 0.1, \rho = 0.3, \rho = 0.5, \rho = 0.7$. The same group that the calculation samples in table I.

Table 1. Different models of risk value and risk reward units

Model	Investment Proportion	Risk	Return of portfolio	Per-risk-Return
Markowitz	0,0.757,0.2427,0	0.000486	0.2152	0.0032
Semi-variance	0,0.7692,0.2308,0	0.000154	0.2144	0.0028
ρ=0.1	0,0.7486,0.2514,0	0.000135	0.2157	0.0039
ρ=0.3	0.68920,0,0,0.3180	0.000130	0.2015	0.0035
ρ=0.5	0.5970,0,0,0.4030	0.00024	0.1825	0.0026
ρ=0.7	0,0.06922,0.3078,0	-0.0002104	0.0612	0.00012

We can see the same group of samples, the risk of method to calculate the half variance than variance method $\rho = 0.1, \rho = 0.3, \rho = 0.5$, weighted model for positive, explain income risk than loss, the possibility of $\rho = 0.7$ risk value is negative, explain in this preference portfolio returns possibility under less than the loss. From $\rho = 0.1$ and $\rho = 0.5$, the comparison of the risk is big, but not necessarily combined income risk reward with a mix of earnings units are related. So, in infrastructure investment portfolio risk returns, the unit is the deciding factors of asset choice.

5 Conclusion

VaR has an unparalleled advantage in risk measurement, in addition to which it can be used in investment decision-making too. The infrastructure construction market is to strengthen national macroeconomic regulation, infrastructure construction enterprises will further accelerate muck, so infrastructure construction enterprise must strengthen its development project risk management, to the competition accounts for the initiative. VAR has the very good measure risk function and easy operation control, infrastructure construction development enterprises not only can choose VAR value as the dynamic index project operation engineering, and based on VAR to original project evaluation index system is improved. On the other hand, China's infrastructure construction market starting time late, market degree still not mature, so many influence factors of infrastructure construction investment risk not appear, so infrastructure construction investment risk management in comprehensive trend for the quantitative measurement method for the VAR management as a Lord of the stage still need to do much preparation and research work. Of course, VAR method is not perfect, and in practical application prove it has some flaws, main performance for:

There are many kinds of the calculation of the VAR method, but various methods calculation results sometimes differ considerably.

VAR will focus on certain credibility locus on the points of the expected losses (i.e. the largest), and points the site was completely ignored, this will make this method does not prevent some extreme events.

In view of these situations, now put forward some theoretical CVAR(Conditional VAR) correction method, it may improve advantages of inherited VAR, also improved VAR shortcomings, its application prospects will be more extensive.

References

1. Wang, Q., Wu, D., Li, J.: Urban infrastructure construction and the influence factors of market financing. Journal of Economic Analysis 7, 33–35 (2009)
2. Morgan, J.P.: Risk Metrics Technical Document, New York (1996)
3. Philippe, J.: Value at Risk, 2nd cdn. McGraw-Hill, New York (2001)
4. Pan, M.S., Chan, K.C., Fok, C.W.: The Distribution of Currency Futures Price Changes: a Two-piece Mixture of Normal approach. International Review of Economics and Finance, 69–78 (April 1995)
5. Edger, E.P.: Chaos and Order in the Capital Markets. Economic Science Press (1999)
6. Yu, S., Zhang, S., Jun, S.: Comparison of VaR Based on GARCH and SV Models. Journal of Management and Sciences of China, 61–66 (May 2004)
7. Li, H.: VAR in project risk management application. Journal of Northeast University of Finance and Economics 7(4) (2001)
8. Xiao, C.: Song however. VAR theory and its application research. Journal of Mathematical Statistics and Management 2(22) (2003)
9. Song, J.: VAR value of three estimation method and comparative management 12 (2002)
10. Liu, J.: Comparative Studies of VaR and CVaR Based on the Extreme Value Theory. The Journal of Quantitative & TechnicalEconomics 3, 521–529 (2007)

The Research and Analysis of Postgraduates' Condition of Consumption

Kai Zhang

Physical Education Department of Tianjin
University of Technology and Education
Tianjin, China
Zhangkai787878@126.com

Abstract. According to the fact that the enrolled postgraduates' PE consumption is currently under-research, the research is carried out by using questionnaire to survey, aimed at holding an inquiry into the enrolled postgraduates' consumption about PE in Tianjin, in addition to which there are also the motives, composition, comportment and level of consumption as well as the influencing factors. The survey indicates that the postgraduates manifest a good sense of consumption about PE, of which, however, the irrational composition and a lower level still exist. Besides, the consequence reveal the fact that they consume mainly for exercising and entertaining, simultaneously considering the entitative consumption more superior, and that boys and doctor students lay more emphasis on its function of social communication compared with girls and doctors more demanding about choosing playground, the environment and quality of sports itself.

Keywords: Tianjin Municipality, Enrolled Postgraduates, PE Consumption.

1 Introduction

With the reform of economic system in China developed and the socialist market economy gradually improved, the demand for PE is increasingly enlarged and the acquaintance of it is progressively deepen, making the consumption of PE a vital element in our daily life. The postgraduates are the talented generation with high quality, in other words, the future masters of the nation. Such factors as life experiences, living environment and cultural background are very decisive of the diverse concepts of consumption they hold against other social communities. The research of postgraduates' consumption about PE and the analysis of its features, motives and factors are aimed at obtaining experience and reference for such study along with guiding them to consume reasonably in PE in order to make such consumption move along.

Q. Zhou (Ed.): ISAEBD 2011, Part I, CCIS 208, pp. 280–285, 2011.
© Springer-Verlag Berlin Heidelberg 2011

2 The Object of Study and the Research Method

2.1 The Object of Study

In the study, 7 colleges and universities and 120 enrolled postgraduates are chosen as the object, including 54 boy students accounting for 45%, 66 girl students accounting for 55%, 83 masters accounting for 69.2%, 37 doctors accounting for 30.8%, with the average age 26.47±4.36.

2.2 The Research Method

Documentary Data Method
   Consult the document on the consumption about PE to meet the need of study. Search into the Chinese Journal Full-text Database to collect loads of related data.
   Questionnaire Method
   According to the design principal of the questionnaire, the designed questions must be filtered via Delphi and the test for validity and credibility must be proceeding. 120 questionnaires are given out with 119 retrieved. Excluding 7 invalid ones, there are 112 valid samples. Validity 93.3%.
   Mathematical Statistics Method
   Using the software SPSS11.5 to analyze the data.

3 The Consequence and Analysis

3.1 The Survey of Postgraduates' Motive of Consumption about PE

The motive of consumption is the driving force to determine consumers' behavior, which is caused by an existing uncomfortable condition, needed but unsatisfied. The indication of the survey is as follows. (Table 1) Postgraduates' Motive and purpose of consumption about PE mainly lie in entertaining, exercising and communicating. The sequence of boys' choice and that of girls also differs in other consumption items, since boys center on social communication while girls tend to pursue the trend of fashion. Beyond that, there are slight differences between the motive of masters and doctors as well, since masters focus on entertaining and exercising while doctors pay attention to entertaining and communicating. Above all, for the motive of consumption, boys and doctors attach more importance to social communication in addition to entertainment.

Table 1. The Statistics on Postgraduates' motive of PE Consumption in Tianjin

	Male		Female		Master		Doctor	
	Sequence	%	Sequence	%	Sequence	%	Sequence	%
Exercising	1	83.3	2	75.8	2	74.7	3	72.9
Entertaining	3	56.1	1	81.8	1	84.3	1	86.5
Social Communication	2	75.8	4	30.3	3	65.1	2	81.1
Studying	4	30.3	5	25.8	5	32.5	5	21.6
Fashion Pursuing	5	25.8	3	56.1	4	43.4	4	37.8

3.2 The Survey of Postgraduates' Composition of Consumption about PE

The composition of consumption is the proportion of various means of consumption that people consume under certain social economic condition. The indication of the survey is as follows. (Table 2) The postgraduates in Tianjin give priority to entitative consumption, with sports equipment becoming boys' most popular choice and sportswear turning into that of girls. The consumption proportion of boys and girls is nearly the same, which reflects that both of the sexes lay stress on the choice of sports equipment and the subjective feeling when exercising with girls thinking highly of the brand and personal appearance. Besides, girls will spend more on training program than boys do and the cost of playground, PE books and tickets from boys will far outweigh that from girls, which shows that females invest more in body training due to the appreciation of beauty and body shaping compared with boys spending more enjoying as well as learning games. Masters and doctors take such entitative consumption as sports equipment and sportswear as the principal thing, too. With masters expending more on playground and training while doctors spending more on books and tickets, masters give first thing to sports participation and doctors emphasize the above as well as equalization, admiration and emulation. In a word, the proportion of postgraduates' entitative consumption in Tianjin is quite high. The fact that the   irrational composition exits cannot be concealed even though the dematerialized consumption like training program counts a lot.

Table 2. The Statistics on Postgraduates' Composition of PE Consumption in Tianjin

	Sports Equipment	Sportswear	Playground	Training Program	Books and CDs	Tickets	Others
Boys	30.2%	29.8%	26.4%	9.4%	7.2%	10.3%	2.7%
Girls	30.1%	41.2%	11.8%	32.4%	2.2%	4.3%	2.1%
Masters	36.2%	39.5%	25.1%	26.4%	3.4%	4.5%	1.4%
Doctors	25.1%	31.4%	12.8%	16.7%	7.0%	11.1%	3.5%

3.3 The Survey of Postgraduates' Sites to Carry Out PE Activities

The indication of the survey is as follows. (Table 3) The primary site for postgraduates to carry out PE activities is the school known as free of charge, next come the charging playground on campus and other free public playground, from which we can briefly see that postgraduates give first place to the free playground at school or in society, leading to a low investment in the site of PE consumption. In choosing the profitable sites to expend, girls and doctors obviously become more active than boys and masters, which explain that the formers require and spend more in choosing the sports playground and environment while the latters make the proportion to select different items of the playground more balanced.

Table 3. The Statistics on Postgraduates' Sites of PE Consumption in Tianjin

Sites	Free Playground at School	Other Public Free Playground	Charged Playground at School	Profitable Sites in Society	Others
Boys	38.6%	18.3%	25.4%	9.3%	8.3%
Girls	40.3%	17.8%	23.2%	16.8%	4.3%
Masters	45.2%	20.0%	27.4%	10.5%	3.6%
Doctors	32.5%	18.6%	19.4%	18.3%	6.2%

3.4 The Survey of Postgraduates' Comportment and Level of Consumption about PE

The comportment of consumption is the psychic tendency most people possess towards a commodity (service) or before consuming, which influences the orientation of consumptive strategy and behavior. The level of consumption is the consumption quantity of both entitative and service means of PE consumption which are averaged according to certain population and can be demonstrated by unit of value (currency). It mirrors the actual degree of satisfaction of the PE consumption requirement that people have in a certain period, i.e. the quantity and quality of the consumables effectively purchased. The survey shows that postgraduates are provided with some ideas of PE consumption because they believe physical exercise exerts such positive effects as exercising, relaxing and amusing. The fact that 86.3% of them are willing to strengthen their health by taking part in PE consumption perfectly proves a positive attitude the current postgraduates have towards the issue. When it comes to the survey of the disposable income and the outcome for PE consumption, people whose disposable fund is between 800 to 1500 RMB accounts for 82.4%, with 61.2% of them spend 800 to 1000 RMB on PE consumption annually, in other words, the monthly expenditure accounts for 5.6% to 8.6% of the disposable income. The Table 2 shows the expenditure of clothing and equipment accounts for 70% of the gross so that the dematerialized expenditure merely accounts for 1.68% to 2.58%, which makes it known that postgraduates' level of consumption, especially the dematerialized one, is still very low.

3.5 The Survey of the Factors Influencing on Postgraduates' Physical Exercise and Consumption

The indication of the survey is as follows. (Table 4) The primary factors influencing on postgraduates' physical exercise and consumption include great study stress, less spare time and fewer playground. The main task for postgraduates is to study research methods in depth and to draw a conclusion from the scientific researches, ultimately enabling the research report and thesis to come into being. With universities' demands for students becoming increasingly strict, the postgraduates are undergoing considerable pressure. At the same time, with the recruit expansion policy carried out, their stress form employment is going up. The double pressure diminishes their spare time, influencing postgraduates' time to exercise and PE consumption. On the other hand, the prerequisite that their disposable fund is fairly ample results in the increasing requirement for playground and environment. It also shows that girls have less interest in buy something related to sports, with 8.4% of them claiming their poor condition to exercise could be the decisive factors that matter. Therefore, it is essential that we enhance the guidance to girls, strengthen their confidence to exercise and develop their interest in PE. Furthermore, doctors have more dominant demands for sports guidance, which tallies well with the case that quite a lot of them tend to choose the profitable playground in society. Compared with masters, doctors need the service and consumption about sports with higher quality.

Table 4. The Statistics on the Factors Influencing on Postgraduates' Physical Exercise and Consumption in Tianjin

	Study Stress	Economic Condition	Playground	Less Spare Time	No Guidance	No Interest	Personal Conditions	Others
Boys	30.6%	16.9%	20.3%	20.4%	7.7%	4.1%	3.6%	2.3%
Girls	31.4%	21.4%	19.6%	22.3%	8.4%	10.5%	8.4%	3.7%
Masters	29.2%	24.3%	22.4%	18.4%	6.4%	6.6%	4.3%	4.1%
Doctors	31.6%	12.5%	18.3%	23.1%	10.0%	6.4%	6.9%	2.2%

4 Conclusion

With the rapid and stable development of China's economy as well as the improved living standard, the PE consumption which was considered a luxurious performance is gradually entering people's life. The survey indicates that the postgraduates manifest a good sense of consumption about PE and that such behavior, as a healthy, positive and modern spending pattern, has been widely adopted by them.

The postgraduates' consumption about PE in Tianjin features not only few disposable funds and low level but also imbalanced composition. Postgraduates' entitative consumption occupies a crucial position, which mainly consists of sportswear and sports equipment. Although their dematerialized consumption like body training enjoys a quite high proportion, the general problem of its low level cannot be concealed. Hence, there's still a very enormous potential for the market of such consumption to develop.

The primary motive for postgraduates to consume about PE is amusing and exercising. However, the purpose and character of different groups among postgraduates obviously differ. Girls tend to pursue the trend of fashion along with beauty, and boys and doctors center on social communication while girls and doctors are more demanding about choosing playground, the environment and quality of sports as well as the subjective experience when exercising.

The Factors influencing on postgraduates' consumption about PE

Postgraduates have a positive attitude towards the issue, forming the concept of paying for health. The consumption about PE has a low rate of the total disposable income, which doesn't match with the attitude. As a result, some measures should be taken efficiently including strengthening guidance, enlarging the proportion, enforcing the idea that it's never too old to exercise, forming the good habit of living and enhancing the sense of PE participation by pursuing physical exercise as the superior way to relieve and amuse.

The spread of activity and culture about PE is the necessary element to build a harmonious society and a harmonious campus. Therefore, the related department and leader should lay great emphasis on it by reinforcing the construction of stadiums to improve sports environment, strengthen sports quality and increase the rate of students participating in PE. Moreover, based on PE teaching department, the training of human talents in PE is to be strengthened. Last but not least, encouraging the construction of the league or club of different levels to let students participate in what they really like and choose the proper pattern is the practical way to satisfy students' demand for PE consumption as well as form a good atmosphere of exercising on campus.

References

1. Wang, Y.b., et al.: The Research of the Postgraduates' Consumption about PE in Western Area. Academic Journal of Xi'an Jiaotong University (Social Science Edition) 5 (2010)
2. Pan, H.w., et al.: The Research of the Postgraduates' Consumption about PE in Chengdu. Journal of Consumption (Theory Edition) 11 (2009)
3. Lin, S.n.: The Research of University Students' Consumption about PE and Influencing Factors. Zhejiang Sports Science 6, 11–13 (2001)
4. Zuo, X.r., et al.: The Research of Sense and Composition of University Students' Consumption about PE. Journal of Chengdu Physical Education 1, 24–27 (2001)
5. Zhang, S.m., Zhang, J.: The Factors Influencing China's Consumption about PE and The Research of Its Solution. Sports Science (2002)

The Investigation and Analysis of Sports Consumption Situation of University Students in Tianjin

Kai Zhang

Physical Education Department of Tianjin University of Technology and Education
Tianjin, China
Zhangkai787878@126.com

Abstract. According to the fact that the university students' PE consumption is under-research, this research, using questionnaire survey, investigates and analyzes the current situation of university students' sports. The result shows that the main motivations for sports consumption of university students are for delighting mood and strengthening constitution and the irrationality of sports consumption structure with a large proportion of material objects. The consumption concepts are gradually built up among students with low levels of sports consumption. Poverty of family and stress from study are the main reasons that affect sports consumption, which leads to students' preference for courts in schools that are free or non-free of charge.

Keywords: Tianjin university students, sports consumption, influencing factor.

1 Introduction

Sports consumption is an activity that people satisfy their needs of sports with consuming or using tangible products and intangible labor products of sports. With the development of the society, sports become an important part in people's life; this is because consuming for health is considered to be a trend. The analysis of the characters, motivations of university students' sports consumption and the factors that affect sports consumption through studying sports consumption situation of them is a good way of improving the constitutions and forming the lifelong sports concepts of university students, moreover, provides scientific proof for college PE teaching reform.

2 Objects and Methods of the Research

2.1 Objects

1200 students with 664 males and 536 females (sports majors and fresh students are not included) from 10 universities of Tianjin (Tianjin University, Nankai University, Tianjin foreign studies University, Tianjin University of technology and education, Tianjin University of science and technology, Tianjin University of commerce,

Q. Zhou (Ed.): ISAEBD 2011, Part I, CCIS 208, pp. 286–291, 2011.

Tianjin institute of urban construction, Tianjin University of agriculture, Tianjin medical University, Tianjin normal University) were tested in this questionnaire survey.

2.2 Methods

Documentation

Abundant of materials related to sports consumption of university students are collected with consulting the relevant domestic documents and retrieving the China Journal Full-text Database.

Questionnaire

In line with the principle of questionnaire design, the questions are screened with Delphi Method and the questionnaires are tested for effectiveness and reliability. 1200 questionnaires are granted and 1158 ones are reclaimed with 68 ineffective ones being rejected and 1090 ones left for the survey of which 621 from male students and 469 from female students. The effective rate is 90.83%.

Mathematical statistics

The effective statistics are analyzed in using of percentage with *SPSS11.0* statistical software.

3   Result and Analysis of the Research

3.1   The Motivations of Sports Consumption of University Students

Table 1 shows that over 50% students' motivation of sports consumption is delighting mood while almost half of them consider that it is strengthening constitution motivates them. The optional orders of other purposes for sports consumption are different between male and female students. Male students pay much attention to the needs for study and social communication, while pursuit for fashion and the needs for study are considered more by female students. The investigation mainly reflects that students have strong demand for sports consumption and the main motivations for sports consumption of them are delighting mood and strengthening constitution.

Table 1. Investigation form of sports consumption motivation of university students in Tianjin

	Strengthening constitution		Delighting mood		Social consumption		Needs for study		Pursuit for fashion	
gender	male	female	male	female	male	female	male	female	male	female
%	44.5	36.7	69.9	59.8	15.7	7.6	17.6	16.3	8.4	18.4
order	2	2	1	1	4	5	3	4	5	3

3.2   Content Structure of Sports Consumption of University Students

Table 2 shows that the consumption of material objects plays a predominant role in sports consumption of university students in Tianjin. Sportswear and sports equipment are ahead of other options. There's a phenomenon of mimicry that university students compare their brands of sportswear with others', which causes high consumption of sportswear. In addition, it is an indispensable factor that PE class requires students for sportswear. The shortage of equipments for practice and necessary protection makes the consumption of sports equipment stay in second place. Male students choose sports drink and fitness training as the third and fourth place where female students choose fitness training and sports drink, which shows that sports drink and fitness training account for a large proportion in university students' sports consumption, and the latter is because that female students pay attention to their own aesthetic character and body shaping. As a whole, the consumption of material objects plays a predominant role, accounting for 60% in sports consumption. Although fitness training accounts a large proportion in consumption of non-material objects and it can tell that university students show a lot of interest in fitness training, there's irrationality of sports consumption structure with a small proportion of non-material objects.

Table 2. Investigation form of sports consumption structure of university students in Tianjin

	sportswear	sports equipment	sports drink	fitness training	Sports book, media	Sports ticket	others
Male	39.56%	24.43%	15.62%	12.24%	6.52%	5.63%	3.65%
Female	40.32%	22.35%	12.34%	14.23%	3.26%	2.12%	1.26%

3.3 Places of Sports for University Students

Table 3 shows that free courts in schools are the main sport places for university students, and then are the courts in schools and public places that are non-free of charge and the consumption in social profitable places accounts for a little proportion. Students live in campus and their financial resource is simplex, which means that they do not have much disposable money. And for the short distance of courts and dormitory and little time spent on the road, students choose free courts in schools where they do the sports. Besides, because there's plenty of sports events in school clubs which, compared with individual activities, has relatively adequate sports equipments and technical guidance from senior students. The fee for renting courts in school is relatively low. So students prefer sport clubs in school for sports consumption than social profitable places.

Table 3. Investigation form of sports consumption place of university students in Tianjin

Place	Free courts in schools	Non-free courts in schools	Courts in public places	Social profitable places	Others
Male	39.25%	26.56%	17.62%	10.2%	8.65%
Female	40.34%	24.73%	18.91%	7.33%	4.23%

3.4   Analysis of Students' Attitude and Sports Consumption Level

Table 4 shows that students have their particular sports consumption concept, they act actively towards sports consumption. About 70%students are willing to spend on physical practice and he consumption concepts are gradually built up among students. 70%students have 300 to700 yuan per month for living expenses, while 80% students consuming 100 to 400 yuan for sports per year. If one year is divided into 10 months, the average consumption for sports is 10 to 40 yuan which account for 3-6% of living expenses per month and apparently shows that level of sports consumption is low. Because a large proportion of living expenses are accounted by food, clothes, learning materials, and without extra income students' sports consumption are mainly affected by these factors. This table shows the same result with table 5.

Table 4. Investigation form of students' attitude and sports consumption level

Content	Options	Male	Female
Agree on investing in physical practice or not	yes	74.6%	68.5%
	no	9.5%	12.6%
	unsure	15.9%	18.9%
Living expenses per month	Below 300yuan	13.6%	15.8%
	300-500yuan	58.6%	60.4%
	500-700yuan	20.5%	17.8%
	Above 700yuan	7.3%	6.0%
Sports consumption of every year	Below 100yuan	2.5%	5.8%
	100-200yuan	21.2%	19.6%
	201-300yuan	35.8%	40.6%
	301-400yuan	29.5%	27.3%
	Above 400yuan	11.0%	6.7%

3.5   Factors that Affected Sports Consumption Place of University Students

Among the factors that affected sports consumption place of university students, the first 3 factors of male and female students are the same, which are poverty of family, stress from study and shortage of courts. The consumers are university students whose financial resources are from their parents with less other resources, which restrict their sports consumption. Poverty of family is the most important factor that affects sports consumption of students, while stress from study is another important one. Sophomores and juniors have a lot of courses while senior students are confronted with the stress of graduation, employment and the postgraduate entrance examination, which leave non-enough time and affect their sports consumption. Because of the expanding enrollment in our country, the construction of sport courts cannot meet the need of so many students, so the shortage of courts also affects their sports consumption. The research also shows that 10.37% female students are not interested in physical practice and 7.64% think that they do not have good condition and confidence. These come into notice that physical educators in universities should guide female students and help to improve their confidence in sports and develop their interest, thus promote the cultivation of physical practice habit and enhance their constitution.

Table 5. Factors that affected sports consumption place of university students in Tianjin

	Poverty of family	Stress from study	Shortage of courts	Shortage of consumption item	No guidance	No interest	Poor self condition	others
Male	28.6%	20.82%	22.90%	8.63%	7.28%	3.01%	2.15%	2.11%
Female	24.65%	20.36%	18.59%	3.65%	9.21%	10.37%	7.64%	4.11%

4 Conclusion

4.1 Students' main motivation of sports consumption is delighting mood and strengthening constitution. Male students pay much attention to the needs for study and social communication, while pursuit for fashion and the needs for study are considered more by female students.

4.2 The sports consumption structure with a large proportion of material objects of university students in Tianjin is irrational.

4.3 Although the consumption concepts are gradually built up among students, the level of sports consumption is low. Poverty of family and stress from study are the main reasons that affect sports consumption.

4.4 Students prefer free courts in school for sports consumption, while students who choose social profitable places are few.

5 Suggestion

5.1 To improve PE teachers' teaching ability, to develop students' interest for sports especially female students', to strengthen the publicity of sport culture and to promote the formation of lifelong sports concepts and the sports consumption concepts.

5.2 To enhance the construction of courts in schools, providing enough places for students' activities.

5.3 To strengthen the construction of sport clubs, providing more ways for students to participate and sport activities and more consumption patterns.

References

1. Liu, Z.: An Analysis of the Factors Influencing Citizens' Consumption Behavior. Journal of Xi'an Institute of Physical Education 1, 25–27 (2001)
2. Zhang, S.m., Zhang, J.: The Factors Influencing China's Consumption about PE and The Research of Its Solution. Sports Science (2002)
3. Wang, Y.b., et al.: The Research of the Postgraduates' Consumption about PE in Western Area. Academic Journal of Xi'an Jiaotong University (Social Science Edition) 5 (2010)
4. Guo, L.: Economic Analysis of consumption in Leisure Time. An Economic Research of the Quantity Economic Technology 4, 15–20 (2004)
5. Zuo, X.r., et al.: The Research of Sense and Composition of University Students' Consumption about PE. Journal of Chengdu Physical Education 1, 24–27 (2001)

Research on Supplier Selection in Supply Chain Management

Xiao-wei Liu and Zhi-wei Kang

School of Management, Liaoning University of Technology, Liaoning Jinzhou, 121001
No. 169, Shi Ying Street, Guta District, Jinzhou City, Liaoning Province, P.R. China
lglxw@sina.com, Jzlglxw64@163.com

Abstract. As is known that supplier has became an important element in competitiveness of enterprises,and the seletion of supplier whether right or wrong has a directly influence on cost ,quality and delivery time of production. By analyzing factors of the influence of supplier selection under supply chain management, the steps for supplier selection, constructing the evaluation index system of supplier selection and method,we have established 6-level indicators that include the supply capacity and some indicators,and 19 Secondary indicators,such as the rate of delivery time.With the methods of AHP and Fuzzy comprehensive evaluation,it researched the supplier seletions of A company,put forward some helpful proposals,such as speeding up the transformation of business ideas,controlling some reasonable limit,finding a comprehensive index system and other actions.

Keywords: Supply Chain, Supplier Selection, Index System, Fuzzy Comprehensive Evaluation.

1 Introduction

More and more business are ware of the importance of supplier in promoting development of their companies.With the fierce market competition environment,some strategic vision of the leaders began to seek a new supply chain management model ,aimed at finished win-win effect. From the supply chain point of view, suppliers is the beginning of entire supply chain,which means it has great influence on other compannies in this supply chain.A lot of companies constract their core competitiveness with the help of suppliers,and by the way of proper management to increase their competitive advantage in the modern market has become the main means.Also supplier seletion has influence on supply chain continuity and coordination.So,companies have to evaluate their supplies with requirement of the introduction of supply chain management to make sure who is the stategic partners.Both of them could achieve the goals of the efficient operation of the supply chain,by the way of incorporation.

Q. Zhou (Ed.): ISAEBD 2011, Part I, CCIS 208, pp. 292–297, 2011.

2 Constract Evaluation Index System and Metods of Supplier Selection

From our research on suppler selection,some main factors are found,such as price,qulity,delivery lead time, delivery on time, the flexible variety, the design capacity and some other special capability. And, raw material cost is effected by price, qulity levels is effected by raw material qulity, inventory levels is effected by delivery lead time when the marke environment is changed,the produce pace is effected by delivery on time, the acceptable of product is decided by flexible variety, the needs of custmers is effected by design capacity and the possibility of being imitated is effected by special capacity.

2.1 Constract Evaluation Index System of Supplier Selection

In the comprehensive study on relevant literature, with indepth business consulting research and the fact in supplier selection, it established evaluation index system with 6-level indicators and 19 secondary indicators included supply capacity. There are 6-level indicators: Supply capacity, Flexible, R & D capabilities, Quality management, Cooperation capacity, Supply prices. There are 19 secondary indicators: On time delivery rate, Supply to meet the rate, Delivery lead time, Quantity flexibility, Time Flexible, R & D expense ratio, Ratio of R & D personnel, Rate of qualified products, Quality improvement program, Quality Management System, Deal with the problem of timely, Income level of cooperation, Prospects for cooperation, The degree of importance, Strategic compatibility, Cultural compatibility, The degree of confidence, The relative price level, Price stability.

2.2 Methods of Supplier Selection in Supply Chain Management

2.2.1 AHP

Analytical Hicrarchy Process (AHP, the Analytical Hierarchy Process),also known as AHP, refers to a complex multi-objective decision problem as a system, the target into multiple objectives or criteria,and then broken down into multiple indicators (or criteria Constraints) and a number of levels,by quantitative methods of qualitative indicators calculated level of a single fuzzy ranking (weights) and the total ranking,as a target (multiple indicators), and more systematic approach to program optimization decision. AHP is a method for more complex and ambiguous decision-making methods.

According to Table Comparative scale, can come up with Matrix A = (aij) n × n, the same time, comparison matrix A are: aij> 0; aij = 1/aji; aii = 1. A counter is a orthogonal matrix, according to Matrix elements obtained by comparing the weight. For A1, ... An eigenvalue obtained by the matrix λ max: AW = maxW, and λ max exists and is unique. Due to the use of mainly tacit knowledge of experts, which can not be completely precise way to judge the methods used to calculate the estimated W and λ max.

$$\lambda_{max} = \frac{1}{n}\sum_{j=1}^{n}(AW_i)W_i \tag{1}$$

2.2.2 Fuzzy Comprehensive Evaluation Method

（1）Determine the index set and Reviews set

Two levels of evaluation index system,the first step has "i"index,the second step has"n" indicators,the review also divide into "m"parts.From AHP,some index weights could be getted.Supposed that, We organized a group of experts to evaluate A supplier,and get the various indicators,and the scores every indicatots get divided by total number of all experts is the fuzzy reviews, named righ（g=1,2,…,ki；h=1,2,…,m）。

（2）To evaluate every indicators,which belong to every indicator set,such as ki in Ui.

From the weights Ai above and review set V={v1；v2；…；vm}, some fuzzy reviews on indicators should be getted,that fuzzy matrix is UixV , Ri=[righ]kixm ,and then by the way of fuzzy change, Qi=Ai·Ri=（qi1,qi2,…,qim）, it could get evaluated results Qi of every indicators set Ui .

（3）put every indicators together to constract review results of Ui

The indicator is U={U1, U2, …, Un},Qi is the fuzzy review,and put themtogether to find fuzzy,Matrix R, which is based on UxV, and Q=A·R=（q1,q2,…,qj）. Weighted algorithm is prominent than other methods, so we decide choose it as the main method.

（4）Determine the total score

If want to make sequence of many plans,it have to change fuzzy review B into a number. So,with the help of experts, a weight W could be getted, and then, use it to calculate the terminal score, S =Σqj·Wj

3 Empirical Analysis in Supplier Selection in Supply Chain

3.1 Company Overview

A company is a production of the main axle rear axle manufacturing enterprises. Covers an area of forty thousand square meters,existing staff 300 people, including 63 engineers and technicians, can be mass "liberation", "Yellow River " and some other major series of hundreds of kinds of models and specifications of the light, medium, heavy, Trucks and agricultural vehicles axle rear axle, while supporting the production of steering knuckle and the axle casing and other products. A company mainly produces the types of Shaft with rear axle axle BJ130, axle JN150, axle and axle HF131C 1605.Company based on market needs, determine from the existing two major suppliers of raw materials M and N, select a strategic partner as the aim is to establish strategic partnership through to achieve the company's sustainable development.

3.2 A Company Evaluation and Analysis of Supplier Selection

Supplier selection by the company related to data analysis, combined with the company's actual situation, the six-level indicators and 19 secondary indicators together, as the company evaluation index system. Using expert scoring method to rate all indicators table3, scoring range is 0 ¬ 10, higher scores indicate greater importance of the index.

(1) The use of AHP to determine weights of indicators at all levels

$$C = \begin{bmatrix} 1 & 8/7 & 8/7 & 8/9 & 1 & 1 \\ 8/7 & 1 & 1 & 7/9 & 7/8 & 7/8 \\ 7/8 & 1 & 1 & 7/9 & 7/8 & 7/8 \\ 9/8 & 9/7 & 9/7 & 1 & 9/8 & 9/8 \\ 1 & 8/7 & 8/7 & 8/9 & 1 & 1 \\ 1 & 8/7 & 8/7 & 8/9 & 1 & 1 \end{bmatrix}$$

λ_{max}=6 W=(0.1702 0.1489 0.1489 0.1915 0.1702 0.1702)

$$CI = \frac{\lambda - n}{n - 1} = 0 \quad RI=1.24 \quad CR = \frac{CI}{RI} = 0 \quad CR<0.1$$

It can determine the matrix consistency, empathy can determine C1, C2, C3, C4, C5, C6 in the form of the matrix has the consistency and coherence through the final inspection.

(2) The use of fuzzy comprehensive evaluation of its evaluation, which reviews set = {very well, good, general}, the corresponding score set = {100,60,20}, and using expert scoring supplier of M Scoring, from the reviews set in Table 1

With the methods of fuzzy comprehensive evaluation,we have got evaluation matrix: R_1, R_2, R_3, R_4, R_5, R_6 .Wih formula CRi=WiRi, we have got that:

CR1 = (0.6043   0.2304   0.1652, CR2= (0.6000   0.2500   0.1500)
CR3= (0.7565   0.1438   0.1000,CR4= (0.7473   0.2003   0.0537)
CR5= (0.7855   0.1500   0.0646,CR6= (0.6067   0.2933   0.1000)
and, with CR= (CR1 CR2 CR3 CR4 CR5 CR6) ,T=WCR= (0.6849   0.2117 0.1036) ,we have got that: the final score of M
S_M=82.264
Similarly, S_N=77.548

3.3 Conlusion and Advice

By the analysis above, the score of M supplier is more than N supplier, so, the company should choice M to be strategic partner.

From the perspective of indicators, main advantage of M suppliers is from 13 secondary indicators:meet the rate, time flexibility, R & D expense ratio, ratio of R & D, product qualification rate, quality improvement plans, deal with the problem of timeliness, cooperation, benefit, emphasis, Strategy compatibility, cultural compatibility, trust, relative price levels reflect the. By contrast,main advantage of N supplier is from 8 secondary indicators it included ratio of supplier R & D, product qualification rate, quality management system, the prospects for cooperation, emphasis, strategic compatibility, cultural compatibility, relative price levels. The

Table 1. Reviews set of secondary indicators of supplier M and N

Secondary indicators	The reviews of supplier M			The reviews of supplier N		
	Very well	good	general	Very well	good	general
On time delivery rate	0.6	0.2	0.2	0.5	0.4	0.1
Supply to meet the rate	0.7	0.2	0.1	0.5	0.3	0.2
Delivery lead time	0.5	0.3	0.2	0.4	0.4	0.2
Quantity flexibility	0.5	0.3	0.2	0.6	0.2	0.2
Time Flexible	0.7	0.2	0.1	0.5	0.3	0.2
R & D expense ratio	0.8	0.1	0.1	0.5	0.3	0.2
Ratio of R & D personnel	0.7	0.2	0.1	0.7	0.2	0.1
Rate of qualified products	0.7	0.2	0.1	0.8	0.1	0.1
Quality improvement program	0.8	0.2	0.0	0.6	0.3	0.1
Quality Management System	0.6	0.3	0.1	0.7	0.2	0.1
Deal with the problem of timely	0.9	0.1	0.0	0.6	0.2	0.2
Income level of cooperation	0.9	0.1	0.0	0.6	0.2	0.2
Prospects for cooperation	0.6	0.2	0.2	0.8	0.1	0.1
The degree of importance	0.8	0.1	0.1	0.7	0.2	0.1
Strategic compatibility	0.9	0.1	0.0	0.9	0.1	0
Cultural compatibility	0.8	0.2	0.0	0.7	0.2	0.1
The degree of confidence	0.7	0.2	0.1	0.6	0.3	0.1
The relative price level	0.7	0.2	0.1	0.7	0.2	0.1
Price stability	0.5	0.4	0.1	0.6	0.2	0.2

result surveys that the level of supplier competitive advantage to its well received is proportional to the number of indicators, the greater the number, the more obvious competitive advantage. Conversely, the fewer the number of competitive advantage also smaller.

Supply Chain Based on the impact of supplier selection factors more directly affect the choice of suppliers to the efficiency of enterprises.In China, Enterprises should change the business concept, combine itself with the entire supply chain, consider the choice of suppliers; establish a comprehensive evaluation index system of supplier; use scientific and rational approach to evaluate suppliers; make a good relationshipwith suppliers ; take effective measures to incent initiatively suppliers to provide better products and services.

References

1. Zhong, M.M.: Research on supplier seletion in supply chain. Hohai University, Nanjing (2006)
2. Jiang, Q., Xie, J.X., Ye, J.: Mathematical model. Higher Education Press, Beijing (2007)
3. Lieckens, K., Vandaele, N.: Reverse logistics network design with stochastic lead time. Computers and Operations Research (2007)
4. Hung, C.C., Li, G.: Products and services of the mode of operation of the supply chain. Logistics Technology (December 2010)
5. Xu, G., Bin, X.J.: Based on improved revenue sharing contract for the supply chain coordination of dual-channel. China Management Science (June 2010)
6. Wu, J.: E-commerce logistics. Tsinghua University Press, Beijing (2009)

The Research on Risk Assessment of New Product Sample Development Stage in Manufacturing Enterprises

Xiao-wei Liu and Xu-yun Liu

School of Management, Liaoning University of Technology,
Liaoning Jinzhou, 121001
No. 169, Shi Ying Street, Guta District, Jinzhou City,
Liaoning Province, P.R. China
lglxw@sina.com, liuxuyun_1986@sina.com

Abstract. The new product development of manufacturing Enterprises is not only complicated, expensive and more difficult, but the risk is high. There will be many uncertainty factors which will lead to the failure of new product development. By analyzing the risk factors of new product sample development stage, an effective risk assessment index system was established, which includes 4 indicators and 14 secondary-level indicators of risk evaluation index system and fuzzy comprehensive evaluation method. It has been applied for SD company to assess the risks of new product development so that SD company carries on the risk assessment and propose countermeasures on new product sample development stage. It will reduce the risk and improve the success rate of new product development, provide a theoretical basis for enterprises to improve their risk management capabilities.

Keywords: Manufacturing Enterprises, New Product Development, Sample Development Stage, Fuzzy Evaluation Method, Risk Assessment.

1 Introduction

New product development in manufacturing enterprise is a series of decision-making process. It refers to choose from research products started to meet the needs of the market to product design, manufacture process design, until the input normal production. The new product development process can be divided into three stages: the new product development conception stage, new product sample development stage, and new product commercial development stage. Manufacturing enterprise new product development risk can be divided into the risk of new product development conception phase, the risk of new product sample development stage and the risk of new product commercial development phase. Research on the risk assessment of new product sample development phase, the measures should be taken to reduce the expense, and with the minimum cost to achieve maximum security.

Q. Zhou (Ed.): ISAEBD 2011, Part I, CCIS 208, pp. 298–303, 2011.

2 Manufacturing Enterprise New Sample Development Phase Risk Assessment Index System and the Model

New product development of manufacturing enterprise risk assessment is to identify manufacturing enterprise new product development process various stages of risk. Risk factors identification key lies in the recognition of manufacturing enterprises that have significant influences of new product development, it could lead to the key risk factors consequences. New product sample development phase of risk factors are technical risks, production risks, risk management and environmental risks.

2.1 Manufacturing Enterprise New Sample Development Phase Risk Assessment Index System

Manufacturing enterprise new product sample development phase of the risk is identified because enterprise new sample development phase of the relevant factors leading to manufacturing enterprise new product development achieve the desired goals of uncertainties. Manufacturing enterprise new sample development phase risk evaluation index mainly includes: technical risks, production risks, management risks, and environmental risks. In manufacturing enterprise new product sample development phase of risk assessment index system, the evaluation index are divided into 4 primary indexes and 14 secondary indexes. Create new products sample development phase of risk assessment index system, see Table 1.

Table 1. Risk assessment index system in new product sample development phase of manufacturing enterprises

Indexes	First-level indexes	Second-level indexes
Risk assessment indexes in sample development stage in new product development of manufacturing enterprises	Technology Risk	Core technology
		Technical personnel
		Supporting technology of equipment
		Ability of associate partnership
	Production Risk	Manufacturing and processing technic
		End product quality
		Production cycle
	Management risk	Coordination of research and development process
		Ability of communication and strain
		Risk decision mechanism
	Environment Risk	Economic development level
		New product patent infringement
		Environmental protection and security in new product
		Industry policy of country

2.2 Manufacturing Enterprise New Sample Development Phase Risk Assessment Model

Weight factor to determine the table and fuzzy comprehensive evaluation method are often used in the application of qualitative and quantitative methods. Weights factor judgment table method is to point to by evaluation expert, later the expert groups develop and complete value factor to determine the table, and then determine the weight value of each expert judgment table. The method of fuzzy comprehensive evaluation method is a kind of fuzzy-based evaluation method. The fuzzy comprehensive evaluation method based on the degree of membership theory to the evaluation of the object into a quantitative evaluation of qualitative evaluation. The specific steps are:

(1) Selected evaluation factors, constitute the evaluation factors. Factor set is a set of relating factors of manufacturing new product development risks. Set U = {U1, U2, ..., Un}, U represent the factor set, Ui (i = 1,2, ..., n) indicated the various risk factors.

(2) Establish the evaluation set. Generally use V showed the sets of New product development of manufacturing enterprises risk factors may be made the object of the evaluation results of various components of total collection, such as V= {V1, V2, ..., Vm}, where Vk (k = 1,2, ..., m) for the various possible results of the assessment. New product development of manufacturing enterprise risk assessment can be divided into V = {high, higher, medium, lower, low}.

(3) Establish the weight set. The various risk factors have a different degree of influence on new products of manufacturer enterprise which generally through the various risk factors Ui (i = 1,2, ..., n) gives a corresponding weight Ai(i=1,2,......,m), the weights of the set A= { a1,a2,......,an } .

(4) To establish the fuzzy relationship matrix, namely to establish the fuzzy relation R which from V to U. Establish the fuzzy relationship matrix R (r_{ij}) with the method of scoring by experts. Then by the experts to evaluate the various risk factors.

$$r_{ij} = \frac{\text{A factor of V in, the experts were divided into a grade}}{\text{The number of evaluation experts}}$$

The relationship of evaluation index set U and set V of the fuzzy is matrix R:

$$R = \begin{pmatrix} r_{11} & r_{12} & \cdots & r_{1m} \\ r_{21} & r_{22} & \cdots & r_{2m} \\ \cdots & \cdots & \cdots & \cdots \\ r_{n1} & r_{n2} & \cdots & r_{nm} \end{pmatrix} \tag{1}$$

Where R_{ik} (i=1,2,......,n; k=1,2,......,m) means a risk assessment on the indexes of i-k-level reviews made by the membership.

(5) Use the fuzzy mathematics method to determine the evaluation results. The fuzzy comprehensive evaluation model is: B = (b1, b2, ..., bn).

$$B = A*R \tag{2}$$

Fuzzy comprehensive evaluation that sets B, b_j (j = 1, 2, ..., n) showed the fuzzy comprehensive evaluation index, fuzzy matrix multiplication of this type carried out operations in accordance with formula. Then the matrix B is normalized, there is:

$$\overline{b}_i = \frac{b_i}{\sum_{i=1}^{n} b_i} \tag{3}$$

$$B = (\overline{b_1}, \overline{b_2}, ..., \overline{b_n}) \tag{4}$$

Evaluation results obtained by calculation, and then based on the maximum subjection principle that manufacturing enterprise, new product development of comprehensive evaluation results value, then determines manufacture enterprise new product development level of risk.

3 Manufacturing Enterprise New Sample Development Phase Risk Assessment

3.1 SD Company Profile

SD company is a subsidiary of Heavy Industry Group Co., Ltd. a large state enterprises which produced and sold bulldozers, concrete machinery, road machinery, engineering machinery parts and other products to large state enterprises. SD company in the introduction, assimilation, on the basis of international advanced technology and constantly changing demands of the market development of new products. The development of new products using advanced hydraulic transmission, hydraulic control technology to control light with a flexible, advanced and reasonable structure, strong power, reliable quality and environmental effects and other characteristics, advantages and features of this new product to meet customer needs. Following the establishment of enterprises based on new product development stages of risk assessment index system, the use of fuzzy comprehensive evaluation of its various stages of new product development, risk assessment analysis.

3.2 Risk Assessment in the Development Phase of New Product Samples

(1) The determination of risk weights in the development phase of new product samples

According to the weights factor judgment method to develop the new product sample development phase primary index weights statistical computing table, acquire samples development phase risk evaluation weights. it is $A_1=$ (technical risk production risk management risk environmental risk)=(0.42 0.28 0.16 0.14). Technical risk evaluation index weights is $A_2=$(0.33 0.29 0.24 0.14). Production risk evaluation index weights is $A_3=$(0.40 0.34 0.26).Management risk evaluation index weights is $A_4=$(0.25 0.35 0.40). Environmental risk evaluation index weights is $A_5=$(0.08 0.32 0.23 0.37).

(2) Fuzzy comprehensive evaluation

From the formula (1), we can get the matrixes:

Technical risk evaluation matrix: Production risk evaluation matrix:

$$R_2 = \begin{pmatrix} 0.04 & 0.1 & 0.6 & 0.14 & 0.12 \\ 0.06 & 0.16 & 0.56 & 0.2 & 0.02 \\ 0.04 & 0.14 & 0.7 & 0.06 & 0.04 \\ 0.02 & 0.06 & 0.72 & 0.12 & 0.08 \end{pmatrix}$$

$$R_3 = \begin{pmatrix} 0.08 & 0.1 & 0.54 & 0.16 & 0.12 \\ 0.06 & 0.08 & 0.52 & 0.18 & 0.16 \\ 0.04 & 0.12 & 0.4 & 0.24 & 0.2 \end{pmatrix}$$

Management risk evaluation matrix: Environmental risk evaluation matrix:

$$R_4 = \begin{pmatrix} 0.02 & 0.06 & 0.28 & 0.44 & 0.2 \\ 0.04 & 0.14 & 0.26 & 0.4 & 0.16 \\ 0.08 & 0.16 & 0.32 & 0.32 & 0.12 \end{pmatrix}$$

$$R_5 = \begin{pmatrix} 0.06 & 0.14 & 0.34 & 0.26 & 0.2 \\ 0.04 & 0.16 & 0.28 & 0.34 & 0.18 \\ 0.1 & 0.2 & 0.36 & 0.22 & 0.12 \\ 0.12 & 0.24 & 0.58 & 0.14 & 0.08 \end{pmatrix}$$

According to the formula $B=A \circ R$, We can draw the technical risk: in sample development stage: $b_2=A_2 \circ R_2$=(0.06 0.16 0.33 0.2 0.12) and B_2=(0.069 0.184 0.379 0.230 0.138) by normalizing b_2, the Production Risk: $b_3=A_3 \circ R_3$=(0.08 0.12 0.4 0.24 0.2) and B_3=(0.077 0.115 0.385 0.231 0.192) by normalizing b_3, the managing Risk: $b_4=A_4 \circ R_4$=(0.08 0.16 0.32 0.35 0.2) and B_4=(0.072 0.144 0.288 0.316 0.180) by normalizing b_4, the environmental risk: $b_5=A_5 \circ R_5$=(0.12 0.24 0.37 0.32 0.18) and B_5=(0.097 0.196 0.301 0.260 0.146) by normalizing b_5.

The risk evaluation weights in new product development sample stage is $A_1 = (0.42$ $0.28\ 0.16\ 0.14)$. Because

$$E2 = \begin{pmatrix} B_2 \\ B_3 \\ B_4 \\ B_5 \end{pmatrix} = \begin{pmatrix} 0.069 & 0.184 & 0.379 & 0.230 & 0.138 \\ 0.077 & 0.115 & 0.385 & 0.231 & 0.192 \\ 0.072 & 0.144 & 0.288 & 0.316 & 0.180 \\ 0.097 & 0.196 & 0.301 & 0.260 & 0.146 \end{pmatrix}$$

From the formula (5), we can get $p_2 = A_1 \circ E_2 = (0.10\ 0.18\ 0.38\ 0.23\ 0.19)$ and $P_2 = (0.092$ $0.167\ 0.352\ 0.213\ 0.176)$ by normalized p_2.

4 Conclusions

According to the maximum membership degree principle, the review of risk in new product development sample stage is V3. we could see that the risk in new product development conception stage is neutral, so the development of new products can be continued. Enterprises in decision-making stage should reinforce the adjustment of technical factors, production factors and environmental factors, Take relevant measures and reduce the influence of the new product development successfully according to the assessment results of adjustment.

References

1. Srivannaboon, S.: Linking bought account Management. Focussing Friend Bought 37(5), 88–96 (2006)
2. Zhang, X.L.: Project risk management. Mechanical Industry Press, Beijing (2008)
3. Chen, Y.: Product innovation project risk assessment methods and application research. Journal of National Defense Science and Technology University Doctoral Dissertation (2007)
4. Zhou, J., Li, D.M.: Project risk assessment methods. Journal of Chinese Science and Technology Information 8, 16–161 (2010)
5. Chen, Y.: Product innovation project risk assessment methods and application research. Journal of National Defense Science and Technology University Doctoral Dissertation (2007)

The Performance Evaluation of Green Supply Chain of Enterprise

Xiao-wei Liu and Zhi-gang Wang

School of Management, Liaoning University of Technology,
Liaoning Jinzhou, 121001
No. 169, Shi Ying Street, Guta District, Jinzhou City,
Liaoning Province, P.R. China
lglxw@sina.com, 59989137@qq.com

Abstract. From the analysis of green supply chain management,we have set up performance evaluation index system and evaluation model of green supply chain about the enterprise. we have determined the eight primary index and 23 secondary indexes and fuzzy comprehensive evaluation model.Take CC enterprise as an example,it apply the established index system and fuzzy comprehensive evaluation model to performance evaluation analysis of green supply chain of the enterprise,It pointed out that the optimization of green supply chain performance about the enterprise is not high.Put forward the advice that the enterprise how to implementation management of green supply chain,the enterprise can use resources and energy reasonably,reduce pollution to the environment,Break the green trade barriers of international, Walk the road of green supply chain management basic on sustainable development.

Keywords: Green supply chain management, Sustainable development, Fuzzy Comprehensive Evaluation, Achievement Evaluation.

1 Introduction

The enterprise have implement the green supply chain management doesn't mean economic loss, because it fit or exceed requirements that the government and environmental groups put on a particular industry, it can reduce costs of material and operating used by the enterprise, So as to strengthen their competitiveness. In fact, the good environmental behavior just is the motor of development of the enterprise instead of obstacles. It also has the extremely vital significance for enterprise by implementing green supply chain management, Through the implementation of green supply chain management, The enterprise can sufficiently meet current and future higher green consumption demand, meanwhile, it can enhance the enterprise the competitive ability by reducing the material cost and operating costs forming higher advantage than rivals competitive, Thus the enterprise can have win and achieved rapid development in the fierce competition.

Q. Zhou (Ed.): ISAEBD 2011, Part I, CCIS 208, pp. 304–309, 2011.
© Springer-Verlag Berlin Heidelberg 2011

2 The Construction of Index System and Evaluation Model

2.1 The Construction of Green Supply Chain Performance Evaluation Index System

Due to the complexity of green supply chain system, it is difficult to use single index to evaluate, so must undertake multi-angle, many from the perspective of evaluation, build hierarchical index system. According to different of the specific problem, different of research objectives, establishment of index system is also different. According to the basic ideas and principles the system evaluation, combining domestic and foreign research results, established hierarchy indicators system. In this the index system, the first index level include pollution to the environment, energy utilization rate, output and treatment, waste resource utilization rate, staff environmental awareness, the cost of each link, enterprise received benefits, customer satisfaction. Meanwhile in primary indicators continue subdivided into secondary indexes, secondary indexes including air pollution, water pollution, soil pollution, noise pollution, energy use sound, energy efficiency, reduce type of energy consumption, output, reproduction utilization, (materials, equipment) utilization, (materials, spare parts) recycle utilization rate of environmental regulations, members of the enterprise, the enterprise staff know degree by environmental education increase in the number of number when, designing and developing cost, manufacturing costs, transportation, marketing costs, recycling costs, customer complaints proportion, customer complaints solve time, customer Suggestions of green products, customer rate of identities, economic value, after-tax net profit.

The optimization performance comprehensive of green supply chain is the comprehensive evaluation to enterprise of green supply chain management, reached the overall conclusions finally using analytic hierarchy process and fuzzy comprehensive evaluation method according to first-order index and secondary indexes.

2.2 The Establishment of Green Supply Chain Performance Evaluation Model

Green supply chain system performance index system is hierarchical, so using analytic hierarchy process and fuzzy comprehensive evaluation method for performance evaluation.

The first step, establish evaluation index elements set, determine the first-order index and secondary indexes use AHP to determine the weights of evaluation indexes.

In determining the invited experts evaluated object's hierarchy should invite relevant expert evaluation panel, these experts composed must possess actual work experience and have deep theoretical foundation, and the evaluation target involved in all aspects of in-depth understanding, to ensure that the real reliability evaluation.

Then construct judgment matrix, through various levels factors binary comparison, centralized element tectonic judgment matrix T. Determine the next layer on a hierarchy of the relative importance of some factors, with certain score.

Tectonic comparative judgment matrix:

$$T = \begin{bmatrix} b_{11} & b_{12} & \cdots & b_{1n} \\ b_{21} & b_{22} & \cdots & b_{2n} \\ \vdots & \vdots & \vdots & \vdots \\ b_{n1} & b_{n2} & \cdots & b_{nn} \end{bmatrix} \tag{1}$$

Using the fuzzy evaluation method allocation

(1) Determines the index set and comments set. Evaluation index is divided into two levels, according to the analysis of method of AHP, so obtained the weight of each index.

(2) Evaluate for each index to, evaluated object relative to each index of the fuzzy transform fuzzy evaluation knowable: $C_i = W_i \cdot R_i = (Ci_1, Ci_2, ..., Cim)$ Thus gets each index evaluation results of domain.

(3) Synthetic each index domain and evaluation results. Index set is: $U = \{U_1, U_2, ..., U_n\}$, Qi is aimed at the fuzzy evaluation index Ui comments，Namely have：$R = [C_1, C_2, ..., C_n]$, $T = [cij]_{nxm}$

$$C = W \cdot R = (C_1, C_2, ..., Cj) \tag{2}$$

(4) Determine total score

The comprehensive fuzzy comments must be integrated into B a number again for several schemes. Therefore, can according to the expert advice to give various comments confirmed a B, set weight W: episode {best, comments can be good, respectively, poor},100,80,60,40,20}} {values so as to obtain enterprise evaluation must into: $T = \Sigma c_j \cdot W_j$.

3   Empirical Analysis of Enterprise Green Supply Chain Performance Evaluation

3.1   CC Enterprise Introduction

CC company mainly produces interior decoration products such as interior ceiling etc, presently it product interior ceiling for many car companies such as China FAW Group, Chery company etc. It product the seat after guard board for audi C6, for audi, chery etc series models supporting exemption fiberglass DVD products etc. The beginning of establishment of CC enterprise successively introduced the world's advanced level of production equipment of German and Italy, and gradually laid the domestic leading material and technical basis. CC enterprise pays great attention to cooperation relationship with each big institutions and research institutions. Recent years CC enterprise not only continue to increase leading products r&d strength, but also strengthened gradually modular products production, and actively carry out such as car carpet, tire cover, battery shield, skylight pull board diversified new product development.

3.2 The Performance Evaluation of Green Supply Chain of CC Enterprise

(1) According to the actual situation of enterprise from environmental pollution degree, energy utilization, employee environment consciousness, etc. According to index system gave the grade using the expert scoring.
(2) Determines the index weight used AHP

$$B = \begin{bmatrix} 1 & 9/8 & 9/8 & 9/7 & 9/8 & 9/7 & 9/7 & 1 \\ 8/9 & 1 & 1 & 8/7 & 1 & 8/7 & 8/7 & 8/9 \\ 8/9 & 1 & 1 & 8/7 & 1 & 8/7 & 8/7 & 8/9 \\ 7/9 & 7/8 & 7/8 & 1 & 7/8 & 1 & 1 & 7/9 \\ 8/9 & 1 & 1 & 8/7 & 1 & 8/7 & 8/7 & 8/9 \\ 7/9 & 7/8 & 7/8 & 1 & 7/8 & 1 & 1 & 7/9 \\ 7/9 & 7/8 & 7/8 & 1 & 7/8 & 1 & 1 & 7/9 \\ 1 & 9/8 & 9/8 & 9/7 & 9/8 & 9/7 & 9/7 & 1 \end{bmatrix}$$

$\lambda_{max=8}$

W=(0.4021 0.3574 0.3574 0.3127 0.3574 0.3127 0.3127 0.4021)

Normalized processing W=(0.1429 0.1270 0.1270 0.1111 0.1270 0.1111 0.1111 0.1429)

$CI = \dfrac{\lambda - n}{n-1} = 0$ RI=1.41 $CR = \dfrac{CI}{RI} = 0$ CR<0.1 From this determine the matrix have accordance

$$B1 = \begin{bmatrix} 1 & 8/6 & 1 & 1 \\ 6/8 & 1 & 6/8 & 6/8 \\ 1 & 8/6 & 1 & 1 \\ 1 & 8/6 & 1 & 1 \end{bmatrix} \quad \lambda_{max=4}$$

W_1(0.5298 0.3974 0.5298 0.5298) Normalized processingW_1(0.2667 0.2000 0.2667 0.2667)

CI=0 RI=0.9 CR=0 CR<0.1 From this determine the matrix have accordance

Similarly, we got known that $B_2, B_3, B_4, B_5, B_6, B_7, B_8$ have accordance.

$$B2 = \begin{bmatrix} 1 & 9/7 \\ 7/9 & 1 \end{bmatrix} \quad B3 = \begin{bmatrix} 1 & 1 & 8/7 \\ 1 & 1 & 8/7 \\ 7/8 & 7/8 & 1 \end{bmatrix} \quad B4 = \begin{bmatrix} 1 & 7/8 \\ 8/7 & 1 \end{bmatrix} \quad B5 = \begin{bmatrix} 1 & 8/7 \\ 7/8 & 1 \end{bmatrix}$$

$$B6 = \begin{bmatrix} 1 & 8/7 & 8/7 & 1 \\ 7/8 & 1 & 1 & 7/8 \\ 7/8 & 1 & 1 & 7/8 \\ 1 & 8/7 & 8/7 & 1 \end{bmatrix} \quad B7 = \begin{bmatrix} 1 & 8/7 & 8/6 & 1 \\ 7/8 & 1 & 7/6 & 7/8 \\ 6/8 & 6/7 & 1 & 6/8 \\ 1 & 8/7 & 8/6 & 1 \end{bmatrix} \quad B8 = \begin{bmatrix} 1 & 1 \\ 1 & 1 \end{bmatrix}$$

Normalized processing finally

$$CI = \sum_{i=1}^{n} WCI_i = 0 \qquad RI = \sum_{i=1}^{n} WRI_i = 0.4023$$

CR=0   CR<0.1 From this we can determine the matrix have accordance
So the weights of evaluate index system is determined.

(3) The evaluation of A enterprise,using the method of expert scoring courts. As Table 1: expert scoring courts shown.

Specific calculation

$$R1 = \begin{bmatrix} 0.1 & 0.3 & 0.3 & 0.2 & 0.1 \\ 0 & 0.5 & 0.3 & 0.1 & 0.1 \\ 0.4 & 0.1 & 0.1 & 0.2 & 0.2 \\ 0.2 & 0.3 & 0.3 & 0.1 & 0.1 \end{bmatrix} \qquad R3 = \begin{bmatrix} 0.5 & 0.2 & 0.3 & 0 & 0 \\ 0.2 & 0.2 & 0.4 & 0.1 & 0.1 \\ 0.2 & 0.4 & 0.1 & 0.2 & 0.1 \end{bmatrix} \qquad R6 = \begin{bmatrix} 0.4 & 0.1 & 0.1 & 0.2 & 0.2 \\ 0.3 & 0.3 & 0.1 & 0.2 & 0.1 \\ 0.5 & 0.4 & 0.1 & 0 & 0 \\ 0.4 & 0.3 & 0.1 & 0.2 & 0 \end{bmatrix}$$

$$R7 = \begin{bmatrix} 0.1 & 0.2 & 0.2 & 0.5 & 0 \\ 0.2 & 0.4 & 0.2 & 0.1 & 0.1 \\ 0.1 & 0.2 & 0.2 & 0.5 & 0 \\ 0.2 & 0.2 & 0.4 & 0.1 & 0.1 \end{bmatrix}$$

$$R4 = \begin{bmatrix} 0.1 & 0.2 & 0.2 & 0.5 & 0 \\ 0.4 & 0.3 & 0.3 & 0 & 0 \end{bmatrix} \quad R2 = \begin{bmatrix} 0.3 & 0.3 & 0.2 & 0.1 & 0.1 \\ 0.3 & 0.2 & 0.2 & 0.1 & 0.2 \end{bmatrix} \quad R5 = \begin{bmatrix} 0.2 & 0.3 & 0.3 & 0.1 & 0.1 \\ 0.2 & 0.4 & 0.1 & 0.2 & 0.1 \end{bmatrix} \quad R8 = \begin{bmatrix} 0.5 & 0.2 & 0.3 & 0 & 0 \\ 0.4 & 0.3 & 0.2 & 0.1 & 0 \end{bmatrix}$$

$C_{R1}=W_1 R_1 =(0.1867\ 0.2867\ 0.2467\ 0.1534\ 0.1267)$ $C_{R2}=W_2 R_2 = (0.2995\ 0.2559\ 0.1996\ 0.0998\ 0.1434)$

$C_{R3}=W_3 R_3 = (0.3041\ 0.2605\ 0.2738\ 0.0955\ 0.0651)$ $C_{R4} = (0.2600\ 0.2533\ 0.2533\ 0.2334\ 0)$

$C_{R5}=W_5 R_5 = (0.2000\ 0.3466\ 0.2067\ 0.1467\ 0.1000)$ $C_{R6}=W_6 R_6 = (0.4000\ 0.2700\ 0.1000\ 0.1533\ 0.0767)$

$C_{R7}=W_7 R_7 = (0.1517\ 0.2483\ 0.2552\ 0.2931\ 0.0517)$ $C_{R8}=W_8 R_8 = (0.4500\ 0.2500\ 0.2500\ 0.0500\ 0.0000)$

$$CR = (CR1\ CR2\ CR3\ CR4\ CR5\ CR6\ CR7\ CR8) = \begin{bmatrix} 0.1867 & 0.2867 & 0.2467 & 0.1534 & 0.1267 \\ 0.2995 & 0.2559 & 0.1996 & 0.0998 & 0.1434 \\ 0.3041 & 0.2605 & 0.2738 & 0.0955 & 0.0651 \\ 0.2600 & 0.2533 & 0.2533 & 0.2334 & 0.0000 \\ 0.2000 & 0.3466 & 0.2067 & 0.1467 & 0.1000 \\ 0.4000 & 0.2700 & 0.1000 & 0.1533 & 0.0767 \\ 0.1517 & 0.2483 & 0.2552 & 0.2931 & 0.0517 \\ 0.4500 & 0.2500 & 0.2500 & 0.0500 & 0.0000 \end{bmatrix}$$

$T_A = WC_R = (0.2832\ 0.2720\ 0.2250\ 0.1480\ 0.0716)$

3.3 The Conclusions and Recommendations

In comment sets (100,80,60,40,20) The optimization performance comprehensive of the enterprise is:$0.2832*100 + 0.2720*80 + 0.2250*60 + 0.1480*40 + 0.0716*20 = 70.9320$.Visibly green supply chain performance optimization of this enterprise is not high.

According to the evaluation the enterprise we have conclusion, The company have the problems such as water pollution, noise pollution, output, sound reproduction utilization, utilization of materials, equipment, members of the enterprise of environmental regulations are familiar, enterprise employees by environmental education when the increase in the number of number, customer complaints ratio, customer complaints solve time, customer Suggestions rate, customers for green products, aimed at the problems the enterprises should improve technology of pollution treatment, reducing emissions of pollutants, improving utilization energy and resource, To strengthen the training of the staff, enhancing employees' consciousness of environmental protection, Strengthen after-sales service, strengthen the communication with customers, And throughout the supply chain establishment of green supply chain partner relationship; Actively implementing lean design, make environmental professionals to join design work stage, when the product design should consider the problems of resource reusable and environmental protection of terminal product.

References

1. Fulei.: The Study of Green Supply Chain Management Based on Sustainable Development (2008)
2. Liu, X.-w., Wu, Z.-g., He, R.-l.: The Cost Management of Construction Project Based on Lean. In: CRIOCM International Research Symposium 2009 on Advancement of Construction Management and Real Estate 2009 (October 2009)
3. Kali, S., Morris, C., Thomas, F.R.: Managerial Economics (2007)
4. Palepu, K.G., Bernard, V.L., Healy, P.M.: Introduction to Business Analysis & Valuation (1998)
5. Liao, Y., Song, W.: The research of operating model of green supply chain, pp. 56–60 (September 2004)
6. Francois, M., Pan, Y., Song, T.: Value chain (2004)

Analysis of Differences in Innovation Capacity and Performance of SMEs Clusters

Haixia Cai and Ruguo Fan

School of Economics & Management, Wuhan University,
Wuhan, China, 430072
caihaixia2003@yahoo.com.cn, rgfanchina@yahoo.com.cn

Abstract. By integrating new growth theory and evolutionary economics theory and using new perspective of open innovation, the paper takes the 54 state-level high-tech industrial development zones as a sample. It analyzes the mechanism between SME clusters' innovation capacity and cluster performance. The empirical results show that innovation input of enterprises in the cluster has the most important impact on the international market of clusters. Open innovation resources as University R & D expenditure, research institution's & D expenditures and provincial technical market transactions contract amount have positive spillovers on the cluster innovation capabilities and therefore affect the cluster performance.

Keywords: innovation capacity, SMEs cluster, performance.

1 Introduction and Literature Review

As the fact that SMEs cluster as an important organizational pattern for innovation has been widely accepted all around the world, many countries, regions and local government make relative policies to promote the SMEs cluster innovation capacity. The Silicon Valley is the typical representative of successful SMEs clusters.

The driven factors of SMEs cluster varies in different development stages. In the initial stage of cluster development, the primary factors of production advantages, namely resource plays an important role. But with the gradual development of the cluster, the primary factors of production contribute to the further development of the cluster gradually reduced, investment has become a major driving force to promote cluster development. However, when the cluster develops to a certain stage, it is hard to maintain the sustainable development of the cluster by only relying on resource driven and investment driven. Since the less developed areas can get comparative advantage by primary production factors such as a leader in acquisition costs, the government can rely on more preferential policies to attract investment. such as SMEs in the southeast coastal areas of China occupy a huge international and domestic market share because of its labor, land, raw materials and low-cost advantage. However, as China's "demographic dividend" and the gradual disappearance of the rise in production costs, SMEs in Southeast Asian countries in recent years to a more affordable price than China and more favorable government policy on China had a

Q. Zhou (Ed.): ISAEBD 2011, Part I, CCIS 208, pp. 310–316, 2011.

real threat. A large number of foreign direct investment moves to Southeast Asian countries. Therefore in order to maintain sustainable competitive advantage of clusters, we must constantly innovate and rely on innovation-driven to upgrade and transform the SMEs clusters.

Although most of the literature consider that SMEs cluster innovation capacity is the key factor in sustained competitive advantage, but few studies have thoroughly investigated the quantitative relationship between them, most of the literature still remain in the theoretical analysis phase. There is no communication between the industry and other innovative institutions which can cause knowledge spillovers. In the present globalization economy, the knowledge update very fast. To maintain the vitality of clusters of innovation, we must constantly update the internal knowledge base and other resources, and timely introduce new information and technology from outside of the cluster.

The paper integrates new growth theory and evolutionary economics theory, takes the new perspective of open innovation, and considers organizations which can cause spillover as key factors, rather than the background elements to examine. It takes the 54 state-level high-tech industrial development zones as the samples to reveal how the SME Clusters capacity and innovation organizations interact with each other, and how to influence the cluster performance.

2 Theory Framework and Assumptions

2.1 Open Innovation Theory Framework

Henry W. Chesbrough considers that some original leaders in the industry failed to benefit from innovation, and even some very brilliant studies did not have much use. This is because most of these companies use "closed Innovation ", which mainly rely on their own creativities and the internal market approach and emphasize that the success of innovation requires a strong control. The old model of innovation is no longer applicable to the new operating environment. Then, Henry W. Chesbrough put forward a new innovation paradigm-open innovation. Open innovation believes that the companies should combine both internal and external market channels in the development of new technologies. In addition, the internal innovation can also be achieved through external market and obtain excess profits.

Compared with the closed model of technological innovation, open innovation believes that the enterprise boundaries can be penetrated. Enterprises can and should take advantage of the innovative ideas of internal and external market. Open innovation will be the creative combination of internal and external under the enterprise structure. Innovative ideas within the enterprise can enter the market through external sources.

The forms of open innovation fall into the following categories: first, the creativity comes from internal and external cooperative enterprises, universities and research institutions to form a joint R & D market, the results of the technology industry and reflect the commercial value in the product. Second, it may come from the transfer of the patent right. Third, open innovation also includes the technology's market-oriented mode of operation, which includes the sale of technology, developing technology with others, investing in the enterprises that use new technologies. Therefore, open innovation is the effective use of internal and external resources in enterprises, research institutions, market innovation network.

In this study, we will consider cluster as a whole enterprise. Open innovation should be taken in order to improve the performance of the cluster. Universities and research institutions around industry cluster are very easy to feel the industry needs and changes. University and research institutes communicate with enterprises in the cluster to form the close cooperation with production and research networks and to transform the scientific and technological information and knowledge into new products as soon as possible. At the same time, by the enterprises' feedback and requests, universities and research institutions can solve the problems during product innovation. Geographic concentration of cluster causes the technology industry competition. The demonstration effect by the technical competition itself or the imitation of spillover effects will strengthen the influence of innovation and progress. What's more, it encourages enterprises to expand the open technical innovation, and promote the level of innovation and Innovation efficiency. Enterprises in the cluster contact with each other closely, complement each other and learn from each other. They make technical progress together by imitation and innovation. The network which includes clusters, universities, research institutions and industry technology exchange provides rich resources for cluster innovation, and it enhances the knowledge transfer ability of clusters.

2.2 Analysis on the Differences of Cluster Innovation Capacity

The performance of SME clusters and its actors SMEs' performance come from its unique innovation capacity. Different innovation capacity bring differences in the performance of SME clusters and enterprises in them. Difference in Innovation capability of clusters both dues to internal factors and external factors. The external factor is to access innovation resources through the Innovation Network, including the formal and informal networks of innovation. Formal innovation network in the cluster typically include cooperation of development with other enterprises or institutions, obtain the technical knowledge through technology licensing, patent notices, etc. Informal innovation networks include communication with other enterprise's employees or employ employers from other enterprises.

Based on above analysis, this paper believes that clusters should take an open attitude towards innovation, and actively absorb external knowledge spillovers of innovation institutions, while strengthening the technology transfer and industrial cooperation. Internal factors are divided into innovation input capacity and innovation output capacity. Innovation input capacity, including funding for R & D expenditures and R & D human capital investment. Many scholars suggest that increasing in internal R & D expenditures is the main access to strengthen the ability of independent R & D and innovation. And the human capital is a key element of successful innovation. There are several indicators to measure the innovation output. Previous studies include the share of sales ratio of innovative products, patent number, the number of innovative products, technical product sales and so on. In this paper, technology product sales are considered to be the cluster's innovation output indicator.

2.3 The Analysis of Cluster Performance

Research on the performance of clusters has a long history. Most of the research is committed to building a complete performance evaluation system. For example, Zhang Shujing (2006) chose the level of cooperation, competition level, innovation capacity, openness level, infrastructure carrying capacity, economies of scale and production capacity to build a cluster Performance Evaluation System which includes seven first class indicators and 23 secondary indicators starting performance of selected secondary cluster. Ding yongfen (2008) divided the performance of the industrial cluster into economic performance and innovation performance, and she thought that the performance of industrial clusters is produced by sharing of resources, competition and cooperation, specialization and cluster opening. Yang Wensheng et al (2008) uses the Balanced Scorecard method in quantitative evaluation of cluster performance. He constructs a Performance Evaluation System from financial, customer, internal operations, learning and growth of the cluster. Mao Jiangxing et al (2008) evaluate the performance of industrial clusters from the national economic output, input and efficiency, which include GDP, the proportion of the industrial structure, investment, exports, consumption, unit GDP energy consumption and energy consumption per unit of industrial added value.

No matter what aspect the performance of SME clusters is measured from, the ultimate result is to improve the cluster production efficiency and performance on the market. Thus, this paper takes industrial output, exports and domestic sales revenue to measure the performance of SME clusters.

3 Empirical Sample Selection

This paper selected the sample of 54 world-class high-tech industry development zones. Since 1988, China established the first national high-tech park of Beijing New Technology Industry Development Experimental Zone, the high-tech park grows rapidly. There are 54 national high-tech development zones, 56 provincial-level high-tech parks. In addition, there are a large number technology parks, university parks, business parks and industrial parks which is set up by cities and counties. In 2008, there are a total of 52,632 enterprises in the China National High-tech Industrial Development Zone. Among them, the number of enterprises with less than 500 employers accounted for 95.51 percent. The total technology revenue income of enterprises which is less than 500 employers accounts for 42.46 percent. the total sales revenue of enterprises with less than 500 employers accounts for 58.28 percent of the total enterprises. (as shown in Table 1). These data suggest that the small and medium enterprises has become the main actor of innovation in the state-level high-tech park. Thus, it is reasonable to take the high-tech industrial and technological development zones as representatives of SME clusters. The data source of empirical analysis is required to "China Torch Statistical Yearbook 2009" and "China Science and Technology Statistical Yearbook 2009".

Table 1. Main Indicator Statistics in National High-tech Park

Employer scale	Enterprises		Technology revenue		Sales revenue	
	No.(person)	percentage	Amount(billion)	percentage	Amount(billion)	percentage
Number ⩾1000	1098	2.09%	2167.95	43.32%	1152.63	25.52%
500 ⩽ No.<1000	1265	2.40%	711.35	14.22%	731.31	16.19%
100⩽ No.<500	7816	14.85%	1223.59	24.45%	1139.21	25.23%
50 ⩽ No.<100	6903	13.12%	332.74	6.65%	819.91	18.16%
No.<50	35550	67.54%	568.36	11.36%	672.81	14.90%
total	52632	100.00%	5003.99	100.00%	4515.87	100.00%

4 Empirical Result Analysis

The paper takes the number of persons that engage into cluster science and technology activities, cluster science and technology activities expenditures, cluster innovation output, cluster technology product sales, university R & D expenditure, research institutions R & D expenditure and technology market transaction contract value in the province as independent variables respectively and industrial production GDP, exports and product sales revenue as the dependent variable to do multiple regression analysis. The regression results are shown in Table 2.

Table 2. Regression Result For the Influence of Cluster Innovation Capacity on Cluster Performance

variables	Industry GDP coefficient	Export coefficient	Domestic sales coefficient
HUINPUT	0.05	137.7391*	0.037568
CAPINPUT	17.33393***	13965.70**	17.23799***
OUTPUT	1.328945**	-391.292	1.071551*
UNIEXP	44.48582***	13362.56**	36.11665***
RESEXP	5.527810**	-1133.23	-3.494306
TEKCON	-1.866256**	2108.124**	-0.717762
R^2	0.818	0.636	0.88
DW	2.08	1.48	2.05

Note: *Represent significant at level of 10%, ** Represent significant at level of 5%, *** Represent significant at level of 1%.

Among the independent variables, all the independent variables have significant impact on the industrial output value except the number of technological activities. The influence of technical market transactions in the province is negative. The reason for this result is due to the imperfections of domestic intellectual property regime.

Technology trade is much more complex than conventional products trade. Not only have you to make the transferee to understand advanced technology, reliability and effectiveness, but also to prevent technology leakage. If there is no intellectual property protection, technology products have no value at all. confidentiality affects the initiative of the supply side of technology and even affect the entire technology market. In recent years, although China's intellectual property system has been improved. However, China's intellectual property rights remain an important factor to constraint for the development of technology in market transactions. In the positive factors, university R&D expenditure has the largest coefficient on the industrial output value. It indicates that increasing funding for university R&D expenditure will increase the University's innovation, and therefore have tremendous spillover effects on cluster innovation.

Among the factors that influence the exports, the number of person in scientific and technological activities, science and technology activities expenditures, university R&D expenditure, technology market transaction contract amount in the province has a significant positive impact, and research institutions R&D expenditure and clusters' innovation output has no significant impact on exports. From Table 2, we observed that the number of researchers only has impact on exports. While although expenditures for scientific and technological activities have positive spillover effect on the performance of the cluster, the impact factor on export is the biggest. This fully demonstrates innovation is particularly important for the performance of international market. When the SMEs of a cluster participates in international market competition, not only they have to face more intense competition than the domestic market and more discerning target customer, but also face more complex and volatile international market environment, international trade barriers, exchange rate policy changes, the target market changes in domestic political and economic situation. In this dynamic competitive environment, companies must increase investment in innovation to maintain the competitive advantage in the international market.

Among factors that have positive impact on sales of domestic product, university R&D expenditure is also the largest. In addition, expenditures for science and technology activities, technical product sales revenue also had a positive impact on domestic sales.

5   Conclusions and Suggestions

By integrating new growth theory and evolutionary economics theory and using new perspective of open innovation, the paper takes the 54 state-level high-tech industrial development zones as a sample. It analyzes the mechanism between SME clusters' innovation capacity and cluster performance. The empirical results show that innovation input of enterprises in the cluster has the most important impact on the international market of clusters. Open innovation resources as University R & D expenditure, research institutions R & D expenditures and provincial technical market transactions contract amount have positive spillovers on the cluster innovation capabilities and therefore affect the cluster performance.

5.1 Encourage Enterprises in the Cluster to Carry Out International Business

SMEs in the cluster rely solely on primary product processing and traditional export development model can not adapt to new developments. Clusters with strong export capacity should focus on strengthening the clusters researchers and research funding to enhance the international competitiveness of the cluster.

5.2 Improve the Absorptive Capacity of SMEs in the Cluster

Due to time and resource constraints, it is necessary to take effective measures to access to knowledge outside and apply it, this is the reason why the paper use "open innovation ". However, not all businesses will benefit from the "open innovation" benefit. Enterprises must be able to have the ability to internalize external knowledge and this ability is called absorption capacity.

5.3 Enhance the Intellectual Property Rights Protection and Improve the Technical Market Transaction System

If there is no intellectual property protection, technology products have no value at all. Therefore, Intellectual property protection system should be further improved, especially the patent system. Intellectual property protection not only makes the trade of technology market more active, but also directly stimulates the cluster engaging in more innovation activities.

References

1. Chesbrough, H.: Open innovation: the new imperative for creating and profiting from technology. Harvard Business School Press, Inc., Cambridge (2003)
2. Johnston, R.: Clusters, a review of their basis and development in Australia. Innovation Management, Policy & Practice 3, 380–391 (2004)
3. Polanyi, M.: The Logic of Tacit Inference, Knowing and Being. Routledge and Kegan Paul, London (1969)
4. Lynn, G.S., Reilly, R.R., Akgun, A.E.: Knowledge Management in New Product Teams: Practices and Outcomes. IEEE Transactions on Engineering and Management 47 (2000)
5. Castellacci, F.: Innovation and the competitiveness of industries: Comparing the mainstream and the evolutionary approaches. Technological Forecasting & Social Change, 984–1006 (2008)

Study on Overall Performance Appraisal of Supply Chain Based on Cooperative View

Libing Shu

Ningbo Institute of Technology, Zhejiang University,
315100 Ningbo, China
shulb@nit.zju.edu.cn

Abstract. The cooperation performance becomes one important component of overall performance of supply chain, as well as financial and operational performance. The key factors influenced the overall performance of supply chain include strength of supply chain, interface management and strength of partnership from cooperative view. Based on the exploration on supply chain partnership, the paper proposes a conceptual model of the overall performance appraisal of supply chain. The model will help to explain the internal influence mechanism of performance of enterprises and their partners.

Keywords: supply chain cooperation, partnership, cooperative performance, overall performance of supply chain.

1 Introduction

The global competition and cooperation have deeply influenced competitive power of an enterprise. In order to strengthen competitive power, many enterprises have developed strategies to manage value chain, which replaces vertical integration with strategic alliance between distributors and suppliers [1]. The supply chain focusing on internal cooperation and external competition has been accepted by all, and has become an interest community led by cooperation and long-term orientation. The supply chain management will transfer from supplier management to supplier development, and change its emphasis from finance and operation to cooperation factors and strategic collaborations. The supply chain partnership has been more and more important since the era of cooperation and competition in supplier chain arrives. Meanwhile, supply chain partnership also has profound influence in performance of supply chain, so the performance appraisal of supply chain takes in more and more cooperative factors.

As performance appraisal in an enterprise, various methods for performance appraisal of supply chain have emerged in endlessly, which goes through a process from appraisal with single factor (financial indicator) to appraisal with various factors. However, the kind of performance appraisal may not be enough to describe performance of a system [2]. We find that all previous perfect performance appraisals of supply chain are limited to financial and operational indicators, failing to pay

Q. Zhou (Ed.): ISAEBD 2011, Part I, CCIS 208, pp. 317–323, 2011.
© Springer-Verlag Berlin Heidelberg 2011

enough attention to cooperative factors. The performance appraisal of cooperation evaluates performance of supply chain from the cooperative relationship and partnership in supply chain. It constitutes one of the three supports of overall performance appraisal on supply chain with financial performance and operational performance. The study attempts to explore overall performance appraisal of supply chain from cooperative view, and constructs relational model of factors of supply chain cooperation influencing performance to reveal the composition of overall performance in supply chain and its internal mechanism, and to provide reference for supply chain cooperation and overall performance appraisal of supply chain.

2   Key Problems in the Supply Chain Partnership

2.1   Supply Chain Partnership and Cooperation Level

Supply chain partnership refers to the relationship established between two independent entities for specific goals. The partnership emphasizes direct and long-term alliance, and encourages the efforts to establish plans and solve various problems generated in the cooperation process together. Supply chain partnership is obviously different from traditional transaction relation, which more emphasizes on mutual trust and cooperation, win-win and long-term results, and non-financial and non-operational indicators including reputation and innovative ability of suppliers [3]. This kind of relationship improves financial and operational performance by decreasing total cost and stock in supply chain and sharing information.

Supplier chain partnership can be divided into three levels including communication, coordination and collaboration, or be divided into three levels including communication layer, negotiation layer and encouragement layer with similar meaning [4]. The research based on five-point scale aimed to find out the most suitable partnership for each situation, and found four best partnership modes including arm's length relation, limited collaboration, multi-department integration and regarding other companies as extension of itself [5].

2.2   Three Key Problems in the Supply Chain Partnership

The initial attempt of supply chain cooperation generated from outsourcing non-core businesses to suppliers, or from cooperation of demand forecasting and stock supplement in middle of 1990s. In the early stage of partnership foundation, people focus on technical system, lead time, creative power and supply chain management style [6]. In fact, the supply chain partnership shall pay attention to three key problems.

Key problem 1: Where does it cooperate? Team consisted of suppliers, producers and dealers improve overall supply chain performance by sharing information so that all participators will be satisfied. A broad communication interface shall be established in supply chain to avoid lacking of internal and external communication and single-point connection [7].

Key problem 2: Who does it cooperative with? The enterprises which want to cooperate with all suppliers and customers can not achieve their goals for the cost of cooperation will surpass its income [8]. Enterprises can get very limited performance if they fail to promote the integration of processes to tactical and strategic level. Every supply chain has specific strategy and culture requiring different leadership styles, so we have to subdivide the supply chains according to differences in customer demands, that is, establishing different supply chains according to customer demands.

Key problem 3: What are risks of cooperation? The maintenance of supply chain needs common contractual conditions to guarantee public shared information and know-how [9]. However, the long-term agreement has risks in itself. The exit barriers are high when one party finds it isn't suitable to establish partnership. As the cost of changing partners is so high that producers may become slaves of suppliers (partnership can not stop easily). The bad performance of suppliers is not the only risk, and producers also have to be worried about the possibility that the suppliers reveal trade secrets to competitors and speculative mind in suppliers.

3 Methods of Overall Performance Appraisal of Supply Chain

Initial supply chain performance appraisal is similar to company appraisal focusing on financial indicators [10]. Enterprises relying on simple financial indicators may ignore good opportunities of constant improvements, and good constructed non-financial and operational indicators can make up the disadvantage. Financial indicators mainly reflect appraisal of external factors on companies, reflecting performance of traditional businesses. Operational performance mainly reflects internal efficiency and performance, which reveals supply chain relationship directly.

Supply chain management in early stage is based on role cooperation, especially related to performance appraisal on various costs, materials, products, and stock management. The performance appraisal based on roles failed to support cooperation of supply chain internally and externally, resulting in many criticisms including excessive emphasis on cost indicators, inconsistent with strategic goals of the organizations, and ignorance of uncertainties in supply chain [11].

As cross-role activities increase, processes with efficient control are more important for the improvement of supply chain performance. The SCOR model reflects supply chain performance by using 11 indicators in five processes including planning, purchasing, production, delivery and reverse logistics to realize the transformation from roles management to processes management [12].

The studies related to roles and processes are start from internal supply chain, and performance appraisal based on functions regards supply chain as black box to appraise overall performance of supply chain from the angle of system functions. The goal of supply chain management is to achieve largest output with lowest cost, or highest income with highest efficiency. The former requires a flexible supply chain including lead time, reliability, capacity, product group and delivery information; and the latter requires a lean supply chain including price, productivity, stock, asset utility, and transaction cost. The best supply chain performance shall be consisted of flexible and lean aspects.

According to pervious single emphasis on price, producers pay more attention to collaboration of suppliers on offering improved service, technological innovation and product design. However, the studies on performance appraisal of cooperative level are still very few. The partnership and strategic alliance in supply chain refer to collaborative and exclusive relationship between the enterprise and upper suppliers & lower customers [13].

So it is far from enough to only appraise performance of buyers or suppliers, and overall performance of supply chain based on partnership is the focus of appraisal. In current studies, the cooperation is separated from performance, and the cooperative performance is not simply sum of cooperation and performance. As a result, the performance appraisal of supply chain seen from cooperative view is a new development direction from financial indicators and operational indicators [13].

4 An Analytical Model of Overall Performance of Supply Chain

4.1 Design of Indicators for Overall Performance of Supply Chain

Based on previous analysis, the study analyzes overall performance of supply chain from three aspects including financial performance, operation performance, and cooperative performance. Although financial performance has been emphasized excessively, recent studies have leaned over backwards. Scholars often ignore financial performance, but the financial performance is the final goal to appraise a company or supply chain. The financial performance can be measured by sales, growth rate of profit and slowdown of cost.

The operational performance mainly discusses efficiency and effectiveness of supply chain, which can be measured by three indicators including flexibility and lead time, quality and quantity, and customer satisfactory. The high-efficiency supply chain obviously has better financial performance. Meanwhile, in order to maintain high-efficiency supply chain, the company needs cooperation from partners besides its own efforts.

The cooperative performance reflects satisfactory between both partners and effects of cooperation. Good partnership is basis of supply chain, which is good for improving financial performance of supply chain. Therefore, on the one hand, cooperative performance directly influences operational performance and influences financial performance indirectly through operational performance; on the other hand, cooperative performance directly influences financial performance.

4.2 Cooperative Factors Influencing Overall Performance of Supply Chain

In different development stages of supply chain, the key factors influencing the successful cooperation of supply chain are different. However, high-level support, efficient communication and integrated coordination are constant factors of successful cooperation of supply chain. Based on efforts of previous researches, the paper proposes that strength of supply chain, interface management and partnership structures are key cooperative factors influencing overall performance of supply chain.

Strength of Supply Chain. Strength of supply chain refers to closeness degree of supply chain partnership, which means that the possibility system maintaining steady status or resisting disturb of certain degree. The supply chain includes four aspects such as technical capacity of members in supply chain, internal and external trust, distribution of income, and cooperative level. The long-term relationship between both parties in supply chain is naturally generated in cooperative level. With the existence of long-term relationship, suppliers have been a part of good supply chain, which reveals constant and positive influence on overall competency of supply chain. High-level trust and coordination in long-term relationship lead to excellent customer responsiveness and performance of other companies. So it can be suggested that strength of supply chain has direct influence on cooperative performance.

Interface Management of Supply Chain. Interface management of supply chain includes interface connecting suppliers and producers, interface connecting various functional departments inside both parties, and interface connecting with environment. Interface management is the very thing that integrates resources on both sides. The interface management between supply chain and environment may have significant influence on overall performance of supply chain. As leaders have better understanding on strategy of supply chain and maintenance of competitive advantage, so they can influence supply chain performance by influencing organization value and management style. The commitment of leadership is very important (always wish to maintain valuable relationship). Therefore, interface management of supply chain has obvious influence on cooperative performance, but also has obvious indirect influence on cooperative performance through strength of supply chain.

Partnership Structure. Partnership structure refers to relative location of producers and suppliers in the supply chain, cooperative means, interactive influence, and integration degree of cultures. It mainly includes cross-role teamwork and communication, mutual dependence, culture inclusiveness and equal status. The mutual dependence mainly reflects in input of mutual beneficial asset, mutual behavior of employees, and expectation and attitude towards future cooperation. Cooperative culture with inclusiveness is good for the promotion of operational efficiency of supply chain and mutual acceptance of employees, resulting in increase in performance of supply chain. Besides, the equal status of both parties can promote long-term cooperation and maintain strategic collaboration to promote performance of supply chain. Therefore, partnership structure has obvious influence on cooperative performance, and also has obvious indirect influence on cooperative performance through strength of supply chain.

4.3 Conceptual Model of Supply Chain Overall Performance

In previous studies, cooperation is regarded as an independent part separated from performance of supply chain. Scholars have suggested many theories and methods of cooperation, but do not explore influence of cooperation on performance of supply chain. Based on relevant studies, the paper puts forward a conceptual model describing influence of cooperation on overall performance of supply chain to make clear the cooperation of supply chain, overall performance of supply chain, and internal mutual relationship between the two (Fig. 1 shows the conceptual model).

The study has put forward a theoretical framework of relation between factors of supply chain cooperation and supply chain performance. Based on the previous performance analysis of supply chain, the paper introduces cooperative performance and divides overall performance of supply chain into three main dimensions such as financial performance, operational performance and cooperative performance. Although in public demonstration and secret planning, the company may have various goals, the financial performance is still the final goal of the company and its supply chain performance. In the performance appraisal of supply chain, cooperative performance and operational performance is the necessary basis for financial performance. The operational performance has been emphasized in previous studies, and the cooperative performance has been developed not long before. A good financial performance can not be separated from good cooperative performance and operational performance. Therefore, the paper has put forwards a simply multi-dimension appraisal framework for overall performance of supply chain.

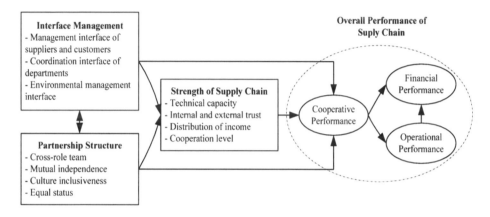

Fig. 1. Conceptual model of supply chain overall performance

5   Conclusions and Discussions

Previous studies on performance appraisal of supply chain only focus on financial performance and operational performance. It is very necessary and valuable to introduce cooperative performance in the new background of cooperation and competition. Furthermore, in the overall performance appraisal of supply chain, cooperative performance and operational performance is the basis of financial performance, which means that cooperative performance and operational performance are intermediate variables, and financial performance is final goal.

The cooperative factors influencing overall performance of supply chain can be summarized as strength of supply chain, interface management of supply chain, and partnership structure. They directly or indirectly influence cooperative performance together and then influence overall performance of supply chain through mutual action. Therefore, it is a key method to promote overall performance of supply chain by adjusting strength of supply chain, integrating interface environment of supply chain, and improving partnership structure.

Performance appraisal of supply chain is an important mean to check cooperation of supply chain and offer feedback of cooperation. The appraisal aims to find something worth to improve for better cooperation in the future and constantly improves cooperative mechanism to promote cooperative performance, instead of choosing, weeding out or punishing suppliers. Therefore, leadership of both parties shall participate in and communicate frankly and frequently in the performance appraisal process to guarantee that real and deep reasons influencing performance can be identified and be improved.

The study has only put forward a conceptual analytical model for supply chain partnership and overall performance of supply chain, and does not conduct necessary empirical analysis on their relationship and reasonability of the model. Therefore, further studies shall be carried out to check the reliability of the conclusion.

Acknowledgment. This work was supported by National Natural Science Foundation of China (No. 70973060).

References

1. Tan, K.C.: A Framework of Supply Chain Management Literature. Eur. J. Purch. Supply Manag. 7, 39–48 (2001)
2. Beamon, B.M.: Measuring Supply Chain Performance. Int. J. Oper. Prod. Manag. 19, 275–292 (1999)
3. Duffy, R., Fearne, A.: The Impact of Supply Chain Partnerships on Supplier Performance. Int. J. Logist. Manag. 15, 57–72 (2004)
4. Christopher, M., Jüttner, U.: Developing Strategic Partnerships in the Supply Chain: a Practitioner Perspective. Eur. J. Purch. Supply Manag. 12, 117–127 (2000)
5. Lambert, D.M., Knemeyer, A.M.: We're in This Together. Harv. Bus. Rev. 12, 114–122 (2004)
6. Hall, R., Andriani, P.: Analyzing Intangible Resources and Managing Knowledge in a Supply Chain Context. Eur. Manag. J. 16, 685–697 (1998)
7. Barratt, M.A.: Understanding the Meaning of Collaboration in the Supply Chain. Supply Chain Manag. 9, 30–42 (2004)
8. Beamon, B.M.: Supply Chain Design and Analysis: Models and Methods. Int. J. Prod. Econ. 55, 281–294 (1998)
9. Feldmann, M., Muller, S.: An Incentive Scheme for True Information Providing in Supply Chains. Omega 31, 63–73 (2003)
10. Neely, A.: The Performance Measurement Revolution: Why Now and What Next? Int. J. Oper. Prod. Manage. 19, 205–228 (1999)
11. Gunasekaran, A., Patel, C., McGaughey, R.E.: A Framework for Supply Chain Performance Measurement. Int. J. Prod. Econ. 87, 333–347 (2004)
12. Chan, F., Qi, H.F.: An Innovative Performance Measurement Method for Supply Chain Management. Supply Chain Manag 8, 209–223 (2003)
13. Gunasekaran, A., Patel, C., Tirtiroglu, E.: Performance Measure and Metrics in a Supply Chain Environment. Int. J. Oper. Prod. Manag. 21, 71–87 (2001)

Study on Behavioral Motivations of Chinese Private Enterprises' Social Responsibility under Perspective of Needs Satisfaction

Libing Shu and Rong Chen

Ningbo Institute of Technology, Zhejiang University,
315100 Ningbo, China
{shulb,chenr}@nit.zju.edu.cn

Abstract. The paper aims to explore the social responsibility behavioral motivations of private enterprises in Chinese market environment. Based on survey of 220 private enterprises in eastern China, it shows that enterprise token on social responsibility is to meet the needs of their subsistence, development, social power, and personal values of entrepreneurs. The needs then will produce corresponding motivations and behaviors. It reveals that there are five different behavioral motivations to bear social responsibilities for different private enterprises, including promotion of entrepreneurs' social status, concerning social values, seeking government support, gathering talented people, and avoiding development risk. Then some suggestions are given to stimulate the internal motivations of private enterprises and promote the cooperation of stakeholders for better social responsibility performance.

Keywords: corporate social responsibility, behavioral motivation, needs satisfaction, private enterprise.

1 Introduction

Corporate social responsibility emerged in the 1950th in western countries. The core idea is that enterprises should not only be responsible for the interests of shareholders to make profits, but also should take on responsibility for employees, society, environment and other benefits related ones. Along with economic globalization, the corporate social responsibility movement also flourishes all over the world. With the reform and open up to the outside of world, the Chinese enterprises rapidly increase the awareness of social responsibility. Chinese companies had the first social responsibility report in 2001. In 2009, a total number of 631 national social responsibility reports were published more than the sum of past years, which indicates that corporate social responsibility in China has gone from the concept to the practice.

Corporate social responsibility is the revolution of the firm nature. [1-2] Friedman, Hayek, Posner, who represent the opponents of corporate social responsibility, believed that the corporate social responsibility goes against the nature of firm. However, taking on social responsibility is still the mainstream both in theory and

Q. Zhou (Ed.): ISAEBD 2011, Part I, CCIS 208, pp. 324–330, 2011.
© Springer-Verlag Berlin Heidelberg 2011

practice. Although some scholars and organizations believe that the social responsibility should be entirely voluntary by the enterprises, there are a lot of arguments about whether corporate social responsibility should include the meaning of voluntary. Lantos [3] divided corporate social responsibility into ethical, altruistic and strategic-type. Jamali [4] thought corporate social responsibility should include mandatory and voluntary type. Corporate social responsibility are multiple motivated based on the observations from the practical view. "Doing well by doing good" and "doing well to do good", which proposed by Drucker [5], also imply the multi-motivations of social responsibility. As the most active economic groups, Chinese private enterprises have paid attention to corporate social responsibilities. This paper analyzed the motivation of corporate social responsibility based on the survey of 220 Chinese private enterprises.

2 Literature Review

As an internal mental process, motivation is often difficult to observe, but can be deduced by the behaviors of task, efforts, activities, and speech. In the past, the study of motivation was largely focused on individuals and has shifted to organizational behavior later on, which is organizational action motivation. Motivations and needs are closely contacting, and needs are the internal conditions of motivation. From the perspective of needs, the behavioral motivation of corporate social responsibility generally has three aspects, including the need for enterprises' survival and development, the need for social power, and the need for entrepreneurs' personal values and social identity.

2.1 The Need for Enterprises' Survival and Development

Economists generally believe that the corporate goal is to pursue of profit maximization, while the basis is to seek long-term survival of enterprises, which requires the managers to take on social responsibility and the resulting social costs. Corporate social responsibility is not an opposite concept to economic responsibility. On the contrary, the economic benefits are always considered as one of the important parts. By taking on the corporate social responsibility, the enterprises can win market reputation and organizational identity. It also can reflect the corporate culture and values orientation, and create better social atmosphere for their development.

From the perspective of internal management, taking on corporate social responsibility can help enterprises develop new resources and the ability to build strong management advantages. From the perspective of external development, corporate social responsibilities communicate the positive information to the outside. It is helpful to create a positive image before customers, investors, bankers and suppliers, which makes them get access to capital, technology, talent and other support easier and better attraction to the best employees. At the same time, corporate social responsibility is necessity to deal with various social contradictions and problems, and avoiding development risk.

2.2 The Need for Obtaining Social Power

The corporate social responsibility is the result of rights and obligations exchange in the process of resources allocation. Berle and Means [6] pointed out that to obtain social power means to take the corresponding social responsibilities at the same time. The "Power - Responsibility Model" [7] means that "corporate social responsibility is from the held social power; and the responsibility is equivalent to the power". In a well-ordered society, the law requires that where the responsibility of decision-making is where the power lies. Accordingly, Davis developed an iron law of responsibility: in the long run, those who cannot fulfill the responsibility will lose their power. After this iron law of responsibility excises, it also can be applied to the organization. It means that the one who avoids corporate social responsibility will lead to a gradual erosion of social power. Drucker also believed that those who wants to gain power must take responsibility, and who is willing to take responsibility can get the power [8].

2.3 The Need for Entrepreneurs' Personal Values and Social Identity

The business managers and entrepreneurs play a key role in corporate taking on corporate social responsibility. Entrepreneurial behavior preferences are decided by ethical and moral view. In the extent of ethics and morality, the effective regulatory system is not from the government's management and legal constraints, but from entrepreneurs' self-discipline. Business development deviated from the normal track which rooted from the lack of morality. Enron's case, Madoff financial fraud and Sanlu milk problem showed that the misconduct of entrepreneurs would lead to serious consequences. Entrepreneurs take responsibility for charitable or public welfare is an effective path to get social value and social identity, as well as to get the public awareness, reputation and support.

3 Questionnaire Design and Data Collection

The questionnaire of this study has refereed to some related researches, and some questions were adapted according to Chinese business context. The samples focus on the typical industries in eastern China, which include manufacturing, textile and garment, construction and real estate, high-tech, and service industries. The survey was carried out from March to April 2009 with the help of Industrial Bureau of Ningbo. A total of 400 questionnaires were issued, and 296 were returned. After strictly screening, 220 valid questionnaires were eventually obtained. The valid response rate was 55%.

The descriptive statistic of respondents shows in Table 1. The established time of all samples is basically subject to uniform distribution. Nearly half of the sampled enterprises are with annual sales less than 5 million and 77.3% are fewer than 30 million. Majority of the enterprises are small manufactories, which is basically consistent with the regional industry. Overall, the distribution of sampled enterprises was various and with a relatively good representation without over concentrated on a particular type of enterprise.

Table 1. Descriptive statistic of respondents N=220

Variable	Items	N	Percent	Variable	Items	N	Percent
Established time	before 1992	23	10.5%	Number of employees	less than 50	130	59.1%
	1993 to 1997	30	13.6%		51~ 300	59	26.8%
	1998 to 2002	78	35.5%		301 ~2000	28	12.7%
	after 2003	89	40.5%		more than 2000	3	1.4%
Sales in 2008	under 5 million	102	46.4%	Industry	manufacturing	83	37.7%
	5~30 million	68	30.9%		textile and cloth	21	9.5%
	30~100 million	38	17.3%		services	32	14.5%
	100~300 million	5	2.3%		high-tech industry	10	4.5%
	over 300 million	7	3.2%		others	74	33.6%

4 Results

4.1 Factor Structure of Corporate Social Responsibility Motivation

We used SPSS software module of exploratory factor analysis to extract the common factors with the principal component method and rotated with varimax. Two items were deleted because of the factor loading lower than 0.50. Finally five common factors including 23 items were retained. The cumulative explanation of variance was up to 67.56%. And the Kaiser-Meyer-Olkin measure of sampling adequacy was 0.900, which totally agreed with the judgment criterion of higher than 0.80 proposed by Kaiser. The approximate Chi-square of Bartlett's test of sphericity was 2980.65 with 253 freedom degrees and significant at level 0.000, which indicated that the sample data was suitable for factor analysis. The abstract of exploratory factor analysis was showed in Table 2.

Table 2. Abstract of exploratory factor analysis

Factor	Factor 1	Factor 2	Factor 3	Factor 4	Factor 5
Motivation	enhancing status of entrepreneur	concerning social value	seeking government support	gathering talented people	avoiding development risk
Cronbach's α	0.893	0.855	0.809	0.855	0.698
Eigenvalue	4.221	3.706	2.749	2.659	2.203
Variance explained	18.35%	16.11%	11.95%	11.56%	9.58%

The results reflected that the questionnaire and measurement showed high construct validity and convergence validity. The Cronbach's α coefficients were 0.893, 0.855, 0.809, 0.855, and 0.698 respectively. The Cronbach's α coefficient of total sample was also up to 0.900. We concluded that the survey tools indicated high reliability from the Cronbach's α coefficient, so the results of reliability and validity test were entirely suitable.

According to the concrete content and meaning of items, we could give a new name of each factor. Here, enhancing status of entrepreneur (F1), concerning social value (F2), seeking government support (F3), gathering talented people (F4), avoiding development risk (F5) were used to rename these five factors separately. We considered these five factors as five dimensions of behavioral motivations for Chinese private enterprise. Among them, the factor of enhancing status of entrepreneur corresponds to the needs for entrepreneur's personal values and social identity. Concerning social values, avoiding development risk and gathering talents correspond to the needs for enterprises' survival and development. The factor of seeking government support corresponds to the needs for gaining social power.

4.2 Classification of Corporate Social Responsibility Motivation

Based on the values of specific items, the weighted means of these five factors were calculated. From the descriptive statistic analysis of these five motivation factors, the mean indicated their relative condition of behavioral motivation of corporate social responsibility for Chinese private enterprises. We found that the strongest motivation of corporate social responsibility was "gathering of talents", followed by "concerning social values". And the motivation of "avoiding development of risk" was the weakest one. And motivations of "enhancing status of entrepreneur" and "seeking government support" were in the middle. We also knew that the standard deviation of each motivation factor was smaller than 0.7. Paired-sample t-test was used to test whether the five motivation factors had statistically significant difference. It clearly displayed in Table 3 that there are significant differences among majority factors. The condition of these factors had extraordinarily significant differences although the difference appeared very small.

Table 3. Paired-samples t-test of motivation factors

Motivation Factors	Mean	F1	F2	F3	F4
Enhancing status of entrepreneur	3.581				
Concerning social value	3.649	0.069 (1.749)			
Seeking government support	3.505	0.076 (1.735)	0.144^{**} (2.907)		
Gathering talented people	3.667	0.086^{*} (2.389)	0.018 (0.518)	0.163^{***} (3.547)	
Avoiding development risk	3.382	0.199^{***} (4.640)	0.267^{***} (5.485)	0.123^{**} (2.818)	0.285^{***} (6.197)

$* \ p < 0.05, \ ** \ p < 0.01, \ *** \ p < 0.001$

The test results in Table 3 showed that private enterprises could be sorted by the motivation intensity of social responsibility. According to the intensity of motivation, it can be divided into three levels which were given in Table 4. "Gathering talented people" and "concerning social value" were the strongest motivation; "enhancing status of entrepreneur" and "seeking government support" were in the middle; and "avoiding development risk" was the weakest one.

Table 4. Level of motivation of corporate social responsibility

Level of motivation	Strong		Medium		Weak
Type of motivation	gathering talented people	concerning social value	enhancing status of entrepreneur	seeking government support	avoiding development risk
Needs of satisfaction	survival and development of enterprise		personal value of entrepreneur	seeking social power	survival and development of enterprise

5 Conclusions and Implications

Corporate social responsibilities are the results of meeting the needs of enterprises' survival and development, social power obtaining, entrepreneurs' personal values and social identity. The paper found that the behavioral motivation of corporate social responsibility had five dimensions, including "enhancing status of entrepreneur", "concerning social value", "seeking government support", "gathering talented people", and "avoiding development risk". Among them, the motivation factor of "enhancing status of entrepreneur" was relevant to the needs for entrepreneurs' personal values and social identity. The three motivation factors of "concerning social value", "seeking government support", and "gathering talented people" were corresponding to the needs of enterprises' survival and development. And the motivation factor of "avoiding development risk" was related to the needs for social power. According to the intensity of motivation for Chinese private enterprises, the behavioral motivation of social responsibility could be divided into three levels, namely, "gathering talented people" and "concerning social value" as the strongest; "enhancing status of entrepreneurs" and "seeking government support" at the middle level; and "avoiding development risk" as the weakest.

Multiple comparisons showed that there were no significant differences of motivation for corporate social responsibilities between small and large & medium enterprises. However, the motivation for corporate social responsibility had positive relation with firm size as a whole. The motivation for corporate social responsibility had partly significant differences for enterprises in different stages. Especially, the motivation of "seeking government support" had most significant difference. Existence and mature enterprises had stronger motivation to take social responsibility to win government support than the enterprises at growth and recession stages. Meanwhile, the enterprises at existence and mature stages also had stronger motivation to enhancing the social status of entrepreneur by taking social responsibilities than the growing enterprises. Enterprises at different stages of life cycle all had obvious motivation to gathering talented people. The motivation of "avoiding development risk" was relatively weak. And the motivation of "seeking government support" was in the middle.

It is a gradual process of taking on corporate social responsibility. The stakeholders, including government, society, associations, and firms should play their roles respectively. The final solution to the problem of social responsibility depends on the attitudes, motivations and behaviors for corporate social responsibility. In order to play a better role and influence of social responsibilities, the firms should initiative the social responsibility at the strategic level. The leading firms could develop appropriate social responsibility strategies, foster entrepreneurship spirits, and strengthen self-discipline. The firms should change their social responsibility behavior gradually, from passive to proactive, random to strategic planning, legal constraints to self-regulation in order to be competitive.

Since the intrinsic motivation is a psychological process, which can not be directly observed, the study on organizational motivation is a challenging task. In this study, the variable selection and questionnaire design may not be comprehensive, and the intrinsic relationship of all the motivation factors and needs does not reveal here. Exploring the inherent relationship and influence mechanism between motivations and needs are important direction for future research.

References

1. Berle, A.A.: Corporate Powers as Powers in Trust. Harv. Bus. Rev. 44, 104–1074 (1931)
2. Dodd, M.E.: For Whom Are Corporate Managers Trustees. Harv. Law Rev. 45, 1145–1163 (1932)
3. Lantos, G.P.: The Boundaries of Strategic Corporate Social Responsibility. J. Consum. Market. 18, 595–630 (2001)
4. Jamali, D.: The Case for Strategic Corporate Social Responsibility in Developing Countries. Bus. Soc. Rev. 112, 11–27 (2007)
5. Drucker, P.: The New Meaning of Corporate Social Responsibility. Calif. Manag. Rev. 26, 53–63 (1984)
6. Berle, A.A., Means, G.C.: The Modern Corporation and Private Property. Transaction Publishers, New Brunswick (1932)
7. Davis, K.: Understanding the Social Responsibility Puzzle: What Does the Businessman Owe to Society? Bus. Horiz. 10, 45–50 (1967)
8. Drucker, P.: Organizational Management. Shanghai Finance University Press, Shanghai (2003) (in Chinese)
9. Churchill, C., Lewis, V.L.: The Five Stages of Small Business Growth. Harv. Bus. Rev. 61, 30–50 (1983)

A Research on Agricultural Products Supply Chain and Food Safety

Hongling Zheng and Lili Lu

The economic management department of Tangshan normal college,
Tangshan, Hebei 063000
honglingzheng@126.com, tstczheng@yahoo.com.cn

Abstract. With the improvement of people's living standard, food safety problems become more sensitive. From the point of view of agricultural products supply chain, this paper analyzes the food safety concern existing in every link of agricultural products supply, and has proposed relevant countermeasures.

Keywords: Agricultural products, supply chain, food safety.

1 Introduction

Hunger breeds discontent and food safety comes to be the first. With the sustainable development of social and economy, people's consumption level has increased characterized by diversified, multispecies and less quantity development direction of consumption structure and an increasingly higher requirement of food demand quality. However, the serial food safety accidents have aroused people's concern with food safety constantly. The food quality safety involves a large range and many influencing factors. Taking agricultural products supply chain as the breakthrough point, this paper has studied the quality safety system of agricultural products supply chain.

2 Food Safety Problems Exist in Agricultural Products Supply Chain

The frequently happened food safety accidents make people realize that unsafe factors run through the overall process of food supply more and more clearly. From production, process, packaging, circulation to consumption, varying degrees of safety concern might exist in each link which both increase the risk of food safety and reduce the benefit of the whole supply chain.

First is the production link. As the headstream, once the production link has safety problems, they will extend into the procedures of the whole supply chain. Therefore, the production link plays a basic and decisive role in the quality safety of agricultural production. Pesticides, fertilizers and waste pollution will bring great hidden danger

Q. Zhou (Ed.): ISAEBD 2011, Part I, CCIS 208, pp. 331–336, 2011.

to food safety. For example, the using of growth regulator and the residue of veterinary drug, etc. will increase safety loophole which may further influence the health of human. Both direct health hazard and the growth of food origin disease will come out after having the polluted agricultural products.

Second is the processing link. At present, problems of small-scale food production of enterprises, backward technology of agricultural production and chaotic management in China are comparative serious. In the first place, the safety awareness of food safety is weak in the process of production in enterprises resulting in that raw materials for food process of some enterprises are unexpectedly expired and deleterious; secondly, the excessively and abusively use of food additives has brought food safety problems; thirdly, problems have bought by the application of new technology, process, and raw materials, such as the application of transgenic technology, modern biotechnology, zymin, etc. in food; and finally, the food process enterprises don't process as the technology required. For instance, the problems of incompletely killed microorganism and unconfirmed hygiene standards of production environment will cause pathogenic microorganism remains in food or microbial corruption occurs during storage and transportation.

Third is the logistics link. On the one hand, due to the backward facilities and technologies of logistics in links of agricultural products supply chain, poor transportation condition as well as the unbuilt cold chain logistics, phenomenon of metamorphism or contaminated of are caused owing to factors of temperature, humidity, time and condition of storage and transportation; on the other hand, the efficiency of postpartum links such as grading, cleaning, precooling and anticorrosive packaging of the majority is low because of backward processing technologies, low intensive processing level, which will result in critical loss in the circulation of fresh and alive agricultural production.

Four is the supervision link. The first problem is that, for a long time, the management of food is bull management. Barriers between different departments and regions, poor communication, overlapping responsibilities of various departments in law enforcement and supervision loopholes or even "vacuum" have appeared in food safety management; secondly, the system of food inspection detection and the evaluation index system of food quality and safety is imperfect and there is large difference between domestic standards and international standards; finally, the construction of food safety credit system need to be strengthened urgently and the construction of food safety supervision net is evidently backward.

Five is the sales and consumptive link. From the perspective of retail link, problems of lack of correspondent food safety detection facilities, imperfection in controlling management of quality guarantee period of goods, substandard storage as well as storage and transportation and container, all these have led to many addle food. And from the perspective of consumptive link, due to the facts that consumers are far from the processes of food production and circulation, for them, the information asymmetry of food safety information exist. It is difficult for consumers to evaluate the quality and safety of food accurately before and after consumption. In addition, as the growth of outer repast consumption and non-seasonal food consumption, the mass food safety issue becomes more serious.

From the important links above, it can be concluded that the agricultural products supply chain is both long and complicated, and food safety concern might exist in any link. The longer the chain, the more the link, the wider the range, the higher frequency and more complicated of food safety issue happens. Problems appear in any link will lead to an increased rate of food risk. Therefore, the primary task of agricultural products supply chain is ensuring food safety.

3 The Food Safety Countermeasure of "from Farmland to Table" Made from the Perspective of Supply Chain

The control of food safety involves the whole process "from farmland to table", including links of production, processing, storage, sales and other middle links. The effective guarantee of food safety needs not only the powerful regulation and interference of governments but also the omnibearing effective measures employed by each relevant parties such as enterprise, scientific research institution, educational institution, medium, consumers, etc. from every link of the industry chain in order to establish an effective food safety system.

3.1 Establish the Green Supply Chain and Ensure Food Safety

The green supply chain is a modern management model which takes into account the environmental impact and resource efficiency comprehensively in the whole supply chain. Based on the green manufacturing theory and management technique of supply chain, involving in supplier, manufacturing plant, retailer and user, the green supply chain fully considers the selected scheme will have a minimum impact (negative effect) on environment in supply process from green purchase and cultivated of headstream to production processing link, up to transportation, storage, packaging, sales, consumption and so on. Thus it has highest resource efficiency.

First is green purchase and cultivated. Food safety should be emphasized from the headstream, stick to experiments and demonstrations, implement seedlings engineering broadly, and study technologies of scaled production of hybrid seeds and breeding as well as seed comprehensive processing in order to greatly develop green agriculture. Select pollution free and robust seedlings from the headstream; increase the use of green raw materials in the production process; conduct green cultivated by adopting green feed, biopesticides and organic fertilizer to vigorously develop intensive ecological aquaculture. Popularize the strategy of "three production and one standard" of agricultural products (pollution-free agricultural products, green food and organic food and agricultural geographic marks); promote the standardized production of agriculture; improve the quality safety level of agricultural products so as to facilitate the agriculture efficiency and increase farmers' income.

Second is green production and processing. In the production processing link, it is supposed to make full use of integrated control technology of agriculture, physics, biology, ecology, etc. to control pests; reduce the using amount of pesticide; formulate scientific and reasonable production craft standards according to the technical requirements required by green food processing; employ clean and sanitary food processing facilities and advanced processing technologies to guarantee the production environment and the sanitation of staff; keep the nutrition constituent of food to the largest extent; do not hold back the properties and ingredients of food additives used in green food to consumers; improve the endurance and stability of products; keep and enhance the nutritional value of products. Meanwhile, for the processed agricultural products, they should be packaged for vacuum, anticorrosive and fresh-keeping by adopting pollution free, no smell and no chemical material materials; optimize the packaging structure; cut down packaging materials; use the packaging materials characterized by safety, degradability and re-utilizing.

Third is green logistics and consumption. Select green transportation, that is, on the basis of planning branches and distribution centers reasonable, try to optimize the delivery routes and advocate deliver jointly; research and develop green logistics technologies actively and the frozen fresh-keeping technology of agricultural products; develop cold chain logistics of agricultural products to make sure the products stay in the low-temperature status required by the postharvest physiological requirements in order to ensure the food quality and reduce food loss. In the consumer phase, green consumption and moderate consumption is advocated vigorously and consumers should resist food with potential safety hazard consciously in consumption.

3.2 Establish a Effective Purchase, Supply and Review System

The division of labor in agricultural supply chain is refined by each passing day that there are as many as dozens of middle links from raw materials to edible food. In order to better control the review of each links of food processing, increase efficiency while ensure the food safety, constructing an effective food safety review management system has become an inevitable choice. Because the close cooperation of the supply chain contributes to the implementation of tracking system, the quality tracking management mechanism can be tried out in production fields which focus on agricultural enterprise, farmer specialized cooperatives and authentication products production base to realize the traceability of quality safety of agricultural products from farmland to table by exploiting technology of information. Every production link should set up production files of agricultural products with cases of complete records of agricultural inputs and pest control, and input information identification in each links of manufacturing, processing, packaging, storage, transportation, sales and so on to guarantee the safety and traceability of food in the overall system of production, logistics and sales.

3.3 Straighten Out the Quality Safety Supervision System of Agricultural Products and Enforce Seamless Quality Safety Supervision of Agricultural Products in Each Node of Supply Chain

Founding a food safety committee composed by relevant functional departments of government aims to coordinate the food safety supervision of departments in charge of government exclusively. It is recommended that the founding is led by quality and technical supervision departments, while other departments differentiate duty and power of each member organizations in accordance with the links of production, processing, sales of agricultural products to achieve seamless docking among supervision departments; establish monitoring and management system in links of planting, cultivation, acquisition, testing, processing, packaging, storage, transport, sale, consumption and other links. The construction of inspection testing system of agricultural products quality is a process of gradual improvement. Therefore, it is supposed to take full advantage of existing resources and gradually perfect the three levels of inspection and testing network integrated by self-test of enterprise, entrusted detection of social intermediary organizations and monitoring of legally qualified professional testing organization in the process of construction; revitalize the integration of stock; strengthen the construction of statutory quality inspection bodies of national and provincial-level agricultural products and give full play to its advantages. In addition, the departments of provincial administrative director of agricultural products quality should organize and coordinate every inspection testing organizations to realize the sharing of resource and data; correspondent legal responsibilities of inspection and testing results are to be shouldered by inspection testing institutes set legally.

3.4 Accelerate the Standardization Process of Quality Safety of Agricultural Products Supply Chain

Set up and improve technology advanced and sound structured system of products quality safety standards, promote the standardization production of agriculture vigorously, and accelerate the development of pollution free agricultural products, green food, organic food and famous agricultural products so as to facilitate the quality safety standardization process of the overall supply chain. The first and foremost thing is to establish and improve the food safety market access system, that is, stick to the principles of quality for the market, accelerating research and establishment of food safety market access, recalling substandard food voluntarily, and compulsory delisting system of illegal enterprise. Second, improve food quality standards and processing technical regulations, and organize enterprises to produce in accordance with standards. Though there are some regulations for production standard system of food safety, it needs further refining; furthermore, the supervision should be strengthened for putting the regulations into practice. Third, standardize the detection and control system of food quality. The food quality control system symbolized by passing certification has played a demonstrative role in improving food quality and safety. And enforce the standardization of food quality inspection and control system is the key to ensure food safety. Finally, improve the standardized food storage and transportation system constantly to safeguard food safety in the process of storage and transportation.

3.5 Intensify the Publicity of Quality Safety of Agricultural Products, Advance the Moral Consciousness and Legal Consciousness of the Whole Society, and Perfect the Early Warning Mechanism of Food Safety of Agricultural Products

Put food safety into the effective supervision of the whole society, establish and improve the complaining and offence reporting system, organize and encourage social institutes, industry organizations and people from all walks of life to participate in the supervision, intensify the supervision on operating enterprises of food manufacturing; meanwhile, popularize knowledge of products quality and food safety greatly, conduct publicity and training work widely and intensively in terms of quality safety knowledge of agricultural products, production technology of pollution free agricultural products, domestic and international quality standards, laws and regulations of agricultural products quality safety, etc. By means of management technology training of agricultural products as well as legal education, let the majority of agricultural products producers and operators set up true quality safety sense and try to improve the food safety consciousness of the whole society.

Moreover, the food safety risk warning and rapid response system is to be established and improved so as to perfect the unexpected food safety emergencies. And conduct analysis on risk evaluation and emergency disposal rehearsal to improve the ability of fast reaction, scientific decision and resolute disposal in terms of significant food pollution accidents, group food poisoning and food safety terrorist events, and enhance the ability to respond to emergencies simultaneously.

Acknowledgment. Fund development projects of Tangshan teachers college 10C04 Guidance program of Tangshan science and technology research and development 10140207c.

References

1. Liao, W.: Solving food safety problems based on food supply chain management. China Social Sciences Report 10 (2010)
2. liang, L.: A study based on food safety perspective. China's Economic and Trade Guide 8 (2009)
3. Han, Y.: A study based on the construction and optimization of safe agricultural products supply chain——analysis from the perspective of positive transfer and reverse traceability on information of supply chain. The World of Survey and Research 1 (2009)
4. Wang, C., Chen, Y.: The recycling economic principle of green supply chain management of agricultural products. Prices Monthly 3 (2008)
5. Tang, Y., Zhu, Y.: Analysis and countermeasures of the status of food safety in China. Food and Nutrition in China 7 (2008)

Study on the Time Problem
of Human Assets Measurement

Kaodui Li[1], Hua Zhang[1], Liping Ji[1], Aiqun Peng[1], Xiaoxian Liu[2], Wu Wan[1],
Bushuang Shen[1], and Jingjin Yu[3]

[1] School of Finance and Economics, Jiangsu University
Zhengjiang, Jiangsu, China 212013
[2] Business School, Jiangnan University
Wuxi, Jiangsu, China 214122
[3] Jingjiang College, Jiangsu University
Zhengjiang, Jiangsu, China 212013
likaodui@ujs.edu.cn, zhanghua2006@ujs.edu.cn,
qingzigao@126.com, zyqpaq@ujs.edu.cn,
liuxx2008@126.com, wanwu@ujs.edu.cn,
1204168553@qq.com, 630065736@qq.com

Abstract. One of the reasons why the human resources accounting is difficult to be implemented is the measurement of human assets. The introduction of the fair value into the measurement of human assets value accounting can effectively eliminate the uncertainly problems of human resources value measurement on the estimates of future time value stream. The value of human assets measured by the fair value can avoid the measurement differences and the difficult-to-operate difficulties caused by the diversification and the complication of measurement models in different theories, which can simplify the human resources accounting and increase the practical feasibility.

Keywords: human assets, human resources value, value stream, fair value, dynamic measurement.

1   The Value Differences between Human Assets and Physical Assets

The biggest difference between human assets and physical assets is the physical asset itself that is the condensation of value, which is the immobilized value created by human labor and has already contained the human knowledge and intelligence. Taking the fixed assets for example, they have contained the fixed value in use when they are obtained. At the same time, they can be also measured quantitatively. And the immobilized value is transferred and used in the using process. The human itself is to create the value, and the value of human resources is the one that creates the value, which refers to the ability to create value. However, the ability that creates value has great uncertainly in itself. And the estimation of value possibly created in future has

Q. Zhou (Ed.): ISAEBD 2011, Part I, CCIS 208, pp. 337–342, 2011.
© Springer-Verlag Berlin Heidelberg 2011

made such evaluation be more ill-founded. Firstly, the created values in different times in future have randomness and are possibly fluctuating. Secondly, the mutation of creating value. For example, an unknown technician may propose a patent that can bring huge benefits to the enterprise after 10 years work. [1] One of the main tasks of human resources value accounting is the measurement of value assets of high-tech workers. But the creation of scientists has greater uncertainty and the estimation of future time value is also an insoluble problem.

In theory, a person's value should be the all benefits created for the enterprise from the employment to withdrawing from the business, which is the most accurate value of human resources. However, the information users couldn't wait for that moment and they need more immediate information to evaluate the business decisions. So they have estimated the creation value of human resources and discounted them, which is just the opposite process compared with the depreciation of original value of fixed assets. The fixed assets have contained the established value when they are obtained. So they shouldn't be included in the current period to calculate the value. Strictly speaking, the real income refers to the fixed assets that are from the beginning to the end of life and the cost is also taken off. But the information users can't also wait for that moment, so the obtained cost value is amortized in the period of benefit. The amortization also has a certain assumption, especially the service life and the depreciation rate. However, the depreciation is for the established value and the discounting is for the future value. In addition to the duration and the discounting rate, the value stream that is estimated periodically is more uncertain. But they are the period and time data in future, how to determine it?

Currently, one of the most important theories of measurement model of human resources value is to choose the salaries or future benefits (Baruch Lev, 1971). Based on this, a series of correction models and adjustment methods are developed, such as "random reward value model", "adjusted stochastic reward model" and so on. This theory suggests that the salary is the price paid for the employee's use value by the enterprise through the equivalence exchange principle. [2-4] However, the salary is just an estimate in future time. The more important thing is that the salary paid for the employees by enterprise isn't consistent with the value created by employees in reality. In addition, there are also some income-based measurement methods of human resources value, such as "economic value method", "company's future revenue model", "discounting method of future net assets" and so on. [5-6] The common aspect between the salary-based measurement method and it is still the estimation of future value stream and the corporate earnings have greater uncertainty than the salaries. Whether the salary-based human resources value measurement or the income-based measurement, etc, they are all the estimation and discounting of the future salaries and excess earnings, which is still a matter of time.

2 Historical Value, Present Value and Fair Value

The accounting measurement firstly requires the reality and the objectivity, which is the advantage of historical cost that can't be replaced. But the reality and the objectivity are relative. The more important thing of reality and objectivity is the usefulness for the present and the historical cost should be said the current value or market value at the moment of obtaining assets. But as time goes on, the historical cost, which is regarded as a static measurement method, has gradually lost the properties of "objectivity and truth" so that it has also lost the usefulness of decision-making. The timely adjustment of the acquisition costs is the fair value, such as the use of market value. The fair value is a present value, which is the one that is in the timely adjustment and whose measurement is dynamic, always objective and real, so it is useful. It could be said that the fair value is a present value adjustment for the historical costs, which is momentary. Then the discounted value of future cash flows is a real-time adjustment for the value in future time, but this discounting has birth defects: one is the selection problem of the discounting rate itself; the other one is the estimation of future earnings. It could be said that these two most important factors that influence the discounted value are both controllable. So the discounting is only regarded as a pre-decision mean of financial management or management accountant and not as a measurement method. Therefore, the employment of discounted value to estimate the human resources value hasn't accurately confirmed the human assets, which can't also be listed in the report to give the readers a convincing evidence so as to prove the measurement of human asset value performed by enterprises is "real and helpful". So the employment of discounted value in the measurement of human resources value accounting can only be limited to the pre-decision of human resources management, which is also the reason that some scholars have classified the human resources accounting into the list of human resources management accounting.

For the investors and the information readers, the useful information must be immediate and the market is undoubtedly the most credible, which is also the reason that the fair value has adjusted the historical cost measurement. It is the same conversely. As for this estimated human resources value, when it is recognized as the asset, the most objective is also the price, which refers to the fair value. Since the value stream in future time is hard to predict and the discounted subjective factors are difficult to eliminate. There are two functions of fair value. One is the present value adjustment of the acquisition costs which are objective. The other one is a present performance of future estimated value. The uncertainty of future value stream can be only determined by the market, which is also the most objective, such as the transfer fee of player in club can be considered as the reference value of human resources value accounting. It could be said that the fair value can not only adjust the past, but the more important is to adjust the future with facing the present.

Although you can take the fair value to measure the human resources value, there are also some problems. The most important thing is the acquisition of fair value. At present, China has only introduced the fair value in new guidelines and there is no criteria fro fair value. The guidance of fair value measurement is also lacked, so it is not possible for the human resources. China is not alone, even the No.157 Financial Accounting Standards issued by the U.S. Financial Accounting Standards Board (FASB) may not contain the fair value measurements of human assets. The International Financial Reporting Standards---Fair Value Measurement (draft) which is issued by the International Accounting Standards Board (IASB) in May, 2009 has tried its best efforts to seek the same results with U.S. FAS 157, which is also not involved in the measurement of human assets. [7-8].

Another problem is that the human resources value accounting and the human resources rights accounting have recognized the cross of assets. This problem can be handled in this way. The human resources which have not confirmed rights are directly employed the fair value measurement and disclosed. As for the human resources which have already confirmed rights when entering the enterprises, the assessment value and the initial recognition capital value are compared and adjusted the human capital reserve (increase or decrease) in the use of fair value for assessment. Then it is only necessary to adjust the human capital reserve not the human capital in the process of assessment and measurement of such human asset value.

3   The Fair Value Measurement of Human Assets

The historical cost, the discounted value and the fair value tend to make the measurement be more objective in the final analysis. The historical cost refers to the past, and the discounted object refers to the future. Only the fair value is the present immediate value. The historical is static and the discounted value is a dynamic discounting of the static state. The fair value performs a moment present value. If the replacement value is considered as a present value adjustment of historical costs and the discounted value is a present value adjustment of future value, then the fair value can be regarded as the present adjustment of historical costs and the estimated value, which is a "universal" adjustment method. The fair value is facing the present to adjust the future and the past. The adjustment method of fair value is the market and the fundamental basis of replacement value is also the market in real terms. At the same time, the discounting rate takes the market as a reference, which is also a market interest rate. They have all used the local market functions and it could be said that the fair value is a comprehensive market view. However, the replacement and the discounting just take a commodity concept (an exchange view). The discounted value compares the future discounted value with the present value. This relationship can be expressed in Figure 1.

The present value refers to the replacement of historical costs and the discounting of future value through the market. The fair value is the market-oriented present value. It is not only a value, but also performs a (fair) process, but this process is the result performed on the past and future through the market. Form this sense, the replacement value and the discounting value are both considered as the fair value, which are the quasi-fair value. The fair value can make the measurement and the disclosure of human resources value more possibilities and practical significance.

The usefulness of human resources information is not only the internal management, but the more important thing is to meet the needs of external information users. Although the human resources cost accounting can be attributed to the financial accounting, it is just a separation of human resources information in the traditional financial accounting to some degree. The significance for the investors is not large from the information that reflects the financial conditions and provides the final operation results. On the contrary, the more useful thing is to provide some basis for analyzing the human resources and some pre-decision information for the enterprise's internal management. For the external users, they need obtain some information which the traditional financial accounting can't provide, that is the information that value accounting has provided. However, in the current academic circle, the value accounting is generally considered to belong to the managerial accounting, which has restricted the original intention of human resources accounting development in some sense. So the disclosure of assets that is measured by the human resources value accounting can better meet the requirements of stakeholders. And the fair value measurement is a timely choice.

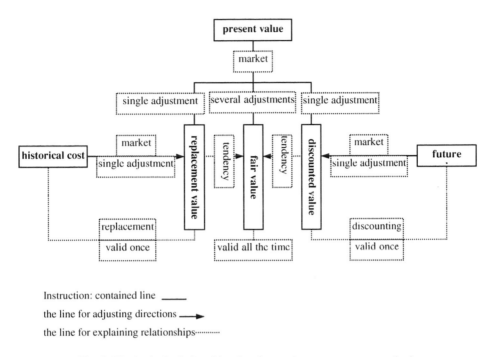

Instruction: contained line ____

the line for adjusting directions ____➤

the line for explaining relationships··········

Fig. 1. The logical relationship of various value measurement methods

4   Conclusion

The conduction of human resources accounting needs to reduce the implementation complexity and uncertainty of human resources accounting to improve the usefulness of the information. The simplification of human resources accounting may induct the fair value measurement in order to eliminate the uncertainty of human resources value measurement and improve the usefulness of the information. The fair value measurement can effectively lift the uncertainty of the estimation of future time value stream in the human resources value measurement and solve the problems that how the value measures and adjusts in the obtained time. Meanwhile, it can also avoid the measurement differences and the difficult-to-operate difficulties caused by the diversification and the complication of measurement models in different theories. In short, the fair value measurement employed for the human assets can simplify the accounting and improve the usefulness of the information. At the same time, it is also easy to carry out the actual development of human resources accounting.

Acknowledgments. The authors gratefully acknowledge the sponsorship from "the 10th College Students' Scientific Research Project *Study on the Time Problem and the Fair Value Measurement of Human Assets*" of Jiangsu University.

References

1. Long, B.S.: Strategic Human Resource Management and the Worker's Experience, p. 266. Baywood Publishing Co., Inc, Can (2007)
2. Lev, B., Schwartz, A.: On the Use of the Economic Concept of Human Capital in Financial Statements. Accounting Review 71(2), 71–103 (1971)
3. Flamholtz, E.G.F.: Human Resource Accounting: Advances in Concepts, Methods and Applications. Kluwer Academic Publishers, Dordrecht (1999)
4. Liu, Z.: Study on the Human Resources Value Accounting Modes. Accounting Research 6, 16–20 (1997) (in Chinese)
5. Schultz, T.W.: Investment in human capital. American Economic Review 51, 1–17 (1961)
6. Flamholtz, E.G.F.: Human Resources Accounting: Advances in Concepts, Methods and Applications. Kluwer Academic Publishers, Dordrecht (1999)
7. Li, K., Che, S., Xu, H.: Discussion on China's establishment of Fair Value Measurement Guidelines. Modern Accounting 3, 29–31 (2010) (in Chinese)
8. IASB: Fair Value Measurement. Exposure Draft ED/2009/5. Comments to be received by 28 September 2009 (2009)

Multi-angle Study on the Folk Borrowing Functions towards the Farm Households Suffering Major Illnesses

Fanrong Kong and Yunjin Tan

School of Economics & Management, HuBei University of Education,
Wuhan 430205 China
kfrong100@yahoo.com.cn,
tanyunjin@whpu.edu.cn

Abstract. By using the methods of investigating and of listing analysis the data from Hong'an and from Xiao Chang , two countries of the Hubei Province in china, we can analysis and review the scale of the folk borrowing of farm households suffering major diseases. From the research, we know that the folk borrowing have a positive effect on the fragile side of livelihood of farm households suffering major illnesses. Based on this survey, we draw several conclusions so that we can put up with some suggestions and counter plans.

Keywords: Folk Borrowing, Major Diseases, Farm Households, Functiongs.

1 Introduction

The folk borrowing is a financing activity among folk people or between folk people and financial organizations. Because the subjects in this research are farm households suffering major illnesses, a special group in the rural area, the folk borrowing has a unique defined category that it only includes the activity of folk borrowing among relatives, friends, and acquaintances. This kind of activity has an influential effect on their livelihood and production in the rural areas of China for a long time. Especially, when this area lives without social security, the folk borrowing has the ability to share the rick. By using the investigative data and the methods of cross table, we can analyze and review the differences of the folk borrowing scale of peasant households who have serious diseases.

2 The Source of the Data and the Effect of the Folk Borrowing to Peasant Households Sufferin Major Illnesses

2.1 The Source of the Data

Hong 'an and Xiao Chang are two poor counties in national level. Between June and October in 2007, our research team began to stratify sampling in these counties by

Q. Zhou (Ed.): ISAEBD 2011, Part I, CCIS 208, pp. 343–347, 2011.
© Springer-Verlag Berlin Heidelberg 2011

two steps. The first one was to investigate 3 towns which were randomly chosen from those counties. In every town, we picked 100 families in 10 villages each in three towns randomly and equidistantly. Finally, we got the samples of 6,077 families (26349 people). According to the standard of major illness, our second step was to filter 316 samples of farm households suffering major illnesses in 2006 from 6,077 samples families in the ratio of 5% to investigate deeply. Finally, we got 176 of 316 peasant households, who borrowed money from relatives, friends, and acquaintances.The total amount of money of these families is 1,751,661 Yuan, 9,953 Yuan per family and 2061 Yuan a person. The min amount is 130 Yuan and the Max amount is 123,000 Yuan.

2.2 The Effect of the Folk Borrowing to Farm Households Suffering Major Illnesses

Comparison of the Usage of folk Borrowing in Different Economic Conditions.

Table 1. Usage of Folk Borrowing of farm households in Different Economic Conditions

situation Usage	See a doctor		Education		house - building		Wedding & funeral		Daily Expend		Others	
	sample	%	sample	%	sample	%	sample	%	sample	%	sample	%
Poverty	85	76	4	4	7	6	5	5	5	5	6	5
plain	43	69	6	10	2	3	2	3	2	3	7	11
Well-off	4	100	0	0	0	0	0	0	0	0	0	0

From table 1, we know that although peasants are in different conditions, they all borrow money. However, rich ones only borrow money for seeing a doctor. Because of the emergency and the sudden of the diseases, they temporarily have the liquidity difficulty and borrow money from relatives and friends,too. The farm households whose economic conditions are plain and poor can borrow money to do all the things above. This difference can tell that it is fundamental for the poor ones to lack money in a long run. What's more, they use majority money to see a doctor. We can conclude in Table 1 that farm houesholds in different economic conditions depend on the Folk Borrowing differently. The poorer, the more they depend on borrowing money. In another word, the Folk Borrowing can help a lot to poor farm households.

Comparative analysis on the scale of the Folk Borrowing of the farm households in serious ill due to different economic conditions.

When suffering compacts from the serious ill, in that of different economic conditions, these peasants may differ in the scale of money borrowing from their relatives or acquaintances. In the survey, we have known from peasants and the village cadre assessments the peasant divided into three levels: wells-off, plain and poverty, whose money borrowing scales are all reflected in the table 1.

In table 1, we can see the poor peasant households as well as the well-off both commit the folk borrowing . While through the inspection result in counting, seriously peasant households with major illnesses hardly differ in the private borrowing scale just because of their economic condition, but the data show, the three groups in folk borrowing scale do have differences. The well-off peasant households hold in the relatively low and high borrowing scale, up to 2000 Yuan at most and start from 20,000 Yuan at least. While the poor and the plain, especially the poor, scatter in all levels of the borrowing scales. It indicates the worse peasant in the economic condition, the more they depend on the folk borrowing.

Comparative analysis on the scales of serious peasant households with major illnesses due to different levels of their medical expenses.

Medical cost is an important portion of the peasant family expenses, to see a doctor, peasants tend to relatives and friends and neighbors for a loan. Table 2 is the use of scale of different levels of the Private Borrowing and Debit due to the medical.

Table 2. Scales of the folk borrowing of samples families due to different economic conditions (unit:¥ a thousand yuan)

Economic condition	Scales of folk borrowing（y）											
	Y≤2		2<y≤7		7<.y≤12		12<y≤20		y>20		In sum	
	sample	%	sample	%	sample	%	sample	%	sample	%	sample	%
poverty	29	26	35	32	14	13	16	15	16	15	110	100
Plain	24	39	21	34	6	10	6	10	5	8	62	100
Well-off	2	50	0	0	0	0	0	0	2	50	4	100
In sum	55	31	56	32	20	11	22	13	23	13	176	100
significancet test	Pearson chi2(8) = 11.3488 Pr = 0.183											

fees. From it, when the cost of medical care does not exceed 3000 Yuan, 77% of families borrowing scale from illness are below 2000; as medical expenses exceed three thousand dollars but no more than ten thousand folk borrowing scale in 2000 are less than 37%, from 2000 to 12000 are of 53%; As medical expenses exceeds 10,000 and no more than 20,000, 57% of families borrow from 2000 to 12 000. 30% of families are of borrowing scale from 12000 to 20,000; When the medical costs is more than 20,000, 46% are above the scale of 20000.

Comparative analysis on the scale of Folk borrowing of peasant households suffering major illnesses facing with the different risks.

Peasants are facing risks, risks to peasants for the defenses are weak, especially when the peasant family's major worker accidently suffers the risk impact of death, disability, and its production ability and daily life will seriously be affected. And

Table 3. Scales of Folk borrowing of peasant households suffering major illnesses due to medical expense level (unit:¥ a thousand yuan)

Medical cost (m)	Scales of Folk borrowing （y）											
	Y≤2		2<y≤7		7<y≤12		12<y≤20		y>20		In sum	
	sample	%	sample	%	sample	%	sample	%	sample	%	sample	%
M≤3	20	77	4	15	0	0	0	0	2	8	26	100
3 < m≤10	33	37	34	38	13	15	5	6	4	5	89	100
10 < m≤20	0	0	14	42	5	15	10	30	4	12	33	100
M>20	2	7	4	14	2	7	7	25	13	46	28	100
合计	55	31	56	32	20	11	22	13	23	13	176	100
significancet test	Pearson chi2(12) = 93.6344 Pr = 0.000											

Table 4. Scale of folk borrowing of farm households suffering major illnesses facing with the risk impact of house main cash bringer accidentally disabled or died (unit:¥ a thousand yuan).

Having risk impact or not	Scales of the folk borrowing （y）											
	Y≤2		2<y≤7		7<y≤12		12<y≤20		y>20		In sum	
	sample	%	sample	%	sample	%	sample	%	Sample	%	sample	%
Having	2	20.0	0	0.0	2	20.0	3	30.0	3	30.0	10	100
Not having	53	31.9	56	33.7	18	10.9	19	11.5	20	12.1	166	100
In sum	55	31.3	56	31.8	20	11.4	22	12.5	23	13.1	176	100
significancet test	Pearson chi2(4)=9.4223 Pr=0.051											

assist from other sources including the Folk borrowing then prove important. Table 3 reflects the scale of the impact of different risk level of families committing the Folk borrowing. From the table, those of suffering risk impact mentioned above have 12000 in loan, and they account for 60% of the sample; while those of not, 65.5% only have loans less than 7000, which means the former bears a larger scale comparing to the latter. The significancet test also shows the relation between the two is 10% of significance.

3   Conclusion and Suggestions

3.1 Conclusions

Through analysis of cross table, we found dependence on the Folk borrowing exists among the peasant suffering seriously ill—such dependence is more obvious to those who are poor and have work force problem from losing the major worker in the family.in easing the peasant's livelihood, Folk borrowing contributes. Otherwise the way Folk borrowing are functioning is meanwhile reflecting two problems in institution: one is the lack of social security from government; the other is the imperfection of the financial and monetary system, not having functioned by helping the peasants dispersing risks.

3.2 Suggestions

Suggestions pointing at solving problems above go in two:

Government should enhance the invest in social security system, perfecting the new type of cooperative medical insurance system in rural area (XINNONGHE in short) and improving the major illness helping policy.

The dependence that exists above may attribute to the imperfection of the established XINNONGHE, for it sets a low compensating rate, too much restrictive conditions, those that all failed to meet peasants' needs, and fail the XINNONGHE's assisting and securing function.

The innovation of financial and monetary products and service, the promotion and R&D of the commercial insurance, and the service that financial market may serve the rural area, all should be strengthened.

Compared with regular financial loans, the folk borrowing have many advantages, as in the convenience, flexibility and security guarantee etc. but formal finance should strengthen the management, marketing and service, innovate financial and monetary products and service that is more competitive than the folk borrowing; as the awareness of the risk aversion at those in the rural poverty-striking area is rather poor, government ought to improve it: publicize and promote commercial insurance business that includes medical services, endowments, accident preventing, etc. thus disperse the risk peasant households may have, and gear up the service financial market would contribute in rural area.

Acknowledgement. This paper, which is supported by the fund of discipline construction of application economics from Hubei University of Education , is one of the results of research project of Ministry of Education on Humanities and Social Sciences(Grant No.10YJDZH001) and the project called "protection for the people in the rural place against the main diseases" (POVILL) which is supported by The EU Framework Program(Grant No.INCO-CT-2005-517657).

Notes

There are three definitions about major illnesses in this research: (1) farm households spend above is above 1,000 Yuan for hospitalization per capital a year; (2) farm households spend above is above 1,000 Yuan for outpatient service per capital a year; (3) member of family has missed 90 days for work because of diseases. If the situation is suitable in one of three above, it will be definite as serious disease.

References

1. Xiong, J., Ding, S.: The Influential Factors and Effects of NCMS in the Western Rural Place. Seek 1 (2010)
2. Liu, Y., Zuo, T., Qi, G.: The research about how the micro-credit relief the fragile peasant family. Rural Economics 4 (2008)
3. Li, X., Ding, S., Chen, Y., Fengli: The analysis of influential factors of medical service for peasants in the rural Place. Journal of Agrotechnical Economics 2 (2009)

A Study on the Reasons of Insufficiency of Entrepreneurship Initiative of Chinese College Students

Xinyu Hu[1] and Yunjin Tan[2]

[1] The Political Department of Wuhan Polytechnic University,
Wuhan 430023 China
hxu@whpu.edu.cn
[2] School of Economics & Management, Hubei University of Education,
Wuhan 430205 China
tanyunjin@whpu.edu.cn

Abstract. The reasons for entrepreneurship insufficiency of university students are complex, which include restraint of Chinese traditional culture, family education in the process of socialization, and the education system for entering a higher education that block the personality and creativity seriously.

Keywords: entrepreneurship of university students, social culture, primary and secondary education.

1 Introduction

The sample showed that the Chinese college graduates from 2007 to 2009 start their own businesses, and compared to just 1% -1.2% [1], which not only far below the level of developed countries in Europe and America, but also behind in India and other developing countries significantly [2]. What's the reasons for this? Recently, from the published literature, there are two aspects of this issue in a discussion of Chinese academe. On one hand, the support of government and society is not enough. On another hand, the serious shortage and prominent defect on entrepreneurship education is obvious [3]. We believe that this view only shows that the reason is lack of initiative and entrepreneurship which is less comprehensive and superficial. Entrepreneurship is a complex system project, therefore the reasons are extensive. Generally, there must be a relatively broad and in-depth perspective.

In 1990s, in order to solve the large surplus labor force and severe underemployment, the Chinese government clearly put forward the policy that an entrepreneurial idea promotes the employment. At the end of 1989, the meeting, named International Conference on Education for the 21st Century, was held in Beijing and the Chinese official put forward the concept of entrepreneurship education. In 1999, Chinese leader Jiang Zemin pointed out in the third National Education Conference: "We should cultivate the sense of undertaking efforts to help people to develop the educated and entrepreneurial skills and foster more and more entrepreneurs in different sectors through the efforts of the education sector". Then, the ideas of strengthening entrepreneurship education to business to promote

Q. Zhou (Ed.): ISAEBD 2011, Part I, CCIS 208, pp. 348–352, 2011.
© Springer-Verlag Berlin Heidelberg 2011

employment are common at all levels of speeches and government documents. After the beginning of this century, facing huge employment pressure of college graduates after enrollment, the Chinese government and Chinese universities realized the importance of entrepreneurship farther and took a number of measures to strengthen entrepreneurship education for students, encouraging their own businesses. However, the effects of these measures are not satisfactory.

The facts have proved that the support and nurture of government is not enough to solve the problem completely, at the same time, there are other deeper reasons on this issue. Next, we will analyze the deep-seated reasons.

2 The Negative Effects of Traditional Culture on Entrepreneurship

China is a country of long history of autocratic feudal agriculture, which under the rule of the feudal dynasty in the stretch for thousands of years, a society that emphasizes the sameness, devoid of personality is the mainstream of the basic value orientation. The concept of valuing loyalty and loyalty to serve the country constitute a core value of Chinese traditional culture. From the Chinese development process, Confucianism, Taoism, Buddhism and Mexico together account for the mainstream of Chinese thoughts and culture. Although the views of four schools are not uniform, their basic values are highly consistent, such as the gentleman personality of Confucian, hermit personality of Taoist, easygoing personality of Buddhis, and heroic character of Mohist. In the long history, Chinese people for generations are affected by these concepts, so that entrepreneurial and creative impulse have been inhibited greatly.

After the founding of the People's Republic of China, although we established basic policies, such as getting traditional culture essence and discarding its dregs, innovation, in the specific implementation process, this approach has not been really implemented. The uniform understanding on what our essence of traditional culture is, what the dross of the traditional culture is, which should be inherited, which should be discarded, has not formed. In addition to the traditional culture itself to the historical development, it is difficult to achieve but long-term unremitting efforts of several generations. Since the founding of the PRC, we have launched a number of ideological and cultural liberation movements, hoping to remove the traditional sense of superstition by scientific ideology and foster the spirit of modern culture, which is not enough. In fact, today after the smooth progress of reform and opening up, in the minds of most Chinese people, the traditional culture still occupy the mainstream position. Because of the strong atmosphere of traditional culture, innovation and entrepreneurship of Chinese students have been greatly inhibited, which constitutes the lack of initiative of the Chinese college students.

3 The Negative Effects of Socialization on Entrepreneurship

From a sociological perspective, the socialization is proper by human beings. Each individual is able to survive only through socialization to master fundamental social and cultural norms. Although a person's socialization process is done by a variety of ways, from whatever point of view, the family of a person in the role of the socialization process is the first and irreplaceable. From the traditional view of Chinese history, the emphasis on children's education of Chinese family is unparalleled to other countries, but under the influence of traditional and customary, the Chinese concept of family education for their children is not scientific, Chinese families in general tamarind into a "dragon". But their "dragon" is one-sided. All the things are beneath contempt, only high school, has become the fundamental value of most families. In their view, the so-called talent is a good academic record, high test scores, a good college and a good job. Therefore, basic education and career aspirations are not included in family education in China. We found that there is convergence of family education and high degree of consistency in China, most parents do not care about the children's attention or interest in nature and do not encourage children to combine their innovation and entrepreneurship to the actual situation of different family environment. Conversely, almost all the families focus on study, examinations and studies.

We must pay our attention that the pervasive concept of family education and socialization process has an extremely negative impact on the students who want to start their own businesses. In essence, entrepreneurship is the creation and innovation which include knowledge, competence, skills and abilities. The entrepreneurial activity is not only influenced by self-esteem, confidence and impact of values, but also by individual behavior, motivation and attitude constraints. The quality, attitude, knowledge, ability and skill formation and training that entrepreneurs should have possess need a very long process, which must be cultivated from an early age. The practice proved that this innovative spirit and creative ability ought to run through the entire educational process,. It's impossible to succeed just through the stage of university education, higher education and business entrepreneurship training. In recent years, entrepreneurship education in colleges and universities is not ideal, because of course, is multifaceted, but it's not nothing to do with these problems. In summary, our basic conclusion is that Chinese college students in the community in the process of family education lead to the lack of initiative to launch a business, another deep-seated reason.

4   The Negative Effects of Primary and Secondary Education on Entrepreneurship

Entrepreneurship education of colleges and universities in China has not shirked the responsibility for low percentage of entrepreneurship. But if we fully attributed to the issue of entrepreneurship education in colleges and universities, it is less scientific and not fair. In the long process of training on entrepreneurship quality, ability and initiative, the role of entrepreneurship education of colleges and universities is important but limited. Chinese scholars neglected the negative effects of primary and secondary education on entrepreneurship, in fact, whether from the visual angle of education or the psychology, the effect of the education ideology, model, methods and contents of primary and secondary schools is enormous in creativity and innovation. In a sense, it can be said, primary and secondary education on entrepreneurship is even more important than the colleges and universities. Because the primary and secondary education is the most important period in spirit of innovation, primary and secondary students are in career aspirations, awareness and development of the formation age, when education and training can not only have a multiplier effect, but also for future growth and development. However, the reality is that innovation and entrepreneurship of the majority of our schools did not like the schools of developed countries in Europe and America. Our elementary and intermediate schools focus on entering, which killed the majority of large commercial awareness and the creation of young talent to their own businesses.

In particular, as the extending of education and improvement of culture, the active entrepreneurial intention of Chinese students has gradually decreased, "the survey showed that the active entrepreneurial intention of students reached the highest point in upper primary and junior middle school to the high school stage, decreased to a significant decline in college." "From primary school to university, the students are gradually inclined to civil servants, public institutions and monopoly-type concentration of state-owned enterprises, high-income and high intelligence industries, as well as big cities and economically developed areas. There is no significant difference on career aspirations of students from the school's impact, different regions, different levels and different types of primary and secondary schools. This fully shows that it is not only common in our tamarind into a "dragon" by family, but also by school [4], and primary and secondary education considers the dragon as entering a higher school. We believe that the exam-oriented education model, only on imparting knowledge, not spoon-feeding education re-thinking Ability, seriously constrains the personality development of students seriously and stifles the creative talents, which is another deep-seated reason.

5 Conclusion

We analyze deep-seated reasons above, of course, we do not deny the support and importance of government, society, and higher education on college students venture entrepreneurial initiative. In fact, the reasons are complex, multifaceted, but we believe that, it is important to strengthen the deeper reasons which cause this phenomenon in particular.

Through the analysis above, we believe that we should spare no effort as follows besides strengthening the support of government and community and improve entrepreneurship education in order to solve the problem above. First, evaluate Chinese traditional culture scientifically and comprehensively. Chinese traditional culture is formed and developed in a long history of feudal system, so its basic value and core kernel is devoid of individuality. We should be well-known of that. We must be true to get traditional culture essence and discard its dregs, completely abandon the passive components of traditional Chinese culture which is not conducive to character development and spirit creation, vigorously promote the market economy values, and nurture sense of innovation and competitiveness of the whole society. Second, giving full role to the socialization outside the family body is a good way to create a wider world for the children. Third, implement the comprehensive development of virtue, wisdom, education, labor policy conscientiously, reform higher test scores in accordance with existing standards for enrollment as the only selection system, with the enrollment system to influence the reform of primary and secondary school, encourage and promote primary and secondary schools to add the concept of the entrepreneurial ability training into the teaching content, lighten the burden of our students in deed, and expand the space for students on independent development, in order to create advantageous conditions for students on the sense of innovation and entrepreneurship.

Acknowledgement. This paper is one of the results of the key research projects of the "Eleventh Five-Year Plan" on education science in Hubei province(Grant No.2010A046).

References

[1] The Max team of research of Chinese student. The report of employment of Chinese student in, vol. 11. Social Science Literature Publishing (2010)
[2] Wu, J.: The low ratio of entrepreneurship of university students,
http://www.chinanews.com/edu/edu-qzcy/news/
2010/03-22/2182256.shtml
[3] Wu, J.: The commentary of education of entrepreneurship of university students. Modern Educational Science 5 (2009)
[4] Tan, Y.: The different angles research of the problem of unemployment in China. The Learned Journal of Hubei University of Education 4 (2010)

Reflections on the Nature of Circular Economy

Fanrong Kong

School of Economics & Management, HuBei University of Education,
Wuhan 430205 China
kfrong100@yahoo.com.cn

Abstract. The establishment of wuhan two-type society has depended on the development of circular economy, a fundamental way to achieve sustainable development of our economic. Only recognize the nature of circular economy can we grasp the direction of its development. Circular economy is the cycle of marketization, of high-end, and of humanism.

Keywords: Circular economy, marketization, Humanization, high-end.

1 Introduction

For many years, the extensive style of economic growth has brought serious resources and environmental pressures for our country. In this context, our country will promote circulation economy strategic, and will change the mode of economic growth, developing circular economy as fundamental way to achieve sustainable development of our economic. Therefore, wuhan city circle has proposed the construction of "resource-saving" and "environmentally-friendly" two-type society. This goal not only embodies the essential characteristics of circulation economy, also can only rely on the development of circular economy can be achieved. But, thinking circular economy is necessary to pay attention to a fact. In the past a long time, people are talking about in the technical level. Circular economy is not the implementation of some technology promotion and not the stack of some projects either. It's clear that recycle economy theory has affected the whole economy operating system in what extent; How can make our economy run on circular economy specified path. Therefore, it is necessary to clarify some problem in theory.

2 The Nature of Circular Economy

2.1 The Circular Economy Is the Cycle of Marketization

Objectively speaking, the backbone of recycling economic principle grew up in ecology and environmentology which is paid little attention for that conomics theory is quite weak. The negative byproducts of this situation is, circular economy advocates often too stress the role of government and technology, but ignore problems-solving from the system level and the market. So, can have very beautiful

Q. Zhou (Ed.): ISAEBD 2011, Part I, CCIS 208, pp. 353–358, 2011.
© Springer-Verlag Berlin Heidelberg 2011

planning, but hard to accept by market; Can have a very touching pilot, but difficult to popularization. Even so, many pilots just talk about "benefit" generally and vaguely, while its profit skirted round.

Since we chose the market as the basic method of economic elements configuration, market may not be avoided when considering an economic development strategy. Otherwise, this strategy will be difficult to carry out. past circular economic study lack this part of research. Therefore, we began to explore from a minimal problems.

Advocates of circular economy always attack the current economic operation mode is "linear economy" and is "the mass production, a large number of consumption and large amount of waste". Of course, it is true. The problem is why the unreasonable way is so popular in the current economic system? Obviously, only to find unreasonable reason, can eliminate unreasonable itself, also can let the market operation conform to the principle of circular economy. So, this is the fundamental task of circular economy.

In the current market economy, the movement of substance is not the process of uniform continuous in human economic system, but is finished through a series of transaction. In a sense, manufacturing also exists such transactions between the former working procedure and the next. We can regard the consumption as a kind of production process, and its "product" is "satisfaction".

Then, material flow in the economic system was abstracted as a series of trading links, mining, etc are links in the specific content. These links linked together, formed the so-called value chain. The value chain guide material flow.

The process of this kind of material from one link to another link, also should be a value added process. For producers, it means the corresponding link can produce acceptable profits. For consumers, this means that consumption of such thing let him feel "value", or he could obtain acceptable consumer surplus. The so-called circular economy, means that exist such value chain, which every link can produce acceptable value. If this value chain leads to the open and close of the market logistics chain, that is the circular economy. This material flow and value generated unity is the basic starting point we insist on when we talk about circular economy.

This value chain which is formed through the transaction will break if a certain part of cannot produce acceptable interests, which can lead to two kind of situations: the first one is, logistics will be diverted. real single value chain don't exist in reality, but be a net by many such chain, market economy is the network which consist of countless transaction relationship. When a link does not produce enough profit, the essence of profit drives capital, to turn to other logistics with capital is diverted. The second one is not diverted, then lead to the abandoned, the garbage is out.

Generally speaking "junk is misplaced resources" while encouraging, but not science. We should consider two kind of situations:

First, market defect resulted in abandoned produce or excessive growth. Or, the externality caused fault of logistics, and cause the value chain rupture and the accumulation of rubbish. In source ,the production process the first industry is usually underestimated and even ignore the environment and ecological cost. For example, extractive industries generally does not take mining subsidence, pollution and ecological restoration into consideration, also don't consider the cost of essence value of natural resources. Forest tree cutting generally doesn't consider the existence value of live trees, planting don't consider the losses of land fertility, fertilizers and pesticides pollution cost. Under the action of general equilibrium or profit homogenisation, the price of primary product is lower than they should have been.

The low prices makes people believe the related resources are abundant. Generating such resources for the wrong place, producers will tend to use more primary products, or the consumer consume more intensive consumptive product. In the international market, the increase of the car's sales of luxurious and fuel consumption general relate with the decrease of oil prices. Furthermore, the whole social material consumption increases promoted abandoned increase. In waste recycled level, cheap primary products is the resistance of this recycle.

Secondly, technical related regeneration or recycling resource is not mature. If this technical immaturity causes regeneration product low quality or high prices, the process of recycle will block in the market. But strictly speaking, technological factors don't be an independent reason to hinder circulation for that they are subjects to the market trends, which will be largely controlled by capital. If cheap of natural resources cause capital turn to excessive use of primary products, r&d of renewable resources field will suffer capital snub.

In sum: in a given system and technical conditions, the garbage is rubbish. Because in a spontaneous market, if the rubbish in some ingredients can generate profits, someone will do this thing. We therefore discuss circular economy, because abandon phenomenon exist unreasonable component, exist potential of further reasonable use material, promoting circulation. Circular economy is studying how to eradicate the barriers between the realization and potential.

The judge has shown direction of circular economy: system innovation and technological innovation. The system innovation is in a more basic position. It can change the behavior of producers and consumers make capital flow to sustainable development. The direction of technology trend is also changed correspondingly. So, system fields should be paid more attentions. Meanwhile, circular economy and must be system ability strong market economy. The government's main mission is to set up complete market system, and formed the ability of executing this system effectively.

2.2 The Circular Economy Is the Cycle of High-End

The so-called high-end, means increase knowledge and technical of circulation industry chain,and the process improve its value-added. Talking about circular economy, the prejudices that cycle economy and "pick garbage" hook should be eliminated, thought it is traditional in the sense of "waste materials" recycle, then consider whether it allow foreign labor or laid-off workers to collect rubbish.

I think the cycle economy is no vitality. It is not difficult to imagine, even if the market price of primary products don't drop any longer, in the long term, a social welfare level rise will always be the purpose of our development, and thus lead to the rise of labor prices. It is the same with the drop of primary product price, It can compress waste value space, and make more and more waste lost their circulation value.

Rising trend of laborer return can't happen in a normal society. Therefore, the development of circular economy is not to use more and more cheaper laborer to collect rubbish. A kind of promising circular economy is as far as possible not to make products into rubbish.

This process must start from producer responsibility and market organization. Due to producers are responsible for the whole life cycle, it faced a choice: recollect the product consumers no longer use, or as waste disposal, and manufacture new products also need to buy raw materials; Or use recycled products to product new goods. In a market economy, interests of course always govern their decision-making. The higher the price of raw materials, the greater the cost of the disposal of rubbish and it is more likely to produce Recycle.

This pressure will cause a series of market and technological revolution. First, the producer will design the products that can use recyclely. Parts of the component after inspecting can be qualified for production of new products or be secondary products at low price, part then generate raw material .

At the other end of the market, in consumers, producers may retain the ownership of the products. Consumers enjoy service supplied by producers, no longer "after-sales service", but "service" period including product, just the same with paying property fee, pay such services on schedule. In this mode, producers explore new profit growth space from three directions. One is the professional service is better than product maintenance by consumers and it make product operate much better, and its life more long. Second one is that good service always encourages consumers to generate new needs, thus brings new opportunities for the enterprise. Third one is that when products scrap, really scrap maybe just a small part, enterprise still owns most of the value of its useful. Of course, one of the difficulties in this mode is how to meet the diversity and personality requirements of the customers, and the pursuit of novel. Its way is to increase possible of product combinations.

High-end also means on the premise of respect for nature: we should take advantage of all kinds of natural forces as much as possible. Recycle economy cannot be understood as merely all kinds of material in the human economic inner recycle. A building, through improve its design ,is able to maximize the use of natural factors such as day-lighting, ventilated, tempering, is actually use natural service continuously. A piece of farmland, if reasonable use, can be in production ,also can produce purify environment, produce landscape effect, water conservation, we can save a lot of investment, energy and raw material if using this continuously nature service.

2.3 The Circular Economy Is the Cycle of Humanism

Along with the advance of circular economy, it will occur that more and more services will substitute for products. Even, the essence of circular economy is a kind of service economy. Every link that the above high-end circular economy involves needs higher skills, therefore, it is a high-end industry, can create a lot of labor chances that pay higher. This is a kind of economic operation mode, which more dependent on human capital, less dependent on consumption of natural resources, therefore, it can be called the human capital intensive economy.

In the more macro level, the circular economy can be understood as a mode , which substitute natural resources for manpower capital, substitute the development of human for depriving of development of nature. Circular economy, the scientific outlook on development and the people-centered development has the close relation. Developing circular economy, is actively implementing the scientific concept of development in actual work. Developing circular economy must be people-oriented, is to put the interests of the people as a whole work starting point and the foothold, constantly satisfy people's various requirements and promote the all-round development of man; The appearance of circular economy is constantly optimize the resources utilization, but its nature is a kind of natural capital substitute for manpower capital the economic operation mode.

This means that social and economic life is reducing materialized ,economy development and improving people's welfare will less dependent on material resources consumption, more dependent on human own efforts, rely on interpersonal services, human social organization and management improvement , the increasing of human knowledge and technology level and the progress of our way of life.

In the economic operation, circulation economy should be full of human caring. The circulation of Circular economy requires requires relying on the increased number of above service flow and quality improvement basic material conditions. In this, then we need to understand a truth: certain material products that can be added services in most cases is no limit, it is the biggest space of sustainable development. Making service instead of material circulation, should be considered as a higher state of cycle.

The most fundamental goal of Circular economy is to create higher welfare for people with little cost. Achieve such a goal does not exist theory and technical difficulties; this is the development track of the many developed countries. We need the optimization of development concept, lifestyle and system, and so on. Many units require office staff to work with wearing suits all throughout the year, this action now whether deserves reflection? A society generally having frugal consciousness, crisis consciousness is a performance of strong, luxury is a kind of social of diabetes. In this issue, the government's role model is extremely important. If the government in building energy-saving, thrift in office, efficient use of regenerate office supplier and public transport, can make a good start.

3 The Functions of the Three Nature of Circle Economy

Based on three characteristics of circle economy, we can divide circle economy to three parts: economy subsystem, social subsystem, and environment subsystem. The aim of economy subsystem is to realize the circle economy happened in primary, secondary, and tertiary industry so that the industry structure can be improved and the economy can increase. The goal of social subsystem is to maintain the social progress and sustain so that people can have a better and secure life, which reflect the characteristic of humanism of circle economy. The purpose of environment subsystem is to use resources eternally and improve the ameliorate the environment so that human can save the resources, reduce the wastes, control the pollution, and protect the surroundings, which reflect the superior of the circle economy.

Acknowledgements. This article is supported by the funds from Hubei University of Education (Grant No: 2009B006).

References

1. Xu, X.: The research for the agriculture circle economy in Oi Tung Estate of Shiga County. Economic Problems 3 (2007)
2. He, D.: Circle economy is a superior type of regional economies. Seek 9 (2006)

The Model of Price Discovery in Fresh Agri-Product Market after Natural Crisis

Lai Wei[1], Hong Chen[2], and Xiaolin Liu[1]

[1] College of Economics and Management, Sichuan Agricultural University,
611134 Chengdu, China
[2] School of Management and Economics, UESTC, 610054 Chengdu, China
wlfuture1969@hotmail.com

Abstract. The paper studies how to use the price discovery model to treat post-disaster reconstruction of fresh agri-product market price under the e-commerce environment. The price discovery model can effectively solve the contradiction between supply and demand in the situation that logistical facilities are greatly influenced by natural disasters. So it can help us from a new perspective to discuss and solve some decision-making problems about the price recovery and reconstruction of fresh agri-product markets. Sichuan Province as an example explains how the price discovery model is achieved. The result shows that even in the situation that infrastructures are severely effected by natural disasters, the price discovery model can help to find abnormal prices of fresh agriculture products after natural crisis and deal with the consequent conflicts, thereby helping the government to regulate and make decisions.

Keywords: price discovery, fresh agri-product market, natural crisis, electronic commerce.

1 Introduction

In May 2008 the Wenchuan Earthquake made Sichuan logistics infrastructure tumble-ed. The transportation of various relief resources and the wounded people made the fragile logistics line for fresh agri-products more blocked. Although this region has achieved a higher degree of deregulation in comparison to other parts of the country, it is not homogeneous in itself. The wholesale market is characterized by regional subsections. In an efficiently working geographic fresh agri-product market regional prices equal the marginal valuation of net benefits at different regional locations. Specifically, prices provide the right incentives for decisions, both in the short- and long-run (Oren et al., 1995). Since regional price differences also reflect the existence of logistics constraints, the direction of flows during off peak and peak periods may influence market power between sub-regions. Logistics cost is not prohibitive within these individual regions, but congestion costs exist interregionally. This outcome may result from logistics constraints, demand and supply conditions, the degree of regional deregulation, or some combination of the three.

Q. Zhou (Ed.): ISAEBD 2011, Part I, CCIS 208, pp. 359–365, 2011.
© Springer-Verlag Berlin Heidelberg 2011

Entering the 21st century, the domestic large fresh produce e-commerce transact-tions gradually into the mainstream, due to zero cost information search, agricultural supplier is always looking for some products of the highest price for gain more profit opportunities. Coordination in the electronic commerce network is an important issue for reliable fresh agri-product supply. Fresh agri-products follow the path of the largest margin and cannot be stored chronically. Every logistics transmission path has a maximal pass capacity that sets an upper limit on the flow on that path. Maximal pass capacity on a single path affects other paths in the logistics network. A change in supply or demand at any node will influence the logistics on the constrained path, which in turn influences on other parallel paths in the logistics network. Load magnitude constraints are another source of congestion on logistics paths. Even when the pass capacity limits are not constraining, load limits can constrain pass capacity of the logistics network. Some argue that free markets cannot deal with such issues and that central coordination and regulation are needed to address these "loop-flow" problems. Most experts reject these arguments, but we still must be aware of the potential inefficiencies of developing competitive markets and sensitive to evidence of their existence, so that corrective action can be appropriately designed and implemented before problems get out of hand.

There are two widely used measures of price discovery for multiple markets that share a common random walk efficient price. Hasbrouck[1] focuses on the variance of the efficient price innovation, and defines one market's information share (IS) as the proportion of the efficient price innovation variance attributable to that market. In contrast, Booth et. al.[2], Chu et. al.[3], and Harris et. al. (2002)[4], adopting the permanent-transitory decomposition technique in Gonzalo and Granger(1995), focus on the composition of the efficient price innovation and measure one market's contribution to price discovery by the component weight of that market in forming the efficient price innovation. Hereafter, we refer to this measure of price discovery as component share (CS). Despite their different focuses, both approaches use co-integration to constrain multiple market prices to share a common efficient price, and both approaches use a reduced form vector error correction (VEC) model for estimation purposes.

For empirical implementations, Hasbrouck[5] suggests sampling at very high frequencies to reduce the contemporaneous correlation in the reduced form residuals between markets that is created by time aggregation. Mark R. et. al [6] by examining the lead-lag relationships between weekly Bloch Benchmark forward prices, spot prices, and lumber futures prices, and find that for the random lengths lumber market the three month Bloch Benchmark prices lead both spot prices and futures prices. Gregory et. al[7] empirically investigate the degree of integration that existed prior to the cost increases that caused emergency conditions in the Western Systems Coordinating Council (WSCC), particularly California, during the summer of 2000.

Price discovery measures are supposed to distinguish which market prices incorporate new information regarding fundamental value more quickly and efficiently. Baillie et. al[8], Lehmann[9] and Hasbrouck[10] construct simple microstructure models with various price discovery lead-lag structures and provide a comparative analysis of the IS and CS. Bingcheng et. al (2007) analyze the structural determinants of two widely used measures of price discovery between multiple markets that trade closely-related securities.

Since September 2008, Sichuan fresh agri-product market has been restructured in an effort to promote development. But the predominant ones among them are (1) reliance on spot market transactions required by the initial market design and the concomitant inability of load serving entities to engage in forward contracting; (2) local market power of some suppliers due to logistics constraints; and (3) a lack of retail price signals reflecting changing cost conditions in fresh agri-product supply. This paper focuses on the first two issues. Specifically, we bring forward the degree of market integration that existed prior to the cost increases that caused emergency conditions since the autumn 2008.

The paper is organized as follows. Section 2 and Section 3 analyze the model of realization and applications respectively. Section 4 offers conclusion and future research.

2 The Model of Realization

A time series is said to be non-stationary if any shock to the system is permanent. On the other hand, shocks to a trend-stationary time series are temporary, and the series will eventually revert to its long-run mean growth rate. It is not apparent that fresh agri-product spot prices should be non-stationary. Some evidence shows that the prices have some trend-stationary characteristics. On the one hand, fresh agri-product prices respond to generation unit outages when could not be sold in time; on the other hand, nominal prices are affected by the rate of inflation but, when the market chain is restored, price reverts back to its original trend. In other words, some shocks to the system have competitive effects on the level of prices. The modeling of a non-stationary time series necessitates more different statistical techniques than the modeling of a trend-stationary series. Therefore, each series must be tested individually for the presence of unit roots.

The consumption of fresh agri-products exhibits seasonality, so does its price. To account for these seasonal effects, seasonal dummy variables for 12 months of the year are created, and each series is regressed against a constant, a deterministic trend and the seasonal dummy variables. Thus, the following model was estimated for each price series:

$$y_{it}=\alpha_0+\alpha_1 t+\beta_1\xi_1+\cdots+\beta_{12}\xi_{12}+\varepsilon_{it}. \tag{1}$$

where y_{it} is the spot price from the ith spot market in time t, t a deterministic time trend, and ξ_j j=1,2, $\cdots$, 12 are monthly dummies. The residuals represent the detrended, seasonally adjusted series of spot prices. In each of the regressions, the time trend is significant at the 1% (most restrictive) level, indicating that both peak and off-peak prices rise over the time period studied.

2.1 Tests for Unit Roots

Through test each de-trended peak and off-peak price series for the presence of unit roots are the Augmented Dickey–Fuller (ADF) procedure as presented in Enders (1995). ADF test statistics are sensitive to the number of lags included in the regression; including too many lags reduces the power of the test to reject the null hypothesis of a unit root since it results in a loss of degrees of freedom, while including too few lags will not capture the actual data generating process and will cause errors to be correlated. The objective of introducing autoregressive terms is, thus, to achieve parsimony. To find the appropriate number of lags for each series, we examine the Ljung–Box Q-statistics for different lag lengths.

2.2 Tests of Granger Causality

If there is arbitrage among different fresh agri-product spot markets, prices in a certain market should respond to price changes in another market. Where this is the case, prices in one market can help predict prices in the other market. Tests of Granger causality will indicate whether lagged values of a certain variables are helpful in forecasting the current values of another variable in the short run.

To perform these tests, the following VAR is specified:

$$SP_t = \gamma_0 + \gamma_1 SP_{t-1} + \cdots + \gamma_q SP_{t-q} + \varepsilon_t . \tag{2}$$

When SP is the vector of de-trended spot prices, A_0 a vector of constants, $\gamma_0, \gamma_1, \gamma_2, \cdots, \gamma_q$ the coefficient vectors, and q is the appropriate autoregressive lag length. VAR model is particularly useful in examining Granger causality among time series variables. However, any test of Granger causality in the context of a VAR is sensitive to different autoregressive lag lengths. Therefore, we estimate the appropriate autoregressive form by evaluating different lag lengths on the basis of the Akaike Information Criterion (AIC) procedure. After specifying the appropriate autoregre-ssive lag lengths, Granger causality can be assessed by testing the joint significance of the lags in the equations for each dependent variable included in the VAR. An F-test is asymptotically valid for testing the joint significance of the lagged variables. If a calculated F-statistic is significant for the lagged variables of a particular series, it can be concluded that the independent variable under examination is Granger caused by the dependent lagged variables.

2.3 Common Features and Structural Characteristics

Correlation (co-movement) between one trend-stationary price series and another is evidence of common long-run influences among markets, because it implies that participants in each market respond to the same information as their actions jointly determine the underlying growth paths of the two series. Testing for long-run correlation between trend-stationary time series involves performing a least squares regression of every original (not de-trended) series on each of the others and testing the coefficients for significance. Rejection of the null hypothesis of zero for the coefficient on a repressor is evidence for a long-run relationship (a common feature) between the two markets, but a stronger version of this test requires that the coefficient not be significantly different from one. This stronger form of long-run integration is necessary for the so-called "law of one price" to hold, and is therefore an indication that the assets being traded in different markets are seen as perfect substitutes. Furthermore, the general results from the previous section may obscure a more fundamental long-run influence on fresh agri-product prices resulting from structural change after natural disasters.

3 Applications

The methods above provide a good approach for the post-disaster reconstruction of the fresh produce under the circumstances of e-commerce. The realization methods include the following steps:

3.1 Empirical Data Acquisition and Processing

In 2000, the first e-commerce website came into existed. By the first half of 2008, all kinds of e-commerce websites relevant to fresh produce, from product promotion to online transactions, had reached more than 20,000. They are playing a very important role in informing the demands of different areas in Sichuan and regulating prices.

Although the earthquake, occurred on the May 12, 2008, caused great casualties and badly damaged the logistical infrastructure and planting and breeding bases across Sichuan, it did no actual harm to the virtual e-commerce trade platform. Through the collection and analysis of the retail and wholesale prices of fresh produce on the e-commerce platform, how to use the aids and support of people all over the country to reconstruct the fresh produce market is the key to the disaster because it is closely related to people's life.

The restoration and reconstruction of the raw agri-products include two different stages. One is relief which is mainly in the first three months after disasters. Like blood transfusion, free fresh produce from foreign countries and our own nation is brought for the victims. Then the second stage—hemopoiesis, namely the self recovery of the market comes. Although there are many unpaid aids on this stage, the price of fresh produce will be gradually directed to the level before the earthquake.

The paper focuses on the clarification of the second stage. At this stage, the data acquisition of e-commerce platform mainly relies on the local market management departments and industry associations. After nearly ten-year construction and improvement of software and hardware infrastructure and e-commerce system, they can basically undertake this task in spite of the low transparency of price information. Compared with the software and hardware equipment, the lack of qualified personnel is the biggest problem. They are required not only to skillfully operate computer software and hardware, ORACAL or SQL SERVER database management system but also to use such large data analysis software as SAS. It is difficult to own such personnel because of the relatively low salary level in agricultural industry.

The 11counties of Sichuan Province in Table 1, which were severely damaged by the Wenchuan Earthquake, are taken as the research subjects.

3.2 Analysis of Results

Through the implementation steps of section 2, some statistical data (Table 2) can be acquired by using relevant software. While there are still unidirectional causality for peak prices or no peak price causality whatsoever, mostly the peak price results

Table 1. The counties of research subjects

	Counties		Counties
1	Wenchuan	7	Dujiangyan
2	Beichuan	8	Pengzhou
3	Qingchuan	9	Jiangyou
4	Maoxian	10	Luzhou
5	Lixian	11	Shifang
6	Mianzhu		

indicate bidirectional causality (at the 5% significance level) for almost every market pair, That is to say, peak prices in most markets are significantly affected by other markets' prices. On the other hand, off-peak prices are not nearly as uniform, indicating a number of purely unidirectional relationships. As with peak prices, some markets exhibit no causality whatsoever in off-peak prices. The significant number of exceptions to bi-directional causality among these markets indicates the possibility of geographic or other constraints that may have prevented effective arbitrage.

Table 2. Augmented Dickey–Fuller tests

Counties	ADF statistic off-peak	Lag length off-peak	ADF statistic peak	Lag length peak
Wenchuan	−7.32	8	−5.31	19
Beichuan	−6.13	9	−7.05	18
Qingchuan	−8.26	9	−6.12	18
Maoxian	−5.03	14	−6.24	12
Lixian	−6.26	9	−6.53	16
Mianzhu	−4.80	15	−5.01	14
Dujiangyan	−5.26	10	−5.88	8
Pengzhou	−5.17	7	−4.92	8
Jiangyou	−6.03	10	−6.82	14
Luzhou	−4.33	11	−5.79	13
Shifang	−4.81	8	−5.69	12

Furthermore, the general results from above may obscure a more fundamental long-run influence on the prices resulting from structural change after natural crisis. The specific regime shift relates to the establishment of the free relief to regulate trade in fresh agri-product for the canton or town after September, 2008. Therefore, we need test for structural change in the relationship between each peak and off-peak pair using a Chow test for a regime shift at this date.

These test results may indicate that the establishment of the equilibrium system of fresh produce market price after natural disasters brought about an important change in the structural relationship between most markets in the network. In order to see how important, researchers need re-estimate the structural VAR, restricting the data set to only the post-natural crisis observations. They would find that the occurrence of natural disasters had a dramatic impact on the degree of integration among market pairs for both peak and off-peak prices. These possible results will play an important role in researching the reconstruction and restoration of a balanced post-disaster fresh produce market price.

4 Conclusions

Based on the characteristics of price transmission and the mutual influence of prices of fresh produce in the e-commerce situation, the paper uses the price discovery theory and takes Sichuan Province for example to discuss the price recovery of fresh produce after natural disasters. The price discovery model can be realized and applied to the reconstruction of equilibrium price chain in the general consumer market chain after natural disasters. Since Sichuan is located in the western part of China and the development of e-commerce is backward and scattered, it will take a long time to establish a unified price database, thus causing difficulties in collecting data. So the main purpose of the paper is to put forward the method and the more empirical researches will be conducted after collecting enough data.

Acknowledgment. The research was sponsored by the Fund of Sichuan Center for Rural Development Research (CR1027) and the Fund for National Natural Science Foundation of China (70773017).

References

1. Hasbrouck, J.: One security, many markets: Determining the contributions to price discovery. Journal of Finance 50, 1175–1199 (1995)
2. Booth, G.G., So, R.W., Tse, Y.: Price discovery in the German equity index derivatives markets. Journal of Futures Markets 19, 619–643 (1999)
3. Chu, Q.C., Hsieh, W.G., Tse, Y.: Price discovery on the S&P 500 index markets: an analysis of spot index, index futures and SPDRs. International Review of Financial Analysis 8, 21–34 (1999)
4. Harris, F.H., Thomas, H., Robert, A.: Security price adjustment across exchanges: an investigation of common factor components for Dow stocks. Journal of Financial Markets 5, 277–308 (2002)
5. Hasbrouck, J.: Intraday price formation in U.S. equity index markets. Journal of Finance 58, 2375–2400 (2003)
6. Manfredo, M.R., Sanders, D.R.: American Agricultural Economics Association Annual Meeting, Long Beach, California, July 23-26 (2006)
7. Dempster, G., Isaacs, J., Smith, N.: Price discovery in restructured electricity markets. Resource and Energy Economics 30, 250–259 (2008)
8. Baillie, R.T., Geoffrey Booth, G., Tse, Y., Zabotina, T.: Price discovery and common factor models. Journal of Financial Markets 5, 309–321 (2002)
9. Lehmann, B.N.: Some desiderata for the measurement of price discovery across markets. Journal of Financial Markets 5, 259–276 (2002)
10. Hasbrouck, J.: Stalking the "efficient price" in market microstructure specifications: an overview. Journal of Financial Markets 5, 329–339 (2002)

The Current Situation of Development and Research on Problems of Self-organization of Youth under the Background of Internet

Fengni Gao, Enyi Zhou, and Shouguo Li

College of Management, Xi'an University of Architecture Technology, China
nini5961@sohu.com

Abstract. Young people are a powerful driving force to promote social progress. With the development of Internet technology, economy and society, the Internet self-organizations of young people have been developing rapidly and increasing to a huge number. Generally speaking, the Internet self-organization of youth is positive, healthy and progressive organization, which can adapt to the sub-cultural phenomenon by satisfying in various degrees the contemporary young people's needs for social interaction, leisure and entertainment which in return form the sub-cultural phenomenon. At the same time, this kind of organization has built a platform to address the problems in relationship and marriage, life, work and participation in various social activities of young people. However, there are still various practical problems in the development of the Internet self-organization, so it is very necessary to research the Internet self-organization of the youth in our country.

Keywords: Internet, Self-organization of Youth, Supervision and Management.

1 Introduction

The youth are not just a simple social group, but also they are a strong driving force to promote social progress in the contemporary society. Hu Jintao points out: "A far-sighted nationality always pays concerned attention to the youth; a far-sighted political party always considers the youth as an important force to promote the development of history and social progress." [1] In the process of social development, the youth's organizations tap the wisdom and intelligence of their great number of members, excellently completing the important task of management on national youth affairs endowed by our Party and country turning to be the main force and vanguard. What is the self-organization of youth? Many domestic scholars have given some different descriptions. Some scholars believe that the self-organization of youth is a kind of non-governmental organization which establishes, develops, operates and manages independently with a certain scale, constitutions and organizational framework.[2] Some other scholars believe that self-organization of youth is one kind of organization which is neither registered in the local civil affairs departments and as

Q. Zhou (Ed.): ISAEBD 2011, Part I, CCIS 208, pp. 366–373, 2011.
© Springer-Verlag Berlin Heidelberg 2011

legal personality, nor registered in office, organization, enterprise and public institution. This kind of organization establishes, develops and operates independently and spontaneously. It is an active organization for youth in social life and a collective that are formed based on the age characteristics or the special interests and needs of the youth in order to realize some certain goal according to certain rules. [3] From the perspective of self-organization, we believe that youth self-organization is a core character which is spontaneously formed by more than three young people who independently establish it, cultivate it and operate it based on a certain interest. Its structure and function are increasingly complex and diversified with each passing day, and it maintains continuous contact with the youth groups in the external environment. Internet self-organization of youth is one kind of spontaneous and independent civil organization sponsored and developed by young people through Internet association based on Internet. It attracts a large number of young people, and it is a new mode of organization and assembly in contemporary youth groups. It only has the features of independence, openness and creativity; it also has the characteristics of sense of time, freshness and attractiveness. With the development of society, young people has more self-conscious, especially since the medium -- Internet was widely used, they have more smooth channel to express their willingness and convenient way to exchange ideas with the people who have the same interests with them. As a result, the Internet self-organization was born, and since then, it has been developing prosperously. The spontaneously formed organizations based on Internet and hobbies are exerting influence on us, and it has changed our way of life, while, some new problems arises, the study on Internet self-organization of youth becomes necessary.

2   Analysis on Current Situation and Characteristics of Young Internet Users in China

According to the "Statistics Report on Twenty-seventh China Internet Development" released by China Internet Information Center, by December 2010, China's Internet users reached 457 million, increasing 7,330 million compared with the end of 2009; Internet penetration rose by 34.3 %, increasing 5.4% compared with 2009. The proportion of Chinese Internet users at the age of 20 to 29 increased from 28.6% in 2009 to 29.8%; the proportion of Internet users at the age of 30 to 39 continued to increase, from 21.5% by the end of 2009 rising to 23.4%. The proportion of Internet users with junior high school degree increased significantly, growing from 26.8% to 32.8%; The proportion of Internet users with a high school degree declined from 40.2% to 35.7% for the first time, decreasing 4.5%.

The number of Chinese Internet users with junior high school degree increased obviously in the year of 2010, and the proportion increased from 26.8% to 32.8%, increasing 6%. The number of Internet users with high school degree decreased for the first time, and the proportion declined from 40.2% to 35.7%, decreasing 4.5%. The Internet users with college degree, and bachelor degree or above maintained the comparatively declining status.

Table 1. [4] The data come from the Statistics Report on Twenty-seventh China Internet Development

Date	The proportion of Chinese Internet users of 20 to 29 years old	The proportion of Internet users of 30 to 39 years old	Total Internet users
			(Billion)
2007	38.10%	20.50%	2.1
2008	31.50%	17.60%	2.98
2009	28.60%	21.50%	3.84
2010	29.80%	23.40%	4.57

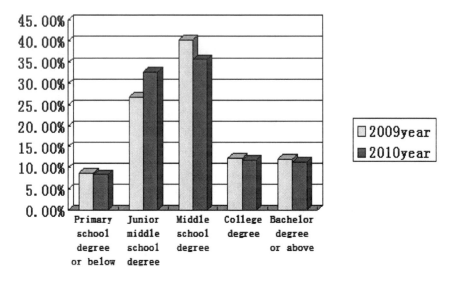

Fig. 1. 2009.12-2010.12 Education Structure users

With the development of the Internet and its combination with telecommunications technologies, the Internet offers more and more services and becomes more and more powerful. "The Internet is no longer a simple tool; it increasingly penetrates into people's daily lives, gradually developing into a virtual community." The virtual space of Internet becomes a new public social area for youth, and the learning, living and Internet working have become the mainstream of part of young people. Thus, the phenomenon of "Internet cluster" and "online community" for young people has become increasingly visible, and Internet organizations and groups taking youth as mainstay emerge endlessly. The Internet self-organization has influenced and changed profoundly on the interaction patterns and collective participation mode of young people, the impact on the philosophy of life, thinking and behavior, entertainment and learning mode growing with each passing day. For example, the services such as "circles" offered by Sina, Sohu and other major portals make the users who have a common interest can contact each other and organize activities more easily.

According to "Statistics Report on China Internet Development ", applications in business in 2010 maintained a rapid development momentum due to large-scale development of power and commercial enterprises and the accumulation of users' habits. The number of customers in business application grew rapidly, and the online shopping customers grew 48.6%, being the fastest growing application of the users. The yearly growth online payment and online banking respectively reached to 45.8% and 48.2%, exceeding greatly the other types of Internet applications. In addition to the instant messaging, search engines, online news, e-mail, and other information and communication functions, the entertainment function of Internet is the main content of young people to use the Internet. From the perspective of Internet applications of the young people, these are obvious: compared with 2009, the applications of information and communication functions such as instant messaging, search engines, blog applications, social Internet sites, online literature, online shopping and BBS forums for young people grew ; while the application of entertainment functions such as online music ,web video and online game which were the important content of young people's daily life before 2009 declined. This phenomenon indicates that Internet application of youth is gradually becoming mature.

3   Analysis on Current Situation and Characteristics of Internet Self-Organization of Youth in China

3.1   Analysis on Current Situation

The birth and development of Internet Self-organization of youth is the result of the economic and social development and the civilization progress. Using the Internet is already a normal life of contemporary youth, and it is a necessary requirement for the development of diversified culture of youth. The self-organization of youth can adapt to the sub-cultural phenomenon by satisfying in various degrees the contemporary young people's needs for social interaction, leisure and entertainment that in return form the sub-cultural phenomenon. At the same time, this kind of organization has built a platform for activities to address the problems in relationship and marriage, life, work and participation in various social activities of young people. Although the contemporary youth share some obvious group features, their growth and life tracks reflect a strong "delicate trend", especially in the last 10 years, new groups such as fan groups, enthusiasts, houseman and house women, self-service tourists have been generated. To sum up, there are several types of Internet self-organization of youth: one is the online Internet group, which is composed by the young people who have the same Internet interests. Its members from all over the country, and they make friends on the sites without involving off-line contacts, such as BBS, blog, Internet society and so on. The other one is a hybrid self-organization, such as public welfare organizations, sports groups, tourist groups, flea markets, marriage-seeking and friends-making, fans groups, etc. These organizations use website, blog, QQ group, MSN Messenger as the base camp or media to discuss, send messages, assembly members before each off-line field activity.

3.2 The Features

Judging from the current development trend, the Internet self-organization of youth gradually begins to form the fundamental nature of realizing the self-organization, but the Internet self-organization of youth is different from the self-organization of youth in reality, it has some special features.

First, the participation rate in Internet self-organization of youth is high, and the membership is complex. Youth is in a special phase for sharing feelings, while their needs cannot be satisfied in the adult society and formal social organizations, thus, they turn to their own organizations. The emergence of Internet self-organization of youth meets the psychological needs of different levels and groups of young people. In particular, it can make up the inferiority complex and marginalization of the young people in the middle layer. Actually, the inferiority complex and marginalization are produced by formal organizations. The Internet self-organization of youth enhances a sense of belonging for the groups of young people, so it can meet the needs of young people's autonomy. What's more, the Internet self-organization of youth itself does not require registration in management department. The main members are connected by interest and predestination, and there are many web sites providing application services with various forms. The applicant can not only join in many different types of self-organization, but also create multiple Internet self-organizations. The equality, freedom and relaxed organizational culture are advocated in the self-organization, and there is no requirement for social status, lifestyle, status and occupation of the members that are required in formal organization. The Internet self-organizations are not influenced by the secular values, so the individual's identity attributes, social attributes and regional property of youth are no longer the barriers to join the online self-organization and participate in the activities in the organization. At the same time, there are few restrictions on members' speech. Each member is the releaser of information and the recipient of information, the member's strong enthusiasm in participation being stimulated in interaction. Therefore, membership of the Internet self-organization is quite complex.

Secondly, Information dissemination in Internet self-organization of youth is fast, simple and efficient. The information dissemination in Internet self-organization of youth has fast process and simple path with the elimination of many transits and the media in the process, so that the organizational structure is simpler, flat with high efficiency compared with the traditional self-organization of youth in the past. According to modern management theory, an organization with a high degree of flattening can eliminate the lengthy linear organized information dissemination channels, the awkward process of organization and operation turning to be more efficient.

Thirdly, structure of the Internet self-organization of youth is loose, operation is still not perfect, lacking in constraints. In the aspect of membership, there is no strict eligibility restriction and regulation in participation and quit for most members in the self-organizations of youth. The cost of register in a variety of Internet groups is relatively low, and the rate of check in and checkout in the Internet organization is quite high. Therefore, the relationship within is looser with more mobility than the organization in the reality. Most of Internet self-organizations of youth belong to the non-governmental organization, and they can be registered freely and virtually, different people can use the virtual identity to realize the register. As for the majority of Internet self-organizations of youth are not the component of the government or the sub-authorities, there is no traditional management system to monitor the organization. Various self-organizations of youth in society have no competent units, so the organization's decisions and actions are free from or nearly free from other effects, the degree of organization being quite lower.

Finally, the Internet self-organization of youth has strong independence, lacking in monitoring. The current Internet self-organization of youth still belongs to the informal organization, and there are many holes in management regulations. According to "Governing Regulations on the Registration of social groups", China's current social groups do not include Internet organization. From this perspective, Internet organizations are illegal social organizations. For example, in December 2006, Civil Affairs Bureau of Chongwen District in Beijing banned the Internet society San Yuan Society for "carrying out activities on behalf of society without registration". San Yuan Society appealed to a higher court, while there is still no result. This case is known as "China's first case of the Internet society" which exposures embarrassment of Internet self-organization in the legislation.

4 The Problems Existing in the Development of Internet Self-Organization of Youth and the Countermeasures

4.1 The Existing Problems

Psychological Components of the contemporary youth have increased, the emotional states becoming more complex, the psychological conflict getting more intensified, which makes them refuse to exchange their emotions such as melancholy, loss and depression with their parents and teachers. Therefore, the self-organization becomes a place for different levels of youth to exchange feelings and ideas and form a platform for mental adjustment and emotional communication, providing opportunity and occasion for members to talk, vent, adjust and stabilize the moods. However, in term of physical and psychological perspective, the physical growth of youth develops fast, the cranial nerve system gets advanced, sexual function turns to be mature, self-consciousness is enhanced, their will and personality have great plasticity, and they have rich emotions that are easy to change and their energy level is high. In terms of social property, the future development space of youth is much larger than the space of the past experience. Different from childhood and old age, transitivity and maximized tendency to the future development are their natures. These characteristics and natures lead in many imbalances and conflicts between the youth groups and the whole social relationships "[5] Thus, on the whole, the Internet self-organization of youth is active, healthy and progressive, having a positive effect on the healthy development of society, while it is also admitted that there are certain problems in very few organizations in the development.

Firstly, the Internet self-organization of youth is likely to become channels for the dissemination of negative information, misleading public opinion. Some online self-organizations of youth have weak sense of social responsibility and they judge things in an extreme and one-sided look way, which make the organization vulnerable to the subjective preferences of individual members and produce a certain tendency. As a result, the organization would be reduced to spread gossip or rumors, and interfere with the normal information communication to mislead young people. It is also possible that a number of people with ulterior motives would create social conflicts, disrupt social order and mislead public opinion.

Second, the Internet self-organizations of youth have weak legal sense, which can make them carelessly violate the legal rights of citizens, disclose personal privacy and encourage network violence. It may be possible that a number of people with ulterior motives to create social conflicts and disrupt public order. For example, the "human flesh search" emerged in recent years.

Third, some organizations of youth are vulnerable to the impact of sectarian ideas and code of brotherhood. Backward forces may trap them, and then the negative culture atmosphere of group would be formed and malformed outlook on world, life and values would be produced, resulting in producing unstable factor that can affect the instability of young people and even social stability and a real or potential factor that can threaten the state and social security.

4.2   The Recommendations on Strengthening the Management

First of all, the appropriate management policies and improving service measures in the Internet self-organization of youth should be introduced as soon as possible. As the Internet self-organization of youth is still in the early stage of development, the management, operation, development level are very uneven. Considered from the government's management perspective, the current laws and regulations related to community management mainly aim at officially registered civil self-organizations, and there is no clear and specific policy and management measure for Internet self-organization. In order to better manage the Internet self-organization of youth, it requires the relevant government departments to introduce management measures on Internet self-organization of youth as soon as possible. The government should regulate the services, management and development issues of Internet self-organization of youth in legislation in order to guide and inspire the healthy growth of the Internet self-organization of youth and to speed up the legislative process of the self-organization. What's more, the relevant government department should place stress on practicality and operability, and make clear the penalties for violations of law. In aspect of the policy guidance and rules standardization, they should allow the corresponding right as much as possible, and avoid direct participation in the organizational activities in order to ensure that the self-organization of youth is a relatively independent organization for youth that truly serve for young people, reflect the aspirations of youth and represent the interests of youth.

Secondly, the network should be occupied by building a platform, making the best use of the situation and applying the advanced culture. Based on the Internet Age, Netizens increase in a great rate and the Internet has changed the production and lifestyle of people. Therefore, the platform and resources support system for Internet self-organization of youth should be built. More self-organizations should be rallied around the organizations for youth within the system through strengthening links, providing services and launching activities in order to establish a new organization system --"multi-concentric circles" to bring together the power and set up healthy communication channels of the Party, League and organizations for youth. Using this platform can serve and guide the contemporary young people in the way they prefer. The network should be occupied with the advanced culture. The members and their activities of the self-organization of youth should be guided and regulated by advanced Internet culture and youth culture. The practical help should be given to the Internet self-organizing of youth that should be guided to conduct legal register and gradually standardize the operation and organization, so that self-organization for youth can be converted to a power to construct the harmonious society.

Finally, the online monitoring should be enhanced and early warning mechanisms should be built in order to integrately manage, guide and regulate the healthy development of online self-organization of youth. As the speech on Internet has great autonomy and rapid information dissemination, the radical speech, negative emotions and distorted propaganda, online violence and malicious attacks on Internet will bring unintended social consequences. Therefore, it is recommended that standardize the mode of supervision of Internet self-organization and establish integrated management through a coalition composed by the Communist Youth League, the Public Security Bureau Internet Supervision, Civil Affairs Bureau and other departments. It is should be ensured that the Internet self-organization of youth develop healthily along the legal line through the functions of early warning monitoring, guidance, persuasion, management services, banning and attacking, which include radical speech correction, negative emotions resolution, the clarification of the distorted truth and the fight against crimes.

References

1. Hu, J.: Creating new results in the New Century - Congratulatory Speech on the Fourteenth National Congress of the Communist Youth League's. China Daily 1(June 20, 1998)
2. An, J.: Comparative Analysis on Generation Logic of Self-organized of youth in America and China. Youth Research (July 2008)
3. Dong, Y., Li, L., Tang, J.: Youth Self Organization A Case Study of Hangzhou. China Youth Study 3, 5–11 (2008)
4. The 27th Statistics Report on China Internet Development
5. Bao, Z.: Modern youth organization, vol. 6. China Youth Press (1991)

Influence of the External Shocks on Price Fluctuations of Agricultural Products of China: An Empirical Analysis Based on the VAR Model

Feng Luo

Business school, Foshan University, Foshan Guangdong 528000
foshanluofeng@yahoo.com.cn

Abstract. This paper has made an empirical analysis of the dynamic effect and contribution degree of various external impact factors on the price fluctuation of domestic agricultural products by applying the VAR model based on the monthly data from January, 2002 to June, 2010. The results indicate that various external impact factors are exerting an increasingly significant effect on the fluctuation of domestic agricultural products. Among the external factors, the transmission of price fluctuation of international agricultural products is the most important one; the contribution degree of petroleum price and international speculation capital rank the second and the third respectively; the contribution degree of external demands and the effective exchange rate of Renminbi are not significant. Finally, this paper proposed some suggestions of controlling the price fluctuation of domestic agricultural products.

Keywords: External Shocks, Agricultural Products, Price Fluctuation, VAR Model.

1   Introduction and Literature Review

With the rapid promotion of industrialization and urbanization in recent years, China's export and import of primary agricultural products are presenting the trend of dramatic increase; the prices of China's agricultural products are not only influenced by domestic factors but also by the financial crisis, oil crisis, fluctuation of exchange rate and other external factors which are exerting an increasingly frequent and complex impact on the agricultural market of China. Under the superimposition effect of the internal and external factors, the price stabilization of agricultural products and the people's living standards in China has suffered tremendous shocks.

The price fluctuation of agricultural products and its causes have always been the key research areas of the academic world. As the integration of the international market is being rapidly promoted, the external factors are exerting an increasingly frequent and strong impact on the world agricultural products thus making the analysis of various shocking mechanism a hot topic of price fluctuation research of domestic agricultural products nowadays. However, most literature lays particular stress on analyzing the price transmitting relation of the futures market of agricultural

Q. Zhou (Ed.): ISAEBD 2011, Part I, CCIS 208, pp. 374–381, 2011.

products outside China (Zhou Yingheng, Zou Lingang, 2007; Zhao Rong, Qiao Juan, 2008) [1]~ [2]. As the amount of imports of primary agricultural products of China is increasing day by day, some scholars have started to study the influence and transmission effect of the external shocks, such as price fluctuation of international agricultural products, fluctuation of exchange rate, world oil crisis, etc on the prices of agricultural products of China. For instance, in view of the violent fluctuations of the prices of agricultural products since 2005, most scholars hold the opinion that the price fluctuation of international agricultural products and other exogenous impact factors exert obvious effect (Cheng Guoqiang, etc 2008; Huang Jikun, 2008; Ding Shouhai, 2009) [3]~[5]. However, the study of Luo Feng and Niu Baojun (2009) has indicated that the price fluctuations of Chinese agricultural products are mainly influenced by domestic prices of the means of production while external factors play a minor role [6]. It is still necessary to further specify the concrete transmission mechanism of various impact factors in terms of theory especially about the influence of idle fund on the agricultural products market; besides, more voices from the government departments lack effective empirical test. Furthermore, there is still lack of comparative analyses of the influence degree with consideration of the external impact factors on price fluctuations of Chinese agricultural products. The innovations of this paper are as follows: first, making a comparative analysis of various external impact factors based on the factors controlling China; second, making a quantitative analysis of the influence of the idle fund which has attracted the major concern of all social sectors in recent years on the price fluctuation of Chinese agricultural products. Therefore, this paper has made an empirical analysis of the dynamic effect route and contribution degree of various external impact factors on the price fluctuation of domestic agricultural products by applying the VAR model based on the monthly data from January, 2002 to June, 2010 to attempt to provide scientific decision-making basis for the government to implement related policies.

2 Research Method, Variable Selection and Data Processing

2.1 Research Method——the VAR Model[8]

The introduction of vector-auto-regression(VAR) model into the economics by Sims(1980) has promoted extensive application of dynamic analysis of the economic system. VAR model is often used to predict interrelated time series system, namely, to analyze the dynamic shocks of random disturbance to the variable system thus explaining the influence formed by various economic shocks to economic variables; the advantage of VAR model lies in that it is unnecessary to make prediction of endogeneity of various variables in advance. However, it is difficult to determine the estimated value of a single parameter in the VAR model; hence it is necessary to observe the impulse response function and variance decomposition in order to draw a conclusion to the VAR model. These two methods have incorporated the economic variables under consideration into a system and can estimate the time lag and influence degree of variable shocks. The impulse response function describes the dynamic reaction of the system to a shock of a certain variable disturbance and judges the time lag relation between variables from the dynamic reaction. The variance decomposition refers to decomposing the predicted mean square error of the system to the contributions made by variable shocks in the system hereby investigating the relative importance of any variable shock in the VAR system. Comparing the changes of this relative importance with time can estimate the function time lags of this variable and also the relative size of each variable, namely, the proportion that the contribution of variable shock takes up in the total contribution.

2.2 Variable Selection and Data Processing

We select the price index of agricultural commodities of Chinese enterprises calculated by the People's Bank of China to measure the price fluctuations of Chinese agricultural products(NCP) and the data source is the website of People's Bank of China(*HTTP*://www.pbc.com); the proxy variables of external shocks reflecting the supply push mechanism are represented by the world oil price (OIL) and the data source is IMF; the proxy variables of domestic shocks are indicated by the prices of the means of agricultural production (SCZL) and the data source is *China Monthly Economic Indicators* issued by the National Bureau of Statistics; the factors reflecting the demands of domestic impact factors are represented by economic growth; but as the monthly data of domestic actual output(GDP) can not be obtained, the growth rate of industrial added value is taken as proxy variable and the data source is the data base of the Macro China website (*HTTP*://edu1.macrochina.com.cn); as for the pull factors of external demands, we have selected the favorable balance of trade (MYSC) in Chinese agricultural products as the proxy variables and the data source is *Statistics of Trade in Agricultural Products* column of the website of the Ministry of Agriculture (*HTTP*://www.agri.gov.cn) ; since the indexes reflecting the price fluctuations of international agricultural products are very difficult to obtain, we have replaced them with the international food price index(GJJG) and the data source is IMF; the exchange rate of the monetary shock channel can be indicated by real effective exchange rate of Renminbi (ERR) and the data source is the website of the Bank for International Settlement(*HTTP*://www.bis.org) ; the federal fund rate(LBLL) of the Federal Reserve are chosen to be the surrogate variable of the international level of interest rate reflecting the international mobility and the data source is the Federal Reserve website (*HTTP*://www.federalreserve.gov) ; Furthermore, we indicate impact factors China's currency by the fluctuation of the broad money M2 and the data source is the website of People's Bank of China. All the data intervals are the year-on-year data from January, 2002 to June, 2010; hence it is unnecessary to deal with various circulation factors, seasonal variation factors and irregular factors.

3 Empirical Analysis and Discussion

3.1 Unit Root Test

In order to avoid the problem of spurious regression, the analysis of time sequence requires making stability test of data sequence and the method of ADF testing is generally adopted. When testing, we should select trend term according to the minimization principle of the akaike information criterion (AIC), determine if the constant term exists and ascertain the order of the optimal lag variables, that is, to set the basic type (c, t, q) of unit roots among which c represents the constant term, t denotes the trend term and q indicates the lag order. The test shows that GDP, OIL, GJJG, SCZL, MYSC, M2 reject the null hypothesis by being under 5% of the significance levels thus being stable variables, that is, they are subject to I (0). However, NCP, LBLL and ERR accepted the null hypothesis by being under 5% of the significance levels thus being unstable variables; selecting the first order difference for each of them leads to the result that they all reject the null hypothesis by being under 1% of the significance levels thus being stable variable, that is, they are all integration of order one, I (1)

Table 1. Test results of unit root of each variable

Variable	ADF statistical value	Test types(c, t, q)	Significant level	stability
GDP	-3.4977	(c, 0, 2)	-2.8909**	Stable
OIL	-3.4977	(c, 0, 2)	-2.8909**	Stable
GJJG	-3.4977	(0, 0, 2)	-2.8909**	Stable
NCP	-1.9936	(c, 0, 1)	-3.5065	Unstable
ΔNCP	-4.4933	(c, 0, 1)	-3.5065***	Stable
LBLL	-1.3854	(c, t, 1)	-3.4977	Unstable
ΔLBLL	-4.8459	(c, t, 1)	-3.4977***	Stable
SCZL	-4.4033	(c, t, 2)	-3.4991***	Stable
ERR	-0.7184	(c, t, 1)	-3.5064	Unstable
ΔERR	-5.0013	(c, t, 1)	3.5064***	Stable
MYSC	-6.7388	(0, t, 1)	-3.4970***	Stable

Notes: *, **, *** represent rejecting the existence of the null hypothesis of unit root under10%, 5% and 1%of the significant levels.

3.2 Determining the Maximum Lag Order

First, select the appropriate lag order generally among the five common indexes, namely, likelihood ratio statistics (LR), final prediction error (FPE), AIC information criterion, SC information criterion and HQ information criterion. It is shown by the test results in Table 2 that FPE, AIC, SC and HQ information principles have all selected Phase 2, hence it is relatively appropriate to select the VAR model of the lagging Phase 2. Second, ascertain if the model can meet the stability conditions of VAR model. The K-order VAR models whose K is bigger than 1 can be adapted to the VAR model in the form of partitioned matrix through matrix transformation and then determine the stability by the roots of characteristic equations. We find that the reciprocals of all the roots of characteristic equations of VAR model are smaller than 1, that is, they are located within the unit circle , which indicates that the VAR(2) model is fully stable. Therefore, k=2 is finally selected as the optimal lag phase.

378   F. Luo

Table 2. Test results of the maximum lag order

Lag	LR	FPE	AIC	SC	HQ
0	NA	5.43E+12	54.86396	55.10285	54.96055
1	1041.305	1.84E+08	44.56504	46.95395	45.53100
2	139.7065	1.70e+08*	44.44404*	48.98296*	46.27936*
3	107.0089*	2.12E+08	44.56329	51.25223	47.26797

3.3 Co-integration Analysis

Through united test, we determine to select Johansen's co-integration test for which only intercept exists and sequence present the determinant linear trend. It is showed by Table 3 that both trace statistic and the max-eigen statistic can indicate that there exists co-integration relationship among 9 variables in the VAR model under the 95% of confidence level. Trace test shows that there are 4 co-integration vectors under the 95% of significant level and the maximum eigenvalue test reveals that the VAR model has 2 co-integration equations under the 95% of the significant level. On the whole, there is co-integration relationship among variables.

Table 3. Co-integration test results of the maximum likelihood value of Johansen

The null hypothesis	Eigenvalue	Trace statistic (P value)	$\lambda-$Max statistic (P value)
None	0.4739	273.6561（0.000）*	62.3055（0.0199）*
At most 1	0.4523	211.3505（0.000）*	58.4105（0.0107）*
At most 2	0.3521	152.9399（0.0004）*	42.1013（0.1298）
At most 3	0.3081	110.8386（0.0031）*	35.7282（0.1426）
At most 4	0.2283	75.1102（0.0178）	25.1482（0.375）
At most 5	0.2080	49.9620（0.0313）	22.6221（0.1902）
At most 6	0.1247	27.3399（0.0936）	12.9295（0.4587）
At most 7	0.1084	14.4103（0.0723）	11.1398（0.1473）
At most 8	0.0331	3.2705（0.0705）	3.2705（0.0705）

Notes: * represents rejecting the null hypothesis under 5% of the significant level.

3.4 Impulse Response Function

In the specific analysis, the change of variable ordering will exert different influences on the impulse response function. In general, the literatures will be ordered according to the following rule: the first variable will not be affected by all the other variables at the same time. However, the shock on the first variable will affect the others. The second variable will affect all the other following variables at the same time except for the first one. However, it will not be affected by the following ones. We can order the variables according to the above rule and the result is as follows: GDP, OIL, GJJG, SCZL, NCP, LBLL, ERR, MYSC, M2.

The results of the impulse response function of Chinese agricultural product price after the positive shock of a standard deviation unit of the other variables shows that all the external impact factors have increased their impacts on the price of Chinese agricultural products: (1) At the very outset, OIL's shock has a negative impact on the price of the agricultural products, later in the middle of the second stage, it begins to have a positive impact and lasts until the fourth stage. At the end of the sixth stage, again it begins to have a negative impact on the price of agricultural products. Generally speaking, oil price has an impact on the price fluctuation of Chinese agricultural products. However, as the pricing mechanism of the Chinese oil varies greatly from countries to countries, the response process manifests itself in a complicated trend. (2) GJJG has a negative impact on the price of Chinese agricultural products at the very outset. However, it soon begins to have a positive impact and reaches it peak at the second stage and lasts until the fifth stage. Then it begins to have a negative impact. (3) LBLL has a negative impact on the price of Chinese agricultural products and reaches its peak at the fourth stage. This indicates international funds do have an important impact on the price of Chinese agricultural products with the further opening up of the Chinese agricultural market. (4) ERR has little impact on the price of Chinese agricultural products at the very outset but later reaches its highest at the third stage and the response amplitude has reached about 0.4. This indicates that the fluctuation of exchange rate does have an important impact on the price of Chinese agricultural products and the fluctuation is high in the first five stages and keeps stable in the later stages. (5) MYSC has a positive impact on the price of Chinese agricultural products and reaches its highest at the second stage. After a short decline it increases its impact again in the fifth stage and keeps stable.

3.5 Variable Decomposition

From the forecast variable decomposition (see in table 4), we can notice that external impact factors gradually increase their impact on the price of Chinese agricultural products. Of all the external impact factors, GJJG has little impact on the price of Chinese agricultural products at the very outset. However, it begins to climb at the second stage and contributes more and more with the passing of time. At the tenth stage, its contribution has toped 10% and 16% at the 24_{th} stage. Therefore it contributes most of all the external impact factors. OIL has an increasing impact on the price of Chinese agricultural products. At the very outset, its percentage is only 1.527% but its contribution has increased obviously at the tenth stage and topped 4% at the 12_{th} stage and 5.5% at the 24_{th} stage. LBLL has little impact on the price of Chinese agricultural products and increases its impact gradually, and then it reaches the highest of 3.78% at the 7_{th} stage. This indicates that LBLL have exerted an impact on the price fluctuation of Chinese agricultural products as the Chinese agricultural market speeds up its opening-up to the world. ERR has a relatively small contribution to the price of Chinese agricultural products. It reaches its most in the 10_{th} stage with only 1.75% and remains stable in the later stages although there is a transitory decline. This indicates that the fluctuation of exchange rate has little impact on the price of Chinese agricultural products. It is very likely that its impact on the price mechanism of Chinese agricultural products is very complicated because of the complexity of RMB's exchange rate. Although MYSC indicating foreign demand has a small impact on the price of Chinese agricultural products, its impact has been on the increase. This indicates international trade environment of Chinese agricultural products has certain impact on the price of Chinese agricultural products.

Table 4. VAR model forecast Variable decomposition——the percentage of factors in forecast variable

Stage	GDP	OIL	GJJG	SCZL	D(NCP)	D(LBLL)	D(ERR)	MYSC	M2
1	0.013	1.527	2.345	3.060	93.054	0.000	0.000	0.000	0.000
2	31.547	2.610	4.528	2.136	56.013	1.022	0.022	1.025	1.095
3	30.346	2.930	5.184	2.597	54.441	1.061	0.355	1.095	1.990
4	29.618	2.816	4.971	2.595	52.036	2.748	1.653	1.057	2.507
5	29.336	2.835	4.939	2.920	51.546	3.215	1.643	1.050	2.516
6	28.731	2.790	5.253	3.357	50.423	3.659	1.696	1.276	2.815
7	28.202	2.829	6.037	3.811	49.396	3.780	1.664	1.464	2.817
8	27.516	2.942	7.198	4.309	47.938	3.775	1.735	1.767	2.821
10	26.756	3.404	10.149	5.164	44.484	3.516	1.754	2.134	2.639
12	26.556	4.107	12.938	5.648	41.033	3.271	1.703	2.312	2.431
14	26.830	4.783	14.568	5.771	38.553	3.179	1.649	2.362	2.306
16	27.253	5.260	15.111	5.703	37.240	3.198	1.608	2.346	2.280
18	27.527	5.494	15.092	5.637	36.770	3.249	1.589	2.324	2.318
20	27.528	5.533	15.093	5.696	36.610	3.272	1.585	2.321	2.363
24	27.068	5.486	16.156	6.132	35.682	3.198	1.581	2.356	2.342

Notes: the shock is ordered as follows:
GDP, OIL, GJJG, SCZL, D(NCP), D(LBLL), D(ERR), MYSC, M2.

4 Conclusions

This paper has conducted an empirical analysis of all the external impact factors that may affect the price fluctuation of Chinese agricultural products based on the VAR model by utilizing the monthly data from January, 2002 to June, 2010. Findings show that all the external impact factors have increased their impacts on the price of Chinese agricultural products among which the trade transmission of international agricultural product price is the most factor and its contribution has reached 16% in the 24th stage; the shock of oil price ranks second and its contribution has increased evidently from the10th stage and reached 5.5% at the 24th stage. Its impact has been stable and continuous since then. Interest rate of international funds ranks third and reaches the highest of 3.78%; the change in the foreign demand and fluctuation of RMB effective exchange rate has exerted little impact on the price of Chinese agricultural products. The policy implication of this paper is that the government should pay special attention to the impact on the price of Chinese agricultural product by the international agricultural product price and oil price. It is government's priority to build and improve the futures market to avoid the price fluctuation of bulk commodities and make use of the price information of the futures market to carry out macro-control in order to improve the foreseeability and pertinency. Secondly, the government should attract foreign funds to conduct long-term investment on Chinese agriculture instead of short-term speculative behavior by means of adjusting the industrial policy.

References

1. Zhou, Y., Zou, L.: Research on Price Relationship Between the Chinese Soybean Futures Market and International Soybean Futures Market — an empirical study based on the VAR model. Agricultural Technical Economy 1, 55–62 (2007)
2. Zhao, R., Qiao, J.: A Comparative Analysis of the Conduction Relationship between Future Price and Spot Price of Sino-American Cotton Trade. China Agricultural University Journal 2, 87–91 (2008)
3. Cheng, G., Hu, B., Xu, X.: An Analysis of the Impacts by the New-round Price Rise of Agricultural Products. Management World 1, 57–62 (2008)
4. Huang, J.: Food Price, Inflation and Countermeasures. China Finance 12, 51–53 (2008)
5. Ding, S.: An Analysis of the Impact on the Chinese Food Price by International Food Price Fluctuation. Economic Science 2, 60–71 (2009)
6. Luo, F., Niu, B.: Transmission Effect on the Price of Chinese Agricultural Product by the International Agricultural Food Price Fluctuation— an empirical study based on the VAR model. International Trade Issue 6, 16–22 (2009)
7. Sims, C.A.: Macroeconomics and reality. Econometrica 48(1), 1–48 (1980)
8. See Sims, for details about the construction of VAR model and specific mathematical description (1980)

Product Quality and Customer Benefit

Pavel Blecharz and Hana Stverkova

VSB – TU Ostrava, Faculty of Economic, Sokolska 33,
701 21 Ostrava, Czech Republic
pavel.blecharz@vsb.cz, hana.stverkova@vsb.cz

Abstract. The article deals with the quality, price and calculating the resulting benefits for the customer. This resulting benefit of the product means the best buy product quality at the chosen scale of quality and price of the selected weight of the product. The resulting benefit is also given in the context of consumer behavior, focusing on ordinal economic theory of utility, where has been confirmed and explained this approach also in theory.

Keywords: quality, weight of quality, utility.

1 Introduction

The quality of the product in general, we consider some comparisons. At the manufacturer we usually compare features and functionalities of the product with their specifications, standards, or possibly to the competition. The quality from a consumer perspective will still be assessed differently.

The current market is quite confusing for customers. From all sides roll new products, aggressive advertising and various promotional events and other activities on consumers. To orientate oneself in the field of terms of product quality is a task that is beyond the capability of any individual. Therefore, in most states act the independent consumer movements, which seek to assist consumers in terms of selecting the best quality at the best price with testing product and comparing them in terms of average price.

2 Quality and Price of a Product

The consumer movement, which carries out consumer tests of selected product groups, provides results in a form that is simple to understand for the layman. And each product is assigned a final overall score. If some consumer prefers a specific function of the product, here are also available individual sub-ratings for each function.

In the Czech Republic is such consumer movement called Dtest, which also publishes a magazine and test results are also available on the websites. Both of them, the magazine and websites are available for a reasonable fee. Similarly is the case in other countries.

Q. Zhou (Ed.): ISAEBD 2011, Part I, CCIS 208, pp. 382–388, 2011.
© Springer-Verlag Berlin Heidelberg 2011

Results for the quality of the tested products were taken from the Dtest magazine, but to the purpose of other calculations and graphics were modified to a higher value for better quality (compared with the original results, which are the opposite). Conversion formula is very simple; from 5.5 point value we subtract the original point value of quality in the Dtest magazine:

Q = 5.5 - original point value

Value 5 is the best quality, while the value 0 is the worst. Classification after conversion:

4-5 - excellent

3-3.9 - above-average, more satisfactory

2-2.9 - average

1-1.9 - below-average, more unsatisfactory

0-0.9 - absolutely unsatisfactory

When the consumer receives the greatest benefit? It's when the highest quality will be obtained and the expended cost will be minimized. But we cannot work directly with the score of quality and price in Table 2. We must first convert the numbers that are equally informative. These will be standardized, dimensionless numbers, where the quality or price takes values from 0 to 1 and when this both indicators will be desirable to maximize value.

For the calculation we will base on a formula that is used in the technique of planned experiments (DOE). The original formula used for comprehensive evaluation criterion OEC for DOE method is as follows (taken from [2]):

$$OEC = (\frac{|Y - w|}{|b - w|}).k_1 + (1 - \frac{|Y - b|}{|b - w|}).k_2 \qquad (1)$$

The first fraction is used directly for the parameter, where a higher value is better (we use it for quality), the second fraction is a parameter with the desired low value (suitable for price), but if the fraction is subtracted from the number 1, this parameter will have the same orientation, i.e. the most desirable value will be the highest value.

So the pointer of benefit to the customer will be the sum of price and quality, which are first converted into dimensionless numbers of the same nature and the best value will be 1, while the worst will be 0. Instead OEC we prefer to use the outcome of the other symbol, to differentiate the sense of variables, and it will be a symbol of QP (quality-price). Regarding the weight of quality and price in the formula, this, of course, will decisively affect the outcome. Therefore, we can compare the quantity QP among the product only for selected weight, for example, the quality will have a weight of 0.6 and the price of 0.4 (the sum of weights is always 1). Survey carried out among customers found range between the scales of quality, where the customer usually moves (Part 3). It was found that most customers prefer the weight for the quality of the 60-75% (i.e. 0.6 to 0.75), which is also used for calculations in Table 2.

Input variables for the calculation are evident in the following table. The best and worst values for quality and price of washing machines were selected from Table 2.

Table 1. Inputs for the calculation

Characteristic	The worst value W	The best value B	The most desirable value	Relative weight k	QP
Quality	1.2	3.6	The highest	k_1	
Price	25060	6990	The lowest	k_2	

w=the worst value for the quality or price
b= the best value for the quality or price
Y= observed value of quality or price of a concrete product
k= weight (importance) of quality or price, giving consumers when purchasing (find with research)

The calculation for the first line and weight of quality of 0.6:

$$QP = (\frac{|2,6-1,2|}{|3,6-1,2|}).0,6 + (1 - \frac{|6990-6990|}{|6990-25060|}).0,4 = 0,75 \tag{2}$$

Other calculations are analogous. All results are listed in Table 2.

Table 2. QP values for the weight of quality of 0.6 and 0.75 – Automatic washing machines [1]

Type of machine	Price CZK	Rating Q	QP (0.6)	QP (0.75)
1) GODDES WFC1025M8S	6990	2.6	0.75	0.69
2) AMICA AWSE10D	8250	1.2	*0.37*	*0.23*
3) ARDO FLSN 125	8890	2.6	0.71	0.66
4) GORENJE WA612SYW	9900	2.3	0.61	0.55
5) SAMSUNG WF7604	11960	3.0	0.74	0.74
6) HOOVER VHD 8143 ZDB	12340	3.1	**0.76**	0.77
7) LG F1222TD	12560	2.9	0.70	0.70
8) ELECTROLUX EWF12483	12680	3.1	0.75	0.77
9) BOSCH WAE2036SBY	13020	3.0	0.72	0.73
10) AEG LAVAMAT 74850	14430	3.3	0.76	0.80
11) WHIRLPOOL AWOE8758	14980	3.1	0.70	0.73
12) PANASONIC NA-14VA1WGN	20060	1.9	0.29	0.29
13) MIELE W 1622	21050	3.6	0.69	**0.81**
14) PANASONIC NA-16VX1WGN	25060	3.0	0.45	0.56

marked in *italics* are the worst values
marked in **bold** are the best value

The table shows that with the change of weight for quality from 0.6 to 0.75 can change the best product for the customer. In our case, Hoover washing machine (or alternatively AEG) can change to the Miele washing machine. The worst product for the customer stays, and it is the machine Amica.

2.1   Weight (Importance) of Quality Survey Conducted among Customer

To determine the importance, weight of quality was conducted the survey in February 2011, when were asked 372 respondents of various ages and professional orientation. It was interviewed 90 people ranging in age from 15 to 30 years, 143 respondents aged 30 - 45 years, 85 of respondents aged 45 - 60 and 54 people in age over 60 years.

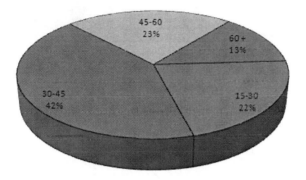

Fig. 1. Age segmentation of respondents

With questioning on a sample of 372 respondents was found that most consumers prefer the weight of quality in the range 0.6 to 0.75. Consumer preferences in individual age groups are shown in the following chart. Exceptions (statistical outliers) are extremely low income category of citizens, or vice versa, grew rich group of entrepreneurs. It should be noted that these results apply to consumer goods like televisions, refrigerators, electric shavers, and also for frequently used goods such as washing powders, etc., not e.g. for food.

Overall, it can be evaluated, that of all respondents, 73% prefer the weight of quality between 0.6 and 0.75, which is shown in the following chart. Taking forty-seven percent prefer the weight of quality 0.6 and twenty-six percent prefer the weight of quality on the level of 0.75. Twenty-seven percent of all respondents prefer lower or higher level of quality.

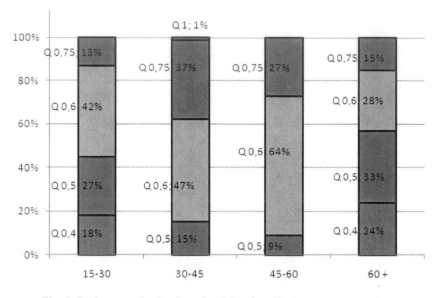

Fig. 2. Preferences distribution of weight of quality by age segmentation

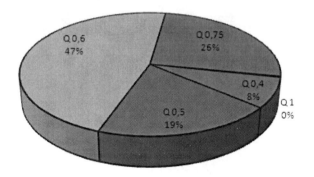

Fig. 3. Separation of preferences according to the weight of quality

2.2 The Economic Interpretation of Benefit to the Customer

The behavior of all economic entities, including individuals, is influenced by comparing the effects of economic activities and expenses that are associated with these activities. The effect is the individual benefit arising from the consumption of goods, in our case washing machines, and expenses associated with the purchase and use of the good. In economic theory it is assumed the rational-thinking individual, who maximizes profit. In our case will be the utility given by the weight of quality, because the benefit stems from consumer preferences, which is limited by his income.

We have to assume that consumer selects from a variety of goods, where his aim is to maximize the benefit associated with these two assumptions [3]:

- the axiom of comparison completeness (every two goods can be compared in term of consumer preferences),
- the axiom of transitivity (for all three baskets there is a preference of the first before the second and the second before the third).

We will build on ordinal version of the utility theory, where this utility is not directly measurable, but it is possible to say that the consumer prefers the situation over another. Curves showing the combination of the same benefit are called indifference curves. The slope of indifference curves are measured by the marginal rate of substitution, which is given by substituting of good Y for X. Consumer is constrained in his decision with his income, so-called budget lines, or a set of market opportunities. The slope of this curve is given by the rate, when the consumer spends all his income in exchange goods X and Y on the market. Optimum of the consumer is given by the rate; the consumer is willing to substitute one good to other, the same as the rate, which can be exchanged on the market. [3]

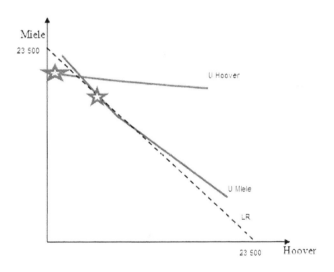

Fig. 4. Optimum of the consumer

With the optimum solution of a consumer is achieved by internal or corner solution. It depends on whether the goods are desirable (goods), undesirable (bads) or indifferent (neuters). In our case are the shapes of indifference curves drawn on the basis of consumer preferences, with the level scale of weight of quality. The budget lines can be moved in parallel position to form a tangent indifference curve, in our case QP curve. In the point, where the budget line is tangent QP curve, is situated the optimum of consumer.

For Miele washing machine is the preference in the shape of indifference - QP curve of the desirable good and it comes to an internal optimum solution for consumers, where the optimum point is the budget line of tangent QP curve.

For Hoover washing machine, the shape of indifference - QP curve based on consumer preferences in term of weight of quality is good rather indifferent, is consumer optimum a corner solution - budget line is tangent indifference - QP curve of Hoover washing machine on the y-axis - the consumer's preference is Miele washing machine. In our case is this corner solution, i.e. the consumer selects this good, that belongs to the axis – i.e. Miele washing machine.

As can be seen from the graph, by comparison of utility, in our case the weight of quality at two washing machines, Hoover and Miele, is confirmed the economic theory and the optimum of consumer based on benefit - a weight of quality and budget line at Miele washing machine. Therefore, the consumer, who prefers the weight of quality 0.6 or 0.75 selects Miele washing machine, because his aim is to maximize of benefit.

3 Conclusions

The approach of calculation of benefit for the customer QP, at the chosen level of weight of quality and price, is characterized by simple calculus, which makes it easy to orientate well in a large group of products. With one number (QP) we quickly find a product, which gives for consumer the highest benefit. Why is benefit the highest, explains the applying of ordinal version of utility theory, when each consumer maximizes his utility - a preference QP. According to a field survey was found, that 73% of respondents prefer a level of quality at the level of 0.6 to 0.75.

The consumer optimum can be with application QP obtained by comparing of the indifference curves of two goods, where is the shape of each curve given by QP values reached at a certain weight of quality and the optimum can be achieved at the point, where the curve of a budget line is a tangent QP curve.

Each customer has his preferences, according to them he can compare goods and maximize his benefit. This article leads to a choice of quality goods with the aim to maximize of benefit based on the influence the weight of quality on the preferences of consumers.

References

1. Dtest 1/2010: Front-loading washing machines, p. 20–21. Civil Consumer Association Test, Prague (2010) ISSN 1210-731X
2. Roy, R.K.: A Primer on the Tachuchi Method. Society of Manufacturing Engineers, Dearborn (1990) ISBN 0-87263-468-X
3. Hořejší, B., Soukupová, J., Macáková, L., Soukup, J.: Microeconomics, 4th Xtns. edn. Management Press, Prague (2009) ISBN 978-80-7261-150-8

Thinking on the Reform of Our Security Investment Fund Management Fees System

Qiutao Shen

College of Management, Shanghai University of Engineering Science,
Shanghai 201620

Abstract. The expenses of our security investment fund management now adopt the single charging mode. This paper from the angle of foreign fund management fees mode, by making an analysis on the existing drawbacks of our current fund management charging manners has put forward the reform directions and countermeasures of our fund management expenses drawing manners.

Keywords: Security investment fund, Management fees mode, Reform direction and countermeasure.

The security investment fund is one of the most dynamic and innovative financial instruments in capital market, which has played a very important role in the process of our security market stepping in maturity. The fund management company controls the fund, whose main incomes are from the fund management fees and the management fees mode is the key system which plays the core motivation role in the process of fund management.

1   The Current Conditions of Our Fund Management Fee

Our current management fee of equity fund adopts the system of drawing annual fixed fees of 1.5% of the fund net value, that is, whether the fund investment is profitable or not, the fund company will draw fund management fees from the fund net assets by the unchangeable rate without any investment management crisis and market crisis to undertake. Thus, the fund management company under the united fixed management fee income system with market monopoly and high fee rate, may not pay out the corresponding hard work with the crisis-free high income to serve the fund beneficiary and create the most valuable return for the beneficiary. It may well be asked: under the environment of market economy, which industry has the absolutely profitable right, but with no any crisis of loss to bear? Which not only disobeys the principle of equity and fairness for market choosing, but the main point of experts being entrusted with financing. Statistics show that, the current drawing manners for fund manager's returns make the fund manager's returns' drawing and fund operating abilities being not proportional.

Q. Zhou (Ed.): ISAEBD 2011, Part I, CCIS 208, pp. 389–394, 2011.

2   The Defects of Our Fund Management Fee Mode

2.1   Administrative Supervisory Mode

In China, the found of investment fund is checked by the supervisory department and the fund management fee criteria is determined by the supervisory section, but this kind of administrative mode is in effect a direct price control. Compared with the participants of fund management market like investment companies and fund holders, the supervisory departments can get no profits from the the fund management fees, so they will not actively try to find and adopt market balanced price. Compared with market, the supervisory department is not a very suitable price decider. And the ideal price level is not static and unique, but is closely related to the service quality and market preference. The administrative mode usually uses a kind of price to apply to all the same funds, therefore, the factors like fund managers' qualities and investors' preferences can entirely not obtain the reflection from the price and thus the price's market adjusting functions have been abolished.

2.2   The Collecting Fixed Fee Rate Being Higher

In America, the total annual fund management fees usually do not exceed the 1% to 1.2% of the fund net assets and the Japan's fund management fees are only equal to the 0.7% of the fund net assets, while at present, our country's fund management fees are calculated and drawn by less than 1.5% of fund assets' net values. To be compared, at present, the total management fees of our country are obviously higher, and added that the returns of our fund managers' are calculated and drawn according to the total net assets, the fund manager mastering larger scale of fund, no matter how bad his operating qualities are, the profits he can obtain are more, and once the operation falls down, it does not matter much, while, at least 1.5% commission of net assets can be obtained, which not only cannot play any stimulating roles, but gives those lazy fund managers a promise of minimum income, which is very unfavorable to the development of our investment fund.

2.3   The Net Fund Values for Counting and Drawing Management Fees Being Operated

Although from the form, the manner of drawing management fees according to the net fund values is international practise, the foreign developed fund market manager's fees are generally also drawn by some proportion of net fund values, with adding day by day and paying by month. But the price of foreign developed security market cannot be controlled, the net fund values can basically truly balance the profitability of fund, therefore, paying the managers' fees by some proportion of net values can properly reflect the contributions managers to fund and form the normalized stimulation and constraint system to the managers. While in the inner security market, the phenomenon of operating market is common and the net fund value can be operated, such as, since there are some relations between our fund net assets and profits, profits may be created when the profitable shares being thrown out and loss may be created when the hung up shares being thrown out and the "clever"managers all know that the profitable shares should not be easily thrown out, since once it is done, a part of assets will be converted to profits and distributed to the fund investors and thus the net fund assets, the base of management fees the managers depend on to count and draw, will decline whether now or in the future.

The fund managers in order to get more management fees may rise up the net fund value, and this time, the net fund value only performances as the floating profits, which cannot truly reflect the fund's profit conditions. While the investors should still pay rewards to the managers for the untrue profits, which is obviously unreasonable and non-understand.

This kind of manners for counting and drawing returns which is not directly related to the fund profitable abilities, makes the fund managers' earnings promised. Although the fund managers in the process of managing the fund have caused direct economic losses to the fund holders, the management fees can still be drawn, which makes the rewards and crisis very unequal.

Moreover, this kind of manners of drawing management fees by some proportion, can hardly find the best balancing point of constraint and simulation between the fund investors and fund managers.

2.4 The Management Fees' Collecting Manner Being Single

In the theoretical analysis, the management fees are divided into two kinds. One is drawing by some proportion of the net fund values and increasing or decreasing with the net fund values. The other is called performance fees, which is generally drawn by some proportion of more than the "basic combination" performance. The fund management fees of our country is counted and drawn by 1.5% fee rate of net fund asset values, without the part of performance stimulation fees.

Why the fund management fee stimulation mode with fixed fee rate has not played the roles to stimulate the fund managers to improve the fund performance and protect the benefits of investors? The main reason is: the agents represented by fund managers own the surplus controlling rights to fund assets, but not has the claiming rights to the fund surplus incomes, while all the risks in the process of fund operation should be beared by the fund holders. The mismatches between surplus claiming rights and risks bearing is the essential feature of fund contract, so the problems of fund managers' "moral risks" will be caused unavoidably.

3 The Reforming Directions and Countermeasures of Fund Management Fees' Drawing Manners

The reforming directions of fund management fee system is gradually marketizing and diversifing under the conditions of enhancing the government supervision. At present, the entrance threshold of fund industry is much higher and the choosing chances of investors are much less, so the competition is not enough. Therefore, it should be done to properly lower the fund entrance threshold of fund management and speed up the development of kinds of trust fund to provide more choices to the investors and create better external environment for the marketization of fund management fee system. In the meanwhile, with the development of our fund industry and the improvement of fund market system, the "universal application" mode of management fee drawing manners must be completely eradicated, and the setting and revision of fund management fees should adopt more active fixing means. The extraction of fund management fee should not only set up the upper limit, but be able to be allowed to adjust the fund management fee rate properly and flexibly according to the difficulty level of fund management and fund management costs the fund scale has confirmed. Moreover, it can be connected with whether to create fortune to fund investors or not, and if the net fund values fall down, the drawing proportion will be decreased, while if the par value cannot even be ensured, the management fees have to be drawn by the minimum criteria. In fact, our fund industry has started the exploration on this aspect, such as collecting the management fees in the norm of value increasing line which has once become the hot issue in market. The so-called value increasing line means the fund managers depending on self investment and risk management create a safe profit increasing track with non-negative increase with time lapse, which is one destination of risk control the fund managers set up by themselves. At present, there are three funds having set up value increasing line, including Boshi Value Increasing, Haifu Income Increasing and Tianzhi Increasing funds. According to the product agreement, the above promise, once the unit net falling down the value increasing line will suspend counting and drawing management fees. This kind of innovative fees collecting mode, in a large part has reduced the investors' investing cost burden, and also contributes to enhance the common beneficial relations between fund managers and investors. The marketization and diversification of fund management fees are not only in favour of selecting superior and eliminating interior among various funds inside the fund industry, but in favour of competing among other self-collecting funds and asset management organizations. Much market pressure should be felt by the fund company and good fund company can get higher management fees with bad get less and worse be closed down. Only this kind of market system can eliminate the interior funds and gradually expand the superior funds' market shares. For the specific drawing fund management fees' manners, the countermeasures needs to be reformed urgently are as follows:

3.1   Changing Current Management Fees' Drawing Manners Being Entirely Counted and Drawn by Net Fund Value

The equity fund at present, is generally counted and drawn by 1.5% annual fee rate of net fund asset value and the drawing manner is according to 1.5% annual fee rate of the former day's net fund asset value with counting day after day, adding day by day till to the end of each month, and paying by month. That is to say, during 365 days of one year, although the equity market is closed, the fund management fees will be drawn as usual. Such counting and drawing manner makes the net fund value being the only reference factor for drawing the fund management fees, while the dividends distributing situation and fund profitable abilities that fund holders care most have no direct influences to the fund managers' benefits. After all, compared to twenty to thirty billion fund shares, reflecting to the changes of net value, the changes of fund profit and loss are much less, and after treated with 1.5% annual fee rate, the changes will be much less. Even since the fund starting net values are not in the same high, the drawn management fees of high profit fund may be less than the low profit fund. Not only profit and loss are not related to the managers' incomes, but the dividends' amounts.

Stressing dividends distribution will always cause the management fees' drawing criteria dropping. Thus it can be seen, the fund management fees are entirely counted and drawn by the fund net value, but not in direct proportion to the fund operating abilities and especially the dividends distributing abilities. The fund management rewards' drawing is related to the operating abilities, which to some extent has influence the development of fund industry.

Proper management fees' drawing manner should carry out according to the net fund value and fund dividends distribution, such as changing the current fixed rate of 1.5%'s net value to two parts of 1.5%, like 0.75%+0.75%. One part is related to net value, as basic management fee, which can show the fund company's pay out to the fund management; The other part is related to the real fund dividends and only can be drawn when distributing dividends. When the net values lose or though high but no dividends, the managers should reduce the management fees. This performance not only can suppress the managers keep high net value but less dividends or no dividends phenomena, but can be taken as the rewards to the fund company's achievements, which show the truth of doing more getting more and to some extent avoid the problems of fund profit transfer and also the fund company in order to rise up the net fund value disregard the value investment idea and expand the fund scale blindly, promoting going up and down.

3.2 Changing the Current Net Confirmation and Counting Manners When Counting and Drawing the Fund Management Fees

At present, in the year when net fund value is floating profit, the managers in the next year should still repeatedly count and draw the last year's floating profit's net value, which damages the fund holders' benefits seriously. The floating profit net value created by managers last year is factually drawn by 1.5% day by day from January 1st to December 31st .but since the dividends to investors cannot be finished at the end of the year, in fact, the last year's floating profits will continue drawing management fees taken as the next year's net value. Just as one company counts to have 100 thousand yuan yuan profits at the end of this year, then year award will be counted and drawn by 100 thousand yuan, but since the profit left to the next year, then the next year will draw rewards from this 100 thousand yuan, is this absurd? All the financial and financing management settle the accounts by year, and the management fee's net value should be parted by year. That is, the net value announced at annual end should not only be the barren number by which the achievements are compared among the fund companies, which has no any senses to the investors. To be specific, the net fund value announced at each year end, should form January 1st of next year, make the net value of counting and drawing management fees returning to par value of 1 yuan.

Marketization and diversification is the reforming direction of our fund management fee system, but it needs a realizing process. The managers should consider to begin with new funds to explore and carry out more active fee rate level and collecting level, which not only can protect the investors' benefits step by step, but further stimulate the excellent fund managers to advance the fund industry to develop healthily.

References

1. Zhou, Q.: Investment Fund Management Research. China's Financial Press (2008)
2. Luo, J.: Comparison Between Chinese and American Securities Investment Fund Management Practices. Finance and Research 11 (2008)
3. Cao, X., Peng, G.: The Effectiveness of Chinese Fund Management Fees. System Engineering 1 (2009)

The Optimization of Small and Medium Manufacturing Enterprises' Production Logistics System Based on TOC

Wang Xinsheng[1], Zhang Jinli[2], and Zhao Haixing[2]

[1] Department of management, Shandong Jiaotong University, Jinan, China
[2] College of mathematics and information science, Qinghai normal university, Xining, China
`hzq-1230@163.com`

Abstract. For small and medium manufacturing enterprise, in particular, multi-species, small and medium volume production enterprises, the management level of production logistics system is the key for the enterprise to utilize sufficiently all production capacity, to reduce the cost, to increase the effectiveness and improve the competitive capacity of product in the market. The problems of production logistics management system in small and medium manufacturing enterprise are analyzed, and based on the principles and procedures of improving the production logistics system performance, optimization design of production logistics management system is done, from factory layout, conveyance system, and balance of production and so on, to improve the management level of production logistics and the operation efficiency and profit. At the same time, according to the real demand of inventory management, the level of inventory management is improved on the basis of the quantitative indention model of the safe inventory and ABC method of inventory logistics. The mechanism of the automatic forecasting and alarming is realized and the upper limit and lower limit of inventory are set up to insure the continuity and stability of the product activity, the overstock and impropriation of the current capital is decreased.

Keywords: Production logistics, Theory of constraints (TOC), Small and medium manufacturing enterprise, Value chain.

1 Introduction

Production logistics management is an important component of production management, and it plays a vital role in the enterprise, besides, raising the level of production logistics management of enterprise is one of the requirements to improve their competitiveness. Therefore, in this case it is necessary to study advanced mode of production logistics management from China's national conditions, improve the efficiency and effectiveness of the enterprise, enhance the competitiveness of Chinese enterprises under the new situation. At present, China already has a large number of advanced "hardware" device environment, but in the aspects of quality, cost, efficiency, effectiveness, etc, the gap with the developed countries is still very large. Domestic manufacturing enterprises have been neglect relatively of logistics management technology, such as the layout of machinery and equipment, the

Q. Zhou (Ed.): ISAEBD 2011, Part I, CCIS 208, pp. 395–401, 2011.

practices of production line design arrangements, methods of the movement of goods, etc, so the logistics of internal enterprise is relatively backward. Production logistics management is the important work of production management of the enterprise, and its flow process decides the production efficiency and production costs of the enterprises and it also the openings of the logistics as a source of corporate third profits.

2 Theories of Constructions

2.1 Theory of Constraints

Theory of Constraints (TOC) is the management philosophy, developed by Israeli physicist, business management consultant, Dr. Goldratt (Dr.Eliyahu M. Goldratt), based on the Optimized Production Technology (OPT) created by him. This theory proposed a number of standardized methods of defining and eliminating constraints in the prosecution and production activities of manufacturing, in order to support the Continuous Improvement. At the same time, TOC is also the development of MRPII and JIT in the concepts and methods. The purpose of the Goldratt to create the Theory of Constraints is to find the internal laws of production under the various conditions, and a scientific logic way of thinking to analyze operating production problems and an effective way to solve problems. One word to express the TOC is that, finding the by the numbers improvement methods to identify the constraints which hinder the achievement of system objectives and eliminate them.

2.2 The Steps of Continuous Improvement of Production the Logistics System Performance under the Theory of Constraints

Bottleneck is the part or the link which hinders the output of overall system, so investing to the non-bottleneck part will not be able to improve production efficiency, and waste of resources. Therefore, to determine the bottleneck has become the foundation work of production logistics control under the Theory of Constraints.

(1) The data for determining the bottleneck resources.

Through the analysis of production operation and the allocation of resources needed only of their own, enterprises can determine the bottleneck resources. The data mainly used in this process are: customer service goals, the list of all the components on the production line, the relative positions of the various processes and their supply points, the production and processing capacities of different located processes, the processing batch of different parts, a different sequence and the inventory levels of different components, the methods of controlling inventory, the productive capacity of existing equipment, etc. The data above have a major impact on the production logistics structure, and through the analysis may enable to find a productivity to make the operation of the facility most efficiently, that is, the uniform logistics amount.

(2) Determine the bottleneck of resources

Based on the above data to identify the impact of the changes of all aspects of production capacity on the production operations management, and identify bottleneck resources.

3   The Production Logistics System and Value Chain of SME

3.1   Types of Production Logistics

In SMEs, there exists the staff flow, capital flow, information flow, the value chain, and logistics. Usually, the "Product Logistics" which is the process from raw materials to finished products are classified into three types: "V", "A" and "T". Where, "V-type logistics" is from one kind raw material to many end-product of different types by processed or transformed; "A-type logistics" is from different kinds of raw material to end-product of one type by processed or transformed; while "T-type logistics" is the deformation of the "A-type logistics", and its ultimate product is various.

3.2   The System of the Production Logistics

Production logistics is the logistics activities in the process of the production, and it refers to the raw materials, purchased parts, auxiliary materials and other materials through the hair and cutting, and then transported to the processing point or storage point of the production line, and further flowed one by one link with the production process, until assembly product is finished to the finished product warehouse (as Figure 1). Production logistics begins from the input of the raw materials and purchased parts to the finished product warehouse, and it runs throughout the entire production process. Only the rational organization of production logistics can enable the production process of enterprises is always at its best. If the production logistics is not smooth, the production of enterprises will be confused, or even halt production.

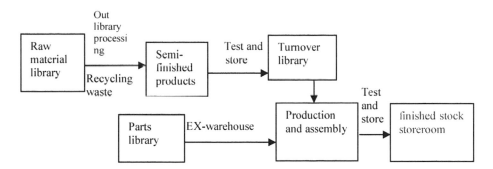

Fig. 1. Production logistics flow chart

3.3   Analysis the Value Chain

The value chain is the whole activities required by the current product passing its basic production process. These activities are consist of two parts: adding value to the product and not adding value to the product, including the whole processes of a product from the most basic raw materials stage to the product delivered to customers, such as an automobile manufacturing, including customer requirements, the conceptual design, product design, prototype manufacturing, testing, stereotypes, production, and the use of post-production after delivery, information feedback and recovery process, and it will pass a lot of workshops, factories, enterprises, and may even have experienced a number of countries and regions. The value chain diagram is a powerful tool to help the analysis of the whole value stream, and it can make usual chaotic value chain into a visual status map of the value chain, making the problems of the value chain emerged out, so that can be applied all relevant industrial engineering methods to eliminate non-value-added waste.

4   The Optimization Design of Logistics System of SME

4.1   The Layout of Factory, Workshop and Equipment

Factory Layout refers to the location of every means of production and their convergence and how to achieve those means of production in the factory. Specifically speaking, that is, to determine the location of machinery, equipment, warehouses, factories and other production means and the building facilities in which achieve production means. Workshop layout is based on the law of the material flow graphs and the principles of workshop layout re-divide and arrange the workshop according to the overall flow and traffic volume of the raw material, products and other materials in the production process. Equipment layout is to arrange the equipment with the same type and workplace centralized to achieve a certain degree process capability. In addition, combined with the principle of group technology to arrange the equipment and the workplace according to a certain part family to improve the equipment utilization and reduce the transport volume and distance.

4.2   The Setup of the Material Handling System

Material handling system is the handling operation which means the material to be transferred between the production process, workshop, and warehouse, in order to ensure continuous production. The design of the material handling system include: access, transport routes identified, equipment selection and the design of the equipment station.

   The relative position of each workshop in the factory and the relative position of each piece of equipment have been established, production logistics routes has also come to be determined. After the adjustment of some workshops, from the total flow of materials to see, the raw material to finished product forms an "O" type. The material handling line avoids the phenomenon of cross, mixed, and going back and forth, meanwhile reduces the stagnation and increases the continuous transport in the entire handling process. A reasonable material handling equipment selection and design of the station apparatus are extremely important to the improvement of the efficiency of the logistics systems, the safety of the transport operations, and the work efficiency.

4.3   The Optimization of the Production Planning and Logistics Organization System

Balanced production means the enterprise and workshops, steps, workplace and other production sectors in the enterprise complete equal, or increasing number of products in equal period of time. From the logistics point of view is that the balance of production logistics flow. The ideal state of the balanced production is "a flow", that is, in the process from the raw material input to the finished output the products are always in the state of flow with not stagnant, non-accumulation, non-stop, not going beyond, rhythmic. The major measures of implement a balanced Production is to develop production plans scientific, and enhance the organization and management of the production logistics system.

(1) The Project Management Based on TOC

The ideology of the TOC formulating plan is that, considering the system resource constraints in the planning period, and firstly to arrange the progress of production operations in the production bottlenecks using the limited capacity scheduling method, then making bottleneck processes as a benchmark to arrange the processes before, during, after the bottleneck processes according to the pull, process order, and driven approach. TOC can optimize the entire plan, at the same time, it can improve the bottleneck processes continuously in order to maximize productivity, and then make the non-bottleneck operations plan are sync with the bottleneck processes.

(2) The Integrated Analysis of MRPII, JIT, TOC

The three kinds of production and management methods: MRPII, JIT and TOC, have their own advantages and disadvantages, and if they complementary advantages and learn from each other, they will produce a very good application effect on enterprise.

The advantage of MRPII is centralized management approach which can facilitate the use of information technology to optimize the entire production operation systems and decision making. Therefore, it can be regarded as production systems of the enterprise for scheduling the master production plan; JIT has a significant effect of reducing make-ready time, manufacturing cycles, inventory and the premium rate, so it can be used to formulate the short-term billboards plan of production cycle or a day. By balancing the logistics of the production process to achieve the maximum output rate, while reducing lead times and in-process inventory; TOC is a management theory about comprehensive application capability management and on-Site operations management, especially through the dynamic control of the DBR system, it is well suited to the requirement of many varieties, small and medium volume production environment. Combining TOC and MRPII to generate a feasible production plan and the monthly production schedule, on the other hand, applying them to the JIT to make up its deficiencies and produce a reasonable workshop billboard plan.

4.4 Inventory Management

Inventory management is an important content in the production logistics management of the enterprise interior, and it plays an important role in ensuring material supply, meeting the requirements of production, storing reasonably, accelerating the material flow, saving material use, reducing cost. The main contents of inventory management are inventory control and warehouse management.

Inventory refers to all the items and resources reserved of an organization. Inventory management refers mainly to monitor inventory levels, determine the inventory levels should be maintained, decide the time to replenish stock and the size of the order. Effective warehouse management will greatly reduce the NBRE and improve the capital turnover rate, thereby improve the economic efficiency of enterprises.

Therefore it should be that planning the warehouse reasonably and strengthening the management of in-out warehouse, especially implementing "the outbound single ingredients" system for the out warehouse, and periodically inventorying and processing the waste.

4.5   The Integration of Production Logistics Information Resources

The management of production logistics information is a useful resource which is an organic whole combined by the logistics and information are combined, and using various options to select, collect and input the relevant data with the logistics planning, business and statistics, through targeted and purposed computer processing output the useful information for management.

Logistics information is large and wide distributed, and the production, processing and application of information are not consistent in form, time, and place; logistics information is strongly dynamic, and the attenuation speed of information is fast; the types of logistics information is various, so it is difficult to classify, research, and screen.

Integrating production logistics information within the enterprise in time can provide a powerful guarantee for formulating rational production plan, controlling the rhythm of the production logistics, compressing inventory, reducing the production cost, making the factory production logistics smoothly and selling market products quickly, etc.

5   Conclusions

The optimization and improving of the production logistics system do not pursue the balance of production capacity but the amount of the balance of the logistics; this requires that bottleneck resources are fully utilized in the whole production process. At the same time, to increase efficiency and reduce logistics costs are taken as a whole system optimization objective, and to achieve these through reasonable technical design, equipment utilization and staff organization. The whole production logistics system can be optimized from the entire production only through a profound understanding of TOC management philosophy, taking advantage of the MRPII and JIT on-site control, implementing the principle of dynamic binding of TOC's ability to manage and on-site job management to the entire process of production planning and control management, combined with the enterprise's own characteristics at the same time, and improving continuously the system in practice.

References

1. Huang, S.: Tactics studying on logistics development of the small and medium-sized enterprises in the central region. Logistics Sci.-Tech. 12, 106–107 (2009)
2. Liu, Q.: The combined application of theory of constraints and MRPII, JIT theory in the logistics. Theory Monthly 05, 168–169 (2007)
3. Qi, E.: Logistics engineering. Tianjin university press (2001)
4. Sun, G., Shao, J.: Production logistics management. Social sciences academic press, London (2006)
5. Wang, L.: Production logistics operation and control study.Tongji university (2007)
6. Wang, Y., Chen, Y., Xu, P.: Study on TPL selecting SMES based on unified credit mode of FTW. Technology Economics 29, 124–128 (2010)
7. Zheng, Y., Essock, E.A.: A local-coloring method for night-vision colorization utilizing image analysis and fusion. Information Fusion 29, 186–199 (2008)
8. Berge B.: 18th IEEE International Conference on Micro Electro Mechanical Systems, MEMS, pp. 227–230 (2005)
9. Peng, R., Chen, J., Zhuang, S.: Design and analysis of a variable-focus optical system based on electrowetting, vol. 28, pp.1141–1146 (2008)
10. Taom, C.: Design of variable-focus optical systems. Defense industry press, Beijing (1998)
11. Young, T.: An essay on the cohesion of Fluids. London: Philos. Trans. R. Soc. 95, 65–87 (1805)

Effects of Combinations Governance on Earnings Management: A Game Analysis among Financial Supervisor, Auditor and Manager

Yunqing Tan[1,2]

[1] School of Business, Shanghai Lixin Univ. of Commerce, Shanghai, China
[2] School of Business, Fudan University, Shanghai, China
tyunq@126.com

Abstract. It's a common view that earnings management from company's managers has threatened the economic development. The datum about suspicious businesses reports mainly provided by audit institutions are the core of financial supervisor anti-earnings management system. Financial supervisor must design an effective anti-earnings management system. This paper constructs a game model among company's managers, auditor and financial supervisor. Under different anti-earnings management policies' combinations, we analyze the loss of social welfare in this model. Findings:(1)The policies' combination of investigating, convicting and punishing earnings management can keep earnings management down effectively;(2)Earnings management must be cracked down;(3)For encouraging auditor of audit institutions to attend anti-earnings management activities, financial supervisor needs to reasonably compensate their anti-earnings management fix cost and enact rewards and penalties system which emphasizes penalties.

Keywords: earnings management, combinations governance, a game analysis.

1 Introduction

Earnings management refers to the intentional manipulation of accruals in order to maximize the managers' utility and/or the market value of the firm. Earnings management has become a well-researched topic in the accounting literature, especially in the years after the many accounting scandals in prominent companies such as Enron and WorldCom. These scandals were even a catalyst for the passage of the U.S. Sarbanes-Oxley act of 2002, which has changed the accounting environment tremendously. Accountants and financial economists have recognized for years that firms use the latitude in accounting rules to manage their reported earnings in a wide variety of contexts. Healy and Wahlen (1999) conclude in their review article on this topic that the evidence is consistent with earnings management "to window dress financial statements prior to public securities offerings, to increase corporate managers' compensation and job security, to avoid violating lending contracts, or to reduce regulatory costs or to increase regulatory benefits." Since that study, evidence of earnings management has only mounted. Cohen, Dey, and Lys (2005) find that

Q. Zhou (Ed.): ISAEBD 2011, Part I, CCIS 208, pp. 402–407, 2011.

earnings management increased steadily from 1997 until 2002, and options and stock-based compensation emerged as a particularly strong predictor of aggressive accounting behavior (see also Gao and Shrieves, 2002; Cheng and Warfield, 2005; Bergstresser and Philippon, 2006). Although earnings management is generally accepted by accounting principles, but it is against the accounting neutrality principles, and there is no doubt to damage the outside investors' interests. Then, more and more papers pay attention to the contract governance to improve earnings management. For example, several studies find that earnings management can be limited by well-designed corporate governance arrangements. Dechow, Sloan, and Sweeney (1996) investigate the relation between outright fraud and board characteristics. Klein (2002) shows that board characteristics (such as audit committee independence) predict lower magnitudes of discretionary accruals. Warfield, Wild, and Wild (1995) find that a high level of managerial ownership is positively related to the explanatory power of reported earnings for stock returns. They also examine the absolute value of discretionary accruals and find that accruals management is inversely related to managerial ownership. Like Klein, they conclude that corporate governance variables may influence the degree to which latitude in accounting rules affects the information of reported earnings. However, Bergstresser and Philippon (2006) find an inconsistent relation between accruals and an index of corporate governance quality. That to say, the expected outcomes can not obtained by corporate governance to control earnings management of enterprises.

In fact, there are various motives for the managers with earnings management, such as strong economic reasons, the interests' motives and psychological factors. In this sense, it is difficult for the issue to governance earnings management problem by controlling single motive of them. Then, in the paper, we will build a game model to analysis effect's analysis of policies' combinations on earnings management among financial supervisor, auditor and company's managers.

Our paper is organized as follows. In the next section, we present our model for the interaction among financial supervisor, auditor and company's managers. Section 3 solve and analyze the model respectively, and section 4 concludes the paper.

2   The Model

2.1   Company Managers' Benefits Function

Company's managers have two choices that they can manipulate earnings or not manipulate earnings. If company's managers manipulate earnings, there are some manipulating earnings management costs, include the participants labor cost, regular commissions of audit institutions, decoration commission, and so on. With earnings management amounts being increase, it is difficult for company's managers to avoid the anti-earnings management actions, earnings management marginal service cost will be increased. In addition to the earnings management services costs from auditor, company's managers may be faced with economic risk and criminal punishment.

Assume that there is a positive relationship between company's managers risk lost (L_1) from being punished and earnings management amounts(X_1, $X_1 \geq 0$), where $L_1 = l_1 X_1$, $l_1 > 0$, l_1 is earnings management penalties proportion. Because earnings management services cost will be increase with the amounts of earnings management, and we assume $TC_1 = \alpha_1 X_1^2 + C_1$, and TC_1 is earnings management service cost, $\alpha_1 > 0$, $C_1 > 0$, C_1 is earnings management fixed costs. Company's managers usually prefer to risk, and underestimate the probability of being investigated and founded. We assume company's managers subjective probability of being investigated and founded is $P = k_1 p$, $0 < k_1 \leq 1$, k_1 is company's managers subjective probability coefficient of being investigated and founded. Because company's managers usually are optimistic, they think the subjective punished proportion might be less than that of the real punished proportion. Then, we assume that the subjective punished proportion is k_2, $0 < k_2 \leq 1$. k_1 and k_2 depend on risk aversion degree of listed companies, and there is a positive relationship between them. To simplify the model, we assume k_1 and k_2 are the model exogenous variables. Then, when company's managers carry out earnings management, their subjective expected net income is as follow:

$$E \prod_1 = (1-P)X_1 - \alpha_1 X_1^2 - C_1 - Pl_1 X_1 \tag{1}$$

When company's managers don't manipulate earnings:

$$E \prod_1 = 0, \quad X_1 = 0$$

2.2 Auditor Benefits Function

Auditor usually also have two choices on investigating and reporting earnings management or not to investigate and report earnings management from company's managers. Denote X_2 as the amounts of being investigated earnings, $(0 \leq X_2 \leq PX_1)$. And financial supervisor give auditor the reward ratio b, and $b \geq 0$. Financial supervisor offer auditor penalty rates l_2, and $l_2 \geq 0$. Denote i_2 as audit services income rates, and $i_2 \geq 0$. Denote B as audit institutions against earnings cost compensation from financial supervisor, and $B \geq 0$. Moreover, for audit institutions without establishment of anti-earnings management and without perfected internal control system, and financial supervisor will ask them for modify and even to withdraw their business license. Denote L_2 as punishment amounts, and $L_2 \geq 0$. If auditor against earnings management cost is TC_2, we assume $TC_2 = \alpha_2 X_2^2 + C_2$ $\alpha_2 > 0$, $C_2 > 0$, C_2 is auditor against earnings management fixed costs. Then, audit institutions with establishment of anti-earnings management benefits function is as follow:

$$E \prod_2 = -\alpha_2 X_2^2 + l_2 X_2 + \left[(1-p)i_2 - pl_2 \right] X_1 - C_2 + B \tag{2}$$

Then, audit institutions without establishment of anti-earnings management benefits function is as follow:

$$E \prod_2^* = \left[(1-p)i_2 - pl_2 \right] X_1 - L_2 \tag{3}$$

2.3 Financial Supervisor Benefits Function

Denote TC_3 as the costs of anti-earnings management of financial supervisor, including expenditure on rewards and input of penalties. Let investigate and penalty cost TC_{31}, and variable costs X_3, $X_3 \geq 0$; fixed costs C_3, $C_3 \geq 0$; then $TC_{31} = X_3 + C_3$. Financial supervisor' expenditure on rewards and penalties against earnings management is TC_{32}; $TC_3 = TC_{31} + TC_{32}$. Denote β as the probability of being investigated and founded from financial supervisor.

When auditor don't investigating and reporting earnings management, financial supervisor variable costs X_3, the being investigated and founded probability p depend on β and X_1, moreover, assume that

$$\frac{dp}{d\left(\beta X_3 / X_1\right)} \geq 0, \frac{d^2 p}{d\left(\beta X_3 / X_1\right)^2} \leq 0$$

Denote S_2 as the decrease cost about audit institutions with establishment of anti-earnings management give the investigating and punishing cost of financial supervisor, and $S_2 = sX_2^2$, $s > \alpha_2$, then,

$$TC_{31} = X_3 - sX_2^2 + C_3$$

$$TC_{32} = p\left(l_1 + l_2\right) X_1 + l_2 X_2 + B - L_2$$

Denote W as the loss of social welfare, and $EW = TC_3 + \gamma X_1$, then

$$EW = p\left(l_1 + l_2\right) X_1 + l_2 X_2 + B - L_2 + X_3 - sX_2^2 + C_3 + \gamma X_1 \qquad (4)$$

When financial supervisor don't investigating earnings management, the loss of social welfare is

$$EW = \gamma X_1 \qquad (5)$$

3 The Solution and Discussion

3.1 How Do the Company Managers Make a Decision?

According to (1), we can obtain:

$$E\prod_1 = \frac{\left[1 - \left(1 + k_2 l_1\right) k_1 p\right]^2}{4\alpha_1} - C_1$$

Obviously, when $2\sqrt{\alpha_1 C_1} > 1 - \left(1 + k_2 l_1\right) k_1 p$, $E\prod_1 < 0$, so company managers don't manipulate earnings. Then we have:

Corollary 1: When financial supervisor don't carry out the anti-earnings management policy and the company managers earnings management cost meets with $2\sqrt{\alpha_1 C_1} > 1$, company managers don't manipulate earnings; when financial supervisor carry out the anti-earnings management policy and company managers earnings management cost meets with $2\sqrt{\alpha_1 C_1} > 1 - (1 + k_2 l_1) k_1 p$, company managers don't manipulate earnings, so anti-earnings management policy portfolios can reduce the amount of earnings management and curbed earnings management efficiently.

3.2 How Do the Auditors Make a Decision?

According to (2) and (3), we can obtain:

$$E \prod_2 = -\alpha_2 X_2^{*2} + l_2 X_2^* - C_2 + B + L_2 \tag{6}$$

When $pX_1 = 0$, $E \prod_2 = -C_2 + B + L_2$ obviously, when $B + L_2 \geq C_2$, Auditor have a choice on investigating and reporting earnings management. Then we have:

Corollary 2: Financial supervisor' policy portfolios on anti-earnings management can make auditor curbed earnings management of company managers.

3.3 How Does the Financial Supervisor Make a Decision?

According to (4) and (5), we can obtain:

$$EW^* = p(l_1 + l_2) X_1^* + l_2 X_2^* + B - L_2 + X_3 - sX_2^{*2} + C_3 + \gamma X_1^*$$

When $X_1^* = 0$, then $X_2^* = 0$, and $EW^* = B - L_2 + X_3 + C_3$

If $X_3^* = 0$, and $B = L_2 = C_3$, and $EW^* = 0$.

If $X_1 > 0$, then $EW^* = \min \left(EW(X_3^*, L_3^*) \right)$, Then we have:

Corollary 3: If the company managers don't manipulate earnings, in order to decrease loss of social welfare, financial supervisor shouldn't input cost of anti-earnings management; when $X_1 > 0$, $X_3 > 0$ and $EW(X_3^*, L_3^*) < 0$, financial supervisor should carry out anti-earnings management policy.

4 Conclude

This paper constructs a game model among company managers, auditor and financial supervisor. Under different anti-earnings management policies' combinations, we analyze the loss of social welfare in this model. The results show:(1) The policies' combination of investigating, convicting and punishing on earnings management can keep earnings management down effectively;(2) Earnings management must be cracked down;(3) For encouraging auditor or audit institutions to attend anti-earnings management activities, the financial supervisor needs to reasonably compensate their anti-earnings management fix cost and enact rewards and penalties system which emphasizes penalties.

Acknowledgments. The work was financially supported by Shanghai Municipal Education Commission key Disciplines Foundation (No.J51701).

References

1. Healy, P., Wahlen, J.: A Review of the Earnings Management Literature and Its Implications for Standard Setting. Accounting Horizons 13(4), 365–383 (1999)
2. Dechow, P.M., Skinner, D.J.: Earnings Management: Reconciling the View s of Accounting Academics, Parishioners, and Regulators. Accounting Horizons 14(2), 235–250 (2000)
3. Lys, T., Watts, R.L.: Lawsuits against Auditors. Journal of Accounting Research 32(3), 65–93 (1994)
4. Myers, J.N., Myers, L.A., Omer, T.C.: Exploring the Term of the Auditor2Client Relationship and the Quality of Earnings: A Case for Mandatory Auditor Rotation? The Accounting Review 78(3), 779–799 (2003)
5. Frankel, R.M., Johnson, M.F., Nelson, K.: The Relation between Auditors' Fees for No audit Services and Earnings Management. The Accounting Review 77(4), 71–105 (2002)
6. Bushman, R.M., Smith, A.J.: Financial Accounting Information and Corporate Governance. Journal of Accounting and Economics 32(123), 237–333 (2001)
7. Francis, J., La Fond, R., Olsson, P.M., Schipper, K.: Costs of Equity and Earnings Attributes. The Accounting Review 79(4), 967–1010 (2004)
8. Chen, C., Chen, S., Su, X.: Profitability Regulation, Earnings Management, and Modified Audit Opinions: Evidence from China. Auditing 20(2), 10–31 (2001)
9. Leuz, C., Nanda, D., Wysocki, P.D.: Earnings Management and Investor Protect ion: an International Comparison. Journal of Financial Economics 69(3), 505–527 (2003)

Financial Development and Changes of China's Foreign Trade Structure

Yujiang Bi[1,2] and Shuangcheng Wang[1,3]

[1] Opening Economy and Trade Research Center, Shanghai Lixin University of Commerce,
Shanghai, 201620, China
[2] School of Economics and Trade, Shanghai Lixin University of Commerce,
Shanghai, 201620, China
[3] School of Mathematics and Information, Shanghai Lixin University of Commerce,
Shanghai, 201620, China
byj163@163.com

Abstract. The purpose of this paper is investigation the relationship between financial development and foreign trade in China using categorized data via SITC (Standard International Trade Classification) one-digit codes. The empirical method is co-integration test. The empirical results provide clear support for the hypothesis that different industries' trade growth has different dependence on financial support. The financial development influenced capital intensive and technological intensive commodities more than others, but price and world economic status influenced primary products' foreign trade notably. The policy implications is government intervention can be called for to help efficient but financially constrained firms to overcome hinders that prevent them from entering international markets and expand their activities abroad.

Keywords: Financial development, Trade structure, SITC, Co-integration test.

1 Introduction

It is widely believed that countries endowed with better financial systems will have special comparative advantages in industries that rely on external finance in production. China's financial industry developed very quickly since the reform and opening-up policy employed. The financial institutes, employees, transaction amounts and the financial instruments all increased very much. Since China's accession to the WTO in 2001, foreign financial subsidiaries obtain more convenient policy to enter China's financial market, and they brought impetus and competitiveness as well. In this period, China's growth in trade has been robust. According to the trade statistics database of Ministry of Commerce of the People's Republic of China, the foreign trade amount in 2008 reached 2560bn USD, China has become the second largest export country in the world. Although the trade amount has decreased 13.9% in 2009 under the impact of the financial crisis, it also reached 2200bn USD, and China has surpassed Germany to become the largest export country and the second largest trading nation.

Q. Zhou (Ed.): ISAEBD 2011, Part I, CCIS 208, pp. 408–414, 2011.

There are a large body of literature showing that financial development promotes growth, especially in financially sensible industries (e.g. Goldsmith,1969; McKinnon,1973; Beck et al.,2000). Researches of Rajan and Zingales(1998) and Braun(2003) also indicated that sectors intensive in external finance and intangible assets grow disproportionately faster in financially developed economies. In a modern society, entrepreneurs and savers both face searching costs when they attempt to deal with each other. Because of asymmetric information costs, financial intermediaries play an important role between savers and entrepreneurs in diversifying their risk in a perfectly competitive environment (Chang et al., 2005).

We argue that financial development should affect the composition of foreign trade for the same reasons that it redistributes production across sectors. Since the industries are different in their needs for external finance support, financial development will determine the cost of outside financial facilities and therefore the development of the industry's export and import. As the second largest trade country, China's trade structure changes definitely have important policy meaning for its trade partners and the world.

The paper is organized as follows: section 2 reviews the literatures which have analyzed the relationships of financial development and international trade. Section 3 calculates the influence effects that financial development on China's categorized foreign trade, as indicated by SITC (Standard International Trade Classification). Section 4 concludes and discusses the results and policy suggestions.

2 Literature Review

Since Goldsmith(1969) introduce the viewpoints about the impact of financial development on economic growth, there are more and more researchers extend the study on the economic effects of financial development, one of the research directions is the effect that financial development on trade growth, especially the growth of export. Among of the studies, Kletzer and Bardhan(1987), Baldwin(1989), Ju and Wei(2005) have built theoretical model to give some canonical analysis about the basis that how the financial development affect the international trade. There are also many empirical researches support the viewpoint (e.g. Beck, 2002; Becker and Greenberg, 2005; Manova, 2005; Berthou, 2006; Bellone et al., 2008).

Goldsmith (1969) pointed out that financial intermediaries ameliorate the allocation of resource across space and time in an uncertain environment to stimulate economic growth. Many studies made deeper analysis about the phases and mechanisms that financial develop influence the foreign trade along the same thoughts. Kletzer and Bardhan (1987) construct a theoretical model to show that countries with less transaction costs have a comparative advantage to develop industries that mainly rely on external finance. Rajan and Zingales (1998) argued that if an industry can develop very well without many external accommodations, the degree of financial development matters little since firms do not need the help of outside financial service.

Chang et al.(2005) explored the possible relevance of financial development and R&D activities in promoting international trade. Ju and Wei (2005) applied the financial contract model of Holmstrom and Tirole (1998) to the Heckscher-Ohlin-Samuelson (HOS) model, in which firms' dependence on external finance is endogenous and the demand for external finance is constrained by financial development. Manova (2008) found that countries with better developed financial systems tend to export relatively more in highly external capital dependent industries and in sectors with fewer tangible assets that can serve as collateral.

Some researchers have done empirical study to test the conclusions coming from theory models. Beck (2002) using a 30-year panel for 65 countries to conclude that countries with a relatively well-developed financial sector have a comparative advantage in manufacturing industries. Berman and Hericourt (2008) studied how financial factors affect both firms' export decisions and the amount exported using a large database containing 5000 firms in 9 economies. Bellone et al. (2008) found that firms enjoyed better ex-ante financial health is more likely to start exporting.

From the literatures above we can see that these studies have established the links between financial development and the growth of export. Some studies believed that the main reason which financial development facilitates export is due to the fact that international trading imposes additional costs. As has been documented by empirical literature, besides costs due to customs and trade regulations, firms also face other fixed and sunk costs such as the costs of acquiring information about the market conditions abroad or establishing distribution channels.

However, we argue that imports also need some additional cost than domestic trade which a bit like that of exports. To import from abroad, firms also need pay some costs such as information collection, business inquiries, and so on. Just like the mechanism that financial development affects the export, financial development will also affect the import. Furthermore, the effect will be different between different industries. If the argue is true, then financial development will have different effects on categorized commodities international trade. Furthermore, financial development will affect a countries' foreign trade structure.

This paper does some validating research on the viewpoint above. We test the effects of financial development on the categorized commodities' foreign trade in China between 1980 and 2009. The commodities are classified by SITC one –digit codes. And co-integration method was used to validate the research.

In contrast to the prior literature, this paper makes a different study in two ways. First, we make the hypothesis that the effects of financial development on different industries are different, and we tested it using China's data. Second, we use the ratio of the sum of one industry's export and import on the total amount of foreign trade to reflect the changing structure of China's foreign trade. We argue that export and import are both very important to economic growth, and financial development would affect both export and import, not only export. It is important to highlight that using disaggregated data helps us to reduce the possible risk of aggregation bias and also helps to capture the sub-sectoral effects which may occur at the industry level.

3 Model Description and Data Resources

According to existing studies, the conventional trade models include the variable that measures the effect of financial development. This study extends this framework to include the measure of world economy size, exchange rate and price level.

The proxy for financial development is denoted as LnFD, which is defined as the logarithm of the amount credited by financial institutions as a share of GDP, we have transform the ratio to an index by making the number in 1980 equal to 100. This measure has been used extensively in the studies on finance and growth (Rajan and Zingales, 1998; Braun, 2003; Beck, 2003; Aghion et al., 2004).

While numerous studies consistently confirm a positive relationship between financial development and international trade, nearly none of them so far has considered the structure adjust effects of financial development especially using categorized data based SITC. The categorized trade structure index is defined as the real amount ratio of categorized industries' foreign trade on total value of China's foreign trade. These variables are denoted as SITCi, i=0, 1, 2....8.

To assess the strength of an independent link between financial development and categorized commodities' foreign trade, we also include a set of control variables. The three control variables (REER, WGDP, Pi,i=ACP,IGP) are considered the main determinants of economic factors but are not directly related to financial development. The change in the main coefficients may suggest whether the argumentation that financial development has different effect on categorized commodities' foreign trade can be conclusive.

Among the control variables, REER is real effective exchange rate of Renminbi. The second is WGDP, which captures the effects coming from external economic environment, it reflect the economic development and market size that affect commodities' foreign trade. The third factor that affects trade volume is price. In this paper, we consider two kinds of price variables. Factory price index of industrial products (ICP, 1980=100) is used in empirical test about foreign trade of industrial production (SITC5-SITC8). Retail price index (ACP, 1980=100) is used in the research of primary commodities' foreign trade (SITC0-SITC4). In this paper LnX denotes the natural logarithm of variable X. Among those variables, the data source of REER and WGDP is International financial statistics (IFS), other variables' data are coming from National Bureau of Statistics of China.

More specifically, we estimate the following models:

$$LnSITC_i = \alpha + \beta LnFD + \gamma LnP_n + \lambda LnREER + \theta LnWGDP + \varepsilon_i$$

Which P_n denotes LnACP or LnICP in empirical test.

Firstly, the Augmented Dickey-Fuller (ADF) unit root tests are employed to test the integration level and the possible co-integration relationships among the variables. We choose the number of lags in the dependent variable by the Akaike Information Criteria (AIC) and Schwarz Criterion (SC) to ensure that the errors are white noise.

Table 1 gives ADF test results for unit root, which prove that all the variables are integrated of order one, that is I(1). This indicates that the first differences of these variables are stationary.

We use both Johansen trace test and maximum eigen value test to find the co-integration relationships among the variables. Johansen test results show that every categorized commodities trade series has one co-integration equation. This means that long run equilibrium relationship exists among these variable series. Table 2 reports the summarized co-integration tests results.

Table 1. Summary of unit root tests

Variable	ADF Statistic	Test equation	Critical values 1%	Critical values 5%	Akaike info criterion	Schwarz criterion
LnSITC0	-2.4867	（C，t，0）	-4.3098	-3.5742	-1.5875	-1.4461
LnSITC1	-2.7873	（C，t，0）	-4.3098	-3.5742	-0.1844	-0.0430
LnSITC2	-0.7491	（C，t，0）	-4.3098	-3.5742	-1.6845	-1.5431
LnSITC3	-2.1259	（C，0，0）	-3.6793	-2.9678	-0.2584	-0.1641
LnSITC4	-3.2318	（C，t，1）	-4.3240	-3.5806	0.6526	0.8430
LnSITC5	-2.7268	（C，t，2）	-4.3393	-3.5875	-1.9086	-1.6686
LnSITC6	-1.9537	（C，t，0）	-4.3098	-3.5742	-2.5878	-2.4464
LnSITC7	-1.1559	（C，t，5）	-4.3943	-3.6122	-2.2231	-1.8305
LnSITC8	-1.0887	（C，t，0）	-4.3098	-3.5742	-1.0621	-0.9207
LnFD	-2.9080	（C，t，1）	-4.3240	-3.5806	-2.7053	-2.5150
LnACP	-0.5549	（C，t，2）	-4.3393	-3.5875	-3.2937	-3.0537
LnICP	-1.3309	（C，t，1）	-4.3240	-3.5806	-2.8769	-2.6866
LnREER	-1.3684	（C，t，0）	-4.3098	-3.5742	-1.5086	-1.3672
LnWGDP	-3.7080	（C，t，1）	-4.3240	-3.5806	-6.1093	-5.9190
dLnSITC0	-3.7581	（C，0，0）	-3.6892	-2.9719	-1.4385	-1.3433
dLnSITC1	-6.6109	（C，0，0）	-3.6892	-2.9719	-0.3601	-0.2650
dLnSITC2	-5.7157	（C，t，1）	-4.3393	-3.5875	-1.8718	-1.6798
dLnSITC3	-4.7449	（C，0，1）	-3.6999	-2.9763	-0.0547	0.0893
dLnSITC4	-5.0307	（C，0，1）	-3.6999	-2.9763	0.7858	0.9298
dLnSITC5	-4.0486	（C，0，4）	-3.7379	-2.9919	-1.9148	-1.6203
dLnSITC6	-5.0044	（C，0，0）	-3.6892	-2.9719	-2.4563	-2.3612
dLnSITC7	-5.5209	（C，0，4）	-3.7379	-2.9919	-2.2851	-1.9906
dLnSITC8	-5.2120	（C，0，0）	-3.6892	-2.9719	-1.0126	-0.9174
dLnFD	-4.2211	（C，0，1）	-3.6999	-2.9763	-2.5436	-2.3996
dLnACP	-2.2441	（0，0，1）	-2.6534	-1.9539*	-3.2349	-3.1389
dLnICP	-1.9191	（0，0，0）	-2.6502	-1.6098	-2.8958	-2.8483
dLnREER	-4.2163	（C，0，0）	-3.6892	-2.9719	-1.3332	-1.2381
dLnWGDP	-3.4249	（C，0，1）	-3.6999	-2.9763	-5.934	-5.7900

Note: dX is difference of variable X. * denotes the 10% critical level. Tests for unit roots have been carried out in Eviews 6.

As a general rule, commodities in SITC classes 0-4 are considered primary products, class 6 and 8 are labor intensive products, and class 5 and 7 are capital intensive or skill intensive products. Class 9 is other uncategorized product of which we has taken no account in this paper. The co-integration test confirmed the results of existing researches (e.g. Beck, 2002; Manova, 2008).

Table 2. Co-integration tests results

	LnFD	LnACP	LnREER	LnWGDP
LnSITC0	1.091813	1.210156	0.906305	6.537537
	(-0.31782)	(-0.15616)	(-0.16768)	(-1.02308)
LnSITC1	-0.91677	0.735969	-0.92851	-1.19119
	(-0.1184)	(-0.05858)	(-0.06339)	(-0.36453)
LnSITC2	0.215469	1.028769	0.048886	0.420587
	(-0.1055)	(1.124536)	(-0.06161)	(-0.06621)
LnSITC3	-2.25528	-0.2646	0.337217	1.756974
	(-0.37118)	(-0.1538)	(-0.20497)	(-0.26003)
LnSITC4	1.874197	5.565586	4.148324	24.33159
	(-1.12133)	(-0.56326)	(-0.6378)	(-3.64086)
	LnFD	LnICP	LnREER	LnWGDP
LnSITC5	1.381319	0.647809	0.597124	2.358188
	(-0.17956)	(-0.08977)	(-0.10421)	(-0.47817)
LnSITC6	-2.56951	-0.22454	-1.52079	0.118043
	(-0.32087)	(-0.14023)	(-0.17117)	(-0.27705)
LnSITC7	5.521501	-0.01374	2.353284	-0.38274
	(-0.92449)	(-0.38607)	(-0.48833)	(-0.78533)
LnSITC8	1.933587	2.28277	1.633025	-2.65635
	(-0.41891)	(-0.1786)	(-0.18816)	(-0.36828)

Notes: Standard error in parentheses.

Among the 9 categorized commodities, financial development has positive influence on 6 categories' foreign trade, most of which is industrialized commodities. The influence degree in classes 4, 5, 7 and 8 is higher than others. Financial development has the maximal influence on the foreign trade on class 7, which degree is 5.5. Besides, financial development has not change the foreign trade model of primary products as a whole. The influence of financial development on the trade of class 1 and 3 is negative.

Except the equations of class 2 and 3, the significant level of coefficients of exchange rate in the equations is relative high. It implies that the change of exchange rate has definitely influence on China's foreign trade. Furthermore, the world economy status also has significant influence on primary commodities foreign trade. However, the influence of world economy scale on industrialized commodities' trade is ambiguous. We can also find that price has relative lower influence on categorized commodities' international trade except class 4 and 8.

We also find that foreign trade of class 5 and 7 are more sensitive to the process of financial development, this is similar to the findings of Manova (2007), Bellone (2008) and Kalina (2008). That is, capital intensive or skill intensive products have relative higher sensitivity to the process of financial development.

4 Discussion and Conclusions

This paper presents evidence of financial development as a source of structure change of foreign trade in China. Although financial development surely has positive effects on some categorized product's trade growth, the degree is not high (e.g. class 1 and class 2). An interesting conclusion of the empirical research is that price is not main factor that affect trade structure changes compared with that of world economy status, which has significant effect on primary products' foreign trade.

This paper has important policy implications as it suggests that, on the process of financial deepening government should pay more attention to the different effects that financial development on the categorized industries. The policy practice should assist all industries obtain equal development opportunities. Furthermore, government can recur to the financial deepening process to change the trade structure except normal industry policy.

Future research in the area should consider the mechanisms that financial development affects the export and import decisions in China, especially using more disaggregated data.

Acknowledgments. We thank the financial support of Leading Academic Discipline Project of Shanghai Municipal Education Commission: International Trade (J51702). National Nature Science Foundation of China (No.60675036).

References

1. Beck, T.: Financial Dependence and International Trade. Review of International Economics 11, 296–316 (2003)
2. Do, Q.T., Andrei, A.: Levchenko. Comparative Advantage, Demand for External Finance, and Financial Development. Journal of Financial Economics 86, 796–834 (2007)
3. Desai, M.A., Foley, C.F., Forbes, K.J.: Financial Constraints and Growth: Multinational and Local Firm Responses to Currency Depreciations. Review of Financial Studies 6, 2857–2888 (2008)
4. Ju, J., Wei, S.J.: Endowment Versus Finance: A Wooden Barrel Theory of International Trade. IMF Working Paper, WP/05/123,(2005)
5. Markusen, J., Venables, A.: The Theory of Endowment, Intra-industry and Multi-national Trade. Journal of International Economics 52, 209–234 (2000)
6. Manova, K.: Credit Constraints, Equity Market Liberalizations and International Trade. Journal of International Economics 76, 33–47 (2008)
7. Manova, K, Zhang, Z.: Export Prices and Heterogeneous Firm Models. Mimeo (2008)
8. Melitz, M.: The Impact of Trade on Intra-Industry Reallocations and Aggregate Industry Productivity. Econometrica 71, 1265–1725 (2003)
9. Rajan, R., Zingales, L.: Financial Dependence and Growth. American Economic Review 88, 559–586 (1998)

Market Effect on the Voluntary Disclosure of Internal Control Information Due to Different Mercerization Degree

Shuwang Zheng[1] and Xianhua Song[2]

[1] Liaoning technical university, professor, 123000 Fuxin, China
[2] Liaoning technical university, master, 125105 Huludao, China
zsw6705@sina.com

Abstract. With the aging of stock market gradually, the role of internal control information has been increasing .Against such a background, the evidence about whether the internal control information provided was recognized will have significant policy implication. Using public companies of three regions listed in Shanghai Stock Exchange as a research sample, this paper tested the market effect on the voluntary disclosure of internal control information based on different mercerization degree. Research results show that the listed companies located in high mercerization regions have bigger changing hands rate after disclosing internal control information voluntarily, but have no significant effect to annual average volatility and risk priority number. The result suggests that mercerization degree could affect the investors' recognition of voluntary disclosure about internal control information.

Keywords: mercerization degree, internal control information, voluntary disclosure, market effect.

1 Introduction

The accounting scandals happened in Enron, WorldCom and other major international companies since 2000 affect the confidence that investors contrary to capital markets. In response to the impact of the lack of internal controls and prevent similar incidents happening again, the U.S. Congress introduced the Sarbanes- Oxley Act in 2002, the bill's introduction caused fundamental changes and profound influences to capital market information disclosure system in USA and China's internal controls. At present, the management of information disclosure about internal control in China is in a transition period; on the one hand, the related departments require the listed companies disclose its internal control systems in its financial reporting, on the other hand, encourages the listed companies that central enterprises holding, financial and other eligible listed companies publicly disclose its self-assessment report about internal control which has been verified by boards and auditors. Under this background, the research about influences that mercerization degree bring to the market effect of information disclosure voluntary will help to expose the root causes

Q. Zhou (Ed.): ISAEBD 2011, Part I, CCIS 208, pp. 415–421, 2011.
© Springer-Verlag Berlin Heidelberg 2011

of instability in the securities market ,and provide empirical experience for the changes of information disclosure system meanwhile.

2 The Literature Review

Joseph Stiglitz, George A. AKerlof and Michael Spence believes that the information that various types of person grasp are different in the market economic activities, the officers who predominate more information are often in a dominant position, while the less are in inferior position. The information asymmetries, which caused by specialization differences and the private information existence, will impact the overall quality of the capital market through adverse selection. However, the disclosure of information can avoid this adverse selection risk to a certain extent, and it will be useful for investors and regulators. Based on this, the information disclosure system of internal control is significant to improve the quality of capital market.

Hermanson (2000) surveyed different person's response to the disclosure of internal control information through sent out questionnaires to American bankers, securities brokers, institutional investors, individual investors and other 9 users of financial statements, the survey results show that the internal control report is widely recognized on its function of improving financial reporting as well as providing additional information. Newson and Deegan (2002) found that the listed companies disclose its internal control information voluntarily will help it to achieve the company's core competencies and global competition strategy through their surveys contrary to multinational companies in Australia, Singapore and South Korea.

Whisenant et al. (2003) analysis the influence about internal control and stock prices, and found that serious internal control deficiencies will lead to negative stock price reaction. Maria et al (2006), who studied the relationship between implicit costs of internal control and effectiveness of internal control through collecting samples in accordance with SEC disclosure requirements, found that disclosure of the internal control deficiencies in the company will cause much higher cost compared with the companies who disclose no defects.

3 The Theoretical Analysis and Hypotheses

3.1 The Theoretical Analysis

The literature has demonstrated that the internal control disclosure will have a series of significant impacts such as stock price's change to the capital markets and the internal control information disclosure system derives from information asymmetry. Accordingly, from the point of signal transmission path, we can say that there has a close relationship between the symmetrical information symmetry degree and mercerization, the higher degree of mercerization will cause high information sharing level while the lower low .In collusion, mercerization, as a key factor to determine information sharing degree, can increase or reduce the market effect caused by internal control disclosure. If we make "the capital market is complete" as the further assumption, stakeholders in the capital market can get all business information like operations because information asymmetric situation does not exist and the information disclosure does not influence the information flow of subjects in the capital markets, then market effects would not exist. However, If narrow the extreme, we can reason out that the disclosure of internal control information voluntarily will lead to much little effects about capital markets in the areas which has higher degree of mercerization , conversely, the smaller is large.

3.2 Variable Definition and Research Hypothesis Offered

(1) Variable definition

The degree of mercerization: it means the progress and degree of the area where the listed companies register. China's current mercerization is so different that the highest mercerization area more than 3 times higher compared with minimum area. This article will use mercerization index which referred in the <China mercerization index – the report about mercerization relative process in 2008 > as the variable to measure mercerization degree. In order to test the hypothesis in this article effectively, in, we selected Shanghai, Hebei and Tibet as measuring samples in 32 provinces, municipalities, autonomous regions (excluding Hong Kong, Macau and Taiwan) due to the difference of mercerization degree.

Market effect: based on the analysis of literature, the article consider market risk, volatility of stock profit and trading volume as the factors to measure market effect influenced by internal control information disclosure. In the three indexes, market risk reflects the intensity of stock profit with the changes of market returns, the theory shows that mercerization degree will reduce the stock risks .Stock gains volatility reflects the vibration amplitude. Stock trading, as a liquidity measure, reflects the willingness of company stock investors to buy or sell. However, it may not seize the investor adverse selection problem because it also contains some irrelevant information such as portfolio adjustment, liquidity impacts, and risk preference change and so on; therefore, we use the total changing hands rate (CHR) as substitutes of total amount of transactions in order to eliminate scale effect.

Disclose internal control information voluntarily: in accordance with internal environment, risk assessment, control activities, information communication, internal supervision, and a secondary 63 indexes, this paper adopts the same methods as "the white paper of internal control about Chinese listed company in 2008" to evaluate the voluntarily degree of listed companies.

(2) Research hypothesis offered

Combined the theoretical analysis with related variables, this article put forward the following hypothesis:

Hypothesis 1: the stock will have lower liquidity if the listed companies which located in the higher mercerization degree regions disclose their internal control information voluntarily. We can calculate that the high liquidity of the stocks belong to the listed companies which located completely capital market is not caused by the internal control information but by the market's own behavior if hypothesis 1 is established.

Hypothesis 2: the stock will have lower volatility if the listed companies which located in the higher mercerization degree regions disclose their internal control information voluntarily. We can calculate that the high volatility of the stocks belong to the listed companies which located completely capital market is not caused by the internal control information but by the market's own behavior if hypothesis 2 is established.

Hypothesis 3: the stock will have lower risk priority number (RPN) if the listed companies which located in the higher mercerization degree regions disclose their internal control information voluntarily.

4 Research Design

4.1 Sample Selection and Data Sources

First of all, choose the companies listed in Shanghai A-share main-board in 2009; Secondly, eliminate all companies outside from Shanghai, Hebei and Tibet; In addition, exclude the financial, insurance, banking and ST companies; At last, eliminate the companies exactly listed in 2009 and the companies that can not collect complete data in RESSET financial research database.According to the above standard, this thesis eventually selected 105 research samples altogether.

Stock's annual average volatility (AAV) returns from mean day-volatility of the stocks in the sample companies; day-volatility, RPN and CHR of the stocks are from the RESSET financial research database; Mercerization index data comes from 'China mercerization index – the report about mercerization relative process in 2008'; the score data of information disclosure degree stems from the sample's annual report and "the white paper of internal control about Chinese listed company in 2008".

4.2 Research Model

This paper uses CHR, AAV and RPN as the comprehensive factors to measure market effects in order to avoid the errors that use single factor may cause, and builds models in allusion to each factor as follows:

Model 1:
$$Ln(ER) = Ln(ER_0) + \left[Ln(ER_{MAI}) - \overline{Ln(ER)}\right] + \left[Ln(ER_{Ln VOLUNTATY} - \overline{Ln(ER)}\right] + Ln(ER_{INTERACTION})$$

Model 2: $VOTILITY = V_0 + (V_{MAI} - \overline{V}) + (V_{Ln(VOLUNTATY)} - \overline{V}) + V_{INTERACTION}$

Model 3: $\beta = \beta_0 + \left(\beta_{mai}. - \overline{\beta}\right) + (\beta_{Ln(VOLUNTATY)} - \overline{\beta}) + \beta_{INTERACTION}$

In model 1, ER_0 is nodal increment, means the part that CHR model cannot explain. ER_{MAI} means the effect that mercerization degree act on CHR. $ER_{Ln VOLUNTATY}$ means the effect that disclosure degree act on CHR. $ER_{INTERACTION}$ means the interaction effect that two factors act on CHR. The Ln before each variable means the logarithmic processing to all data.

The variables in model 2 and model 3 are similar with model 1.

4.3 Empirical Test and Results Analysis

(1) Descriptive statistics analysis

Table 1. Descriptive statistics results

MI	CHR			AAV			RPN		
	MAX	MEAN	MIN	MAX	MEAN	MIN	MAX	MEAN	MIN
2.34	7.31	6.51	4.87	0.04	0.03	0.02	1.38	1.05	0.43
1.86	7.34	6.98	6.58	0.04	0.03	0.02	1.49	1.17	0.77
0.92	7.45	7.18	6.60	0.04	0.03	0.03	1.28	0.99	0.74

Table 1 show the descriptive statistics results of market effects index after the company disclose internal control information voluntarily in 2009. We can find that the CHR and AAV reflect the theory prospects while RPN not. For example, the MAX, MEAN, MIN of the CHR and AAV in the region of higher MI is Significantly bigger than lower MI.

Table 2. Tests of Between-Subjects Effects

Dependent Variable	Source	Type III Sum of Squares	df	Mean Square	F	Sig.
CHR R Squared =0.999 (Adjusted R Squared = 0.997)	Corrected Model	32.21	58	.56	548.72	.000
	Intercept	1495.61	1	1495.61	1477721.24	.000
	MI	1.02	2	.51	505.48	.000
	disclosure	27.51	46	.60	590.93	.000
	interaction	.09	10	.01	8.82	.000
	Error	.05	46	.001		
	Total	4600.73	105			
	Corrected Total	32.26	104			
AAV R Squared =0.760 (Adjusted R Squared = 0.457)	Corrected Model	.002(a)	58	0.0000287	2.51	.001
	Intercept	.027	1	.027	2379.09	.000
	MI	0.0000255	2	0.0000127	1.12	.336
	disclosure	.001	46	0.0000283	2.48	.001
	interaction	.000	10	0.0000288	2.52	.016
	Error	.001	46	0.0000114		
	Total	.083	105			
	Corrected Total	.002	104			
RPN R Squared =0.654 (Adjusted R Squared = 0.218)	Corrected Model	1.808(a)	58	.031	1.501	.078
	Intercept	36.12	1	36.12	1739.24	.000
	MI	.04	2	.018	.850	.434
	disclosure	1.53	46	.033	1.61	.056
	interaction	.133	10	.013	.64	.772
	Error	.955	46	.021		
	Total	121.08	105			
	Corrected Total	2.76	104			

(2) Significant test and analysis

The first part of table 2 shows that the F-statistic of mercerization degree, disclose voluntarily and the interaction of two factors were 505.483, 590.927, 8.819, the corresponding significance probability were less than 0.05. The result shows that the differences between these three roles and CHR are significant. The mean of pairwise multiple comparisons should use Tamhance results because homogeneity of variance test rejected the null hypothesis, and therefore the question does not have the homogeneity of variance. T test results show in Table 3. From table 3 we can find that the CHR caused by high mercerization degree and medium degree, low degree is significant; while the difference between medium degree and low degree does not exists significant differences.

Similarly, the last two parts of table 2 show that the influence of AAV caused by mercerization degree does not pass the F-statistic, but disclosure and the interaction passes; all of the three factors does not pass the F-statistic contrary to RPN. We can also find that there were no significant differences between the different mercerization degree and different AAV, RPN.

Table 3. Multiple Comparisons

Dependent Variable	(I) MI	(J) MI	Mean Difference (I-J)(*)	Std. Error	Sig.
CHR	2.50	6.41	0.1932	0.17	0.66
Tamhane		10.41	0.6679(*)	0.166	0.027
The mean difference is	6.41	2.50	-0.1932	0.1708	0.660
significant at the .05 level.		10.41	0.4747(*)	0.0938	0
	10.41	2.50	-0.6679(*)	0.1656	0.027
		6.41	-0.4747(*)	0.0938	0
AAV	2.50	6.41	0.0005	0.0021	0.995
Tamhane		10.41	0.0033	0.0017	0.321
The mean difference is	6.41	2.50	-0.0005	0.0021	0.995
significant at the .05 level.		10.41	0.0028	0.0014	0.182
	10.41	2.50	-0.0033	0.0017	0.321
		6.41	-0.0028	0.0014	0.182
RPN	2.50	6.41	-0.1856	0.1045	0.301
Tamhane		10.41	-0.0642	0.0871	0.875
The mean difference is	6.41	2.50	0.1856	0.1045	0.301
significant at the .05 level.		10.41	0.1215	0.0620	0.203
	10.41	2.50	0.0642	0.0871	0.875
		6.41	-0.1215	0.0620	0.203

5   Conclusions and Significance

This paper examines the difference of market effects under different MI after the listed companies disclose their information voluntarily with empirical research method. The results show that the mercerization degree, internal control information disclosure voluntarily and the interaction of two factors will affect the CHR significantly. The mercerization degree, as a single variable, can not affect AAV significantly, while the interaction with disclosure voluntarily could affect. Both single and double variables can not affect RPN significantly.

The results show that investors in capital market recognize the internal control information of listed companies that located in high mercerization regions more compared with who located in low regions. The relative reasonable explanation is that these companies are considered to be more credible because they are affected more external environment constraint. With the development of disclosure system about internal control reports gradually, only rise the mercerization steady, the information disclosure behavior of the listed companies could be more and more accept by investors.

References

1. Hermanson, H.M.: An analysis of the demand for reporting on internal control. Accounting Horizons (2000)
2. Newson, M., Craig, D.: Global expectations and their association with corporate social disclosure practices in Australia, Singapore and South Korea. The International Journal of Accounting (2002)
3. Willis, D.M., Lightle Susan, S.: Management reports on internal control. Journal of Accountancy (2000)
4. Wesley, M.S., Luiz, A.: The voluntary disclosure of financial information on the internet and the firm value effect in companies across Latin America. SSRN working Paper (2004)
5. Whisenant, J.S., Sankaraguruswamy, S., Raghunanadan, K.: Market reactions to disclosure of reportable events. Auditing: A Journal of Practice and Theory (2003)
6. Krishnan: Audit committee quality and internal control-an empirical analysis. The Accounting Review (2005)
7. Lang, M., Lundholm,R.: Cross-sectional determinants of analyst ratings of corporate disclosures. Journal of Accounting Research (autumn) (1993)
8. Bin, L., Jing, R.: Why do Listed Companies Disclose the Auditor's Internal Control Reports voluntarily?-An Empirical Study Based on Signaling Theory in China. Accounting Research (2009)
9. Chen, G., Liu, Y.: The Market Respond of the Information Disclosure of Internal Control. Systems Engineering (2007)

CO₂ Emissions Embodied in China's Export to U.S.: Analysis on the Top Ten Export Goods

Yinghua Meng

Open Economy and Trade Research Center,
Shanghai Lixin University of Commerce
Shanghai, P.R. China
mymgy@yahoo.com.cn

Abstract. Trade creates a mechanism for consumers to shift environmental pollution associated with their consumption to other countries. Applied an input–output approach, the article estimates the amount of CO2 embodied in Sino–U.S. Export trade during 2002–2009, It was found that the CO2 emissions of China's top ten export goods constitute over 75% of CO2 emissions of all export goods, and the most carbon-intensity export sector is office machines and automatic data-processing machines, miscellaneous manufactured articles, and telecommunications and sound-recording and reproducing apparatus and equipment; in addition, the less carbon-intensity export sector is textile yarn, fabrics and related products, furniture, and parts thereof; bedding, mattresses, mattress supports, cushions and similar stuffed furnishings, and articles of apparel and clothing accessories.

Keywords: Sino-US Trade, Embodied CO2 Emissions, Export.

1 Introduction

In China, trade surplus have reached 262 billion dollars in 2007, and among those trade partners, Sino-US trade surplus already achieved 163 billion dollars. Now U.S. has been the second largest trade partner of China and the one that contributed most to China's trade surplus. Even though Sino-US trade is such an important topic, little research has been investigated in the issues of the environment problem of Sino-US trade.

International trade is a main reason for green gas emission. Since 20th 90s, many literatures have discussed the topics of embodied carbon in international trade, and almost all of the these literatures have come to a common conclusions that international trade is one of the mechanism of transferring carbon emission, in addition, developed countries are the main exporter of embodied carbon. Wyckoff and Roop (1994) believed that among the largest 6 OCED countries in 1984-1986, it is about 13 percent of their carbon emission reflected in their import of manufacturing. Ahmad and Wyckoff (2003) have investigated the embodied carbon in international trade for 24 countries.

Machado et al. (2001) have computed the embodied carbon in international trade for Brazil from 1970 to 1992, and considered that most developed countries were

Q. Zhou (Ed.): ISAEBD 2011, Part I, CCIS 208, pp. 422–428, 2011.

transferring much of their carbon emission to developing countries by outsourcing their manufacturing to developing countries and import the related goods. Weber and Matthews (2007) have studied the issue of carbon emission in international trade for U.S. from 1997 to 2004. In all, we can conclude that most of the literatures only aimed at the developed countries, and neglect the issue on developing countries, since most of the carbon is released by developing countries, so it is very important to discuss more carefully on developing countries. In addition, among developing counties, China is second largest carbon emission counties of the world. On recent years, some countries and organizations condemned China have released too much carbon in the process of development. As a result, it is important to accurately estimate how much carbon has been released in China. However, from the point of consuming, China is not only the responsibility country for carbon emission, some of China's export goods consumed by other countries, such as U.S., JAPAN, should also be responsibility for this environment problem. In addition, in 2009, U.S. have passed a law, it will levied high carbon tax on imported goods for some high-energy consuming product and primary goods, such as steel and aluminum.

Under this background, the most important work to do for evaluating how much tax will be levied for China's export to U.S. is the computing research for embodied carbon of Sino-USA trade. And this paper wills analysis the CO_2 emissions embodied in the top ten export goods of China's export to U.S.

2 Literature Review

At present, most literatures on China's carbon emission believed that China's export constitute one of the main factors for carbon emission, in addition, among China's export counties, developed countries are taking more responsible for China's carbon emission. IEA (2007) believed that the carbon emission embodied in China' export was already occupied 34% of its total carbon emission. Wang and Watson(2007) considered that China have been export 1.1 billion tons of embodied carbon in 2004, about 23% of its total carbon emission, in addition, export goods produced about 1.49 billion tons of carbon. Li and Hewitt (2008) investigated the embodied carbon in Sino-UK trade, and found that China have emitted 186MT carbon for demand of consuming of UK. Xu et al. (2009) found that the embodied carbon reflected in China's export to USA is about 12%-17 %(8%-12%) of its total carbon emission for 2002(2007) respectively.

The main method of computing the embodied carbon in international trade is by using trade value multiply the intensity coefficient of carbon emission accordingly. But since we can not judge how much carbon have been emitted from the finished product, because carbon is also emitted on the process of producing the inputs. So the method of input-output is widely used in this field to sum up the total carbon emission reflected in the finished product. By using this method, we can compute and analyze the direct and indirect carbon emission reflected in all of the processing period.

From 20th 50s, input-output table was widely introduced in analyzing the economy. Up till now, China has made 5 basic input-output tables (1987, 1992, 1997, 2002 and 2007). But till now, less work is done on computing the embodied carbon in international trade of China, among those literatures, the most distinguished work was done by Shui and Harriss(2006).they used EIO-LCA(Economic Input Output-Life Cycle Assessment) developed by Carnegie Mellon University to evaluated the carbon emission reflected in Sino-US trade from 1997-2003.

This paper is contributing to the existing literatures by classifying and computing the carbon emission reflected in top ten goods of China's export to U.S., in addition, in order to remedy the problem of lacking enough sample, we use improvement of technology, price index and exchange rate to enlarge the basic sample data to full range of research period.

3 Method and Data Source

3.1 Economic Input-Output Life Cycle Assessment

We use the intensity coefficient of carbon emission from the EIO-LCA software, and the method in this software is base on the input-output method. The principle of input-output method is as follows:

The input–output analysis was introduced by Leontief in the 1930s and has been applied to analyze the economic–environmental relationships since the 1960s. This strategy allows both direct and indirect environmental impact. This method has been applied to estimate the embodied energy, CO_2 emissions, pollutants associated with products sold in national or international markets.

As originally formalized by Leontief in his groundbreaking work, the total output of an economy, x, can be expressed as the sum of intermediate consumption, Ax, and final consumption, y:

$$x=Ax+y \tag{1}$$

Where A is the economy's direct requirements matrix and y is the demand for which the supply-chain output, x, is to be derived. The matrix A describes the relationship between all sectors of the economy. When solved for total output, this equation yields:

$$x=(I-A)^{-1}y \tag{2}$$

When coupled with an environmental matrix, C, which shows the environmental emissions caused by each sector in the model, the total amount of emissions can be calculated as:

$$c=C(I-A)^{-1}y \tag{3}$$

c representing the sector-wise total supply-chain emissions to meet the final demand y.

3.2 Data Source

1. Carbon Intensity Coefficients.
We use China's input-output table of 122 sectors in 2002 and EIO-LCA software, we compute the carbon intensity coefficients "c" of the top ten China's export goods to U.S. And the CO2 emission factors for the China exports to US on the basic year

(2002) are derived from the EIO-LCA software developed by Green Design Initiative at Carnegie Mellon University.

Since the production technology have been changed a lot from 2002, so in order to have a more accurately evaluation of the carbon intensity coefficients of the other year, we use improvement of technology, price index and exchange rate to extend the basic sample data of 2002 to full range of research period. See table 1.

Table 1. Amended Parameter for Carbon Intensity Coefficients (2002-2009)

	2002	2003	2004	2005	2006	2007	2008	2009
improvement of technology [a]	1.000	1.034	1.025	0.982	0.962	0.931	0.972	0.972
exchange rate	8.277	8.277	8.277	8.192	7.972	7.604	6.945	6.831
price index	1.000	1.012	1.051	1.07	1.087	1.139	1.206	1.197

Sources: a. computing base on average energy consuming per 10,000 Yuan. Exchange rate and price index is from China Statistical Yearbook.

3.3 Trade Data

Data of China's export to U.S. are from US Census Bureau. Firstly, we list the top ten goods of China's export to U.S. as follows. We refer them to symbol A-J:

(A)SITC65 -- Textile yarn, fabrics, made-up articles, n.e.s., and related products; (B)SITC 69 -- Manufactures of metals, n.e.s.;(C) SITC 74 -- General industrial machinery and equipment, n.e.s., and machine parts, n.e.s.;(D) SITC 75 -- Office machines and automatic data-processing machines;(E) SITC 76 -- Telecommunications and sound-recording and reproducing apparatus and equipment; (F) SITC 77 -- Electrical machinery, apparatus and appliances, n.e.s., and electrical parts thereof (including non-electrical counterparts, n.e.s., of electrical household-type equipment); (G) SITC 82 -- Furniture, and parts thereof; bedding, mattresses, mattress supports, cushions and similar stuffed furnishings; (H)SITC 84 -- Articles of apparel and clothing accessories; (I) SITC 85 – Footwear; (J) SITC 89 -- Miscellaneous manufactured articles, n.e.s.

Secondly, since the data of China's export to USA from US Census Bureau is Customs Value, and it exclude the US import duties, freight, insurance and other charges incurred in bringing the merchandise to the U.S., we assume that Chinese export data record custom value of the goods produced in China. We were aware that the same monetary value of goods produced in one country will represent different quantities of goods of the same category produced in another. Therefore purchasing power parity (PPP), which compares the prices of a basket of common household goods between countries, must also be taken into consideration. Thus, relative purchasing power parity (RPPP) was used to translate the US dollar values documented by the US Census Bureau to the actual quantity of Chinese exports in the condition of using emission factors derived from the EIO-LCA. RPPP is a ratio between the exchange rate of a US dollar relative to Chinese currency RMB and PPP conversion factor (Shui and Harriss, 2006). Table 2 presents the RPPP values we used for estimating the CO2 embodiment in Chinese exports to the U.S. for the years 2002–2009.

Table 2. China's RPPP during 2002-2009

Year	Exchange rate (RMB/US$)	PPP conversion factor(LCU/US$)
2002	8.277	4.147
2003	8.277	4.102
2004	8.277	4.15
2005	8.192	4.087
2006	7.972	4.017
2007	7.604	4.091
2008	6.945	4.171
2009	6.831	4.171

Sources: China's exchange rate is from China Statistical Yearbook; PPP conversion factor is from UN millennium development goals database. LCU=local currency unit.

Then, the CO_2 emissions embodied in the Chinese exports to the U.S. were estimated from:

$$[CO2]_{j,y} = X_{j,y} \times C_{j,y} \times (CPI_{2002}/CPI_y) \times RPPP_y \tag{4}$$

where $[CO_2]_{j,y}$, with units of MMT, represents the total CO_2 emissions embodied in Chinese exports in the year y; $X_{j,y}$ refers to China's export value to USA; $C_{j,y}$ refers to carbon intensity coefficients, which is computing from EIO-LCA software; CPI_{2002} and CPI_y refers to customer price index in year 2002 and y respectively; $RPPP_y$ refers to relatively purchase power parity in year t.

4   Estimates Results

The regression results are in table 3. From table 3, we can see that the difference between different export sectors is very great. The most emission of embodied carbon is from the following three products: Office machines and automatic data-processing machines (SITC 75); Miscellaneous manufactured articles, n.e.s. (SITC 89); and Telecommunications and sound-recording and reproducing apparatus and equipment (SITC 76). In order to decrease more carbon emission during China's export to U.S., also prevent U.S. will levy high carbon tax on these export goods, we should improve the production technology of these three products, or choose substitute goods to produce and export. On the contrary, the less emission of embodied carbon is from

Table 3. The Embodied Carbon Emission of China's Export to USA. MMT

	2002	2003	2004	2005	2006	2007	2008	2009
A	13.82	19.36	23.96	29.78	31.62	28.74	23.1	19.09
B	44.49	56.06	71.92	83.07	93.64	86.42	70.98	52.29
C	21.9	29.04	38.14	45.6	55.2	54.06	45.06	36.01
D	102.33	165.79	244.51	273.69	288.83	233.24	181.03	172.93
E	70.88	88.04	124.26	164.35	185.83	188.32	152.44	131.19
F	66.23	80.19	101.06	112.98	124.19	113.33	94.79	80.14
G	37.58	49.41	60.35	68.79	72.76	63.86	47.261	37.41
H	39.51	49.14	57.54	79.51	84.79	82.00	64.16	60.65
I	55.25	59.66	62.76	66.38	66.6	55.89	44.67	39.35
J	126.91	148.49	163.31	175.15	177.87	173.61	140.32	116.15
Total	578.87	745.16	947.81	1099.31	1181.33	1079.47	863.82	745.20

Notes: A-J refers to the top ten goods that China's export to U.S.: SITC 65,69,74,75,76,77,82,84,85,89.

Table 4. Embodied Carbon in All China's Export Goods and China's Export to U.S.

	All China's export goods(1)	China's CO2 emissions if China does not export to the U.S.(2)	Embodied carbon in China's export to USA (3)=(1)-(2)
2002	3376.15	2769.83	606.32
2003	3983.12	3220.96	762.16
2004	4753.33	3754.40	998.93
2005	5322.69	4128.65	1194.04
2006	6231.52	4887.11	1344.41
2007	6722.38	5337.43	1384.95

Source: The U.S. Information Administration.

the following three products: textile yarn, fabrics, made-up articles, n.e.s., and related products (SITC65); furniture, and parts thereof; bedding, mattresses, mattress supports, cushions and similar stuffed furnishings (SITC 82); and articles of apparel and clothing accessories (SITC 84).

In addition, we compare our above results with the results of The U.S. Information Administration. from table 4, we can conclude that the embodied carbon of top ten goods that China's export to U.S. has already occupy 75% of embodied carbon in all China's export goods to U.S.. So if we can control the emission of embodied carbon in top ten goods that China's export to U.S., we can effectively deal with the law of carbon tax of U.S.

Acknowledgments. Supported by Leading Academic Discipline Project of Shanghai Municipal Education Commission: International Trade (J51702).

References

1. Hayami, H., Kiji, T.: An input–output analysis on Japan–China environmental problem: compilation of the input–output table for the analysis of energy and air pollutants. Journal of Applied Input–Output Analysis 4, 23–47 (1997)
2. Li, Y., Hewitt, C.N.: The effect of trade between China and the UK on national and global carbon dioxide emissions. Energy Policy 36(6), 1907–1914 (2008)
3. Machado, G., Schaeffer, R., Worrel, E.: Energy and carbon embodied in the international trade of Brazil: an input–output approach. Ecological Economics 39, 409–424 (2001)
4. Shui, B., Harriss, R.C.: The role of CO2 embodiment in U.S.–China trade. Energy Policy 34(18), 4063–4068 (2006)
5. Wyckoff, A.W., Roop, J.M.: The embodiment of carbon in imports of manufactured products. Energy Policy 22(3), 187–194 (1994)
6. Weber, C.L., Matthews, H.S.: Embodied environmental emissions in U.S. international trade, 1997–2004. Environmental Science and Technology 41, 4875–4881 (2007)

Determined Factors of International Trade in Cultural Goods of China: A Panel Data Analysis

Yinghua Meng

Open Economy and Trade Research Center,
Shanghai Lixin University of Commerce
Shanghai, P.R. China
mymgy@yahoo.com.cn

Abstract. We use gravity model to estimate the determined factors of international trade in China's Cultural Goods. Except for antiques and other visual arts, most of cultural goods have negative relations with distance variable. Most of China's import in cultural goods are from developed countries, and highly influenced by exporters market conditions, such as architecture, design and jewellery. China's import of cultural goods is not influenced by China's purchasing power; but most of China's export in cultural goods is highly influenced by importer's purchasing power. Because of different traits of culture goods, China's GDP and population variable have different effects on China's trade in culture goods. In addition, the productiveof cultural goods has little effect on China's import of culture goods, but has a positive effect on China's export of other visual arts, jewellery, film and video, architecture and design.

Keywords: Trade in Cultural Goods, China, Gravity Equation.

1 Introduction

At the last 20 years, broadcasting, television, news press, publish, film and other culture industry have create great wealth, at the same time, the growth of these industries foster the development of international trade in cultural goods quickly.

Although China has a very long history and plentiful of diversified culture, China's international trade in cultural goods should have reached a high level, but in fact, Cultural enterprise of China have disadvantage in exporting their cultural goods, more specific, most of their export goods are hardware related with entertainment and education, software products are hardly access to reach another country. Secondly, most cultural goods of trade are highly concentrated on processing products, the production of original cultural goods are very few. Thirdly, China's trade pairs in cultural goods are only limited to some developed countries, less likely to trade with most developing countries of the world. So, we should ask, what China should do to increase its advantage in its production and export capability of cultural goods?

In order to enlarge China's trade in cultural goods, the most important thing is that we should analysis and point out the determined factors of the China's trade in cultural goods. With UNESCO (2009), this report clearly illuminates a new classified

Q. Zhou (Ed.): ISAEBD 2011, Part I, CCIS 208, pp. 429–435, 2011.
© Springer-Verlag Berlin Heidelberg 2011

and computation framework for international trade in cultural goods. We use the method of UNESCO (2009) to collect the data, and then we plan to use trade gravity model to empirical test the main determined factors of the international trade in cultural goods.

2 Literature Review

In recent years, researches in trade in service have made great progresses in constructing theory and empirical model. Since trade in cultural goods is part of trade in service, so these work have benefited a lot for our discussing. For example, in constructing the mode of trade in service, different traits in service (Markusen, 1989; van Marrewijk, 1996; Francois, 1990), market structure (Kierzkowski, 1986; Francois & Wooton, 2001a, 2001b) and mode of supply (Markusen, 1989; Wong et al, 2006) have been incorporated in their theory model. In empirical literatures, most researchers considered that trade in service is influenced by GDP per capita, market scale, economic freedom, FDI scale. But trade in cultural goods also has its distinctive traits, such as the importance of historic and cultural resource in increasing the competitive advantage of trade in cultural goods; cultural goods can be classified into copied goods and goods that can not be copied. So, with a view to finding the main determined factors of the international trade in cultural goods, we should firstly clear understand the traits of international trade in cultural goods.

First, people doubt if the traditional trade theory can be applicable to trade in cultural goods. Mas-Colell (1999) believe that Comparative Advantage Theory can be use to explain the fact of trade in cultural goods. Schulze (1999) thinks that Comparative Advantage Theory can be used to explain the cultural goods that can be copied, but can not be applicable to cultural goods that can not be copied. Hoskins and McFadyen (1995) consider the first mover advantage and Economies of Scale is the main reason why USA can occupy most of the market in trade in cultural goods. Throsby (1999) thinks that most of trade in cultural goods are intra-industry trade, and can be analyze with the theory of demand preference similarity.

3 Empirical Analysis

At first, we construct the basic gravity model and add the interested variable into the equation for empirical study.

3.1 Regress Model

The gravity model is the workhorse model for empirical analysis of the relation between trade costs and trade flows. The gravity model explains bilateral trade as a function of the trading partner's market size, and bilateral trade costs relative to all other trading partners. Commonly used measures of such costs are the distance between the trading partners, whether or not they have a common border, whether or not they share a common language and whether or not one or both are members of a regional trade agreement. In the following, in order to emphasis the main determined factors of trade in China's cultural goods, we define the actual gravity model as follows:

$$Log(Tradeijt)=Cijt+Log(GDPit)+Log(GDPjt)+Log(POPit)+Log(POPjt)+ \\ Log(DISTij)+ +FTAij+Log(CULt)+uijt \tag{1}$$

The variable's meaning in the gravity equation are presented below: GDPit: gross GDP of country i in year t; GDPjt: gross GDP of China in year t; POPit: population of country i in year t; POPjt :population of China in year t; DISTij: distance between country i's capital and China's economic zone; FTAij: If country i is membership of ASEAN, then=1,else=0; CULt: Productive efficiency of cultural goods in China in year t; Tradeijt: export value of cultural goods from China to country i in year t; Cijt: intercept; uij: white noise.

3.2 Data

1. Cultural goods.

The first computation framework of cultural goods is released in 1986 by UNESCO, and the new revised version is released in 2007, in this paper, our measuring method of cultural goods is base on the latter new framework.

According to UNESCO (2007), trade in cultural goods is classified into 8 series as follows (bracket is HS classified number): A. Cultural and Natural Heritage: Antiques (970500, 970600). B. Performance and Celebration: Musical instruments (830610,920110,920120,920190,920210,920290,920510,920590,920600,920710,920 790,920810,920890); Recorded media1 (852321, 852329, 852351, 852359, 852380, 490400). C. Visual Arts and Crafts: Paintings (970110, 970190, 491191); Other visual arts (970200, 970300, 392640, 442010, 442090, 691310, 691390, 701890, 830621, 830629, 960110, 960190); Craft(580500, 580610, 580620, 580631, 580632, 580639, 580640, 580810, 580890, 580900, 581010, 581091, 581092, 581099, 581100600240, 600290, 600310, 600320, 600330, 600340, 600390, 600410, 600490); Jewellery(711311, 711319, 711320, 711411, 711419, 711420, 711610, 711620); Photography(370510, 370590). D. Books and Press: Books (490110, 490191, 490199); Newspaper (490210, 490290); Other Printed Matter (490300, 490591, 490510, 490599, 490900, 491000). E. Audio-visual and Interactive Media: Film and Video (370610, 370690, 950410). F. Design and Creative Services: Architecture and design (490600). G. Tourism. H. Sports and Recreation.

According to the above classification and HS07 number, we can compute the A-F cultural goods with UN COMTRADE database. In this database, we only collect 2007-2009 trade data, so considering disposal the abnormal data, we choose China's trade partner country with as follows: Australia, Austria, Belgium, Brazil, Canada, Colombia, Denmark, Finland, France, Germany, Italy, Japan, Rep. of Korea, Malaysia, Mexico, Netherlands, Singapore, South Africa, Spain, Sweden, Thailand, United Kingdom, and USA.

2. Other data and source

We use the variable of value added of cultural industry per capita to refer to the productive efficiency of cultural goods in China. And data source of value added of cultural industry and population is from China Statistical Yearbook. Considering the lag effect of productive efficiency on trade, we compute the data from 2006-2008 accordingly. FTA variable refers to if the trade partner is the membership of ASEAN, data source of population and GDP are from UN basic stat. database, the distance between trade partner's capital and Shanghai is calculated from the net: http://www.hjqing.com/find/jingwei/

4   Estimates Results

This section applies the gravity model for estimating the main determined factors of China's export of cultural goods. We use the eviews 6.0 to run the regression model. The results presented in Table1 almost support our hypothesis; almost all the variable coefficients get their expected values and are significant at the 1% level: Except for antiques and other visual arts, most of cultural goods have negative relations with distance variable. The correlation coefficient of most of cultural goods is positive with importer's GDP and is negative with importer's population; the coefficient of China's GDP is positive with the China's export of visual arts, jewellery and architecture and design, but is positive with China's export of film and video. China's population is negative with China's export of craft, jewellery, film and video, but is positive with other visual arts, architecture and design. The productive efficiency of cultural goods in China has obvious positive effects on China's export of other visual arts, jewellery, film and video, architecture and design.

In addition, when we discuss more in specific culture goods, we can conclude that: 1. Antiques. Antiques are valuable, and can not be produced again. So China's export of antiques is correlated with the of importer's purchase power, that is to say, China's export of antiques is positive correlated with the importer's GDP and negative correlated with the importer's population. In addition, there is no obvious relationship between China's export and China's GDP (or population) and productive efficiency of cultural goods; FTA variable can foster China's export of antiques. 2. Musical instruments. Musical instruments are manufacturing products, so trade cost can be easily affected by transport distance, as a result, China's export of the above two products are negative correlated with the distance variable. Secondly, with the growth of economy, people will demand more inspirit products. So the export of the above two product is positive correlated with importer's GDP. In addition, export of China's musical instruments has no relationship with China's GDP (or population) and importer's population, but China's export of recorded media1 is negative correlated with importer's population. FTA variable can foster export of the above two products. Productive efficiency of cultural goods in China have no relationship with export of the above two products.3. Paintings. In foreign countries, the price of the paintings is very high, so China's exports of paintings are obvious affected by importer's purchase power. China's export of the above two products is positive correlated with FTA variable, and there is no relationship between export of the above two products and China's GDP (or population), productive efficiency of cultural goods and distance variable.

Table 1. The Regression results of Gravity Equation

Variable	Antiques	Musical instruments	Recorded media1	Paintings
DIST	0.45***	-0.1***	-0.56***	0.21
	(-9.98)	(-6.17)	(-2.82)	(1.39)
POPj	0.08	-0.1	-0.28	0.59
	(0)	(0)	(0)	(0)
POPi	-0.22***	-0.06	-0.36*	-0.64***
	(-6.46)	(-1.55)	(-1.86)	(-4.4)
GDPi	1.38***	1.05***	1.54***	1.52***
	(41.42)	(28.65)	(6.85)	(9.27)
GDPj	2.09	0.9	-0.98	3.94
	(0)	(0)	(0)	(0)
FTA	0.53***	0.82***	3.47***	1.47***
	(3.1)	(22.6)	(6.12)	(3.42)
CUL	-3.56	-0.57	1.72	-3.07
	(0)	(0)	(0)	(0)
R2	0.89	0.75	0.62	0.64
N	69	69	68	69

The t-value is presented in parentheses. Values marked (***), (**) and (*) are significant at the 1% and 5% and 10% levels, respectively.

Table 2. The Regression results of Gravity Equation (continue)

Variable	Other visual arts	Craft	Jewellery	Photography
DIST	0.08*	-0.1***	-0.87***	0.83
	(1.79)	(-1.8)	(-41.68)	(1.56)
POPj	1.8***	-1.18***	-2.68***	-35.4
	(36.57)	(0)	(-54.97)	(0)
POPi	-0.41***	0.6***	-1.01***	-2.44***
	(-112.23)	(8.07)	(-18.4)	(-3.12)
GDPi	1.43***	0.34***	2.76***	3.03***
	(44.34)	(4.65)	(28.63)	(3.64)
GDPj	-0.52***	0.89	-2.18***	-23.22
	(-18.36)	(0)	(-18.65)	(0)
FTA	1.6***	1.27***	3.73***	3.71**
	(6.72)	(5.61)	(28.66)	(2.25)
CUL	0.55***	-0.77	1.55***	22.7
	(26.64)	(0)	(16.14)	(0)
R2	0.96	0.87	0.89	0.51
N	69	69	69	50

Table 3. The Regression results of Gravity Equation (continue)

Variable	Books	Newspaper	Other Printed Matter	Film and Video	Architecture and design
DIST	0.25 (1.44)	-0.67* (-1.78)	-0.22*** (-2.71)	-0.33*** (-7.02)	-0.84 (-1.44)
POPj	0.2 (0)	-0.97 (0)	-2.68 (0)	-11.37*** (-17.35)	9.9** (2.2)
POPi	-0.38** (-2.2)	-0.48 (-1.15)	-0.49*** (-5.81)	0.18 (0.82)	-1.22*** (-6.1)
GDPi	1.54*** (7.9)	2.07*** (4.51)	1.66*** (15.9)	1.95*** (7.48)	2.34*** (11.76)
GDPj	1.16 (0)	-1.44 (0)	1.37 (0)	3.07*** (9.33)	-8.65*** (-2.54)
FTA	1.62*** (3.19)	2.78*** (2.58)	0.92*** (3.94)	1.21*** (10)	1.17 (1.12)
CUL	-0.45 (0)	1.92 (0)	-0.33 (0)	0.75*** (3.12)	5.32*** (2.83)
R2	0.61	0.41	0.86	0.86	0.88
N	69	60	69	68	40

4. Other visual arts. Most of this kind of products are handmade, and can not be produced in large scale, with the increasing of China's GDP, instead of export to other countries, more products will be sell domestic, so export of these products are negative correlated with China's GDP. In addition, with longer distance, people are willing to cost more money to buy these products, so when this effect overweight the effect of transport cost, export of other visual arts are positive correlated with the distance variable. Productive efficiency of cultural goods is positive correlated with export of this kind of product. 5. Craft. This kind of products is standard manufacturing product, and can be produced at large scale, like other manufacturing goods, export of craft is negative correlated with the distance variable. Export of craft is negative correlated with China's population, which is because with the increasing of China's population, more craft is sale at China instead of exporting to other counties. With more importers' population, more import demand is created, so export of craft is positive correlated with importer's population. There is no relationship between China's GDP and productive efficiency of cultural goods in China. 6. Jewellery. Jewellery is very expensive, and the raw material is very limited. More China's population and GDP can increase the domestic demand of jewellery, so export of jewellery is negative correlated with China's GDP and population. In addition, export of jewellery also is affected by importer's purchase power, so export of jewellery is positive with importer's GDP and negative with importer's population. The technique of making jewellery is very skillful, so with the improvement of productive efficiency of cultural goods, more good jewellery are produced, and more export of these jewellery as a result. 7. Photography. Contrast with Japan and USA, China's technique in producing photography products is very poor, and with the enhancement of China's GDP, China's population is more inclined to buy foreign products. So China's export of photography is effected by importer's purchase power,

in addition, FTA variable also can increase China's export of this product. 8. Newspaper. Newspaper has its fixed reading customer, and cheaper when contrasts with books. So, there is no relationship between export of newspaper and China's population (or GDP) or importer's population. But export of newspaper is positive correlated with importer's GDP, and this is because with the more GDP, more information are needed, as a result, they increase the import of newspapers from China. There is no relationship between export of China's newspaper and productive efficiency of cultural goods in China. 9. Other Printed Matter is similar with books. But export of other printed matter is negative correlated with distance variable. 10. Film and Video. Film and video is primarily produced for domestic demand, and is a kind of product that can be consumed by most civilians. With the increasing of China's GDP, China are more capable to produce more good films and videos, so export volumes will increase as a result. With the decreasing of purchase power, it reduce the incentive of producing more good films and videos, so China's export of film and video is negative correlated with China's population and is positive correlated with importer's GDP. There is no relationship between importer's populations. FTA variable and productive efficiency of cultural goods have a positive effect on China's export of film and video. Because export of film and video are exported by disk and other saving media, so, like export of most goods, export of film and video is negative correlated with distance variable. 11. Architecture and design. Architecture and design are very technical products, and always related to copyrights. Increasing of China's population can enhance the demand for architecture and design and can provide more designer, so more architecture and design will be exported to other countries, in addition, increasing of China's GDP can enlarge the domestic demand of architecture and design, but number of such designs is limited, so China's GDP is negative related to export of architecture and design. The price of architecture and design is very high, so importer's purchase power can influence the export of such products. Distance and FTA variable have no effects on the China's export. Productive efficiency of cultural goods in China can promote China's export of such goods.

Acknowledgments. Supported by Leading Academic Discipline Project of Shanghai Municipal Education Commission: International Trade (J51702).

References

1. Mas-Colell, A.: Should Cultural Goods Be Treated Differently? Journal of Cultural Economics 23(1), 87–93 (1999)
2. Marvasti, A.: International Trade in Cultural Goods: A Cross-Sectional Analysis. Journal of Cultural Economics 18, 135–148 (1994)
3. UNESCO: The 2009 UNESCO Framework for Cultural Statistics (FCS). UNESCO Institute for Statistics, Canada (2009)

Farmers on Rice Straw Recycling Intend Research

Xiaomei Zhang and Chunqiu Zhao

Graduate collage of Northeast Agriculture University,
No.59, Mucai Street, Xiangfang District
Harbin, Heilongjiang 150030, China
251914614@qq.com

Abstract. This text based on PuYang farm in Heilongjiang province of rice straw recycling farmers willingness of survey, Using descriptive statistics and data proportion type statistics, Analyzed farmer on the influence factors of straw recycling results indicate that: farmer's cultural degree; Understanding of straw recycling levels; Farmers and family's attitude; Funds, equipment, technical factors; Farmer's gender, age. Those factors affecting farmers on obviously rice straw recycling will.

Keywords: recycling, straw, farmer, intend.

1 Introduction

The current state in the new energy issues, there are many new policy in these new policy support recycling, will become the first choice scheme to substitute rice straw recycling other non-renewable resources, not only can reduce pollution to the environment but also increased the economic income, Therefore to improve farmers on straw recycling of knowledge, improving farmer straw recycling intend.

2 Survey Program and Sample Distribution

This study selected PuYang farm in Heilongjiang province, this farm take the rice as the main kinds of plants, farmers on the rice planting has rich experience, farmers depend on plant rice as the main economic source also, so choose the region for respondents more representative.

This investigation range is PuYang farm, through the questionnaire survey manner, Total 66 entries, retrieve the questionnaires of 60, sample effective rate was 92%.

Table 1 shows, among respondents farmers, male52, account 87% of the total, female 8, account 13% of the total. Householders average age is about 38 years old, 2 people was 18-29 years of age, accounting 5% of the total, 51 people was 30-50 years of age, accounting for 85%, 7 people over the age of 51, account 10% of the surveyed household, the survey of households in elementary school cultural degree have 11 people, account 18% of the surveyed household, in middle school culture have 33 people, account 55% of the surveyed household, in high school culture degree have 10 people, account 16% of the total. There are 6 people above senior high school

Q. Zhou (Ed.): ISAEBD 2011, Part I, CCIS 208, pp. 436–441, 2011.

Table 1. The basic situation of interviews farmers

		Number	Proportion（%）
Features	male	52	87%
	female	8	13%
Age	18-29	2	5%
	30-50	51	85%
	51 years old above	7	10%
cultural degree	Elementary school	11	18%
	Middle school	33	55%
	High school	10	16%
	Above senior high school	6	11%

Note: Data are rounded part of the ratio.

degree, account 11% of the total, the overall distribution is more reasonable sample, and the reality was consistent.

3 Farmer's Current Situation to the Straw Recycling Waste

Table 2 shows, this farm take the rice as the main kinds of plants, all of farmers depend on sale rice to increase economic benefit, in this farm every farmer's plant scale are large, in 1-10 planting scale of 9 people, account 17% of the total, in 11-20 planting scale of 24 people, account 40% of the total, in 21 30 planting scale of 20 people, account 13% of the total, in 30 planting scale of 7 people, account 13% of the total, The farm scale very large, such as take the straw stalk recycling utilization so benefits will be greater than before without recycling.

Table 2. The Straw scale of planting and growing purposes

(Unit : 10000square meter)			
		Number	Proportion（%）
Planting scale	1—10	9	17%
	11—20	24	40%
	21—30	20	30%
	30以上	7	13%

Note: Data are rounded part of the ratio.

Table 3 shows, farmers recycling knowledge sources, from the agricultural promotion seminar have 28 people, account 46% of the total. From the older generation imparting have 10 people, account 18% of the total. From network have 22 people, account 36% of the total. Farmers use common tools have 53 people, account

88% of the total; farmers use mechanized farm tools have 7 people, account 12% of the total. In handling way, there are 13 people put straw crushing do livestock feed, account 21% of the total, there are 9 people smashing counters-field, account 16% of the total, there are 38 people burning the straw, account 63% of the total. Farmers of straw recycling knowledge does not understand, and use of equipment is common tools, can not very well to protect the rice straw, The biggest problem is that most shattering wasted straw, not only the recycling into resources, have become the environment pollution sources.

Table 3. Farmer's straw recycling knowledge sources, Using equipment, Processing mode

		Number	Proportion（%）
Sources	From agricultural promotion seminar	28	46%
	From older	10	18%
	From Internet	22	36%
Equipment	Common tools	53	88%
	Mechanized farm	7	12%
Handling	After mashing do livestock feed	13	21%
	After smashing counters-field	9	16%
	Burn	38	63%

Note: Data are rounded part of the ratio.

Table 4. Farmers accept guidance, Farmers on the government's proposals

		Number	Proportion (%)
Get help situation	Received	3	5%
	No received	57	95%
Advise	In the policies need help	18	30%
	In the funds need help	17	28%
	In the equipment need help	11	23%
	In the technology need help	14	19%

Note: Data are rounded part of the ratio.

Table 4 shows, Received popularization personnel guidance have 3 people, account 5% of the total, no have received popularization personnel guidance 57 people, account 95% of the total, nobody initiative attended agricultural promotion seminar, In the suggestion, there are 18 people In the policies need help, account 30% of the total, there are 17 people in the funds need help, account 28% of the total, there are 11 people in the equipment need help, account 23% of the total, there are 14 people in the technology need help, account 19% of the total. Farmers don't attend agricultural lecture, cause of every aspect need help, and so the author thinks that farmers must be strengthen families with straw recycling of agricultural knowledge of promotion.

Table 5 shows, there are 46 people said family support funding for straw recycling, account 76% of the total, there are 14 people said family does not support funding for straw recycling, account 24% of the total. On the expansion, there are 43 people have expanded intend, account 71% of the total, there are 17 people no have extension intend. The potential value in straw, there are 36 people understand, account 60% of the total, there are 24 people do not know that. If farmer completely mastery of the straw recycling technology so economic benefits would have increased significantly.

Table 5. Farmer family's attitude in Straw recycling investment, Farmer's desire to expand and understand to potential value

		Number	Proportion (%)
Farmers attitude	Support	46	76%
	Don't support	14	24%
Desire on expand	Interested	43	71%
	No interested	17	29%
Straw's potential value	Understand	36	60%
	No understand	24	40%

Note: Data are rounded part of the ratio.

Table 6. The farmer's attitude about environmental protection

		Number	Proportion (%)
The harm to human	Know	13	21%
	Don't know	47	79%
The harm to plant	Know	8	14%
	Don't know	52	86%
The harm to the environment	Know	7	12%
	Don't know	53	88%
Will become a Environments	Yes	28	30%
	Do my best	43	70%

Note: Data are rounded part of the ratio.

Table 6 shows, 13 people realized the environmental pollution was harmful to human beings, account 21% of the total, 47 people do not know that, account 79% of the total. 8 people realized that the environment pollution was harmful to rice, account 14% of the total, 52 people don't know that, account 86% of the total. 7 people realized that the environment pollution harm straw total of don't know the 12% of the total, 53 people do not realized that, account 88% of the total. when farmer was asked will to do a environmentalists, 28 people said will be a environmentalists, account 30% of the total, 43 people said that may be do their best to protect the environment, account 70% of the total.

4   Farmers on Rice Straw Recycling Intend to Analysis

Farmers grow rice aimed at achieving economic income. Due to farmers don't understand straw recycling technology makes economic income decrease, only when farmer understand straw recycling benefit they will actively learn the straw recycling technology. But there are many main factors influenced farmer to do rice stalk recycling.

4.1   The Farmer's Culture of Straw and Degree of Recycling Knowledge Familiar

As shown(table 1), Some farmers only junior middle school culture level, not familiar with recycling technology on straw make farmer do not realize the benefits of straw recycling. Therefore must organize farmers enter into the agricultural extension to learn the knowledge of straw recycling in lectures, to improving farmer of straw recycling actively intend.

4.2   Farmers and Family Attitude and in Funds, Equipment, Technical Factors

As shown (table 7), Farmers aware of straw recycling with low levels, enthusiasm is poor, family could not support, all of reasons to causing the farmer put straw wasted, so to really let farmers understand the benefits of recycling, and active learning straw recycling technology.

4.3   Farmer's Gender and Age

As shown(table 1), Mainly adopt the basic planting technology, because male householder on new technology don't understand cause the rice yield decreased, so straw output is also will decrease, therefore must improve male farmer's recycling technology, make male householder realize recycling advantage, Thus improving farmer on rice straw recycling will.

Table 7. Farmer with Family's attitude on straw recycling attitude and difficult obstacles of source samples

		Number	Proportion (%)
Farmer's attitude	Identity	10	16%
	Indifference	50	84%
The attitude of families	Support1	6	16%
	Don't support	6	10%
	Indifference	38	64%
The barrier	From the tools	7	11%
	From equipment	51	85%
	From the ground	2	4%

Note: Data are rounded part of the ratio.

5   The Conclusion and Suggestion

The farm most farmer don't understand straw recycling economic value, didn't realize recycling benefit, think that must be through the display in straw recycling increased income of farmers to inspire the farmer's economic desire, organization of popularizing agricultural lectures, arrange promotion personnel guidance and answer farmers in the technical difficulties enable farmers learn straw recycling technology, take the farmer who with outstanding achievements as model, make broad farmers learn from him, in order to improve farmers on rice straw recycling will.

References

1. Torgerson, R., Reynolds, B., Gray, T.: Evolution of cooperative Thought,Theory and Purpose. Journal of Co-operative 13, 1-20.4 (1998)
2. Ecology and ecnomy. Weller. Muller 29 (1999)
3. Tsutsumi, M., Seya, H.: Hedonic approaches based on spatial econometrics and spatial statistics: Application to evaluation of project benefits. J. Geogr. Syst. 11(4), 357–380 (2009)
4. LeSage, J.P., Pace, R.K.: Introduction to spatial econometrics. CRC press, Taylor and Francis Group, Boca Raton (2009)
5. Sathre, R., Gustavsson, L.: Process-based analysis of added value in forest product Industries. Forest Policy and Economics 11(1), 65–75 (2009)

Recycling of Livestock Manure Farmers Intend Research

Xiaomei Zhang and Chunqiu Zhao

Graduate collage of Northeast Agriculture University,
No.59, Mucai Street, Xiangfang District
Harbin, Heilongjiang 150030, China
251914614@qq.com

Abstract. This article is based on XinFu county in Heilongjiang Province on the recycling of livestock manure will survey, empirical analysis of household recycling of livestock manure results show that the influencing factors: farmer age, education level, farmer's subjective consciousness significantly affect the farmers on the wishes of recycling animal wastes. Proposed the implementation of large-scale recycling of animal waste in rural areas need to strengthen professional and technical training for farmers to promote waste recycling knowledge, in order to improve recycling, increase the farmers income.

Keywords: cyclic utilization, excrement of animal's, intend.

1 Introduction

To develop agriculture in the country' policy, just now there are some region to become model, these areas become not only formed a complete set of recycling system model outside, still development scale production and professional management, thus not only it is favorable to the environment protection for farmers, but also in economic branches. Therefore vigorously promoted on rural livestock waste recycling knowledge technique is very important.

2 Survey Program and Sample Distribution

This study selected the XinFu town of Heilongjiang Province for the survey, because most farmers breed livestock in the region, manure production and more, and also has a strong representation of aquaculture, livestock's aquaculture has become the farmers Second source of income, more conducive to the actual nature of the investigation.

The scope of this survey is the XinFu rural township, by way of questionnaire survey households, a total of 65 questionnaires, 60 were recovered, and the sample rate was 92%.

Table 1 shows, in the surveyed of household, 32 males, 53% of the total, 28 females and 47% of the total. The average age of household was about 30 years old, 20 people was 18-29 years of age, accounting 30% of the total, 38 people was 30-50 years of age, accounting for 63%, 2 people over the age of 51,account 7% of the surveyed household, the survey of households in elementary school cultural degree

Q. Zhou (Ed.): ISAEBD 2011, Part I, CCIS 208, pp. 442–447, 2011.

have 23 people, account 38% of the surveyed household, in middle school culture have 35 people, account 58% of the surveyed household, in high school culture degree have 2 people, account 4% of the total. The overall distribution is more reasonable sample, and the reality was consistent.

Table 1. Basic Overview of Head of Household

		Number	Proportion
Householder features	Male	32	53%
	Female	28	47%
Householder Age	18——29	20	30%
	30——50	38	63%
	51 years old above	2	7%
Cultural degree	Elementary school	23	38%
	Middle school	35	58%
	High school	2	4%

Note: Data are rounded part of the ratio.

3 Farmer's Current Situation on the Recycling Waste

As shown in table 2, farmers recycling knowledge sources, from the village of agricultural extension meeting have 1 people, account 2% of the total. From the older

Table 2. Recycling Knowledge Sources, Using Equipment, Processing Place and Utilization Direction Samples

		Number	Proportion
Sources	From farm promotion seminar	1	2%
	From older	33	58%
	From Internet	4	7%
	Don't know	22	38%
Equipment	Common tools	47	78%
	Mechanized farm	13	22%
Place	Home	23	38%
	Village designated location	13	21%
	Field	24	41%
Use directions	Agricultural fertilizers	46	76%
	Biogas utilization	1	2%
	Other uses	2	3%
	Throw away	11	19%

Note: Data are rounded part of the ratio.

generation imparting have 33 people, account 55% of the total. From network have 4 people, account 10% of the total. 22 do not understand, account 33% of the total. Farmers use normal tools have 47 people, account 78% of the total. Using mechanized farm has 13 people, account 22% of the total. Handling excrement in their yard were 23 people 38%, in the village of designated place handling excrement were 13 people, account 21 % of the total, In the field of handling excrement were 24 people 41% of total. As the feces of chemical fertilizer have 46 people, account 76% of total, take the feces as methane gas have 1 people, account 2% of total, take the feces for other uses have 2 people, account 3% of total, there are 11 people throw away the feces, account 19% of total. On recycling knowledge farmers own very little, so make favorable resources wasted.

As shown in table 3, received popularization personnel guidance have 4 people, account 7% of the total, not received popularization personnel guidance have 56 people account 93% of the total. Attended the promotion conference have 6 people account 10% of the total, with 54 people have never been there, account 90% of the total. there are 1 people need help from the township government ,account 2% of the total, there are 1 people need help in the funds, account 2% of the total, there are 1 people need help in the machinery, account 2% of the total, there are 57 people need help in the technical, account 94% of the total. Farmers did not take part in recycling promotion conference will lead all aspects need help, so the author thinks must strengthen families feces recycling of agricultural knowledge of promotion.

Table 3. Farmer Gets Help and Advice to the Township of Samples

		Number	Proportion
Get help situation	Received	4	7%
	No received	56	93%
Advise	In the policies need help	1	2%
	In the funds need help	1	2%
	In the equipment need help	1	2%
	In the technology need help	57	94%

Note: data scale to all take the integer part.

Table 4 shows, 9 people earning under 10,000 Yuan, account 16% of the total, and 43 people earning under 2-3 million, account 71% of the total, 8 people earning under 4-5 million, account 13% of the total. 2 people have intended to expend the breeding scale, account 3% of the total, there are 58 people do not have the intention to expend, account 97% of the total. The farmers who had the sale feces experience were 2 people; account 3% of the total, no sale experience was 58 people, account 97% of the total. Due to farmers don't understand recycling value, most farmer income between 2--3 million in share access most of the farmers.

Table 4. Farmer's Income, Expand Intention, Sale Feces Experience

		Number	Proportion
Average annual income	10000 within	9	16%
	2——3 million	43	71%
	4——5 million	8	13%
The desire	Have the willingness	3	4%
	No intention	57	96%
Experience	Sale	2	3%
	Never	58	97%

Note: data scale to all take the integer part.

Table 5 shows, 46 people had aware of the environmental pollution, account 76% of the total. 14 people don't aware the environmental pollution, account 24% of the total, the damage to human beings had 13 people aware of that, account 21% of the total, 47 people don't aware of the damage to human beings, account 79% of the total. 16 people aware that the environmental pollution was harmful to the livestock, account 27 of the total, 44 people don't aware that environmental pollution was harmful to the livestock, account 73% of the total, 55 people realized that the feces was harmful to the environment, account 92% of the total, 5 people not realized that the feces was harmful to the environment, account 8% of the total, when farmer was asked will to do a environmentalists, 40 people said will be a environmentalists, account 67% the total, 20 people said that may be do their best to protect the environment, account 33% of the total.

Table 5. The Farmer's Attitude about Environmental Protection

		Number	Proportion
Environmental pollution	Understand	46	76%
	Don't understand	14	24%
The harm to human	Know	13	21%
	Don't know	47	79%
The harm to livestock	Know	16	27%
	Don't know	44	73%
The harm to the environment	Know	55	92%
	Don't know	5	8%
Will become a Environments	Yes	40	67%
	Do my best	20	33%

Note: data scale to all take the integer part.

4 Farmers on Excrement of Animals Recycling Intend to Analysis

Farmers raise cattle is to bring economic benefits, increasing economic income, then recycling manure can increase the income, but there are many main factors influenced farmer to do feces recycling.

4.1 The Farmer's Gender and Age

After investigation cattle breeding work most by the male householder management, age at roughly 30 to 50 between, (such as shown in table 1) Men more understand the recycling cattle, feces men also understand, therefore must be teach this kind of person the recycling knowledge.

4.2 The Cultural Degree and Peasant Technical Level

Some people have the junior high school level, account 58% of the total, (such as table 1), culture knowledge lacks is causing the farmers don't understand the new knowledge another factor, Some farmers behind the technology to get the best effect recycling, reducing the recycling benefits.

4.3 The Owners and Farmers of Feces Recycling Family Attitude

As table 6 shows that 50% of farmers willing to learn recycling knowledge, family also maintain support attitude, but also has 20% of farmers keep indifference attitude, attitude directly affect the farmer's enthusiasm, so change the attitude will peasant farmers on recycling increase the positive intend feces.

Table 6. Farmer with Family's Attitude on Recycling Attitude and Difficult Obstacles of Source Samples

		Number	Proportion
Farmer's attitude	Identity	20	33%
	Indifference	40	67%
The attitude of families	Support	18	30%
	Don't support	5	9%
	Indifference	37	61%
The barrier	From the tools	6	10%
	From equipment	53	88%
	From the ground	1	2%

Note: data scale to all take the integer part.

5   The Conclusion and Suggestion

Research results indicate that, some farmers have realized feces recycling can bring economic benefits, but not fully aware of feces recycling of technical knowledge, therefore to improve farmers on the willingness of feces cycle using the key lies in:

Ascend the cultural degree, popularize peasant agricultural knowledge; the popularization of agro-techniques; regular visits to farmers; understand progress and difficult situation and help to solve the problem, recommended successful farmers case, let farmers learn from each other successful experience; form good recycling study ethos to improve farmers on recycling will.

References

1. Cook, M.: The Future of U.S. Agricultural Cooperatives: A Neo-institutional Approach. American Journal of Agricultural Economics 7, 1144–1152 (1995)
2. Sathre, R., Gustavsson, L.: Process-based analysis of added value in forest product Industries. Forest Policy and Economics 11(1), 65–75 (2009)
3. LeSage, J.P., Pace, R.K.: Introduction to spatial econometrics. CRC press, Taylor and Francis Group, Boca Raton (2009)
4. Tsutsumi, M., Seya, H.: Hedonic approaches based on spatial econometrics and spatial statistics: Application to evaluation of project benefits. J. Geogr. Syst. 11(4), 357–380 (2009)

Positive Research on Information Disclosure of Internal Control Defects

Min Qu, Yongjun Guan, Xiuna Liu, and Aijun Zhou

Finance & Economics Department, Guangxi University of Technology,
268, Dong-Huan Road, Liuzhou, Guangxi, China

Abstract. In this paper, we take 33 companies which disclosed internal control defects in their annals reporter from 2006 to 2010 in Shanghai stock market. and select another 54 companies for control sample ,we found, the number of segment in the report and the size of corporate affect the information disclose of internal control deficiency. Finally, we come up with some suggestions for policy maker.

Keywords: Inner Control Deficiency, Information Disclosure, Positive Research.

1 Introduction

Internal control information disclosure refers to release the company's internal control operation status information to society through certain media published for the listed company. According to the COSO report, Establishing and maintaining effective internal control system is the responsibility of the enterprise management, management authorities must ensure proper design internal controls and effective implementation of internal control. For this purpose, management authority should be regularly evaluate the effectiveness of internal control design and implementation according to certain standards, and provide the assessment information to external users. In 2002, the United States congress issued act about public company accounting reform and investor protection, in the act, Mentioned the responsibility of financial reporting for company and the internal control evaluation for management, emphasized the full and effective responsibility of management in establishing and maintaining the internal control system and the corresponding control program The management of issuer's effectiveness evaluation about internal control system and the control program of recent fiscal years; the accounting company of corporate annual audit should test and evaluate the internal control of the company and provide the evaluation report. Meanwhile in the act, also demanded the CEO and CFO of the company must submit to the SEC the legality of the financial report and fair expression of guarantee. In December 2000 China securities regulatory commission (CSRC) issued the "information disclose preparing rules of public companies ",in 2003 the commercial bank disclosure special provisions was issued, these acts required securities companies, commercial Banks reporting the integrity, reasonableness and effectiveness explanations of the internal control. And also should entrust the certified public accountants evaluating its internal control systems,

Q. Zhou (Ed.): ISAEBD 2011, Part I, CCIS 208, pp. 448–454, 2011.

especially the risk management system integrity, reasonableness and effectiveness, and put forward Suggestions on improvement, and issue the evaluation report. Evaluation reports submitted to China securities regulatory commission and the securities exchange together with the annual report. Certified public accountants employed pointed out that the internal control of company have a serious defect in "three-properties", board of supervisors should explain the opinion that explicitly, and separately disclosed. For non-financial category listed companies, our country has been not publish corresponding system requiring mandatory disclosure in the annals of internal control information, that's to say, the listed company's internal control information has been in voluntary disclosure form. In this case, the listed companies tend to disclose the good things, the existing problems of the internal control problems hasn't disclosed, this paper, we will explore the reasons.

2 Literature Review

Generally speaking, internal control flaw can be divided into significant defect, substantive loopholes and general defects. Significant defects refer to control flaw or control flaw collection of interim report would lead to the annual or not irrelevant error cannot be prevented. Substantive vulnerability refer to control flaw or control flaw collection of interim report would lead to the major annual or error cannot be prevented, Except for a significant flaws or substantive loophole internal control ,namely for general defects. In internal control flaw information disclosure research, foreign scholars have formed abundant achievements. Krishnan[1] Inspected 128 companies from 1994 to 2000 which discloses the control flaw, she found the audit committee quality has a positive relationship with the internal control quality. Chan Farrell and Lee[2] found that that that company disclosing the internal control substantive flaws according to 404 rules had he more earnings quality management and lower investment returns compare with other companies. Ashbaugh Skaife Collins and Kinney[3] Found that the company disclosing the internal control defective was more complex in operation, especially more quantity of foreign operations division, a lot of merger and reorganization, holding large inventory and fast growth company size; Small companies and the company reported losses often disclose the internal control defects, the auditor resignation positively related to the disclosure of internal control defects; the reason that management aren't will to disclose the internal control defect is management reputation and management compensation. Bryan and Lilien[4] found that the company disclosing the internal control substantial loopholes has some characteristics in small scale, the poor performance, high values, and usually a auditor change and financial report. De Franco Guan and Lu[5] In 3 days, found the accumulative total excess returns (the CAR) is - 1.8% for the company that disclose the internal control flawed. Ge and McVay[6] found that weak internal control usually has a positive relation with   the resources input in the accounting control.

Krishnan and Visvanathan[7] found that the internal control defects has no significant relationship with the audit committee meeting, the proportion of financial experts in audit committee, audit fees. Doyle Ge and McVay[8] base on 779 companies from 2002 to 2005 which disclose the internal control substantive loopholes, and found substantial loopholes companies has such characteristics as small in scale, profitability, low operation complex, growing at a faster pace, These companies face less internal control resource input, complicated accounting problems.

Andrew J.Leone[9] found that the influence factors of internal control disclosure have some characteristics in organized structure complexity, organizational changes and internal control investment, and also, he provided some evidence.

3 Model

3.1 Data

The Company disclosing the internal control defects come from Shanghai stock market between2006-2010, we got 33 companies, in order to conduct the multiple regression analysis in use of logit Model, we select one or two peer companies in the industry as a control sample of companies, a total of 54 control samples selected.

3.2 Dependant Variables

The dependant variables were the motivation of listed company in disclosing the internal control defects, it was dummy variables denoted by ICD_DISCLOSURE, For the company disclosing internal control defects, ICD_DISCLOSURE was 1, For the control sample company ,ICD_DISCLOSURE was 0。

3.3 Independent Variables and Control Variables

Table 1. Independent Variable and Control Variable

Variable	Variable code	Expected symbols	Definition
Independent Variable	SEGMENTS	+	The number of segments
	GROWTH	+	average percentage increase in sales in the last 3 years
	SIZE	-	Log (market value of the company), the company's market value of the data obtained from CSMAR
	INST_CON	+	The percentage of the top ten shareholders of shares held by institutional investors and institutional investors on December 31

Table 1. (continued)

Control variable	FOREIGN _SALES	+	There are Foreign sales in the annual report are to 1, otherwise 0
	INVENTORY	+	the average percentage of total assets inventory in the first 2 years
	M&A	+	There are merger, acquisition 1, otherwise.0
	RESTRUCTURE	+	There are reorganization 1, otherwise 0
	AUDITOR _RESIGN	+	There are changing the accounting firm 1, otherwise 0
	AUDITOR	+	The accounting form was the Big 4 1, otherwise 0

4 Results

4.1 Descriptive Analysis

Table 2. Descriptive Analysis

	Mean	Std. Dev.	25%	Median	75%
		SEGMENTS			
ICD sample	3.7879**	2.0426	2.0000	3.0000	4.5000
Control sample	2.7963	1.3512	2.0000	3.0000	4.0000
		GROWTH			
ICD sample	1.0692**	5.3279	-0.0614	0.1124	0.4111
Control sample	0.3297	0.4025	0.1247	0.2136	0.4294
		SIZE			
ICD sample	9.0109***	0.3962	8.7481	8.9515	9.2370
Control sample	9.1703	0.3642	8.8930	9.1238	9.3695
		INST_CON			
ICD sample	0.1139**	0.1004	0.0598	0.0842	0.1217
Control sample	0.0901	0.0391	0.0664	0.0821	0.1072
		FOREIGN_SALES			
ICD sample	0.3333	0.4787	0.0000	0.0000	1.0000
Control sample	0.4259	0.4991	0.0000	0.0000	1.0000

Table 2. (*continued*)

	INVENTORY				
ICD sample	0.1165	0.1105	0.0243	0.0930	0.1535
Control sample	0.1656	0.1886	0.0540	0.1217	0.1947
	M&A				
ICD sample	0.3939	0.4962	0.0000	0.0000	1.0000
Control sample	0.4259	0.4991	0.0000	0.0000	1.0000
	RESTRUCTURE				
ICD sample	0.1515*	0.3641	0.0000	0.0000	0.0000
Control sample	0.0370	0.1906	0.0000	0.0000	0.0000
	AUDITOR_RESIGN				
ICD sample	0.0303	0.1741	0.0000	0.0000	0.0000
Control sample	0.1296	0.3391	0.0000	0.0000	0.0000
	AUDITOR				
ICD sample	0.0606	0.2423	0.0000	0.0000	0.0000
Control sample	0.0926	0.2926	0.0000	0.0000	0.0000

4.2 Regression Analysis

We use the following logistic regression model

$$ICD\_DISCLOSURE = b_0 + b_1 SEGMENTS + b_2 GROWTH + b_3 SIZE + b_4 INST\_CON + b_5 FOREIGN\_SALES + b_6 INVENTORY + b_7 M\&A + b_8 RESTRUCTURE + b_9 AUDITOR\_RESIGN + b_{10} AUDITOR + e$$

Table 3 shows, the more the number of SEGMENTS Segment reporting year, the more prone to internal control deficiencies, which is expected to sign the same, but also through a significant test. The company's sales growth (GROWTH) consistent with the expected sign, but did not pass the significance test. Size of the company (SIZE) consistent with the expected sign, through a significant test, indicating that the smaller size of the company, the smaller investment in the internal control, the more prone to internal control deficiencies. The ratio between top ten shareholders of shares held by institutional investors and the number of institutional investors (INST_CON), foreign sales (FOREIGN_SALES), the ratio of inventories to total assets (INVENTORY), mergers and acquisitions (M & A), recombinant (RESTRUCTURE), auditor change (AUDITOR_RESIGN), auditor (AUDITOR) consistent with the expected sign, but not through the test of significance, indicating for the selected samples, the impact of these factors is not significant.

Table 3. Logistic Regression results and Collinearity Statistics Test

Independent variable	Expected symbols	Results			Collinearity Statistics	
		coefficient	Wald	Sig.	Tolerance	VIF
Constant	+/-	12.751	2.920	0.087		
SEGMENTS	+	0.469	5.745	0.017	0.951	1.051
GROWTH	+	0.057	0.200	0.655	0.888	1.126
SIZE	-	-1.607	3.810	0.051	0.846	1.182
INST _CON	+	5.189	1.535	0.215	0.933	1.072
FREIGN _SALES	+	-0.451	0.624	0.429	0.861	1.161
INVENTORY	+	-3.268	2.124	0.145	0.930	1.075
M&A	+	-0.087	0.025	0.875	0.940	1.063
RESTRUCTU RE	+	1.433	2.430	0.119	0.961	1.041
AUDITOR _RESIGN	+	-1.885	2.571	0.109	0.938	1.066
AUDITOR	+	-0.141	0.020	0.889	0.837	1.195

5 Concluding Remarks

According to the result, we found that the impact factor disclosing the internal control for the company were the number of segments reporting in the report and the size of the company, in the current weakening of the internal control situation, the regulatory measures within the control of information disclosure of listed companies should be mandatory disclosure of internal control information, , regulators should focus on the disclosure of internal Control defects to strengthen the supervision of listed companies and establish the appropriate channels to encourage the investing public supervision.

References

1. Krishnan, J.: Audit committee quality and internal control an empirical analysis. The Accounting Review 80, 649–675 (2005)
2. Chan, K.C., Farrell, B.R., Lee, P.: Earnings Management and Return-Earnings Association of Firms Reporting Material Internal Control Weaknesses Under Section 404 of the Sarbanes-Oxley Act(R). Working Paper Series (2005), http://papers.ssrn.com/
3. Ashbaugh-Skaife, H., Collins, D.W., Kinney Jr., W.R.: The Discovery and Reporting of Internal Control Deficiencies Prior to SOX-Mandated Audits. Journal of Accounting and Economics (2005)
4. Bryan, S.H., Lilien, S.B.: Characteristics of Firms with Material Weaknesses in Internal Control: An Assessment of Section 404 of Sarbanes Oxley. Working paper, Wake Forest University and City University of New York (2005)
5. De Franco, G., Guan, Y., Lu, H.: The Wealth Change and Redistribution Effects of Sarbanes-Oxley Internal Control Disclosures. Working paper, University of Toronto (2005)

454   M. Qu et al.

6. Ge, W., Mcvay, S.: The disclosure of material weaknesses in internal control after The Sarbanes-Oxley Act. Accounting Horizons (2005) (forthcoming)
7. Krishnan, G.V., Visvanathan, G.: Reporting Internal Control Deficiencies in the Post-Sarbanes-Oxley Era The Role of Auditors and Corporate Governance. Working paper, George Mason University (2005)
8. Doyle, J., Ge, W., McVay, S.: Determinants of Weaknesses in Internal Control Over Financial Reporting. Journal of Accounting & Economics 9, 44(12), 31, 193–223 (2007)
9. Leone, A.J.: Factors related to internal control disclosure: A discussion of Ashbaugh, Collins, and Kinney and Doyle, G. and McVay. Journal of Accounting and Economics (2007), http://www.elsevier.Com/locate/jae

Positive Research on Economics Consequence of the Stock Option Incentive Plan

Yongjun Guan, Min Qu, Xiaojing Liu, and Xiuna Liu

Finance & Economics Department, Guangxi University of Technology,
268, Dong-Huan Road, Liuzhou, Guangxi, China

Abstract. In this paper, the economics consequence of 202 listed companies, which have announced Stock option incentive plan in Shenzhen and Shanghai A-Share markets after the year of 2006, is tested by event study, considering the market reaction. Moreover, to what extent the different incentives levels from Stock option incentive plan affect the anticipated performance is analyzed empirically through the use of multi-linear regression model. The results demonstrate that the Stock option incentive plan announced by the listed companies in China produced a positive impact on the stock prices, and there is a significant economics consequence while investors have a higher expectancy on effects of the incentives towards the companies with higher profit growth and higher growth capacity. And the investors in China more focus on the event of Stock option incentive of the listed companies, so that they ignore the specific incentive levels of the Stock option incentive plans.

Keywords: Stock Option Incentive Plan, Event Study, Economics consequence.

1 Introduction

New "Company Law" and "Securities Law" put into practice on January 1st, 2006. In this year, the Split Share Reform was strengthened, and the obstacles for implementing Stock option incentive system were eliminated. In the multiple background, the China Securities Regulatory Commission promulgated the "Management Measures of Stock option incentive of the Listed Company" (here in after referred to as "Management Measures") and "the Implementation of Stock option incentive of State Holding listed Company (Domestic)", opening up a stage of the implementation of Stock option incentive in domestic listed companies, arousing enormous imaginative zone for benefits. As of April 30th, 2007, 95% of the listed companies completed the reform. Also, 202 domestic listed companies had announced a draft of Stock option incentive from the enactment of "management measure" to the end of April in 2007.

Generally speaking, the impact of the Stock option incentive plan on the stock price is mainly manifested in two aspects: one is the impact on investors to anticipate the performance improvement of listed companies; the other is the impact on actual performance of the listed companies. In the beginning of implementing the Stock option incentive, the plan strengthens the investors' expectancy of performance

Q. Zhou (Ed.): ISAEBD 2011, Part I, CCIS 208, pp. 455–461, 2011.

improvement in the company and has more positive impact on stock price. When come to the economics consequence of Stock option incentive of the listed companies, many scholars have engaged in the theoretical and empirical verification and reached two points: the first view is that there is a significant positive correlation between Stock option incentive and enterprise performance, which is the conclusion of most scholars; another view is that there is little correlation between them, or even not relevant. In these studies, most of scholars incline to the view of accounting performance and seldom study the factors of economics consequence with the view of market. However, the study of domestic companies in China, which is based on the change of company performance prior to 2006, focuses on the impact of Stock option incentive on the actual performance of listed companies. Since Stock option incentive of the listed companies lack of consummate incentive plans and system backgrounds prior to 2006, and therefore there is no response from literature that research investors to the Stock option incentive plan in China. Under such background, this thesis uses the event study to examine the economics consequence of the Stock option incentive of the listed companies, which announced the introduction of incentive plans after 2006. As it is a relatively short time for the listed companies to carry out Stock option incentive, the impact of company Stock option incentive on actual performance is not obvious. Thus, this thesis emphasizes on whether incentive plans have affected the investors' anticipation of performance improvement of listed companies, which is mainly represented in whether the stock price have increased obviously after the announcement of the Stock option incentive plan. Our empirical research shows that the economics consequence of Stock option incentive does indeed exist. In other words, investors expect that Stock option incentive can reduce moral risk of the brokerage, which results from the principal-agent relationship and can have a long-term effect. Following this, the relationship between expected performance (namely the cumulative abnormal return rate), the Stock option incentive level and financial indexes is tested by multi-linear regression model. The results demonstrate that the correlation coefficient of them is positive. In addition, the coefficient values of profitability and growth ability are relative high, showing that investors have a higher expectancy on effects of the incentives towards the companies with higher profit growth and higher growth capacity.

2 Economics Consequence of Stock Option Incentive Plan Based on Event Study

2.1 Data Sources and Sample Selection

The study objects in this thesis are the Stock option incentive plan of the listed companies in Shanghai and Shenzhen Stock Markets after the promulgation of "Management Measures" (Trial) on January 1st, 2006. The data required for empirical study arise from TianRuan database and Wind database, in which the first announcement date is arranged by company bulletin and annual reports on cninfo.com. Additionally, the accounting data of the study derive from TianRuan database. Based on the needs of the study, the treating process of samples is as follows:

2.2 The Test of the Economics Consequence of Stock Option Incentive

According to the time window, which is from 20 days before the announcement date to 20 days after the announcement date, this thesis intends to study market reaction to the Stock option incentive announcement, calculate AAR and CAR and make the statistical test. The results are shown in Table 1.

Table 1. -20 to 20的AAR（%）Test

Date	AAR	T-Value	P-Value	Date	AAR	T-Value	P-Value
-20	-0.06	-0.167	0.868	1	1.31	1.818	0.075*
-19	-0.45	-1.442	0.156	2	-0.2	-0.54	0.591
-18	0.37	1.053	0.298	3	-0.06	-0.138	0.891
-17	0.4	1.194	0.238	4	0.57	1.114	0.271
-16	-0.46	-1.201	0.236	5	-0.5	-1.059	0.295
-15	0.14	0.358	0.722	6	-0.17	-0.387	0.701
-14	0.48	1.601	0.116	7	0.11	0.317	0.753
-13	-0.54	-1.412	0.164	8	-0.23	-0.58	0.564
-12	-0.37	-1.404	0.166	9	1.06	2.305	0.026**
-11	-0.39	-0.915	0.365	20	-0.42	-1.175	0.246
-10	0.27	0.718	0.476	11	0.14	0.308	0.759
-9	0.65	1.597	0.117	12	-0.36	-1.064	0.292
-8	0.72	1.629	0.11	13	0.19	0.395	0.694
-7	0.08	0.226	0.822	14	-0.21	-0.482	0.632
-6	0.09	0.231	0.818	15	0.58	1.293	0.202
-5	-0.14	-0.433	0.667	16	-0.42	-0.989	0.328
-4	-0.4	-1.025	0.31	17	0.37	0.818	0.417
-3	-0.06	-0.135	0.893	18	-0.47	-1.402	0.167
-2	0.57	1.314	0.195	19	-0.26	-0.65	0.519
-1	0.64	1.376	0.175	20	0.9	1.82	0.075*
0	2.66	4.747	1.9E-05***				

Note: *、 **、 ***indicate the significance of the level 20%, 5% and 1% respectively, with the method dual-tail T-test

It can be seen from Table 1 that the value of abnormal return rate was not high and fluctuates between positive and negative 1 prior to the announcement date. Also, the absolute value of abnormal return rate was less than 0.1% on the date of -20, -7, -6, -3, where the results were not significant. However, the abnormal return rate was 2.66% at the announcement date, which was significantly more than any abnormal return rate before the announcement date. Moreover, the result at the level 1% was significantly positive on the announcement date. Then, there was not significant difference among the symbol of the abnormal return rates after the announcement date and the values were obviously less than the value at the announcement date, while only three days ,results in the statistic were significant.

The CAR curve shows that the cumulative abnormal return has been rising from 3 days prior to announcement date of the Stock option incentive. Moreover, the rising range of the time 0 was the most significant. The upward trend stopped one day after the announcement date, and the return rate fluctuated between 5% and 6% in the period (2, 20). Then we will use the accumulated method to calculate the cumulative abnormal return rate of (CAR) of each interval to get the reactions of the stock price at different phase.

As shown in Table 2, the cumulative abnormal return rates of the window phases (-1, 1), (5 ,5), (-10,10), (-15,15), (-20,20) were significantly positive, in which the first three windows phase were significant at level 1%, and the last two window phases were significant at the level 5%. In addition, the cumulative abnormal return rates of two window phases, (-20, -2) and (2, 20), were positive, with the low value and not significant results in the statistic.

Consequently, the Stock option incentive plan of the listed companies in China has a positive impact on the stock price. This shows that investors in China possess a positive attitude to the Stock option incentive. That is, investors anticipate that Stock option incentive can release the contradiction of principal-agent relationship between owners and managers. The results of CAR in the (-20, -2) and (2,20) were not significant, which indicated that there was no leaking information before the announcement date and that positive anticipation date did not last after announcement.

Table 2. Cumulative Abnormal Return Rate of Different Window Phases and the Statistics

Time Window	CAR (%)	T-Value	P-Value
(-1, 1)	4.62	5.045	6.93E-06***
(-5, 5)	4.4	2.715	0.009***
(-10, 10)	6.55	3.079	0.003***
(-15, 15)	6.2	2.645	0.011**
(-20, 20)	6.1	2.058	0.045**
(-20, -2)	0.89	0.548	0.586
(2, 20)	0.59	0.28	0.781

Note:*, **, ***indicate the significance of the level 20%，5%，1% respectively，with the method dual-tail T-test.

3   Economics Consequence of Stock Option Incentive Plan Based on Multi-linear Regression Model

3.1   Research Methods and Sample Selection

The event study method, though concise and intuitive, only can indicate the Stock option incentive announcement, the event affecting the anticipated performance, but cannot demonstrate the different incentive levels from Stock option incentive plan affecting the anticipated performance. In order to verify how much different incentives levels of plans affect the anticipated performance, a multi-linear regression analysis is employed based on the abnormal return method in this thesis. The cross section study method used in the multi-linear equation, which mainly based on some sample selection and window selection, is to set up a regression equation between accounting event and abnormal return. And then, the magnitude and figure of the regression coefficient and the degree of significance are utilized to estimate the information content of certain accounting event and the effects on the stock market. The hypothesis is that the accounting event conveys certain information, affecting the re-anticipation in the market potentially. As a result, the responsive coefficient, which the stock price reacts to the accounting event, would change relevantly, reflecting the adjustment of the market to the original expectancy.

In the last paragraph, after discretion, the sample includes 102 companies which have announced Stock option incentive plans. However, among them there are four companies which did not acclaim the degree of Stock option incentive in the plan, so these four companies are excluded in the empirical analysis process in this paragraph and the resulting study sample includes only 45 companies.

3.2 Study the Variable Definition and Model Construction

Given that the implementation of Stock option incentive studied in this thesis is still on the starting stage, among which some are not yet carried into execution. As a result, in the analysis, we take the anticipated CAR of investors as the place of the enterprise performance. And take the percentage of granted amount of stocks among the total issued stocks in the feature of Stock option incentive plan instead of the level indicators of the Stock option incentive, for the fact that, in the Stock option incentive plan announced by the listed companies in China, the percentage of amount of granted stocks taking up in the whole issued stocks is publicized.

Based on the assumption, the following model is established:

$$CAR_{(t1,t2)} = \beta_0 + \beta_1 \times EQUITY\_INCENTIVES + \beta_2 \times ROA + \beta_3 \times D/A$$
$$+ \beta_4 \times B/M + \beta_5 \times LNASSET + \varepsilon \tag{1}$$

Table 3 shows the variable definition in the multi-linear regression model.

3.3 Empirical Results

As it shown in the regression results of the table 4, the regression coefficient between equity-based incentive level and CAR is positive, which demonstrates that there is a positive correlation between them. However, the coefficient value is only 0.105, which claims that the correlation of them is not very tight. Besides, it can be seen from the regression coefficient between control variables and CARs that there are positive correlations between CAR and ROA, D/A, B/M and LNASSET, among which the regression correlations of ROA and B/M are great, so that the profitability and growth capacity of the corporate are strong. As a result, the investors would hold a high expectancy towards the promoting impacts of the Stock option incentive level on the enterprise performance. However, it could also be seen from the regression results mentioned above that those of all the variables are not significant statistically.

Table 3. Variable Definition

Variable		Abbrev	Definition
Explained Variable	Cumulative Abnormal Return Rate	$CAR_{(t1,t2)}$	The sum of CAR from t1 to t2, and the time window in this thesis is (-20, 20)
Explaining Variable	Stock option incentive Level	EQUITY_INCENTIVES	The proportion of the incentive amount to total shares
Control Variable	Return Rate on total Asset	ROA	net profit/ (total assets at the beginning plus total assets at the end of year) /2
	Asset-liability Ratio	D/A	Liabilities at the end of year/total assets at the end of year
	Price per Book Value	B/M	Total market value at the end of year/net assets at the end of year
	Asset Scale	LNASSET	Natural logarithm of the asset scale at the end of year

Table 4. Regression Result

Variables	Coefficient	Value-T	Value-P
Intercept	-27.472	-0.378	0.707
EQUITY_INCENTIVES	0.205	0.079	0.937
ROA	0.854	1.159	0.253
D/A	0.173	0.589	0.559
B/M	1.055	1.363	0.181
LNASSET	0.412	0.116	0.908
R^2	0.130	——	——
Adjusted R^2	0.018	——	——
F-test Value	1.164	——	——

4   Concluding Remarks

The thesis select the listed companies, which have announced Stock option incentive drafts after the implementation of "Management Measure" (Trial) on Jan. 1st, 2006 as the research objects. And we respectively use Event Study Method and Multi-linear Regression Method to empirically test the economics consequence of the Stock option incentive drafts announced by the listed companies in China with the market view. The test results show that: the investors in China more focus on the event of Stock option incentive of the listed companies, and they ignore the specific incentive levels of the Stock option incentive plans. The drawbacks of the study in this thesis are that: when selecting the samples, only the companies announcing after 2006 had the complete Stock option incentive plans, so that the samples included 102 companies during the research. However, for some of the plans were lacking statistics about the Stock option incentive level, the sample in the regression was reduced to only 45 companies. Thus, when analyzing the effect of the difference, which derived from the features of the Stock option incentive plan and the statistics of the cross sections in the companies, on the CAR, none of the regression results passed the statistical examination. Therefore, the author thought, as the development of Stock option incentive progresses and the sample number of the listed companies in China could be increasing to reach the statistical requirement, the research results of this thesis should be tested again then.

References

1. Kato, H.K., Lemmon, M., Luo, M., Schallheim, J.: An empirical examination of the costs and benefits of executive stock options: Evidence from Japan. Journal of Financial Economics 78, 435–461 (2005)
2. Chauvin, K.W., Shenoy, C.: Stock price decreases prior to executive stock option grants. Journal of Corporate Finance 7, 53–76 (2001)
3. Chen, Y., Liao, G.-M., Wang, T.: Empirical Analysis of Incentive Effect of Chinese Listed Companies. Management World 2, 158–159 (2005)
4. Yu, H.-l.: Empirical Test of Effect of Management Stock option incentive of Stated-owned Listed Companies. Economic Science 1, 108–116 (2006)
5. Zhang, J.-r., Zhao, J.-w., Zhang, J.: Empirical Analysis of the Correlation between Management Incentives and Enterprise Performance of the Listed companies. Accounting Research 9, 29–34 (2003)
6. Song, Z.-g.: Further Discussion of the Correlation between Management Incentives and Enterprise Performance of the Listed companies. Xi'an Finance 5, 30–32 (2006)

Enhancing the Effectiveness of the 4-Year Accounting Practice Programme: Students and Instructors Engagement Strategies

Hua Duan

Biochemical Engineering College of Beijing Union University, No.18, Fatou Xili 3 Qu,
Chaoyang District, Beijing, China
zhenzhen8991_cn@hotmail.com

Abstract. The paper includes three parts. At first, the contents and importance of accounting practice courses are introduced. The second part is the literature review. In the final and the most important part, three investigations are made and analyzed to enhance the effectiveness of the accounting practice programme. According to the analysis, the conclusions are obtained that accounting practice courses have great significance for developing the learning and working abilities of the students. In order to achieve the goal, it is essential that a reasonable proportion of different practice methods, teachers with adequate practical experiences, and financial support of the college.

Keywords: effectiveness, accounting practice programme, accounting practice methods.

1 Introduction

Accounting is a technical discipline including accounting theory and accounting practice. It has not only a complete theoretical system, but also has a set of standard operating procedures and professional methods. Theory courses include basic accounting, intermediate accounting and senior accounting. Basic accounting means accounting principles. Intermediate accounting includes financial accounting, cost accounting, and computerized accounting and so on. Senior accounting includes financial management, management accounting etc. In accounting theory courses students can learn accounting theories and principles, develop their good study habits and ways of thinking. But if there aren't practice courses, the students can not truly apply the accounting theory. In accounting practice courses, students can learn basic accounting processing, develop their operating capacity, actual problem-analyzed and problem-solving abilities.

I would like to introduce the contents and importance of accounting practice courses. That is the reason why I chose the title to research.

Practice courses include practical training in universities and outside practice. In the practice courses, normally, teachers will spend some time in teaching about the basic principles of operation and process. Then, the forms of practical training in my college include manual accounting training, computerized accounting training and

Q. Zhou (Ed.): ISAEBD 2011, Part I, CCIS 208, pp. 462–466, 2011.

ERP training. ERP means enterprise resource planning. It is an information system that takes management accounting as its core. ERP is applied to identify and plan enterprise resources in order to obtain customer orders, complete the processing and delivery, the final payment by customers. As regards outside practice in our university, the fourth year students will be required two months outside accounting practice in some enterprises. That will help them to prepare for their work in the near future.

The percentage of practice courses is more than about 50 percent in my college. The specific proportion varies according to different accounting practice courses. Thus, as a teacher of accounting, it is significant to provide good practice courses. Moreover, in my college, most of the teachers who teach accounting courses lack of practical experiences in enterprises. In such circumstances, it is very necessary to research how to teach accounting practice courses.

2 Literature Review

The debates surrounding the development of accounting education continue to focus on the ubiquitous view that accounting practice and the role of the professional is changing but accounting education is not reflecting this change (Patten and Williams, 1990; Albrecht and Sack, 2000). The AECC Position Statement No.1 (AECC 1990) was instrumental in summarizing the vision of the desired professional profile of future accountants. This statement, in conjunction with the Bedford Report, the White Paper and the AICPA statements, formed a solid basis for a large number of curricular innovations and research studies. The Bedford Report (AAA, 1986) concluded that accounting courses should 'aim to develop the students' capacities for analysis, synthesis, problem solving and communication.' Of particular concern was the misleading way in which accounting problems are presented to students as being well-structured and well defined (Sterling, 1980; Mayer-Sommer, 1990). A comment in the Bedford Report drew attention to the influence of accounting regulation on teaching styles: 'the current pedagogy also emphasizes problems with specific solutions rather than cases with alternative solutions.' As part of the calls for change in accounting education, prescriptions emerged for educators to move to case-based methods, seminars, role-plays, and simulations for actively involving students in the learning process (AAA, 1986; AECC, 1990; IFAC, 1996; Adler and Milne, 1997a; Hassall et al., 1998a). And similar calls have come from educationalists more generally who were concerned that undergraduate education was overemphasizing the technical capacities of students' knowledge to the detriment of more generic 'life-long' skills and attitudes (e.g., Biggs, 1989; Gibbs, 1992; Ramsden, 1992; Candy et al., 1994). Accounting academics indicate that the analysis of case studies, linked to oral and written assessments, was the preferred pedagogical approach to promote synthesis and evaluation of content and to develop professional skills in higher level courses (Ainsworth and Plumlee, 1993; Hassall et al., 1998b). In response to the calls for change, case studies are now being increasingly used in the teaching of accounting in higher education and they have also been added to the examination structure of many accountancy professional bodies.

3 Methodology

3.1 Research Question

In what ways can students and instructors engage to enhance the effectiveness of the accounting practice programme.

3.2 Investigation

Investigation 1. Investigation one is about the percentages among four different forms of accounting practical training in my college.

We mentioned four practical training above, which are manual accounting training, computerized accounting training, ERP and outside practice. Among them, now, in our college, the largest percentage is Manual accounting training, which is about 45%. The percentage of the other three is about 55%. Specific percentages are follows:

Table 1. The percentages among four different forms of accounting practical training

	manual accounting training	Computerized accounting training	ERP	outside practice	Total
weeks	13 weeks	7 weeks	1 week	8 weeks	29 weeks
percentage	45%	24%	3%	28%	100%

Investigation 2. Investigation two is about the percentages between teachers have accounting practical experiences and teachers lack accounting practical experiences in my college.

There are 16 teachers in accounting teaching office of economics and management department in my college. Among them, 5 teachers had practical experiences in some enterprises. Nevertheless, other 10 teachers have been working in my college since they graduated from their university. They never worked outside our college. Specific percentages between the two groups are follows:

Table 2. The percentages between teachers have practical experiences and teachers lack practical experiences

	Teachers have practical experiences	Teachers lack practical experiences	Total
number	5	11	16
percentage	31%	69%	100%

Investigation 3. Investigation three is about accounting labs in my college.

There are only two exclusive accounting labs. One is a manual accounting laboratory, the other is an ERP laboratory which was established in 2005 and never added new facilities since then. There is no exclusive computerized accounting laboratory. We had to give students computerized accounting training in computer labs. Thus, the time of this training has been limited. As for outside practice, steady outside accounting training bases haven't been set up. Between my college and some enterprises, there were no long-term stable cooperative relations. The following is the number of accounting labs in my college.

Table 3. The percentages among different type accounting labs .

	manual accounting laboratory	computerized accounting laboratory	ERP laboratory	outside accounting training bases
number	1	0	1	0

3.3 Analysis

From the above investigation, we know that in comparison with computerized accounting, ERP and corporate practice, the percentage of manual accounting training is too high in my university. At present, computerized accounting and ERP have been applied widely in most of the enterprises in China. In such circumstances, only giving students more computerized accounting training, ERP and corporate practice can they better meet the social real demands for accounting professionals. So, the first thing we should do is reducing the percentage of manual accounting training. At the same time, Increase the percentage of computerized accounting, ERP and corporate practice.

The investigation also reflects that most of the teachers lack adequate practical experiences in my department, which can not fully meet the needs of practical teaching. It is very important that the instructors' practical training should be strengthened, so that they will be competent for practice teaching. On the one hand, from 2009, accounting teachers were required to carry out six months of full-time business accounting practices. On the other hand, professional accountants should be invited to my college in order to guide the accounting teaching practice, so students can see the accounting methods applied to deal with the real economic and business transactions. In this way, the interests of students in learning accounting will be improved. Teachers can also be guided in accounting practice courses.

As regards accounting labs in the investigation, we learn about that the accounting practice courses in my college have insufficient supports. There are some important things that are needed to do for the leaders and teachers of my college. Firstly, we should complete the old accounting simulation laboratory, equipped with full-time laboratory assistant, who will be responsible for collection and safekeeping of practical information required, especially in a wide variety of original documents and accounting cases. Secondly, we also need to establish exclusive computerized accounting lab, equipped with accounting software, skills assessment software, and other assisted teaching software to meet the needs of teaching and practice. Finally, we will conduct social practice activities outside our college, even if it has some difficulty in it. We should try our best to create conditions to ensure the practical teaching activities carried out, such as the establishment of stable college-enterprises cooperation, so that there are outside accounting training bases for students to visit and learn. Despite of establishment of accounting lab, funds, technology, space, and other resources should be provided to support the accounting practice courses.

3.4 Results

Accounting practice courses have great significance for developing the learning and working abilities of the students, which can promote quality education, achieve training objectives.

In order to improve accounting practice courses, it is essential that a reasonable proportion of different practice methods, teachers with adequate practical experiences, and financial support of the college.

References

1. Accounting Education Change Commission (AECC): Objectives of education for accountants. position statement number one. Issues in Accounting Education 5(2), 307–312 (1990)
2. American Accounting Association (AAA) Committee on the Future Structure, Content, and Scope of Accounting Education (The Bedford Committee), future accounting education: preparing for the expanding profession. Issues in Accounting Education 1(1), 168–195 (1986)
3. Gibbs, G.: Improving the Quality of Student Learning. Technical and Education Services Ltd., Bristol (1992)
4. International Federation of Accountants (IFAC): Prequalification Education Assessment of Professional Competence and Experience Requirements of Professional Accountants. International Education Guideline No. 9. IFAC, Washington DC(1996)
5. Mayer-Sommer, A.P.: Substance and strategy in the accounting curriculum. Issues in Accounting Education 5(1), 129–142 (1990)
6. Milne, M.J., McConnell, P.J.: Problem-based learning: a pedagogy for using cased material in accounting education. Accounting Education, an International Journal 10(1), 61–82 (2001)
7. Patten, R.J., Williams, D.Z.: There's trouble – right here in our accounting programs. the challenge to accounting education. Issues in Accounting Education 5(2), 175–179 (1990)
8. Ramsden, P.: Learning to Teach in Higher Education. Routledge, London (1992)
9. Sterling, R.: Schools of Accounting. A look at the Issues. American Institute of Certified Public Accountants, New York (1980)

Present Situation and Countermeasures of Sustainable Development of Sports Industry in Jiangxi Province

Xuejun Cai[1] and Guojing Xiong[2]

[1] School of Education, Nanchang University, Jiangxi Province, China
caixuejun@ncu.edu.cn
[2] School of Economy and Management, Nanchang University, Jiangxi Province, China
xiongguojing@ncu.edu.cn

Abstract. Sports industry, as an newly emerging industry, has become one of the world's most promising sunrise industry. The sports industry management system should be rationalized and policies to support the development of sports industry should be formulated. Enterprise management, macro guidance and control efforts of the sports industry should be strengthened. The sports industry should be nurtured as the new economic growth point of national economy. Government should establish a relatively complete sports market system, further standardize and improve the fitness entertainment market, sports goods market, and sports intermediary market, and actively cultivate Jiangxi sports betting market, the sports media market, sports insurance market and competitive performance market, thereby promote the sports industry in Jiangxi Province to develop rapidly and sustainably.

Keywords: Sports Industry, Strategy, Sports Market, Poyang Lake Economy Ecological Region.

1 Introduction

As a result of continued socialization, life, market-orienting, sports industry has important values in increasing employment opportunities, adjusting the national industrial structure and promoting GDP growth. It also plays a dual role in implementing the concept of scientific development and building a harmonious society. The Sports industry, as a sunrise industry with huge potential, is becoming increasingly significant impact on the national economic and social development, and on the overall development of society. Its important role can not be ignored. To develop the sports industry not only can stimulate economic growth, promote industrial restructuring, expand employment opportunities, but also it play a significant role in improving the quality and quality of life.

China is in the key stages of development, which per capita GDP acrosses from $ 1,000 to $3,000, with the improvement of people's material and cultural living standards, people obtain health to sports, it has become a fashion. Thus, sports industry is not only one of the industries that supported and developed by the state,

Q. Zhou (Ed.): ISAEBD 2011, Part I, CCIS 208, pp. 467–474, 2011.

but also industrial categories with higher returns. For example, since the 2008 Olympic Games, Beijing, Shanghai and Guangzhou take the sports industry as a pillar (mainstay)industry with social and economic development of, and promote the rapid development of many related industries in tertiary industry. Stick to the guiding principles of sports development to keep pace with the times, and promote economy and society' coordinated development, build the Trinity's new sports development model which combines of competitive sports, social sports and sports industry, and the operation mechanism of the social, industrial, self-government. Comprehensive survey of Status and Problems ofsports industry in Jiangxi Province, it is necessary to plan comprehensively for the over-all layout and long-term development of the province's sports industry.

2   The Status and Lack of Sports Industry Development of Jiangxi Province

2.1   The Current Situation of Mass Sports industry Development in Jiangxi Province

Since the reform and open policy, the Jiangxi economy has continued the fast growth, higher than the national average level. The economic development and per capita disposable income continued to improve, builted a solid economic basis and provided the preconditions for the sports industry development. The momentum of economic development of Jiangxi Province was more fierce in recent years, GDP growth rate had higher than that of the national average. Primary, secondary and tertiary industries accounted for 10.6%, 46.8% and 42.6% of the GDP, the added value of Tertiary industry was 14.2918 trillion yuan, Rose by 0.8 percentage points. The proportion of tertiary industry increases gradually, such as the pulling effects of the industry chain provide a good development to the development of the sports industry. The average level of economic growth has achieved double-digit in the last years in Jiangxi Province,along with the increase in urban and rural incomes and with the acceleration of urbanization(Construction in the city), consumption of the sports industry will must be pulled and be growing consumer population can be growing. The sports population of Jiangxi Province has reached 28.2% of the national average, the sports population of Jiangxi Province in 2010 will expect to exceed 13 million, and as the economy goes on to keep a steady growth, the development prospects of the sports industry is getting better and better.

According to statistics, since December 2000 Jiangxi Computer Sports Lottery has been listed,and has issued a total of more than 50 billion yuanr,aising the national total of nearly 20 billion yuan of sports lottery public welfare fund. Jiangxi sports lottery has become an important source of funds and place of national public-spirited business as well as new sources of local taxes, provided more than 7,000 jobs to the community, and it had made great contributions to the country and sports in Jiangxi Province.

Table 1. 2003 - 2009, sales of sports lottery in Jiangxi Province(a hundred million yuan)

Year	2003	2004	2005	2006	2007	2008	2009
Sales	3	2. 56	8. 2	6. 6	8. 87	9. 33	12. 6
Chest	0. 91	0. 896	2. 8	2. 3	1. 3	1. 33	1. 73
National Ranking	18	19	15	19	17	22	15

Source: "Jiangxi Sports Yearbook" (2004 -2010)

Table 2. 2003 - 2009 the proportion of three industries in Jiangxi Province in the table (%)

Year	2003	2004	2005	2006	2007	2008	2009
Primary Industry	20. 0	20. 4	19. 0	17. 0	16. 6	16. 4	10. 6
Secondary Industry	43. 4	45. 6	47. 2	50. 2	51. 7	52. 7	46. 8
Tertiary Industry	36. 6	34. 0	33. 8	32. 8	31. 7	30. 9	42. 6

Source: "Statistical Yearbook of Jiangxi Province" (2004 -2010)

From Table 2, we can know, the proportion of three industries in Jiangxi Province has been adjusted to control, the primary industry has weakened, the proportion of second and tertiary industries are generally more than 80%, Moreover, that of the tertiary industry rises by a super-to-rise trend.As the sports industry in Jiangxi Province turns into a fast development stage,The sports industry which mainly to fitness, entertainment, competitive performance, technical training, sports goods, sports lottery has begun with the scale.

2.2 Insufficient Development of the Sports Industry in Jiangxi Province

(1) Economic underdevelopment, low levels of urbanization. According to statistics, GDP of Jiangxi Province reached 758.92 billion yuan, only accounted for 2.26% of national GDP in 2009. Per capita disposable income of urban residents of Jiangxi Province was 14,022 yuan, lower than the national average 18%. Jiangxi province economy is still in low level comparing the whole country. Physical output value only covers about 0.16% of zone total output, is more consumedly low than the national average of 0.7%,it ranked 25th in the country.

Seen from Table 3, the disposable income of urban residents of the national and Jiangxi Province was up, as well as the overall growth rate, moreover, the disposable income of urban residents in Jiangxi was significantly lower than the disposable income of urban residents in the countr. But the growth rate of the disposable income of urban residents in Jiangxi was slightly higher than the national urban growth rate of disposable income.

(2) Irrational industrial structure, the capital market system of the sports industry is to be perfect. Current and even for a long period of time, the body pillars of sports industry should be located in Event Industry, fitness and entertainment, Intangible asset development and management industry. The positioning of these three pillars of the industry is decided by its huge market potential.Defects in the structure of the sports industry of Jiangxi Province,which is not enough in the bulk

Table 3. 2003 - 2009 National and the disposable income of urban residents in Jiangxi Province and the growth rate

	year	2003	2004	2005	2006	2007	2008	2009
country	Disposable income (yuan)	8472	9942	10493	11759	13786	15781	17175
	Revenue growth (%)	9. 0	7. 7	9. 6	10. 4	12. 2	8. 4	9. 8
Jiangxi	Disposable income (yuan)	6901	7560	8620	9551	11222	12866	14022
	Revenue growth (%)	7. 8	5. 6	12. 2	9. 3	12. 7	8. 8	9. 7

Source: "National Statistical Yearbook" and the "Statistical Yearbook of Jiangxi Province" (2004 -2010)
Among them: after deducting price factor, increase in income is than the ratio of real growth last year.

growth of industrial development, there is no advantage to form a pillar,the reason is mainly that the scale of sports enterprises is generally small, the development lack of sustainable energy, the market is less competitive.At the same time, defects in the structure of the sports industry also reflected in the absence of the body estate market,although there are some exchange transactions, the real standardized sport labor market and sport technology market have not formed.

(3) Sports Goods Manufacturing immature, sports industry market level is not high. Sports consumption generally classified as sports consumption in kind, watch-type sports consumption and participatory sports consumption.Seeing from the current situation,the proportion of sports consumption in kind is significantly higher. Aggregate is not large, the level is not high, less competitive, self-development is not perfect,these issues are incompatible with the rapid development of Jiangxi Economic andsports.The sports goods manufacturers in Jiangxi are few,the size of the business is small, organizational forms are not standardized, backward mode of operation, the number and variety is single, marketing tools and methods are obsolete, the products lack of brand, less competitive, the share is low.Manufacturers are still in the workshop-style production status, they invest inadequately in new product development, Jiangxi lacks internationally competitive large-scale leading enterprises Sports Industry Group, Jiangxi sports enterprises have not a listed company.

(4) Shortage of sports industry professionals,the quality of management teams is generally low. To develop the sports industry, Construction of qualified personnel is the most critical, the serious lack of sports industry management and operational personnel are a major bottleneck of restricting the development of sports industry. At this stage, the number and capacity of the sports industry professional management are far short of needs.from the inside of Sports system, unit organization of the sports industry is not standardized, institutions are not perfect, lack high-quality sports marketing executives, some cities and counties do not even have sports management or professional and technical personnel. From the external environment, the quality of employees is not high in the business units of the community sports industry, the management who not only really understands sports, but also understands the anagement talent is very exile.

3 Models and Countermeasures of Sports Industry in Jiangxi Pronvince

3.1 Optimizing the Structure of the Sports Industry, and Improving the Quality and Efficiency in the Sports Industry

Optimizing the structure of the sports industry is the root path that raises the sports industry growth mass and efficiency, also the foundation that promotes an athletics industry booming development. Seting up a sports market system of completing categories, reasonable Structures and completeing Functions, which is an requirement that optimizing sports industry structure and it is also a foundation that developing industries. Analysising From the structure, sports market is a marketfor the body to Physical fitness and entertainment market, competition performance market, Sports intangible asset markets and sports talent market, sports consulting market. it Drives relevant sports markets,such as sport goods market, sports lottery market, advertising market and tourism market. Changeing ideas positivly, free training in the economic conditions, relying on the technical advantages of sports department, opening or guiding to hold various types of training courses, clubs, special schools, the training mainly contents Martial arts gymnasium, sports dance, swimming, badminton to charge fees to remedy the lack of training funds. With contest athletics to arouse mass sports, amateur training, building venues, talent cultivation and the rapid growth of sports consumer market. Encouraging social and enterprise to Invest profit or nonprofit sports facilities, promoting the mode of "diversification of property rights".

3.2 Perfecting Management of Post Qualification, Strengthening Efforts to Introducing Talents and Cultivating of the Sports Industry

By selecting management, training existing sports industry talents and employing sports business talents, the sports department should build a sports Industry talent team of good management, extensive knowledge and reasonable structure, promoting sustained and rapid development of sports industry.To strengthen business training of sports industry professional employees,specially the discovery of management personnel, training of the sports industry economic talents.Strengthening in-service training of the management of the sports industry development,improving the quality and viability of their business.Creating a pilot of sports talent market, promoting the flow of sports technical personnel, management personnel, social organization talent management and sports guidance personnel, sports agent talent. Cultivating and standardizing sports talent market, improving personnel evaluation system and incentive mechanism.Introduction of various kinds of high-level , high-quality, senior management personnel from home and abroad.It recommends and transferrs number of operators who understand management, and enrichs the sports industry management team, improves their management level. To strengthen mutual communication of sports department, institutions of higher learning and sports entrepreneur, support qualified institutions to add professional and courses of sports industry, training experts in the sports industry according to market.

3.3 Deepening Reform of Sports Management System, Exploring and Innovating Model of Sports Market Management

The perfect policy specification manages and laws and regulations to promote the development of sports industry, which are not only advantageous to athletics industrial healthy deveolp,also are assure the inevitable request of athletics industry mass. It enlarges a policy to strength,creats a good environment for athletics industrial. Necessary policy support should be given from the public finance, taxation, financing, etc. Through mergers, alliances,restructure, to form a group large-scale sports enterprises with well-known brands, strongsenseof innovation, modern enterprise management, diversified investment. In the area of tax policy,it should promote the development of sports industry through the differences in tax rates and reduction of tax policy. Strengthening the management Supervising and controling of the sports market,Maintaining the order in the sports market,improving the business activities of special projects and sports intermediary market regulations; Establishing a market access system of transparent andStandardized management;Establishing a sports market of reasonable structure,regulate development,reasonable competition for operators, full choice for consumers.

3.4 Speeding Up the Process of Urbanization and Modernization, Promoting Sports Socialization and Industrialization

Urbanization is not only the compulsory process of economic development, but also an important part of modern. Urbanization is conducive to fostering and developing the sports market, especially fitness entertainment market, and competition performance market. At present, urbanization of Jiangxi Province is Lower than the national average urbanization rate of 2 percentage points, it is expecting to higher than the national average at the end of the next five-year plan. Depending on the development of urban industrialization to physical capital accumulation, it is good for the virtuous circle to Form sports industrialization and modernization in the city. Therefore, useing regional advantages to accelerate the economic growth of the cities to construct sports industrialization and urbanization, modern circulation sustainable development system. Gradually, they form capital city as the center's sports radiation circle, provincial city as the supporting point, county city sports industry chain and rural town sports life nets, form cycle mechanism of mutually promoting common development.

3.5 Giving Full Play to Locational Advantage, Promoting Coordinated Development of Sports Industry in Jiangxi Province

Overall planning, integration of resources, formulation and choose a sports industry development mode that is suitable for oneself and scientific and effective. Making efforts to explore development breakthrough, cultivating and developing characteristic sports market, make the sports industry in jiangxi province develop towards scientific, effective, rapid and sustainable. Making full use of intangible assets in sports industry, seizing the historic opportunity development of Poyang Lake Economy Ecological Region, Developing sports goods industry, sports entertainment industry, sports complete performance industry, sports lottery industry, sports tourism industry, forming a new way of development for Jiangxi province-item sports industry. They should act the ring Poyang Lake Economic Region as the initial developing centre of jiangxi sports industry,the government should give them key support in resources and policy.With its elevation of agglomeration benefits and economic benefits, progressively increasing support and motivating the diffusion effects of central.Exerting regional advantages and resources, according to local conditions, creating sports service products andsports industry development belt which have distinctive characteristics. Sports can converg with culture and tourism. Employment can interact with fitness, leisure and entertainment.

4 Conclusions

Applying market mechanism to deploy reasonablely and usei efficiently, improving sports undertakings for the social service performance and overcoming theconflict with inadequate investment and wasting of resources.Various kinds of public sports stadiums should accelerate to management type, implementing an enterprise management. Various sports training base and sports school training grounds should open to the society, break enclosed self-service system, and pay for the use gradually and Independent operation. They focus on the development of sports competition demonstration industry and fitness entertainment industry, enlarge sports lottery, keep with development advantages of lottery sales soar, introduce and hold high level of sports competitions at home and abroad actively, activate the sports competition performance market,improve the commercialization of sports contest performance. In addition, they should establish a broker system competition as soon as possible, encourage the community to undertake sports or sponsoring sporting events in ways such as charter, specify, naming, specializing, to provide a way of seting their image, thereby stimulating relevant advertising, brokerage, media, insurance and etc, building competition performance industry chain.To promote popularization and living fashion of the sports consumption, further expand sports consumer groups.

Strengthening the regulations construction of sports market access, the market competition and market supervision and management. Speeding up the development planning of formulated perfect sports industry, combined with the fact of various areas, it provides good policy and regulation environment for the development of the sports industry. To plan scientific and reasonable sports industry layout and develop sports industry. Setting up the sports development and promotion mode of government support, association supervision, enterprise dominant, the market operation, strengthening the connection between the enterprises and intermediary organizations, conducting sports agent pilot and sports service authentication. establishing sports cooperative development platform through various forms and channels, be ensure sponsors and intermediary organizations rights. They should encourage an independent economic entity, entity to do industry, according to the needs of the market, to invest and operate.They should expand financing channels, encourage private and foreign investment into sports industry. Through establishing reasonable tax polic, proeing and standardizing sports market, strengthening market supervision, to guide enterprises to operate in accordance with law, honestly and trustworthy, safeguard consumers' rights. The rapid rise of Poyang Lake Economic Zone is quickly rising, which provides a good opportunity for the development of Jiangxi province. The sports industry structure of poyang lake (reasonable layout) should be constructed, thereby the rapid development of the sports industry leads other provinces and jiangxi province to promote the overall development rapidly and healthily.

Acknowledgement. This study was partially supported by the Jiangxi Province Office of Sports Social Science Foundation Grant # 2009010. Corresponding author: Xiong Guojing. Tel.: +86791-8025371. E-mail address: xiongguojing@ncu.edu.cn

References

1. Li, L., Yang, J., Yang, T., Xu, L.-h.: A Research on the Sustainable Development of Evaluation Index System of Regional Sports Industry. Journal of Jilin Institute of Physical Education 33(9), 26–29 (2010)
2. Ge, B., Song, H., Wang, Y.: Analysis on the Influential Factor of the Sports Industry Development. Journal of Jilin Institute of Physical Education 40(4), 17–18 (2004)
3. Meng, Z.-R., Yang, T.-l.: A Discussion on the Necessity of the Research of the Developing Strategy for the Sports Industry in Beijing. Journal of Capital Institute of Physical Education 18(1), 41–43 (2006)
4. Wang, C.-j., Zhou, F.-x., Meng, X.-h.: Research of Sports Industry Sustainable Development Based on the Vision of Technical Economic in China. Journal of Xi an Physical Education University 27(5), 551–554 (2010)
5. Zhu, X.-h.: Analysis of Sports Industry s Sustainable Development Factors in Our Country. Journal of Xi an Institute of Physical Education 122(2), 9–28 (2005)
6. Deng, G.: Strategic Research on the Sustainable Development of the Sports Industry of Jiangsu Province, Vol. 27(5), 58–61 (2006)
7. Li, G.-y.: An Evaluation of Modern Sports Industry in China in the View of Sustainable Growth. Journal of Capital Institute of Physical Education 18(5), 83–85 (2006)

Ski Industry Effects of Opening Skiing Lessons in Heilongjiang Province University and College

Liang Zhang

Sports Department
Northeast Agricultural University
No.59, Mucai Street, Xiangfang District,
150030, Haerbin, China

Abstract. Heilongjiang Province is Located in North China, with advantaged resource of ice storm. Opening Skiing Lessons in Heilongjiang University and College is a new action implementation of sunshine athletic sports. It not only satisfied the nee d of contemporary undergraduate, but also make winter sports richer and colorful. As far as ski industry is concerned, university and college open skiing lessons broaden the consumption market of ski industry and provide potential management and technical talent for ski industry, which is helpful to propote the sound and rapid development of ski industry.

Keywords: skiing, ski industry.

1 Introduction

Heilongjiang province situates at our country's north, which owns the source of advantaged snow and ice. The cold weather is breeding the specific way of body-building—snow-ice sports. It is full of Romance, passion, excitement and challenge to place yourself into the world of snow and ice, which agglomerates affinities of the time and nature.Ice-snow spots have already become one of the most popular winter sports in North America and Europe. With the improvement of domestic living standards, people have had new views about the need of sport-entertainment and body-building culture, the excitement of the skiing itself and the function of building strong body. And skiing has gradually removed the coat of noble game recent years, become a very popular sport among the mass of the people. With the special geographical position and the source and snow and ice, it makes undergraduates to crush into the world of snow and ice by establishing skiing courses in colleges. It is good for improving undergraduates' physical and psychological health and forming healthy personality to get across the creative sports with the aid of natural advantage, to find enjoyment of snow-ice sports get them, and to ask for knowledge and health from snow-ice, exercise will and edify sentiment Meanwhile, undergraduates are also the potential consumers and talents in support. As a result, it is important for the sustainable development of skiing industry to improve the cognition and desire of participation of snow-ice sports.

Q. Zhou (Ed.): ISAEBD 2011, Part I, CCIS 208, pp. 475–479, 2011.

2 The Development Tendency of Skiing Industry in Heilongjiang Province

2.1 Analyzing of the Present Situation

Heilongjiang Province has a very long history about skiing industry. And Yuquan skiing field was the earliest skiing traveling base in our country, and was even honored as "Hometown of skiing in China " in the 1930s.The development of skiing industry in Heilongjiang Province has good foundation and condition, had come into a fast-development period in the beginning of 20th century. It have successfully held World university Student Winter Games in 2009,has already built more than 80 skiing fields recently, which takes up more than 60 percent among the total skiing fields in our whole country. Besides, it now has more than 200 different kinds of snow ways, more than 200 pieces of rope ways, more than 60,000 couples of skiing equipment, more than 1,500 coaches in different classes. The reception number of skiing traveling has a yearly average 20 percent grow. And the number of skiing traveling has broken through 6000,000,most of which just has the purpose of traveling to go skiing fields to watch snow or to try to ski. The guests out-of-town are even ski at the first time, also may be the only time of skiing, the proportion of skiing people is decreasing. From the view of the time of reception, skiing people always choose holidays and the period of winter vocation to ski, skiing fields are is full relatively. But there are little people in the workdays from the end of November to the beginning of January.

Yabuli skiing field, the biggest skiing field in China, has been the brand symbol of winter traveling in Heilongjiang Province, which has led to the development of winter traveling economy in Heilongjiang Province. And skiing traveling has been the hit product of winter traveling and the new growth point of traveling economy in Heilongjiang Province. However, there is gaps between competitive skiing sports and skiing industry in China. Comparing with competitive skiing in China, common skiing drops behind a lot. Comparing with other countries, skiing industry is just in the beginning ,no matter development time, scale of skiing fields or   participation population.

2.2 The Difference between Internal and Overseas

With large numbers of skiing resorts appear , foreign companies which are focus on selling skiing equipment have already taken step in China. As far as it's concerned, the equipment sell in the market is still foreign brands these days. Irregular market, failure of industrial structure, and poor management, all these weak points make us aware that development and mastery for skiing resorts, equipment and related technologies are still right here waiting for development .

Although the ski industry of our country is developing rapidly , when compared with those countries which stepped early in the area, such as Japan South Korea in Asia , Chile and Argentina in South America, we find shortages not only in our skiing resorts and infrastructure but also in the service of related industries, such as the convenient transportation ,the comfortable shopping experience, the remarkable living environment ,the prefect facilities of health care ,the modern entertainment city and the famous attractions accompanied.

Otherwise, in case of the shortages of the infrastructure and the service of related industries, we are faced with the big pressure from Japan and South Korea in terms of the development of foreign tourist market .It is reported that there are more than 100 skiing resorts in the mountains of northern Japan ,there are 12 skiing resorts with international standards in South Korea. And the quantity is expanding anyway. However, as the spending in our country is much lower than that of Europe and Japan, so neighboring countries still like to come to our country for skiing.

Skiing in China is currently still at the level of fashion ,when people really understand many of its benefits and participate in it ,skiing in winter will become an important part of Chinese people's life .

3 The Motivation of Our Province Colleges and Universities Setting Up Ski Lessons

3.1 Teaching of Setting Up Ski Lesson Is the Need for Reform

The freezing of our province is up to 5 months ,during this period ,various sports activities in our province in college must be reduce ,school sports have entered hibernation.

For the "Teaching of Physical Education Curriculum Guidelines" and "Hundreds of millions of students to carry out the sun on the sports notice" of the instructions ,the province should increase winter sports university teaching ,and enable students to understand the importance of physical training in winter ,and tap their inner power to participate in outdoor sports in winter to stimulate students interest in snow sports ,broaden the potential content of snow ,rational use of ice and snow resources ,abundant snow and ice sports items ,so that more students can participate in this campaign and hone their own in the snow world to improve health .College Student Section is to implement the Sunshine ski sports a new initiative to fill the gaps in university teaching in the winter sports ,this will inspire students to participate in snow sports .Most of the skiing resorts in our province is located in the remote mountain ,so it's a good chance for students to leave school and get close to nature .And it's also a chance to improve students' adaptability ,self-care ability ,team spirit .Besides ,it has a positive effect in improving students' environmental awareness.

3.2 Setting Up Ski Lessons Is the Aspirations of College Students

Skiing is an ancient and new sports, as China's economic developed rapidly, it has gradually faded "noble sport" cloak and become a favorite sport by the general public. College students are the people who are thinking of new things and dare to cognitive new things. The survey of nearly 900 college students in our province attitudes and participation in sports ,results are as follows ,84.5% of students want to ski, 74.7% support to open ski lessons ,69.5% want to have ski lessons, and 91.3%have never learned skiing or don't acquire to skiing .So we can see the majority of students are really interested in skiing. This shows that it is feasible to set up ski lesson. At the same time, we regret that although skiing is a kind of unique ,charismatic and highly valuable training sports in the north , as much as 91.3% of the students have never learned skiing or don't acquire to skiing. This shows that the province of setting up ski lesson is necessary.

4   The Influence of Setting Skiing Course in Universities to the Development of Skinning Industry in Our Province

University students, reflecting the state's mental outlook and future direction are the pillars of the country in the contemporary era. Setting skiing course are not only benefit to the health of college students but also conducive to the development of skinning industry.

4.1   Setting Skiing Course in Universities Could Expand the Skinning Consumer Market

In Heilongjiang province, there are more than seven hundred and six thousand students studying in the twenty seven universities. Setting skiing course in these universities could attract more students to participate in skiing sport. This will become a huge consumer group in skinning industry. Good arrangements could solve the problem of depressed state of the skinning market from the the end of November to the June the next year. Because of the special status of the university students, setting skiing course could produce a promotional effect. In the end, they will attract more and more people to take part in this sport warmly. Meanwhile because of the passion of the young college students, more and more people will became loyal skiing fans.

4.2   The Loyal Skiing Fans of Students Are the Potential Managers of Skiing Industry

Most of the managers of sports industry are retired athletes or coaches now. Most of them are only familiar with the sport itself for the lack of understanding of the market and its laws. Setting skiing course in universities could enhance their understanding toward skiing sport and skiing industry. This will be attracting more students to participate in this game, improving the quality of managers, meeting the needs of skiers, improving the service quality and promoting the development of the skiing industry. Frequent communication and cooperation with foreign friends will improve the skiing industry in our province's competitiveness in the world and this will promote the commercialization of skiing industry in our province.

4.3   The Loyal Skiing Fans of Students Are the Potential Technology Professionals

Because of the high quality of college students and their professional learning in a certain direction, technology professionals could be trained in skiing industry among the students. For example, some of them focus on the resort area of infrastructure, some specializes in the design of ski clothing and others specialize in the manufacture of ski equipment. The technological innovation and competitiveness of skiing industry will be improved by these people in China.

4.4 The Loyal Skiing Fans of Students Are Helpful for the Formation of the Skiing Industry Chain

Most college students engaged in different professions and direction of learning. By the exchange of the skiing sport, the communication between different professionals including skiing industry could be strengthened. Different chain of skiing industry could also bring coordinated development by communication between different professionals. For example, coordinated development could be obtained by the communications among the entertainment industry, the tourism industry, the transportation and related services.

5   Results and Discussions

Setting skiing course in the universities of Heilongjiang province is a new initiative for the implement of sunshine sports. both to meet the needs of contemporary college students, make the winter sports more colorful ,effectively improve students' physical and psychological health, and has a positive role to improve students' adapting ability, ability of self-dependence, sense of cooperation . On the ski industry, setting up ski lessons expanded the consumer market for the ski industry development, provides a potential talents of management and technical talents, which is beneficial to the formation of ski industry chain, to improve our province's competitiveness of the ski industry in the world, but also to promote the ski industry healthy and rapid development.

References

1. Zi, j., M.S.: The impact analysis about Chinese ski movement on the ski industry. Lanzhou university master degree theses (2007)
2. Cui, X.: The conception of The northeast university start skiing elective course. Snow sports. [4] (2006)
3. You, n.: The current situation and development trend of Ski Industry in our country. Shenyang Institute of Physical Education. [2] (2006)
4. 2010 The Planning Project of Philosophy and Social Sciences in Heilongjiang Province, 10B059 approval number (2010)

Research on Chinese Economic Development and the Decoupling of Energy Consumption from Consumer Perspective

Jianping Hou and Lei Ma

School of Economics & Management, Xi'an Technological University,
Xi'an ,710032, China

Abstract. Chinese current industrial development is in the medium-term, the current dominant industry structure is still industry with large consumption of energy. According to 'decoupling' and 're-hook' basic principles, based on economic development and energy consumption relative 'decoupled' and 're-hook' concept model, Chinese consumption amount to analyze the relationship and energy consumption, And the various stages of 'decoupling' the identification and analysis of the phenomenon. Studies suggest that in a certain stage of Chinese total consumption and energy consumption in the 'relative decoupling' and 'expansive re-hook'.

Keywords: Consumption, Economic development, Energy consumption, Decoupling.

1 Introduction

In 2003, Britain proposed the concept of low-carbon economy, transition to a low carbon economy is the economic growth and greenhouse gas emissions, relations between the 'decoupling' process. In 1960s, Foreign scholars through long-term observation, Found in the course of economic development, Total consumption of materials(TEC) in economic development with the total economy early growing together growth, appear at a later stage of the reverse change, So as to realize the economic growth material consumption decreased, called the 'decoupling' theory. Since then, about 'decoupling' concept has been engaged in discussions.

Chinese current industrial development is in the medium-term, Large consumption of energy and mineral resources. Look from the relative amounts, Chinese economic development and energy consumption has been 'decoupled'. In this paper, Based on Chinese since reform and opening up the consumption amount (resident's consumption and government consumption), Energy intensity indicators, Perspective on the economy through consumption and energy consumption analysis of the relationship between the decoupling.

Q. Zhou (Ed.): ISAEBD 2011, Part I, CCIS 208, pp. 480–486, 2011.

2 Decoupling Cheory

2.1 The Concept of Decoupling

The 20th century in the 1970s and 80s a lot of economic growth deviate from the material consumption. Many scholars from different angles of this 'decoupling' phenomenon described, Studies suggest that 'decoupling' reflects the economic growth and material consumption does not change the substance of sync. The 'decoupling' theory is that economic development, utilization of resources and environmental pressure on the relationship between the performance for two relations: first is the resource utilization and environmental pressure increases along with the economic development, second is of resource utilization and environmental pressure and not with the development of economy and increase, and even less. In some cases the material consumption decline after period of time (namely 'decoupling') rising again (called 're-hook').

Based on the 'decoupling' concept, WU Yuming (2008) study China regional economic growth and environmental coupling coordination development; Chen Baiming, Du Hongliang (2006) analyzes the cultivated land occupied and GDP growth between the decoupling relationship; Yu Fawei (2008) analysis of Chinese grain production and irrigation water between the decoupling relationship; Wang Chongmei (2009) Study on Chinese economic growth and energy consumption decoupling relationship.

2.2 Decoupled Classification

Decoupling major can be divided into two types: Relative decoupling and absolute decoupling. The former refers to the economic development, the resources use or for environmental pressure at relatively low rate increase; Absolute decoupling of economic development, resource utilization and decrease the growth rate of environmental pressures. Relative decoupling happen first, but ultimately transform for the absolute decoupling. Relative decoupling point conversion to absolute decoupling, is a resource/environmental turning point. Decoupling reflect driving force (such as GDP growth) and pressure (environmental pollution) in the same period of growth changes. The two phenomena of mutual transformation between relations as shown in figure 1.

Zhao Yiping (2006) Using TEC (energy consumption) and GDP (economic development) between the fluctuation relation of 'decoupling' and 'complex hook' concept description. According to TEC and GDP change relations, 'decoupling' and 're-hook' can be divided into six types: relative decoupling, expansion re-hooks, strong re-hook, recession re-hook, recession decoupling, absolute decoupling (Figure 2).

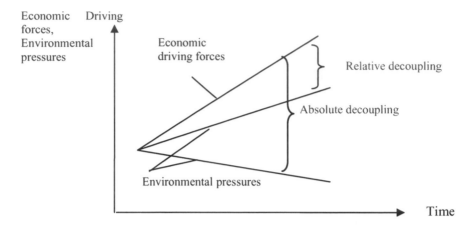

Fig. 1. Relative Decoupling and Absolute Decoupling Relationship

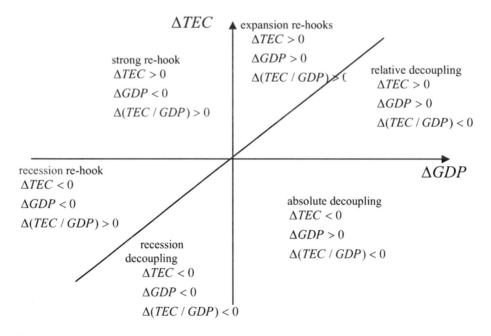

Fig. 2. Economic Development and Energy Consumption with the Relative Decoupling Re-hook Conceptual Model

Figure 2 shows that 'decoupling' and 're-hook' is not only the attention to ΔGDP, ΔTEC, and analysis of changes of $\Delta(TEC/GDP)$, if $\Delta(TEC/GDP)$ less than 0 decoupling, greater than 0 for re-hook. The most ideal state is an absolute decoupling.

3 Empirical Study

3.1 Data Sources and Processing

This paper uses total consumption (TCE) instead of a conceptual model of gross domestic product (GDP), select the total domestic consumption (TCE) (including household consumption and government consumption), total energy consumption (TEC) and unit energy consumption of that energy intensity (TEC/TCE) as a research index. Collected data from the 1980-2009 year.

To eliminate the impact of inflation on nominal economic variable---gross domestic consumption (TCE) was to index treatment (to the level of consumption in 1979 as the base index $k=1$), 2009 calculated level of consumption is 9.37, To see the index formula (1).

$$TCE_i = TC_i / k_i \qquad (1)$$

TCE_i for the first i years of practical domestic consumption amount, TC_i for the name of the first i in domestic consumption amount, k_i for the first i years of consumer price index (in 1979 as a benchmark). Calculate ΔTEC, ΔTCE and $\Delta(TEC/TCE)$ by the Chinese response relationship between consumption and the energy index value, the results shown in Table 1.

3.2 Analysis of Causes of Change

From table 1, In 1980—2009 Chinese consumer index and energy consumption relationship with decoupling relationship were divided into four stages:

(1) In 1980, 1985-1998 and 2008 Chinese consumption (ΔTCE) and energy consumption (ΔTEC) rate were greater than zero, $\Delta(TEC/TCE)$ was less than zero, that the long-term energy consumption growth and consumption growth in the 'relative decoupling' state.

1980 China was the reform and opening up, the total spending levels were significantly increased, the level of the progressive development of industrialization. 1985-1998, Chinese rapid economic development, people's living standards and a substantial increase in the level of consumption. The year of 2008 although because of financial crisis, the growth rate of total consumption compared with previous years growth slowdown, environmental protection consciousness enhancement, the consumption of energy resources is slow.

(2) In 1981 Chinese consumption (ΔTCE) rate was greater than zero, energy consumption (ΔTEC) rate and $\Delta(TEC/TCE)$ were less than zero, that energy consumption and consumption growth in the 'absolute decoupling' state.

Table 1. Chinese Consumer Index and Energy Consumption Relationship with Decoupling Relationship

YEAR	ΔTEC	ΔTCE	$\Delta(TEC/TCE)$	Decoupling type
1980	1687	126.3387	-0.40705	relative decoupling
1981	-828	87.38086	-0.96096	absolute decoupling
1982	2620	98.51604	0.191189	expansion re-hooks
1983	3973	79.52502	0.759392	expansion re-hooks
1984	4864	148.9847	0.50779	expansion re-hooks
1985	5778	280.9298	-0.14378	relative decoupling
1986	4168	303.6477	-0.68384	relative decoupling
1987	5782	300.8884	-0.16985	relative decoupling
1988	6365	688.8137	-1.75482	relative decoupling
1989	3937	651.5149	-1.63363	relative decoupling
1990	1769	238.8286	-0.44652	relative decoupling
1991	5080	410.8277	-0.34891	relative decoupling
1992	5387	471.4968	-0.41422	relative decoupling
1993	6823	1134.262	-1.58901	relative decoupling
1994	6744	2113.067	-2.587	relative decoupling
1995	8439	1614.594	-1.04075	relative decoupling
1996	4016	1050.461	-0.65057	relative decoupling
1997	717	607.8595	-0.4518	relative decoupling
1998	275	157.9283	-0.10385	relative decoupling
1999	4385	-49.9204	0.372637	strong re-hook
2000	4962	243.553	0.176092	expansion re-hooks
2001	4875	335.186	0.089803	expansion re-hooks
2002	9025	39.87939	0.62376	expansion re-hooks
2003	24361	144.5859	1.630633	expansion re-hooks
2004	29664	591.0601	1.506901	expansion re-hooks
2005	22541	727.0799	0.777393	expansion re-hooks
2006	22679	572.0687	0.874202	expansion re-hooks
2007	21832	865.6988	0.459639	expansion re-hooks
2008	10940	1095.043	-0.42152	relative decoupling
2009	15199	-97.2512	0.950643	strong re-hook

(3) In 1982-1984 and 2000-2007, Chinese consumption (ΔTCE) rate was greater than zero energy consumption (ΔTEC) rate and $\Delta(TEC/TCE)$ were greater than zero, that hat energy consumption and consumption growth in the 'expansive re-hook' state.

1982-1984 China vigorously developing heavy industry, energy-intensive, consumption amount although have certain scope increase, but less than energy consumption growth. In the 21st century, with the market economy and opening-up pattern of the establishment, development of social productive forces, supply shortages disappeared, began to form a competitive market, The resulting 'expansive re-hook' phenomenon

(4) In the year of 1999 and 2009 Chinese consumption (ΔTCE) rate was less than zero, energy consumption (ΔTEC) rate and $\Delta(TEC/TCE)$ were greater than zero, that energy consumption and consumption growth in the 'strong re-hook' state.

To sum up, from the early 1980s began China consumption and the amount of energy consumption has been in 'relative decoupling' the relationship state, in recent years continuous appeared 'expansion re-hooks ' trend.

To sum up, from the early 1980s began China consumption and the amount of energy consumption has been in 'relative decoupling' the relationship state, in recent years continuous appeared 'expansion re-hooks ' trend.

4 Conclusion

'Relative decoupling' and 'expansion re-hooks' is the main feature of the relationship of Chinese consumer and the amount of energy consumption. At present, China is a higher level of well-off society in building critical period, heavy industrialization, urbanization, and international development exacerbated the trend of rapidly rising energy demand, China faces continue to appear to 'expansion re-hook' of the crisis. Improve energy efficiency and reduce greenhouse gas emissions, is the first principle of Chinese energy policy. China must adopt a energy policy of give priority to energy conservation. Efficiency mainly' energy policy, increasing clean-coal combustion technique to popularize strength. In view of changes in the international environment, focus on strengthening the development and utilization of renewable energy, energy structure to the development strategy of rapid upgrade, comprehensive to ensure stable energy supply and sustainable development of the national economy.

References

1. Zhuang, G.: China: To Low-carbon Economy to Address the Challenge of Climate Change. Environmental Economy 1, 69–71 (2007)
2. Carter, A.P.: The Economics of Technological change. Scientific American 214, 25–31 (1966)
3. Azar, C., Holmberg, J., Karlsson, S.: Decoupling-past Trends and Prospects for the Future. Ministry of the Environment of Sweden (2002)
4. Deng, H., Duan, N.: Evaluation Mode of Decoupling and its Impact on Circular Economy. China Population, Resources and Environment 6, 44–47 (2004)

5. Wu, Y.: Analyzing Coupled Regional Economic Growth and Environmental Conservation in China. Resources Science 1, 25–30 (2008)
6. Chen, B., Du, H.: Analyzing Decoupling Relationship Between Arable Land Occupation and GDP Growth. Resources Science 9, 36–42 (2006)
7. Yu, F.: Chinese grain Production and Irrigation Water Decoupling Relation Analysis. Chinese Rural Economy 10, 34–44 (2008)
8. Wang, C.: Decoupling Analysis of China Economic Growth and Energy Consumption. China Population, Resources and Environment 3, 35–37 (2010)
9. Yu, F.: Between Economic Development and Resources and the Environment Decoupling an Empirical Study. Journal of Inner Mongolia Finance and Economics College 3, 29–34 (2009)
10. Zhao, Y.: Responsive Relationship Between Economic Development and Energy Consumption in China - a practical research based on comparative de-link and re-link theory. Science Research Management 3, 128–134 (2006)
11. 2010 China Statistical Yearbook. China Statistics Press, Beijing (2010)

The Empirical Study of Individual Housing Loan Credit Risk Based on Proximal Support Vector Machine

Jianping Hou and Qiang Xue

School of Economics & Management, Xi'an Technological University,
Xi'an ,710032, China

Abstract. The purpose of this paper is to reduce the default rate of personal housing loan and accurately predict whether or not the borrower defaults. Based on the data of individual housing loan, this paper employs a proximal support vector machine (PSVM) to explore the credit risk factors. Then the paper constructed the credit risk assessment system of individual housing loan. The data of individual housing loan was from China Construction Bank of Shaanxi branch in Xi'an market. The empirical results not only show that PSVM can accurately predict credit risk assessment of personal housing loan, but also can quickly and accurately judge whether or not the borrower break a contract.

Keywords: PSVM, Credit risks, Housing loan.

1 Introduction

With the amount of China's personal housing loan increase unceasingly, the credit risk exposed gradually. It is very important to study the influence factors and to reduce the credit risk. The default influence factors of personal housing loan have gradually become a spotlight since the 1970s. Domestic and foreign scholars have studied default influence factors. Bart Lambrecht (1997) thought that the most significant default influence were loan to Value, wages, marital status and interest rate[1]. Morton (1975) thought that is support population, LTV and occupation[2]. George (1978) thought that is the borrower past credit rating and occupation[3]. Kau (1995) thought that the higher the LTV, the default probability is more higher[4]. Quercia (1992) thought that the default rate decrease over time[5]. Many scholars used the Logistic model to do empirical study in china.

Based on the indexes system of individual housing loan credit risk and PSVM model, the empirical study are shown as follows: This paper put the borrower's index as attribute matrix and put whether the borrower does break a contract or not as the discriminant matrix. We use 260 samples in training set to get optimal hyperplane and then use 40 samples in test set to predict the result. The result show that combined with PSVM Model, this paper gets credit risk assessment for individual housing loan, which has highly predictive accuracy when it has been tested and evaluated.

Q. Zhou (Ed.): ISAEBD 2011, Part I, CCIS 208, pp. 487–493, 2011.

2 Model

Vapnik introduced SVM into machine learning area in 1992. PSVM is an improved version of SVM, which has become the standard tool in machine learning and data mining area.

We assume that use a n-1 dimensional optimal hyperplane separate the n-dimensional real space R^n. SVM classifies points by assigning them to one of two disjoint halfspaces, points are classified by assigning them to the closest of two parallel planes that are pushed apart as far as possible (see Figure 1). Make sure the maximum margin between sample data and optimal hyperplane. The margin is $\dfrac{2}{\|w\|}$, which equivalent to make $\dfrac{1}{2}\|w\|^2$ minimum. The standard SVM with a linear kernel is given by the following quadratic program with parameter $v > 0$:

$$\min_{(w,\gamma,y)\in R^{n+1+m}} ve'y+\frac{1}{2}\|w\|^2$$
$$s.t.\begin{cases} D(Aw-e\gamma)+ y \geq e \\ \qquad\qquad y \geq 0 \end{cases} \qquad (1)$$

Where $A \in R^{m\times n}, D \in \{-1,+1\}^{m\times1}, e = 1^{m\times1}$, e is unit column vector, v is weighting factors, y is slack variable, w is interface normal vectors, γ is bias vector.

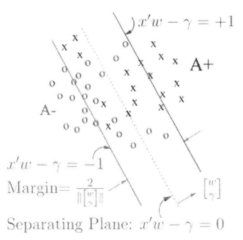

Fig. 1. Proximal support vector machine classification principle

PSVM is improved based on SVM. The linear PSVM can easily handle large datasets. PSVM use three parallel hyperplanes approximatively separate all samples into two groups. The rest of the two hyperplanes are two kind of clustering center. Similarly, the optimization problem is replaced by the following problem:

$$\min_{(w,\gamma,y)\in R^{n+1+m}} v\frac{1}{2}\|y\|^2 + \frac{1}{2}(w'w+\gamma^2)$$
$$s.t. \quad D(Aw-e\gamma)+y=e \tag{2}$$

3 Construct Risk Evaluation Index System

This paper has evaluated the credit risk of personal housing loan in four dimensions: borrower, loans, housing and area. The risk evaluation index system has 17 indexes.

Table 1. Credit Risk Assessment System of Individual Housing Loan

Dimension	variable code	variable name	Quantitative method
Borrower	X1	Sex	Male = 1, female = 2
	X2	Age	Actual age
	X3	Educational level	Below High school = 1, High school or technical secondary school =2, College school=3, Undergraduate=4, Postgraduate or above =5
	X4	Census register	Xian = 1, Other places= 2
	X5	Marital status	Unmarried = 1, Married with children = 2, Married childless = 3, Divorce = 4
	X6	Career	Private entrepreneurs and individual engaged in commerce =1, Business, service personnel = 2, Management personnel and concerned personnel =3, All kinds of professional and technical personnel = 4, State organs, organization, enterprise or business unit principal = 5, Military = 6, The inconvenience classification of other employees = 7
	X7	Professional title	No title = 1, Primary = 2, Intermediate = 3, Senior = 4
	X8	Family Monthly Income	Thousand
	X9	Family debt ratio	%
Loans	X10	Loan contract amount	Ten thousand Yuan
	X11	Loan Period	Year
	X12	Loan to value	%
	X13	Loan interest rate	Annual percentage rate
	X14	Payment method	Matching interest repayment law =1, Matching principal repayment law =2
Housing	X15	Floor space	Square meter
	X16	Housing price	Thousand
Area	X17	House price index	%

4 Empirical Study

This paper had extracted customer information from China construction bank of Shaanxi branch in 2005-2008, the quantity respectively is 2156, 3589, 7828 and 10021. According to strict screening standard, we had randomly extracted normal sample 150 and default sample 150. The effective sample aggregate capacity is 300.

We put the data sample into training set and test set and each sample contained the attributes matrix and the test matrix. We assume that classifying m points in the n-dimensional real space R^n, represents by the $m \times n$ matrix A. Each line of matrix A represents a sample. Each column of matrix A represents the sample's index attribute, which is the borrower's index in table 1.   Judging matrix D is a column vector in the m-dimensional, which represents whether or not the borrower break a contract. Value -1 represented the borrower defaults, 1 is normal.

300 valid samples are randomly divided into training set 260 and testing set 40. We use the training set obtain the optimal hyperplane and its parameter are w and γ. Put w and γ into the discrimination function, which obtain the test set's judging matrix D'. Careful comparison of D and D', then calculate prediction accuracy of the test set. The flow diagram is in figure 2.

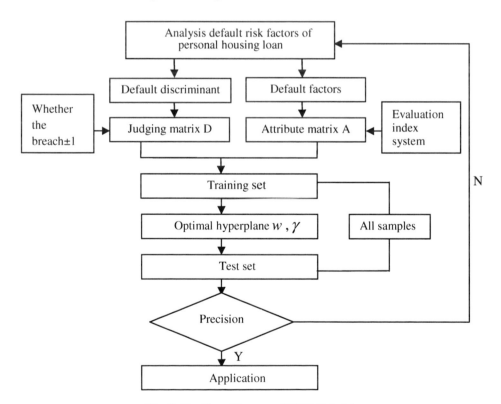

Fig. 2. The Flow Diagram of PSVM Model

All computational results are based on our design procedure of MATLAB code. The optimal hyperplanes values are as shown in Table 2.

Table 2. The Value of Optimal Hyperplanes w

variable code	variable name	The value of Optimal hyperplanes w
X1	Sex	-0.064
X2	Age	-0.016
X3	Educational level	-0.629
X4	census register	0.037
X5	marital status	-0.301
X6	career	0.207
X7	professional title	0.174
X8	Family Monthly Income	0.025
X9	Family debt ratio	0.135
X10	Loan contract amount	-0.305
X11	Loan Period	-0.103
X12	loan to value	0.595
X13	loan interest rate	1.951
X14	Payment method	0.553
X15	floor space	-0.112
X16	Housing price	-0.040
X17	House price index	1.440
	constant γ	0.774

Put w and γ into the discrimination function (see formulation (3)). Then forecasting test set. The discrimination function is as follow:

$$y = \text{sgn}(w \cdot x + \gamma) = \begin{cases} -1, & for \ w \cdot x + \gamma < 0 \\ +1, & for \ w \cdot x + \gamma > 0 \end{cases} \tag{3}$$

Where sgn is symbols function, w is hyperplane's normal vector, γ is offset, x is the borrower's index attribute vector. Compared with predicted value and real value, accuracy is depicted in table 3.

The forecast accuracy is 82.5%, so we think PSVM can accurately predict credit risk assessment of personal housing loan.

5 Discussion

(1)In this paper the first type of error rate (2.5%) is far below the second type of error rate (15%). The reason is that the bank may preliminary screening borrowers, according to their credit risk evaluation system and experience. The bank eliminated obviously default borrowers, the first type of error will not occur or little. So the PSVM model is efficient in reducing the first type of error under unchanged total model accuracy.

(2)The training data is usually noisy, so we cannot guarantee that there exists a target function properly mapping training data. The borrower's solvency may depend on some unknown factor in detecting credit risk of personal housing loan.

(3)Many factors may affect the forecast accuracy, such as system error and artificial operation error, difficult to obtain data of ignore tax and housing transaction cost, etc.

Table 3. The comparison between prediction and the real value

The number	Predictive value	Real value	Judge	The number	Predictive value	Real value	Judge
1	-1	-1	✓	21	-1	-1	✓
2	-1	-1	✓	22	-1	1	×
3	-1	-1	✓	23	1	1	✓
4	-1	-1	✓	24	-1	1	✓
5	1	1	✓	25	-1	-1	✓
6	-1	-1	✓	26	-1	1	×
7	-1	-1	✓	27	1	1	✓
8	-1	1	×	28	-1	-1	✓
9	1	-1	×	29	-1	-1	✓
10	1	1	✓	30	1	1	✓
11	-1	-1	✓	31	1	1	✓
12	-1	-1	✓	32	-1	-1	✓
13	-1	-1	✓	33	1	1	✓
14	-1	1	×	34	-1	-1	✓
15	-1	-1	✓	35	-1	1	×
16	-1	-1	✓	36	1	1	✓
17	-1	-1	✓	37	-1	1	×
18	-1	-1	✓	38	-1	-1	✓
19	-1	-1	✓	39	-1	-1	✓
20	-1	-1	✓	40	1	1	✓
Accuracy					82.5%		

Note: ✓ is predicting correctly, × is prediction error

6 Conclusion

This paper had used PSVM model predict credit risk assessment system of personal housing loan, the conclusions are as follows:

(1)The forecast accuracy is 82.5%, PSVM model can quickly and accurately judge whether or not the borrower break a contract. The 17 indexes comprehensively reflect the borrower's feature information, which offer reference to commercial Banks.

(2)We should pay attention to classification error rates when evaluate prediction accuracy. The serious mistakes were regard as the first type of error in statistics, because the first type of error's probability can be controlled by the size of α value. But the second type of error's probability β can't be controlled. In this paper the first type of error refers to the bank wrongly identify default customer as normal customer. The bank may extend loans to the bad credit customer, which is the loan crisis's root. The second type of error refers to the bank wrongly identify normal customer as default customer. The bank will lose normal customer and loan business will reduce. Obviously, the first type of error loss more severe, the bank should focus on prevention and control in practice.

(3)As a new kind of machine learning method, the approximate support vector machine (PSVM) model base on a speed, accuracy and stability. Especially in resolving low dimensional data classification problem, the training speed is quick and does not affect the classified quality, which effectively improved the classifier performance.

Acknowledgement. Supported by the National Natural Science Foundation (70673054), Headmaster Fund of Xi'an Technological University (XAGDXZJJ0823), and Philosophy Social Science Characteristic Discipline Construction Project of Shaanxi Ordinary University.

References

1. Lambrecht, B., Perraudin, W., Satchell, S.: Time to Default in the UK Mortgage Market. Economic Modelling 10, 485–499 (1997)
2. Morton, T.G.: A Discriminant Function Analysis of Residential Mortgage Delinquency and Foreclosure. Areuea. 3, 73–90 (1975)
3. George, W., Gau, A.: Taxonomic Model for the Risk-Rating of Residential Mortgages. Business 51(4), 687–706 (1978)
4. Kau, K.: An Overview of the Option-Theoretic Pricing of Mortgages. Housing Research 6(2), 217–244 (1995)
5. Quercia, S.: Residential Mortgage Default: A Review of the Literature. Housing Research 3(2), 341–379 (1992)
6. Wang, f., Jia: An Empirical Study of the Factors Influencing Residential Mortgage Defaults: The Case of Hangzhou. China Economic Quarterly 4(3), 739–752 (2005)
7. Wang, x.: Research on Risk Management of Commercial Bank of Family House Mortgage Loan Based on Logistic regression. Finance and Economy 12, 109–110 (2008)
8. Tian, k.: The Risk Management of Our Commercial Bank's Personal Housing Mortgage. Technology Information 27, 418–420 (2008)
9. Fung, G., Mangasarian, O.L.: Proximal Support Vector Machine Classifiers. KDD, San Francisco (2001)
10. Vapnik, V.N.: The Nature of Statistical Learning Theory, 2nd edn. Springer, New York (2000)

Research on Degree of Bubbles and Fundamental Value of Real Estate in China and Hong Kong

ChunQing Xu[*], YiXiang Tian, and YongKai Ma

School of Management, University of Electronic and Science Technology of China,
Chengdu, China
Lihx176@163.com

Abstract. In order to study degree of real estate bubbles of China, we proposed a model of fundamental value of real estate based on partial equilibrium analysis and law of average profit rate. We made up for some imperfections of ZhiGang Yuan's model, and then empirically studied the degree of real estate bubbles of China and Hong Kong. We find that the current degree of real estate bubbles of China is not high compared to that of Hong Kong in the period of its real estate peak time, and is not rapidly expanding. The degree of real estate bubbles is generally low in inland of China, and is relatively high in some coastal areas.

Keywords: real estate price, bubbles, degree of bubbles, fundamental value of real estate.

1 Introduction

Real estate bubbles are price phenomenon led by group speculative activities. Real estate bubbles can lead to that real estate price soars far away from its fundamental value, and then collapses suddenly. The collapses of real estate bubbles can cause serious and long time harm to the macro-economy, so it is important to study detection methods of real estate bubbles and test the degree of real estate bubbles exactly.

Real estate price of China has been growing rapidly since 1998. The average growth rate of housing price was 13.2% from 2004 to 2007. For domestic and international reasons, real estate price of China changed its rising trend and went down in December 2007. After more than a year real estate price of China continued its rising trend in the first half of 2009. The rapid growth of real estate price of China attracts more and more attention of all social sectors. In 1985 banks of Hong Kong began to loan in the way of mortgaging property. This led to the cycle effect of wealth. Real estate price grew rapidly especially since 1990s. The average growth rate of housing price of Hong Kong was 17.2% from 1992 to 1997. There were severe real estate bubbles in the real estate market of Hong Kong. Real estate bubbles collapsed in the impact of Asian financial crisis in 1997. This seriously harmed macro-economy of Hong Kong. How serious are the current real estate bubbles of China? What about real estate bubbles of every province city in China? Are the current real estate bubbles of China serious compared to that of Hong Kong in 1997? These questions need to be answered by theoretical workers.

---

[*] Corresponding author.

Q. Zhou (Ed.): ISAEBD 2011, Part I, CCIS 208, pp. 494–501, 2011.

2   Literature Review

Theoretical workers have put forth many detection methods of real estate bubbles, which fall into three categories: indirect method, indicator method, and direct method.

Indirect method is that real estate bubbles are assessed by the trend of change of some variables and testing hypothesis using proper model[1][2]. We can study real estate bubbles qualitatively by using indirect method, but it is difficult for this method to study degree of real estate bubbles quantitatively.

Indicator method is that rationality of real estate price is tested by ratio of some variables[3][4]. These indicators are ratio of housing price to income, housing vacancy rates, and so on. This method was widely used. But this method is too simple, and national situations in different countries differ, the reliability of this method is not high if it is used alone.

Direct method is a very useful method studying real estate bubbles quantitatively. Real estate price is divided into two parts: fundamental value of real estate (or equilibrium price of real estate), and the discrepancy between fundamental value of real estate and real estate price. Degree of real estate bubbles is defined as the discrepancy divided by fundamental value of real estate. There are different methods calculating fundamental value of real estate. Discounted cash flow analysis is a way calculating fundamental value of real estate[5][6]. But there is considerable subjectivity in selecting expected rate of return. Besides, it is difficult to determine the yield of real estate in future periods. Econometrics is another way calculating fundamental of real estate[7][8]. Fundamental value of real estate can be taken as the function of disposable income, interest rate, rate of employment, production cost, and so on. This method is strongly affected by variables selected in the function. ZhiGang Yuan and others proposed a model of fundamental value of real estate based on partial equilibrium analysis[9]. Their model was used by ChunHai Jiang to study degree of real estate bubbles of China from 1991 to 2003[10]. This is a good way for us to study fundamental value of real estate, but it has some imperfections.

This paper improves ZhiGang Yuan's model of fundamental value of real estate based on partial equilibrium analysis and law of average rate of profit, and makes up for some imperfections of the model, and then empirically studies the degree of real estate bubbles of China and Hong Kong. The seriousness of current real estate bubbles of China is quantitatively studied by comparing degree of real estate bubbles of China and Hong Kong.

3   Degree of Bubbles and Fundamental Value of Real Estate

Without financial intermediary, ZhiGang Yuan and others took real estate price based on partial equilibrium analysis as fundamental value of real estate[9]. But in their theory profit rate of each period is not average social profit rate, and they neglect the difference between average social profit rate and bank rate. ZhiGang Yuan and others took a quadratic function of area of housing built as cost function. Although this practice embodies the concept of increase in marginal cost, their cost function is simple, and it is difficult to estimate the parameter of this cost function. Because this parameter is affected by all kind of factors, and changes with time, it is difficult to use econometrics method to estimate this parameter. ChunHai Jiang replaced this parameter with unit cost of buildings completed when he empirically studied fundamental value of real estate of China[10], but this practice lacks of support of economic significance. Based on above reasons, we improve ZhiGang Yuan's model as follow.

Because there is no financial intermediary, housing buyers only depend on their disposable income, YD, to buy housing, and real estate developers develop housing by their own funds. P is real estate price, and H is area of housing bought by consumer. First, we suppose that general goods, G, and housing with total value, PH, can all confer utility, and the utility function is logarithm, addition separability. Secondly, we suppose that the discount rate of utility of each period is 1, so total expected utility is simply the sum of utility of each period. Housing buyers bound by their disposable income select suitable area of housing to maximize expected utility:

$$\underset{H_{t+i}}{Max} E_t U^s = \sum_{i=0}^{\infty} [\ln G_{t+i} + \ln(E_t P_{t+i} \cdot H_{t+i})] \qquad (1)$$

$$\text{s.t.} : G_{t+i} + E_t P_{t+i} \cdot H_{t+i} = YD_{t+i} \qquad (2)$$

The first order of programming condition of above optimum programming is:

$$(E_t P_{t+i} \cdot H_{t+i})^s = \frac{YD}{2} \qquad (3)$$

Because real estate developers only depend on their own funds, B , their profit of each period equals income of selling houses minus cost of building houses, and minus opportunity cost of their own funds. First, we suppose that opportunity cost of real estate developers is bank rate, r_1 , times B. Secondly we suppose that the discount rate of profit of each period is 1, so total expected profit is simply the sum of profit of each period. Ordinary cost function (CES, Douglas function) is assumed to have strict homogeneity and additivity, therefore the assumption that elasticity of substitution keeps constant comes into existence. But this only applies to the production that has one input in feedstock and one output in production. The assumption that elasticity of substitution keeps constant does not hold up for the production that has multiple inputs in feedstock and multiple outputs in production. This was proved by Uzawa and McFadden as early as in 1963. Christensen and Jorgenson put forward cost function of transcendental logarithm[11]. Because this cost function does not have the property that elasticity of substitution keeps constant, it was widely used. The production developing housing can be taken as the one that has multiple inputs in feedstock and one output in production, so this paper supposes that the assumption that elasticity of substitution keeps constant does not hold up, and we select cost function of real estate developers as follow:

$$TC = cH \ln H + kH \qquad (4)$$

In above equation, TC is total cost, c and k are parameters. Real estate developers select suitable area of housing built to maximize their expected profit:

$$\underset{H_{t+i}}{Max} E_t \prod^s = \sum_{i=0}^{\infty} (E_t P_{t+i} \cdot H_{t+i} - cH_{t+i} \ln H_{t+i} - kH_{t+i} - r_1 B) \qquad (5)$$

$$\text{s.t. :} \ cH_{t+i}\ln H_{t+i} + kH_{t+i} = B \tag{6}$$

The first order of programming condition of above optimum programming is:

$$(E_t P_{t+i})^s = (c\ln H_{t+i} + c + k)(1+r_1) \tag{7}$$

Equilibrium price of real estate, P^*, derived from equation (3) and equation (7) is:

$$
\begin{aligned}
P^* &= (E_t P_{t+i})^s \\
&= (c\ln \frac{YD}{2P^*} + c + k)(1+r_1)
\end{aligned}
\tag{8}
$$

In this case, the marginal utility of general goods and housing are equal for housing buyers. Because of profiteering, capital will transfer from trades of low profit rate to trades of high profit rate, consequently, the profit rate of different trades tends to equal. This objective necessity is the law of average profit rate. This law is a useful tool for us to study fundamental value of real estate. We can suppose that profit rate of real estate developers is average social profit rate to get a theoretical reference for real estate price.

$$P^*_{t+i} H_{t+i} - B = Br_2 \tag{9}$$

In equation (9), r_2 is average social profit rate. According to equation (3), (6), (7), and (9), equation (8) can be expressed as:

$$P^* = \frac{(1+r_2)k}{1+r_1-(r_2-r_1)\ln\dfrac{YD}{2P^*}}(1+r_1) \tag{10}$$

Equation (10) is the function of fundamental value of real estate. Using the computer, we can calculate fundamental value of real estate according to this equation. Compared with ZhiGang Yuan's model of fundamental value of real estate, this model has some important advantages. Not only marginal utility of general goods equals to marginal utility of real estate for housing buyers, but also profit rate of real estate developers for each period is average social profit rate. Bank rate and average social profit rate are not taken as the same. The estimation of the parameter, k, in this cost function has the support of economic significance. According to equation (4), the average cost of real estate developers is $c\ln H + k$, and the parameter, k, is the part that does not vary with the change of H. Because labor cost and material cost needed to build unit area of housing are relatively fixed, unit cost of buildings completed has the character of parameter, k. So we use unit cost of buildings completed as the estimated value of the parameter, k. The data of unit cost of buildings completed can be found in Chinese Statistics Yearbook.

P is real estate price, and the degree of real estate bubbles, θ, is defined as:

$$\theta = \frac{P-P^*}{P^*} \cdot 100\% \tag{11}$$

High degree of real estate bubbles implies low stability of real estate market system. How low should degree of real estate bubbles be when the real estate market system keeps stability? There is not a clear line, because the computational methods of degree of real estate bubbles are different. As for the method computing degree of real estate bubbles in this paper, we can compare the data of the areas that real estate bubbles had been collapsed for us to study the seriousness of current real estate bubbles of China.

4   Empirical Research on Degree of Real Estate Bubbles

Referring to ChunHai Jiang's method, we replace r_1 in equation (10) by one-year deposit rate of commercial bank. Because the left of equation (2) represents total expenses that housing buyers buy housing and general goods, we replace the variable, YD, in equation (10) by per capita consumption expenditures of urban households. We use unit cost of buildings completed as estimated value of the parameter, k.

ZhiHong Tang proposed a model of average social profit rate based on classical growth function[12]. But according to this model, it will bring great deviation to estimate the share of capital in total output. We estimate average social profit rate base on its common definition. Namely, average social profit rate is total social profit divided by aggregate social capital. We replace total social profit by total social operating surplus. Perpetual inventory method was mostly used to estimate Chinese aggregate social capital. HaoJie Shan used this method to calculate Chinese aggregate social capital from 1952 to 2006 after collecting a lot of related references [13]. We use HaoJie Shan's research results and calculate Chinese aggregate social capital in 2007 and 2008.

Table 1. Degree of real estate bubbles of China from 1994 to 2008 (the unit of P, k and P^* is Yuan per square meter, and the currency is RMB)

Year	P	k	YD (Yuan)	r_2 (%)	r_1 (%)	P^*	θ (%)
1994	1408	797	3496	13.07	10.98	913.8	54.08
1995	1591	911	4283	12.90	10.98	1043.8	52.42
1996	1806	1111	4839	12.83	9.2	1285.1	40.53
1997	1997	1175	5160	12.14	7.2	1364.2	46.39
1998	2063	1218	5425	10.89	5.0	1409.0	46.42
1999	2053	1152	5854	10.46	3.0	1354.5	51.57
2000	2112	1139	6280	10.41	1.8	1361.1	55.17
2001	2170	1128	6860	10.15	1.8	1347.3	61.06
2002	2250	1184	7703	10.37	1.6	1421.4	58.29
2003	2359	1273	8472	10.73	1.58	1537.5	53.43
2004	2778	1402	9422	13.41	1.61	1770.8	56.88
2005	3168	1451	10493	16.40	1.8	1930.9	64.07
2006	3367	1564	11760	17.14	1.9	2113.4	59.32
2007	3864	1657	13786	17.95	2.8	2270.9	70.15
2008	3800	1795	15781	16.89	3.9	2405.9	57.95

Chinese data we used was derived from Chinese Statistics Yearbook published by National Bureau of Statistics from 1995 to 2008, and data of Hong Kong was derived from Hong Kong Statistics Yearbook. We can not find data similar to total social operating surplus in Hong Kong Statistics Yearbook, so we can not calculate average social profit rate of Hong Kong as we calculate average social profit rate of China. Because of profiteering, capital is not only transferable among different trades but also transferable among different areas. Hong Kong is connected with Chinese mainland, and has close economic trade contact with Chinese mainland, so we replace average social profit rate of Hong Kong by average social profit rate of China to calculate degree of real estate bubbles, θ, of Hong Kong.

Calculations and data we used are in table 1 and table 2. Data of per capita consumption expenditures of urban households are calculated by dividing consumption expenditures of urban households by urban population. Real estate price of Hong Kong is weighted average real estate price, and the weighted factor is trading volume. According to equation (10), the larger average social profit rate is, the smaller degree of real estate bubble is. Because we replace average social profit rate of Hong Kong by average social profit rate of China, in order to try to avoid the problem that the calculation of θ become larger than its real value, we also use the largest value of average social profit rate of China from 1994 to 2008 to calculate degree of real estate bubbles, θ_1, of Hong Kong, which is listed in table 2.

Table 2. Degree of real estate bubbles of Hong Kong from 1994 to 2008 (the unit of P, k and P^* are Yuan per square meter, and the currency is Hong Kong dollar)

Year	p	k	YD (Yuan)	r_2 (%)	r_1 (%)	P^*	θ (%)	θ_1 (%)
1994	48435	10111	112610	13.07	3.92	13115	269.31	232.07
1995	44746	12454	122239	12.90	5.61	15529	188.14	159.56
1996	45968	14561	128609	12.83	5.1	18117	153.73	129.48
1997	61878	15148	137772	12.14	6.03	18387	236.53	199.45
1998	43634	17960	127048	10.89	5.59	21083	106.96	82.43
1999	36500	22062	122385	10.46	4.81	25573	42.73	26.98
2000	32873	20926	123151	10.41	5.54	24125	36.26	20.55
2001	28987	19788	123622	10.15	3.58	22779	27.25	11.61
2002	25888	22175	119662	10.37	1.61	26337	-1.71	-12.27
2003	23214	19944	115273	10.73	0.82	24149	-3.87	-14.03
2004	30853	20348	123585	13.41	0.15	26056	18.41	10.42
2005	37230	21155	129972	16.40	2.42	27846	33.70	30.57
2006	38873	18386	139318	17.14	3.72	24852	56.42	54.25
2007	42194	21159	155053	17.95	3.65	28892	46.04	46.04
2008	49489	21331	160986	16.89	0.23	29856	65.76	62.83

In table 1, the lowest θ of China was 40.53% in 1996, and the highest θ of China was 70.15% in 2007. Comparing the θ of China in 2007 and 2004, we find that its growth rate was not high in spite of real estate price of China growing fast since 2004.

In table 2, degree of real estate bubbles, θ, of Hong Kong reached 269.31% (θ_1 was 232.07%) in 1994. Although degree of real estate bubbles of Hong Kong was very high at that time, real estate bubbles did not collapse because there were no strong outside factors like the Asian Financial Crises. But when θ of Hong Kong got up to 236.53% (θ_1 was 199.45%) in 1997, the Asian Financial Crises happened. This led to the collapse of real estate bubbles of Hong Kong. From 1997 to 2003, real estate price of Hong Kong sharply declined.

Based on the above analysis, we find that the current degree of real estate bubbles of China is not serious compared to that of Hong Kong in the period of its real estate peak time, and is not rapidly expanding. If there are no especially strong outside factors, the case like real estate market of Hong Kong in 1997 will be hard to happen. How about degree of real estate bubbles of China by regions? Using the same method, we study degree of real estate bubbles of some provinces and cities in 2007 when degree of real estate bubbles of China were the highest, which are in table 3.

In table 3, the degree of real estate bubbles in inland of China is generally low, for example, degree of real estate bubbles of Jiangxi province, Hebei province, Xi'an city, Wuhan city, and Harbin city, are much lower than the general level of China. But degree of real estate bubbles of some coastal areas is relatively high, for example, Zhejiang province, Fujian province, Shanghai city, and Ningbo city. What needs to be stressed is that degree of real estate bubbles of Xiamen city was even high up to 348.37%. So degree of real estate bubble of some coastal areas needs to get enough attention in order to avoid the case that happened in Hainan province and Beihai city in the early 1990s.

Table 3. Degree of real estate bubbles of some provinces and cities in 2007 (the unit of p, k and P^* are Yuan per square meter, and the currency is RMB)

Province and City	P	k	r_1 (%)	r_2 (%)	YD (Yuan)	P^*	θ (%)
Zhejiang	5786	2010	2.8	17.95	14091	2752	110.24
Fujian	4682	1379	2.8	17.95	13006	1973	137.30
Shandong	2904	1468	2.8	17.95	12633	2071	40.22
Jiangxi	2072	1006	2.8	17.95	9200	1432	44.69
Hebei	2586	1647	2.8	17.95	9941	2206	17.22
Sichuan	2841	1041	2.8	17.95	12720	1550	83.29
Qingdao	5202	2096	2.8	17.95	13376	2831	83.75
Shanghai	8360	3096	2.8	17.95	23623	4292	94.78
Xiamen	8250	1217	2.8	17.95	16380	1840	348.37
Ningbo	6252	2070	2.8	17.95	17018	2850	119.37
Jinan	3775	2014	2.8	17.95	12390	2706	39.50
Xi'an	3381	2091	2.8	17.95	13541	2830	19.47
Wuhan	4670	2658	2.8	17.95	17290	3600	29.72
Harbin	3057	1547	2.8	17.95	11006	2122	44.06

5 Conclusions

This paper gives out a new theoretical reference for real estate price. Using our theory to study degree of real estate bubbles of China and Hong Kong, we find that although real estate price of China has been growing fast since 2004, the degree of real estate bubbles of China is not high compared to that of Hong Kong in the period of its real estate peak time, and is not rapidly expanding. The degree of real estate bubbles is generally low in inland of China, and is relatively high in some coastal areas, especially Xiamen city. Since the early 1990s, the ability of Chinese government in controlling real estate market has been improving constantly. The income level of Chinese people grows fast, and the demand for housing also grows fast. Real estate market of China is laggard, but developing fast at the current time. Because of these reasons, although real estate price of China has been growing fast since 2004, the degree of real estate bubbles of China is not serious, and will not bring serious harm to the healthy development of real estate market of China at the current time. It can be predicted that the case like Hong Kong real estate market in 1997 will be hard to happen, if there are no especially strong outside factors.

Acknowledgement. Funds project is the national natural science funds(70672104).

References

1. Shiller, R.J.: Do Stock Prices Move too much to be Justified by Subsequent Changes in ividends? American Economic Review 71, 421–436 (1981)
2. Kenneth, D.W.: A Specification test for Speculative Bubbles. National Bureau of Economic Research Working Paper 11, 1–44 (1986)
3. Zhang, C., Luo, S., Yu, X.: Review on Testing Method of Real Estate Bubbles. Real Estate of China 8, 22–24 (2005)
4. Li, P.: Research on Degree of real estate bubbles of China. Statistic and Decision 24, 82–85 (2007)
5. Holt, C., Monnin, P.: Fundamental Real Estate Price: A Empirical Estimation with International Data. Journal of Real Estate Finance and Economics 36, 427–450 (2008)
6. Fraser, P., Hoesli, M.: Housing Price and Bubbles in New Zealand. Journal of Real Estate Finance and Economics 37, 71–91 (2008)
7. Eddie, C.M., Hui, S.Y.: Housing Price Bubbles in Hong Kong, Beijing and Shanghai: A Comparative Study. Journal of Real Estate Finance and Economics 33, 299–327 (2006)
8. Case, k.E., Shiller, R.J.: Forecasting prices and excess returns in housing market. AREUEA Journal 18, 253–273 (1990)
9. Yuan, Z., Fan, X.: Analysis on rational bubbles of real estate. Economic Research 3, 35–42 (2003)
10. Jiang, C.: A Case Study of Speculation Bubble on China's Real Estate Market. Management World 12, 71–84 (2005)
11. Christensen, L.R., Jorgenson, D.W.: Transcendental Logarithmic Production Frontiers. Review of Economics Statistics 55, 188–197 (1973)
12. Tang, Z.: Estimation of average profit rate of China. Economic Research 5, 61–65 (1999)
13. Shan, H.: Another Estimation of aggregate social capital, K, of China: 1952-2006. Quantitative & Technical economics Research 10, 17–32 (2008)

Research on Chinese Capital Account Liberalization under Soft Constraints

Heng Sun

School of Business, Shandong University at Weihai, Weihai, 264209, China
sunheng2007@gmail.com

Abstract. This paper will discuss some unfavorable restraint factors influencing Chinese capital account liberalization progress. It will employ theoretical and empirical method to analyze the restraints of foreign reserve increase, foreign exchange administrative regime, imperfect industrial structure and changeable monetary policy to this liberalization with data (1993-2010) and chart. Then, it suggests some basic principles of progressive liberalization, flexible deregulation and differential administration At last, suggestive proposals of controlling foreign reserve quantity, establishing a flexible and effective exchange rate regime, accelerating the reform of industrial structure and setting up an emergent adjustment mechanism will be given. The innovative part of this paper is the establishment of emergent foreign reserve pool.

Keywords: Capital Account Liberalization, Soft Constraints, Emergent Foreign Reserve Pool.

1 Introduction

With the development of international financial integration since the 1980s, many developing countries made a significant progress in capital account liberalization. However, many countries have been faced with some financial problems due to economic development level and stage, economic structure and development model, financial market maturity and government economic control ability in different nations in the process of capital account liberalization. The common realization can be agreed upon right now: capital account liberalization should undergo a gradual, orderly and reiterative process; every nation should liberalize its capital account carefully and progressively based on its domestic macroeconomic situation.

2 Analysis on Macroeconomic Soft Constraints to Capital Account Liberalization

In the process of capital account liberalization after current account liberalization at the end of 1996 in China, international capital inflow increased greatly and quickly. On one hand this can complement the domestic need for capital in the period of fast development; on the other hand, it brought some noticeable problems, like fast

Q. Zhou (Ed.): ISAEBD 2011, Part I, CCIS 208, pp. 502–508, 2011.
© Springer-Verlag Berlin Heidelberg 2011

increase of foreign reserve, RMB appreciation, asynchronous development between industrial structure and economic development, monetary policy independency of central bank, etc. These factors (here is called soft constraints because they can be eliminated by institutional innovation and effective management) actually hinder the further development of Chinese economy.

2.1 Fast Increase of Foreign Reserve Leading to Imbalance of International BP (Balance of Payment)

Chinese foreign reserve was $1.296 billion negative which means China owed a foreign debt. However, Chinese foreign reserve increased to $11.093 billion ten years later in 1990, 124 times as much as ten years before; while foreign reserve continued increasing to $165.574 billion in the end of 2000, 15 times as much as in 1990; this figure goes on increasing to $2.8473 trillion in 2010, which doubled the figure of 2000. The whole process of foreign reserve increase trend from 1993 to 2010 can be obtained in Fig. 1 below.

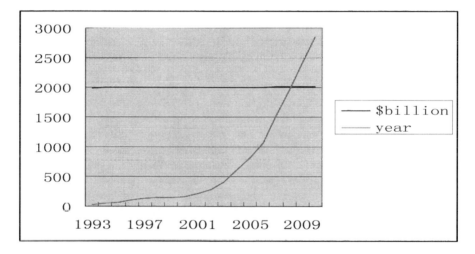

Fig. 1. Foreign Reserve Increase Trend in China from 1993 to 2010. X-axis stands for the years from 1993 to 2010, while Y-axis for Foreign reserve in billion US dollars.

In fact, Chinese foreign reserve exceeded Japan and became No. 1 foreign reserve country in 2006. The dramatic increase of foreign reserve mainly results from two reasons: one is that government encourages foreign trade businesses to earn foreign currencies to a large extent by policy incentives; the other is that the nation strengthens the introduction of FDI (foreign direct investment) and QFII (qualified foreign institutional investor) which lead to a great amount of foreign capital inflow through current account and capital & financial account. However, with the fast increase of foreign reserve and foreign currency supply exceeding demand, RMB continues to be stable with no appreciation which, therefore, reinforces RMB appreciation expectation continuously since 2003; the foreign capital inflow in this year amounted to $403.251 billion, $116.844 billion more than previous year which exceeds the total amount of foreign reserve in 1996 (current account liberalization this year). Therefore, the foreign reserve stock can only be adjusted through encouraging capital outflow and administrating these two accounts. That is to say the fast increase of foreign reserve has brought heavy burden to capital account management. I will probably result in financial system issues if this problem is not solved as soon as possible.

2.2 Foreign Exchange Control System Resulting in Burden of Capital Account Management

There still exists "Money Exchange" system in foreign exchange regulations in China right now. The SAFE only exams and administrates the capital inflow in exchange settlement based on the ostensible authenticity. But this administrative system can not prevent abnormal inflow of international hot money completely in reality because it has two weak points. For example, the authenticity of hot money inflow can not be verified clearly since the reporting mechanism and verifying mechanism are done separately by different sectors in exchange settlement. This administrative mode can lead to illegal and constant inflow of foreign exchange either through current account or through capital account, which makes it harder to effectively control the foreign exchange amount particularly when the RMB appreciation pressure and constant current account surplus are not eliminated. If the capital outflow control in capital account is deregulated in the near future, the quantitative control of foreign exchange will be more difficult to deal with.

Moreover, foreign reserve administration is also faced with some problems. Under the circumstances of holding great amount of foreign reserve and constant RMB appreciation, the total value of foreign reserve will dramatically decrease if the value of reserve currency or the reserve currency value against domestic currency value changes. The greater the reserve currency exchange rate fluctuates, the bigger change the total value of foreign reserve is faced with. It has been difficult for China to find a diversified solution to foreign reserve administration. USD which fluctuates greatly in international financial crisis accounts for a large proportion in foreign reserve. In addition, liquidity management of foreign reserve is restricted by overseas investment, which increases foreign reserve management costs and decreases the liquidity of foreign reserve in terms of the high overseas investment risk.

2.3 Unreasonable Industrial Structure Causing the Change of Capital Flow Direction

The unreasonable industrial structure has been an essential problem to hinder Chinese economic development. China has been implementing the development mode of intensive labor-oriented industry for a long time; therefore, the export is also based on the production of labor-intensive industry. Undoubtedly, this development mode increases employment rate, but it has unfavorable impacts on the development of national economy and foreign trade in the long run. Chinese labor cost keeps increasing with profit margin narrowing for exported products which affects the export scale and volume recently. This means that the price of export goods dominated in foreign currency will increase greatly in the process of RMB constant appreciation. Furthermore, the insufficient demand resulted from international financial crisis in both of domestic market and foreign market directly heats Chinese foreign trade. So the current account surplus will probably turn to decrease or to be negative if the industrial structure is not readjusted. If this happens, the deficit of current account should be balanced through capital account financing. Therefore, capital account management will undertake more managing task.

2.4 The Unstable Monetary Policy Leading to the Difficult Management of Capital Account

The unstable monetary policy may result in the change of investment expectations and international capital flow changes. People's bank of China escalated reserve ratio for five times to high breaking record of 17.5% in the second half of 2008 in order to restrain the inflation expectations. Later, central bank employed expansionary monetary policy positively to deal with global financial crisis, tuning down financial institution reserve ratio on September 25, October 15, December 5 and December 25 respectively. Large deposit banks' reserve ration tuned down 2% while the small-medium-sized banks tuned down 4 percent of the reserve ratio. The frequent unprecedented adjustment of reserve ration fostered the inflation to a great extent. In return, the central bank escalated 3% of depositary financial institutions' deposit reserve ratio on January 18, February 25, May 10, November 16, November 29 and December 20 respectively in 2010 to control overheated economy and mounting inflation. As we know, the great frequent interest rate changes may directly lead to large quantity of international capital inflow and outflow which bring great trouble to the capital account administration.

3   The Principles for Liberalizing Capital Account in New Situation

Financial market must be integrated with international market if a country wants to make more profits from it, while the capital account liberalization can meet this requirement. To avoid the negative effect from the capital account liberalization, reasonable and effective management method should be employed on basis of a effective and scientific principle during the liberalization.

3.1   Progressive Liberalization

The capital account liberalization is closely correlated with financial market safety of a country. China is still an underdeveloped country, so the capital account should be liberalized step by step. And this has been agreed upon by domestic and overseas scholars. However, there is still a debate on the liberalization sequencing. In my opinion, the liberalization of capital account should be based on stable situation of macro economy, financial market and interest rate.

3.2 Flexible Control

The economic development can be influenced by some unfavorable factors inside or outside the country, for instance, global or regional financial crises, unsteady development of trade partner countries, so it is necessary to employ regulating way or deregulating way in the progress of capital account liberalization accordingly to stabilize the domestic financial market.

3.3 Differential Administration

The implementation of capital account liberalization should depend upon domestic economic situation. Differential controlling way of capital account liberalization will be adopted in different circumstances, like development of macro economy, development of state-owned economy and private economy, individual income and credit status, and so on. For example, when the current account and capital account have large quantity of surplus, the corporate sectors' overseas investment should be enforced, more foreign high quality goods should be imported and considerable restrictions on individual overseas investment should be lifted. Otherwise, some restraints should be brought into effects.

4 Various Adoptive Ways for Facilitating Capital Account Liberalization

The complete capital account liberalization can not be done in a short period of time. Some restraints will influence the liberalization progress. However, some essential methods and strategies can be employed to decrease economic upheaval caused by the capital account liberalization in a large part and to make the liberalization go smoothly.

4.1 Strengthening the Administration of Foreign Reserve

A. Controlling the foreign reserve quantity. There have been both continuous surpluses in current account and capital account since 1999 in China, which leads to foreign reserve increase. Therefore, many kinds of measures must be taken to channel the capital outflow, for example, increasing overseas investment, strengthening government procurement, implementing overseas merging and acquisition, participating in the international cooperation, purchasing overseas intellectual property rights, softening the restrictive terms for individual overseas investment, etc. Foreign reserve pressure as well as inflation pressure can be released through these methods.

B. Enforcing the diversification of reserve currency. The depreciation risk of reserve currency caused by using single reserve currency can be avoided in doing so. Chinese foreign reserve mostly focuses on US dollar assets; as a result, foreign reserve value will be diminished once facing US dollar depreciation. And this is necessarily the case when RMB has been appreciating against US dollar since July of 2005. Managing foreign reserve in the way of investment portfolio not only can lower the risk resulted from US dollar depreciation, but may decrease the unfavorable impact on Chinese monetary policy if US monetary policy changes.

C. Seizing the opportunity to do away with Money Exchange mechanism. Money Exchange mechanism is a compulsive managing method when China was lack of foreign reserve. But China is accelerating the capital account liberalization and the disadvantages of this method have been revealed because it is hard for enterprises to dispatch foreign funds, furthermore, it brings the unnecessary administration task and cost to the foreign exchange administration. It is the best way to abolish Money Exchange mechanism as soon as possible and to make the foreign exchange administration concentrate on the capital flow supervision and regulation.

4.2 Controlling the Quantity and Direction of Foreign Capital Flow Effectively

The foreign capital here means the subjective capital. This kind of foreign capital inflow and outflow not only have strong impact on the quantity of foreign reserve, but also give a heavy blow to virtual economy, including to the capital market and real estate market etc. This blow may lead to a national bubble economy. Controlling the subjective capital flow should do as follows: first, controlling its overflow to the stock market; second, preventing it from flowing into capital market through foreign trade indirectly.

4.3 Establishing a Flexible and Effective Administrative Mode

The RMB floating mode should be reinforced with flexible management. The key to foreign exchange administration should be: first, a necessary measurement should be taken to sustain the stability of exchange rate when the exchange rate is attacked by abnormal factors and fluctuates dramatically; second, adequate adjustment of currency basket should be made to change the currencies weight when foreign economic communication suddenly changes or a certain pegged currency meets with serious crisis. These can make RMB exchange rate regime more flexible.

4.4 Accelerating Chinese Industrial Structure

Optimizing industrial structure should do as follows. First, it is essential to decrease the absolute proportion of primary industry and increasing the proportion of secondary industry and service industry gradually. Second, it is inevitable to change labor-intensive development mode into capital-intensive and technology-intensive development mode. Third, it is necessary to cultivate and store more versatile and innovative talents with strong ability to apply theoretical and practical knowledge, to communicate in dealing with foreign business affairs and to cooperate with teams.

4.5 Setting Up an Emergent Adjustment Mechanism

Setting up an emergent foreign exchange reserve pool and singling out a sum of foreign reserve as reserve fund for emergent use which can be employed to intervene foreign exchange market and to stabilize RMB value and financial market. The sum of foreign reserve can be deposited to several big commercial banks by means of current deposit so as to maintain its value and withdraw when needed.

References

1. Zhang, Q.: Study on International Capital Flow and Foex Control Policy in China. Zhejiang Finance 8, 5–7 (2008)
2. Zhang, Z.: Capital Account of Opening China—Development of Sequencing Theory and Its Enlightenment for China. International Economic Review 2(1), 5–15 (2003)
3. SAFE, http://www.safe.gov.cn

Influence of Economic Growth, Population and Wages on Employment of China's Three Industries

Yucheng Liu and Guangrong Tong

Economics and Management School, Wuhan University, Wuchang,
430072 Wuhan, P.R. China
yuchengliu@whu.edu.cn

Abstract. This paper explored the relationship between economic growth, population, wages and employment using the economic data of China's three industries (1978--2009). The paper analyzed the long-term equilibrium relation of the employment in the three industries through cointegration test and Granger causality test and explored the impulse responses of the employment to the structural shocks by using the SVAR (Structural Vector Autoregression) model. The results show that there exists a long-term equilibrium between employment, economic growth, population and wages and the employment in the three industries all show various degrees of responses to the structural impulses. The rise of the wages will cause negative effects to the employment and the employment elasticity in the three industries are totally different.

Keywords: employment in the three industries, per capita GDP, economically active population, wages of the employed workers, SVAR model.

1 Introduction

In recent years, there have been a number of studies that are concerned with the employment of China's three industries, which can be divided into two classes. The first class of studies mainly focus on the totality of the three industries. For instances, Guomei Yu [1] found that there existed a correlationship between GDP and employment and the employment in primary industry negatively correlated with GDP. Aijun Fan, et al. [2] showed that the export trade promoted the growth of employment of secondary and tertiary industry. Tao Qin [3] thought that China's unemployment was mainly structural unemployment and the employment elasticity of secondary industry was the biggest. Hong Xia [4] argued that the urbanization level negatively (positively) correlated to the employment level of primary (secondary or tertiary) industry. The second class of studies mainly focus on a certain industry. For examples, Mingxia YE, et al. [5] found that tertiary industry had the strongest level of absorbing labor force. Jian Jin, et al. [6] showed that the employment in primary industry occupied a large portion in employment structure, but its GDP employment elasticity declined year by year. Haiying MA, et al. [7] studied the effect of absorbing labor force in tertiary industry and found that the employment growth elasticity of tertiary industry was relatively high.

Q. Zhou (Ed.): ISAEBD 2011, Part I, CCIS 208, pp. 509–515, 2011.
© Springer-Verlag Berlin Heidelberg 2011

However, the above studies don't consider the effects to the employment caused by external impacts. In fact, in economic practice the external impacts difinitely affect the employment. Based on the economic data of China's three industries (1978--2009) and the SVAR model, this paper will explore the relation between economic growth, population, wages and employment in the three industries and the impulse response of employment to the structural shocks.

The paper includes 5 parts: Part 2 introduces the variables and the sources of data; Part 3 describes the SVAR model; Part 4 is the empirical analysis and test. Part 5 gives the conclusions.

2 Variables and Data Resources

From the economic variables that influence the employment, we select the alternative variables as follows

Ni: The employment quantity of the i-th industry (i=1, 2, 3).
PGDP: The per capita GDP based on the price of 1978.
EP: The economically active population.
Wi: The total wages of the employed workers in the i-th industriy (i=1, 2, 3) based on the price of 1978.
LNNi, LNPGDP, LNEP and LNWi: The logarithms of Ni, PGDP, EP and Wi.
DLNNi, DLNPGDP, DLNEP and DLNWi: The one-order differences of LNNi, LNPGDP, LNEP and LNWi.

PGDP, EP and Wi represent the economic growth, the change of the population and the change of the wages respectively in our study. The data of the variables come from China Statistical Yearbook (1978--2009), the Statistics Bulletin of the National Economic and Social Development of China (1978--2009) and China Economic Information Network.

To eliminate the heteroscedasticity of the sequences, we perform logarithmic trasformation for the variables Ni, PGDP, EP and Wi. To test the stationarity and causality of the variables LNNi, LNPGDP, LNEP and LNWi, we perform ADF Test(Augmented Dickey-Fuller Test) and the Pairwise Granger Causality Test for them. The results of ADF test show that LNNi, LNPGDP, LNEP and LNWi are not stationary while their one-order differences are all stationary. The Pairwise Granger Causality Test shows that there exists causality between them. Therefore,we select DLNNi, DLNPGDP, DLNEP and DLNWi (i=1, 2, 3) as our research variables.

3 Introduction of Model

The SVAR model, which is originally established by Sims [11], is the developmental result of the VAR (Vector Autoregression) model and resolves the identificational restriction of traditional dynamic simultaneous equations through the analysis of impulse response. The VAR model is superior in handling the analysis and prediction of multiple related economic indexes, but it has a fatal defect, i.e., it can't give a definite form of the current relationship between variables. The SVAR model introduces the current relationship between variables into the model, so it resolves the defect of the VAR model. In general, the SVAR(p) model can be expressed as

$$C_0 Y_t = \Gamma_1 Y_{t-1} + \Gamma_2 Y_{t-2} + \cdots + \Gamma_p Y_{t-p} + \mu_t = \sum_{i=1}^{p} \Gamma_i Y_{t-i} + \mu_t . \tag{1}$$

The VAR（p）model constituted by Y_t and its lagging vectors is expressed as

$$Y_t = \sum_{i=1}^{p} \Phi_i Y_{t-i} + \varepsilon_t . \tag{2}$$

Here, t=1,2,···,M, M denotes the sample size, C_0 and Γ_i (i=1, 2, ..., p) are the vectors of coefficients of equation (1), μ_t is the vector of structural shocks, ε_t is the vector of the disturbances of the VAR model. By mathematical transformations, we get

$$A(L)\varepsilon_t = B(L)\mu_t . \tag{3}$$

Here, A(L) and B(L) are the vectors of the lagging operators. Through equation (3), we construct the relationship between the disturbance terms of the VAR model and the potential structural shocks of the SVAR model.

According to the selection of variables in Part 2, the endogenous vectors of our SVAR models are

$$Y_{it} = (DLNNi, DLNPGDP, DLNEP, DLNWi)^T . \tag{4}$$

Here, i=1, 2, 3, T denotes the transposition of the vector. Based on the combined selection of various criterions such as LR（Sequential Modified Likelihood-ratio Test Statistic）, FPE（Final Prediction Error）, SC（Schwarz Information Criterion）, AIC（Akaike Information Criterion）, HQ（Hannan-Quinn Information Criterion）, etc. and considered the effectiveness of the parametres of the model and the sample size of the variables, we determine that the optimal lagging numbers of the three SVAR models are 5, 4 and 4 respectively. In practical estimation, we suppose that the expression form of the estimated equation is

$$A\hat{e}_t = B\mu_t, t=1,2,\cdots,M . \tag{5}$$

Here, M=30, A and B are the restraint matrices, e_t is a vector of the disturbance terms of the VAR model. μ_t is a vector of the structural shocks of the SVAR model and complies with Gauss Normal Distribution $VMN(0_4, I_4)$.

4 Empirical Analysis and Test

We will explore the long-term equilibrium relationship between economic growth, population, wages and employment by using the cointegration test and causality test. Meanwhile, we will study the impulse responses of the employment to the structural shocks through the SVAR model.

4.1 Johansen Cointegration Test and Granger Causality Test

As LNN_i, LNPGDP, LNEP and LNW_i (i=1, 2, 3) are not stationary and their one-order differences are all stationary, we assume that there are cointegration effects between them. Johansen Cointegration Test (1991) and EG Test (Engle-Granger Two-stage Test, 1987) show that the following cointegration equations are feasible (standard error in parentheses)

$$LNN1= -1.99*LNPGDP+0.81*LNEP-0.09*LNW1-0.15*TIME . \tag{6}$$
$$(0.11) \qquad\quad (0.05) \qquad (0.04) \qquad (0.01)$$

$$LNN2=10.84*LNPGDP+7.19*LNEP-0.94*LNW2-0.99*TIME . \tag{7}$$
$$(1.29) \qquad\quad (0.64) \qquad (0.31) \qquad (0.11)$$

$$LNN3=5.20*LNPGDP-0.95*LNEP-3.48*LNW3-0.04*TIME . \tag{8}$$
$$(0.40) \qquad\quad (0.31) \qquad (0.35) \qquad (0.04)$$

Equations (6)~(8) show that, in the long run, LNN1 negatively correlates with LNPGDP while LNN2 or LNN3 positively correlates with LNPGDP, which is in accordance with Guomei Yu [1]. This shows that, with the growth of economy and when PGDP reaches a certain stage, the labor force will gradually transfer to secondary and tertiary industries and N1 will gradually reduce. The PGDP employment elasticities of the three industries are -1.99, 10.84 and 5.20 respectively, which is in accordance with Tao Qin [3]. As LNN1 and LNN2 all positively correlate with LNEP, the increase of EP will bring a certain increment to N1 and N2. However, the increase of EP will negatively influence N3. We think that maybe the high mobility of the employees of tertiary industry causes the result. The rise of the wages will negatively influence the employment of the three industries. We think that the rise of the wages causes the crowding-out effect to the employment and leads to the decrease of the employees, which shows that the three industries cannot resist the pressure of the rising cost at present.

The long-term equilibrium relationship between variables only shows the superficial statistic correlationship. Through Granger Causality Test, we can find the causality of the variables. The results of Granger Causality Test tell us, at 5% significance level, LNPGDP, LNEP and LNW1 Granger Cause LNN1, LNN2 Granger Causes LNEP, LNW3 Granger Causes LNEP, LNPGDP Granger Causes LNEP and LNW2 Granger Causes LNN2.

4.2 Estimations and Impulse Responses of the SVAR Models

Firstly, we construct a VAR model with DLNNi, DLNPGDP, DLNEP and DLNWi (i=1, 2, 3) being as the endogenous variables. Then, we will identify the SVAR models. In recent years, several methods have been offered by some researchers, e.g., Sims [8] proposed the method of triangle recursion in 1980, Sims [9] and Bernanke [10] offered the nonrecursive method in 1986, Amisano & Giannini [11] presented the method of the AB model in 1997, etc.. We choose the method of the AB model to identify the SVAR model, i.e., we let B be an unit matrix and let all the main diagonal elements of the matrix A be ones. By estimating, we obtain three A matrices of the three SVAR models as follows

$$
A1: \begin{pmatrix} 1 & 45.73 & -35.13 & 0 \\ -80.59 & 1 & 53.11 & 0 \\ 71.28 & 74.15 & 1 & -43.40 \\ 0 & 59.16 & 26.28 & 1 \end{pmatrix}, A2: \begin{pmatrix} 1 & -33.86 & -54.31 & 0 \\ -62.71 & 1 & 31.30 & 0 \\ -4.41 & 34.14 & 1 & -26.75 \\ 0 & -37.87 & 7.41 & 1 \end{pmatrix},
$$

$$
(9)
$$

$$
A3: \begin{pmatrix} 1 & -75.96 & 29.68 & 0 \\ -40.03 & 1 & 25.61 & 0 \\ -13.76 & 138.91 & 1 & -51.45 \\ 0 & 21.92 & 50.04 & 1 \end{pmatrix}
$$

Based on the estimations of the A-matrices of the three SVAR models, we study 10 periods of impulse respone functions of DLNNi and provide the results as follows:

(1) The impulse responses of DLNN1 to the structural shocks of DLNPGDP, DLNEP and DLNW1: A shock of a positive standard deviation of DLNPGDP will lead to a reversed response of DLN1 at the current period, and DLNN1 will decrease and reach the short-term low point of -0.012 and then slowly upswing. After about 5.5 years, the reversed response will disappear. DLNN1 don't response to the shock of DLNEP at the current period and a year later will generate a positive response which will disappear after about 1.5 years. A shock of DLNW1 will lead to a positive response of DLLN1 at the current period and DLNN1 will reach the short-term high point of 0.009 and then falls quickly. After about 0.5 year, the response will disappear.

(2) The impulse responses of DLNN2 to the structural shocks of DLNPGDP, DLNEP and DLNW2: A shock of a positive standard deviation of DLNPGDP will lead to a reversed response of DLNN2 at the current period and DLNN2 will decrease and reach the short-term low point of -0.016 and then quickly upswing. After about 3 years, the reversed response will disappear. DLNN1 only gives a weak response to the shock of DLNEP at the current period and will generate a reversed response after 1 year and reach the short-term low point of -0.012. Then,DLNN2 will quickly upswing and the response will disappear after about 4 years. A shock of a positive standard deviation of DLNW2 will lead to a positive response of DLN2 at the current period and DLNN1 will quickly upswing and reach the short-term high point of 0.019 and then fall quickly. After about 3 years, the response will disappear.

(3) The impulse responses of DLNN3 to the structural shocks of DLNPGDP, DLNEP and DLNW3: a shock of a positive standard deviation of DLNPGDP will lead to a reversed response -0.025 of DLNN3 at the current period and, then, DLNN1 will quickly upswing. The reversed response will disappear after about 1.5 years. A shock of a positive standard deviation of DLNEP only leads to a weak response of DLNN3 at the current period. However, DLNN1 will generate a positive response after 1 year and reach the short-term high point of 0.009. Then DLNN3 will fall quickly and the response will disappear after about 1.5 years. A shock of a positive standard deviation of DLNW2 will lead to a positive response of DLNN3 at the current period and DLNN3 will quickly upswing and reach the short-term high point of 0.011 and , then, fall quickly. After about 0.5 year, the response will disappear.

5 Conclusions

This paper empirically analyzed the relationship between economic growth, populaion, wages and employment, using the economic data of China's three industries (1978--2009). The results of the cointegration analysis show that there exists a steady relationship between economic growth, populaion, wages and employment in the long run; the employment in primary (secondary or tertiary) industry is negatively (positively) related to the economic growth; secondary industry has the biggest economic growth-employment elasticity and population-employment elasticty, while tertiary industry has the biggest wages-employment elasticity; the rise of wages will cause negative effect to the employment of all the three industries. In addition, the Granger Causality Test shows that the changes of economic growth, population or wages will lead to the change of employment in primary and secondary industries and the combined change of economic growth, populaion and wages will lead to the changes of the employment in all the three industries.

The analysis of the impulse response based on the SVAR model shows that the shock of the economic growth will lead to a long-term response of the employment in primary industry, whereas in secondary and tertiary industries the responses are effective for about 3 and 1.5 years respectively; the responses of the employment in the three industries to the structural shock of the population are effective for a long time; the responses of employment in primary and tertiary industries to the structural shocks of the wages are effective for a short time while the response of employment in secondary is effective for a long time.

From a policy point of view, our findings have important consequences for policy making. For instance, the analysis of the impulse responses suggests that the state should comprehensively consider the influence of increment speed of national economy to the employment of the three industries in medium and long term and give appropriate policy supports to primary industry. The cointegration analysis reminds us that it may be not a good choice to attract the labor force by purely increasing the wages of employees in the long term. In addition, this paper is the first to explore the impulse responses of employment in the three industries to the structural shocks of economic growth, population and wages by using the SVAR model. However, our research is only on the basis of macrodata and static analysis and don't consider the spatial influence and regional difference. Exploring the relationship between employment, economic growth, population and wages by using the panel data and spatial econometrics method is an issue left for future research.

References

1. Yu, G.: Statistic Analysis of GDP and Employees of Three Industries. Jonural of Anhui University of Technology 2, 49–51 (2004)
2. Fan, A., Liu, W.: Influence of Export Trade to Flow of Labor Force of China's Tertiary Industry. International Economic Research 5, 50–74 (2008)
3. Qin, T.: An Analysis of the Influence of China's Three Main Industries on the Problem of Employment of Our Country. Economic Survey 2, 46–49 (2007)
4. Xia, H.: Correlation of Urbanization and Structure of Employment in Tertiary Indutry. Research on Economics and Management 5, 85–90 (2008)
5. Ye, M., Chen, J., Xiong, Y.: Empirical Research on Employment Potential of Tertiary Industries in China. The Theory and Pracice of Finance and Economics 2, 117–120 (2007)
6. Jin, J., Chen, Q., Zhang, F.: Industrial Characteristics of Employment in Primary Industry. Journal of Anhui Agricltural Science 13, 4074–4075 (2007)
7. Ma, H., Wang, L.: Research on Effects of Cycle Stability and Employment Ab-sorption of China's Tertiary Industry. China Soft Science 7, 144–150 (2009)
8. Sims, C.A.: Macroeconomics and Reality. Econometrica 48, 1–48 (1980)
9. Sims, C.A.: Are Forecasting Models Usable for Policy Analysis? Quarterly Review 10, 2–16 (1986)
10. Bernanke, B.: Alternative Explanations of the Money-income Correlation. In: Carnegie-Rochester Conference Series on Public Policy. North-Holland, Amsterdam (1986)
11. Amisano, G., Giannini, C.: Topics in Structural VAR Econometrics. Springer, Berlin (1997)

Study on PPP Contract-Models for Urban Rail Transit (URT) Projects in China

Guanguan Hua

Dept of Construction Management and Real Estate,
School of Economics and Management, Tongji University,
1239 Si Ping Road, Shanghai 200092, China
augustin.hua@gmail.com

Abstract. As an alternative to public financing, PPP (Public Private Partnership) is testified far more than a pure financing method. Aimed to introduce PPP into URT sector, in this thesis I analyzed several possible PPP contract-models which are applicable to deliver URT (Urban Rail Transit) projects in China. Detailed model structures were analyzed, together with allocation of risks (to Public vs. Private sector). In addition, contract-models were analyzed intergraded with land-development thinking. At the end, a comparison of analyzed PPP contract-models was made. As part of conclusion, BTO can be the most possible model applied in China, because it can definitely lighten public financial pressure.

Keywords: URT (Urban Rail Transit), PPP (Public Private Partnership), SPC (special purpose company), Financing, Refinancing.

1 Possible PPP Contract-Models

The background to develop PPP contract-model is that public sector (government) in China has heavy financial pressure, while social private investors would like to invest and involve in URT field to win profits. It is aimed that detailed illumination of PPP contract-models can be introduced to all levels' governments, stimulating massive development of URT systems in China.

1.1 BTO (Build-Transfer-Operate)

After the selection of eligible private partners, SPC (special purpose company) will be founded purely by this consortium. SPC is in absolute charge of financing, construction, operation, also purchase of trains and telecom-systems, while public sector has no financial investment but only does supervision and coordination [1]. When construction work is completed, a check-up will be carried out by SPC and then by public sector. If quality and functions of URT project match specification, the project will be transferred from SPC to public sector. According to BTO contract, public sector will then endue SPC with the right to operate URT line, together with the right to develop and operate URT stations, also adjacent lands along the URT line. At the same time, SPC will take the daily maintenance work of URT line.

Q. Zhou (Ed.): ISAEBD 2011, Part I, CCIS 208, pp. 516–523, 2011.
© Springer-Verlag Berlin Heidelberg 2011

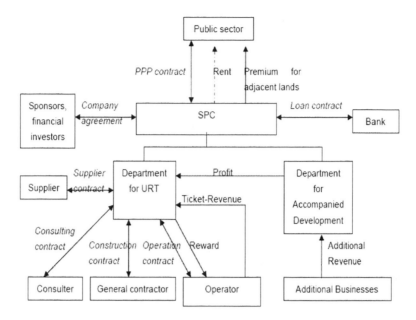

Fig. 1. Main Structure of B-T-O Contract-model

In this model, public sector invests neither in construction, financing, nor in operation and maintenance stage. Private sector can win back investment and subsequent return through ticket and other revenues from accompanied development. For public sector, two methods can be applied to oversee and control the profit of private sector. The first is to regulate ticket-price, and the second is to endue SPC with operation right and charge a "rent" for using URT assets. Through these two methods, it can prevent private sector to win excessive profit. The right to develop then operate URT stations and adjacent lands are called "supporting policies". Such policies are main source for SPC to refinance.

How to quantify the rent and how long is the charge period? In principle, the rent should not be a heavy burden to private sector. So at beginning stage of URT operation, the rent can be symbolistic or can be released. During this period, passenger volume is below the forecasting figure, partly because URT-net is not complete and the effect of "Economies of Scale" can not form. Operation work is just warming up, which means the operation efficiency is not high. The most important factor is that accompanied development is still under construction and has no outcome yet. After URT-net becomes mature, public sector can start charge rent.

When doing URT construction, SPC can also develop adjacent lands, e.g. real estate. SPC is encouraged to develop residential blocks at first, which will bring URT with considerable passengers in future. Land development must be as a part of entire URT project. Otherwise, the procurement of lands in China needs a complicated procedure like auction. Before signing PPP contract, SPC needs to submit his plan of to development adjacent lands. This plan is as appendix to be included in PPP contract. Before development, SPC need to pay land premium. That means adjacent lands of URT lines are reserved for potential SPC, but not cost free.

Through residential development, private sector can get considerable revenue to maintain URT's operation and get return on investment. After concession expires, in the case both public and private sectors are satisfied to each other, another contract eg. merely for operation and maintenance is possible.

In this model, public sector has no financial input and is hands-off in detail works, except supervision and coordination. Private sector can deliver URT project themselves and can win profit through accompanied development. This is a win-win situation. Certainly, there are also difficulties during execution, like how to identify maturity period from beginning period. Subsequently, how to define appropriate rent-level. In addition, it is difficult to define the scope of to-be developed lands, also not easy to forecast commercial revenues from accompanied development.

1.2 SB-O-T (Subsidize in Build-Operation-Transfer)

The whole URT project will be divided into two parts: Part A: investment and construction of tunnel, viaduct, station and rail; Part B: investment on vehicles, telecom devices and operation together with maintenance. Here, "subsidize in building" means the first part will be in the charge of State-owned Company. The second part will be undertaken by SPC which is purely founded by private investors. After the completion of construction and purchase work, the whole URT line will be operated by SPC. The assets of part A will be provided to SPC, at the price of charging a symbolistic rent or even released [2]. By this means, through ticket-revenue (and if necessary, together with accompanied development), private sector can win back investment and subsequent reasonable return. Between public and SPC, a concession contract will be signed, in which service, safety and other standards will be framed. The duration of such concession depends on the amount of private

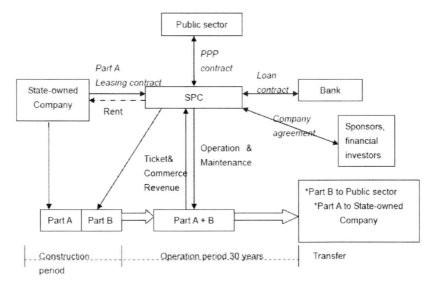

Fig. 2. Main Structure of SB-O-T Contract-model [3]

investment, in general, 30 years. After expiration of concession duration, SPC will hand over all assets to public sector without cost. Of course, then an operation and maintenance contract is possible between public and private sectors.

The same as in BTO model, the rent for assets A is an instrument to control over-profit of private sector. During growing period, rent can be released, in order to help private sector warm up and raise operation efficiency. Also, more profits at beginning can make private sector more confident and encourage him to fulfill his work.

During maturity period, a rent will be charged from private sector, which has two functions. Apart from the control of over-profit, rent can also pay back part of public investment on Part A.

1.3   B-SO-T (Build-Subsidize in Operation-Transfer)

In B-SO-T contract-model, government and private investors will form SPC, which means public sector will involve the capital investment, but in operation period. Based upon forecasted passenger volume and regulation of ticket-price, public sector estimates SPC's operation cost and revenue. To possible deficit, which is theoretically calculated, public sector will directly provide SPC with financial subsidy [2].

All these are only principles in theory. One certain figure as annual increase of travelers will be assumed in advance, which is critical for the adjustment of subsidy. For instance, such a figure can be "a%", as the average annual increase of travelers [2]. In practice, if real passenger volume is beyond or below forecast by extent of a%, public sector and SPC will share the related profit or loss. To public sector, it is equal to reduce or increase annual subsidy to SPC, which is estimated based on theoretic deficit "d". The share-proportion of public sector and SPC is agreed in advance and needs to be included in PPP contract. For instance, the share proportion of public sector and SPC is 1: 1. Situation I, real passenger volume in this year is 1+a%+b% and regulated ticket-price is c. Situation II, real passenger volume and regulated price is respective (1-a%-b %) and c'. The amount of subsidy in these two years and calculation process will be seen in the following table.

Table 1. Amount of Subsidy to SPC, in B-SO-T Contract-model

Situation	Forecasting figure of passenger volume	Annual increase of passenger volume	Real passenger volume	Regulated ticket-price	Theoretic deficit	Amount of Subsidy to SPC
I	1	a%	1+a%+b%	c	d	d-b%*c*50%
II	1	a%	1-a%-b%	c'	d	d+b%*c'*50%

Definitely, the forecasting figure of passenger volume is not always the same, but will be adjusted according to real situation every 3 years, for a more precise subsidy [1]. After the expiration of concession period, SPC will hand over all URT assets to public sector.

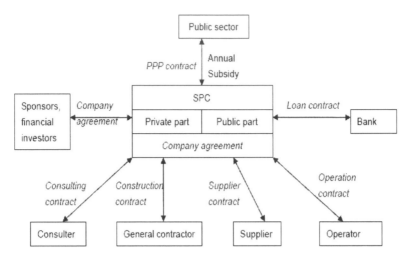

Fig. 3. Main structure of B-SO-T model [4]

The main character of this model is that public sector participates into SPC and additionally supports SPC with annual subsidy during operation. To a certain extent, this kind of cooperation reduces risks of private investors at financing, construction, operation, etc., because the risks are partly shared with public sector. Thus, with B-SO-T model, private investors are more encouraged to participate into investment of URT project.

1.4 BLT (Build-Lease-Transfer)

Similar but not the same as in SB-O-T model, URT project will be divided into two parts: Part A: investment and construction of tunnel, viaduct, station and rail; Part B: investment on trains, conduction devices and maintenance. Part A will be implemented by public sector or state-owned companies, while Part B is in the charge of SPC that is founded purely by private investors. When construction is finished, SPC will lease assets of Part B to public sector, who will fulfill the operation work. And SPC has responsibility to carry out maintenance work. In the form of lease-rent, public sector will pay SPC for his investment on part B and also the ongoing work of maintenance. This rent consists of grant and unfixed payment depends on fare box revenue. After expiration of concession period, assets of part B will be transferred to public sector. Then, if possible, a pure maintenance contract may be signed between public and private sector [5].

Besides professional URT Operation Company, this model is also attractive to those private investors, who have no URT operation experience but are experienced for mechanical and electrical projects. For instance, large production company for URT vehicles and telecom technique may have interest to Part B.

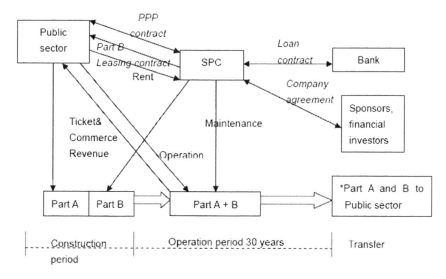

Fig. 4. Main structure of BLT model

2   Comparison of PPP Contract-Models

After developing main structures of above four PPP contract-models for URT projects, I tried to make a comparison table including several key aspects, aimed to form my final conclusion.

Table 2. Comparison of PPP Contract-models, Used for URT Projects

Criterion	Characters			
	BTO	SB-O-T	B-SO-T	BLT
Who founds SPC	Private consortium	Private consortium	public and private consortium	Private consortium
Ownership of SPC and its assets	100% public ownership of assets (transferred); 100% private ownership of SPC	100% public ownership of Part A; 100% private ownership of Part B and SPC	X% public ownership, (100-X)% private ownership	100% public ownership of Part A; 100% private ownership of Part B and SPC
Operation	SPC/Private sector	SPC/Private sector	SPC/public and private sector	public sector

Table 2. (*continued*)

Sub-contractors	optional, contracting by SPC (open tendering)	optional, contracting by Public sector (Part A); contracting by SPC (Part B)	optional, contracting by SPC (open tendering)	optional, contracting by Public sector (Part A); contracting by SPC (Part B)
Financing	by private investors' equity + external capital	Part A: by Public sector, own and external capitals; Part B: by private investors' equity + external capital	by public and private investors' equity + external capital	Part A: by Public sector, own and external capitals; Part B: by private investors' equity + external capital
Refinancing	passengers pay fees to SPC + Profit from accompanied development	passengers pay fees to SPC	passengers pay fees to SPC + subsidy form public sector	passengers pay fees to public sector, public sector pay rent to SPC
Risk distribution Public	*Public sector:* when selecting private consortium, framing PPP contract, service standards and supporting policies;	*Public sector:* when selecting private consortium, framing PPP contract, service standards and technical risks, financing risks at Part A;	x% *public risk,*	*Public sector:* when selecting private consortium, framing PPP contract, service standards and technical risks, financing risks at Part A, demand risk, operation risk, possible risk due to maintenance of private sector;
Risk distribution Private	*Private sector:* technical risks, financing risks, demand risk, operation risk, political risk, risk of insufficient profit from accompanied development	*Private sector:* demand risk, technical and financing risks of Part B, operation risk	(100-X)% *private risk* with respect to equity of SPC; bankruptcy risk of SPC usually is rather theoretical	*Private sector:* technical and financing risks of Part B, risk of uncertain return on investment

Table 2. (*continued*)

Operation efficiency	highest, profit motivation due to private operation	highest, profit motivation due to private operation	high, profit motivation due to private participation	low, pure public operation
Financial pressure of government	low	higher	high	highest

3 Conclusion

Seeing from above table, every contract-model has its merits and shortages. Aimed to lighten financial pressure of government, BTO is the best model. Another highlight of this model is the accompanied development. However, in this execution, public sector has little involvement (implying little control ability), while private sector has too many responsibilities and corresponding risks. Once private sector is in plight at one certain step, the whole project may be in danger.

Thus, the application of PPP contract-models needs to match real situation of cities, above all, local economic and administrative capability. That is the reason why the State Council set strict key preconditions to control the approval of URT projects.

References

1. Zhu, W., An, R.: Discussion on Adoption of PPP Financing Mode for the Construction of Urban Mass Transit. Railway Transport and Economy (1) (2005)
2. Wang, H.: On Metro Financing and Investment - Innovation and Application of PPP, p. 25. China Finance Publishing House, Beijing (2006)
3. Sun, B.: The Research for Quasi-profit Infrastructure PPP Mode. Tongji University, Shanghai (2006)
4. Weber, B., Alfen, H.W., Maser, S.: Projektfinanzierung und PPP, p. 37. Bank-Verlag GmbH, Koeln (2006)
5. Cai, Y.: Innovation and Application of PPP Mode in Urban Rail Transit Projects. Urban Rapid Rail Transit 20(1) (2007)
6. 2008-2010 Research on Chinese Urban Rail transit and Analysis on investment perspective, Abstract section. China Investment Consulting Net (January 2008), http://www.ocn.com.cn/

Study on Ticket Pricing-System for Urban Rail Transit (URT) Projects in China

Guanguan Hua

Dept of Construction Management and Real Estate,
School of Economics and Management, Tongji University,
1239 Si Ping Road, Shanghai 200092, China
augustin.hua@gmail.com

Abstract. Aimed to identify an appropriate ticket pricing-system for URT project in China, in this thesis I analyzed several economic characters which can influence pricing system itself and then detailed analyzed four possible pricing systems, respectively from view of cost, competitive market, marginal profit, and social comprehensive benefit. At the end, the conclusion is given that pricing system based upon social comprehensive benefit is reasonable, to ensure benefit of operation company and the whole society. As extension, possible concerns when applying this system in realistic were also mentioned for further thinking.

Keywords: Ticket Pricing-system, URT (Urban Rail Transit), Refinancing, Revenue.

1 Economic Characters

Today, Urban Rail Transit (URT) is a massive developing traffic tool overall China. Well known that both financing and refinancing are important to the success (establishment and operation) of the Urban Rail Transit (URT) project itself. Financing is easy to understand, to finance the establishment of the project, while refinancing means in a simple word how to win revenue after project establishment to pay off before financed capital. In this thesis, the most discussed refinancing way is tickets revenue.

Before the discussion of ticket pricing system for URT projects, it is indispensable to learn about URTs economic characters, which have big influence to the financing and refinancing aspect of project. In below paragraphs, 3 main economic characters of URT will be listed, and they are "club goods", "positive externality" and "commonweal".

1.1 Club Goods

Club goods, also known as collective goods, is a type of goods in economics, sometimes classified as a subtype of public goods that are excludable but non-rivalrous, at least until reaching a critical point where congestion occurs [1].

Q. Zhou (Ed.): ISAEBD 2011, Part I, CCIS 208, pp. 524–530, 2011.
© Springer-Verlag Berlin Heidelberg 2011

Table 1. Private and public goods[2]

	Excludable	Non-excludable
Rivalrous	*Private goods* food, clothing, toys, furniture, cars	*Common goods (Common-pool resources)* water, fish, hunting game
Non-rivalrous	*Club goods* cable television	*Public goods* national defense, free-to-air television, air

Urban rail transit is a kind of club goods, which has characters of non-rivalness and excludability. Firstly, the sole aim to take a URT is to travel from one place to another. So before the URT becomes too crowded (a critical point), while one passenger takes URT, other passengers can also take it, which means non-rivalrous. Of course, before the critical point (too crowded) is a precondition. Secondly, not all passengers can use the service of URT. Before they take it, they need to buy a ticket. That means who does not buy a URT-ticket, can not share the service of URT and is excluded from such a right. This is URT's excludable character.

Public goods can be naturally available or it is often provided by government, although it is not always the case. Oppositely, private goods are mainly provided by private. For club goods, just like urban rail transit, they can be provided either by government or by private, with or without subsidies.

1.2 Positive Externality

In economics, an externality is an impact (positive or negative) on any party not involved in a given economic transaction. Take an example of positive externality, someone plants a beautiful garden in front of his house and may provide benefits to others living in this area, and even financial benefits in the form of increased property values for all property owners [3].

When talking about transportation, negative externalities are dominating, like noise, air pollution, land consumption, etc. However, urban rail transit has distinctive merits on all these aspects, especially when comparing to conventional traffic system. Here, when considering externalities, URT should not be compared with doing nothing, but with the consequence of doing nothing. Doing nothing means the current traffic problems will only be disposed, by means of building more new roads, which causes much more adverse influence to both traffic and urbanization. It can be then a vicious circle. Certainly, the large scale of URT's construction work can also bring some negative effects, like noise. But in long term, when URT-net reaches its maturity, it brings more comprehensive benefits than its negative influence.

Thus, it is said that urban rail transit has main positive externalities, such as a newly built metro line can increase the value of adjoining lands, especially in developing countries which are in process of urbanization. Another example, URT line can promote the development of commercial utilities, like shops and gas-station, which raise living-quality of people living there. Also, more people will take URT instead of driving cars or taking buses, which reduces emission of harmful gas and decreases further air pollution.

Once externality exists, no matter positive or negative, free market will be disturbed and loses the power to allocate resources effectively. It needs then intervention from government. One solution of externality is to get an agreement between all involved parties [4].

1.3 Commonweal Character

Urban rail transit is one kind of biggest infrastructures and has great effect on urban planning and development. On the other hand, URT is one kind of public transport (note here, not means public goods), which is characterized by commonweal. The reason is that the price of public transport can not be purely derived from marginal cost, because the average cost is usually higher than the marginal cost. To URT, a high ticket-price is definitely impossible, because it may exclude a bulk of common people to take URT, and then all advantages of URT can not realize and then this new traffic system will loss its sense. Thus, considering huge social benefit, URT should be a commonweal product or service, which people can use at a low price. In most cases, authorities have to regulate the market, in the way of providing URT operation with subsidies.

2 Models of Pricing System

Ticket-price of URT can be seen as the sale price of URT transportation (a service rather than a product). The price level of ticket definitely influences passenger flow and then the survival and development of URT operation. Also, price level of ticket concerns the benefit of public sector (authority), because he may provide subsidy for operation in the case of deficit. In addition, URT system has a clear commonweal character, which determines ticket pricing must consider besides the benefit of operation partner also social benefit.

Thus, the pricing system seems complicated and must take account of following factors: operation cost of URT; ticket-price of alternative transportation tools; local economic level and peoples' living standard; political factors like price regulation, subsidy for transportation, etc [5].

Considering above factors, an appropriate ticket-price of URT can be worked out, under consideration of both benefit of operation partner and whole society. Several pricing systems will be analyzed in turn as following:

2.1 Pricing System Based Upon Cost

This system is widely used to price a product in most industries and by most corporations. Price of product depends on the production cost and plus some profit.

$$P = (1+i+i')*C/ (Q* Sav) [6].$$

P–Price/p*km (p-person)
i–profit rate
i'–rate of all taxes   (1)
C–operation cost of Operation Company
Q–forecasted passenger volume
Sav–average transported distance per person

When estimating costs, proportion of fixed and variable costs, short-term and long-term costs should be considered. Occasional cost can not be counted into general operation cost. Otherwise, the price will be incorrect.

This pricing model starts from Operation Company's aspect, aimed to win profit through operation. However, it ignores market factors, especially at keen competitions. If to price URT ticket in this way, the price seems too high and URT transportation service becomes less attractive.

2.2 Pricing System Based on Perfectly Competitive Market

This pricing model does not take account of operation cost, but depends on the function of Demand-Supply relationship. The final price (Po) should be the one which is accepted by most URT passengers. At pricing, the relationship of demand and supply, also other alternative transportation modes will be considered [7].

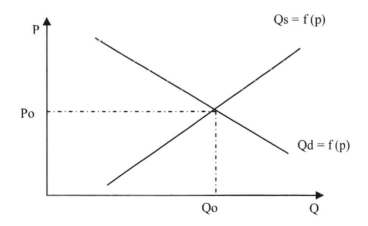

Fig. 1. Demand-Supply in perfectly competitive market

Here, to URT projects, 100% market pricing is not suitable. With control from neither public nor private partner, social benefit can not be ensured.

2.3 Pricing System Based Upon Marginal Cost-Marginal Revenue Theory

Marginal Revenue (MR) is the extra revenue that an additional unit of product will bring to a firm. It can also be described as the change in total revenue/change in number of units sold. In a perfectly competitive market, marginal revenue is equal to price [8].

In economics and finance, marginal cost is the change in total cost that arises when the quantity produced changes by one unit [9].

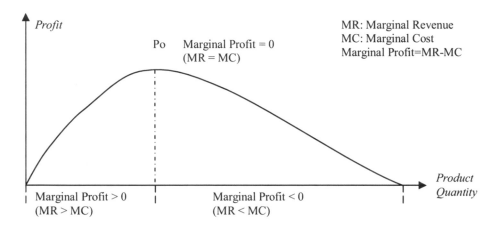

Fig. 2. The Relationship of Marginal Revenue and Marginal Cost of a Product

Seeing from above figure, for each unit sold, marginal profit equals marginal revenue minus marginal cost. Then, if marginal revenue is more than marginal cost, marginal profit is positive; and if marginal revenue is less than marginal cost, marginal profit is negative. When marginal revenue equals marginal cost, marginal profit is zero. Since total profit increases when marginal profit is positive and total profit decreases when marginal profit is negative, it must reach a maximum where marginal profit is zero - or where marginal cost equals marginal revenue [10].

So a company can get its maximal profit on the point that marginal cost equals marginal revenue. Try to use this theory on URT products. Obviously, it is unsuitable to price the URT product or service at the marginal cost. Before URT vehicles become too crowded, as a critical point, one more passenger will cause almost no cost. This means marginal cost of URT product is equal to zero. Thus, it is not realistic to price URT (transport service) zero. This kind of pricing model is not feasible.

2.4 Pricing System Based Upon Social Comprehensive Benefit

This model is not only for Operation Company or for public sector (authority), but for comprehensive benefit of the whole society. This comprehensive benefit consists of benefit of passengers and Operation Company, commonweal, urban development, thinking about environment, investment atmosphere, etc. Under such thinking, public sector (authority) needs to provide financial support (as subsidy), to ensure the smooth operation of URT. In a lot of PPP projects, besides subsidy, public sector also constitute supporting policies, helping SPC (special purpose company) or private partner attain other commercial revenue. Under such principle, the ticket-price represents no real price, but only a discount price with function of all kinds financial supports.

$$S+Rc+Q* Sav*P=C+I \ [7].\tag{2}$$

S–subsidy from public sector
Rc–profit from other commercial revenue, due
    to supporting policy
Q–forecasted passenger volume
Sav–average transportation distance
P–price/p*km (p–person)
C–operation cost of Operation Company
I–profit of Operation Company

It can be seen from above formula, the more profit from other additional businesses, the less subsidy from public sector. The real situation in China determines that public sector has to frame favorable policies, to support SPC or Operation Company to balance operation cost and various revenues, due to the discount ticket-price. This pricing system will do a great help, not only to the development of URT system, but also to the integral society.

3 Conclusion

Seeing from above analysis, in realistic, pricing system based upon cost, based upon perfectly competitive market, or based upon Marginal Cost–Marginal Revenue theory is not suitable to price the URT ticket. Conversely, it is reasonable to price the URT ticket, when taking comprehensive benefit of the whole society into consideration. However, how to quantify the amount of subsidy, how to identify the amount of other commercial revenue, how to define reasonable profit of operation company, etc are the real questions to be solved. In real situation, public listening on price, price regulation mechanism are both used to adjust URT ticket price at interval, to ensure the benefit of both operation company and society can be protected.

References

1. Buchanan, J.M.: An Economic Theory of Clubs. Economica 32, 1–14 (1965)
2. Samuelson, P.A.: The Pure Theory of Public Expenditure, P, pp. 387–389 (1954)
3. Johnson, P.M.: A Glossary of Political Economy Terms, http://www.auburn.edu/~johnspm/gloss/externality
4. Hu, K., Ying, Y.: Analysis and Thinking of financing on Urban Rail Transit (April 2006)
5. Zhang, F., Qian, C.: General Instruction to Urban Rail Transit, p. 150. Press of Southwest Jiaotong University, Chengdu (2007)
6. Ji, L., Zhang, G.: Operation and Organization of Urban Rail Transit, p. 120. China Railway Publishing House, Beijing (2003)
7. Mao, B.: Operations and Management for Urban Rail Transit, pp. 294–295. China Communications Press, Beijing (2003)

8. http://www.economist.com/research/Economics/
   alphabetic.cfm?LETTER=M#marginal;
   http://en.wikipedia.org/wiki/Marginal_revenue
9. http://www.economist.com/research/Economics/
   alphabetic.cfm?LETTER=M#marginal,
   http://en.wikipedia.org/wiki/Marginal_cost
10. http://en.wikipedia.org/wiki/
    Profit_maximization#Marginal_Cost-Marginal_Revenue_Method

Research on the Trust Game Model of Stockholders Harmonious Management: From the Social Capital Viewpoint

Xinan Li

Henan University of Economics and Law, Zhengzhou,
450002, P.R. China
xinan6758@163.com

Abstract. According to some of the problems that exist in corporate governance, we use game theory methods, raise Social relations network of the corporate governance from the perspective of social capital mutual trust and harmonious cooperation. On the basis of Company harmony and all of the relevant stockholders to get the state of an orderly, coordinated and complementary, establishment of a trust game model, should help supervision try to solve the various problems that exist in corporate governance and achieve the harmonious management of the company.

Keywords: Harmonious managemen, Corporate governance, Trust Game.

1 Introduction

The social capital first appeared in the sociological research, Pierre Bourdieu in the 1970s In 1988, Coleman in the "American Journal of Sociology," the "social capital as a condition of human capital development," the academic of sociology in the United States first use the concept of social capital, carry out an deep-going research and discuss. The same as the material and human capital, Social capital is not a complete substitute for certain activities, but only link with certain specific activities together. Some of the specific form of social capital can enhance the community's efficiency of operations through the promotion of cooperation. Network, trust and reciprocity are essential elements of social capital. Social capital is indispensable factors that obtain material capital, human capital, in fact, it is the decisive factor.

With the development of companies, modern companies showing important feature, such as scattered of shareholding structure, ownership and management separation. The ownership and management of company are separation, operating of the objective function and shareholders of target function may become inconsistent. If both the objective function is inconsistent, and the information asymmetry, the cost of supervision will lead to significant improvements. Corporate governance company stockholders through a series of internal and external mechanisms for the implementation of the common governance. The goal of corporate governance is resolving commissioned agent of asymmetric information and internal control

Q. Zhou (Ed.): ISAEBD 2011, Part I, CCIS 208, pp. 531–537, 2011.
© Springer-Verlag Berlin Heidelberg 2011

problems, not only maximize the interests of shareholders, but also to ensure scientific decision-making companies. Therefore, to slove the corporate governance issues, harmonious management company has become the focus of attention.

2   The Game Model of Stockholders Harmonious Management

The so-called harmonious means that the internal things, and the synergy, coordinate, adapt between the various components, it is reflect social factors that interact with each other. In this sense, harmony refers a certain state that the coordination of the social factors determine by relations of production.

Company governance harmony refers to all of the relevant stockholders with company to achieve an state that orderly, coordinated and complementary, common development. In this state, social capital and corporate governance support each other. Social capital refers to the relationship such as trust, reciprocity, norms and networks between the stockholders, and governance is based on trust, reciprocity, norm,the relation of cooperation between principal and agent.such as fig.1:

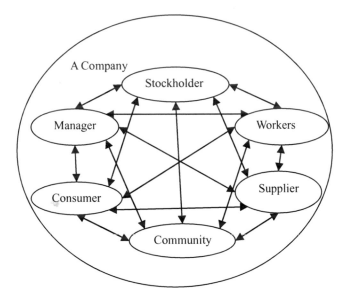

Fig. 1. Stockholders'relations

Any cooperation must has two conditions, the one is trust, and the other is reciprocity. Under Social Capital Perspective, the cooperative game model of stockholders harmonious management as follows:

2.1   Model Assumptions

The player in cooperative game are stockholders, managers (M), shareholders (SH), employees (E), creditors (CR), customers (CU), suppliers (SP) and communities

(CO). They are in the network of social capital, put their own special assets into company , share the risks together, operating activities together , maintain long-term cooperation relationship with the company, achieving a win-win situation. Stockholders are mutual cooperation action to achieve a harmonious management of the company that on the basis of the extent of trust that on their understanding and the extent to worry about the collapse of trust.

Although different stockholders have their own interests, the company claims and that they are seeking to control the actual shares.

Assumed the rent that surplus of the power with demand and control is V , the stockholders's extent of trust is γ_i , with the other stockholders, if exist the implementation of opportunism ,the extent of worried that the collapse of trust is f_i , the parties have reached profit by trust is x_i , the effectiveness that the parties results from trust is $u(x_i)$. If implementation of opportunism , the effectiveness that collapse of trust with various parties (that is threat points)is v_i , abovementioned $i = M, SH, E, CR, CU, SP, CO$. The extent of trust v_i is exogenous variable that impact by institution, time, economy and the other variables. If implementation of opportunism , will make collapse of trust, it have a positive impact to the party of trust i , in ability from achieving benefit. f_i is the trust side's sectional avoid to the result of the collapse of trust, decision by the individual utility function. v_i is the level of minimum acceptable to the side of trust i , it also is utility that the party i last successful acquisition.

Let

$$u'(x_i) = x_i - v_i \tag{1}$$

$u'(x_i)$ is the pure profit(marginal utility) that can be acquired by the i .

2.2 Model Construction

According to the negotiations theorem of Nash, if this four of theorem can be satisfied: (1) individual rational, (2) does not change the result of the utility function by linear transformation , (3) symmetry, (4) the independence of does not link with choose, it is the only solution for that, approsched is $\max \prod_{i=M}^{s} (x_i - v_i) \cdot \prod_{i=M}^{s} (x_i - v_i)$ is the maximization of stockholders. The binding force of game is involved by the parties is when access to the effectiveness of reached trust more than collapse of trust, that is $x_i \geq v_i > 0$.

According to the promoting negotiations theorem of Nash, on the basis of negotiations theorem of Nash, introduce the extent of trust (γ_i) and the extent of worry about the collapse of the trust (f_i).

$$\sum_{i=M}^{s} \gamma_i = 1, \partial x_i / \partial \gamma_i > 0, \lim_{\gamma_i \to 0} x_i = v_i = 0 \tag{2}$$

$$\lim_{\gamma_i \to 1} x_i = x; f_i = u_i(x_i)/u_i'(x_i) \tag{3}$$

When meet the five theorem, the trust of the stockholders under the restrictions $\sum_{i=M}^{S} x_i = x$, select x_i in order to maximize $\prod_{i=M}^{S} u_i^{\gamma_i}$. Make the objective function $\sum_{i=M}^{S} u_i^{\gamma_i}$ to transform, let natural logarithm for the new function $\sum_{i=M}^{S} \gamma_i \ln u_i$, combine the restrain conditions $\sum_{i=M}^{S} x_i = x$, Construction the function of *Langrange* :

$$L = \sum_{i=M}^{S} \gamma_i \ln u_i + \lambda \left(\sum_{i=M}^{S} x_i - x \right) \qquad (\lambda \text{ is parameter}) \tag{4}$$

Let,

$$\gamma_i \frac{u_i'}{u_i} - \lambda = 0 \tag{5}$$

then

$$\gamma_i \frac{u_i'}{u_i} = \gamma_j \frac{u_j'}{u_j} (i \neq j) \tag{6}$$

2.3 Model Analyze

By the $f_i = u_i(x_i)/u_i'(x_i)$ reliance on x_i, suppose $u_i(x_i)$ is concave function, assume $u_i'(x_i) > 0$, $u_i''(x_i) < 0$, then to $u_i'(x_i) > 0$, there is a result that

$$\frac{\partial f_i}{\partial x_i} = \frac{[u_i'(x_i)]^2 - u_i(x_i)u_i''(x_i)}{[u_i'(x_i)]^2} > 0 \tag{7}$$

therefore , we get Proposition I.

Proposition I : In corporate governance, the stockholders's extent of worry about collapse of the trust recrease ,in pace with they increase obtain from the results.

For simplicity's sake, assume that only 1 and 2 for both trust and their extent of trust are γ_1 and γ_2 , If 1 obtains the net profit from to the trust is x_i , 2 obtains the net profit from to the trust is $v - x_i$; this can be found :

$$\frac{x_i}{v - x_i} = \theta \frac{\gamma_1}{\gamma_2} \qquad (\theta > 0) \tag{8}$$

Let

$$y = \gamma_1 \Big/ \gamma_2 \tag{9}$$

We have

$$x_1 = \frac{\theta v_y}{1 + \theta_y} \tag{10}$$

on the type of derivatives with y ,

$$\frac{\partial x_1}{\partial y} = \frac{v\theta}{(1 - \theta y)^2} > 0 \tag{11}$$

and so we get Proposition II.

Proposition II : In corporate governance, the stockholders' relative trust the stronger, they obtained the higher net income from the result of trust.

Satisfy

$$f_i / \gamma_i = f_j / \gamma_j , \tag{12}$$

$i, j = M, SH, E, CR, CU, SP, CO, i \neq j$ in the best solution; According to the definition with f_i ,

$$f_i = u_i(x_i) / u_i'(x_i) \tag{13}$$

we have

$$\frac{u^*_i}{u^*_j} = \frac{\gamma_i}{\gamma_j} \times \frac{u_i'}{u_j'} \tag{14}$$

u^*_i is achieved object of effectiveness, that is the best solution with i , thus we can obtain Proposition III.

Proposition III : In corporate governance, comparison of the effectiveness of all stockholders, and the optimal solution depends on their degree of trust in the Department of marginal utility evaluation over.

2.4 Model Apply

Company is concluded "net lease" that between the stockholders, the stockholders in the company, invest of social capital, physical capital, human capital, or influenced by the company's activities, in order to obtain benefit or compensation that is unable to obtain by the cooperation of production units personal. Stockholder participation in corporate governance by the extent of trust through social capital, and follow the principle of cooperation. Such as: Fig.2

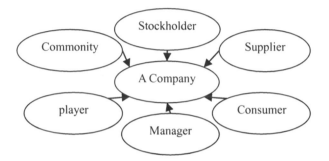

Fig. 2. Stockholders' corporate governance through social capital of trust

3 Conclusion

According to the conclusion of the trust Game Analysis, try to solve the various problems that exist in corporate governance :

First, the controlling shareholders of listed companies exist the tendency to abuse affiliated transactions, and against the interests of small shareholders. Deeper reason is that the state shares surge of bad ruler forsaken by the lack of protection of rights and interests of small shareholders controlling shareholder of the restraint mechanism. Social capital can be used to enhance the transparency of corporate information, establishing and improving confidence in the vulnerable groups of stockholders.

Second, China's listed companies stockholder governance mechanisms are relatively weak, The difference was larger. Use of the advantages of social capital and trust in the network, effectively encourage the participation of stockholders, and appropriate participation corporate governance and management .Game dynamic trust and achieve a harmonious management of the company. Enterprises can build competitive advantage in human resources through the development of social capital.

Third, although the overall situation of China's information disclosure of listed companies has improved, but the authenticity of the information disclosed. Social capital applies to corporate governance issues facing the internal control, the free-rider problem, adverse selection and moral hazard problem.

The main interest of the company parties to blend different cultures are intertwined, appear the specific form of corporate governance culture. Positive and progressive, mutual cooperation and strict discipline, good corporate governance culture will help raise the efficiency of corporate governance.

Acknowledgements. Support under the following programmes: Humane Social Science Fund Project of Chinese Ministry of Education (NO:10YJA790099); Henan Province Science Project(082102360031); the Henan department of education Science Foundation (Grant No.2009-JD-014; 2008A630001; 2009B63002 ; 2011A630001); Sponsored by (2008HASTIT021).

References

1. Zhou, H.-y.: Social capital:the compare with Bourdieu, Coleman and Putnam. Compare with Economic and Social Systems 4, 46–53 (2003)
2. Chen, Q.-g., Cheng, X.: The study of "Social capital" theory to a new progress. Guizhou Financial Services Institute Journal 5, 79–82 (2003)
3. Hua, Z.-y.: Corporate governance:social capital research embedded. Western Finance 4, 45–48 (2006)
4. Yao, X.-t., Xi, y.-m.: A majority of the public thinks, Social network theory and its application in the research application. Journal of Xi'an Jiaotong University 4, 19–23 (2003)
5. Zhang, C.-j., Wen, Z.-m.: Game cooperation with the stockholders of the company's and financial management harmony. Modern Management Science 9, 25–28 (2005)

Research on Behavior Interaction between the Owner and Entrepreneu

Xinan Li and Chunhua Li

Henan University of Economics and Law, Zhengzhou,
450002, P.R. China
xinan6758@163.com

Abstract. This article establishes a dynamic game of incomplete information model, studies how Psychological Contract (PC) influence entrepreneurs' behavior after PC violation is perceived, tries to explains why the owner has driven to exposure their PC style as well as the inclination. Comparing with existing research, this thesis incorporates results of entrepreneurs' PC into economic framework, adds utility change from implied contract into utility function of explicit contracts to analyze entrepreneurs' behavior and mutual effect between entrepreneurs and owners, which makes our research close to reality as well as enhances interpretability of entrepreneurs' behavior.

Keywords: Psychological contract(PC), Incomplete information, Entrepreneur's behavior.

1 Introduction

Psychological contract (PC) is one of the hottest topics that academic circles studies, and many famous scholars have made very big contributions out in theory research or demonstration research here [1-6]. Though these analyses have shown that the entrepreneur's psychological contract is inclined to relational one [7] and empirical study has testified the influence of psychological contract on work attitude of top management [7], while, in order to enhance the forecast force towards entrepreneur's behavior, making theoretical analysis suit the behavior interaction between both sides in reality, the following questions should be answered: how would the type choose of the owner's psychological contract influence the behavior of entrepreneur? How such influence has effect on the behavior choose of entrepreneur? All these questions include a game between the owner and entrepreneur. Therefore, this article builds an incomplete and dynamic game model to find the answer.

2 The Theoretical Hypothesises and Model Consruction

According to the previous research, the following hypothesis is put forward before game analysis:

Q. Zhou (Ed.): ISAEBD 2011, Part I, CCIS 208, pp. 538–544, 2011.
© Springer-Verlag Berlin Heidelberg 2011

Hypothesis 1: It is the common knowledge that the type of the entrepreneur's psychological contract is relational one.

Hypothesis 2: Though the part who make psychological contract with the entrepreneur includes stakeholders, while, in order to simplify the analysis, we choose the owner as the representative of stakeholders, and take the owner p and the entrepreneur A as two sides of the game.

Hypothesis 3: Once the enterprise makes judge that the owner deviated from relational psychological contract, he or she would think his or her psychological contract be breached, certain psychological effects such as disappointment and negative emotion arises. In order to implant such effects into our economic model, we assume that these psychological effects would directly result in profit loss of the owner (the client). Meanwhile, we assume that the behavior of entrepreneur satisfy the Rabin's basic assumptions of "to return a favor with a favor", that is: (1) People are willing to sacrifice their own material well-being to help those who are being kind. (2) People are willing to sacrifice their own material well-being to punish those who are being unkind. (3) Both motivations (1) and (2) have a greater effect on behavior as the material cost of sacrificing becomes smaller.

Hypothesis 4: The owner's psychological contract is private information, there exists two types, one is transactional contract, and the other is relational one. So the entrepreneur can only guess the type of the owner's psychological contract through his behavior, and then decide his own best behavior. We assume that the entrepreneur judges the owner's type through payoffs the owner paid to him or her.

The payoff modes the owner paid to the entrepreneur have two possibilities. One is material payoff, the rewards related with performance, is equal to basic wages adds performance, we note it as: $S_m = S(\pi) = \alpha + \beta\pi$. The other is kind payoff, the owner not only provides material payoff (rewards related with performance), but gives enough careness, more chance for entrepreneur, etc.. Such payoff is noted as: $S_k = S_m + C_s = S(\pi) + C_s$, here C_s may be seemed as additional cost the owner paid to the entrepreneur. In other words, the behavior group of the owner $A_p = \{material;\ kind\}$, the corresponding rewards is S_m and S_k, here $S_m < S_k$.

Hypothesis 5: The entrepreneur judges the type of the owner's psychological contract according to look into the reward modes the owner provided to him. As the type of the entrepreneur's psychological contract is relational one, and it is known by the owner as well. Therefore, it is the best wish of the entrepreneur to be paid with kind rewards by the owner; in return, the entrepreneur is loyalty to the owner. In consequence, if the entrepreneur thinks the owner as kind, he would make judge that the type of the owner's psychological contract is relational, and then he would be loyalty. If the entrepreneur thinks the owner as material, he would make judge that the type of the owner's psychological contract is transactional, and then he would only play his own part. Meanwhile, the entrepreneur would think the owner goes against the psychological contract between two sides, and then negative emotion or retaliatory behavior would be emerged. All these can be seen as rules of the game.

Hypothesis 6: As analysis above, the behavior group of the entrepreneur is $A_a =$ $\{be \quad loyal, \quad be \quad conscientious\}$ .The entrepreneur would make more effort if he is loyal (the cost is counted as c_e), the performance he make would increase from π to $\pi + s_a \cdot s_a$ is the performance added because of the loyalty of the entrepreneur. The change of the effect of the entrepreneur is different when he chooses "be conscientious" according to different type of the owner. According to Rabin's assumptions of "to return a favor with a favor", negative emotion emerges, which leads to the effect of the entrepreneur decreases(counted as C_n). At the same time, the conscientious entrepreneur would give up some investment programs or good chance for the owner, which leads to profit loss of the owner (counted as S_b). On the contrary, if conscientious entrepreneur is provided kind rewards by excusatory the owner, he would not only appreciate the kindness of the owner, but also feel ashamed or for being not loyal, which leads to negative effect(counted as C_b), and meanwhile, the entrepreneur makes amend for his fault by good deeds, to stop some detrimental behavior, which makes profit increase(counted as S_d).

3 Game Analysis

According to 6 Hypotheses, we construct a two-step game between the owner and the entrepreneur, the sequences of the game is as follows.

Firstly, "Nature" chooses the type of the owner, we use $\theta_p \in \Theta(\Theta=\{\theta_r, \ \theta_t\})$ to represent space of the owner's type, in which θ_r represents relational, θ_t represents transactional. The owner knows well his own type, but the entrepreneur only knows the transcendental possibility $P(\theta)$, in other words, the entrepreneur knows that the possibility of the type of the owner is relational, $P(\theta_t)$ is equal to μ, that is $P(\theta = \theta_t) = \mu$, and the possibility of the type of the owner is transactional, $P(\theta_r)$ is equal to $1 - \mu$, that is $P(\theta = \theta_r) = 1 - \mu$.

Secondly, after the choice of the "Nature", the owner begins to decide to provide S_m or S_k to the entrepreneur. It is worthy to note that as the owner has predicted that his behavior would be used by the entrepreneur, therefore he has the motion to behave under the guise of transiting favorable information, in other words, it is possible for the owner who is transactional provide S_k not S_m to cover his real type.

Lastly, the entrepreneur revises the transcendental possibility $P(\theta)$ after he watched the owner's behavior, and then chooses optimum behavior from A_a. If he judges that the owner is transactional psychological contract, he would choose to be conscientious about his work, or he would choose to be loyal.

3.1 The Process of the Game

There are two steps of the game, in the first step(t=1), the owner promises to entrepreneur, he would be provided with attractive rewards on condition that he makes effort to work, which comes to be one item of the psychological contract of the entrepreneur. The entrepreneur knows his own type well, but doesn't know whether the owner is transactional or relational, he thinks the transcendental possibility that the owner is transactional one is μ, and the transcendental possibility that the owner is relational is $1-\mu$.

Assume that the owner transits the information about his type by prepaying to the entrepreneur. If the real type of the owner is transactional, the corresponding payment to the two rewards mode are $-S_m$ and $-S_k - C_0$; and if the real type of the owner is relational, the corresponding payment to the two rewards mode are $-S_m - C_0$ and $-S_k$, here C_0 can be understood as disguise cost, the corresponding payment of the entrepreneur in step one is S_m and S_k according to the rewards gained from the owner.

If $C_0 > C_s$, then $-S_m > -S_k - C_0$, that is, the optimum reward the transactional owner would choose to pay, in the first step, to the entrepreneur is $S = S_m$, while the optimum reward the relational owner would choose to pay to the entrepreneur is $S = S_k$; and if $C_0 < C_s$, the optimum rewards the owner pay to the entrepreneur is S_m, no matter what the type of the owner.

In the second step (t=2): if the entrepreneur chooses to be loyal, the payment of the two sides is $(\pi + S_a, \ S_m - C_e)$ when the owner is transactional one; the payment of the two sides is $(\pi + S_a, \ S_k - C_e)$ when the owner is relational one. If the entrepreneur chooses to be conscientious, the payment of the two sides is $(\pi - S_b, \ S_m - C_n)$ when the owner is transactional one; the payment of the two sides is $(\pi - S_b + S_a, \ S_k - C_b)$ when the owner is relational one.

It can be testified, on the condition of complete information, the entrepreneur would choose to be conscientious if the owner is transactional, and while the entrepreneur would choose to be loyal if the owner is relational. The extended statement of this game is as the following Figure.

3.2 Analysis and Discussion

According to the descriptions above, we make discussion that under what condition that the entrepreneur choose to be loyal to the owner, the relational owner or the transactional owner to be pretend and under what condition that both sides has the motion to expose their real type.

(1) The condition the entrepreneur choose to be loyal to the owner

The payment of the entrepreneur who chooses to be loyal to the owner is $S_m - C_e$ given that the owner is transactional according to figure 1; while payment of the entrepreneur is $S_k - C_e$ given the owner is relational. On the other side, the payment of the conscientious entrepreneur are $S_m - C_n$ and $S_k - C_b$ respectively. If

$$\mu\left(S_m - c_e\right) + \left(1-\mu\right)\left(S_k - c_e\right) \geq \mu\left(S_m - c_n\right) + \left(1-\mu\right)\left(S_k - c_b\right) \tag{1}$$

That is $\mu \leq \dfrac{c_b - c_e}{c_b - c_n}$ ($C_e \geq C_n$), the entrepreneur would choose to be loyal, or he would choose to be conscientious.

(2) The condition the relational entrepreneur has the motion to pretend to be transactional.

As the hypothesis, the entrepreneur knows that the owner is transactional ($\tilde{p}\left(\theta_t \middle| s_m\right)=1$) if $S = S_m$, and he knows the owner is relational ($\tilde{p}\left(\theta_t \middle| s_k\right)=0$) if $S = S_k$. Given this posteriori, it is easy to know, the entrepreneur would choose to be conscientious, not loyal, iff $S = S_m$, because the payment he choose conscientious is smaller than that he choose to be loyal, that is $S_m - C_e < S_k - C_n$ ($C_n \leq C_e$).

For transactional owner, if he chooses to provide S_m, his payment of the first stage is $-S_m$, the payment of the second stage is $\pi - S_b$, total payment is $\pi - S_m - S_b$. While, if he pretends to be relational to pay S_k, his payment of the first stage is $-S_k - C_0$, the payment of the second stage is $\pi + S_a$, total payment is $\pi - S_k + S_a - C_0$.

So, if the payment of pretending is larger than that he behaves honestly; the transactional owner has the motion to pretend to be relational. That is

$$\pi - S_k + S_a - C_0 > \pi - S_m - S_b$$
$$\Rightarrow S_a + S_b > C_0 + C_s \tag{2}$$

(3) The condition the transactional entrepreneur has the motion to pretend to be relational

For relational owner, if he choose to provide S_k, his payment of the first stage is $-S_k$, the payment of the second stage is $\pi + S_a$, total payment is $\pi + S_a - S_k$. while, if he pretends to be transactional to pay $-S_m$, his his payment of the first stage is $-S_m - C_0$, the payment of the second stage is $\pi - S_b + S_a$, total payment is $\pi + S_a - S_b - S_m - C_0$. If

$$\pi + S_a - S_b - S_m - C_0 > \pi + S_a - S_k$$
$$\Rightarrow S_d + C_s - C_0 > S_a + S_b \tag{3}$$

That is, when the data (equal to the loss retained because the conscientious entrepreneur stop unfavour behavior to the owner as he was provided kind rewards, adds support cost, and detract guise cost) is larger than performance added because of the loyalty of the entrepreneur to the owner, relational own we has the motion to pretend to be transactional.

(4) The condition both sides has the motion to expose their real type

From the analysis above (if $C_0 + C_s > S_a + S_b$, transactional owner doesn't pretend, and if $S_a + S_b > S_d + C_s - C_0$, relational owner doesn't pretend), it is easy to find that when guise cost is larger than half of the conscientious entrepreneur stop unflavored behavior as he was provided kind rewards, that is $C_0 > \dfrac{S_d}{2}$, both sides has the motion to expose their real type.

3.3 Equilibrium of the Game

Then, to discuss the equilibrium of the game when $\mu \le \dfrac{C_b - C_e}{C_b - C_n}$ and $\mu > \dfrac{C_b - C_e}{C_b - C_n}$

(1)As $\mu \le \dfrac{C_b - C_e}{C_b - C_n}$, when $S_a + S_b < C_0 + C_s$ and $S_a + S_b + C_0 > S_d + C_s$, that is $S_d + C_s - C_0 < S_a + S_b < C_0 + C_s$, it can be proved that there exists the only perfect Bayesian equilibrium (Separate Equilibrium) : $\theta_t \to S = S_m$, $\theta_r \to S = S_k$, $\tilde{p}(\theta_t \mid S = S_k) = 1$, $\tilde{p}(\theta_t \mid S = S_m) = 0$. It means that transactional owner would choose to provide material reward to the entrepreneur ($S = S_m$), and relational owner would choose to provide kind reward to the entrepreneur ($S = S_k$), if watch $S = S_k$, the entrepreneur would choose to be loyal ($\tilde{p}(\theta_t \mid S = S_m) = 0$), but if watch $S = S_m$, he would be conscientious (because $\tilde{p}(\theta_t \mid S = S_k) = 1$). here, Space lacks for a detailed description of it.

(2) As $\mu > \dfrac{C_b - C_e}{C_b - C_n}$, when satisfy $S_a + S_b < C_0 + C_s$ and $S_a + S_b < S_d + C_s - C_0$, it can be proved that there exists the only perfect Bayesian equilibrium : $\theta_t \to S = S_m$, $\theta_r \to S = S_m$, $\tilde{p}(\theta_t \mid S = S_k) = 1$ .which means that both relational and transactional owner would choose to pay material reward ($S = S_m$) to the entrepreneur, if watch $S = S_k$, the entrepreneur would choose to be loyal(based on $\tilde{p}(\theta_t \mid S = S_k) = 1$). Here, the process of the proof is omitted too.

4 Conclusion and Suggestion

The game analysis of this paper proves that the owner is possible to reveal his real type when disguise cost is larger than half of the regained loss as conscientious entrepreneur come to his senses. The behavior of the owner is decided by many factors such as the added profit S_a from loyalty entrepreneur, profit loss S_b as the entrepreneur choose to be conscientious, regained profit S_d as the entrepreneur stop sabotage, disguise cost C_0 of the owner, etc.. On the other hand, the behavior of the entrepreneur depends on the priori probability of the rewards that the owner would pay to him, the priori probability is related with effort cost C_e, violation cost C_n and excusatory cost of the entrepreneur. Given that $\mu \leq \dfrac{C_b - C_e}{C_b - C_n}$ ($C_e \geq C_n$), the entrepreneur chooses to be loyal, or he would be conscientious.

The findings above provide some suggestions for the owner to build more healthy relations with the entrepreneur. Relational payoffs to the entrepreneurs from the owner would get loyalty of the entrepreneurs in return, or the entrepreneur would only choose only conscientious to the owner. The organization tends to make transactional psychological contract with temporary or common employees in the ordinary course of things, and make relational contract with core employees. But if the organization changes to make relational contract with all its members regardless of their status, the organization would acquire more rewards because of the loyal behavior of its members.

Acknowledgements. Support under the following programmes: Humane Social Science Fund Project of Chinese Ministry of Education (NO:10YJA790099); Henan Province Science Project(082102360031); the Henan department of education Science Foundation (Grant No.2009-JD-014; 2008A630001; 2009B63002 ; 2011A630001); Sponsored by (2008HASTIT021).

References

1. Schein, E.H.: Organizational Psychology. Prentice-Hall, Englewood Cliffs (1980)
2. Rousseau, D.M.: Psychological and Implied Contracts in Organizations. Employee Rights and Responsibilities Journal 2, 121–139 (1989)
3. Robinson, S.L., Kraatz, M.S., Rousseau, D.M.: Changing Obligations and the Psychological Contract: A Longitudinal Study. Academy of Management Journal 37(1), 137–152 (1994)
4. Turnley, W.H., Feldman, D.C.: Psychological Contract Violations During Corporate Restructuring. Human Resource Management 37, 71–83 (1998)
5. Chen, J.-z., Fang, l.-l., et al.: Value intervention in Counseling. Journal of Developments in Psychology 3 (2001)
6. Tang, Y.: Managerial Level, Attitude and Psychological Contract: An Empirical Study in China's Context. Nankai Business Review 6, 73–78 (2004)
7. Monge, P., Contractor, N.: Theories of Communication networks. Oxford University Press, New York (2003)

The Diffusion of the Activity-Based Costing Method: A Comparison between France and China

Gregory Wegmann

Department of Business Administration, LEG-FARGO, UMR CNRS 5118
University of Burgundy
France
Gregory.Wegmann@u-bourgogne.fr

Abstract. In France, like in the USA, the Activity-based Costing method (ABC) was considered as a remedy for the crisis of management accounting. Now, the level of diffusion in France is as important as in the Anglo-Saxon countries. Not surprisingly, the ABC method is more developed in western countries than in China. Chinese scholars began to do researches on ABC in the 1990s and at the beginnings of the 21st century, we can observe some ABC implementations in Chinese manufacturing enterprises and then in the service industries. But, we can also find a similarity between the Chinese and French situations. In France, we have observed some resistances to the Anglo-Saxon way of manage firms and at the beginnings, a tool like ABC has been strongly criticised.

Keywords: Management accounting, Activity-based Costing method, Chinese-French comparison.

1   The ABC Method in Western Countries

1.1   Introduction about the ABC Method in Western Countries

Traditional management accounting practices have been under attack for their failure to provide detailed and timely information (Kaplan, 1984; Cooper & Kaplan, 1991; Gosselin, 1997). Since the work of Johnson and Kaplan (1987) on the "Relevance Lost" of management accounting practices, the Anglo-Saxon scholars have been very dynamic about the study of the diffusion of cost and management accounting innovations (Chenhall & Langfield-Smith, 1998; Anderson & Young, 1999; Cooper & Kaplan, 1991; Johnson, 1992; Gosselin, 1997).

The ABC method was designed in the United-States during the 80's (Cooper and Kaplan, 1988)[1]. It is a refined cost system which enables classifying more costs as direct, to expend the number of indirect-cost pools and to identify cost drivers. ABC favours better costs allocations using smaller cost pools called activities. Using cost drivers, the costs of these activities are the basis for assigning costs to other cost objects such as products or services. With the historical research of Johnson and Kaplan, we

---

[1] General Electric experimented with a kind of ABC during the 60's.

Q. Zhou (Ed.): ISAEBD 2011, Part I, CCIS 208, pp. 545–553, 2011.
© Springer-Verlag Berlin Heidelberg 2011

understand the context from which ABC arose. Looking for management accounting methods which could clarify the decision making process, Johnson and Kaplan suggest: First, to analyse more deeply the organization activities and processes and second, to link together the strategic management and the operational one. The ABC method was conceived at first to correct misleading overhead allocations. It was a response to the inaccurate standard costing American methods. But several scholars, like Lebas (1999) in France, explain that rapidly, the ABC method has gained managerial (ABM) and strategic dimensions (Jones and Dugdale, 2002).

1.2 The Impact of Cultural Differences on Management Accounting Principles and Techniques

An important fact is that the Management Control theory is built on a North-American reference grounded on strong hypotheses about the representation of the firm. It fits more with contractual and disciplinary approaches of the firm (Agency and Transaction Costs theories) where the objectives of the management control activities are to reduce conflicts and provide control, to tie the strategy to the resources allocation and to facilitate the firm's internal coherence (Jensen and Meckling, 1992; Brickley et al. (1997)).

The situation is clearly different in countries like France, Germany or Northern countries of Europe where the cultural features are specific. For instance, French and German managers see the checking behind control, while the Anglo-Saxons see steering there. In the French tradition, management accounting is mainly used to identify the costs of a product, an activity or a process whereas in the North American approach, management accounting is used in a cybernetic process, by which the standards are compared with the real data and the deviations are identified and decomposed. Firms from Northern countries of Europe are more sensitive to knowledge-based approach of management (Argyris and Schön (1978) : Organizational Learning Theory) where the participative approaches are favoured. How to allocate the indirect costs was the major problem for French and German management accounting pioneers. This problem led them to build an accounting technique very similar to the ABC method (method of the homogeneous sections).

1.3 The Diffusion of ABC in the Western Countries

ABC was initially popularized in the USA in the mid-1980s (Jones and Dugdale, 2002). It was then diffused gradually in many other western countries throughout the 1990s (Bjornenak, 1997; Malmi, 1999). We can say that today, it is a widely developed method in these countries. But differences in the diffusion were strong. U.K., Australian and Scandinavian firms followed the ABC adoption in U.S. in its early days without too much gap in the implementation time frame. It was not the same situation in France.

The major problems associated with the introduction of ABC system have been enumerated as follow (Green and Amenkhienan, 1992): the increased amount of detailed information needed the increased paperwork, the difficulty in cost driver identification, and the insufficient support by top management.

2   ABC Implementation in France

2.1   The Beginnings

Until 1999, France had a highly detailed legislation covering how firms should managerially account for their transactions. Today, the situation is quite similar as in the other European countries.

The first series of French inscriptions on ABC date back to the late 1980s (Lorino, 1989 and 1991; Mevellec, 1991; Lebas, 1991). In France, like in the USA, ABC was therefore problematized as a remedy for the crisis of management accounting. From 1991 to 1996, French scholars dedicated large amounts of their writings to the method's costing aspects, among which the general architecture of the system and the translation/adaptation of specific concepts, such as "cost driver", required to operate it. Thirty-five articles on ABC were published over this period. Bescos and Mendoza (1994) published the first book relating several ABC implementations in French companies. Other publications followed.

2.2   Criticisms and Evolutions

A few months after its importation by a network of pioneers, ABC faced a major controversy. It concerned its innovative character in comparison with an older French method: the *"Sections Homogènes" (the homogenous sections)*. When implemented and used "correctly", ABC and the *"Sections Homogènes"* gave similar results in terms of cost calculation.

ABC has been in a second time a mode of modelling the functioning of organizations: According to Mevellec (1995, p. 38), "Such an approach is a lot more ambitious than a simple cost calculation technique…" One of the first French books about ABC (Lorino, 1991) suggests using ABC as a way to link strategy to operational management; and Chauvey and Naro (2004) described the strategic potential of ABC.

2.3   ABC in France: The Facts about Its Diffusion

We find several studies dedicated to ABC diffusion in France: De La Villarmois and Tondeur (1996), Bescos et al. (2002), Alcouffe (2004), Godowski (2004) and Rahmouni (2008). Bescos et al. (2002) found a rate of adoption of 23%, Alcouffe (2004) a rate of 16% whereas Bescos et al. (2002) found an equivalent level of adoption between Canada (22.6%) and France (23%) (7% in Japan). French managers express a good opinion on the ABC method, thanks to professional journals. But they frequently hesitate to entirely adopt the method. They prefer limited experiments. Alcouffe (2004) used the « innovations diffusion theory » (Roger, 1983, 1995) to the subject of ABC diffusion. Godowski (2004) studied the ABC diffusion in the French banking system. But a more recent inquiry (Rahmouni, 2008), finds a higher rate of adoption: 33.8% implemented and 18.2% in progress.

Table 1. Compared level of diffusion of ABC in France (Rahmouni, 2008, p. 217)

ABC system	Rahmouni (2008)	Bescos et al. (2002)
In progress	33.3 %	23 %
In project	18.2 %	23 %
Not retained	48.5 %	54 %
Total	100 % (66 French firms)	100 % (122 French firms)

Now, the level of diffusion in France seems as important as in Anglo-Saxon countries. It could be even more important than for instance in Ireland and New Zealand (p. 226). More precisely, the inquiry of Rahmouni (p. 227) reports that 30.2% of the firms of services use ABC, whereas this is the case for 39.1% of the industrial firms. Concerning the firms of services, 22.8% of them delivering services to firms or customers are using ABC, whereas it is the case for 62.5% of the banks and insurances. About the firms that have the project to implement ABC, 23.2% of them are delivering services whereas only 8.7% are industrial ones; which means that the future of the ABC method in France concerns more especially the activities of services. Maybe it could be explained by the high level of competition in those sectors in such a country like France. In most of the cases (82%), the ABC method covers all the processes of the firms. The first objective of the method is to calculate the commercial costs and the customers' profitabilities, than the administrative (73%), research and development (64%) and information systems costs (59%).

Now, we present the Chinese situation.

3   ABC Implementation in China

3.1   Introduction

The popularity of ABC in the West and its widespread coverage in the Chinese management accounting textbooks has made it an attractive costing method for academics and practitioners in China. Since the understanding of success and / or failure of ABC implementation has primarily been generated through empirical research in developed countries, it is rare to learn whether ABC technics can be implemented successfully in organizations in countries such as China.

Chinese scholars began to do researches on ABC in 1990s, and made some achievements (Pan and Zhou, 2002). After introducing the concepts (cost objects, activities, cost drivers, ...), they began to examine the implementation and some detailed calculations, first in Chinese manufacturing enterprises, second in service industries (Ou and Wang, 2000; Wang et al, 2000; Lin and Liu, 2001; Pan et al, 2003; Zhang et al, 2006; Yong & Liu, 2009; Yang and Chen, 2009). With more experiences of ABC in China, some researchers began to make investigations and try to discover the influence of industrial factors and enterprises scale on the implementation (Zhu and Chen, 2000; Hu, 2001; Pan et al, 2004). The results of these investigations show that in Hong Kong, it was not very long since many companies have begun to get in touch with ABC. They also put in evidence that the scale of the companies of these applied ABC was much larger than the others, and that the main motivation for using ABC was to get more accurate cost information. In mainland China, ABC has been hardly implemented, but some Activity-based Management (ABM) ideas have been used in some experiences.

3.2 ABC Diffusion in Mainland of China

We describe here the situation of ABC in China for the past ten years from three aspects: the rate of adoption, the sectors of diffusion, and the main factors explaining the diffusion of ABC.

Hu (2001) collects 531 reports on firms' advanced management accounting experiences. His reports concern at least 27 provinces/cities and dozens of industries. Eliminating reports on regional industries and non-profit organizations, he keeps 397 valid ones. Using them, he does statistical analyses on cost management and ABC/ABM methods. Among these 397 reports, there are 189 firms that use all kinds of cost management methods. The cost management methods he examines include ABC, Target Costing, Life Cycle Costing, PDCA (Plan, Do, Check and Action) method, and Quality Cost Management.

Table 2 shows Hu's statistics results.

Table 2. Statistics about the adoption of cost management methods in China

	ABC	Target Costing	Life Cycle Costing	PDCA	Quality Cost Management	Others	Total
Firms distribution	6	161	2	2	10	8	189
Percentage	3.17%	85.19%	1.06%	1.06%	5.29%	4.23%	100%

The ABC rate of adoption is very low. According to Hu (2001), ABC and similar experiences are mostly experimental, for instance for one department, product design, or for quality management. ABC similar experiences usually exist with Target Costing. Frequently, we observe a kind of activities analysis when a firm use this Japanese approach. The ideas developed with ABM can also be seen in some management experiences. To explain this situation, we can argue that the production and operational environments in China are not yet enough matured so that ABC could be widened developed. Before using ABC, the firms judge whether the method can bring them benefits and help them to analyze and solve problems. Even if ABC not only applies for high-tech manufacturing firms, the level of processes complexity has to be enough so that such a refined and time consuming technic could be relevant. The ABC diffusion, like in France, seems to need time and we have to carefully observe the further evolutions.

The implementation of ABC is concentrated on manufacturing industries, especially advanced or high-tech industrial companies. But Wang et al. (1999) find that ABC is not only suitable for high-tech manufacturing firms, but also for some non-high-tech ones, such as Xi'an Agricultural Machine Factory, in which the volume differences between products were large and the ratio of manufacturing overheads versus direct costs is high. They also argue that there are successful ABC applications in some foreign non-manufacturing industries, such as finance/insurance, sales and health industries. More recently, some researchers argue that ABC could be implemented in many other areas, such as colleges and universities (Gan and Tao, 2007), restaurants (Li and Shao, 2007), commercial banks (Chen, 2009; Deng and Wei, 2010) and coal mining industries (Li and Wang, 2010).

According to Su et al. (2007), the size of the company, the management system, the competitive pressure and the cost structure, have significant influences on the diffusion of ABC ideas in Chinese companies; but the field sector and the company's strategy seem to have no influence. More precisely, the scales of the company, the degree of centralization of its management and the percentage of overheads in the total costs, have a positive correlation with the probability that this company tends to adopt and apply ABC. Meanwhile, a company in a strongly competitive market is less likely to adopt ABC than a company in a low intensity competitive market. Moreover, Pan et al. (2004) find that employees tend to lower their evaluation of ABC if their performance is to be connected with this method. They also find that the quality of the ABC software would have a great influence on the application of the method.

Finally, Zhu and Chen (2000) explain that the most significant motivation to implement ABC is to acquire more precise cost information and data, and that the biggest difficulty lies in the information collect. They add that the main reasons of not applying ABC are the lack of training staff and the satisfactory with current systems.

A well described experience of ABC implementation takes place in Xu Ji Electric Co. Ltd (Liu and Pan, 2007). The ABC project was initiated in 2001 mainly because overheads produced inaccurate product costing and divisional profitability information, and impeded Xu Ji's ability to compete pricing. The first ABC report was produced in June 2003. Despite some unresolved issues, the experience permits to reduce the total expenditures, to increase the sale revenues, to cut the labor costs and to enhance the productivity.

4 Discussion and Conclusion

Not surprisingly, the ABC method is at this time more developed in western countries than in China. Even if some internal and external factors explain for a part the low level of ABC adoption in China, the "cultural" dimension could be a major determinant. On that point, we can find a similarity between the Chinese and French situations. In France, we have observed some resistances to the Anglo-Saxon way of manage firms and at the beginnings, a tool like ABC has been strongly criticised. But today, the globalization phenomenon has impacted the French firms, which could explain the increase of the level of adoption of such a technic as ABC. Maybe China will experience the same evolution as France in a next future.

For a further research, we would like to study a Chinese-French joint venture where the ABC method has been settled. We could also extend our compared analysis to other management accounting tools like the Balanced Scorecard.

References

1. Alcouffe, S.: Diffusion and adoption of management innovations in Accounting and Management Accounting: the case of the ABC in France, Ph.D. dissertation, HEC (High School of Management), France (2004)
2. Anderson, S.W., Young, S.M.: The Impact of Contextual and Process Factors on the Evaluation of Activity-Based Costing Systems. Accounting Organization and Society 24(7), 525–559 (1999)
3. Argyris, C., Schön, D.A.: Organizational Learning. Addison-Wesley Publishing Company, Readings (1978)
4. Bescos, P.L., Mendoza, C.: The Performance Management (translated), Editions Comptables Malhesherbes, Paris (1994)
5. Bescos, P.-L., Cauvin, E., Gosselin, M., Yoshikawa, T.: Activity-based Costing and Activity-based Management: A comparison between Canada and France (translated), Comptabilité – Contrôle – Audit, pp. 209–228, 229–244 (May 2002)
6. Bjørnenak, T.: Diffusion and accounting: the case of ABC in Norway. Management Accounting Research 8(1), 3–17 (1997)
7. Brickley, J.A., et al.: Managerial Economics and Organizational Architecture. McGraw Hill, New York (1997)
8. Chauvey, J.-N., Naro, G.: Contributions of the ABC method to the strategic analysis: Learnings from a research-action study (translated). Finance Contrôle Stratégie (Finance Control Strategy) 7(3), 63–89 (2004)
9. Chen, T.: Activity-based Costing Implementation Study in Commercial Banks (translated). Journal of Anhui Vocational College of Electronics & Information Technology (2009)
10. Chenhall, R.H., Langfield-Smith, K.: The relationship between strategic priorities, management techniques and management accounting: An empirical investigation using a systems approach. Accounting, Organizations and Society 23(3), 243–264 (1998)
11. Cooper, R., Kaplan, R.S.: Measure Costs Right: Make the Right Decisions. Harvard Business Review 66(5), 96–103 (1988)
12. Cooper, R., Kaplan, R.S.: The Design of Cost Management Systems: Text, Cases and Readings. Prentice-Hall, New York (1991)
13. De La Villarmois, O., Tondeur, H.: ABC in France. The determinants of the implementation (translated). In: 17th Congress of the French Association of Accounting (May 1996)
14. Deng, Wei: Activity-based Costing Implementation in Commercial Banks (translated). Corporative Economy, Science and Teconology (China) 1 (2010)
15. Gan, Tao: Discussion on Activity-based Costing in Colleges and Universities Cost Computation (translated). Vocational Education and Economic Research (China) 5(2), 26–29 (2007)
16. Godowski, C.: The assimilation process of the ABC approaches in the Banking system (translated). Comptabilité - Contrôle – Audit (Accounting Control Audit) 10(2), 179–196 (2004)
17. Gosselin, M.: The effect of strategy and organizational structure on the adoption and implementation of activity-based costing. Accounting, Organizations and Society 22(2), 105–122 (1997)
18. Green, F.B., Amenkhienan, F.E.: Accounting Innovations: A Cross-Sectional Survey of Manufacturing Firms. Journal of Cost Management for the Manufacturing Industry, 58–64 (Spring 1992)
19. Hu, Y.M.: The spontaneous formation and development of ABC, ABM in Chinese organisations (translated). Accounting Research (China) 3, 33–38 (2001)

20. Jensen, M.C., Meckling, W.H.: Specific and General Knowledge, and Organizational Structure. In: Werin, L., Wijkander, H. (dir.) (eds.) Contract Economics. Blackwell, Malden (1992)
21. Johnson, H.T., Kaplan, R.S.: Relevance Lost: The Rise and Fall of Management Accounting. Harvard Business School Press, Boston (1987)
22. Johnson, H.T.: Relevance Regained: From Top-Down Control to Bottom-up Empowerment. The Free Press, New York (1992)
23. Jones, C., Dugdale, D.: The ABC bandwagon and the juggernaut of modernity. Accounting Organizations and Society 27, 121–163 (2002)
24. Kaplan, R.S.: The evolution of management accounting. The Accounting Review, 390–418 (1984)
25. Lebas, M.: Management accounting based on activities, analysis and management of activities (translated). Revue Française de Comptabilité (French Review of Accounting) 226, 47–63 (1991)
26. Lebas, M.: Why ABC? Accounting Based on Causality Rather than Activity-Based Costing. European Management Journal 17(5), 501–511 (1999)
27. Li, C.Z., Wang, H.Y.: Activity-based Costing Implementation in Coal Mining Enterprises (translated). Business Economics (China) 1, 92–93 (2010)
28. Li, J., Shao, X.Z.: Activity-based Costing and its Implementation in Restaurant Management (translated). Journal of Zhejiang International Maritime College 3(4), 36–39 (2007)
29. Lin, B., Liu, Y.G.: Case Study of Activity-based Costing Implementation in Chinese Railway Transportation Enterprises (translated). Accounting Research (China) 2 (2001)
30. Lana, Y.J.L., Pan, F.: The implementation of activity-based costing in China: an innovation action research approach. The British Accounting Review 39(3), 249–264 (2007)
31. Lorino, P.: Strategic Cost Management (translated), Dunod, Paris (1991)
32. Lorino, P.: The economist and the manager (translated), La Decouverte, Paris (1989)
33. Malmi, T.: Activity-based costing diffusion across organizations: an exploratory empirical analysis of Finnish firms. Accounting, Organizations and Society 24, 649–672 (1999)
34. Mevellec, P.: Management tools: The relevance regained (translated), Editions Comptables Malesherbes, Paris (1991)
35. Mevellec, P.: Activity based costing: A double meaning question. Comptabilité – Contrôle – Audit (Accounting Control Audit) 1, 62–80 (1995)
36. Ou, P.Y., Wang, X.P.: Activity-based Costing Method and the Implementation in Chinese Advanced Manufacturing Enterprises (translated). Accounting Research (China) 2 (2000)
37. Pan, F., Zhou, W.L.: Activity-based Costing in China: Yesterday, Today and Tomorrow (translated). Shanghai Accounting 8, 3–5 (2002)
38. Pan, F., Tong, W.H., Yang, H.H.: Study on Activity-based Costing Design in Manufacturing Departments (translated). Shanghai Accounting 5, 8–11 (2003)
39. Pan, F., Tong, W.H., Yang, H.H.: The Application Study on Activity-based Costing in Non-manufacturing Departments (I) & (II) (translated). Shanghai Accounting 9&10, 6-8, 6-9 (2003)
40. Pan, F., Tong, W.H., Yang, H.H.: The perception of Chinese enterprises on ABC (translated). Journal of Shanghai University of Finance and Economics 1 (2004)
41. Rahmouni, A.: The settling of the ABC method in the French firms: features and adoption and success variables (translated), Ph.D. dissertation, University of Nice, France (September 2008)
42. Su, W.B., et al.: Which Factors Affect the Adoption and Application of ABC in China? An Empirical Research (translated). Nanjing University Business Review 15, 116–130 (2007)

43. Wang, P.X., Han, X.M., Lei, Q.L.: The applicability of activity-based costing and activity-based management in China (translated). Accounting Research (China) 8 (1999)
44. Wang, P.X., Han, X.M., Lei, Q.L.: Discussion on Activity-based Costing Implementation in Chinese Enterprises (translated). Chinese Accounting & Finance Research 2 (2000)
45. Yang, W.P., Chen, W.W.: The Application Study on Activity-based Costing Calculation and Design, and Case Analysis in Chinese Insurance Companies (translated). Economic Research Guide (China) 7, 86–88 (2009)
46. Yong, S.Y., Liu, Y.G.: The Application Study on Activity-based Costing in Telecommunication Enterprises: Based on a Case Study on a Branch Office of China Rail Communications Corporation (translated). Communication of Finance and Accounting (China) 5, 24–26 (2009)
47. Zhang, R., et al.: The Application Study on Activity-based Costing in Cigarette Manufacturing Industry (translated). Accounting Research (China) 6, 59–65 (2006)
48. Zhu, Y., Chen, G.M.: Survey and Analysis of ABC Application in Hong Kong (translated). Accounting Research (China) 8, 60–65 (2000)

A Comparative Analysis of Credit Risk Management Models for Banking Industry Using Simulation

Hsin-Hung Chen[1], Ben-Chang Shia[2], and Hsiu-Yu Lee[1]

[1] Department of Business Administration, Cheng Shiu University
No.840, Chengcing Rd., Niaosong Dist., Kaohsiung City 83347, Taiwan
mchen@csu.edu.tw, shirley3801329@yahoo.com.tw
[2] Department of Statistics and Information Science, Fu Jen Catholic University
025674@mail.fju.edu.tw

Abstract. Risk management is an issue that has become increasingly important. Basel II Accord has been widely discussed since it was proposed. However, the comparative analysis of CreditMetrics with Basel II Accord has not been found in previous literatures. The objective of this study is to compare CreditMetrics with Basel II Accord using empirical data and simulation programs. Moreover, the fitness of the standard for Basel II Accord which proposed the minimum requirement of 8% of capital to risk-weighted assets is discussed in this study. The records of the data system in a bank listed by the Taiwan Stock Exchange Corporation (TSEC) were used as the empirical data in this research. The results showed that the expected loss calculated by the 8% capital ratio defined in Basel II is clearly lower than the Credit VaR obtained from the CreditMetrics model.

Keywords: Basel II Accord, CreditMetrics, credit risk, Value-at-Risk (VaR).

1 Introduction

Risk management is an issue that has become increasingly important. Financial institutions compete aggressively for more market shares and customers, and consequently, they take on more risks [1]. Therefore, the implementation of risk management within financial institutions is crucial. The risk management attempts to reduce and manage the risks, increase the benefits, and avoid harm from taking risks due to default of loan accounts [2]. In the financial sector and banking industry, risk management is an issue of high interest due to the financial crises of the last two decades [3]. These crises occurred for various reasons but according to the Basle Committee, which is the international banking supervisory body, the largest source of serious banking problems is credit risk which caused by counterparty default. Serious financial scandals and crises such as the Russian Default and the Tequila crisis are related to credit risk [1]. Scandals of that type in the 1990s are estimated to have cost at least $125 billion within the United States. Another indicator of the crucial importance of credit risk is the fact that in recent years there has been a steady increase of defaults and bankruptcies and a decline in the creditworthiness of financial institutions' counterparties [4] and [5]. In 2008, the events of sub-prime mortgage and global

Q. Zhou (Ed.): ISAEBD 2011, Part I, CCIS 208, pp. 554–562, 2011.
© Springer-Verlag Berlin Heidelberg 2011

financial distress occurred. These reasons provided the motivation for the present authors to explore the issue of credit risk in this study.

In order to improve credit risk management and financial stability for banking industry, the Bank for International Settlements (BIS) [6], an international organization that fosters cooperation toward monetary and financial stability, proposed the 1988 Basel Capital Accord (Basel I) and the New Basel Capital Accord in 2001 (Basel II). The major difference between the two capital accords is that Basel II provides more flexibility and risk sensitivity in credit risk management than Basel I. Basel II consists of three mutually reinforcing pillars: Pillar 1 — minimum capital requirements, Pillar 2 — supervisory review process, and Pillar 3 — market discipline [7].

Besides Basel I and Basel II proposed by BIS, J.P. Morgan published CreditMetrics to evaluate credit risk of loan portfolios in 1997. CreditMetrics' approach is based on credit migration analysis, i.e. the probability of moving from one credit quality to another, including default, within a given time horizon, which is often taken arbitrarily as 1 year. While interest rates are assumed to evolve in a deterministic fashion, the changes in value are related to the eventual migrations in credit quality of the loan account or obligor upgrades and downgrades as well as default [8].

Basel II Accord has been widely discussed since it was proposed. For example, Lamy [9] discussed the treatment of credit risk in the new Basel Accord and the results revealed that the new Basel Accord should encourage A-rated banks to act as liquidity providers in economic slowdown phases. The issue of credit risk also has been investigated frequently [10], [11] and[12]. However, CreditMetrics' approach was rarely discussed by empirical analysis. The study of Crouhy et al. [8] has introduced and reviewed the CreditMetrics approach as well as other credit risk measurement models, but there was no empirical analysis in that article. Moreover, the comparative analysis of CreditMetrics with Basel II Accord has not been found in previous literature. Therefore, the objective of this study is to compare CreditMetrics with Basel II Accord using empirical data. And the fitness of the standard for Basel II Accord which proposed the minimum requirement of 8% of capital to risk-weighted assets is discussed in this study. The records of the data system in a bank listed by the Taiwan Stock Exchange Corporation (TSEC) are used as the empirical data in this research.

The remainder of this paper is organized as follows. Section 2 introduces the Basel II proposed by BIS. Section 3 reviews the CreditMetrics approach proposed by JP Morgan. Section 4 presents the results of empirical analysis including the object of analysis. Section 5 discusses the managerial implications of the analytical results, and the last section provides conclusions and suggestions.

2   The New Basel Capital Accord (BASEL II)

According to Saunders and Allen [13], the 1988 Basel International Bank Capital Accord (Basel I) was essential because it sought to develop a single capital requirement for credit risk across the major banking countries of the world. A major focus of Basel I was to differentiate the credit risk of bank, and mortgage obligations (accorded lower risk weights) from nonblank private sector or commercial loan obligations (accorded the highest risk weight). All commercial loans implicitly required an 8 percent total capital requirement, regardless of the innate creditworthiness of the borrower, its external credit rating, the collateral offered, or the covenants extended. As a result, there was little or no attempt to discriminate the credit risk exposure within the commercial loan classification. Since the capital requirement was set too low for high-risk/low-quality business loans and too high for low-risk/high-quality loans, the incorrect estimation of commercial lending risk created an inducement for banks to shift portfolios toward loans that were more underpriced from a regulatory risk capital perspective. An example is banks tended to retain the most credit risky tranches of securitized loan portfolios [14]. Therefore, the Basel I had the disadvantage which lead to encourage a long-term deterioration in the overall credit quality of bank portfolios. The proposed objective of the new Basel Capital Accord of 2001 (Basel II) is to correct the inaccurate estimation of credit risk inherent in Basel I and incorporate more risk-sensitive credit exposure measures into bank capital requirements.

Hammes and Shapiro[15] define several key drivers motivating Basel II, that includes (1) the structural changes in the credit markets, (2) opportunities to remove inefficiencies in the lending market, and (3) ballooning debt levels during the economic upturn, with a potential debt crisis in an economic downturn.

Banks can choose from Basel II that follows a three-step (potentially evolutionary) paradigm. The first is the basic standardized model, second is the internal ratings-based (IRB) model foundation approach, and the third is the advanced internal ratings-based model. The standardized model is based on external credit ratings assigned by independent ratings agencies (such as Moody's, Standard and Poor's and Fitch IBCA). Both internal and advance internal ratings approaches require the bank to formulate and use its own internal ratings system. The risk weight assigned to each commercial obligation is based on the ratings assignment (either external or internal). Thus, higher (lower) rated means obligors have high (low) credit quality and have lower (higher) risk weights and therefore have lower (higher) capital requirements. For that reason, Saunders and Allen [13] attempted to eliminate the incentives of Basel II to engage in risk shifting and regulatory arbitrage.

In contrast to the market risk alteration of Basel I which is only concerned with unexpected losses, Basel II assimilates both expected and unexpected losses into capital requirements. Hence, loan loss reserves are considered as portion of capital that cushions expected credit losses, whereas economic capital covers unexpected losses. The new capital requirements in Basel II are applied on both consolidated and unconsolidated basis to holding companies of banking firms. When Basel II is completely adopted, overall regulatory capital levels, on average are targeted by the BIS to remain unchanged for the system as a whole. However, recent tests conducted by 138 banks in 25 countries have led to a downward classification of the capital levels required to cover credit risk and operational risk [6].

Basel II Accord has been widely discussed since it was proposed. Other than the study of Lamy[9] mentioned in the previous section, Safakli[16] examined the issue of credit risk for the banking sectors of the Northern Cyprus. The author suggested that necessary preparations of technological, administrative, know-how and qualified personnel should be made in accordance with Basel II framework. Jacobson et al. [17] investigated the issue of the credit risks of retail and small and medium size enterprises (SMEs). Under Basel II, retail and SME credit received special treatment because of a supposedly smaller exposure to systemic risk. However, the research of Jacobson et al. [17] found that retail and SME portfolios were usually riskier than corporate credit. Special treatment under Basel II was thus not justified and should be reconsidered.

3 Approach of CreditMetrics

CreditMetrics was first introduced in 1997 by Gupton, Finger and Bhatia of J.P. Morgan and its co-sponsors (Bank of America, KMV, Union Bank of Switzerland, and others) as a Value-at-Risk (VaR) framework to apply to the valuation and risk of non-tradable assets such as loans and privately placed bonds. As mentioned before, because loans are not publicly traded, CreditMetrics observed neither the loan's market value nor the volatility of the loan value over the horizon of interest. Nevertheless, using (1) the available data on a borrower's credit rating, (2) the probability that the rating will change over the next year (the rating transition matrix), (3) the recovery rates on defaulted loans, and (4) the credit spreads and yields in the bond (or loan) market, it is possible to compute a hypothetical market value and volatility of the loan value for any non-traded loan or bond, and VaR estimation for individual loans and the loan portfolio.

There are four steps for evaluating credit VaR for a bond or loan that was summarized by Crouhy et al. [8]. The first step is to specify a rating system with rating categories, in conjunction with the probabilities of migrating from one credit quality to another over the credit risk horizon. This transition matrix is the key component of the credit VaR model proposed by Gupton et al. [18]. The second step is to specify the risk horizon. The third phase consists of specifying the forward discount curve at the risk horizon for each credit category. Then finally, this information is translated into the forward distribution of the changes in portfolio value consecutive to credit migration.

Kalapodas and Thomson [1] pointed out that the CreditMetrics model has several advantages. As a portfolio model, it enables credit risk analysts to identify the nature of the contribution of each asset to portfolio risk, the distribution of credit exposures among the ratings and the overall performance of the portfolio. It also provides the opportunity to restructure the distribution of credit exposures among different ratings in the portfolio in order to adjust its risk. However, Kalapodas and Thomson[1] indicated that the model is not without its limitations. It is a highly demanding model, involving many inputs and complicated mathematics, and its computation is time-consuming.

4 Empirical Analysis

In this study, the empirical data is taken from the corporate loan database of a bank listed in Taiwan Stock Exchange Corporation (TSEC), and the empirical sample is the 347 loan accounts at the bank in 2009 that belong to public companies.

To evaluate the credit Value-at-Risk (VaR) of the portfolio, the approach of CreditMetrics was used. Moreover, to objectively select the samples which can represent the 347 loan accounts in the bank, this study first conducted a cluster analysis using the SPSS 14.0 software, and the Nearest-Neighbor Method (NNM), to divide the sample into five clusters according to credit rating and industry type. The classification of the cluster sample is presented in Table 1. Next, based on the proportion of the cluster sample in the total corporations, 20 loan accounts were randomly selected for empirical practice.

Table 1. The distribution of loan account after cluster analysis

Cluster	Number of loan account	Percentage
1	36	10.37%
2	57	16.43%
3	120	34.58%
4	76	21.90%
5	58	16.72%
Total	347	100%

The loan accounts randomly selected were all one-year kind of unsecured loan; the loan interest rate and default recovery rate are calculated according to their credit rating system which is similar to CreditMetrics introduced in Section 3. With the above data, the Credit VaR was analyzed. First, we conducted Monte Carlo simulation 10,000 times to generate 10,000 loan asset portfolios from the cluster sample. Next, we calculated the mean and standard deviation (SD) of the 10,000 loan asset portfolios, which are NT$3.458 billion and NT$417 million, respectively.

With these data, we were able to calculate the percentile Credit VaR. In our estimation by simulating the values of 10,000 loan asset portfolios from the cluster sample, the significance level of 1% refers to a 100th position in the ranking of the values in ascending order. Moreover, the difference between the 100th loan asset portfolio value and the mean represents the Credit VaR under the 1% significance level. By this method, we calculated the percentile loan asset portfolio values under the significance levels of 1%, 5%, 50%, 95% and 99%, as well as the loan asset portfolio values under the same significance levels assuming normal distributions of loan values, and conducted a comparison of the two sets of values, as presented in Table 2.

Table 2. The values of loan asset portfolio of Monte Carlo simulation
— randomly selected sample   (million NT$)

Significance level	1%	5%	50%	95%	99%
percentile method	2411	2893	3793	3918	3947
assuming normality	2486	2769	3458	4146	4429

As shown in Table 2, under the significance levels of 1% and 5%, the percentile of Credit VaR are NT$1.047 billion and NT$565 million, and the Credit VaR of assumed normality are NT$972 million and NT$689 million. Although under the significance level of 5%, the Credit VaR of assumed normality is higher than the percentile Credit VaR, but under the significance level of 1%, it is lower than the latter. This demonstrates that under the significance level of 1%, the estimation of Credit VaR under the assumption of normality is more conservative than the percentile estimation.

In addition to the VaR measurement based on the randomly selected samples with cluster analysis, the study further applied the concept of stress testing and selected a sample of 20 listed companies with the greatest loan amount in the objective bank of this study.

The mean and SD of the loan asset portfolios' values of this sample are NT$11.328 billion and NT$1.361 billion, respectively. As shown in Table 3, the percentile Credit VaR of the 20 biggest loan asset portfolio under the significance levels of 1% and 5% are NT$2.255 billion and NT$1.726 billion, respectively, exceeding the Credit VaR of the loan asset portfolio selected by cluster analysis under the same significance levels by NT$1.208 billion and NT$1.161 billion. The Credit VaR of assumed normality are NT$3.171 billion and NT$2.246 billion under the significance levels of 1% and 5%. The analyzed results showed that banks should take into account the concept of stress testing and select the greatest loan asset portfolio to obtain the Credit VaR as the most conservative estimation.

Table 3. The values of loan asset portfolio of Monte Carlo simulation
− stress testing

Significance level	1%	5%	50%	95%	99%
percentile method	9073	9602	12355	12632	12672
assuming normality	8157	9082	11328	13574	14499

(million NT$)

Finally, this study compared the Credit VaR obtained by the formula for calculating risk in the CreditMetrics model and capital requirement defined by the New Basel Capital Accord (Basel II).

Below is the Basel II formula for calculating the minimum capital requirement (CR) to risk-weighted assets:

$$CR = RWA*8\% \tag{1}$$

and the risk-weighted assets (RWA) is calculated by the formula below:

$$RWA = RW*EAD \tag{2}$$

where EAD is the assets exposure at default, and RW is the risk weight which is calculated by the formula below:

$$RW = \left(\frac{LGD}{50}\right)*BRW \tag{3}$$

where LGD is the percent of the loss given default, and BRW is the benchmark risk weight calculated by the following formula:

$$BRW = 976.5*N(1.118*G(PD)+1.228)*1+0.047*\left(\frac{(1-PD)}{PD^{0.44}}\right) \tag{4}$$

The term N(.) denotes the cumulative distribution function for a standard normal random variable, and the term G(.) denotes the inverse cumulative distribution function for a standard normal random variable. Using the formula, the RWA of the cluster sample and the loan asset portfolio with the greatest outstanding balance are calculated as NT$8.614 billion and NT$34.901 billion, respectively. At the minimum capital ratio of 8%, the unexpected loss would be NT$689 million and NT$1.912 billion. Table 4 presents a comparison of these results with those obtained from the CreditMetrics model.

Table 4. Comparison of credit risks evaluated by BASEL II and the CreditMetrics approach (million NT$)

Sample	Basel II	CreditMetrics model 1	CreditMetrics model 2
Randomly selected	689	1,047	972
Stress testing	1,912	2,255	3,171

Note 1: CreditMetrics model 1 uses percentile method under the significance levels of 1%.
Note 2: CreditMetrics model 2 assumes normal distributions of loan values under the significance levels of 1%.

The above table shows that the expected loss calculated by the 8% capital ratio defined in Basel II is clearly lower than the Credit VaR obtained from the CreditMetrics model under the significance levels of 1%. This could be caused by that the CreditMetrics model that takes into account the risk of the loan assets being downgraded or upgraded. Moreover, the evaluation methods of the relationships in the various assets within a portfolio are different for CreditMetrics model and Basel II.

5   Managerial Implications

In the old Basel Capital Accord (Basel I), the credit risk faced by banks is measured by the total outstanding balance, in that, the total outstanding balance is multiplied by 8% to obtain the minimum equity capital required to guarantee the potential loss from credit risk. However, this approach overlooks the difference in default probability between individual borrowers. As a result, in 1988, the Basel Committee generally graded credit risk and established a set of risk weights, a first attempt at enforcing banks to consider the relationship between actual credit risk and capital requirements as a whole. Nevertheless, the classification of risk weights was rather unsophisticated, allowing certain banks to exploit the weaknesses of the regulation by making portfolio adjustments, somewhat defeating the purpose of the 1988 version. Basel II, implemented in early 2007, includes significant revisions and represents a considerable improvement in the regulation of credit risk in banking. However, the Accord still regards credit risk individually, and overlooks the effect of credit portfolios on overall credit risk. In light of the above, this study tried to establish a process for measuring the

Credit VaR of loan asset portfolios, using the data available from a bank in Taiwan and following the example of Gupton et al. [18] in measuring the Credit VaR of investment portfolios with CreditMetrics, and offer banks suggestions for its utilization.

This study makes an important managerial contribution to the Bank for International Settlements (BIS) and other financial institutions. For BIS, it is suggested to reconsider the standard of 8% for minimum capital requirement of credit loans. The ratio may need to increase to a higher standard such as 9% or 10%. For general financial institutions, credit risk managers have to notice that if the credit risk is evaluated by meeting the standard of Basel II Accord because it may be underestimated. After the events of sub-prime mortgage and global financial distress in 2008, this issue should be noticed. Although the CreditMetics model was proposed in 1997 which was earlier than Basel II proposed in 2001, its evaluating process is more complicated than Basel II Accord. Nevertheless, the CreditMetics model considered the risk and probability of the loan assets being downgraded or upgraded. It may be a more precise method to estimate credit risk than the approach in Basel II Accord.

6 Conclusions

Basel II, implemented in early 2007, includes significant revisions and represents a considerable improvement in the regulation of credit risk in banking. However, the Accord still regards credit risk individually, and overlooks the effect of credit portfolios on overall credit risk. Moreover, it did not consider the risk and probability of the loan assets being downgraded or upgraded in the future. On the other hand, J.P. Morgan published CreditMetrics to evaluate credit risk of loan portfolios in 1997. It is a more complicated and precise method to evaluate credit risk, but little research has explored the advantages and characteristics of CreditMetrics. This study is the first research to compare the results of credit risk evaluation by the CreditMetrics model and Basel II Accord. The results showed that the expected loss calculated by the minimum capital requirement ratio defined in Basel II is clearly lower than the Credit VaR obtained from the CreditMetrics model. Managerial implications for BIS and other financial institutions were then discussed. The data system of loan accounts in a bank listed by the Taiwan Stock Exchange Corporation (TSEC) was used as the empirical data in this study. Future study can extend the research to analyze the credit risk of loan accounts in banking industry of other countries using the CreditMetrics model and Basel II Accord and compare the results with that of present study.

References

1. Kalapodas, E., Thomson, M.E.: Credit risk assessment: a challenge for financial institutions. Journal of Management Mathematics 17, 25–46 (2006)
2. Waring, A., Glendon, I.A.: Managing Risk. International Thomson Business Press, UK (1998)
3. Galindo, J., Tamayo, P.: Credit risk assessment using statistical and machine learning methods as an ingredient for financial intermediaries risk modeling. Computational Economics 15, 107–143 (2000)
4. Brady, B.: Ratings Performance 2001. Standard & Poor's, New York (2002)

5. Tillman, V.: Ratings Performance 1999. Standard & Poor's, New York (2000)
6. Bank for International Settlements.: The new Basel Capital Accord. Basel Committee on Banking Supervision Document (2001)
7. Gup, B.E.: The New Basel Capital Accord. Thomson, New York (2004)
8. Crouhy, M., Galai, D., Mark, R.: A comparative analysis of current credit risk models. Journal of Banking & Finance 24, 59–117 (2000)
9. Lamy, M.F.: The treatment of credit risk in the Basel Accord and financial stability. International Journal of Business 11, 159–170 (2006)
10. Fare, R., Grosskopf, S., Weber, W.L.: The effect of risk-based capital requirements on profit efficiency in banking. Applied Economics 36, 1731–1743 (2004)
11. Thompson, M.A.: Are adjustments in the default risk premium asymmetric. Applied Economics 39, 2693–2698 (2007)
12. Chen, Y.H., Wang, K., Tu, A.H.: Default correlation at the sovereign level: evidence from some Latin American markets. Applied Economics 41, 1466–4283 (2009)
13. Saunders, A., Allen, L.: Credit Risk Measurement: New Approaches to Value-at-Risk and other Paradigms. John Wiley & Sons, New York (2002)
14. Jones, D.: Emerging problems with the Basel Capital Accord: Regulatory capital arbitrage and related issues. Journal of Banking & Finance 24, 35–58 (2000)
15. Hammes, W., Shapiro, M.: The implications of the New Capital Adequacy Rules for portfolio management of credit assets. Journal of Banking & Finance 25, 97–114 (2001)
16. Safakli, O.V.: Credit risk assessment for the banking sector of northern Cyprus. Banks and Bank System 2, 21–31 (2007)
17. Jacobson, T., Linde, J., Roszbach, K.: Credit risk versus capital requirements under Basel II: Are loans and retail credit really different? Journal of Financial Services Research 28, 43–75 (2005)
18. Gupton, G.M., Finger, C.C., Bhatia, M.: CreditMetrics. RiskMetrics Technology Document. J.P. Morgan, San Francisco (1997)

Review of Institutions and Economic Growth Empirical Research

Yi Lin[1] and Xiaoman Chen[2]

[1] School of Public Administration, Southwest Jiaotong University,
610031 ChengDu, China
fisher.818@163.com
[2] College of Mobile Telecommunications, ChongQing
University of Posts and Telecom, 401520 ChongQing, China
mike2121@sina.com

Abstract. To study further the relationship between institutions and economic growth, this paper reviewed the existing empirical researches in this area. These empirical literatures have provided compelling evidence for a causal link between a cluster of "good" institutions and more rapid long run economic growth. However, many questions would limit further research, such as coarseness of quantitative institutions, defects of instrumental variables and so on. Derived through two simple models, these questions could be proved. Finally, it gives three improved suggestions to the sample of study in China. These suggestions can help researchers understand better how economic growth arises in response to institution changing in China.

Keywords: Institutions, Economic Growth, Instrumental Variables.

1 Introduction

Since the last century, there is a remarkable and exciting revival of interest in the empirical analysis of how a broad series of institutions affects economic growth. These papers focus on variation in "institutional quality" to identify whether a causal effect runs from institutions to growth. We used table form to summarize it in section 2.

Although these studies have abundant results, the corresponding issues still exist. The coarseness of quantitative institutions, and the defects of instrumental variables, will limit further progress. We analyzed these issues concretely in section 3.

In section 4, we give three suggestions with the sample for the study in China: (1) modify the theoretical framework; (2) emphasis on the political institutions; and (3) explore all levels of the institutions to influence the economic growth. They can help us understand better how economical change arises in response to changing institutions in China. Finally, section 5 is the paper conclusion.

Q. Zhou (Ed.): ISAEBD 2011, Part I, CCIS 208, pp. 563–569, 2011.
© Springer-Verlag Berlin Heidelberg 2011

2 Review of Empirical Research

2.1 Foreign Research

The foreign research belongs to cross-country mostly. Table 1 lists fourteen widely cited literatures. Most of them have used influential institutional quality measures or instrumental variables to address the endogenous of institutional measures.

All of these literatures usually using economic outcomes (mostly GDP) as the dependent variables, and using the quantitative indicators to be able to measure the "good or bad" of institutions as independent variables. The measures used by the institutions (set) are unified, that can make cross-country research feasible. All studies indicate that: the strengthening of the protection degree of private property rights, improvement of the bureaucratic institutions and financial markets, enhancement of law rules level, etc, are all related closely more rapid to economic growth.

Table 1. Foreign empirical research representative papers (1 SD is one standard deviation)

Author	Institutions	Instrument	The main conclusion
Knack&Keefer (1995) [1]	ICRG[1]; BERI[2]	No instrument	1 SD increase in ICRG increase GDP per capita growth rate by 1.2%
Mauro (1995) [2]	Bureaucratic efficiency[3]	Ethnolinguistic fractionalization[1]	1 SD increase in B.E. index increases GDP per capita growth by 3%
Knack&Keefer (1997) [3]	Trust	Ethnolinguistic homogeneity[2];	1 SD increase in trust increases GDP per capita income growth by 1.2%
Clague et al (1999) [4]	CIM[4]	Colonial origin[3]	1 SD increase in CIM increases growth by 1.74%
Hall&Jones (1999) [5]	Social infrastructure[5]	Predicted trade share[4]; Distance from equator[5]	1% increase in S.I. index increases output per worker by 5.14%
Rodrik (1999) [6]	Political institutions	Colonial origin	1 SD increase in FH increases average wages by 36.72%
AJR (2001) [7]	Expropriation risk[6];	Settler mortality[6]	1 SD increase in expropriation risk increases GDP per worker by 309%
AJR (2002) [8]	Executive constraints[7]	Settler mortality	1 SD increase in expropriation risk increases GDP per capita by 118%
Bockstette et al (2002) [9]	Social infrastructure	State antiquity	1% increase in S.I. index increases output per worker by 1.8%
Rodrik et al (2004) [10]	Rule of law	See Hall&Jones	1 SD increase in rule of law index increases GDP per capita by 205%
Jones&Olken (2005) [11]	Democratization[8]	No instrument	1 SD increase in democratization increase annual growth by 2.1%
Cavalcanti et al (2005) [12]	Social infrastructure	See Hall&Jones	Countries with the same institutions have different levels of growth
Shaw et al (2007) [13]	Bureaucratic efficiency	Predicted trade share	1 SD increase in B.E. index increases GDP per capita growth by 3%
Persson et al (2009) [14]	Democratic capital	No instrument	Democratic capital can promoting economic growth

2.2 Domestic Research

Table 2 is part of representative results of domestic empirical research. The main feature is: the indicators are almost economic institutions; the role of the political institutions has been virtually ignored. It may have two reasons: first and foremost, the political institutions are difficult to quantify, such as the degree of democracy, the extent of government executive constraints, has a subjective measurement basically. It's difficult to be precise and objective as economic institutions. Last but not the least is that, most scholars believe that the economic institution is a decisive factor in Chinese economic growth from reform and opening up, while contemporary political institutions are relatively stable or slow evolution. Of course, all studies have reached a consensus: the improvement of the economic institutions can significantly improve Chinese economy.

Table 2. Domestic empirical research representative papers

Author	Institutions	Instrument	The main conclusion
Jin Yuguo (2001) [15]	Non-nationalization; Market; Opening; Government revenue	No instrument	Market institution has the greatest contribution to Chinese growth
Wang Wenbo et al (2002) [16]	See Jin Yuguo	No instrument	Economic institutions increases 1%, growth increases 0.23%
Shen Kunrong et al (2005) [17]	Fiscal decentralization	No instrument	F.D. can promote economic growth
Xu Xianxiang et al (2005) [18]	Social infrastructure	Private industry output	S.I. can explain the difference of growth between the provinces
Liu Wenge et al (2008) [19]	Non-nationalization; State-controlled funds; Opening	No instrument	Economic institutions increases 1%, growth increases 0.15%
Fang Ying et al (2008) [20]	Property rights protection	Primary school enrollment	P.R.P. has 4.23% marginal contribution to growth
Li Yankai et al (2009) [21]	Property changes; Opening	No instrument	All institutions can promoting economic growth in China
Wang Liying et al (2010) [22]	Property rights; Opening	No instrument	All institutions can promoting economic growth in China

3 Problems of Existing Empirical Research

3.1 Coarseness of Quantitative Institutions

Firstly, the problem is subjectivity of institution indicators, which derived from subjective evaluation of professional organizations (e.g. ICRG), resulting in that objectivity is slightly weak; Secondly, the randomness of weights, such as the ICRG components and respective weights: ICRG=0.5×political indicators+0.25×financial indicators+0.25×economic composite index. It doesn't take into account differences among countries apparently. To illustrate, consider equation (1):

$$Y_i = \beta_0 + \beta X_i + \mu_i . \tag{1}$$

Y_i is economic growth indicators, X_i is institutions (set) quantization (we don't consider the control variables, it doesn't affect conclusions). We suppose X_i contains n species specific institutions $(X_{i1}, X_{i2},..., X_{in})$. (1) transforms to equation (2):

$$Y_i=\beta_0+\beta_1 X_{i1}+\beta_2 X_{i2}+...+\beta_n X_{in}+\mu_i . \tag{2}$$

β_1, β_2,..., β_n stand for n species institutions impact on their respective economic growth in X_i. Therefore, we need to assume equation (3):

$$X_i=\gamma_1 X_{i1}+\gamma_2 X_{i2}+...+\gamma_n X_{in} . \tag{3}$$

γ_1, γ_2,..., γ_n represent respectively the weight in X_i about $(X_{i1}, X_{i2},..., X_{in})$. So (1) transforms to equation (4):

$$Y_i=\beta_0+\beta\gamma_1 X_{i1}+\beta\gamma_2 X_{i2}+...+\beta\gamma_n X_{in}+\mu_i . \tag{4}$$

Actually, (1) is used usually, combined (2) and (4), which is equivalent to imposing a restriction, namely: $\beta=\beta_1/\gamma_1=\beta_2/\gamma_2=...=\beta_n/\gamma_n$. The weight is often given in advance, so this restriction is unlikely to meet in fact. Although it can be resolved by using principal component analysis, but the randomness of weights is still there when measuring secondary indicators in institutions (set).

3.2 Defects of Instrumental Variables

The institution X_i is endogenous, so:

$$X_i=\lambda_0+\lambda Z_i+\varepsilon_i . \tag{5}$$

Z_i is instrumental variable, according with $Cov(Z_i, \mu_i)=0$ and $Cov(Z_i, X_i)\neq 0$. It makes that natural instrumental variable is very rare in reality. Looking at foreign and domestic research, the scarcity of instrumental variables is a common feature: the usual practice is to add the lag item, while the constraints of instrumental variables also often not fully met in fact. To illustrate, according to equation (5), we have:

$$X_{i1}=\lambda_{01}+\lambda_1 Z_i+\varepsilon_{i1},\ X_{i2}=\lambda_{02}+\lambda_2 Z_i+\varepsilon_{i2},...,\ X_{in}=\lambda_{0n}+\lambda_n Z_i+\varepsilon_{in} . \tag{6}$$

Therefore, (3) spreads out as follows:

$$X_i=\gamma_1\lambda_{01}+\gamma_2\lambda_{02}+...+\gamma_n\lambda_{0n}+(\gamma_1\lambda_1+\gamma_2\lambda_2+...+\gamma_n\lambda_n)Z_i+\gamma_1\varepsilon_{i1}+\gamma_2\varepsilon_{i2}+...\gamma_n\varepsilon_{in} . \tag{7}$$

Equation (7) means what two constraints are met that Z_i and each of $(X_{i1}, X_{i2}, ..., X_{in})$. This limitation is too harsh clearly. Also, a "perfect" instrumental variable doesn't exist basically. Such as Glaeser et al (2004) [23] believed that "settler mortality" may be relevant to the distribution of endemic disease at that time, that can't distinguish which determine economic growth whether to institutions or the distribution of epidemic. Albouy (2008) [24] also pointed out that settler mortality data wasn't comparable in different regions, and thus believed that this instrumental variable is invalid. It's clear that the harsh conditions instrumental variables are likely to make a larger bias in empirical research.

4 Enlightenment to China from Research

4.1 Modify the Theoretical Framework

Chinese economic growth is mainly due to the economic institutions reform, but come out on the premise of relatively stable political institutions. The government played a key role in guiding. In addition, the legal institution of maintaining economic order is another security condition to promote economic growth. Hence, the existing theoretical framework is necessary to modify: attempt the economic, political and legal institutions into the framework of the macro-institution jointly, fully explore the relationship between the institutions and economic growth.

4.2 Emphasis on the Political Institutions

In fact, Chinese political institutions have always been constantly deepened, therefore, neglecting the role of the political institutions is to be wrong of discussing in domestic empirical studies. With the reform and opening up, the evolution of the political institutions slow will have inevitably with rapid changes of economic institutions, recent years for particular, Chinese political development has been lagging behind economic growth. Therefore, the impact of the political institutions should be greater emphasized.

4.3 Explore All Levels of the Institutions to Influence the Economic Growth

The coarseness of institutions measurement and the heterogeneity of countries limit exploration that the specific institution impact on economic growth in cross-country studies. So we proposed to use data of a single country to research. Chinese reform and opening up is the natural sample of this idea. In addition, there may be some inner links among the economic, political and legal institutions. Therefore, this kind of research is an interesting challenge.

5 Conclusion

This paper summarized the problems that may exist in empirical research between institutions and economic growths, put forward proposals to their relationship, and provide a wider field of vision. We believe our suggestions can help make progress on the above issues, and can help us better understand how economical change arises in response to changing institutions in China.

References

1. Knack, S., Keefer, P.: Institutions and Economic Performance: Cross-country Tests Using Alternative Institutional Measures. Economics and Politics 7, 207–227 (1995)
2. Mauro, P.: Corruption and Growth. Quarterly Journal of Economics 110, 681–712 (1995)
3. Knack, S., Keefer, P.: Does Social Capital Have an Economic Payoff? A Cross-country Investigation. Quarterly Journal of Economics 112, 1251–1288 (1997)

4. Clague, C., Keefer, P., Knack, S., Olson, M.: Contract-Intensive Money: Contract Enforcement, Property Rights, and Economic Performance. Journal of Economic Growth 6, 185–211 (1999)
5. Hall, R.E., Jones, C.I.: Why Do Some Countries Produce so much more Output per Worker than Others? Quarterly Journal of Economics 114, 83–116 (1999)
6. Rodrk, D.: Democracies Pay Higher Wages. Quarterly Journal of Economic 8, 707–738 (1999)
7. Acemoglu, D., Johnson, S., Robinson, J.A.: The Colonial Origins of Comparative Development: An Empirical Investigation. American Economic Review 91, 1369–1401 (2001)
8. Acemoglu, D., Johnson, S., Robinson, J.A.: Reversal of Fortune: Geography and Institutions in the Making of the Modern World Income Distribution. Quarterly Journal of Economics 117, 1237–1294 (2002)
9. Bockstette, V., Chanda, A., Putterman, L.: States and Markets: The Advantage of an Early Start. Journal of Economic Growth 7, 347–369 (2002)
10. Rodrik, D., Subramanian, A., Trebbi, F.: Institutions Rule: The Primacy of Institutions over Geography and Integration in Economic Development. Journal of Economic Growth 9, 131–165 (2004)
11. Jones, B.F., Olken, B.A.: Do Leaders Matter? National Leadership and Growth Since World War II. Quarterly Journal of Economics 120, 835–864 (2005)
12. Cavalcanti, T.V., Novo, Á.A.: Institutions and Economic Development: How Strong is the Relation? Empirical Economics 30, 263–276 (2005)
13. Shaw, P., Katsaiti, M.S., Jurgilas, M.: Corruption and Growth under Weak Identification. NBER Working Paper (2007)
14. Persson, T., Tabellini, G.: Democratic Capital: the Nexus of Political and Economic Change. American Economic Journal 1, 88–126 (2009)
15. Jin, Y.: The Contribution of Macro-institutional Changes to Growth in Economy Transformation Period of China. Finance and Economics, 24–28 (2001) (in Chinese)
16. Wang, W., Chen, C., Xu, H.: An Empirical Analysis on China's Economic Growth Model Containing International Factors. Modern Economic Science 2, 33–37 (2002) (in Chinese)
17. Shen, K., Fu, W.: The Relationship between China's Decentralized System in Finance and Regional Economic Growth. Management World, 31–39 (2005) (in Chinese)
18. Xu, X., Li, X.: Endogenous Institutions and Provincial Disparity in China. China Economic Quarterly s1, 81–100 (2005) (in Chinese)
19. Liu, W., Gao, W., Zhang, S.: The Measurement of Institutional Transition and China's Economic Growth: An Empirical Analysis Based on the Data of China During the Period of 1952-2006. Economist 6, 48–55 (2008) (in Chinese)
20. Fang, Y., Zhao, Y.: In Search of Instruments for Institutions: Estimating the Impact of Institutions on Chinese Economic Performance (2008) (in Chinese)
21. Li, Y., Han, Y.: Institutional Change and China's Economic Growth. Research on Economics and Management 6, 26–33 (2009) (in Chinese)
22. Wang, L., Liu, H.: Endogenous Institutions, Government Efficiency and Economic Growth: A Category Test. Economists 1, 20–26 (2010) (in Chinese)
23. Glaeser, E.L., La Porta, R., Lopez-de-Silanes, F., Shleifer, A.: Do Institutions Cause Growth? Journal of Economic Growth 9, 271–303 (2004)
24. Albouy, D.Y.: The Colonial Origins of Comparative Development: An Investigation of the Settler Mortality Data, NBER (2008)

Appendix I: Notes on Institution Measures

1. Combines: protection against expropriation risk; rule of law; repudiation of contracts by government; corruption in government; and quality of bureaucracy. Source: International Country Risk Guide dataset.
2. Combines: contract enforceability; infrastructure quality; nationalization potential; and bureaucratic delays. Source: Business Environments Risk Intelligence.
3. Combines: judiciary system; red tape; and corruption indices.
4. Ratio of non-currency money to total money supply. An objective measure of enforceability of contracts and the security of property rights. Source: International Financial Statistics.
5. Institutions and government policies that provide incentives for individuals and firms in an economy.
6. A measure of risk of expropriation of foreign private investment by government. Source: Political Risk Services.
7. 1-7 category scale, higher score means more constraints on the executive. Source: Polity III.
8. Using the "polity" variable to distinguish a dictator or a democrats. Source: Polity IV.

Appendix II: Notes on Instruments

1. Measures probability that two randomly selected persons from a given country will not belong to the same ethnolinguistic group. Source: Taylor&Hudson (1972).
2. Percentage of a country's population belonging to the largest ethnic group. Source: Sullivan (1991).
3. Dummy variable indicating whether country was a British, French, German, Spanish, Italian, Belgian, Dutch or Portuguese colony. Source: La Porta et al (1999).
4. Log value, based on a gravity trade model that only uses a country's population and geographical features. Source: Frankel&Romer (1999).
5. Center of county or province within a country that contains the most people. Source: Global Demography Project, University of California, Santa Barbara.
6. Log estimated mortality for European settlers during European colonization (before 1850). Source: Curtin (1989).

Application of ActiveX Technology in the Remote Dynamic Monitoring System Based on B/S

Xiaohui Mo[1,2] and Yi Zhang[1]

[1] Department of Information Technology,
Jinling Institute of Technology
[2] Department of Automation, Southest University
Nanjing, China
{mxh,zhangyi}@jit.edu.cn

Abstract. For the purpose of implementing industry remote Dynamic monitor based on the web in the MIS, the structure of system is the thin client model as Browser/Server, the html files which embraced ActiveX controls are downloaded on the client, the method of ActiveX control is called to access data port, and the remote data on the client are transferred by the way of ADO. In the paper, an application example is given according to the working experience, which introduces how to apply the technology of ActiveX and ADO to B/S system structure. It is proved by practice that efficient and secure internet application software can be developed by adopting this system structure.

Keywords: B/S, ActiveX, ADO, Dynamic Monitor System.

1 Introduction

With the rapidly development of internet/intranet technology, the network environment is constantly updated, and the browser technology is becoming more perfect, it is imperative to build remote dynamic monitoring system based on B/S. The purpose of research and development for the system is to require it to breakthrough the current closed situation of the general monitoring system, and browse the dynamic situation with browser on intranet everywhere, and make the level of automation, operation management, economic and human investment and other aspects of enterprise in the higher cost performance.

Recent years, with the functional requirements improving of internet/intranet, many new technologies emergence to expand internet capabilities, it makes possible for those assumptions, the ActiveX technology based on the Component Object Model (COM) and Windows 32-bit application program interface (Win32API) is especially eye-catching[1]. In the paper, we discuss an application method of ActiveX technology in the development of dynamic remote monitoring system in a steel plant for readers to learn.

Q. Zhou (Ed.): ISAEBD 2011, Part I, CCIS 208, pp. 570–575, 2011.
© Springer-Verlag Berlin Heidelberg 2011

2 Key Technologies of System Development

2.1 ActiveX Technology

ActiveX is the technology that Microsoft provide the majority of developers to integrate the computer desktop environment and internet, and its substantial resources together [2-3]. As a technology for internet application development, ActiveX is widely used in Web servers and clients in all aspects. ActiveX control technology is the core technology of ActiveX which will be used to compile some interface program or complex program block(contains lots of graphics, images, etc.) in accordance with requirements of ActiveX control. The program is ActiveX control. In fact, ActiveX control is a program which accord the specification of ActiveX control. These programs usually are stored on the server with exe,dll,ocx suffix. they can run on the server for other programs call, and also can be automatically downloaded to the client to run, thereby they can enhance the browsing speed.

2.2 ADO Technology

ADO (ActiveX Data Objects) is the database access component of ActiveX which is the latest product of Microsoft for database realease on the inernet, it can shield complexity of remote data access with high speed.

There are seven separate objects and four collections in ADO model. These objects of ADO greatly simplify the complexity of database access, and make database access easier. ADO supports VBScript, JavaScript and other scripting language with remote data service characteristics, especially for database access on the internet/intranet environment. It is particularly important for the monitoring system with B/S structure.

3 Application of ActiveX Technology in System

3.1 Use ActiveX Control to Achieve Web Dynamic Display

In Web pages of the system, we need to show curves, bar graphs, components and other graphics. The status of those graphics can be changed by real-time data. It is difficult to achieve dynamic graphics display by ASP and other pure Web technology, but ActiveX control technology is very suitable for internet/intranet applications [4].

First, ActiveX control can be developed in multiple languages, such as VC, Delphi, VB and so on. ActiveX controls developed by these high-level languages are embedded in Web pages, they not only increase the flexibility of Web page development, more importantly, greatly expand Web features. they make some functions only achieved by high-level language to be realized easily in the Web pages.

Secondly, after the ActiveX control on internet/intranet is automatically downloaded to the local, it will become the local computer's resources for future use. it can divorce from the Web server to be executed by IE as an independent process.

So we arrange the database access and the graphical display capabilities to the ActiveX controls to implement. Web server only needs to embed ActiveX controls in HTML pages for IE browser download. After the control is downloaded to the client computer, the control will connect the network database to read real-time data and generate graphics based on the data[5-6]. Because the refresh timer function is added in the control, so the dynamic graphical display can be realized. It is shown in Fig. 1.

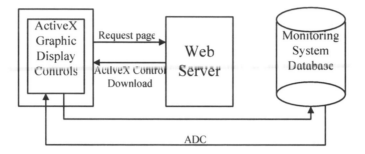

Fig. 1. Web dynamic graphic display bsaed on ActiveX control

Controls use ADO to access database. Because ADO can use connection string to connect database, so we only define connection string in design. ADO control is downloaded to the local computer without database configuration with more versatility. So it is more suitable to access database for distributed users on the intranet.

Because the graphical display and refresh function run locally, Intranet only transport the real-time data, so this way reduces network data traffic, and ActiveX can provide better graphical user interface, and allows the realization of dynamic graphics for better result . In addition to graphics, we also use this way to do various operations in the database such as query, modify and so on. this way is much faster rate than the ASP.

3.2   Example of ActiveX Control Development in Delphi

As an excellent development tool, Delphi provides a powerful component development technology, ActiveX controls can be easily compiled by it. ActiveX controls can be developed in two ways: First, make a single VCL (Visual Component Library) control in delphi directly into ActiveX control. Secondly, package multiple VCL to constitute functional complex ActiveX control by ActiveForm.

ActiveX controls compiled by ActiveForm are very convenient, you can put in visual controls or non-visual controls in ActiveForm. We can use controls to compile more complex programs, and then add properties, methods, and events to the ActiveX type library. These properties, methods, and events associated with properties, methods, and events of ActiveForm allow users to operate their controls on the ActiveForm. ActiveX compiled into ActiveX controls with OCX Suffix can be easily embedded in Web pages.

Figure 2 is ActiveX TrendControl which use to display field data trend and bar graphs in the system. it reads real-time data of database on the server through ADO, and then convert the data to display with trend curve and bar graphs[7-8]. It can display four data at the same time. As it involves complex graphs, we use ActiveForm to develop it. ActiveForm of the TrendControl includes the following main Delphi controls:

- ADOTable is used to access table on the database server by ADO mode.
- DBEdit shows data accessed by the TADOTable.
- DataSource shows data source interface between TADOTable and TDBEdit.
- Image is used to draw trend curve.
- Guage is used to display bar graphs.
- Timer is used to produce dynamic effects.

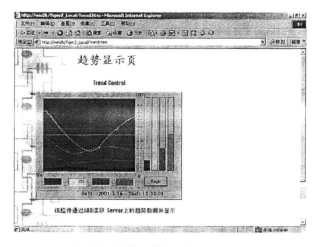

Fig. 2. TrendControl control

In the application of the system, we also use ActiveForm technology of Delphi to develop data query controls, statistical controls, report controls, etc. they make the client better interactivity and achieve the data release. In these controls, we all use ADOConnection, ADOQuery, ADOTable and other controls of Delphi, they connect database through ADO mode. Next, we briefly outline the method of their implementation:

(1) Data Query Control: This control provides users with a data query interface. Users can query data by time, sector classification. In the development of such control, we use some database display controls of Delphi, such as DBGrid, BNavigator, DBEdit, etc. These controls can provide a good user interaction, so that the data query become more convenient. Data query use SQL statements to achieve, it can be easily inserted in the ADOQuery.

(2) Statistical Control: The control has statistics, summary and rendering graphics functions according to different data categories. In addition to have data query control functions, it also need to achieve a certain of statistical computing and graphics rendering capabilities. Statistics and summary are achieved by SQL statement. Graphics rendering can be used by Delphi's DBChart or some graphics display ActiveX control.

(3) Report Control: It is used to implement generation, printing of various types of report in the client. The Formula One Control is used to generate and print Excel report independently. As various reports have different formats, when we use Formula One to develop the report controls, there are two options: First, use program to generate the corresponding report, This method is more complicated. The other is that the base table is defined by artificial, data put in it by program. This method is simple. However, before the client program running, the client need to download the base table to local or read the base table from remote server firstly.

The following simple example use the ActiveX control TrendControl. Ocx of the system.

```
< OBJECT ID="Syspic"
CLASSID="CLSID:795BA425-2FA3 -11D3 -8BEA -00105A5ED4E"
CODEBASE="http://99.98.97.5/trend/TrendControl.ocx#version=1,0,0,0"
WIDTH="798"  HEIGHT="658" ALIGN="center"
</OBJECT>
```

Here, the ClassID and file path or URL of OCX must be provided. Before the client browse this page, it will search ClassID in the local registry firstly. If there is no updated version, the control is not necessary to be downloaded. Otherwise, the control will be searched according to the path specified by CODEBASE and be downloaded to the client, so the client can access dynamic real-time information and historical information via IE. Also the ID of tag OBJTCT is the name of the OCX object, it is used to access and set properties, and call the object methods, etc.

4 Questions in Development of ActiveX Control

According to the development practice, in the development of ActiveX control, we should pay attention to the following questions:

(1) the Size of Control: If the control is too large, it will affect browsing speed at the first time. In order to reduce the size of graphical controls, we should avoid some graphical interface which are provided by the development environment, while try to use API functions (Win32GDI) of Windows to draw the graphics. Of course, it will increase the difficulty of the development. we should specific treatment to specific circumstances.

(2) the Universal of Control: First, the control should fit requirements of different Web users. it requires to use windows common technology to develop the control, it can also run in a pure Windows environment. Secondly, the common functions should be taken into account in the control development. For the similar functionality, you can use a control to achieve, which can reduce the number of controls, and also reduces the number of control downloads on the network.

(3) the Maintainability of Control: the control should be considered upgrad, maintenance and other issues in the system development. Control need to provide more flexible methods and properties. When the system structure changes, the control should continue to be used.

Considering the above questions, although the control development will increase the difficulty, but it makes the system structure optimized to facilitate the development of the system, and can bring good maintainability.

Acknowledgments. The heading should be treated as a 3rd level heading and should not be assigned a number.

5 Conclusions

In Comparison with the other remote supervisory control methods, the paper shows the advantages of B/S structure based on ActiveX technique in remote dynamic monitoring system, and gives an example of practical application. It is proved by practice that efficient and secure internet application software can be developed by adopting this system structure.

Acknowledgments. The project is supported by the Natural Foundation of the Jiangsu Higher Education Institutions of China under Grants No. 09kjd510009.

References

1. Microsoft Corporation. ActiveX Controls (Internet Explorer_ActiveX Controls), http://msdn.microsoft.com/workshop/components/activex/activex_node_entry.asp
2. Zimmerman, S.: Designing ActiveX Components: Implementing Internet Communication, http://www.Microsoft.com/msdnonline
3. Zimmerman, S.: Designing ActiveX Components with the MFC Doeument/View Model, http://www.Microsoft.com/msdnonline
4. Tall, E., Ginsburg, M.: Late Night Activex. Ziff-Davis Press, New York (1996)
5. Zhang, L., Zhong, C.Q., Zhang, L.Y., et al.: Development of dynamic acqustion system of industrial field temperature data on WWW. Journal of Dalian University of Technology 44, 906–911 (2004)
6. Qiu, P., Chen, J.-h., Chang, Q.: Study of XML&SQL Server and Application in Distributed Integration. Measurement and Instruments. 17, 4369–4372 (2007)
7. Blake, B., Hamilton, G., Hoyt, J.: Using Component-Based Development and Web Technologies to Support a Distributed Data Management System. Annals of Software Engineering 13, 13–34 (2002)
8. Qiu, B., Gooi, H.B., Liu, Y.L., et al.: Internet-based SCADA display system. IEEE Computer Applications in Power 15, 14–19 (2002)

Implementation of Distance Education Platform Based on Virtual Reality for the Deaf

Yi Zhang and Xiaohui Mo

Department of Information Technology, Jinling Institute of Technology
Nanjing, China
{zhangyi,mxh}@jit.edu.cn

Abstract. With the issue of increasing concern deaf education, the special education people begin to focus on teaching quality. In this paper our aim is to design a distance education platform using VRML. Its main tasks including it analysis that the deaf education exists the problems and virtual reality technologies apply in the distance education, points out construction programmers and implementation process of the deaf distance education. Through introducing virtual reality technology-related knowledge, points out a B/ (W-A) /D system structure. The separations and functions of each module in the scalable modularization structure and the key technology of implement the system are expounded in detail finally. The virtual reality technology to improve the teaching of deaf education has an important significance.

Keywords: Deaf, VRML, Distance Education, B/ (W-A) /D.

1 Introduction

As for the deaf education this problem concerns the increased year by year, people for special education teaching quality also begin to pay close attention to. In recent years, presents a constructivist theory as a foundation, aiming at the characteristics of virtual learning for the deaf interactive platform solution. This scheme is the purpose of the application of virtual reality technology, having a new communication mechanism and rich resource of the real and virtual situation, through the visual sensory stimulation, the deaf can be immersive virtual scenario with a virtual role in the exchange and simulation study, complete the real world need to complete some of the communication, so as to solve the current task deaf teaching some difficult to resolve the psychological, environment, resources, etc [1][2].

2 Deaf Classroom Teaching Characteristics and Problems

With the normal demand for higher education in sharp contrast, China's higher education of persons with disabilities one of the few currently focus on several special education college or university's Department of Special Education. Most colleges and universities are able-bodied people as the object of education, the educational

Q. Zhou (Ed.): ISAEBD 2011, Part I, CCIS 208, pp. 576–583, 2011.

environment, it is difficult for existing facilities and resources for audio-visual barriers and obstacles to serious action to provide learning support services for persons with disabilities can only recruit a small number of physical disabilities, life can take care of themselves, does not affect reported in professional learning, and scored student to meet the requirements of persons with disabilities. However, for people with disabilities overcome the obstacles of higher learning to provide effective support services, not only on the school environment, facilities and equipment and other hardware to make corresponding improvements, and need to be able to effectively help the different types and degrees of disabilities to overcome barriers to learning teachers, courses and institutions. For the purposes of colleges and universities to further expand and improve the higher education of persons with disabilities, obviously subject to various factors [3].

According to the actual situation of the deaf, take full advantage of strengths and policy advantages, integrated around the existing resources will be deaf education and employment of persons with disabilities the combination of welfare, focusing on the development of lifelong education system built to explore creating a broader platform. The main building based on the local educational institutions teaching points, the use of modern means of distance education and open educational methods, to provide all kinds of deaf education. In this process, gradually exploring the deaf training distance education mode and teaching mode, management mode and operation mechanism, set up a series of learning needs to adapt to the deaf, including lifelong learning needs of deaf people's courses, professional and training programs, efforts to highlight the teaching resources and learning support services, distance education characteristics of the deaf, opened up so that more deaf people to accept a higher level, higher-quality new way of education, the formation of distance education for the deaf.

3 Distance Education Platform the Theoretical Basis

Virtual reality technology is 90 years since the 20th century, the rise of a new information technology, is a new form of human-computer interface. What it seeks is the traditional needs of people use a computer from a keyboard and mouse to operate the equipment of its people are into computers to create artificial environments. Users with complex fixed equipment (such as data gloves, helmets, etc.) to the natural methods of interaction with the virtual environment, mutual influence, to gain experience with the real-world equivalent, as well as experience in the real world is difficult to experience [4].

Virtual reality has many potential uses because it appeals to our intuitive use of information. In education it can allow for the creation of full environments that would present the experience of hands-on study without needing to leave the classroom. In medicine it can allow students and researchers to treat virtual patients as training and, in combination with advanced robotics, perform surgery at a distance. Engineers can create, modify and test designs in a virtual space, and soldiers can train in virtual war zones. Psychologists and therapists may also utilize virtual reality for treatment purposes, especially in the treatment of trauma disorders. The composition of the field of virtual reality system shown in Figure 1.4.

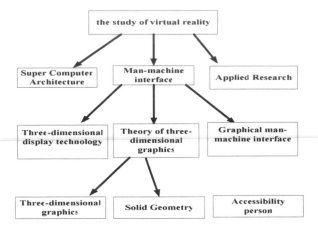

Fig. 1. The composition of the field of virtual reality system diagram

Using virtual reality technology to build a distance education platform is the direction of emerging technologies, especially in the field of educational technology, virtual reality technology to build a real teaching environment, laboratory environment and the virtual learning environment platform skills training. This platform to classroom teaching completion will no longer restricted to tangible classroom, classroom teaching activities of the space and time to get the intangible expansion [5][6]. It provided for the deaf vivid, realistic learning environment, students can become a participant in the virtual environment, in a virtual environment to play a role, which is to mobilize the enthusiasm of the deaf to learn to break through the teaching focus, difficult, deaf culture human skills will play an active role.

4   Distance Education Platform Design and Implementation

4.1 Design Philosophy

Distance education system and all the design of virtual reality system several principles should be followed it.

(1) System Security

Enhance operating system security, database security, network security and information transmission management system itself security.

(2) System Accessibility

For system design good user interface, through full communication with the system users, system users to learn more about the work content, work flow, focused care about. Then summarized, well-designed interface to meet user requirements [7].

(3) Ensure System Stability

Reasonable choice of software development life cycle, iterative development model, in the development process of repeated authentication software features to ensure system stability.

(4) Ensure System Scalability

Full account of the changing data needs increase, the system according to modular design, each module is independent, the module communication interface between the left, making the software platform is very easy to upgrade. When some modules need to be upgraded, and some modules do not need to upgrade, just need to upgrade the module can be changed without the other modules of the software platform to make any changes.

4.2 System Architecture Design

System design it is necessary to conform to current application needs, but also functions as possible to adapt to future expansion. It is necessary to meet the special nature of the industry but also has some versatility, not only from the perspective of the user to consider the availability of the system programmer's point of view but also from the feasibility of system development, the development cycle, cost, software quality problems. Therefore, the overall design of the system is a system realized the need to address the core issue.

Distance education platform to be adopted this three-tier B / (W-A) / D (Browser / (Webserver-ApplicationServer) / Dataserver structure. Taking into account the current majority of distance education software and virtual reality systems using C / S structure is conducive to inherit the traditional software system design ideas, and B / (W-A) / D structure is the development trend of the current computer system, so make sure that the distance education system is based on three-tier B / (W-A) / D structure.

As shown in figure 2 (dashed line indicates no cross.)

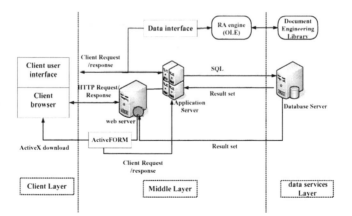

Fig. 2. System structure

Figure 2 with three-tier B / (W-A) / D strengths to achieve good results. Both can handle complex business rules, and also enhance the flexibility of the system (which can be cross-platform, such as Unix-Windows), open, implementation, and Internet standards, establish a complete information network, to achieve the greatest range of resource sharing, improved work and decision-making efficiency.

Three-tier structures were client layer, business logic layer and data services layer.
(1) Client Layer (presentation layer)

Client layer provides a user-friendly, intuitive interface. Student input through the user interface, handling all kinds of information, and complete the work subjects. You can also through the client browser view class teachering progress, teaching schedule, and the job is completed and so on.

(2) Business Logic Layer

In the B / (W-A) / D application environment, the business logic layer by the WEB server (Webserver) and application server (ApplicationServer) together to complete. Business logic layer is the core of the entire application, while the component object is equal to its heart. WEB server accepts a standard HTTP browser request and the request to the application server. Run in application server business logic (BusinessLogic) and data logic (DataLogic), this logic are encapsulated in several components, the components responsible for handling requests that the application layer to complete the business and data logic and database computing tasks and interaction, and the results are returned to the user in the presentation layer display. Business logic processing layer is originally placed in the client's business logic separate, centralized place application server, part of the share for all users.

(3) Data Services Layer

Data services layer for the application server provides data sources. And above the two-tier architecture, the database no longer maintain a connection for each active client, but the number of customers through the application of the logical components of a shared database server connections, thereby reducing connection times, improved server performance data and personal security, but also reduce network hardware investment.

4.3 System Software and Hardware Deployment

(1) Hardware Deployment

Because the system structure using B / (W-A) / D structure, the use of web publishing in ways that greatly facilitate the data reporting and integration. Its hardware structure and website work system similar to the top to bottom are: server, interface board, the transmission network, the customer terminal. Maximum use of existing resources, local area network, does not increase the cost of the hardware and software investment.

Server by way of web publishing, making the students computer terminal access to a central server through the Internet directly, for data reporting, information query and distance learning.

(2) Software Deployment

System data Center software architecture, including a central server and various teaching and the individual user software structure.The teaching points and individual users do not need software, just visit the website you can use online resources and online e-learning. All data are stored on a central server in the background database. Workflow of the system shown in Figure 3.

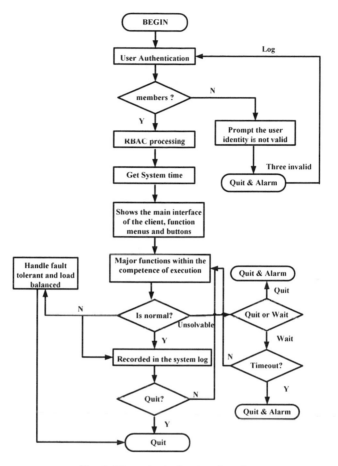

Fig. 3. Flow chart of system functions

4.4 System Module Division

(1) Rights Management module
The highest management authority can be granted permissions to users, such as changes to recover, and authority. User permissions, access to the system operation are also different.such as students, only homework in distance education authority, and no other students in their operations to see the permissions, but there is the teaching point of view of teachers teaching their own point of authority for all student work.

(2) Virtual Reality Module
Through the virtual learning environment, teaching the true display of the scene, creating a personalized learning environment for deaf students to the natural, friendly atmosphere for learning. In particular, the virtual display through sign language, deaf students can appreciate the distance education a familiar feeling, because they can not hear and to overcome the inconvenience, thereby enhancing the effectiveness of

learning and interest. The main idea of virtual reality technology is embodied in this section[8][9].

(3) Teaching Statistics Module

Learning or teaching students to achieve statistical operation, understanding what time distance students complete the course, and now how much time has been spent, what happened to complete the work, should inform them seize the time to learn.

(4) Course Learning Modules

The study participants according to their account and password to access the course module, the module provides all the learning courses. Students according to their professional and determined by the school curriculum independently choose the course open, the various stages of completion operations, and to submit, and classroom teachers into the system through their own permission to communicate with the students, answer questions, and conduct job correcting, and timely return to operating results and other operations, to realize the remote education purpose.

(5) Database Management Module

Database management module by the data backup module, data recovery module, back-end database, and several other modules. All kinds of information will continue to change as well as manual omissions that may occur, therefore, the system provides data backup and data recovery features that help owners complete the change has entered the data in the database, and does not need one by one to find errors. Its function is similar to the database automatically updates, especially for such small Access2000 database (stand-alone database application Access2000), does not have this feature, so this module is to protect the system data is an important guarantee the right.

(6) Print Function Module

The initial settings for printing, such as paper, network printing and so on.

(7) Web Information Distribution Module

Providing schools and education anywhere point of view and to download relevant information and automatically update the progress of teaching diagram. In addition to system administrators, other users and do not have information on the teaching point set upload permissions, but the conditions have to modify their own login authentication permissions. Also publish notice, such as notices of meetings, test notification.

(8) System Logs Module

Record number of key operations mainly to help users clear of the last operation, but also to be informed of who carried out the operation, clear responsibilities, regular cleaning by the system administrator in the system log records.

(9) Other Information Module

Distance education system, mainly various types of information resources, such as key guidance, teaching experiments, offline job, teaching files, online discussion and more.

5 Conclusions

Virtual reality technology based distance education platform for the realization of the deaf is a new teaching methods to try. Through Distance Education platform to inspire passion for learning the deaf, by providing a safe private space for learning to overcome the psychological barriers to the deaf and deaf to actively guide the spontaneous, self-confidence, freedom, self-learning attitude. Because of its authenticity, interactive, immersive, customizable, security features, thereby helping to overcome the deficiencies in teaching the deaf. we believe that with the continuous development of virtual reality technology, its practical value will better play.

Acknowledgment. The research was supported by 2009 Education Scientific Research Subject of the Eleventh Five-year Plan of Nanjing City, China (No: L09/005).

References

1. Lee, T.Y.: Investigating confidence and efficacy of special education pre-service teachers in traditional and alternative teacher education programs in Taiwan. Unpublished doctoral dissertation, University of Oklahoma, Norman, OK, U.S.A (2000)
2. Chenyunying: Making Special Education Compusory and Inclusive in China. Cambridge Journal of Education 26(1) (1996)
3. Benford, S.D., et al.: Embodiments, avatars, clones and agents for multi-user, multi-sensory virtual worlds. Multiedia System 5(2), 93–104 (1997)
4. Nddeau, D.R.: Tutorial.:Building virtual worlds wih VRML. IEEE Computer Graphics & Applications 19, 18–29 (1999)
5. Kalawsky, P.S.: Exploiting Virtual Reality Techniques in Education and Training.Technological Issues. AGOCG
6. Cheng, C., Zhang, M., Pan, Z.: Multi-resolution Modeling for Virtual Design. International Journal of Virtual Reality 4(4), 52–56 (2000)
7. Geroimenko, V., MikePhilliPs: Multi-User VRML Environment for Teaehing VRML: Immersive Collaborative Learning. In: Proeeedings of the 1999 International Conference on Informatlon Visualization (1999)
8. Hamada, Y., Shimada, N., Shirai, Y.: Hand shape estimation under complex backgrounds for sign language recognition. In: Proc. of Symposium on Face and Gesture Recognition, Seoul, Korea, pp. 589–594 (2004)
9. Lucio, I., Luca, C.: Employing Virtual Humans for Education and Training in X3D/VRML Worlds. Computers & Education 6(5), 23–25 (2005)

An Analysis on the Employment Effect of Raising Remuneration of Labor: A Study Based on Labor Market Imbalance

Xi Wang and Kaiming Ge

School of Management, Shanghai University of Engineering Science,
Shanghai 201620, China

Abstract. This paper made an analysis on the employment effect of raising labor remuneration in a labor market, where real wage received by labor is lower than their contribution. A labor demand and supply model was established to make this research. Besides, a fixed effect model was used to test propositions drawn from the model. It can be concluded that rising remuneration of labor have no negative effect on employment in China where negative distortion in labor market exits. Moreover, rising remuneration of labor can stimulate domestic demand, which is beneficial to employment and the realization of labor market equilibrium. This research give up the hypothesis that labor market in China is equilibrium, and the conclusion is more accurate and meaningful.

Keywords: imbalanced market remuneration of labor, negative distortion of labor market, employment effect, panel data.

1 Introduction

The proportion of residents' consumption expense to GDP in China has declined dramatically Since 90 decade of past century. Fixed asset investment and export become the most important drivers of economic growth in our country. However, the strategic role of expanding domestic consumption demand has been paid more and more attention to after international financial crisis of 2007. Only by increasing residents' income and improving social security system, can domestic consumption demand increase and become an important driver of economic growth. As a result, the reform on labor and wage institutions, aimed at increasing residents' income and social security level, has been carried out in recent years. The improving of labors' remuneration and minimum wage standard also raised doubts about its negative effects on employment, although they are welcomed by workers.

The existing research was conducted based on the hypothesis that labor market in China is a balanced market, and wage is determined by worker's marginal productivity. However, the most apparent characteristic of labor market in our country is that there is a large amount of surplus work force. This paper will make an analysis of the employment effect of raising remuneration of labor based on the imbalance characteristic of labor market in our country.

Q. Zhou (Ed.): ISAEBD 2011, Part I, CCIS 208, pp. 584–589, 2011.
© Springer-Verlag Berlin Heidelberg 2011

2   The Imbalance Characteristic of Labor Market in China

Walras' concept of general equilibrium price considered that labor market can be cleared automatically if labor resources are distributed based on the wage and workers can flow freely. In a balanced labor market described by Walras, wage is determined by marginal productivity of labor. If wage is improved to the level which is higher than the equilibrium wage, employment rate will decrease.

Is labor market in China a balanced market as described by Walras? Capital resources in China is scarce compared with labor resources, so labor demand is constrained by economic scale, which lead to an excessive supply of labor.

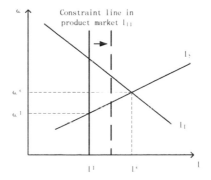

Fig. 1. The constraint from product market in an imbalanced labor market

As shown in figure 1, Labor market is balanced if aggregate demand in product market is large enough to absorb all potential labor force, labor can flow freely, and wage can adjusted freely. In such circumstances, equilibrium wage and employment are determined by the labor demand curve L_D and labor supply curve L_S. Equilibrium wage is ω^*, which is determined by productivity of labor. Equilibrium employment is L^*. However, employment will be constraint by aggregate demand in product market, if aggregate demand in product market is not enough to absorb call potential labor force. Assume that labor demand determined by effective demand in product market is $L_d(GDP)$, which is lower than equilibrium employment is L^*. Real labor demand curve is labor demand curve L_{DI} determined by output in product market. So Real wage is ω^I, lower than equilibrium wage ω^*. Real employment is L^I, lower than equilibrium employment L^*.

Under this circumstance, there will be no notable negative effects on employment, as real wage rises with the increase of minimum wage standard. In addition, real labor demand curve L_{DI} will move to the right and real employment will rise followed along with the increase of wage if aggregate demand in product market is expand with the increase of wage level. Based on the studies and analyses mentioned above, we can draw several conclusions as follows:

Proposition 1: There is relatively surplus labor supply in China, so real remuneration of labor is lower than their marginal productivity.

Proposition 2: The rise of minimum wage standard and the increase of average wage level will have no notable negative effect on employment, if there is negative distortion in labor market.

Proposition 3: Employment will increase followed along with the rise of wage, if output in product market can be expand with the rise of wage.

3 Instruction of Sample, Data and Software

Liaoning, Heilongjiang, Shanghai, Zhejiang, Fujian, Guangdong, Hubei, Hunan, Gansu, Shanxi are selected as study samples. Study period is from 1990 to 2009. All the data used in the paper come from China Statistical Yearbook each year, Statistical Yearbook of each province and city, and the announcements when local government adjusted minimum wage standard. Soft ware used in the research is Eviews6.0.

4 Measurement of the Distortion Level in Labor Market

This paper will measure the level of distortion in labor market by the index of labor market distortion degree (*lmd*). Labor market distortion degree is the gap between real wage and equilibrium wage. There is negative distortion in labor market if real wage is lower than equilibrium level. On the opposite, the distortion is positive. Equilibrium wage is determined by the real contribution of labor in production.

Table 1. Measurement of labor market distortion of 10 representative provinces and cities

district	Marginal productivity of labor	Proportion of labor remuneration to GDP	labor market distortion degree (*lmd*)
Liaoning	0.76	0.46	-0.3
Heilongjiang	0.71	0.44	-0.27
Shanghai	0.66	0.35	-0.31
Zhejiang	0.75	0.44	-0.31
Fujian	0.81	0.5	-0.31
Guangdong	0.8	0.49	-0.31
Hubei	0.77	0.55	-0.22
Hunan	0.62	0.57	-0.05
Gansu	0.5	0.49	-0.01
Shanxi	0.48	0.45	-0.03

As shown in table 1, various degrees of negative distortion are existed in ten provinces and cities. Proposition 1 is verified. Among these 10 provinces and cities, the level of negative distortion of labor market is the highest in Shanghai, Zhejiang, Fujian, and Guangdong, which are the regions of net labor import.

5 Study on the Employment Effect of Changing Remuneration of Labor

The following part of this chapter will make a study on the employment effect of changing average wages and adjusting minimum wage using panel data of 10 sample cities from 1995 to 2009. The model shown as below is used.

$$logY_{it}=c+\alpha logX_{it}+\beta Z_{it}*logX_{it}+\gamma_1 loggdp_{it}+\gamma_2 logpopulation_{it}. \qquad (1)$$

In equation (1), $employment_{it}$ is a dependant variable, which is the number of labor employed in the province or city of i at the end of the year of t. X_{it} is independent variable, which is the index relevant to the level of wage, including $wage_{it}$ that is the average wage, $mwage_{it}$ that is the minimum wage, and $mwage/wage_{it}$ which is minimum wage divided by average wage. Two controlling variables are included in equation 1 in order to eliminate the influence of aggregate demand and supply in product market, as well as total labor supply on employment. One is gdp_{it}. The other is $populatioin_{it}$. A cross term named $Z_{it}*X_{it}$ is included in order to inspect the relation between employment effect of raising wages and labor market imbalance. Z_{it} is a dummy variable, Z_{it} equals to 1 when the level of negative labor market imbalance is higher than average. Otherwise, Z_{it} equals to 0. Detailed explanations about every variable are shown in table 2.

Table 2. Detailed explanations about every variable

	Variable	Explanation about the variable
Dependant Variable	$employment_{it}$	Logarithm of the number of people employed
Independent Variables	$wage_{it}$	Logarithm of average wage
	$mwage_{it}$	Logarithm of minimum wage (choosing the highest minimum wage standard in this province or city)
	$mwage/wage_{it}$	Minimum wage divided by average wage
	Z_{it}	A dummy variable. Z_{it} equals to 1, if lmd is less than -0.21. Otherwise, Z_{it} equals to 0.
Controlling Variables	gdp_{it}	Logarithm of GDP (deflated by price level in 1990)
	$populatioin_{it}$	Logarithm of the number of population

Based on equation 1 and analysis above, four models are created to make tests about employment effect of changing average wages and adjusting minimum wage standard. Fixed effect model is chosen in making regression analysis. Results are shown in table 3.

It can be concluded from model 1 that employment is not decreased with the rise of remuneration of labor. However, employment is significantly increased with the rise of remuneration of labor in regions where level of labor market imbalance is higher than average. In model 2, the coefficient of $mwage/wage_{it}$ is positive ($p<0.05$), which means that employment will increase if the gap between minimum wage and average wage is narrowed.

Table 3. Results of regression analysis

	Model 1	Model 2	Model 3	Model 4
$wage_{it}$	0.0138	0.0211		
$mwage_{it}$			0.0202	0.0079**
$wage_{it} * Z_{it}$	0.0076**	0.0186**		
$mwage_{it} * Z_{it}$			0.0119**	0.0328**
$mwage/wage_{it}$		0.2825*		0.2150**
$mwage/wage_{it}* Z_{it}$		-0.3354		-0.3523
gdp_{it}	0.3098**	0.3256**	0.3036**	0.3263**
$populatioin_{it}$	0.6950**	0.5885**	0.6992**	0.5216**
$Ajusted\ R^2$	0.99	0.99	0.99	0.99

(Note: ** means the coefficient is significant at probability of 5%, * means the coefficient is significant at the probability of 10%.)

It can be concluded from model 3 that employment is not decreased with the rise of minimum wage standard. However, employment is significantly increased with the rise of minimum wage standard in regions where level of labor market imbalance is higher than average. In addition, it can be proved in model 4 that employment will increase with the narrowing of the gap between minimum wage and average wage. Proposition 2 is verified.

It can be drawn from the above analysis that real remuneration received by labor is lower than their contribution in production in an imbalanced labor market with the existence of surplus labor force. Under this circumstance, raising remuneration of labor may expand employment instead of reducing employment. This is because dispensable income and consuming capacity of residents can be increased with the rise of remuneration of labor, which can expand aggregate demand in product market, and increase employment. Proposition 3 is verified. Besides, reducing the income gap by rising minimum wage standard can improve marginal propensity to consume of the whole society, which is beneficial to promote economic growth and employment.

6   Conclusions and Suggestions

It is proved in this paper that real remuneration of labor is lower than their marginal contribution to economic growth. Thus, rising average wage and minimum wage standard will expand aggregate demand in product market and employment. This conclusion is very important in reforming wage and income distribution system.

(1) It is essential to raise average wage and minimum wage standard in regions where negative distortions in labor market exist.
(2) The rise of average wage and minimum wage standard must be accompanied with the increasing of labor productivity.

(3) It is essential to narrow the gap between minimum wage standard and average wage in order to reduce income gap with the increase of average wage in the society.

Acknowledgement. This paper is sponsored by Social Science and Humanity Research Project of The Ministry of Education in China in 2011. The project is RMB Exchange Rate Friction and Policy Choice in Transition. (Grant No.10YJA790054).

References

1. Lemos, S.: Minimum Wage Effects in a Developing Country. Labour Economics. 16(2), 224–237 (2009)
2. Brown, C., Curtis, G., Andrew, K.: The Effect of the Minimum Wage on Employment and Unemployment. Journal of Economic Literature. 20(2), 487–528 (1982)
3. Shi, J.: The Employment Effects of Minimum Wage Standards in China: Based on the National and Regional Empirical Research. Contemporary Economy & Management 31(12), 8–11 (2009)
4. Ding, S.: An Analysis of Minimum Wage Effects on the Labor Market —Effect of Interaction with the Law of the PRC on Employment Contracts. Chinese Social Science 1, 85–102 (2010)
5. Yuan, Z.: Application of non-Walraslan Equilibrium Theory in China. Shanghai People's Publishing House, Shanghai (2006)

Research of Strategy of Shandong Sports Tourism's Development Depending on the Eleventh National Games

Li Yan, Yu Cao, Xiaomei Zhou, Yiming Liu, Fang Han, Li Li, and Yajing Wang

Tourist Management Department, University of Jinan, Jinan, P.R. China

Abstract. In order to provide relevant theoretical help for Shandong sports Tourism's development, taking Shandong sports tourism as the research object, this paper analyzed the advantages and the problems of Shandong sports tourism, studied the influences of the Eleventh National Games and on this basis looked for the countermeasures of Shandong sports Tourism. The authors believe that the only outlet is to combine government's macro-control, self-improvement of the sports tourism, and taking the opportunity of the Eleventh National Games with each other.

Keywords: Shandong, sports tourism, the Eleventh National Games, development.

1 Introduction

1.1 Sports Tourism

In a broad sense, sports tourism is a tourism based on all kinds of sports, namely the sum total of relationships of a variety of physical recreation, physical exercise, sports competition, sports rehabilitation which tourists engage in and sports-to-culture activities related to tourist sports, sports tourism enterprises and the society. In a narrow sense, it is a social activity aimed at promoting social material and spiritual civilization, enriching social cultural life. In order to adapt and meet the needs of tourists of various sports, make a harmonious development of body and mind by kinds of sports programs. To its social nature, sports tourism is a kind of social economic and cultural activity in no matter a broad sense or a narrow one, and also an important part of sports' industrialization and commercialization.

1.2 The Eleventh National Games

In October, 2009, the Eleventh National Games are held in Jinan. The magnificent sports meeting contributed to Shandong's economics, society, environment, and so on.

1.2.1 Promote the Development of Tertiary Industry
During National Games, a large number of media, visitors, and viewers gather in Jinan, leading to various economic activities and increasing extra consumer demand.

Q. Zhou (Ed.): ISAEBD 2011, Part I, CCIS 208, pp. 590–596, 2011.

They mainly centralize in transportation, tourism. catering, post and telecommunications, sports and health industry, convention and exhibition industry, social services, commerce, education, arts and culture industries, broadcasting, film and television industry, finance and insurance, media and other fields, greatly leading the development of tertiary industry in Shandong.

1.2.2 Give Publicity to Qilu Culture, Show Characteristics of the Springs

The Games holding in Jinan is a great opportunity to give publicity to Qilu Culture. Through the window of the Games, the whole country and the world can get a better understanding of Jinan and Shandong. It is a chance to show that Jinan is a civilized, open, simple and harmonious modern city. This opportunity should be taken advantage of to expend Jinan's business card of Springs' City recognition.

1.2.3 Improve the Nation's Fitness and Development of Sports Career

Shandong Province calls out the slogan "nationwide body-building goes with the National. Games and the Olympic Games ", brings the development of masses sports career into the Eleventh National Games' purpose, carries out a series of nationwide body- building activities and develops one point three ways project and "nationwide sports body- building" project. The Eleventh National Games is significant to raise awareness of fitness, spread body- building knowledge, set off a fitness craze and to enhance people's health. The Eleventh National Games leaves a large number of fitness facilities and stadiums, giving an important guarantee to nationwide body-building activities.

1.2.4 Promote Spiritual Civilization

During the Eleventh National Games, the masses carry out spiritual civilization "Welcome the National Games, deliver civilization, new spirit" spiritual civilization activities, the civilized education expanding, the civilized order developing, spiritual civilization community building, key areas' improvement, springs volunteers' dedication, leading immaturity. Thus forms a united progressive, civilized, harmonious social atmosphere and provides a good social environment for economic and social development of Jinan.

2 The Eleventh National Games' Influences to Shandong Sports Tourism

2.1 Scale Effect of Industry Development

The Eleventh National Games drive the cooperation of the sports institutions and the tourism institutions and contribute to the scale development of sports tourism. Its influence mainly manifest in: first, the cooperation of the sports institutions and the tourism institutions will be further deepened, and sports tourism-related organization management and government support will be increased; second, investment to sports tourism will be a hot spot of the future areas of tourism investment; Third, the combination of sports and tourism will provide more space and options for the city management of the city's image.

2.2 Spreading Effect of the City's Image

The successful host of the Olympics in Beijing improves China' international image and status, makes more people to travel in China. The propagation to China and then attracts more people to travel in China. The propagations and reports running through the Eleventh National Games reinforce the understanding of Shandong of potential tourists, improve Shandong' s visibility and reputation and have a contribution to expanding the tourism market. Among all the most important is its large-scale free market spread.

2.3 Intensified Effect of Sports Awareness

The Eleventh National Games inspire the masses' enthusiasm for participation in sports activities and helps to promote the development of sports tourism market. Nowadays, People's leisure manners change a lot. They are satisfied with the traditional leisure lifestyle no more and begin to participate in some sports tourism items which can promote health, restore physical energy, enhance physical exercise, such as hiking, swimming, skiing and enjoying large-scale competitions. The upsurge enthusiasm of the public and positive healthy attitude will lead popular sports forward. Meanwhile, the watch and participation, the civil sporting events, national and international sports events will greatly increase. People's enthusiasm for the sports will be the catalyst for the development of sports tourism.

2.4 The Expansion Effect of Source Markets

The international experience shows that the organization of major sports events can bring an objective effect of promoting the diversity of source markets. According to statistics, there is one in every four tourists seek participation in sports activities when traveling. The successful host of the Eleventh National Games brings a sharp raise of temperature of sports which means the expansion of the demand of sports market. The awareness of the nationwide body-building promotes consumption of sports and civilian leisures and affordable-type sports grow up. Meanwhile, with the increase in consumption levels, people pay more attention to recreational activities of middle and high levels. As the kinds of the sports increases, the consumers have more options and this will bring quantities of tourists, which will provide a good opportunity to extend Shandong's sports tourism market.

2.5 The Ensuring Effect of Infrastructure

The Eleventh National Games' holding leads to the construction of the major part of the city and urban green environment. After the Eleventh National Games, the passion for the public sports tourism grows constantly in Shandong Province. More tourist destinations notice it and for the sake of attracting sports tourists, they begin the construction of sports facilities and carry out various featured sports tourism projects. Jinan City is also active in urban infrastructure construction, and overall renovation and construction on tourist facilities, transportation, environmental protection, and communication and competition venues. The great strength to the construction of urban infrastructure will offer infrastructure guarantee for Shandong sports tourism.

2.6   The Perfecting Effect of the Product Structure

The Eleventh National Games' holding promotes the systematic and innovative development of Shandong sports tourism products. It plays a positive role in standing the form of sports tourism products and perfecting sports tourism industry structure. At present, the exploit of Shandong's sports tourism remains to be scattered and sports tourism products of high quality are few. The Eleventh National Games' successful holding pulls the product development of various watch type, participation type, and culture recreational type based on the Eleventh National Games.

3   Strategy for the Development of Sports Tourism in Shandong Province

3.1   Government's Macro-Control

3.1.1   Setting Up Specific Administrative Agencies for the Developing of Sports Tourism

Special administrative agencies for sports tourism are supposed to be established by relevant departments to have concrete guide and management on sports tourism. Policies should be formulated to develop and preserve the sports tourism resources and efforts should be made to enhance the standardized and international management of sports tourism market. Moreover, involved departments should pay attention to the cultivation of talents on sports tourism, the relevant problems to sports tourism development.

3.1.2   Formulating Scientific Plan on Sports Tourism Development

Policy-makers and relevant workers in sports industry should base on current tourist sites and give full play to its strengths on natural resources as well as human and cultural resources; and formulate plans for developing sports tourism, including annual plan, five-year plan and long-term plan. Plans should be formulated on the basis of market economy and sports tourism should be included into the whole tourism plan, so as to establish a unified tourism market system across Shandong Province. If necessary, policy-makers could take "proper leading" into consideration.

3.1.3   Strengthening the Publicity Effects

Manners of propagating should be improved and various methods of propagation could be employed including films and television, songs, advertisements and Internet to increase the propagating influence, expand the coverage, raise its scientific content as well as to enhance real effects of propagation on sports tourism.

3.1.4   Improving Expertise Training for Sports Tourism

At present, there is a shortage of expertise on the whole who have a good knowledge not only about tourism but also about sports. And the situation is worse in Shandong Province. To turn Shandong Province into a province which is famous for its sports tourism home and abroad, a group of specific talents on sports tourism who are well-qualified, high-leveled and capable should be trained, through various dimensions and methods including sports tourism guiders, coaches on sports tourism projects and intelligents for the design and development of sports tourism products, thereby raising the overall competence of the Shandong tourism group.

3.1.5 Formulating Long-Term Plan for the Sustainable Development of Sports Tourism

With the regard of developing the sports tourism resources, the principle of long term, caution, and sustainability should be followed and more attention should be paid to the presence of culture as well as human's living environment. The long-term plan for development of sports tourism should be in line with both the local regions' normal social development and social morale regulations to protect the natural resources. The long-term development of China's sports tourism should be focused on the theme of ecotourism to precede green development, thus contributing to the sustainable development of sports tourism.

3.2   Self-improvement and Self-development of the Sports Tourism

3.2.1   Improving the Construction of Sports Tourism Infrastructure and Other Related Facilities

As the host province of the Eleventh National Games, it will have great influence to achieving the developing tasks in advance of a great number of ?including Jinan, Qingdao, Weihai and some other ?In addition,it will also accelerate the construction and of transportation, hotels, communication and some other infrastructure construction and help to build a internationally high-leveled sports stadiums. Though, from the perspective of long-term development of sports tourism, constant progress should be made in promoting on the development of infrastructure and relevant facilities to provide tourists with much more improved touring services.

3.2.2   Establishing and Improving the System for Sports Tourism Products

It's necessary to establish and improve a comprehensive system for sports tourism products which is based on various forms of resources and could meet the demands of different market groups. For instance golf tourism and spring tourism could be developed for the Japanese or Korean visitors, vocational tourism of swimming in summer for the Russian visitors and touring along seaside for visitors from other domestic regions.

Depended upon the characteristic of the sports resources in Shandong Province, touring on a bike, in a car or with exploration and other various forms of sports touring activities would be introduced, It could host high-leveled sporting events and attract sports training camps to settle down in Shandong, thus facilitating the optimization and upgrading of industrial structure of sports tourism.

3.2.3   Emphasizing on the Local Characteristics of Sports Tourism in Shandong Province

Characteristics are the key to its attractiveness of sports tourism. Designs on the touring lines, activities and sites should be conformed to its local conditions, instead of overlooking its human and cultural strengths as well as its natural advantages. Unique natural and human and cultural conditions in Shandong Province should be taken full advantage of to creatively develop the sports tourism products with characteristics. For instance, to develop characteristic projects including beach volleyball, sand football, diving, surfing, waterskiing along the "golden coast" in the eastern costal cities such as Qingdao, Weihai, Rizhao, Yantai; to add programs such as rock-climbing, exploration, umbrella-jumping, and so on. These types of tourism products can meet sports tourists' meets of various vacations, ages and educations.

3.2.4 Employing a Variety of Promoting Strategies

It is important for people engaged in sports tourism to employ various methods to strengthen the propagation on Shandong sports tourism, thereby enabling tourists to recognize and accept this new type of tourism through public opinion. Positive propagation could strengthen the communities' and people's concepts on sports tourism so that the sports tourism could begin from a relative high point and operate within social regulations, which would give full play to its role in economic and social development and thus spur economic development and improve people's living quality.

3.3 Taking the Opportunity to Develop Sports Tourism

3.3.1 Taking Full Advantage of the Sporting Stadium

The newly-built stadiums for the Eleventh National Games could be included into the development of touring line as emerging resources so that the city's touring product system could be enriched and more creative. There will be new changes in spatial architecture of the city's touring system; in particular, the rising of the Olympic Stadium of the eastern region is likely to change the current landscape architecture of Jinan's tourism, transferring the focus of tourism attracting system. In addition, there will also have several new spotlights in industrial distribution of tourism attracting system, for instance, which is exemplified that resources of sports affairs could be made use of to further develop new types of programs, such as meeting, exhibition, show and so forth. This is not only improvements of tourism attracting system, but also a good opportunity to develop modern urban sports tourism.

3.3.2 Enhancing the Spreading of Images of Urban Sports System

As the National Games is the largest and most influential comprehensive sports through China, during the four years before hosting the National Games, Shandong Province has become the spotlight of the whole country and was even concerned by several countries around the world. The tremendous media effect during the Eleventh National Games ,particularly the praise effect caused by domestic and international tourists will change its relative weaknesses in sports tourism to a large extent and increase tourists enthusiasm and expectations for traveling in Shandong Province, particularly it could substantially raise the good fame and prestige of Shandong's touring brand. Shandong should take this chance to demonstrate the new image combining tourism propagation with Shandong Province's reform and opening up to the domestic and international visitors through media including newspapers, magazines, radios and televisions.

3.3.3 Making Greater Efforts to Nurture Mass Sports Tourism Market

With the help of the propagation of the National Sports Games, the government and relevant departments could spur the public's participating enthusiasm and raise the public's recognition toward sports tourism. Furthermore, continuous propagation should also be proceeded to strive for potential consumers as well as to make sports tourism penetrate people's mind, thereby nurturing wide mass sports tourism market.

4 Conclusion

In a word, the hosting of the Eleventh National Games has provided unprecedented opportunities for the development of Shandong Province's sports tourism. Our province should formulate feasible strategies on the basis of the current state of Shandong's sports tourism and finally make sports tourism a spotlight of Shandong Province tourism.

Acknowledgments. The authors would like to express their thanks to the Shandong University Scientific Research Project and the Jinan University Social Science Research Project for the financial support under the grants of J9WJO1-2 and X0938.

References

1. Sun, C.: Current State of Sports Tourism and Research on Its Relevant Development. Modernization of the Business Sphere 556, 37–40 (2008)
2. Jia, L., Cheng, Y.: Impacts upon Jinan's Economy and Society of the Eleventh National Games. Neijiang Science and Technology 07, 134 (2009)
3. Zheng, Y.: Research on the Development of Dalian Sports Tourism in the Post-Olympics era. Learning Theory 13, 56–58 (2009)
4. Wang, B.: Beijing Olympic Games' Effect and Countermeasures on China Tourism. Sports Science 2, 77–78 (2007)
5. Chang, H.: Situation and Prospects of Sports Tourism in China. Sports Culture Guide 1, 33–34 (2003)
6. He, Q.: Situation, Problems and Countermeasures of Sports Tourism. Journal of Shanxi Normal University Physical Education Institute 20, 24–25 (2005)

Brief Analysis on Green Service of Economy Hotel

Lin Liu

Tourism & Cuisine School, Harbin
University of Commerce, Harbin, China
bestlyn@163.com

Abstract. Limited service is such a characteristic of economy hotel which meets the consumers' requests and fits the development trend of hotel industry. So economy hotel becomes a new force which rises suddenly in the fierce market competition. Nowadays, the new development trend of hotel industry is protecting environment, saving resources and constructing green hotel. The owners of economy hotel need to accept new concept and carry out green service with its own advantages in order to have further development.

Keywords: economy hotel, green service, environment.

1 Introduction

People have paid unprecedented attention to the following problems such as limited resources, climate change and environment pollution in recent years. So the concepts of environmental protection and economy are accepted and chosen as people's life attitudes and lifestyles. Under the circumstances, green hotel becomes popular for the development of hotel industry. In China, GB/T14308-2010 Star-rating Standard of Tourist Hotel has been implemented. It promotes the course of establishing green hotels for all star-rated hotels in China because of its new environmental protection requirements. And such a course is becoming an outbreak of "green revolution" in hotel industry. However, establishing a green hotel needs to carry out green service which may promote green marketing and realize green management authentically. Facing such a new development trend of hotel industry, the owners of economy hotel had better make effective use of the advantages of the hotel to construct green hotel and carry out green service in order to get long-term development for the hotel.

2 Relative Definition

2.1 Hotel Service

Hotel service can be defined from the standpoint of service provider. And it has its broad or narrow sense. Broadly speaking, hotel service means all the effort that hotel staff has put into work to meet the guests' needs. And in this case, hotel service has the same meaning with hotel product, including tangible product and intangible

Q. Zhou (Ed.): ISAEBD 2011, Part I, CCIS 208, pp. 597–601, 2011.
© Springer-Verlag Berlin Heidelberg 2011

product. Tangible product refers to the product that satisfies the guests' material demands, such as food product, accommodation product. And intangible product means the product that meets the guests' spirit needs. The narrow definition of hotel service is also called intangible service which means the effort that hotel staff has put into work only to satisfy the guests' spirit needs. The following discussion of this paper is made on the basis of broad definition of hotel service.

2.2 Limited Service

Limited service is just the opposite of full service which is offered by high-ranking hotel. It is defined as the basic hotel service that only meets the guests' accommodation needs. It simplifies or cancels the supporting services of full service such as catering, entertaining and shopping. Its prime product is accommodation product. Although the function is relatively simple, it emphasizes the availability of the service and pays attention to the excellence of service quality.

2.3 Green Service

Green service refers to the hotel service which is under the guidance of sustainable development throughout the course of offering service. There are four layers of meaning in this concept. They are the following: First, it advocates the reasonable use of resources, effective environmental protection measures and getting economic, environmental and social benefits simultaneously. Second, it should be under the guidance of sustainable development, not only the course of offering service but also before-offering and after-offering. Third, it meets the guests' needs and provides green service product. Fourth, it makes the guests realize the importance of environmental protection and choose green service consumption which has the least negative effects to the environment.

3 Meaning of Carrying Out Green Service

3.1 Conforming to the Trend of Environmental Protection

Nowadays, the global resources are consumed excessively and the ecological environment becomes increasingly serious. In China, the contradiction between growth of economy and restriction of resources and environment has become more and more obvious. Therefore, paying attention to environmental protection has become the theme of the times. In such a situation, we must insist on the concept of sustainable development and seek for the adaptation of social development and the environment, the harmony of economic construction and the environment. We'd try to have consensus of protecting the environment, saving energy and reducing pollution. Comparing with the star-rated hotel, economy hotel has less environmental pollution, resources waste and energy consumption. This is more helpful to fit with the trend of constructing green hotel and offering green service.

3.2 Enlarging Market Share

More and more people are concerned about their health, the impact of their consumption behavior and how to minimize the impact on the worsening natural environment. So, it is quite in fashion to stay in green hotel and accept green service. For economy hotel, offering green service may expand its market share because it will attract more new guests, especially those eco-concerned guests who only have experiences of staying in other kinds of hotels. In China, the brand economy hotel has just an 8% market share while it is 70% in developed countries in Europe and America. It indicates that our economy hotel has huge development potential in market competition. On the other hand, being green hotel and offering green service may help our economy hotel break green barriers, get competition qualification and realize chain operation in the international market.

3.3 Reducing Operating Costs

The energy price has risen constantly in recent years because limited energy is not enough for people's increasing demands. However, hotel operation needs a large number of energy such as water, electricity. So the hotel has to pay more for the energy and operating costs. But offering green service is an effective way to reduce operating costs and increase profits by adopting advanced technology, updating products, reducing daily consumption and transforming related institution. It is also an effective way to change the status of high energy consumption, serious pollution and high emission of high-ranking hotel.

3.4 Promoting Hotel Image

The course of offering green service to the guests by economy hotel is not only good for its operation, but also for protecting local environment, saving resources and reducing social stress and burden. This not only helps the hotel gain the guests' respect and trust but also promotes the hotel reputation and public image. Meanwhile, this course is a good role model for economy hotel business partners because it may promote their green transformation of products and services.

4 Advantages of Carrying Out Green Service

4.1 Ideas of Establishing

Economy hotel is constructed to offer product that is less expensive, clean, comfortable and safe to business people and FIT according to the change of market demand. It insists on operating at lower costs since the beginning of construction in order to keep lower room rate. It requires us to save both investment costs and operation costs and emphasize simplicity, energy saving and consumption reduction on every detail of establishment and operation. And this is just the connotation of green service. Therefore, economy hotel has more advantageous concept of investment and operation mode than high-ranking hotel to carry out green service.

4.2 Service Features

The most important feature of economy hotel service is "limited service". Comparing with full service which is offered by high-ranking hotel, limited service is characterized by distributing resources more reasonably and utilizing resources more effectively. It coincides with the requirements of green service better. Economy hotel emphasizes the principle of simple and efficient on the staffing. And the employee should be qualified for more than one post. That guarantees the maximum possibility of costs and resources saving while offering excellent and professional service to the guests.

4.3 Customer Groups Characteristics

The customer groups of economy hotel are more likely to be business people and FIT. Most of them are the young and the middle-aged. On the one hand, they usually have new ideas, strong sense of social responsibility and awareness of unexpected development so they can understand why the hotel carries out green service and are willing to cooperate. Even some eco-concerned guests may only choose to stay in green hotel which offers green service. On the other hand, the customer groups of economy hotel care more about the room rate so they are more easily to consume and accept green service under the guidance of the hotel.

5 Measures of Carrying Out Green Service

5.1 Establishing Green Service Concept

Only the staff of economy hotel has realized the importance of environmental protection and the necessities of carrying out green service could they gradually establish green service concept and work under its guidance. And this is the only source of carrying out green service in economy hotel. The owners of the hotel need to take effective measures such as constant staff training and taking part in public welfare activities for educational propaganda in order to help staff establish green service concept.

5.2 Emphasizing Green Service Design

Broadly speaking, green service design is equal to green product design. And for most economy hotels, guest room is the main product. The following are the steps to design green guest room. First of all, design the overall planning of the hotel itself. The examples are as follows: Try to make full use of natural lighting while designing the layout of the hotel. Choose new materials which are energy saving, waterproof and soundproof as building materials. While planning water supply system, choose water-saving utensils and equipment such as variable frequency and constant pressure water supply equipment, temperature sensor-controlled tap for public area, reclaimed water disposal equipment, boiler backwater circulating equipment. Secondly, design the decoration and fitment of the guest room. It can be exemplified by the following: Choose the latest environmental-friendly lacquer and ornament materials. Install energy-saving lighting device, water-saving equipment and energy control facilities, such as energy-saving lamp, sensor-controlled water valve and energy-limiting system. Once more, design daily necessities in the guest room. For example, adopt more environment-friendly and recyclable packaging and select the recyclable materials.

5.3 Advocating Green Service Consumption

Green service consumption refers to the total consumption and advocacy of green service which is made by the guests who advocate "green, healthy and natural" service. Economy hotel guests can't be accustomed to green service consumption in one day. They need time to understand and accept green service and also the guidance of the hotel. For example, place green card in the guest room to guide them for less times of changing the linen. Also we may reward the guests' environmental protection behavior. Take the following for examples: If the guest doesn't use one-time gratis washing supplies in Home Inn, he may get the awarded score. And the guest can have preferential rate if he pays for the electricity and water charge himself in Green Tree Shell.

6 Conclusion

Now the competition of hotel industry has entered a "green competition" stage since environment and energy problems become worse. As a new member of hotel industry, economy hotel can offer green service more easily than high-ranking hotel because of its ideas of establishing, service features and customer groups characteristics. Therefore, it is necessary for the owners and staff of economy hotel to establish green service concept, emphasize green service design and advocate green service consumption in order to conform to the trend of environmental protection, enlarge market share, reduce operating costs and promote hotel image. And only in this way can the owners of economy hotel take the opportunity of the change of consuming demand to keep good competitiveness.

References

1. Li, Y., Zong, C.: Research on Measures of Creating Green Economy Hotels Under the Concept of Circular economy. Commercial Research 4, 189 (2010)
2. Zhao, X.: Discussion on Hotel Operation Based on Low Carbon Economy. China CIO News 11, 137 (2010)
3. Hu, Z.: On Green Service. Journal of Southwest Jiaotong University (Social Sciences) 2, 66 (2004)

Research on Moral Hazard of Tourism Enterprise on the Basis of Game Theory

Lin Liu

Tourism & Cuisine School, Harbin
University of Commerce, Harbin, China
bestlyn@163.com

Abstract. The moral hazard of tourism enterprise has become a problem in the development of tourism industry. Based on game theory, this paper constructs a game model for the government and the tourism enterprise. It makes the following conclusion after analyzing the game model. If the government strengthens the restraint and increases the penalty for the tourism enterprise which has moral hazard, the tourism enterprise will choose the operation without moral risk voluntarily.

Keywords: moral hazard, game, government, tourism enterprise.

1 Introduction

Moral hazard is such a conception which advanced by western economists in economy and philosophy category. It refers to the behavior of economic agents who damage the interests of others because of seeking their maximum utility when they don't need to take overall responsibility for the consequences of their actions. Moral hazard is common in economic activities mainly on incomplete contracts and asymmetric information. It also exists in tourism industry. Based on game theory, this paper constructs a game model of restricting moral hazard of the tourism enterprise.

2 Main Manifestation of Moral Hazard of Tourism Enterprise

Moral hazard of tourism enterprise influences the following main subjects in tourism market.

First, tourism administration department. The tourism enterprise may not obey laws and regulations of tourism, carry out obligations of protecting environment and undertake social responsibilities in the operation in order to realize maximum interests. Take the following for examples: The operation of the travel agency is beyond the legally-operated scope. The registered capital is used for any other purposes after capital verification. The course of developing tourism attractions pays no attention to the protection of resources and environment.

Q. Zhou (Ed.): ISAEBD 2011, Part I, CCIS 208, pp. 602–606, 2011.

Second, tourist. The following are the influences of moral hazard of tourism enterprise on tourists. Regarding the signing contract with travel agency, it is usually unequal and incomplete. And even sometimes the travel agency may break the contract. Talking of service, it is often provided with great randomness. For example, the tour guide changes the itinerary without tourists' permission. Also the timeliness of provided service is poor. For instance, it takes a long time to queue at the scenic spots. So is its efficiency. For example, no bellman takes care of your baggage in the hotel. Also there is effect on price. On the one hand, fraudulent pricing is serious. The souvenir shop or the hotel may make false quotation while the travel agency makes fuzzy quotation for sales promotion. On the other hand, price discrimination exits in operation. For example, the travel agency may charge more for the old, the child and even the teacher.

Third, partner. For the partner, the problem of back money has been one of main effects caused by moral hazard of tourism enterprise. Back money refers to the tourism enterprise which is the purchaser refuses to pay the supplier the owed money. It is most serious in travel agency industry. Meanwhile, problems of default and illegitimate competition are worth considering. All of these problems increase cooperation costs, lower cooperation efficiency and obstruct the cooperation.

Fourth, employee. Moral hazard of tourism enterprise also affects the employee. For example, the tourism enterprise underpays or defaults the salary, reduces employee benefits, offer no help for career planning and promotion space.

3   Game Model of Restricting Moral Hazard of Tourism Enterprise

The reasons of forming moral hazard of tourism enterprise are various. And the fundamental reason is asymmetric information. To be more specific, this kind of asymmetric information can also be called action style asymmetric information. In this condition, both parties of signing the contract know the relevant information. But one of the parties takes advantage of the information which the other party knows nothing about after signing and causes loss for the other party. This kind of action may be indolent or failing in his duties. Moral hazard of tourism enterprise may disrupt tourism market order and restrict the healthy development of tourism industry. Therefore, it is urgent for local government to regulate the action of tourism enterprise. And the main method of is through legislative process by the government.

3.1   Model Hypothesis

Suppose there are only two participants in this model, namely the government and the tourism enterprise. For the government, it may choose to impose restraint and impose no restraint. And the tourism enterprise may have no moral hazard or have moral hazard. And once the government imposes restraint on moral hazard of the tourism enterprise, the restraint will be effective. The government has no information on the action of the tourism enterprise before making decision, and vice versa. But they have known mutual strategy and profit function exactly. In this case, this model is a complete information static game.

3.2   Model Analysis

In this model, k_1 is the income which the tourism enterprise gets with no moral hazard. k_2 is the income which the tourism enterprise gets with moral hazard. s_1 is the additional costs for the tourism enterprise with no moral hazard. s is the costs of imposing restraint on the tourism enterprise by the government. s_p equals the penalty which should be paid by the tourism enterprise with moral hazard. P equals probability of being imposed restraint by the government. Meanwhile, y is for the probability of imposing restraint and 1-y is the probability of imposing no restraint by the government. x equals the probability of having no moral hazard and 1−x equals the probability of having. Therefore, the following table may show decision-making behavior of both the government and the tourist enterprise:

Table 1. Game Matrix of Government and Tourism Enterprise

Tourism Enterprise \ Government	imposing restraint (y)	imposing no restraint (1-y)
having no moral hazard (x)	k_1-s_1 ,-s	k_1-s_1 ,0
having with moral hazard (1-x)	k_2-ps_p ,ps_p-s	k_2 ,0

The following are some logical hypotheses which are listed for the convenience of the research. First, suppose the costs of imposing restraint is more than the penalty, ps_p>s. Second, the penalty is greater than additional costs for the tourism enterprise with no moral hazard, ps_p>s_1. Otherwise the tourism enterprise may decide to have moral hazard for economic interests. Third, the income which the tourism enterprise gets with no moral hazard is less comparing to the income which the tourism enterprise gets with moral hazard, k_1-s_1<k_2. That is why the tourism enterprise has the motivation to have moral hazard. Fourth, the income which the tourism enterprise gets with no moral hazard is more than the balance of paying the penalty for the tourism enterprises with moral hazard, k_1-s_1<k_2-ps_p. It demonstrates the effectiveness of the policy.

3.3   Model Solution

According to table 1 and the above hypotheses, it is evident that if the tourism enterprise has no moral hazard, the government may impose no restraint as the best strategy. And when the government imposes no restraint, the tourism enterprise may choose to have moral hazard. In this condition, the best strategy for the government is to impose restraint. But in this condition, the tourism enterprise may choose to have moral hazard again. Thus, the interests of both parties can't be realized. So there is no pure strategy Nash equilibrium, the government and the tourism enterprise will take mixed strategy.

When y is certain, the expected returns of the tourism enterprise which has no moral hazard (x=1) and which has no moral hazard (x=0) are the following:

$$\pi(y, 1) = (k_1 - s_1) y + (k_1 - s_1) (1 - y) . \tag{1}$$

$$\pi(y, 0) = (k_2 - ps_P) y + k_2 (1 - y) . \tag{2}$$

From the equilibrium condition, we get: $\pi(y, 1) = \pi(y, 0)$, namely, (1)= (2). So,

$$(k_1 - s_1) y + (k_1 - s_1) (1 - y) = (k_2 - ps_P) y + k_2 (1 - y) .$$

The solution on y of the above formula is also the best probability of imposing restraint by the government in equilibrium.

$$y^* = \frac{k_2 - k_1 + s_1}{ps_P}$$

When x is certain, the expected returns of the government which imposes restraint (y=1) and which imposes no restraint (y=0) are the following:

$$\pi(1, x) = sx + (ps_p - s) (1 - x). \tag{3}$$

$$\pi(0, x) = 0 . \tag{4}$$

From the equilibrium condition, we get: $\pi(1, x) = \pi(0, x)$, namely, (3)= (4). So,

$$sx + (ps_p - s) (1 - x) = 0.$$

For the tourism enterprise, the solution on x of the above formula is also the best probability of having no moral hazard in equilibrium.

$$x^* = \frac{ps_p - s}{ps_p}$$

So $(\frac{ps_p - s}{ps_p}, \frac{k_2 - k_1 + s_1}{ps})$ is the solution of this mixed strategy Nash equilibrium model. This solution indicates the following. For the tourism enterprise, if the probability of imposing restraint is less than y^*, the best strategy for the tourism enterprise is having moral hazard, and vice versa. For the government, if the probability of having no moral hazard is less than x^*, the best strategy for the government is imposing no restraint, and vice versa. Moreover, the two parties can be in game equilibrium when x equals x^* and y equals y^*.

3.4 Revelation

So the inspiration of this game model is the following. In order that the tourism enterprise may have no moral hazard on his initiative, the government needs to increase p——the probability of imposing restraint and s_P——the penalty, reduces s——supervisory costs. Because it is a positive correlation between x* and p, s_P, while negative correlation between x* and s. In other words, the higher probability of imposing restraint and more penalty, or the lower supervisory costs, the higher probability of having no moral hazard for the tourism enterprise. While the more penalty, the lower probability of imposing restraint by the government.

4   Conclusion

If the tourism enterprise has no moral hazard in the operation, the healthy development of tourism market can be improved effectively. And it can also promote the development potential of tourism. Since asymmetric information is the fundamental reason that the tourism enterprise has moral hazard, the government needs to take administrative and legal means to regulate the action of the tourism enterprise. Through the game analysis of the government and the tourism enterprise, it is obvious that the government strengthens the restraint and charges more penalties for the tourism enterprise which has moral hazard may promote his operation with no moral hazard. So it is effective for the government to regulate moral hazard of the tourism enterprise.

References

1. Han, J.: Information Economics. Beijing Library Press, Beijing (2000)
2. Yang, X.: A Study on Tourism Credit. Doctoral dissertation (2005)
3. Shen, J.: Game analysis on Government Regulation for Enterprise Implementation of Ecotourism Environmental Protection Planning. Pioneering with Science & Technology Monthly 6, 78 (2009)

Author Index